LIVING
LANGUAGES

LIVING LANGUAGES

CONTEXTS FOR READING AND WRITING

EDITED BY

NANCY BUFFINGTON
Youngstown State University

MARVIN DIOGENES
University of Arizona

CLYDE MONEYHUN
Youngstown State University

A BLAIR PRESS BOOK

PRENTICE HALL, UPPER SADDLE RIVER, NJ 07458

Library of Congress Cataloging-in-Publication Data

Living languages : contexts for reading and writing / edited by Nancy
  Buffington, Marvin Diogenes, Clyde Moneyhun.
    p.   cm.
  Includes index.
  ISBN 0-13-668963-9
    1. Readers—Language and languages.   2. Language and languages
  —Problems, exercises, etc.   3. English language—Rhetoric.
  4. College readers.   I. Buffington, Nancy.   II. Diogenes, Marvin.
  III. Moneyhun, Clyde.
  PE1127.L47L59   1997
  808'.0427—DC21   96–45326
                                                                 CIP

Publisher: Nancy Perry
Acquisitions Editor: Mary Jo Southern
Editorial/production supervision: Alison D. Gnerre
Manufacturing Buyer: Mary Ann Gloriande
Cover design: Karen Salzbach
Cover art: Joan Miro; *Painting*, 1949; oil on canvas: 50 1/4" × 6' 4"; courtesy of
the Morton G. Neumann Family Collection; 1997 Artists Rights Society (ARS),
NY/ADAGP, Paris

Acknowledgments appear on pages 459–60, which constitute a continuation
of the copyright page.

A Blair Press Book
 © 1997 by Prentice-Hall, Inc.
Simon & Schuster/A Viacom Company
Upper Saddle River, New Jersey 07458

Printed in the United States of America

10 9 8 7 6 5 4 3 2 1

ISBN 0-13-668963-9

Prentice-Hall International (UK), Limited, *London*
Prentice Hall of Australia Pty. Limited, *Sydney*
Prentice Hall Canada, Inc. *Toronto*
Prentice Hall Hispanoamericana, S.A., *Mexico*
Prentice Hall of India Private Limited, *New Delhi*
Prentice Hall of Japan, Inc., *Tokyo*
Simon & Schuster Asia Pte. Ltd., *Singapore*
Editora Prentice-Hall do Brasil, Ltda., *Rio de Janeiro*

To the Instructor

Living Languages is a thematic reader with activities and assignments designed for use in college composition courses. The selections focus on how we live our lives through language—how we create our worlds with language and are in turn shaped by worlds of language—so that languages can be said to take on a life of their own in their influence on us. The text as a whole builds on students' previous experiences and knowledge of language in the home and school and introduces them to the special uses of language in higher education, in professional life, and in the wider culture.

Students come to the college classroom as experts in certain kinds of language use. Higher education challenges them to expand their linguistic repertoire if they are to function effectively in new and different contexts. *Living Languages* helps students create roles for themselves within these new linguistic "worlds" by privileging the concept of immersion into discourses. Discourses are discussed in terms of conventions rather than rules, so students can see that discourses are constructed and negotiated by the people using them.

The Readings

The nature of its readings distinguishes *Living Languages* from other language readers. Selections focus on language use and the individual's interaction through language with social, cultural, educational, and political environments. The readings show writers in dynamic relationships with their cultures, using language to define themselves as individuals, family members, students, workers, professionals, and citizens. In brief, the readings highlight how the writers act in language to change themselves and their worlds.

The selections, at least half of them never before anthologized in a composition reader, represent the work of a diverse group of writers:

scholars and educators from many fields, poets and novelists, social critics, politicians, journalists. Many of the writers speak from the special perspective of membership in a so-called non-mainstream group, such as an ethnic, racial, or class minority. Women writers and their particular views of language and its uses and abuses are also a central feature of the book. Language is presented through all the readings as an important medium for the expression of cultural difference as well as a means to intercultural communication. We believe that such selections can illuminate the positions of all students, including those who see themselves as members of a "mainstream" culture.

The Organization

An important feature of *Living Languages* is the way the readings guide students through a complete course in the uses of language, expanding their knowledge and experience of language as the locus of self-definition and cultural expression. At the same time, the book is flexible enough for instructors to adapt it to their own syllabi and teaching methods. Individual reading selections are freestanding and independent, and instructors can pick and choose among activities and assignments.

The readings are divided into thematic chapters (and further divided into units) that lead students from language uses they have mastered to language uses that may be new to them: "Languages of Home and Community," "Leaving Home: Languages in Conflict," "Languages of Academic Discourse," "Languages of Professional Life," "Languages of Cultural Criticism," "Languages of Personal Exploration," and "Languages of Literary Expression." Within every chapter are two units of several essays each.

The Activities

Chapters in *Living Languages* are introduced by brief essays that prepare students for the content of the readings in the chapter, and the readings are then preceded by two kinds of activities: "Before You Read" activities that help students access prior knowledge on the chapter's themes and "After You Read" activities that help students follow up on what they learn from the readings. Each reading is accompanied by activities that ask students to work both "with" the text and "beyond" the text, linking it to issues in their lives and the world.

The emphasis of this pedagogical apparatus is less on "reading comprehension" as an isolated skill and more on students' real engagement with the issues in the readings. The various activities ("Before You Read," "After You Read," "Working with the Text," "Working beyond the Text") have been written to give instructors maximum flexibility in using them. Some activities ask for close discussions of the readings, including rhetorical analysis. Others ask students to relate the issues raised by the readings to their life experiences. Still others call for research outside the confines of the readings, either textual research in the library (including journals and newspapers) or informal "ethnographic" research in the students' lived worlds (including popular culture). Few spell out specific tasks; most can be adapted for various uses: in-class discussions, small-group work, homework assignments, even whole essay assignments.

The Instructor's Manual

Living Languages is accompanied by a useful instructor's manual. It contains an introduction that sketches recent trends in reading and writing pedagogy, and it offers a collection of in-class and at-home activities that take a process approach to both reading and writing. The activities described, for example, include "prior knowledge" exercises, interactive journals, and group writing projects. The manual also offers several sample syllabi to help instructors structure an entire composition course around the book's readings and apparatus; the syllabi illustrate a range of thematic and pedagogical progressions. Finally, there is a special section of activities that ask students to work with all the essays in individual units, if the instructor chooses to have students read all the essays in the unit. Taken as a whole, the manual demonstrates the flexibility and adaptability of the reader.

Acknowledgments

Special thanks to our research assistant Kevin Farkas, whose many contributions were indispensable.

Marvin would like to thank his wife Merle Turchik for her avid proofreading and for her support throughout the process of putting the book together.

We are grateful to the following reviewers for their helpful suggestions: Duncan Carter, Portland State University; Kitty Chen Dean, Nassau Community College; James Egan, University of Akron; Joel Hansen, University of Michigan; John Heyda, Miami University—Middletown; Bob Hughes, Highline Community College; Andrew Pawelczak, Passaic Community College; Thomas Recchio, University of Connecticut—Storrs; Elizabeth Renfro, California State University—Chico; and Richard Veit, University of North Carolina at Wilmington.

Thanks also to Alison Gnerre, our production editor at Prentice

Hall, who shepherded the book through the process from final manuscript to printed page.

A simple "thanks" won't be enough for our Blair Press editor, Nancy Perry. She believed in the project from the beginning; she offered material and moral support as we got started; she showed patience and good humor as we labored to finish the manuscript; and she made invaluable editorial suggestions that strengthened both the form and the content of the book.

TO THE STUDENT

Composition instructors often use "readers," or anthologies, in their courses, and *Living Languages* is the one your instructor has chosen for this course. Like most readers, it offers essays arranged in chapters according to their content. However, the content of this reader's essays is special. All of the essays are about how we use language in various contexts: home, school, work, and so on. If you glance at the table of contents, you'll see the focus of each chapter. You obviously won't have time during the course to read all the essays in the book. Your instructor will probably choose, but you may also be given the opportunity to select what you read. Of course, you may decide to read any or all of the essays on your own if you become interested in the subjects of particular chapters.

Like most readers, *Living Languages* has questions, activities, and assignments to accompany the essays. At the beginning of each chapter, you'll see two kinds of activities:

- "Before You Read" activities that will help you think about the ideas in the chapter's essays before you even read them. The principle behind these activities is that you already know a lot about some of the chapters' subjects, and clarifying what you already know can help you absorb new knowledge.
- "After You Read" activities that will help you use the essays as a springboard to other learning. Some of these activities, for example, ask you to find other materials to read that deal with the same subjects as the chapters.

In addition to these activities, there are two kinds of questions that follow every reading:

- "Working with the Text" questions that help you think about what you've read by pointing to specific passages in the essays. These questions ask you to reread the essays with a specific purpose in mind.

- "Working beyond the Text" questions that ask you to think about the ideas in the essays in different contexts, especially the context of your own life. You may be asked to compare the author's ideas to your own experiences or to do some research on your own.

Almost any of the questions, activities, and assignments may be used in any number of ways. Your instructor may use them, for example, as either group or individual activities, as either in-class discussion questions or at-home writing assignments. In addition, your instructor will almost certainly ask you to do other kinds of in-class activities and other kinds of writing assignments.

Whatever kinds of reading and writing you do in this course, remember that the goal of the editors of this book is to help you think about the living presence of language in your life. It's been said that what water is for fish, language is for human beings, only more. We live in it, love in it, work in it. We get what we need through language, we learn what life means through language, we make ourselves understood through language. This book tries to take what we all do naturally and almost unconsciously in our everyday lives and draw your attention to it. Through understanding how language works in our lives, we may come to know ourselves and those around us better.

CONTENTS

CHAPTER 7   Languages of Literary Expression   395

Rhetorical Contents

DEFINITION

PROCESS

CLASSIFICATION

CAUSE AND EFFECT

ARGUMENT

DOCUMENTED ESSAY

1

LANGUAGES OF HOME

AND COMMUNITY

INTRODUCTION

We learn our first language not in a classroom but at home, not from a teacher but from a family and a community. Some of us learn a "mainstream" language, not just English but a "standard" form of English. Others learn a language other than English or a form of English not considered standard. Still others learn several languages at once, becoming "bilingual" and "bicultural."

No matter what language we learn in our home and community, along with a language we learn rules about how to use it: when to speak and when not to speak, which words to use and which not to use, what subjects are appropriate with which listeners. Parents and other members of our community are constantly correcting us: "Nobody asked you for an opinion," "Good little girls don't talk that way," "No yelling at the dinner table." Sometimes we test the limits of these rules, especially when we use the unauthorized language of adults and older brothers and sisters, or the language of people from outside the community. But like it or not, we do learn the languages of home and community, and along with them the culture, the values, and the customs of home and community.

We also learn to take joy in language. We love puns, the stupider the better, and nonsense words, knock-knock jokes, limericks, TV commercial jingles, and the qualities of language we later learn to call rhyme and meter: "*John* and *Mary* sitting in a *tree*, K-I-S-S-I-N-G." We experiment with the possibilities of language, making up wild stories with impossible events and creatures and never-before-heard words. We may be read to and may learn to read to ourselves before we ever leave home for school—another source of delight in language.

The selections in this chapter explore the languages we learn in the home and community, for better or worse: the joys and possibilities and connectedness to community, but also the limits and punishments and shame we sometimes experience because of language learned in the home. Why is it important to think about these things, listen to what others say about them, remember what we know about them from our own lives? The languages we learn in our homes and communities are the foundation for other languages we learn when we

1

enter the larger worlds of school and work. Before we examine the way we use language outside the home, we should try to understand both the limitations and the gifts of the languages we learn in our homes and communities.

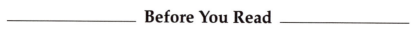

Before You Read

Before you read any combination of essays in this chapter, you might prepare by doing any of the activities below as either class or small group discussions, or as formal or informal writing assignments. They are designed to help you find out what you already know about the issues discussed by the authors in the chapter, so you have some background for understanding what the authors say.

1. What stories does your family tell about the use of language by you or your siblings when you were children? What were your first words, for example, or the first jokes you learned to tell? What were you proud of being able to do?
2. What is the relation of your family's language to other languages used in the United States? Is it the language of a particular ethnic group, social class, or geographical region, for example? Is it a "mainstream" or a "marginal" language or somewhere in between?
3. As Americans, we all belong to a broad American culture, but we all also belong to one or more "subcultures" because of who we are, where we live, how old we are, and so on. Which subculture or subcultures would you say you belong to? What kind of language is characteristic of your subculture(s)? Be prepared to give specific examples.
4. How would you assess your language abilities? What are your strengths and weaknesses? Do you feel confident or shy about your ability to express your ideas and feelings? Do you have different abilities in different situations? How do your abilities help or hinder your work in school?

After You Read

After you read any combination of essays in this chapter, you might follow up by doing any of the activities below as either class or small group discussions, or as formal or informal writing assignments. They are designed to help you extend what you have learned from the authors in the chapter by discovering new perspectives on the chapter's themes on your own.

1. There is a lot of research about specific styles of English and how they are affected by ethnicity, class, and gender. What are the different styles of English spoken by members of different ethnic groups, for example? How does middle-class English differ from working-class English? How does men's speech differ from women's speech? Choose a specific area of research in different styles of English and research it in the library. Relate what you discover to the ideas of several of the writers in this chapter who write about the language of particular ethnicities, classes, or genders.

2. Several of the writers in this chapter discuss the special position occupied by people who belong to a culture that speaks a language other than English, and the pressures to speak English from the "mainstream" English-speaking majority. Today, as in the past, many states and even the federal government are considering or have already established "English-only" laws that would require the use of English in schools, government documents, and so on, to the exclusion of all other languages. Research some aspect of English-only initiatives in the United States: their place in American history, for example, or the most recent efforts around the country.

3. Interview one or more classmates or friends about the language (or languages) they speak in the home. Ask for specific examples of their language and its role in their lives. Compare what they say to ideas from any of the essays you read in this chapter.

Unit One

Learning the Rules

Talking Back

bell hooks

bell hooks is the pen name of Gloria Watkins, a writer, teacher, feminist, and black activist. In her many collections of essays, including *Talking Back, Feminist Theory: from margin to center,* and, most recently, *Teaching to Transgress,* hooks often uses details from her personal life to explain her political beliefs. In the following essay from *Talking Back* (1989), hooks discusses the rules of speech she learned (and broke) during her upbringing in rural Kentucky.

In the world of the southern black community I grew up in, "back 1 talk" and "talking back" meant speaking as an equal to an authority figure. It meant daring to disagree and sometimes it just meant having an opinion. In the "old school," children were meant to be seen and not heard. My great-grandparents, grandparents, and parents were all from the old school. To make yourself heard if you were a child was to invite punishment, the back-hand lick, the slap across the face that would catch you unaware, or the feel of switches stinging your arms and legs.

To speak then when one was not spoken to was a courageous 2 act—an act of risk and daring. And yet it was hard not to speak in warm rooms where heated discussions began at the crack of dawn, women's voices filling the air, giving orders, making threats, fussing. Black men may have excelled in the art of poetic preaching in the male-dominated church, but in the church of the home, where the everyday rules of how to live and how to act were established, it was black women who preached. There, black women spoke in a language so rich, so poetic, that it felt to me like being shut off from life, smothered to death if one were not allowed to participate.

It was in that world of woman talk (the men were often silent, 3 often absent) that was born in me the craving to speak, to have a voice, and not just any voice but one that could be identified as belonging to me. To make my voice, I had to speak, to hear myself talk—and talk I did—darting in and out of grown folks' conversations and dialogues, answering questions that were not directed at me, endlessly asking questions, making speeches. Needless to say, the punishments for these acts of speech seemed endless. They were intended to silence me—the child—and more particularly the girl child. Had I been a boy, they might have encouraged me to speak believing that I might some-day be called to preach. There was no "calling" for talking girls, no le-gitimized rewarded speech. The punishments I received for "talking back" were intended to suppress all possibility that I would create my own speech. That speech was to be suppressed so that the "right speech of womanhood" would emerge.

Within feminist circles, silence is often seen as the sexist "right 4 speech of womanhood"—the sign of woman's submission to patriar-chal authority. This emphasis on woman's silence may be an accurate remembering of what has taken place in the households of women from WASP backgrounds in the United States, but in black communi-ties (and diverse ethnic communities), women have not been silent. Their voices can be heard. Certainly for black women, our struggle has not been to emerge from silence into speech but to change the nature and direction of our speech, to make a speech that compels listeners, one that is heard.

Our speech, "the right speech of womanhood," was often the solil- 5 oquy, the talking into thin air, the talking to ears that do not hear you—the talk that is simply not listened to. Unlike the black male preacher whose speech was to be heard, who was to be listened to, whose words were to be remembered, the voices of black women—giving orders, making threats, fussing—could be tuned out, could be-come a kind of background music, audible but not acknowledged as significant speech. Dialogue—the sharing of speech and recognition—took place not between mother and child or mother and male author-ity figure but among black women. I can remember watching fasci-nated as our mother talked with her mother, sisters, and women friends. The intimacy and intensity of their speech—the satisfaction they received from talking to one another, the pleasure, the joy. It was in this world of woman speech, loud talk, angry words, women with tongues quick and sharp, tender sweet tongues, touching our world with their words, that I made speech my birthright—and the right to voice, to authorship, a privilege I would not be denied. It was in that world and because of it that I came to dream of writing, to write.

Writing was a way to capture speech, to hold onto it, keep it close. 6 And so I wrote down bits and pieces of conversations, confessing in cheap diaries that soon fell apart from too much handling, expressing the intensity of my sorrow, the anguish of speech—for I was always saying the wrong thing, asking the wrong questions. I could not con-fine my speech to the necessary corners and concerns of life. I hid these writings under my bed, in pillow stuffings, among faded underwear. When my sisters found and read them, they ridiculed and mocked me—poking fun. I felt violated, ashamed, as if the secret parts of my self had been exposed, brought into the open, and hung like newly clean laundry, out in the air for everyone to see. The fear of exposure, the fear that one's deepest emotions and innermost thoughts will be dismissed as mere nonsense, felt by so many young girls keeping diaries, holding and hiding speech, seems to me now one of the barriers that women have always needed and still need to destroy so that we are no longer pushed into secrecy or silence.

Despite my feelings of violation, of exposure, I continued to speak and write, choosing my hiding places well, learning to destroy work when no safe place could be found. I was never taught absolute silence, I was taught that it was important to speak but to talk a talk that was in itself a silence. Taught to speak and yet beware of the betrayal of too much heard speech, I experienced intense confusion and deep anxiety in my efforts to speak and write. Reciting poems at Sunday afternoon church service might be rewarded. Writing a poem (when one's time could be "better" spent sweeping, ironing, learning to cook) was luxurious activity, indulged in at the expense of others. Questioning authority, raising issues that were not deemed appropriate subjects brought pain, punishments—like telling mama I wanted to die before her because I could not live without her—that was crazy talk, crazy speech, the kind that would lead you to end up in a mental institution. "Little girl," I would be told, "if you don't stop all this crazy talk and crazy acting you are going to end up right out there at Western State."

Madness, not just physical abuse, was the punishment for too much talk if you were female. Yet even as this fear of madness haunted me, hanging over my writing like a monstrous shadow, I could not stop the words, making thought, writing speech. For this terrible madness which I feared, which I was sure was the destiny of daring women born to intense speech (after all, the authorities emphasized this point daily), was not as threatening as imposed silence, as suppressed speech.

Safety and sanity were to be sacrificed if I was to experience defiant speech. Though I risked them both, deep-seated fears and anxieties characterized my childhood days. I would speak but I would not ride a bike, play hardball, or hold the gray kitten. Writing about the ways we are traumatized in our growing-up years, psychoanalyst Alice Miller makes the point in *For Your Own Good* that it is not clear why childhood wounds become for some folk an opportunity to grow, to move forward rather than backward in the process of self-realization. Certainly, when I reflect on the trials of my growing-up years, the many punishments, I can see now that in resistance I learned to be vigilant in the nourishment of my spirit, to be tough, to courageously protect that spirit from forces that would break it.

While punishing me, my parents often spoke about the necessity 10 of breaking my spirit. Now when I ponder the silences, the voices that are not heard, the voices of those wounded and/or oppressed individuals who do not speak or write, I contemplate the acts of persecution, torture—the terrorism that breaks spirits, that makes creativity impossible. I write these words to bear witness to the primacy of resistance struggle in any situation of domination (even within family life); to the strength and power that emerges from sustained resistance and the profound conviction that these forces can be healing, can protect us from dehumanization and despair.

These early trials, wherein I learned to stand my ground, to keep 11 my spirit intact, came vividly to mind after I published *Ain't I A Woman* and the book was sharply and harshly criticized. While I had expected a climate of critical dialogue, I was not expecting a critical avalanche that had the power in its intensity to crush the spirit, to push one into silence. Since that time, I have heard stories about black women, about women of color, who write and publish (even when the work is quite successful) having nervous breakdowns, being made mad because they cannot bear the harsh responses of family, friends, and unknown critics, or becoming silent, unproductive. Surely, the absence of a humane critical response has tremendous impact on the writer from any oppressed, colonized group who endeavors to speak. For us, true speaking is not solely an expression of creative power; it is an act of resistance, a political gesture that challenges politics of domination that would render us nameless and voiceless. As such, it is a courageous act—as such, it represents a threat. To those who wield oppressive power, that which is threatening must necessarily be wiped out, annihilated, silenced.

Recently, efforts by black women writers to call attention to our 12 work serve to highlight both our presence and absence. Whenever I peruse women's bookstores, I am struck not by the rapidly growing body of feminist writing by black women, but by the paucity of available published material. Those of us who write and are published remain few in number. The context of silence is varied and multi-dimensional. Most obvious are the ways racism, sexism, and class exploitation act to suppress and silence. Less obvious are the inner struggles, the efforts made to gain the necessary confidence to write, to re-write, to fully develop craft and skill—and the extent to which such efforts fail.

Although I have wanted writing to be my life-work since child- 13 hood, it has been difficult for me to claim "writer" as part of that which identifies and shapes my everyday reality. Even after publishing books, I would often speak of wanting to be a writer as though these works did not exist. And though I would be told, "you are a writer," I was not yet ready to fully affirm this truth. Part of myself was still held captive by domineering forces of history, of familial life that had charted a map of silence, of right speech. I had not completely let go of the fear of saying the wrong thing, of being punished. Somewhere in the deep recesses of my mind, I believed I could avoid both responsibility and punishment if I did not declare myself a writer.

One of the many reasons I chose to write using the pseudonym bell hooks, a family name (mother to Sarah Oldham, grandmother to Rosa Bell Oldham, great-grandmother to me), was to construct a writer-identity that would challenge and subdue all impulses leading me away from speech into silence. I was a young girl buying bubble gum at the corner store when I first really heard the full name bell hooks. I had just "talked back" to a grown person. Even now I can recall the surprised look, the mocking tones that informed me I must be kin to bell hooks—a sharp-tongued woman, a woman who spoke her mind, a woman who was not afraid to talk back. I claimed this legacy of defiance, of will, of courage, affirming my link to female ancestors who were bold and daring in their speech. Unlike my bold and daring mother and grandmother, who were not supportive of talking back, even though they were assertive and powerful in their speech, bell hooks as I discovered, claimed, and invented her was my ally, my support. 14

That initial act of talking back outside the home was empowering. It was the first of many acts of defiant speech that would make it possible for me to emerge as an independent thinker and writer. In retrospect, "talking back" became for me a rite of initiation, testing my courage, strengthening my commitment, preparing me for the days ahead—the days when writing, rejection notices, periods of silence, publication, ongoing development seem impossible but necessary. 15

Moving from silence into speech is for the oppressed, the colonized, the exploited, and those who stand and struggle side by side a gesture of defiance that heals, that makes new life and new growth possible. It is that act of speech, of "talking back," that is no mere gesture of empty words, that is the expression of our movement from object to subject—the liberated voice. 16

Working with the Text

1. bell hooks traces certain tendencies in her adult life, especially the writing career she has chosen, to roots in her family life. How does she relate the habit of "talking back" to her career as a writer? How are the definitions of "talking back" different for her parents, for her as a child, for her as an adult?

2. Even after publishing books, hooks says she still has trouble thinking of herself as a writer: "Part of myself was still held captive by domineering forces of history, of familial life that had charted a map of silence, of right speech." What does she mean by this?

3. hooks seems to understand the risks involved in making secret thoughts public, but seems to want to do it anyway. In what situations has she made her thoughts known? What were the risks involved? Why does she still take the risk?

4. hooks opens her essay with three paragraphs of personal narrative, but beginning in the fourth paragraph ("Within feminist circles . . ."), she makes it clear that her life experiences have broader meanings for all women, especially black women. What is the relation between hooks' life experiences and the broader themes she explores? How does her use of personal narrative help her express her broader themes?

Working beyond the Text

1. In hooks' childhood home there were very particular rules for speaking. What were they? How were they made clear to her and enforced? How does she seem to feel about them? What are the rules about speaking in your home? How did you learn these rules? How do you feel about them?

2. hooks took another name in order to write. Why? Whose name is it and what significance does it have for her? Do you "put on another self" when you write? How is the self you present in your writing different from the self you present to your family, to your friends?

3. hooks describes the feeling of being crushed by criticism after having dared to speak out. What does she say about it? Can you remember a time when you have spoken out or put strong personal feelings into writing and then been criticized in a way that made you feel "wiped out, annihilated, silenced"? What was the situation? How did you react?

4. hooks contrasts black men's "poetic preaching in the male-dominated church" and black women's authority "in the church of the home, where the everyday rules of how to live and how to act were established." Have you noticed a similar contrast in men's and women's language? That is, do women and men have different language rights in different places?

The Pleasures of Remembrance: Raking in Circles and Other Unexpected Delights

Julie Jung

Julie Jung is a Ph.D. candidate in Rhetoric and Composition at the University of Arizona. Born in 1966, the youngest of five children in a Catholic family, she earned a B.A. in Mathematics and an M.A. in Composition. Perhaps this unusual combination of scholarly interests relates to the two language styles of her father and mother, the one analytical and argumentative, the other sensitive and narrative. In this essay Jung examines the influence of those very different languages styles on her own development as a writer.

A few weeks ago, a friend and colleague of mine asked me to visit 1 her sophomore composition class to talk about women's ways of writing. I balked at the invitation, perhaps because I'm not sure there are such things as women's ways of writing, but more I suppose because I didn't know what I would say.

"I haven't done very much research on that issue, "I told her. "The 2 only thing I'd be able to talk about is my own experience."

She smiled and said that would be fine. So, it was while talking to 3 this bright and articulate group of second-year writers that I surprised myself. I began talking about my dad.

It was the norm in my family that all five children, regardless of 4 age or gender, shared in doing what few chores were required of us, and, on one particular fall day, when I was about eight, it was my turn to rake leaves. I can remember trekking outside into the yard where three enormous maple trees stood, and where infinite numbers of orange, yellow, and red leaves blanketed the grass that was our front lawn. Holding a tool made for grownup hands, I began to rake, and, after some effort, I got a pretty nifty rhythm going—in, shake, out, and in again. After about twenty minutes, I heard a voice behind me ask:

"Why are you raking in circles?" 5

Before I could answer, my dad took the rake from my hands and, 6 in his usual methodical manner, showed me how, by raking in columns and rows, I could maximize my efforts.

"You see," he said, "This is much more logical. Now you won't 7 ruin your piles trying to step out of them."

He returned the rake to me and I, watching him wide eyed—who 8 was this man who was home on a Saturday?—vowed to make my raking more logical.

It was in this fashion that I was a daughter to my father. I listened 9 to him, was awed by him, feared him. He was never home much: a workaholic, he spent most of his time trying to get his computer software company off the ground. He'd be home on an occasional Sunday afternoon, but these infrequent lapses into relaxation he reserved for lying on the couch, simultaneously reading a book, watching old war movies, and eating salted pistachios.

When I was about twelve, I can remember his coming to pick me 10 up at one of my weekend softball games. For some reason I cannot recall, my mom, who usually sat through entire games in a lounge chair along the third base line, with a newspaper in her lap and our family dog Tina by her side, could not be at this game. And it was late in the eighth inning, my team at bat, when I heard the left fielder say, "Who is *that*?" I turned slowly, following her voice, knowing before my eyes registered him that "that" would be my dad. And indeed it was. I recognized the pose instantly. He was wearing one of his then fashionable three-piece suits, his right hand in his pocket, the other supporting him as he leaned against the fence. Behind him, parked diagonally to take up two parking spaces, was his Porsche—the same one he slept in the very night he bought it, the same one he was forced to sell when his company began to go under. I saw his face before he saw mine, and I was immediately grateful that my uneventful turn at bat had already come and gone. For his face bore that familiar expression of evaluation, silently taking in the scene before him, immediately assessing that the right fielder was playing too far in and the batter had better keep her back foot planted if she wanted to get on base. I turned to my teammates and answered, finally, "That's my dad." Thirteen faces turned toward me in a mixture of awe and horror. They were impressed with his suit, his car, his confidence. I could see that. But there was also pity there, and fear. I could see that, too. Dads were men who on Saturdays wore t-shirts and jeans, sat in the bleachers and drank Pepsis, coached us on how to throw like a boy, and cheered when we finally hit the ball out of the infield. But this tall and serious man in the suit at the fence, clearly this mystery was no dad—this was a father.

My dad had this kind of effect on people: he could make his presence felt. So much so, in fact, that when I was growing up, friends refused to sleep over because they were afraid of him. But if my dad's mere bodily existence could instill fear in little children, it was his language that awed, especially me. And it was this kind of presence, this power to awe, that I, over time, began to want for myself. I began drinking coffee when I was nine because it was after dinner that my parents—or rather, my dad—talked. So wonderful was my father's language that I didn't want to leave the table, and so I drank coffee to get a glimpse into his world outside of home. He spoke of his company, the men who worked for him, his chance to expand into Denver and Dallas. Now, years later, it's not the content of these talks that I remember, but rather the way he expressed it. His voice was direct, cool, logical. My dad is the only person I know who, upon answering the phone, says "Hello" like a statement, not a question. In my father's language, there is no room for doubt. For him, the right answer is always right there, obvious and clear.

By the time my dad and I got around to having our first conversation, when I was seventeen, I was ready. Having internalized his language, I knew how to organize my thoughts in a linear manner that served the development of my logical argument. I knew how to support my points not with emotion but with data. I had learned how to anticipate his next question and create detours around my weak points. And when I nervously finished delivering my argument, my dad, sitting across from me on the living room couch, smiled. "Yes," he said. "I agree. You were right to quit that job." Oh, the euphoria. I had done it. I had pleased him. I had won.

It should not be surprising, then, that when I went off to college, I 13 succeeded. I could write well. Like my father, my mostly male teachers were pleased with my language because it echoed their own. "Insightful, organized, and well argued," they'd often write at the bottom of my drafts. I was nothing as a writer if not organized.

And then something happened, something changed for me. Dur- 14 ing my second year of graduate school, I met writers who kept talking about voice. I would look at them and wonder what they were talking about. "What's the big deal with voice?" I'd ask. "Argument and organization matter most, don't they?" By the looks on their faces, I could tell there was something I didn't get, or rather, didn't have. And although I can't pinpoint the exact date, it was around this time that I realized that I, as a writer, didn't have my own voice.

Since that time, I've been struggling to find it, or to remember it, 15 unsure of how to proceed but sensing that it might be found in those places where I write about what pleases me, excites me, gets me moving. Searching for my voice also means that I have an alternative to my father's, which gives me a kind of subversive power. Now I can step outside his language when it fails to please me. Like last summer, when my father tried to engage me in one of his verbal wrestling matches. His language is like a chess game or a Platonic dialogue—it depends on someone messing up, driving herself into a corner, contradicting herself. Not wanting to engage, I leave that room, but my father, in need of a sparring partner, turns to my newly reborn Christian sister, who, weak from a recent bitter divorce, is vulnerable.

"Why are you so into God now?" he asks. 16

It's not a question; it's a set up, and she knows it, but what can she 17 do? She's been sucked in. So she tries her best, but in the course of speaking her experience, she is eventually forced to defend it, and in so doing, she loses her voice. All of this is mere speculation, by the way. I am not there, in that room, with Dad and Terry. I am in the kitchen, where I tell make-believe stories to my three-year-old niece and we eat bleu-cheese deviled eggs and laugh.

As a writer, I doubt that I will ever lose the language of my father. 18 And I don't think I want to, necessarily. It comes in handy, for writing dissertations and taking in-class essay exams, for example. But I do now want to realize that in so valuing his voice, I have ignored the language of my mother. And it was she who taught me about stories. Eating peanut butter on crackers in the afternoon after school, we tell each other about our days. I speak of Maria Romer's new boyfriend, my disappointment over not making the volleyball team, my horrors over learning about Nazi Germany. She listens well, asks me questions to flesh out the details of my experience. And when it's her turn to speak, she tells me about her bridge game, though I don't understand a word. She spreads peanut butter onto another saltine and reminisces about her school days, feeling inferior to her older, smarter sister Alice, and hating math. She remembers the time she got in trouble for locking her math teacher—an eighty-year-old nun—in a coat closet.

"What happened then, Mom?" I ask, simultaneously horrified and 19 delighted to learn of my mother's secret rebellious streak.

She answers my questions and we eat more crackers, never de- 20 fending the value of our experiences but instead finding value in the telling. It is the conversation that binds us, that connects me to her. Though we never say so, we both sense these moments are special and rare, and so we share our stories with an urgency that fuels the excitement. Soon my older brothers will bust through the back door, smelling of grass and football. They will attack the refrigerator and fight over who gets the last cherry popsicle. My mom will flash me a knowing smile—one that reassures me we will talk again soon—and then slowly, reluctantly she will rise from the table to admonish my brothers for what I know must be the zillionth unheard time.

I have often wondered why talking with mom was so easy and 21 talking with my dad so difficult. Rereading this I see that the *kinds* of talk were different. With my mom, it was conversation. With my dad, argument. Early on, I see I associated school with my dad's brand of talk, and, not surprisingly, school conversations, like those with my dad, scared me, and so I refused to talk. I was, in fact, so afraid of speaking that, rather than interrupt my teacher and ask if I could go to the restroom, I wet my pants while the whole class sat in a circle listening to her read *The Little Engine that Could*. That was in the first grade. And I only peed my pants two more times before my mom succeeded in convincing me that it was indeed okay to SPEAK UP.

Finding my voice, as a writer, as a speaker, has in many ways been 22 a bodily struggle for me. Lately I've been paying a lot of attention to voices, mostly spoken—which ones I like, which ones I don't—hoping that perhaps if I can find one that pleases me I might be able to find my own. The voice of Melanie Griffith, for example, I can do without. ("Don't lie about your age—defy it.") Please. Too stereotypically feminine. And Sylvester Stallone. ("I am the law.") The flip side. Too stereotypically male. But Lauren Bacall, save that degrading milk ad, has got something going there. Sassy. Smart. Confident. And Hakeem Olajuwon pleases me. That big body coupled with a voice so sweet and gentle. Is it the contradiction I find interesting?

I've been listening to my own spoken voice, too. There's my an- 23 swering machine. "You've reached—. Please leave a message and I'll call you back soon." Too much Stallone. Not enough Olajuwon. But there's a reason. I'm trying to ward off those obscene phone calls. And then there's my voice in conference with my favorite teacher. She's going over my paper, and I interrupt her to ask, "So, do you like it?" Too much Griffith. Not enough Bacall.

And there are, of course, those out-of-body experiences I have 24 while teaching writing. There I am, at the front of the room, droning on and on about something and for a moment I drift out of my body and hear my own voice and for one split second I can hear myself, really hear myself, and I think, "My voice. It sounds so weird, like I actually know what I'm talking about." But when I come back into my body, I'm confused. I stop midsentence, turn to a friendly face in the front row and ask, "What was I saying?"

When I was very young, I used to look into the mirror for long 25 stretches of time and say over and over again, "This is me. This is me. This is me." I wasn't evaluating my face—my brothers did that for me—I was just trying to know myself. I don't do that "mirror thing" anymore. It seems bizarre, and besides, I can't seem to do it without noticing the deepening creases alongside my mouth or the shaggy condition of my hair.

I think that to write and to speak publicly—to voice yourself—is to 26 risk an unexpected future. And for too long, I have equated risk and evaluation: if I speak, if I write, what will *they* think? What will *they* say? Fearing negative, hurtful feedback, I decided very early on that I would speak only when I knew I was right. Thus, I have not only internalized my father's language, but I have also become my harshest critic, silencing myself when others would have me speak. And although I'm getting better at claiming my right to speak in my language, my father is always there, lurking, waiting to jump in when I pause to take a breath. The best I can do, I suppose, is try to balance him out with my mother. And like them—they divorced after twenty some odd years of marriage—I find this balance difficult to achieve. But it's a struggle worth undertaking, I think. And I try to enact this balance every time I write by normalizing, even finding pleasure in, those out-of-body experiences, by listening hard to what I write, and by being willing to say—without fear of harsh evaluation: "This is *for* me. This is *by* me. This *is* me."

Working with the Text

1. Jung talks about "internalizing" the language of others, especially her father, without really thinking about it. Why does she internalize, and learn to speak in, her father's voice?
2. What is "voice," as Jung defines it? Why does it become important to her to find her "voice"? What are the difficulties of finding her own voice?

3. Jung begins to value ways of speaking other than her father's way, while at the same time continuing to find uses for that masculine voice. What other ways does she discover and explore? What value does she find there? What value does she continue to find in her father's way?

4. Why do you think Jung begins her essay by referring to the experience of visiting a friend's sophomore composition class? What do the ideas in her essay have to do with such a class?

5. Physical descriptions of people, especially of Jung's father and mother and herself, are very important in the essay. Examine the descriptions of how people look, dress, stand, and talk. What ideas are being communicated in these descriptions?

Working beyond the Text

1. Jung describes both the experiences of winning an argument with her father and giving up on an argument with him. What are the two situations? How are they different? Have you ever felt the pleasure of winning or the feeling of giving up because you didn't want to argue? What was the situation? How are the two experiences different?

2. Jung talks about looking for models to find a "voice": her father, her mother, Sylvester Stallone, Lauren Bacall. What qualities does she see in each model she analyzes? What models would you like to imitate, and why?

3. Like many feminists, Jung identifies two different ways of speaking with men and women. At the same time, she sees both tendencies within her own "voice." What are the two styles she discusses, and which is associated with which gender? Do you see tendencies toward both styles in your own ways of speaking in different situations? When do you use one style, and when do you use the other?

Bryn Mawr Commencement Address

Ursula Le Guin

Ursula Le Guin, born in 1929, is a well-known writer of fantasy and science fiction, poetry, and children's books. Her novels include *A Wizard of Earthsea*, *The Tombs of Atuan*, and *The Farthest Shore*. In this excerpt from a speech to the graduating class of a prestigious women's college (published in her book *Dancing at the Edge of the World* in 1989), Le Guin outlines the different "tongues" she learned in her home and in the world, and counsels young women to find their own tongue, as she did.

Thinking about what I should say to you made me think about 1
what we learn in college; and what we unlearn in college; and then
how we learn to unlearn what we learned in college and relearn what
we unlearned in college, and so on. And I thought how I have learned,
more or less well, three languages, all of them English; and how one of
these languages is the one I went to college to learn. I thought I was
going to study French and Italian, and I did, but what I learned was
the language of power—social power; I shall call it the father tongue.

This is the public discourse, and one dialect of it is speechmak- 2
ing—by politicians, commencement speakers, or the old man who
used to get up early in a village in Central California a couple of hundred years ago and say things very loudly on the order of "People
need to be getting up now, there are things we might be doing, the re-
pairs on the sweathouse aren't finished and the tarweed is in seed over
on Bald Hill; this is a good time of day for doing things, and there'll be
plenty of time for lying around when it gets hot this afternoon." So
everybody would get up grumbling slightly, and some of them would
go pick tarweed—probably the women. This is the effect, ideally, of
the public discourse. It makes something happen, makes somebody—
usually somebody else—do something, or at least it gratifies the ego of
the speaker. The difference between our politics and that of a native
Californian people is clear in the style of the public discourse. The difference wasn't clear to the White invaders, who insisted on calling any
Indian who made a speech a "chief," because they couldn't comprehend, they wouldn't admit, an authority without supremacy—a non-
dominating authority. But it is such an authority that I possess for the
brief—we all hope it is decently brief—time I speak to you. I have no
right to speak to you. What I have is the responsibility you have given
me to speak to you.

The political tongue speaks aloud—and look how radio and tele- 3
vision have brought the language of politics right back where it belongs—but the dialect of the father tongue that you and I learned best
in college is a written one. It doesn't speak itself. It only lectures. It
began to develop when printing made written language common
rather than rare, five hundred years ago or so, and with electronic processing and copying it continues to develop and proliferate so powerfully, so dominatingly, that many believe this dialect—the expository
and particularly the scientific discourse—is the *highest* form of language, the true language, of which all other uses of words are primitive vestiges.

And it is indeed an excellent dialect. Newton's *Principia* was writ- 4
ten in it in Latin, and Descartes wrote Latin and French in it, establishing some of its basic vocabulary, and Kant wrote German in it, and
Marx, Darwin, Freud, Boas, Foucault—all the great scientists and social
thinkers wrote it. It is the language of thought that seeks objectivity.

I do not say it is the language of rational thought. Reason is a fac- 5
ulty far larger than mere objective thought. When either the political
or the scientific discourse announces itself as the voice of reason, it is
playing God, and should be spanked and stood in the corner. The essential gesture of the father tongue is not reasoning but distancing—
making a gap, a space, between the subject or self and the object or
other. Enormous energy is generated by that rending, that forcing of a
gap between Man and World. So the continuous growth of technology
and science fuels itself; the Industrial Revolution began with splitting
the world-atom, and still by breaking the continuum into unequal
parts we keep the imbalance from which our society draws the power
that enables it to dominate every other culture, so that everywhere
now everybody speaks the same language in laboratories and government buildings and headquarters and offices of business, and those
who don't know it or won't speak it are silent, or silenced, or unheard.

You came here to college to learn the language of power—to be 6
empowered. If you want to succeed in business, government, law, engineering, science, education, the media, if you want to succeed, you
have to be fluent in the language in which "success" is a meaningful
word.

White man speak with forked tongue; White man speak di- 7
chotomy. His language expresses the values of the split world, valuing
the positive and devaluing the negative in each redivision: subject/ob-
ject, self/other, mind/body, dominant/submissive, active/passive,
Man/Nature, man/woman, and so on. The father tongue is spoken
from above. It goes one way. No answer is expected, or heard.

In our Constitution and the works of law, philosophy, social 8
thought, and science, in its everyday uses in the service of justice and
clarity, what I call the father tongue is immensely noble and indispens-
ably useful. When it claims a privileged relationship to reality, it becomes dangerous and potentially destructive. It describes with exquisite accuracy the continuing destruction of the planet's ecosystem by its
speakers. This word from its vocabulary, "ecosystem," is a word unnecessary except in a discourse that excludes its speakers from the
ecosystem in a subject/object dichotomy of terminal irresponsibility.

The language of the fathers, of Man Ascending, Man the Con- 9
queror, Civilized Man, is not your native tongue. It isn't anybody's native tongue. You didn't even hear the father tongue your first few
years, except on the radio or TV, and then you didn't listen, and neither did your little brother, because it was some old politician with
hairs in his nose yammering. And you and your brother had better
things to do. You had another kind of power to learn. You were learning your mother tongue.

Using the father tongue, I can speak of the mother tongue only, in- 10
evitably, to distance it—to exclude it. It is the other, inferior. It is prim-

itive: inaccurate, unclear, coarse, limited, trivial, banal. It's repetitive, the same over and over, like the work called women's work; earthbound, housebound. It's vulgar, the vulgar tongue, common, common speech, colloquial, low, ordinary, plebeian, like the work ordinary people do, the lives common people live. The mother tongue, spoken or written, expects an answer. It is conversation, a word the root of which means "turning together." The mother tongue is language not as mere communication but as relation, relationship. It connects. It goes two ways, many ways, an exchange, a network. Its power is not in dividing but in binding, not in distancing but in uniting. It is written, but not by scribes and secretaries for posterity; it flies from the mouth on the breath that is our life and is gone, like the outbreath, utterly gone and yet returning, repeated, the breath the same again always, everywhere, and we all know it by heart. John have you got your umbrella I think it's going to rain. Can you come play with me? If I told you once I told you a hundred times. Things here just aren't the same without Mother, I will now sign your affectionate brother James. Oh what am I going to do? So I said to her I said if he thinks she's going to stand for that but then there's his arthritis poor thing and no work. I love you. I hate you. I hate liver. Joan dear did you feed the sheep, don't just stand around mooning. Tell me what they said, tell me what you did. Oh how my feet do hurt. My heart is breaking. Touch me here, touch me again. Once bit twice shy. You look like what the cat dragged in. What a beautiful night. Good morning, hello, goodbye, have a nice day, thanks. God damn you to hell you lying cheat. Pass the soy sauce please. Oh shit. Is it grandma's own sweet pretty dear? What am I going to tell her? There there don't cry. Go to sleep now, go to sleep. . . . Don't go to sleep!

It is a language always on the verge of silence and often on the [11] verge of song. It is the language stories are told in. It is the language spoken by all children and most women, and so I call it the mother tongue, for we learn it from our mothers and speak it to our kids. I'm trying to use it here in public where it isn't appropriate, not suited to the occasion, but I want to speak it to you because we are women and I can't say what I want to say about women in the language of capital M Man. If I try to be objective I will say, "This is higher and that is lower," I'll make a commencement speech about being successful in the battle of life, I'll lie to you; and I don't want to.

Early this spring I met a musician, the composer Pauline Oliveros, [12] a beautiful woman like a grey rock in a streambed; and to a group of us, women, who were beginning to quarrel over theories in abstract, objective language—and I with my splendid Eastern-women's-college training in the father tongue was in the thick of the fight and going for the kill—to us, Pauline, who is sparing with words, said after clearing her throat, "Offer your experience as your truth." There was a short silence. When we started talking again, we didn't talk objectively, and we didn't fight. We went back to feeling our way into ideas, using the whole intellect not half of it, talking with one another, which involves listening. We tried to offer our experience to one another. Not claiming something: offering something.

How, after all, can one experience deny, negate, disprove, another 13 experience? Even if I've had a lot more of it, *your* experience is your truth. How can one being prove another being wrong? Even if you're a lot younger and smarter than me, *my* being is my truth. I can offer it; you don't have to take it. People can't contradict each other, only words can: words separated from experience for use as weapons, words that make the wound, the split between subject and object, exposing and exploiting the object but disguising and defending the subject.

People crave objectivity because to be subjective is to be embod- 14 ied, to be a body, vulnerable, violable. Men especially aren't used to that; they're trained not to offer but to attack. It's often easier for women to trust one another, to try to speak our experience in our own language, the language we talk to each other in, the mother tongue; so we empower one another.

But you and I have learned to use the mother tongue only at home 15 or safe among friends, and many men learn not to speak it at all. They're taught that there's no safe place for them. From adolescence on, they talk a kind of degraded version of the father tongue with each other—sports scores, job technicalities, sex technicalities, and TV politics. At home, to women and children talking mother tongue, they respond with a grunt and turn on the ball game. They have let themselves be silenced, and dimly they know it, and so resent speakers of the mother tongue; women babble, gabble all the time. . . . Can't listen to that stuff.

Our schools and colleges, institutions of the patriarchy, generally 16 teach us to listen to people in power, men or women speaking the father tongue; and so they teach us not to listen to the mother tongue, to what the powerless say, poor men, women, children: not to hear that as valid discourse.

I am trying to unlearn these lessons, along with other lessons I was 17 taught by my society, particularly lessons concerning the minds, work, works, and being of women. I am a slow unlearner. But I love my unteachers—the feminist thinkers and writers and talkers and poets and artists and singers and critics and friends, from Wollstonecraft and Woolf through the furies and glories of the seventies and eighties—I celebrate here and now the women who for two centuries have worked for our freedom, the unteachers, the unmasters, the unconquerors, the unwarriors, women who have at risk and at high cost offered their experience as truth. "Let us NOT praise famous women!"

Virginia Woolf scribbled in a margin when she was writing *Three Guineas*, and she's right, but still I have to praise these women and thank them for setting me free in my old age to learn my own language.

The third language, my native tongue, which I will never know 18 though I've spent my life learning it: I'll say some words now in this language. First a name, just a person's name, you've heard it before. Sojourner Truth. That name is a language in itself. But Sojourner Truth spoke the unlearned language; about a hundred years ago, talking it in a public place, she said, "I have been forty years a slave and forty years free and would be here forty years more to have equal rights for all." Along at the end of her talk she said, "I wanted to tell you a mite about Woman's Rights, and so I came out and said so. I am sittin' among you to watch; and every once and awhile I will come out and tell you what time of night it is." She said, "Now I will do a little singing. I have not heard any singing since I came here."[1]

Singing is one of the names of the language we never learn, and 19 here for Sojourner Truth is a little singing. It was written by Joy Harjo of the Creek people and is called "The Blanket Around Her."[2]

> maybe it is her birth
> which she holds close to herself
> or her death
> which is just as inseparable
> and the white wind
> that encircles her is a part
> just as
> > the blue sky
> hanging in turquoise from her neck
>
> oh woman
> remember who you are
> woman
> it is the whole earth

So what am I talking about with this "unlearned language"—po- 20 etry, literature? Yes, but it can be speeches and science, any use of language when it is spoken, written, read, heard as art, the way dancing is the body moving as art. In Sojourner Truth's words you hear the coming together, the marriage of the public discourse and the private experience, making a power, a beautiful thing, the true discourse of

---

[1]Sojourner Truth, in *The Norton Anthology of Literature by Women*, ed. Sandra M. Gilbert and Susan Gubar (New York: W. W. Norton & Co., 1985), pp. 255–56.

[2]Joy Harjo, "The Blanket Around Her," in *That's What She Said: Contemporary Poetry and Fiction by Native American Women*, ed. Rayna Green (Bloomington: Indiana University Press, 1984), p. 127.

reason. This is a wedding and welding back together of the alienated consciousness that I've been calling the father tongue and the undifferentiated engagement that I've been calling the mother tongue. This is their baby, this baby talk, the language you can spend your life trying to learn.

We learn this tongue first, like the mother tongue, just by hearing it or reading it; and even in our overcrowded, underfunded public high schools they still teach *A Tale of Two Cities* and *Uncle Tom's Cabin*; and in college you can take four solid years of literature, and even creative writing courses. But. It is all taught as if it were a dialect of the father tongue. 21

Literature takes shape and life in the body, in the womb of the mother tongue: always: and the Fathers of Culture get anxious about paternity. They start talking about legitimacy. They steal the baby. They ensure by every means that the artist, the writer, is male. This involves intellectual abortion by centuries of women artists, infanticide of works by women writers, and a whole medical corps of sterilizing critics working to purify the Canon, to reduce the subject matter and style of literature to something Ernest Hemingway could have understood. 22

But this is our native tongue, this is our language they're stealing: we can read it and we can write it, and what we bring to it is what it needs, the woman's tongue, that earth and savor, that relatedness, which speaks dark in the mother tongue but clear as sunlight in women's poetry, and in our novels and stories, our letters, our journals, our speeches. If Sojourner Truth, forty years a slave, knew she had the right to speak that speech, how about you? Will you let yourself be silenced? Will you listen to what men tell you, or will you listen to what women are saying? I say the Canon has been spiked, and while the Eliots speak only to the Lowells and the Lowells speak only to God, Denise Levertov comes stepping westward quietly, speaking to us.[3] 23

> There is no savor
> more sweet, more salt
>
> than to be glad to be
> what, woman
>
> and who, myself,
> I am, a shadow
>
> that grows longer as the sun
> moves, drawn out

[3]Denise Levertov, "Stepping Westward," in *Norton Anthology*, p. 1951.

on a thread of wonder.
If I bear burdens

they begin to be remembered
as gifts, goods, a basket

of bread that hurts
my shoulders but closes me

in fragrance. I can
eat as I go.

As I've been using the word "truth" in the sense of "trying hard 24
not to lie," so I use the words "literature," "art," in the sense of "living
well, living with skill, grace, energy"—like carrying a basket of bread
and smelling it and eating as you go. I don't mean only certain special
products made by specially gifted people living in specially privileged
garrets, studios, and ivory towers—"High" Art; I mean also all the low
arts, the ones men don't want. For instance, the art of making order
where people live. In our culture this activity is not considered an art,
it is not even considered work. "Do you work?"—and she, having
stopped mopping the kitchen and picked up the baby to come answer
the door, says, "No, I don't work." People who make order where people live are by doing so stigmatized as unfit for "higher" pursuits; so
women mostly do it, and among women, poor, uneducated, or old
women more often than rich, educated, and young ones. Even so,
many people want very much to keep house but can't, because they're
poor and haven't got a house to keep, or the time and money it takes,
or even the experience of ever having seen a decent house, a clean
room, except on TV. Most men are prevented from housework by intense cultural bias; many women actually hire another woman to do it
for them because they're scared of getting trapped in it, ending up like
the woman they hire, or like that woman we all know who's been
pushed so far over by cultural bias that she can't stand up, and crawls
around the house scrubbing and waxing and spraying germ killer on
the kids. But even on her kneebones, where you and I will never join
her, even she has been practicing as best she knows how a great, ancient, complex, and necessary art. That our society devalues it is evidence of the barbarity, the aesthetic and ethical bankruptcy, of our society.

As housekeeping is an art, so is cooking and all it involves—it in- 25
volves, after all, agriculture, hunting, herding. . . . So is the making of
clothing and all it involves. . . . And so on; you see how I want to
revalue the word "art" so that when I come back as I do now to talking
about words it is in the context of the great arts of living, of the woman
carrying the basket of bread, bearing gifts, goods. Art not as some ejac-
ulative act of ego but as a way, a skillful and powerful way of being in

the world. I come back to words because words are my way of being
in the world, but meaning by language as art a matter infinitely larger
than the so-called High forms. Here is a poem that tries to translate six
words by Hélène Cixous, who wrote *The Laugh of the Medusa*; she said,
"*Je suis là où ça parle,*" and I squeezed those six words like a lovely
lemon and got out all the juice I could, plus a drop of Oregon vodka.

> I'm there where
> it's talking
> Where that speaks I
> am in that talking place
>   Where
> that says
> my being is
>   Where
> my being there
> is speaking
> I am
>   And so
> laughing
> in a stone ear

The stone ear that won't listen, won't hear us, and blames us for its 26
being stone. . . . Women can babble and chatter like monkeys in the
wilderness, but the farms and orchards and gardens of language, the
wheatfields of art—men have claimed these, fenced them off: No Tres-
passing, it's a man's world, they say. And I say,

> oh woman
> remember who you are
> woman
> it is the whole earth

We are told, in words and not in words, we are told by their deafness,
by their stone ears, that our experience, the life experience of women,
is not valuable to men—therefore not valuable to society, to humanity.
We are valued by men only as an element of their experience, as things
experienced; anything we may say, anything we may do, is recognized
only if said or done in their service.

One thing we incontestably do is have babies. So we have babies 27
as the male priests, lawmakers, and doctors tell us to have them, when
and where to have them, how often, and how to have them; so that is
all under control. But we are *not to talk about* having babies, because
that is not part of the experience of men and so nothing to do with reality, with civilization, and no concern of art.—A rending scream in
another room. And Prince Andrey comes in and sees his poor little

wife dead bearing his son—Or Levin goes out into his fields and thanks his God for the birth of his son—And we know how Prince Andrey feels and how Levin feels and even how God feels, but we don't know what happened. Something happened, something was done, which we know nothing about. But what was it? Even in novels by women we are only just beginning to find out what it is that happens in the other room—what women do.

Freud famously said, "What we shall never know is what a 28 woman wants." Having paused thoughtfully over the syntax of that sentence, in which WE are plural but "a woman" apparently has no plural, no individuality—as we might read that a cow must be milked twice a day or a gerbil is a nice pet—WE might go on then to consider whether WE know anything about, whether WE have ever noticed, whether WE have ever asked a woman what she *does*—what women do.

Many anthropologists, some historians, and others have indeed 29 been asking one another this question for some years now, with pale and affrighted faces—and they are beginning also to answer it. More power to them. The social sciences show us that speakers of the father tongue are capable of understanding and discussing the doings of the mothers, if they will admit the validity of the mother tongue and listen to what women say.

But in society as a whole the patriarchal mythology of what "a 30 woman" does persists almost unexamined, and shapes the lives of women. "What are you going to do when you get out of school?" "Oh, well, just like any other woman, I guess I want a home and family"— and that's fine, but what is this home and family just like other women's? Dad at work, mom home, two kids eating apple pie? This family, which our media and now our government declare to be normal and impose as normative, this nuclear family now accounts for seven percent of the arrangements women live in in America. Ninety-three percent of women don't live that way. They don't do that. Many wouldn't if you gave it to them with bells on. Those who want that, who believe it's their one true destiny—what's their chance of achieving it? They're on the road to Heartbreak House.

But the only alternative offered by the patriarchal mythology is 31 that of the Failed Woman—the old maid, the barren woman, the castrating bitch, the frigid wife, the lezzie, the libber, the Unfeminine, so beloved of misogynists both male and female.

Now indeed there are women who want to be female men; their 32 role model is Margaret Thatcher, and they're ready to dress for success, carry designer briefcases, kill for promotion, and drink the Right Scotch. They want to buy into the man's world, whatever the cost. And if that's true desire, not just compulsion born of fear, O.K.; if you can't lick 'em join 'em. My problem with that is that I can't see it as a good life even for men, who invented it and make all the rules. There's power in it, but not the kind of power I respect, not the kind of power that sets anybody free. I hate to see an intelligent woman voluntarily double herself up to get under the bottom line. Talk about crawling! And when she talks, what can she talk but father tongue? If she's the mouthpiece for the man's world, what has she got to say for herself?

Some women manage it—they may collude, but they don't sell out 33 as women; and we know that when they speak for those who, in the man's world, are the others: women, children, the poor . . . .

But it is dangerous to put on Daddy's clothes, though not, per- 34 haps, as dangerous as it is to sit on Daddy's knees.

There's no way you can offer your experience as your truth if you 35 deny your experience, if you try to be a mythical creature, the dummy woman who sits there on Big Daddy's lap. Whose voice will come out of her prettily hinged jaw? Who is it says yes all the time? Oh yes, yes, I will. Oh I don't know, you decide. Oh I can't do that. Yes hit me, yes rape me, yes save me, oh yes. That is how A Woman talks, the one in What-we-shall-never-know-is-what-A-Woman-wants.

A Woman's place, need I say, is in the home, plus at her volunteer 36 work or the job where she's glad to get sixty cents for doing what men get paid a dollar for but that's because she's always on pregnancy leave but childcare? No! A Woman is home caring for her children! even if she can't. Trapped in this well-built trap, A Woman blames her mother for luring her into it, while ensuring that her own daughter never gets out; she recoils from the idea of sisterhood and doesn't be-lieve women have friends, because it probably means something un-natural, and anyhow, A Woman is afraid of women. She's a male con-struct, and she's afraid women will deconstruct her. She's afraid of everything, because she can't change. Thighs forever thin and shining hair and shining teeth and she's my Mom, too, all seven percent of her. And she never grows old.

There are old women—little old ladies, as people always say; little 37 bits, fragments of the great dummy statue goddess A Woman. No-body hears if old women say yes or no, nobody pays them sixty cents for anything. Old men run things. Old men run the show, press the buttons, make the wars, make the money. In the man's world, the old man's world, the young men run and run and run until they drop, and some of the young women run with them. But old women live in the cracks, between the walls, like roaches, like mice, a rustling sound, a squeaking. Better lock up the cheese, boys. It's terrible, you turn up a corner of civilization and there are all these old women running around on the wrong side—

I say to you, you know, you're going to get old. And you can't 38 hear me. I squeak between the walls. I've walked through the mirror and am on the other side, where things are all backwards. You may look with a good will and a generous heart, but you can't see anything in the mirror but your own face; and I, looking from the dark side and seeing your beautiful young faces, see that that's how it should be.

But when you look at yourself in the mirror, I hope you see your- 39 self. Not one of the myths. Not a failed man—a person who can never succeed because success is basically defined as being male—and not a failed goddess, a person desperately trying to hide herself in the dummy Woman, the image of men's desires and fears. I hope you look away from those myths and into your own eyes, and see your own strength. You're going to need it. I hope you don't try to take your strength from men, or from a man. Secondhand experience breaks down a block from the car lot. I hope you'll take and make your own soul; that you'll feel your life for yourself pain by pain and joy by joy; that you'll feed your life, eat, "eat as you go"—you who nourish, be nourished!

If being a cog in the machine or a puppet manipulated by others 40 isn't what you want, you can find out what you want, your needs, de- sires, truths, powers, by accepting your own experience as a woman, as this woman, this body, this person, your hungry self. On the maps drawn by men there is an immense white area, terra incognita, where most women live. That country is all yours to explore, to inhabit, to describe.

But none of us lives there alone. Being human isn't something peo- 41 ple can bring off alone; we need other people in order to be people. We need one another.

If a woman sees other women as Medusa, fears them, turns a stone 42 ear to them, these days, all her hair may begin to stand up on end hiss- ing, *Listen, listen, listen!* Listen to other women, your sisters, your mothers, your grandmothers—if you don't hear them how will you ever understand what your daughter says to you?

And the men who can talk, converse with you, not trying to talk 43 through the dummy Yes-Woman, the men who can accept your expe- rience as valid—when you find such a man love him, honor him! But don't obey him. I don't think we have any right to obedience. I think we have a responsibility to freedom.

And especially to freedom of speech. Obedience is silent. It does 44 not answer. It is contained. Here is a disobedient woman speaking, Wendy Rose of the Hopi and Miwok people, saying in a poem called "The Parts of a Poet,"[4]

> parts of me are pinned
> to earth, parts of me

---

[4]Wendy Rose, "The Parts of a Poet," in *That's What She Said*, p. 204.

undermine song, parts
of me spread on the water,
parts of me form a rainbow
bridge, parts of me follow
the sandfish, parts of me
are a woman who judges.

Now this is what I want: I want to hear your judgments. I am sick 45
of the silence of women. I want to hear you speaking all the languages,
offering your experience as your truth, as human truth, talking about
working, about making, about unmaking, about eating, about cooking,
about feeding, about taking in seed and giving out life, about killing,
about feeling, about thinking; about what women do; about what men
do; about war, about peace; about who presses the buttons and what
buttons get pressed and whether pressing buttons is in the long run a
fit occupation for human beings. There's a lot of things I want to hear
you talk about.

This is what I don't want: I don't want what men have. I'm glad to 46
let them do their work and talk their talk. But I do not want and will
not have them saying or thinking or telling us that theirs is the only fit
work or speech for human beings. Let them not take our work, our
words, from us. If they can, if they will, let them work with us and talk
with us. We can all talk mother tongue, we can all talk father tongue,
and together we can try to hear and speak that language which may be
our truest way of being in the world, we who speak for a world that
has no words but ours.

I know that many men and even women are afraid and angry 47
when women do speak, because in this barbaric society, when women
speak truly they speak subversively—they can't help it: if you're un-
derneath, if you're kept down, you break out, you subvert. We are vol-
canoes. When we women offer our experience as our truth, as human
truth, all the maps change. There are new mountains.

That's what I want—to hear you erupting. You young Mount St. 48
Helenses who don't know the power in you—I want to hear you. I want
to listen to you talking to each other and to us all: whether you're writing an article or a poem or a letter or teaching a class or talking with
friends or reading a novel or making a speech or proposing a law or giving a judgment or singing the baby to sleep or discussing the fate of na-
tions, I want to hear you. Speak with a woman's tongue. Come out and
tell us what time of night it is! Don't let us sink back into silence. If we
don't tell our truth, who will? Who'll speak for my children, and yours?

So I end with the end of a poem by Linda Hogan of the Chickasaw 49
people, called "The Women Speaking."[5]

---

[5]Linda Hogan, "The Women Speaking," in ibid., p. 172.

Daughters, the women are speaking.
They arrive
over the wise distances
on perfect feet.
Daughters, I love you.

Working with the Text

1. Le Guin describes three different languages in her essay. What are they? What are the characteristics of each one? How are they different from each other?
2. What does Le Guin mean when she says that the "mother tongue" is "the language of all children and most women"?
3. Which does Le Guin say is more "powerful," the mother tongue or the father tongue? What are the consequences of this difference in power? That is, since one is more powerful than the other, what is it able to do to the other?
4. Which of the three languages or "tongues" that Le Guin defines do you think she is trying to use in her essay? Or does she use aspects of all three? Explain your answer by analyzing specific passages.

Working beyond the Text

1. According to Le Guin, when, where, and why is each of the three "tongues" she identifies spoken? Do you see the three languages functioning in your own life in any ways? In what situations?
2. What and where is Bryn Mawr? To whom is Le Guin speaking and at what occasion? Look for every passage in the essay where Le Guin directly addresses the audience. How does speaking to that audience help shape Le Guin's message and the way she expresses it?
3. Le Guin makes allusions to many writers and their works: Newton, Marx, Darwin, Freud, Boas, Foucault, Wollstonecraft, Woolf, Sojourner Truth, Medusa, *Three Guineas*, Joy Harjo, *A Tale of Two Cities*, *Uncle Tom's Cabin*, Ernest Hemingway, Linda Hogan. Which names do you recognize, and which might you look up? (You might make a visit to the library.) How might any of the allusions help communicate some part of Le Guin's thesis?
4. Le Guin asserts that one dialect of "the father tongue" is "speechmaking." What speeches have you made in your life? How did you feel about them? Would you agree that you adopted "the father tongue" as Le Guin defines it?

UNIT TWO

CREATING A SELF

How to Tame a Wild Tongue
Gloria Anzaldúa

Gloria Anzaldúa describes herself as a "Chicana tejana lesbian-feminist poet and fiction writer." She is the author of *Borderlands/La Frontera: The New Mestiza* and editor of the important collections of minority women's writing *This Bridge Called My Back* and *Making Face, Making Soul/Hacienda Caras.* In the essay that follows, which is a chapter from *Borderlands/La Frontera* (1987), Anzaldúa talks about learning to speak in the midst of forces trying to keep her silent.

"We're going to have to control your tongue," the dentist says, 1 pulling out all the metal from my mouth. Silver bits plop and tinkle into the basin. My mouth is a motherlode.

The dentist is cleaning out my roots. I get a whiff of the stench 2 when I gasp. "I can't cap that tooth yet, you're still draining," he says.

"We're going to have to do something about your tongue," I hear 3 the anger rising in his voice. My tongue keeps pushing out the wads of cotton, pushing back the drills, the long thin needles. "I've never seen anything as strong or as stubborn," he says. And I think, how do you tame a wild tongue, train it to be quiet, how do you bridle and saddle it? How do you make it lie down?

> "Who is to say that robbing a people of
> its language is less violent than war?"
> —Ray Gwyn Smith[1]

I remember being caught speaking Spanish at recess—that was 4 good for three licks on the knuckles with a sharp ruler. I remember being sent to the corner of the classroom for "talking back" to the Anglo teacher when all I was trying to do was tell her how to pronounce my name. "If you want to be American, speak 'American.' If you don't like it, go back to Mexico where you belong."

---

[1]Ray Gwyn Smith, *Moorland Is Cold Country,* unpublished book.

"I want you to speak English. *Pa' hallar buen trabajo tienes que saber* 5
*hablar el inglés bien. Qué vale toda tu educación si todavía hables inglés con
un* 'accent,'" my mother would say, mortified that I spoke English like
a Mexican. At Pan American University, I, and all Chicano students
were required to take two speech classes. Their purpose: to get rid of
our accents.

Attacks on one's form of expression with the intent to censor are a 6
violation of the First Amendment. *El Anglo con cara de inocente nos ar-
rancó la lengua.* Wild tongues can't be tamed, they can only be cut out.

Overcoming the Tradition of Silence

Ahogadas, escupimos el oscuro.
Peleando con nuestra propia sombra
el silencio nos sepulta.

En boca cerrada no entran moscas. "Flies don't enter a closed mouth" 7
is a saying I kept hearing when I was a child. *Ser habladora* was to be a
gossip and a liar, to talk too much. *Muchachitas bien criadas,* well-bred
girls don't answer back. *Es una falta de respeto* to talk back to one's
mother or father. I remember one of the sins I'd recite to the priest in
the confession box the few times I went to confession: talking back to
my mother, *hablar pa' 'tras, replar. Hocicona, repelona, chismosa,* having a
big mouth, questioning, carrying tales are all signs of being *mal criada.*
In my culture they are all words that are derogatory if applied to
women—I've never heard them applied to men.

The first time I heard two women, a Puerto Rican and a Cuban, 8
say the word *"nosotras,"* I was shocked. I had not known the word existed. Chicanos use *nosotros* whether we're male or female. We are
robbed of our female being by the masculine plural. Language is a
male discourse.

> And our tongues have become
> dry   the wilderness has
> dried out our tongues   and
> we have forgotten speech.
>   —Irena Klepfisz[2]

Even our own people, other Spanish speakers *nos quieren poner* 9
candados en la boca. They would hold us back with their bag of *reglas de
academia.*

---

[2]Irena Klepfisz, *"Di rayze aheym*/The Journey Home," in *The Tribe of Dina: A Jewish Women's Anthology,* Melanie Kaye/Kantrowitz and Irena Klepfisz, eds. (Montpelier, VT: Sinister Wisdom
Books, 1986), 49.

Oyé como ladra: el lenguaje de la frontera

Quien tiene boca se equivoca.
—Mexican saying

"*Pocho,* cultural traitor, you're speaking the oppressor's language 10
by speaking English, you're ruining the Spanish language," I have
been accused by various Latinos and Latinas. Chicano Spanish is considered by the purist and by most Latinos deficient, a mutilation of
Spanish.

But Chicano Spanish is a border tongue which developed natu- 11
rally. Change, *evolución, enriquecimiento de palabras nuevas por invención
o adopción* have created variants of Chicano Spanish, *un nuevo lenguaje.
Un lenguaje que corresponde a un modo de vivir.* Chicano Spanish is not
incorrect; it is a living language.

For a people who are neither Spanish nor live in a country in 12
which Spanish is the first language; for a people who live in a country
in which English is the reigning tongue but who are not Anglo; for a
people who cannot identify with either standard (formal, Castillian)
Spanish nor standard English, what recourse is left to them but to create their own language? A language which they can connect their
identity to, one capable of communicating the realities and values true
to themselves—a language with terms that are neither *español ni inglés,*
but both. We speak a *patois,* a forked tongue, a variation of two languages.

Chicano Spanish sprang out of the Chicanos' need to identify our- 13
selves as a distinct people. We needed a language with which we
could communicate with ourselves, a secret language. For some of us,
language is a homeland closer than the Southwest—for many Chicanos today live in the Midwest and the East. And because we are a
complex, heterogeneous people, we speak many languages. Some of
the languages we speak are:

1. Standard English
2. Working class and slang English
3. Standard Spanish
4. Standard Mexican Spanish
5. North Mexican Spanish dialect
6. Chicano Spanish (Texas, New Mexico, Arizona and California
   have regional variations)
7. Tex-Mex
8. *Pachuco* (called *caló*)

My "home" tongues are the languages I speak with my sister and 14
brothers, with my friends. They are the last five listed, with 6 and 7

being closest to my heart. From school, the media and job situations, I've picked up standard and working class English. From Mamagrande Locha and from reading Spanish and Mexican literature, I've picked up Standard Spanish and Standard Mexican Spanish. From *los recién llegados*, Mexican immigrants, and *braceros*, I learned the North Mexican dialect. With Mexicans I'll try to speak either Standard Mexican Spanish or the North Mexican dialect. From my parents and Chicanos living in the Valley, I picked up Chicano Texas Spanish, and I speak it with my mom, younger brother (who married a Mexican and who rarely mixes Spanish with English), and aunts and older relatives.

With Chicanas from *Nuevo México* or *Arizona* I will speak Chicano 15 Spanish a little, but often they don't understand what I'm saying. With most California Chicanas I speak entirely in English (unless I forget). When I first moved to San Francisco, I'd rattle off something in Spanish, unintentionally embarrassing them. Often it is only with another Chicana *tejana* that I can talk freely.

Words distorted by English are known as anglicisms or *pochismos*. 16 The *pocho* is an anglicized Mexican or American of Mexican origin who speaks Spanish with an accent characteristic of North Americans and who distorts and reconstructs the language according to the influence of English.[3] Tex-Mex, or Spanglish, comes most naturally to me. I may switch back and forth from English to Spanish in the same sentence or in the same word. With my sister and my brother Nune and with Chicano *tejano* contemporaries I speak in Tex-Mex.

From kids and people my own age I picked up *Pachuco. Pachuco* 17 (the language of the zoot suiters) is a language of rebellion, both against Standard Spanish and Standard English. It is a secret language. Adults of the culture and outsiders cannot understand it. It is made up of slang words from both English and Spanish. *Ruca* means girl or woman, *vato* means guy or dude, *chale* means no, *simón* means yes, *churro* is sure, talk is *periquiar, pigionear* means petting, *que gacho* means how nerdy, *ponte áquila* means watch out, death is called *la pelona*. Through lack of practice and not having others who can speak it, I've lost most of the *Pachuco* tongue.

Chicano Spanish

Chicanos, after 250 years of Spanish/Anglo colonization have de- 18 veloped significant differences in the Spanish we speak. We collapse two adjacent vowels into a single syllable and sometimes shift the stress in certain words such as *maíz/maiz, cohete/cuete*. We leave out certain

[3]R.C. Ortega, *Dialectología Del Barrio*, trans. Hortencia S. Alwan (Los Angeles, CA: R.C. Ortega Publisher & Bookseller, 1977), 132.

consonants when they appear between vowels: *lado/lao, mojado/mojao*.
Chicanos from South Texas pronounce *f* as *j* as in *jue (fue)*. Chicanos use
"archaisms," words that are no longer in the Spanish language, words
that have been evolved out. We say *semos, truje, haiga, ansina,* and *naiden*.
We retain the "archaic" *j*, as in *jalar*, that derives from an earlier *h*, (the
French *halar* or the Germanic *halon* which was lost to standard Spanish
in the 16th century), but which is still found in several regional dialects
such as the one spoken in South Texas. (Due to geography, Chicanos
from the Valley of South Texas were cut off linguistically from other
Spanish speakers. We tend to use words that the Spaniards brought
over from Medieval Spain. The majority of the Spanish colonizers in
Mexico and the Southwest came from Extremadura—Hernán Cortés
was one of them—and Andalucía. Andalucians pronounce *ll* like a *y*,
and their *d*'s tend to be absorbed by adjacent vowels: *tirado* becomes
tirao. They brought *el lenguaje popular, dialectos y regionalismos*.[4])

Chicanos and other Spanish speakers also shift *ll* to *y* and *z* to *s*.[5] We   19
leave out initial syllables, saying *tar* for *estar, toy* for *estoy, hora* for *ahora*
(*cubanos* and *puertorriqueños* also leave out initial letters of some words.)
We also leave out the final syllable such as *pa* for *para*. The intervocalic
y, the *ll* as in *tortilla, ella, botella*, gets replaced by *tortia* or *tortiya, ea, botea*.
We add an additional syllable at the beginning of certain words: *atocar*
for *tocar, agastar* for *gastar*. Sometimes we'll say *lavaste las vacijas*, other
times *lavates* (substituting the *ates* verb endings for the *aste*).

We use anglicisms, words borrowed from English: *bola* from ball,   20
carpeta from carpet, *máchina de lavar* (instead of *lavadora*) from washing
rnachine. Tex-Mex argot, created by adding a Spanish sound at the beginning or end of an English word such as *cookiar* for cook, *watchar* for
watch, *parkiar* for park, and *rapiar* for rape, is the result of the pressures on Spanish speakers to adapt to English.

We don't use the word *vosotros/as* or its accompanying verb form.   21
We don't say *claro* (to mean yes), *imagínate*, or *me emociona*, unless we
picked up Spanish from Latinas, out of a book, or in a classroom.
Other Spanish-speaking groups are going through the same, or similar, development in their Spanish.

Linguistic Terrorism

> *Deslenguadas. Somos los del español deficiente*. We are your linguis-
> tic nightmare, your linguistic aberration, your linguistic *mestisaje*, the
> subject of your *burla*. Because we speak with tongues of fire we are

---

[4] Eduardo Hernandéz-Chávez, Andrew D. Cohen, and Anthony F. Beltramo, *El Lenguaje de los Chicanos: Regional and Social Characteristics of Language Used By Mexican Americans* (Arlington, VA: Center for Applied Linguistics, 1975), 39.

[5] Hernandéz-Chávez, xvii.

culturally crucified. Racially, culturally and linguistically *somos huér-fanos*—we speak an orphan tongue.

Chicanas who grew up speaking Chicano Spanish have internal- 22 ized the belief that we speak poor Spanish. It is illegitimate, a bastard language. And because we internalize how our language has been used against us by the dominant culture, we use our language differences against each other.

Chicana feminists often skirt around each other with suspicion 23 and hesitation. For the longest time I couldn't figure it out. Then it dawned on me. To be close to another Chicana is like looking into the mirror. We are afraid of what we'll see there. *Pena.* Shame. Low estimation of self. In childhood we are told that our language is wrong. Repeated attacks on our native tongue diminish our sense of self. The attacks continue throughout our lives.

Chicanas feel uncomfortable talking in Spanish to Latinas, afraid 24 of their censure. Their language was not outlawed in their countries. They had a whole lifetime of being immersed in their native tongue; generations, centuries in which Spanish was a first language, taught in school, heard on radio and TV, and read in the newspaper.

If a person, Chicana or Latina, has a low estimation of my native 25 tongue, she also has a low estimation of me. Often with *mexicanas y latinas* we'll speak English as a neutral language. Even among Chicanas we tend to speak English at parties or conferences. Yet, at the same time, we're afraid the other will think we're *agringadas* because we don't speak Chicano Spanish. We oppress each other trying to out-Chicano each other, vying to be the "real" Chicanas, to speak like Chicanos. There is no one Chicano language just as there is no one Chicano experience. A monolingual Chicana whose first language is English or Spanish is just as much a Chicana as one who speaks several variants of Spanish. A Chicana from Michigan or Chicago or Detroit is just as much a Chicana as one from the Southwest. Chicano Spanish is as diverse linguistically as it is regionally.

By the end of this century, Spanish speakers will comprise the 26 biggest minority group in the U.S., a country where students in high schools and colleges are encouraged to take French classes because French is considered more "cultured." But for a language to remain alive it must be used.[6] By the end of this century English, and not Spanish, will be the mother tongue of most Chicanos and Latinos.

So, if you want to really hurt me, talk badly about my language. 27 Ethnic identity is twin skin to linguistic identity—I am my language.

[6]Irena Klepfisz, "Secular Jewish Identity: Yidishkayt in America," in *The Tribe of Dina,* Kaye/Kantrowitz and Klepfisz, eds., 43.

Until I can take pride in my language, I cannot take pride in myself. Until I can accept as legitimate Chicano Texas Spanish, Tex-Mex and all the other languages I speak, I cannot accept the legitimacy of myself. Until I am free to write bilingually and to switch codes without having always to translate, while I still have to speak English or Spanish when I would rather speak Spanglish, and as long as I have to accommodate the English speakers rather than having them accommodate me, my tongue will be illegitimate.

I will no longer be made to feel ashamed of existing. I will have 28 my voice: Indian, Spanish, white. I will have my serpent's tongue—my woman's voice, my sexual voice, my poet's voice. I will overcome the tradition of silence.

> My fingers
> move sly against your palm
> Like women everywhere, we speak in code. . . .
> —Melanie Kaye/Kantrowitz[7]

"Vistas," corridos, y comida: *My Native Tongue*

In the 1960s, I read my first Chicano novel. It was *City of Night* by 29 John Rechy, a gay Texan, son of a Scottish father and a Mexican mother. For days I walked around in stunned amazement that a Chicano could write and could get published. When I read *I Am Joaquín*[8] I was surprised to see a bilingual book by a Chicano in print. When I saw poetry written in Tex-Mex for the first time, a feeling of pure joy flashed through me. I felt like we really existed as a people. In 1971, when I started teaching High School English to Chicano students, I tried to supplement required texts with works by Chicanos, only to be reprimanded and forbidden to do so by the principal. He claimed that I was supposed to teach "American" and English literature. At the risk of being fired, I swore my students to secrecy and slipped in Chicano short stories, poems, a play. In graduate school, while working toward a Ph.D., I had to "argue" with one advisor after the other, semester after semester, before I was allowed to make Chicano literature an area of focus.

Even before I read books by Chicanos or Mexicans, it was the 30 Mexican movies I saw at the drive-in—the Thursday night specials of $1.00 a carload—that gave me a sense of belonging. *"Vámonos a las vistas,"* my mother would call out and we'd all—grandmother, brothers,

---

[7]Melanie Kaye/Kantrowitz, "Sign," in *We Speak in Code: Poems and Other Writings* (Pittsburgh, PA: Motheroot Publications, Inc., 1980), 85.

[8]Rodolfo Gonzales, *I Am Joaquín/Yo Soy Joaquín* (New York, NY: Bantam Books, 1972). It was first published in 1967.

sister and cousins—squeeze into the car. We'd wolf down cheese and bologna white bread sandwiches while watching Pedro Infante in melodramatic tearjerkers like *Nosotros los pobres,* the first "real" Mexican movie (that was not an imitation of European movies). I remember seeing *Cuando los hijos se van* and surmising that all Mexican movies played up the love a mother has for her children and what ungrateful sons and daughters suffer when they are not devoted to their mothers. I remember the singing-type "westerns" of Jorge Negrete and Miquel Aceves Mejía. When watching Mexican movies, I felt a sense of homecoming as well as alienation. People who were to amount to something didn't go to Mexican movies, or *bailes* or tune their radios to *bolero, rancherita,* and *corrido* music.

The whole time I was growing up, there was *norteño* music, some- 31 times called North Mexican border music, or Tex-Mex music, or Chicano music, or *cantina* (bar) music. I grew up listening to *conjuntos,* three- or four-piece bands made up of folk musicians playing guitar, *baja sexto,* drums and button accordian, which Chicanos had borrowed from the German immigrants who had come to Central Texas and Mexico to farm and build breweries. In the Rio Grande Valley, Steve Jordan and Little Joe Hernández were popular, and Flaco Jiménez was the accordian king. The rhythms of Tex-Mex music are those of the polka, also adapted from the Germans, who in turn had borrowed the polka from the Czechs and Bohemians.

I remember the hot, sultry evenings when *corridos*—songs of love 32 and death on the Texas-Mexican borderlands—reverberated out of cheap amplifiers from the local *cantinas* and wafted in through my bedroom window.

Corridos first became widely used along the South Texas/Mexi- 33 can border during the early conflict between Chicanos and Anglos. The *corridos* are usually about Mexican heroes who do valiant deeds against the Anglo oppressors. Pancho Villa's song, *"La cucaracha,"* is the most famous one. *Corridos* of John F. Kennedy and his death are still very popular in the Valley. Older Chicanos remember Lydia Mendoza, one of the great border *corrido* singers who was called *la Gloria de Tejas.* Her *"El tango negro,"* sung during the Great Depression, made her a singer of the people. The ever present *corridos* narrated one hundred years of border history, bringing news of events as well as entertaining. These folk musicians and folk songs are our chief cultural mythmakers, and they made our hard lives seem bearable.

I grew up feeling ambivalent about our music. Country-western 34 and rock-and-roll had more status. In the 50s and 60s, for the slightly educated and *agringado* Chicanos, there existed a sense of shame at being caught listening to our music. Yet I couldn't stop my feet from thumping to the music, could not stop humming the words, nor hide from myself the exhilaration I felt when I heard it.

There are more subtle ways that we internalize identification, es- 35 pecially in the forms of images and emotions. For me food and certain smells are tied to my identity, to my homeland. Woodsmoke curling up to an immense blue sky; woodsmoke perfuming my grandmother's clothes, her skin. The stench of cow manure and the yellow patches on the ground; the crack of a .22 rifle and the reek of cordite. Homemade white cheese sizzling in a pan, melting inside a folded *tortilla*. My sister Hilda's hot, spicy *menudo, chile colorado* making it deep red, pieces of *panza* and hominy floating on top. My brother Carito barbequing *fajitas* in the backyard. Even now and 3,000 miles away, I can see my mother spicing the ground beef, pork and venison with *chile*. My mouth salivates at the thought of the hot steaming *tamales* I would be eating if I were home.

Si le preguntas a mi mamá, "¿Qué eres?"

> Identity is the essential core of who
> we are as individuals, the conscious
> experience of the self inside.
> —Kaufman[9]

Nosotros los Chicanos straddle the borderlands. On one side of us, 36 we are constantly exposed to the Spanish of the Mexicans, on the other side we hear the Anglos' incessant clamoring so that we forget our language. Among ourselves we don't say *nosotros los americanos, o nosotros los españoles, o nosotros los hispanos.* We say *nosotros los mexicanos* (by *mexicanos* we do not mean citizens of Mexico; we do not mean a national identity, but a racial one). We distinguish between *mexicanos del otro lado* and *mexicanos de este lado.* Deep in our hearts we believe that being Mexican has nothing to do with which country one lives in. Being Mexican is a state of soul—not one of mind, not one of citizenship. Neither eagle nor serpent, but both. And like the ocean, neither animal respects borders.

> *Dime con quien andas y te diré quien eres.*
> (Tell me who your friends are and I'll tell you who
> you are.)
> —Mexican saying

[9]Kaufman, 68.

Si le preguntas a mi mamá, "¿Qué eres?" te dirá. "Soy Mexicana." My 37
brothers and sisters say the same. I sometimes will answer *"soy mexi-cana"* and at others will say *"soy Chicana" o "soy tejana."* But I identified
as *"Raza"* before I ever identified as *"mexicana"* or *"Chicana"*.

As a culture, we call ourselves Spanish when referring to our- 38
selves as a linguistic group and when copping out. It is then that we
forget our predominant Indian genes. We are 70-80% Indian.[10] We call
ourselves Hispanic[11] or Spanish-American or Latin-American or Latin
when linking ourselves to other Spanish-speaking peoples of the West-ern hemisphere and when copping out. We call ourselves Mexican-American[12] to signify we are neither Mexican nor American, but more
the noun "American" than the adjective "Mexican" (and when cop-ping out).

Chicanos and other people of color suffer economically for not ac- 39
culturating. This voluntary (yet forced) alienation makes for psycho-logical conflict, a kind of dual identity—we don't identify with the
Anglo-American cultural values and we don't totally identify with the
Mexican cultural values. We are a synergy of the two cultures with
various degrees of Mexicanness or Angloness. I have so internalized
the borderland conflict that sometimes I feel like one cancels out the
other and we are zero, nothing, no one. *A reces no soy nada ni nadie. Pero
hasta cuando no lo soy, lo soy.*

When not copping out, when we know we are more than nothing, 40
we call ourselves Mexican, referring to race and ancestry; *mestizo* when
affirming both our Indian and Spanish (but we hardly ever own our
Black ancestry); Chicano when referring to a politically aware people
born and/or raised in the U.S.; *Raza* when referring to Chicanos; *te-janos* when we are Chicanos from Texas.

Chicanos did not know we were a people until 1965 when Cesar 41
Chavez and the farmworkers united and *I Am Joaquín* was published
and *la Raza Unida* party was formed in Texas. With that recognition,
we became a distinct people. Something momentous happened to the
Chicano soul—we became aware of our reality and acquired a name
and a language (Chicano Spanish) that reflected that reality. Now that
we had a name, some of the fragmented pieces began to fall together—who we were, what we were, how we had evolved. We began to get
glimpses of what we might eventually become.

Yet the struggle of identities continues, the struggle of borders is 42
our reality still. One day the inner struggle will cease and a true inte-

[10]Chávez, 88–90.

[11]"Hispanic" is derived from *Hispanis* (*España,* a name given to the Iberian Peninsula in ancient
times when it was part of the Roman Empire) and is a term designated by the U.S. government to
make it easier to handle us on paper.

[12]The Treaty of Guadalupe Hidalgo created the Mexican-American in 1848.

gration take place. In the meantime, *tenémos que hacer la lucha. ¿Quién está protegiendo los ranchos de mi gente? ¿Quién está tratando de cerrar la fisura entre la india y el blanco en nuestra sangre? El Chicano, si, el Chicano que anda como un ladrón en su propia casa.*

Los Chicanos, how patient we seem, how very patient. There is [43] the quiet of the Indian about us.[13] We know how to survive. When other races have given up their tongue, we've kept ours. We know what it is to live under the hammer blow of the dominant *norteamericano* culture. But more than we count the blows, we count the days the weeks the years the centuries the eons until the white laws and commerce and customs will rot in the deserts they've created, lie bleached. *Humildes* yet proud, *quietos* yet wild, *nosotros los mexicanos-Chicanos* will walk by the crumbling ashes as we go about our business. Stubborn, persevering, impenetrable as stone, yet possessing a malleability that renders us unbreakable, we, the *mestizas* and *mestizos,* will remain.

Working with the Text

1. Anzaldúa begins by writing about her dentist trying to control the author's tongue during a dental procedure. Why do you suppose she begins with this episode? How does it relate to her message in the essay as a whole?

2. What does Anzaldúa mean by having a "wild tongue"? And how does she say that the world attempts to "tame" it? Give examples from the essay of her tongue's "wildness" and of the world's attempts to "tame" it.

3. As a Hispanic, Anzaldúa feels pressure from both "Anglos" and other Hispanics. What kinds of pressures do these two groups put on those Anzaldúa defines as Chicano/a or mestizo/a? Point to specific passages where she describes these pressures.

4. Anzaldúa reflects on ways in which her "wild tongue" is tamed both as an ethnic minority and as a woman. Point to passages in which she emphasizes her special position as not only a minority but also a woman, and discuss the ways in which her experiences as a Chicana might differ from those of a Chicano.

5. From the second paragraph of her essay, Anzaldúa uses Spanish, and she continues to use Spanish throughout the essay. Why, do you think? Why does she take the chance, knowing that a portion of her audience speaks no Spanish?

---

[13]Anglos, in order to alleviate their guilt for dispossessing the Chicano, stressed the Spanish part of us and perpetuated the myth of the Spanish Southwest. We have accepted the fiction that we are Hispanic, that is Spanish, in order to accommodate ourselves to the dominant culture and its abhorrence of Indians. Chávez, 88–91.

Working beyond the Text

1. Anzaldúa states, "If a person . . . has a low estimation of my native tongue, she also has a low estimation of me." What does she mean by this? In your own experience, do you think that this statement is true? Explain what you mean with examples from your own experience or knowledge.

2. Anzaldúa discusses the many ethnic labels that people might try to give her or that she might give herself: Mexican, Hispanic, Chicana, Latina. What are the differences in meaning among the different ethnic labels? What labels are given to your ethnic group? Which do you prefer and why? What is so important about these words?

3. Anzaldúa makes a list of words peculiar to *Pachuco* Spanish, such as *ruca* for woman, *vato* for man, *chale* for no, *simón* for yes, and so on. You almost certainly belong to some group that has its own special vocabulary, words that people from outside the group would not understand. Make a list of the words and give their definitions. Why does your group use such words? Do other people consider such language "bad" language?

The Language We Know

Simon Ortiz

Born in 1941, Simon Ortiz is an award-winning poet and short story writer who also teaches creative writing. An Acoma Pueblo Indian from New Mexico, he is considered an important Native American writer. His works include *Naked in the Wind, Going for the Rain,* and *Fight Back: For the Sake of the People, for the Sake of the Land.* Much of his writing describes the difficulty and beauty of Native American life. In this essay, included in a 1987 anthology entitled *I Tell You Now: Autobiographical Essays by Native American Writers,* Ortiz speaks of the Native American language he learned to speak as a child and describes the attempts made by public school teachers to "Americanize" him through teaching him English.

I don't remember a world without language. From the time of my earliest childhood, there was language. Always language, and imagination, speculation, utters of sound. Words, beginnings of words. What would I be without language? My existence has been determined by language, not only the spoken but the unspoken, the language of speech and the language of motion. I can't remember a world without memory. Memory, immediate and far away in the past, something in the sinew, blood, ageless cell. Although I don't recall the exact moment I spoke or tried to speak, I know the feeling of something tugging at the core of the mind, something unutterable uttered into existence. It is language that brings us into existence. It is language that brings us into being in order to know life.

My childhood was the oral tradition of the Acoma Pueblo people—Aaquumeh hano—which included my immediate family of three older sisters, two younger sisters, two younger brothers, and my mother and father. My world was our world of the Aaquumeh in Mc-Cartys, one of the two villages descended from the ageless mother pueblo of Acoma. My world was our Eagle clan-people among other clans. I grew up in Deetziyamah, which is the Aaquumeh name for McCartys, which is posted at the exit off the present interstate highway in western New Mexico. I grew up within a people who farmed small garden plots and fields, who were mostly poor and not well schooled in the American system's education. The language I spoke was that of a struggling people who held ferociously to a heritage, culture, language, and land despite the odds posed them by the forces surrounding them since A.D. 1540, the advent of Euro-American colonization. When I began school in 1948 at the BIA (Bureau of Indian Affairs) day school in our village, I was armed with the basic ABC's and the phrases "Good morning, Miss Oleman" and "May I please be excused to go to the bathroom," but it was an older language that was my fundamental strength.

In my childhood, the language we all spoke was Acoma, and it was a struggle to maintain it against the outright threats of corporal punishment, ostracism, and the invocation that it would impede our progress towards Americanization. Children in school were punished and looked upon with disdain if they did not speak and learn English quickly and smoothly, and so I learned it. It has occurred to me that I learned English simply because I was forced to, as so many other Indian children were. But I know, also, there was another reason, and this was that I loved language, the sound, meaning, and magic of language. Language opened up vistas of the world around me, and it allowed me to discover knowledge that would not be possible for me to know without the use of language. Later, when I began to experiment with and explore language in poetry and fiction, I allowed that a portion of that impetus was because I had come to know English through forceful acculturation. Nevertheless, the underlying force was the beauty and poetic power of language in its many forms that instilled in me the desire to become a user of language as a writer, singer, and storyteller. Significantly, it was the Acoma language, which I don't use enough of today, that inspired me to become a writer. The concepts, values, and philosophy contained in my original language and the struggle it has faced have determined my life and vision as a writer.

In Deetziyamah, I discovered the world of the Acoma land and 4
people firsthand through my parents, sisters, and brothers, and my
own perceptions, voiced through all that encompasses the oral tradition, which is ageless for any culture. It is a small village, even smaller
years ago, and like other Indian communities it is wealthy with its
knowledge of daily event, history, and social system, all that make up
a people who have a many-dimensioned heritage. Our family lived in
a two-room home (built by my grandfather some years after he and
my grandmother moved with their daughters from Old Acoma),
which my father added rooms to later. I remember my father's work at
enlarging our home for our growing family. He was a skilled
stoneworker, like many other men of an older Pueblo generation who
worked with sandstone and mud mortar to build their homes and
pueblos. It takes time, persistence, patience, and the belief that the
walls that come to stand will do so for a long, long time, perhaps even
forever. I like to think that by helping to mix mud and carry stone for
my father and other elders I managed to bring that influence into my
consciousness as a writer.

Both my mother and my father were good storytellers and singers 5
(as my mother is to this day—my father died in 1978), and for their
generation, which was born soon after the turn of the century, they
were relatively educated in the American system. Catholic missionaries had taken both of them as children to a parochial boarding school
far from Acoma, and they imparted their discipline for study and
quest for education to us children when we started school. But it was
their indigenous sense of gaining knowledge that was most meaningful to me. Acquiring knowledge about life was above all the most important item; it was a value that one had to have in order to be fulfilled
personally and on behalf of his community. And this they insisted
upon imparting through the oral tradition as they told their children
about our native history and our community and culture and our "stories." These stories were common knowledge of act, event, and behavior in a close-knit pueblo. It was knowledge about how one was to
make a living through work that benefited his family and everyone
else.

Because we were a subsistence farming people, or at least tried to 6
be, I learned to plant, hoe weeds, irrigate and cultivate corn, chili,
pumpkins, beans. Through counsel and advice I came to know that the
rain which provided water was a blessing, gift, and symbol and that it
was the land which provided for our lives. It was the stories and songs
which provided the knowledge that I was woven into the intricate
web that was my Acoma life. In our garden and our cornfields I
learned about the seasons, growth cycles of cultivated plants, what
one had to think and feel about the land; and at home I became aware
of how we must care for each other: All of this was encompassed in an

intricate relationship which had to be maintained in order that life continue. After supper on many occasions my father would bring out his drum and sing as we, the children, danced to themes about the rain, hunting, land and people. It was all that is contained within the language of oral tradition that made me explicitly aware of a yet unarticulated urge to write, to tell what I had learned and was learning and what it all meant to me.

My grandfather was old already when I came to know him. I was 7 only one of his many grandchildren, but I would go with him to get wood for our households, to the garden to chop weeds, and to his sheep camp to help care for his sheep. I don't remember his exact words, but I know they were about how we must sacredly concern ourselves with the people and the holy earth. I know his words were about how we must regard ourselves and others with compassion and love; I know that his knowledge was vast, as a medicine man and an elder of his kiva, and I listened as a boy should. My grandfather represented for me a link to the past that is important for me to hold in my memory because it is not only memory but knowledge that substantiates my present existence. He and the grandmothers and grandfathers before him thought about us as they lived, confirmed in their belief of a continuing life, and they brought our present beings into existence by the beliefs they held. The consciousness of that belief is what informs my present concerns with language, poetry, and fiction.

My first poem was for Mother's Day when I was in the fifth grade, 8 and it was the first poem that was ever published, too, in the Skull Valley School newsletter. Of course I don't remember how the juvenile poem went, but it must have been certain in its expression of love and reverence for the woman who was the most important person in my young life. The poem didn't signal any prophecy of my future as a poet, but it must have come from the forming idea that there were things one could do with language and writing. My mother, years later, remembers how I was a child who always told stories—that is, tall tales—who always had explanations for things probably better left unspoken, and she says that I also liked to perform in school plays. In remembering, I do know that I was coming to that age when the emotions and thoughts in me began to moil to the surface. There was much to experience and express in that age when youth has a precociousness that is broken easily or made to flourish. We were a poor family, always on the verge of financial disaster, though our parents always managed to feed us and keep us in clothing. We had the problems, unfortunately ordinary, of many Indian families who face poverty on a daily basis, never enough of anything, the feeling of a denigrating self-consciousness, alcoholism in the family and community, the feeling that something was falling apart though we tried desperately to hold it all together.

My father worked for the railroad for many years as a laborer and 9 later as a welder. We moved to Skull Valley, Arizona, for one year in the early 1950s, and it was then that I first came in touch with a non-Indian, non-Acoma world. Skull Valley was a farming and ranching community, and my younger brothers and sisters and I went to a one-room school. I had never really had much contact with white people except from a careful and suspicious distance, but now here I was, totally surrounded by them, and there was nothing to do but bear the experience and learn from it. Although I perceived there was not much difference between *them* and *us* in certain respects, there was a distinct feeling that we were not the same either. This thought had been inculcated in me, especially by an Acoma expression—*Gaimuu Mericano*—that spoke of the "fortune" of being an American. In later years as a social activist and committed writer, I would try to offer a strong positive view of our collective Indianness through my writing. Nevertheless, my father was an inadequately paid laborer, and we were far from our home land for economic-social reasons, and my feelings and thoughts about that experience during that time would become a part of how I became a writer.

Soon after, I went away from my home and family to go to 10 boarding school, first in Santa Fe and then in Albuquerque. This was in the 1950s, and this had been the case for the past half-century for Indians: We had to leave home in order to become truly American by joining the mainstream, which was deemed to be the proper course of our lives. On top of this was termination, a U.S. government policy which dictated that Indians sever their relationship to the federal government and remove themselves from their lands and go to American cities for jobs and education. It was an era which bespoke the intent of U.S. public policy that Indians were no longer to be Indians. Naturally, I did not perceive this in any analytical or purposeful sense; rather, I felt an unspoken anxiety and resentment against unseen forces that determined our destiny to be un-Indian, embarrassed and uncomfortable with our grandparents' customs and strictly held values. We were to set our goals as American working men and women, singlemindedly industrious, patriotic, and unquestioning, building for a future which ensured that the United States was the greatest nation in the world. I felt fearfully uneasy with this, for by then I felt the loneliness, alienation, and isolation imposed upon me by the separation from my family, home, and community.

Something was happening; I could see that in my years at Catholic 11 school and the U.S. Indian school. I remembered my grandparents' and parents' words: Educate yourself in order to help your people. In that era and the generation who had the same experience I had, there was an unspoken vow: We were caught in a system inexorably, and we had to learn that system well in order to fight back. Without the motive of a fight-back we would not be able to survive as the people our heritage had lovingly bequeathed us. My diaries and notebooks began then, and though none have survived to the present, I know they contained the varied moods of a youth filled with loneliness, anger, and discomfort that seemed to have unknown causes. Yet at the same time, I realize now, I was coming to know myself clearly in a way that I would later articulate in writing. My love of language, which allowed me to deal with the world, to delve into it, to experiment and discover, held for me a vision of awe and wonder, and by then grammar teachers had noticed I was a good speller, used verbs and tenses correctly, and wrote complete sentences. Although I imagine that they might have surmised this as unusual for an Indian student whose original language was not English, I am grateful for their perception and attention.

During the latter part of that era in the 1950s of Indian termination 12 and the Cold War, a portion of which still exists today, there were the beginnings of a bolder and more vocalized resistance against the current U.S. public policies of repression, racism, and cultural ethnocide. It seemed to be inspired by the civil rights movement led by black people in the United States and by decolonization and liberation struggles worldwide. Indian people were being relocated from their rural homelands at an astonishingly devastating rate, yet at the same time they resisted the U.S. effort by maintaining determined ties with their heritage, returning often to their native communities, and establishing Indian centers in the cities they were removed to. Indian rural communities, such as Acoma Pueblo, insisted on their land claims and began to initiate legal battles in the areas of natural and social, political and economic human rights. By the retention and the inspiration of our native heritage, values, philosophies, and language, we would know ourselves as a strong and enduring people. Having a modest and latent consciousness of this as a teenager, I began to write about the experience of being Indian in America. Although I had only a romanticized image of what a writer was, which came from the pulp rendered by American popular literature, and I really didn't know anything about writing, I sincerely felt a need to say things, to speak, to release the energy of the impulse to help my people.

My writing in my late teens and early adulthood was fashioned 13 after the American short stories and poetry taught in the high schools of the 1940s and 1950s, but by the 1960s, after I had gone to college and dropped out and served in the military, I began to develop topics and themes from my Indian background. The experience in my village of Deetziyamah and Acoma Pueblo was readily accessible. I had grown up within the oral tradition of speech, social and religious ritual, elders' counsel and advice, countless and endless stories, everyday event, and the visual art that was symbolically representative of life all around. My mother was a potter of the well-known Acoma clayware, a traditional art form that had been passed to her from her mother and the generations of mothers before. My father carved figures from wood and did beadwork. This was not unusual, as Indian people know; there was always some kind of artistic endeavor that people set themselves to, although they did not necessarily articulate it as "Art" in the sense of Western civilization. One lived and expressed an artful life, whether it was in ceremonial singing and dancing, architecture, painting, speaking, or in the way one's social-cultural life was structured. When I turned my attention to my own heritage, I did so because this was my identity, the substance of who I was, and I wanted to write about what that meant. My desire was to write about the integrity and dignity of an Indian identity, and at the same time I wanted to look at what this was within the context of an America that had too often denied its Indian heritage.

To a great extent my writing has a natural political-cultural bent 14 simply because I was nurtured intellectually and emotionally within an atmosphere of Indian resistance. Aacquu did not die in 1598 when it was burned and razed by European conquerors, nor did the people become hopeless when their children were taken away to U.S. schools far from home and new ways were imposed upon them. The *Aaquumeh hano*, despite losing much of their land and surrounded by a foreign civilization, have not lost sight of their native heritage. This is the factual case with most other Indian peoples, and the clear explanation for this has been the fight-back we have found it necessary to wage. At times, in the past, it was outright armed struggle, like that of present-day Indians in Central and South America with whom we must identify; currently, it is often in the legal arena, and it is in the field of literature. In 1981, when I was invited to the White House for an event celebrating American poets and poetry, I did not immediately accept the invitation. I questioned myself about the possibility that I was merely being exploited as an Indian, and I hedged against accepting. But then I recalled the elders going among our people in the poor days of the 1950s, asking for donations—a dollar here and there, a sheep, perhaps a piece of pottery—in order to finance a trip to the nation's capital. They were to make another countless appeal on behalf of our people, to demand justice, to reclaim lost land even though there was only spare hope they would be successful. I went to the White House realizing that I was to do no less than they and those who had fought in the Pueblo Revolt of 1680, and I read my poems and sang songs that were later described as "guttural" by a Washington, D.C., newspaper. I suppose it is more or less understandable why such a view of Indian literature is held by many, and it is also clear why there should be a political stand taken in my writing and those of my sister and brother Indian writers.

The 1960s and afterward have been an invigorating and liberating 15 period for Indian people. It has been only a little more than twenty years since Indian writers began to write and publish extensively, but we are writing and publishing more and more; we can only go forward. We come from an ageless, continuing oral tradition that informs us of our values, concepts, and notions as native people, and it is amazing how much of this tradition is ingrained so deeply in our contemporary writing, considering the brutal efforts of cultural repression that was not long ago outright U.S. policy. We were not to speak our languages, practice our spiritual beliefs, or accept the values of our past generations; and we were discouraged from pressing for our natural rights as Indian human beings. In spite of the fact that there is to some extent the same repression today, we persist and insist in living, believing, hoping, loving, speaking, and writing as Indians. This is embodied in the language we know and share in our writing. We have always had this language, and it is the language, spoken and unspoken, that determines our existence, that brought our grandmothers and grandfathers and ourselves into being in order that there be a continuing life.

Working with the Text

1. Ortiz has an ambivalent attitude toward learning English. Why would he have reservations about learning it but at the same time be glad he learned it? Point to passages in which he expresses and explains these mixed feelings.
2. The title of this essay is "The Language We Know," and Ortiz does discuss many aspects of the languages he knows. However, he also includes details from his life that seem to have little to do with language. What are some of these other details? What is the connection between those other details and the details about language?
3. Ortiz has complicated things to say about the way language makes knowledge of our world possible. "It is language that brings us into being in order to know life." Where else in the essay does he explain this idea? What does he mean by it?
4. Who do you think is the audience Ortiz has in mind for this essay? Native Americans or non-Native Americans? College educated or relatively uneducated? Informed on the subject he writes about or not very well informed? How can you determine this? Point to specific aspects of the essay to form a portrait of Ortiz's audience.

Working beyond the Text

1. Ortiz says that when he went to school, getting caught speaking his Native American language would lead to "punishment, ostracism, and the invoca-

tion that it would impede our progress toward Americanization." In your own experience, what types of language use (English or otherwise) led teachers to punish students or led students to ostracize each other? Why?

2. An oral tradition is strongly associated with Native Americans, but every culture and every family has some kind of oral tradition. What is the oral tradition in your family or culture? What kinds of stories do you tend to tell, and why? You might narrate a favorite story and tell why it is repeated in your family.

3. What do you know or what can you find out about Native American languages? (You might make a visit to the library.) For example, how many Native American languages are spoken today, where, and by how many people? How do Native American languages differ from each other? What dictionaries, grammar books, and literature are written in what Native American languages?

The Girl Who Wouldn't Sing

Kit Yuen Quan

Kit Yuen Quan immigrated to the United States from Hong Kong as a small child and was raised speaking Chinese and English in San Francisco's Chinatown. In this essay, first published in Gloria Anzaldúa's 1990 anthology of writings by women of color entitled *Making Face, Making Soul/Haciendo Caras,* Quan tells about a life complicated by the conflicting expectations of traditional old-world parents and contemporary American society, and by the feeling of being a stranger in both the Chinese-speaking and the English-speaking worlds.

It was really hard deciding how to talk about language because I had to go through my blocks with language. I stumble upon these blocks whenever I have to write, speak in public or voice my opinions in a group of native English speakers with academic backgrounds. All of a sudden as I scramble for words, I freeze and am unable to think clearly. Minutes pass as I struggle to retrieve my thoughts until I finally manage to say something. But it never comes close to expressing what I mean. I think it's because I'm afraid to show who I really am. I cannot bear the thought of the humiliation and ridicule. And I dread having to use a language that has often betrayed my meaning. Saying what I need to say using my own words usually threatens the status quo.

People assume that I don't have a language problem because I can speak English, even when I ask them to take into account that English is my second language. This is the usual reaction I have gotten while working in the feminist movement. It's true that my language problems are different from those of a recent immigrant who cannot work outside of Chinatown because she or he doesn't speak enough English. Unlike my parents, I don't speak with a heavy accent. After twenty years of living in this country, watching American television and going through its school system, I have acquired adequate English skills to function fairly well. I can pass as long as I don't have to write anything or say what I really think around those whom I see as being more educated and articulate than I am. I can spend the rest of my life avoiding jobs that require extensive reading and writing skills. I can join the segment of the population that reads only out of necessity rather than for information, appreciation or enlightenment.

It's difficult for people to accept that I believe I have a literacy 3 problem because they do not understand the nature of my blocks with language. Learning anything new terrifies me, especially if it involves words or writing. I get this overwhelming fear, this heart-stopping panic that I won't understand it. I won't know how to do it. My body tenses up and I forget to breathe if there is a word in a sentence that I don't know or several sentences in a paragraph containing unfamiliar words. My confidence dwindles and I start to feel the ground falling from under me. In my frustration I feel like crying, running out or smashing something, but that would give me away, expose my defect. So I tune out or nod my head as if there is nothing wrong. I've had to cover it up in order to survive, get jobs, pass classes and at times to work and live with people who do not care to understand my reality.

Living with this fear leaves me exhausted. I feel backed against a 4 wall of self-doubt, pushed into a corner, defeated, unable to stretch or take advantage of opportunities. Beyond just being able to read and write well enough to get by, I need to be able to learn, understand, communicate, to articulate my thoughts and feelings, and participate fully without feeling ashamed of who I am and where I come from.

When I first arrived in San Francisco from Hong Kong at age 5 seven and a half, the only English I knew was the alphabet and a few simple words: cat, dog, table, chair. I sat in classrooms for two to three years without understanding what was being said, and cried while the girl next to me filled in my spelling book for me. In music class when other kids volunteered to go up in front of the class to play musical instruments, I'd never raise my hand. I wouldn't sing. The teacher probably wondered why there were always three Chinese girls in one row who wouldn't sing. In art class, I was so traumatized that I couldn't be creative. While other kids moved about freely in school, seeming to flow from one activity to the next, I was disoriented, out of step, feeling hopelessly behind. I went into a "survivor mode" and couldn't participate in activities.

I remember one incident in particular in the fourth grade during a 6
kickball game. I had just missed the ball when Kevin, the class jock,
came running across the yard and kicked me in the butt. Had I been
able to speak English, I might have screamed my head off or called for
the teacher, but I just stood there trying to numb out the pain, feeling
everyone's eyes on me. I wasn't sure it wasn't all part of the game.

At home I spoke the *sam yup* dialect of Cantonese with my par- 7
ents, who were completely unaware of the severity of my problems at
school. In their eyes I was very lucky to be going to school in America.
My father had had only a high school education before he had to start
working. And we children would not have had any chance to go to
college had we stayed in Hong Kong. We had flown over the Pacific
Ocean three times between the time I was seven and a half and eight
and a half because they were so torn about leaving their home to reset-
tle in a foreign country and culture. At the dinner table after a day of
toiling at their jobs and struggling with English, they aired their frustrations about the racism and discrimination they were feeling everywhere: at their jobs, on the bus, at the supermarket. Although they
didn't feel very hopeful about their own lives, they were comforted by
the fact that my brother and I were getting a good education. Both my
parents had made incredible sacrifices for my education. Life would
be easier for us, with more opportunities and options, because we
would know the language. We would be able to talk back or fight back
if need be. All we had to do was study hard and apply ourselves. So
every day after school I would load my bag full of textbooks and walk
up two hills to where we lived the first few years after we landed here.
I remember opening each book and reading out loud a paragraph or
two, skipping over words I didn't know until I gave up in frustration.

My parents thought that by mastering the English language, I 8
would be able to attain the Chinese American dream: a college education, a good-paying job, a house in the suburbs, a Chinese husband
and children. They felt intimidated and powerless in American society
and so clung tightly to me to fulfill their hopes and dreams. When I
objected to these expectations using my limited Chinese, I received
endless lectures. I felt smothered by their traditional values of how a
Chinese girl should behave and this was reason enough not to learn
more Chinese. Gradually language came to represent our two or more
opposing sets of values. If I asserted my individuality, wanted to go
out with my friends, had opinions of my own, or disagreed with their
plans for me, I was accused of becoming too smart for my own good
now that I had grown wings. *"Cheun neuih,* stupid girl. Don't think
you're better than your parents just because you know more English.
You don't know anything! We've eaten more salt than you've eaten
rice." Everything I heard in Chinese was a dictate. It was always one
more thing I wasn't supposed to do or be, one more way I wasn't sup-

posed to think. At school I felt stupid for not knowing the language. At home I was under attack for my rebellious views. The situation became intolerable after I came out to my parents as a lesbian.

When I ran away from home at sixteen, I sought refuge in the 9 women's community working part-time at a feminist bookstore. I felt like I had no family, no home, no identity or culture I could claim. In between hiding from my parents and crashing at various women's houses, I hung out in the Mission playing pool with other young dykes, got high, or took to the streets when I felt like I was going to explode. Sometimes at night I found myself sitting at the counter of some greasy spoon Chinese restaurant longing for a home-cooked meal. I was lonely for someone to talk to who could understand how I felt, but I didn't even have the words to communicate what I felt.

At the bookstore, I was discovering a whole other world: women, 10 dykes, feminists, authors, political activists, artists—people who read and talked about what they were reading. As exciting as it all was, I didn't understand what people were talking about. What was political theory? What was literary criticism? Words flew over my head like planes over a runway. In order to communicate with other feminists, most of whom were white or middle class or both, educated, and at least ten years older than me, I had to learn feminist rhetoric.

Given my uprooted and transplanted state, I have a difficult time 11 explaining to other people how I feel about language. Usually they don't understand or will even dispute what I'm saying. A lot of times I'll think it's because I don't have the right words, I haven't read enough books, or I don't know the language. That's how I felt all the time while working at a feminist bookstore. It wasn't only white, educated people who didn't understand how I felt. Women of color or Third World women who had class privilege and came from literary backgrounds thought the problem was more my age and my lack of political development. I often felt beaten down by these kinds of attitudes while still thinking that my not being understood was the result of my inability to communicate rather than an unreceptive environment.

Even though feminist rhetoric does give me words to describe 12 how I'm being oppressed, it still reflects the same racist, classist standards of the dominant society and of colleges and universities. I get frustrated because I constantly feel I'm being put down for what I'm saying or how I talk. For example, in a collective meeting with other women, I spoke about how I felt as a working class person and why I felt different from them. I told them they felt "middle class" to me because of the way they behaved and because of the values they had, that their "political vision" didn't include people with my experience and concerns. I tried to say all of this using feminist rhetoric, but when I used the term "working class," someone would argue, "You can't use that term. . . ." Because they were educated they thought they owned the language and so could say, "You can't use 'middle class,' you can't use 'working class,' because nowadays everybody is working class and it's just a matter of whether you're poor or comfortable." They did not listen to the point I was trying to make. They didn't care that I was sitting there in the circle stumbling along, struggling to explain how I felt oppressed by them and the structure and policies of the organization. Instead of listening to why I felt that way, they invalidated me for the way I used language and excluded me by defending themselves and their positions and claiming that my issues and feelings were "personal" and that I should just get over them.

Another example of my feeling excluded is when people in a room 13 make all sorts of literary allusions. They make me feel like I should have read those books. They throw around metaphors that leave me feeling lost and confused. I don't get to throw in my metaphors. Instead of acknowledging our different backgrounds and trying to include me in the discussion, they choose to ignore my feelings of isolation. I find that among feminists, white and colored, especially those who pride themselves on being progressive political activists with credentials, there's an assumption that if a person just read more, studied more, she would find the right words, the right way to use them, and even the right thoughts. A lot of times my language and the language of other working class, non-academic people become the target of scrutiny and criticism when others don't want to hear what we have to say. They convince themselves we're using the wrong words: "What definition are you using?" "What do you mean by that?" And then we get into debate about what was meant, we get lost in semantics and then we really don't know what we're saying.

Why should I try to use all of these different words when I'm 14 being manipulated and suppressed by those whose rhetoric is more developed, whether it's feminist, academic, or leftist?

Those of us who feel invisible or misunderstood when we try to 15 name what is oppressing us within supposedly feminist or progressive groups need to realize that our language is legitimate and valid. It comes from our families, our cultures, our class backgrounds, our experiences of different and conflicting realities. And we don't need to read another book to justify it. If I want to say *I'm working class,* I should be able to *say* I'm working class without having to read or quote Marx. But just saying that I'm working class never gives me enough of the understanding that I want. Because our experiences and feelings are far too complex to be capsulized in abstractions like "oppression," "sexism," "racism," etc., there is no right combination of these terms which can express why we feel oppressed.

I knew that I needed to go some place where some of my experi- 16 ences with language would be mirrored. Through the Refugee

Women's Program in the Tenderloin district of San Francisco, I started to tutor two Cambodian refugee girls. The Buth family had been in the U.S. for one and a half years. They lived, twelve people to a room, in an apartment building on Eddy Street half a block from the porno theaters. I went to their home one evening a week and on Sundays took the girls to the children's library. The doorbells in the building were out of order, so visitors had to wait to be let in by someone on their way out. Often I stood on their doorsteps watching the street life. The fragrant smell of jasmine rice wafting from the windows of the apartment building mixed with the smell of booze and piss on the street. Newspapers, candy wrappers and all kinds of garbage swept up by the wind colored the sidewalks. Cars honked and sped past while Asian, Black and white kids played up and down the street. Mothers carrying their babies weaved through loose gatherings of drunk men and prostitutes near the corner store. Around me I heard a medley of languages: Vietnamese, Chinese, Cambodian, English, Black English, Laotian.

Sometimes, I arrived to find Yan and Eng sitting on the steps be- 17 hind the security gate waiting to let me in. Some days they wore their school clothes, while on other days they were barefooted and wore their traditional sarongs. As we climbed the stairs up to their apartment, we inhaled fish sauce and curry and rice. Six-year-old Eng would chatter and giggle but Yan was quieter and more reserved. Although she was only eight years old, I couldn't help but feel like I was in the company of a serious adult. I immediately identified with her. I noticed how, whenever I gave them something to do, they didn't want to do it on their own. For example, they often got excited when I brought them books, but they wouldn't want to read by themselves. They became quiet and withdrawn when I asked them questions. Their answer was always a timid "I don't know," and they never asked a question or made a request. So I read with them. We did everything together. I didn't want them to feel like they were supposed to automatically know what to do, because I remembered how badly that used to make me feel.

Play time was the best part of our time together. All the little kids 18 joined in and sometimes even their older brothers. Everybody was so excited that they forgot they were learning English. As we played jigsaw sentences and word concentration and chickens and whales, I became a little kid again, except this time I wasn't alone and unhappy. When they made Mother's Day cards, I made a Mother's Day card. When they drew pictures of our field trip to the beach, I sketched pictures of us at the beach. When we made origami frogs and jumped them all over the floor, I went home and made dinosaurs, kangaroos, spiders, crabs and lobsters. Week after week, I added to my repertoire until I could feel that little kid who used to sit like the piece of unmolded clay in front of her in art class turn into a wide-eyed origami enthusiast.

As we studied and played in the middle of the room surrounded 19 by the rest of the family who were sleeping, nursing, doing homework, playing cards, talking, laughing or crying, Yan would frequently interrupt our lesson to answer her mother. Sometimes it was a long conversation, but I didn't mind because English was their second language. They spoke only Cambodian with their family. If they laughed at something on television, it was usually at the picture and not at the dialogue. English was used for schoolwork and to talk to me. They did not try to express their thoughts and feelings in English. When they spoke to each other, they were not alone or isolated. Whether they were living in a refugee camp in the Philippines or in Thailand or in a one-room apartment on Eddy Street, they were connected to each other through their language and their culture. They had survived war, losing family members, their country and their home, but in speaking their language, they were able to love and comfort each other. Sitting there on the bamboo mat next to the little girls, Eng and her younger sister Oeun, listening to their sweet little voices talking and singing, I understood for the first time what it was like to be a child with a voice and it made me remember my first love, the Chinese language.

While searching for an address, I came across a postcard of the San 20 Francisco-Oakland Bay Bridge. I immediately recognized it as the postcard I had sent to my schoolmate in Hong Kong when I first got here. On the back was my eight-and-a-half-year-old handwriting.

In English it says: 21

> Dear Kam Yee, I received your letter. You asked if I've been to school yet. Yes, I've already found a school. My family has decided to stay in America. My living surroundings are very nice. Please don't worry about me. I'm sorry it has taken so long for me to return your letter. Okay lets talk some more next time. Please give my regards to your parents and your family. I wish you happiness. Signed: Your classmate, Yuen Kit, August 30th.

The card, stamped "Return To Sender," is postmarked 1970. Al- 22 though I have sketchy memories of my early school days in Hong Kong, I still remember the day when Kam Yee and I found each other. The bell rang signaling the end of class. Sitting up straight in our chairs, we had recited "Goodbye, teacher" in a chorus. While the others were rushing out the door to their next class, I rose from my desk and slowly put away my books. Over my left shoulder I saw Kam Yee watching me. We smiled at each other as I walked over to her desk. I had finally made a friend. Soon after that my family left Hong Kong and I wrote my last Chinese letter.

All the time that I was feeling stupid and overwhelmed by lan- 23 guage, could I have been having the Chinese blues? By the time I was seven, I was reading the Chinese newspaper. I remember because there were a lot of reports of raped and mutilated women's bodies found in plastic bags on the side of quiet roads. It was a thrill when my father would send me to the newsstand on the corner to get his newspaper. Passing street vendors peddling sweets and fruit, I would run as quickly as I could. From a block away I could smell the stinky odor of *dauh fuh fa,* my favorite snack of slippery, warm, soft tofu in sweet syrup.

Up until a year ago, I could only recognize some of the Chinese 24 characters on store signs, restaurant menus and Chinese newspapers on Stockton and Powell Streets, but I always felt a tingle of excitement whenever I recognized a word or knew its sound, like oil sizzling in a wok just waiting for something to fry.

On Saturdays I sit with my Chinese language teacher on one of the 25 stone benches lining the overpass where the financial district meets Chinatown and links Portsmouth Square to the Holiday Inn Hotel. We have been meeting once a week for me to practice speaking, reading and writing Chinese using whatever material we can find. Sometimes I read a bilingual Chinese American weekly newspaper called the East West Journal, other times Chinese folk tales for young readers from the Chinatown Children's Library, or bilingual brochures describing free services offered by non-profit Chinatown community agencies, and sometimes even Chinese translations of Pacific Bell Telephone inserts. I look forward to these sessions where I reach inward to recover all those lost sounds that once were the roots of my childhood imagination. This exercise in trying to use my eight-year-old vocabulary to verbalize my thoughts as an adult is as scary as it is exhilarating. At one time Chinese was poetry to me. Words, their sounds and their rhythms, conjured up images that pulled me in and gave me a physical sense of their meanings. The Chinese characters that I wrote and practiced were pictographs of water, grass, birds, fire, heart and mouth. With my calligraphy brush made of pig's hair, I made the rain fall and the wind blow.

Now, speaking Chinese with my father is the closest I have felt to 26 coming home. In a thin but sage-like voice, he reflects on a lifetime of hard work and broken dreams and we slowly reconnect as father and daughter. As we sit across the kitchen table from one another, his old and tattered Chinese dictionary by his side, he tells me of the loving relationship he had with his mother, who encouraged him in his interest in writing and the movies. Although our immigrant experiences are generations apart and have been impacted differently by American culture, in his words I see the core of who I am. I cannot express my feelings fully in either Chinese or English or make him understand my choices. Though I am still grappling with accepting the enormous love behind the sacrifices he has made to give me a better life, I realize that with my ability to move in two different worlds I am the fruit of his labor.

For 85 cents, I can have unlimited refills of tea and *gai mei baau* at   27 The Sweet Fragrance Cafe on Broadway across from the World Theatre. After the first bite, the coconut sugar and butter ooze down my palm. Behind the pastry counter, my favorite clerk is consolidating trays of walnut cupcakes. Pointing to some round fried bread covered with sesame seeds, she urges the customer with "Four for a dollar, very fresh!"

Whole families from grandparents to babies sleeping soundly on   28 mothers' backs come here for porridge, pastries and coffee. Mothers stroll in to get sweets for little ones waiting at home. Old women carrying their own mugs from home come in to chat with their buddies. Workers wearing aprons smeared with pig's blood or fresh fish scales drop in for a bite during their break. Chinese husbands sit for hours complaining and gossiping not unlike the old women in the park.

A waitress brings bowls of beef stew noodles and pork liver por-   29 ridge. Smokers snub out their cigarettes as they pick up their chopsticks. The man across from me is counting sons and daughters on the fingers of his left hand: one son, another son, my wife, one daughter. He must have family in China waiting to immigrate.

The regulars congregate at the back tables, shouting opinions from   30 one end of the long table to the other. The Chinese are notorious for their loud conversations at close range that can easily be mistaken for arguments and fights until someone breaks into laughter or gives his companion a friendly punch. Here the drama of life is always unfolding in all different dialects. I may not understand a lot of it, but the chuckling, the hand gestures, the raising of voices in protest and in accusation, and the laughter all flow like music, like a Cantonese opera.

Twenty years seems like a long time, but it has taken all twenty   31 years for me to understand my language blocks and to find ways to help myself learn. I have had to create my own literacy program. I had to recognize that the school system failed to meet my needs as an immigrant and that this society and its institutions doesn't reflect or validate my experiences. I have to let myself grieve over the loss of my native language and all the years wasted in classrooms staring into space or dozing off when I was feeling depressed and hopeless. My various activities now help to remind me that my relationship with language is more complex than just speaking enough English to get by. In creative activity and in anything that requires words, I'm still eight years old. Sometimes I open a book and I still feel I can't read. It may take days or weeks for me to work up the nerve to open that book again. But I do open it and it gets a little easier each time that I work through the fear. As long as there are bakeries in Chinatown and as long as I have 85 cents, I know I have a way back to myself.

Working with the Text

1. Quan says that though she has lost something of her Chinese language and culture in the United States, "As long as there are bakeries in Chinatown and as long as I have 85 cents, I know I have a way back to myself." What does she mean?

2. Quan lacks confidence in her ability to speak and write English, and says she also has "limited Chinese." Both these conditions restrain or limit her life in various ways. What does she find herself unable to do? What does she learn to do about the situation?

3. Explain what Quan means when she says, "I had to recognize that the school system failed to meet my needs as an immigrant and that this society and its institutions doesn't reflect or validate my experiences." Relate these ideas to specific examples or illustrations in the essay.

4. Quan ends her essay, before the final paragraph, with a four-paragraph description of the Sweet Fragrance Cafe. Why? What might be the purpose of the description? What ideas might Quan intend to communicate with it? How do the ideas relate to the rest of the essay?

Working beyond the Text

1. Quan associates terrible emotions with having to speak in public, with having to write in school, and with having to read things she doesn't understand. These experiences are accompanied by feelings of "dread," "humiliation," "ridicule," "terror," and "overwhelming fear." Why does she feel these things? Have you ever felt any such emotions when you had to speak, read, or write? What was the situation?

2. Language is something that both separates Quan from her parents and connects her to them. In what ways? Many people experience a similar kind of separation from and connection to parents. Have you? If so, what form has it taken?

3. Quan talks about being able to "pass" among people who she imagines are "more educated and articulate" than she is. What does she mean? Why does she try to "pass"? What does she fear about not "passing"? What other people, perhaps including yourself, try to "pass," and in what ways?

4. Quan says that her home culture and poor education make her feel "excluded" in the world beyond her home. Excluded in what ways? Have you ever felt "excluded" in similar ways? When and why?

2

LEAVING HOME:

LANGUAGES IN CONFLICT

INTRODUCTION

One of the most vivid memories of many students' first year of college is sitting in class, struggling to pay attention, and not understanding a thing the teacher is talking about. Words fly out from the teacher's mouth: ontology, epistemology, teleology; feudalism, patriarchy, dialectical materialism; paradigm, red shift, Doppler effect; idealism, existentialism, phenomenology. The assigned readings may leave students feeling the same way their classes do: exhausted and frustrated, wondering whether they are really college material after all. Worst of all, everybody else seems to be doing fine, taking notes during lectures, asking intelligent questions, answering the questions the teacher asks.

Most students entering college have been fairly successful in school, or at least more successful than the classmates they left behind at graduation. They have no reason to wonder if they are in some ways "illiterate" by college standards. That is, though they are perfectly able as speakers, readers, and writers in some contexts, students may lack a kind of "academic literacy" that their teachers take for granted. Take a simple word like "capitalism," for example. A dictionary, even if a student tried to use it, might say something about an economic system involving private property. But it would tell nothing about the history of capitalism in Europe in the eighteenth and nineteenth centuries, the profound changes it brought about in our society, or the socialist revolutions fought against it from time to time. Most of all, the student would know little about the bad reputation of capitalism in many academic circles, especially if he or she comes from a cultural background in which the features of capitalism are highly valued. Little in the student's background would have prepared him or her to be "literate" in this sense.

In the essays in this chapter, writers talk about leaving home with a set of language skills and find that those skills are inadequate or actually in conflict with the new world of language they enter. For some people, the hardest transition is going into the first grade, especially when a language other than English is spoken in the home. For other people it's leaving the neighborhood for junior high or high school. For still others, it's leaving high school, where they have been successful with reading and writing skills that may have limited use in college. If they attend a university, they may discover that teachers may assume they know things they don't or expect them to have values and beliefs they don't possess.

For the writers in this chapter, encountering new languages beyond home and community can create problems of identity and loyalty. Will the new language and culture replace the old ones, and will a new cultural identity replace the old one? Will refusal to learn the new language lead to failure in school and in the larger world? What sorts of solutions might there be to these dilemmas?

Before You Read

Before you read any combination of essays in this chapter, you might prepare by doing any of the activities below as either class or small group discussions, or as formal or informal writing assignments. They are designed to help you find out what you already know about the issues discussed by the authors in the chapter, so you have some background for understanding what the authors say.

1. What are your strongest early memories of learning language in school? For example, do you remember learning to form letters and words? Do you remember learning the parts of speech and how to understand a sentence? Do you remember the first book you read for school? What do your memories suggest about the way we learn language in schools?

2. What in your life experience either prepared you or failed to prepare you for understanding the kind of language used in school? How can students be better prepared for understanding school language before they leave home for the first time as children?

3. Think about how "everyday language" is different from "school language." What does everyday language do that school language can't do? What does school language do that everyday language can't do?

4. Imagine many situations in which you might want to show that you "belong" (for example, on the job, in the classroom, writing an essay for class, in a supermarket, applying for a job, talking with friends). What styles of language would you use in each situation? Why?

After You Read

After you read any combination of essays in this chapter, you might follow up by doing any of the activities below as either class or small group discussions, or as formal or informal writing assignments. They are designed to help you extend what you have learned from the authors in the chapter by discovering new perspectives on the chapter's themes on your own.

1. How should children be taught how to read and write? What would be the features of an ideal language education, based on your experiences and the experiences of the writers in this chapter?

2. What special problems are faced by immigrants to the United States who do not speak English? You might interview a family member, friend, or classmate whose first language is not English, asking what problems they had and how they solved them (or failed to solve them). How do their experiences compare to any of those recounted by the writers in this chapter?

3. Using one of the essays in this chapter as a model, discuss a specific situation in which you felt a sense of belonging or alienation because of your use of (or inability to use) a certain kind of language. Tell the story of that situation, and try to explain the link between language and the sense of belonging or alienation in that situation.

4. Several of the writers in this chapter discuss their names: how their names changed in different settings, who had power over the names they would be known by, how names are an essential part of their sense of self and self-esteem. What names have you been known by, and in what situations? What do the various names tell about who you are and what different worlds you inhabit?

UNIT ONE

NEW LANGUAGES, NEW SELVES

Zami: A New Spelling of My Name

Audre Lorde

Audre Lorde was born in New York City and raised in Harlem. Her parents emigrated to the United States from Grenada. She is the author of many books of poetry, essays, and autobiography. *Zami: A New Spelling of My Name* is the story of her childhood and young adulthood, and in this excerpt from it she tells of her first experiences in school as a child too precocious to succeed in conventional ways.

When I was five years old and still legally blind, I started school in 1
a sight-conservation class in the local public school on 135th Street and
Lenox Avenue. On the corner was a blue wooden booth where white
women gave away free milk to Black mothers with children. I used to
long for some Hearst Free Milk Fund milk, in those cute little bottles
with their red and white tops, but my mother never allowed me to
have any, because she said it was charity, which was bad and demeaning, and besides the milk was warm and might make me sick.

The school was right across the avenue from the catholic school 2
where my two older sisters went, and this public school had been used
as a threat against them for as long as I could remember. If they didn't
behave and get good marks in schoolwork and deportment, they
could be "transferred." A "transfer" carried the same dire implications
as "deportation" came to imply decades later.

Of course everybody knew that public school kids did nothing but 3
"fight," and you could get "beaten up" every day after school, instead
of being marched out of the schoolhouse door in two neat rows like little robots, silent but safe and unattacked, to the corner where the
mothers waited.

But the catholic school had no kindergarten, and certainly not one 4
for blind children.

Despite my nearsightedness, or maybe because of it, I learned to 5
read at the same time I learned to talk, which was only about a year or
so before I started school. Perhaps *learn* isn't the right word to use for
my beginning to talk, because to this day I don't know if I didn't talk
earlier because I didn't know how, or if I didn't talk because I had
nothing to say that I would be allowed to say without punishment.
Self-preservation starts very early in West Indian families.

I learned how to read from Mrs. Augusta Baker, the children's li- 6
brarian at the old 135th Street branch library, which has just recently
been torn down to make way for a new library building to house the
Schomburg Collection on African-American History and Culture. If
that was the only good deed that lady ever did in her life, may she rest
in peace. Because that deed saved my life, if not sooner, then later,
when sometimes the only thing I had to hold on to was knowing I
could read, and that that could get me through.

My mother was pinching my ear off one bright afternoon, while I 7
lay spreadeagled on the floor of the Children's Room like a furious little brown toad, screaming bloody murder and embarrassing my
mother to death. I know it must have been spring or early fall, because
without the protection of a heavy coat, I can still feel the stinging sore-
ness in the flesh of my upper arm. There, where my mother's sharp
fingers had already tried to pinch me into silence. To escape those inexorable fingers I had hurled myself to the floor, roaring with pain as I
could see them advancing toward my ears again. We were waiting to
pick up my two older sisters from story hour, held upstairs on another
floor of the dry-smelling quiet library. My shrieks pierced the reveren-
tial stillness.

Suddenly, I looked up, and there was a library lady standing over 8
me. My mother's hands had dropped to her sides. From the floor
where I was lying, Mrs. Baker seemed like yet another mile-high
woman about to do me in. She had immense, light, hooded eyes and a
very quiet voice that said, not damnation for my noise, but "Would
you like to hear a story, little girl?"

Part of my fury was because I had not been allowed to go to that 9
secret feast called story hour since I was too young, and now here was
this strange lady offering me my own story.

I didn't dare to look at my mother, half-afraid she might say no, I 10
was too bad for stories. Still bewildered by this sudden change of
events, I climbed up upon the stool which Mrs. Baker pulled over for
me, and gave her my full attention. This was a new experience for me
and I was insatiably curious.

Mrs. Baker read me *Madeline,* and *Horton Hatches the Egg,* both of 11
which rhymed and had huge lovely pictures which I could see from
behind my newly acquired eyeglasses, fastened around the back of my
rambunctious head by a black elastic band running from earpiece to

earpiece. She also read me another storybook about a bear named Herbert who ate up an entire family, one by one, starting with the parents. By the time she had finished that one, I was sold on reading for the rest of my life.

I took the books from Mrs. Baker's hands after she was finished 12 reading, and traced the large black letters with my fingers, while I peered again at the beautiful bright colors of the pictures. Right then I decided I was going to find out how to do that myself. I pointed to the black marks which I could now distinguish as separate letters, different from my sisters' more grown-up books, whose smaller print made the pages only one grey blur for me. I said, quite loudly, for whoever was listening to hear, "I want to read."

My mother's surprised relief outweighed whatever annoyance she 13 was still feeling at what she called my whelpish carryings-on. From the background where she had been hovering while Mrs. Baker read, my mother moved forward quickly, mollified and impressed. I had spoken. She scooped me up from the low stool, and to my surprise, kissed me, right in front of everybody in the library, including Mrs. Baker.

This was an unprecedented and unusual display of affection in 14 public, the cause of which I did not comprehend. But it was a warm and happy feeling. For once, obviously, I had done something right.

My mother set me back upon the stool and turned to Mrs. Baker, 15 smiling.

"Will wonders never cease to perform!" Her excitement startled 16 me back into cautious silence.

Not only had I been sitting still for longer than my mother would 17 have thought possible, and sitting quietly. I had also spoken rather than screamed, something that my mother, after four years and a lot of worry, had despaired that I would ever do. Even one intelligible word was a very rare event for me. And although the doctors at the clinic had clipped the little membrane under my tongue so I was no longer tongue-tied, and had assured my mother that I was not retarded, she still had her terrors and her doubts. She was genuinely happy for any possible alternative to what she was afraid might be a dumb child. The ear-pinching was forgotten. My mother accepted the alphabet and picture books Mrs. Baker gave her for me, and I was on my way.

I sat at the kitchen table with my mother, tracing letters and call- 18 ing their names. Soon she taught me how to say the alphabet forwards and backwards as it was done in Grenada. Although she had never gone beyond the seventh grade, she had been put in charge of teaching the first grade children their letters during her last year at Mr. Taylor's School in Grenville. She told me stories about his strictness as she taught me how to print my name.

I did not like the tail of the Y hanging down below the line in Au- 19
drey, and would always forget to put it on, which used to disturb my
mother greatly. I used to love the evenness of AUDRELORDE at four
years of age, but I remembered to put on the Y because it pleased my
mother, and because, as she always insisted to me, that was the way it
had to be because that was the way it was. No deviation was allowed
from her interpretations of correct.

So by the time I arrived at the sight-conservation kindergarten, 20
braided, scrubbed, and bespectacled, I was able to read large-print
books and write my name with regular pencil. Then came my first rude
awakening about school. Ability had nothing to do with expectation.

There were only seven or eight of us little Black children in a big 21
classroom, all with various serious deficiencies of sight. Some of us
were cross-eyed, some of us were nearsighted, and one little girl had a
patch over one of her eyes.

We were given special short wide notebooks to write in, with very 22
widely spaced lines on yellow paper. They looked like my sister's
music notebooks. We were also given thick black crayons to write with.
Now you don't grow up fat, Black, nearly blind, and ambidextrous in a
West Indian household, particularly my parents' household, and survive without being or becoming fairly rigid fairly fast. And having
been roundly spanked on several occasions for having made that mistake at home, I knew quite well that crayons were not what you wrote
with, and music books were definitely not what you wrote in.

I raised my hand. When the teacher asked me what I wanted, I 23
asked for some regular paper to write on and a pencil. That was my
undoing. "We don't have any pencils here," I was told.

Our first task was to copy down the first letter of our names in 24
those notebooks with our black crayons. Our teacher went around the
room and wrote the required letter into each one of our notebooks.
When she came around to me, she printed a large A in the upper left
corner of the first page of my notebook, and handed me the crayon.

"I can't," I said, knowing full well that what you do with black 25
crayons is scribble on the wall and get your backass beaten, or color
around the edges of pictures, but not write. To write, you needed a
pencil. "I can't!" I said, terrified, and started to cry.

"Imagine that, a big girl like you. Such a shame, I'll have to tell 26
your mother that you won't even try. And such a big girl like you!"

And it was true. Although young, I was the biggest child by far in 27
the whole class, a fact that had not escaped the attention of the little
boy was sat behind me, and who was already whispering "fatty,
fatty!" whenever the teacher's back was turned.

"Now just try, dear. I'm sure you can try to print your A. Mother 28
will be so pleased to see that at least you tried." She patted my stiff
braids and turned to the next desk.

Well, of course, she had said the magic words, because I would   29
have walked over rice on my knees to please Mother. I took her nasty
old soft smudgy crayon and pretended that it was a nice neat pencil
with a fine point, elegantly sharpened that morning outside the bathroom door by my father, with the little penknife that he always carried
around in his bathrobe pocket.

I bent my head down close to the desk that smelled like old spittle   30
and rubber erasers, and on that ridiculous yellow paper with those
laughably wide spaces I printed my best AUDRE. I had never been too
good at keeping between straight lines no matter what their width, so
it slanted down across the page something like this: A

             U

               D

                 R

                   E

The notebooks were short and there was no more room for anything
else on that page. So I turned the page over, and wrote again, earnestly
and laboriously, biting my lip, L

             O

               R

                 D

                   E

half-showing off, half-eager to please.

By this time, Miss Teacher had returned to the front of the room.   31

"Now when you're finished drawing your letter, children," she   32
said, "Just raise your hand high." And her voice smiled a big smile.
It is surprising to me that I can still hear her voice but I can't see her
face, and I don't know whether she was Black or white. I can remember the way she smelled, but not the color of her hand upon my
desk.

Well, when I heard that, my hand flew up in the air, wagging fran-   33
tically. There was one thing my sisters had warned me about school in
great detail: you must never talk in school unless you raised your
hand. So I raised my hand, anxious to be recognized. I could imagine
what teacher would say to my mother when she came to fetch me
home at noon. My mother would know that her warning to me to "be
good" had in truth been heeded.

Miss Teacher came down the aisle and stood beside my desk,   34
looking down at my book. All of a sudden the air around her hand beside my notebook grew very still and frightening.

"Well I never!" Her voice was sharp. "I thought I told you to draw   35
this letter? You don't even want to try and do as you are told. Now I
want you to turn that page over and draw your letter like everyone . . ."
and turning to the next page, she saw my second name sprawled
down across the page.

There was a moment of icy silence, and I knew I had done some- 36 thing terribly wrong. But this time, I had no idea what it could be that would get her so angry, certainly not being proud of writing my name.

She broke the silence with a wicked edge to her voice. "I see." she 37 said. "I see we have a young lady who does not want to do as she is told. We will have to tell her mother about that." And the rest of the class snickered, as the teacher tore the page out of my notebook.

"Now I am going to give you one more chance," she said, as she 38 printed another fierce A at the head of the new page. "Now you copy that letter exactly the way it is, and the rest of the class will have to wait for you." She placed the crayon squarely back into my fingers.

By this time I had no idea at all what this lady wanted from me, 39 and so I cried and cried for the rest of the morning until my mother came to fetch me home at noon. I cried on the street while we stopped to pick up my sisters, and for most of the way home, until my mother threatened to box my ears for me if I didn't stop embarrassing her on the street.

That afternoon, after Phyllis and Helen were back in school, and I 40 was helping her dust, I told my mother how they had given me crayons to write with and how the teacher didn't want me to write my name. When my father came home that evening, the two of them went into counsel. It was decided that my mother would speak to the teacher the next morning when she brought me to school, in order to find out what I had done wrong. This decision was passed on to me, ominously, because of course I must have done something wrong to have made Miss Teacher so angry with me.

The next morning at school, the teacher told my mother that she 41 did not think that I was ready yet for kindergarten, because I couldn't follow directions, and I wouldn't do as I was told.

My mother knew very well I could follow directions, because she 42 herself had spent a good deal of effort and arm-power making it very painful for me whenever I did not follow directions. And she also be-lieved that a large part of the function of school was to make me learn how to do what I was told to do. In her private opinion, if this school could not do that, then it was not much of a school and she was going to find a school that could. In other words, my mother had made up her mind that school was where I belonged.

That same morning, she took me off across the street to the 43 catholic school, where she persuaded the nuns to put me into the first grade, since I could read already, and write my name on regular paper with a real pencil. If I sat in the first row I could see the blackboard. My mother also told the nuns that unlike my two sisters, who were models of deportment, I was very unruly, and that they should spank me whenever I needed it. Mother Josepha, the principal, agreed, and I started school.

My first grade teacher was named Sister Mary of Perpetual Help, 44
and she was a disciplinarian of the first order, right after my mother's
own heart. A week after I started school she sent a note home to my
mother asking her not to dress me in so many layers of clothing because
then I couldn't feel the strap on my behind when I was punished.

Sister Mary of Perpetual Help ran the first grade with an iron 45
hand in the shape of a cross. She couldn't have been more than eighteen. She was big, and blond, I think, since we never got to see the
nuns' hair in those days. But her eyebrows were blonde, and she was
supposed to be totally dedicated, like all the other Sisters of the
Blessed Sacrament, to caring for the Colored and Indian children of
America. Caring for was not always caring about. And it always felt
like Sister MPH hated either teaching or little children.

She had divided up the class into two groups, the Fairies and the 46
Brownies. In this day of heightened sensitivity to racism and color
usage, I don't have to tell you which were the good students and
which were the baddies. I always wound up in the Brownies, because
either I talked too much, or I broke my glasses, or I perpetrated some
other awful infraction of the endless rules of good behavior.

But for two glorious times that year, I made it into the Fairies for 47
brief periods of time. One was put into the Brownies if one misbe-
haved, or couldn't learn to read. I had learned to read already, but I
couldn't tell my numbers. Whenever Sister MPH would call a few of
us up to the front of the room for our reading lesson, she would say,
"All right, children, now turn to page six in your readers." or, "Turn to
page nineteen, please, and begin at the top of the page."

Well, I didn't know what page to turn to, and I was ashamed of 48
not being able to read my numbers, so when my turn came to read I
couldn't, because I didn't have the right place. After the prompting of
a few words, she would go on to the next reader, and soon I wound up
in the Brownies.

This was around the second month of school, in October. My new 49
seatmate was Alvin, and he was the worst boy in the whole class. His
clothes were dirty and he smelled unwashed, and rumor had it he had
once called Sister MPH a bad name, but that couldn't have been possible because he would have been suspended permanently from school.

Alvin used to browbeat me into lending him my pencil to draw 50
endless pictures of airplanes dropping huge penile bombs. He would
always promise to give me the pictures when he was finished. But of
course, whenever he was finished, he would decide that the picture
was too good for a girl, so he would have to keep it, and make me another. Yet I never stopped hoping for one of them, because he drew
airplanes very well.

He also would scratch his head and shake out the dandruff onto 51
our joint spelling book or reader, and then tell me the flakes of dan-

druff were dead lice. I believed him in this, also, and was constantly terrified of catching cooties. But Alvin and I worked out our own system together for reading. He couldn't read, but he knew all his numbers, and I could read words, but I couldn't find the right page.

The Brownies were never called up to the front of the room; we 52 had to read in anonymity from our double seats, where we scrunched over at the edges, ordinarily, to leave room in the middle for our two guardian angels to sit. But whenever we had to share a book our guardian angels had to jump around us and sit on the outside edge of our seats. Therefore, Alvin would show me the right pages to turn to when Sister called them out, and I would whisper the right words to him whenever it came his turn to read. Inside of a week after we devised this scheme of things, we had gotten out of the Brownies together. Since we shared a reader, we always went up together to read with the Fairies, so we had a really good thing going there for a while.

But Alvin began to get sick around Thanksgiving, and was absent 53 a lot, and he didn't come back to school at all after Christmas. I used to miss his dive-bomber pictures, but most of all I missed his page numbers. After a few times of being called up by myself and not being able to read, I landed back in the Brownies again.

Years later I found out that Alvin had died of tuberculosis over 54 Christmas, and that was why we all had been X-rayed in the auditorium after Mass on the first day back to school from Christmas vacation.

I spent a few more weeks in the Brownies with my mouth almost 55 shut during reading lesson, unless the day's story fell on page eight, or ten, or twenty, which were the three numbers I knew.

Then, over one weekend, we had our first writing assignment. We 56 were to look in our parents' newspaper and cut out words we knew the meaning of, and make them into simple sentences. We could only use one "the." It felt like an easy task, since I was already reading the comics by this time.

On Sunday morning after church, when I usually did my home- 57 work, I noticed an ad for White Rose Salada Tea on the back of the *New York Times Magazine* which my father was reading at the time. It had the most gorgeous white rose on a red background, and I decided I must have that rose for my picture—our sentences were to be illustrated. I searched through the paper until I found an "I," and then a "like," which I dutifully clipped out along with my rose, and the words "White," "Rose," "Salada," and "Tea." I knew the brand-name well because it was my mother's favorite tea.

On Monday morning, we all stood our sentence papers up on the 58 chalk-channels, leaning them against the blackboards. And there among the twenty odd "The boy ran," "it was cold," was "I like White Rose Salada Tea" and my beautiful rose on a red background.

That was too much coming from a Brownie. Sister Mary of PH 59 frowned.

"This was to be our own work, children," she said. "Who helped 60 you with your sentence, Audre?" I told her I had done it alone.

"Our guardian angels weep when we don't tell the truth, Audre. I 61 want a note from your mother tomorrow telling me that you are sorry for lying to the baby Jesus."

I told the story at home, and the next day I brought a note from 62 my father saying that the sentence had indeed been my own work. Triumphantly, I gathered up my books and moved back over to the Fairies.

The thing that I remember best about being in the first grade was 63 how uncomfortable it was, always having to leave room for my guardian angel on those tiny seats, and moving back and forth across the room from Brownies to Fairies and back again.

This time I stayed in the Fairies for a long time, because I finally 64 started to recognize my numbers. I stayed there until the day I broke my glasses. I had taken them off to clean them in the bathroom and they slipped out of my hand. I was never to do that, and so I was in disgrace. My eyeglasses came from the eye clinic of the medical center, and it took three days to get a new pair made. We could not afford to buy more than one pair at a time, nor did it occur to my parents that such an extravagance might be necessary. I was almost sightless without them, but my punishment for having broken them was that I had to go to school anyway, even though I could see nothing. My sisters delivered me to my classroom with a note from my mother saying I had broken my glasses despite the fact they were tied to me by the strip of elastic.

I was never supposed to take my glasses off except just before get- 65 ting into bed, but I was endlessly curious about these magical circles of glass that were rapidly becoming a part of me, transforming my universe, and remaining movable. I was always trying to examine them with my naked, nearsighted eyes, usually dropping them in the process.

Since I could not see at all to do any work from the blackboard, 66 Sister Mary of PH made me sit in the back of the room on the window seat with a dunce cap on. She had the rest of the class offer up a prayer for my poor mother who had such a naughty girl who broke her glasses and caused her parents such needless extra expense to replace them. She also had them offer up a special prayer for me to stop being such a wicked-hearted child.

I amused myself by counting the rainbows of color that danced 67 like a halo around the lamp on Sister Mary of PH's desk, watching the starburst patterns of light that the incandescent light bulb became without my glasses. But I missed them, and not being able to see. I never once gave a thought to the days when I believed that bulbs were starburst patterns of color, because that was what all light looked like to me.

It must have been close to summer by this time. As I sat with the 68 dunce cap on, I can remember the sun pouring through the classroom window hot upon my back, as the rest of the class dutifully intoned their Hail Marys for my soul, and I played secret games with the distorted rainbows of light, until Sister noticed and made me stop blinking my eyes so fast.

Working with the Text

1. When Lorde first starts school, she finds that some rules for behavior are familiar from home and others are not. In what ways are her teachers' expectations similar to her mother's, and in what ways do her teachers treat her differently from the manner in which her mother treats her? How does not understanding the school rules for behavior get her into trouble?

2. In Lorde's first grade class, students were divided into two groups, the Fairies and the Brownies. What is the difference between the two groups? What does Lorde mean when she says, "In this day of heightened sensitivity to racism and color usage, I don't have to tell you which were the good students and which were the baddies"?

3. In her early school experiences, Lorde is actually punished for knowing more and being able to do more than her teachers feel she should. Why is her first teacher angry when she writes her whole name instead of just her first initial? What is her second teacher's reaction to her first writing project: "I like White Rose Salada Tea"? What does Lorde appear to be saying about teacher expectations and student abilities?

4. Lorde's tone is quite sarcastic in places in the essay, almost humorous, as when she describes the Catholic school children "being marched out of the schoolhouse door in two neat rows like little robots, silent but safe and unattacked." Can you find other examples of Lorde's sarcastic humor?

Working beyond the Text

1. What are your earliest memories of school? Did you have trouble, as Lorde did, adjusting to the new and different expectations of school? Or was it a fairly smooth transition?

2. Lorde remembers the librarian Mrs. Baker reading her *Madeline, Horton Hatches the Egg,* and a story about Herbert the bear: "By the time she had finished that one, I was sold on reading for the rest of my life." What are your earliest memories of reading and writing? What were your reactions to your early reading and writing? Why do you think you responded this way?

3. Contrast Lorde's first experiences with reading and writing (with the librarian Mrs. Baker and with her mother) with her experiences at school (first at public school, then at a Catholic school). What is she saying about the effect of school on children's attitudes toward reading, writing, and learning? Do you agree with her? Why?

Exile

Eva Hoffman

Eva Hoffman was born in Poland in 1945. Together with her parents and sister, Hoffman emigrated from Cracow, Poland to Vancouver, Canada in the aftermath of World War II. She worked in the United States as a literature professor and an editor. In this chapter from her autobiography, *Lost in Translation: A Life in a New Language* (1989), Hoffman tells the story of her first days as a "newcomer," a Polish-speaking Jew in English-only Canadian schools, and of losing one language before truly acquiring another.

We are in Montreal, in an echoing, dark train station, and we are 1 huddled on a bench waiting for someone to give us some guidance. Timidly, I walk a few steps away from my parents to explore this terra incognita, and I come back with snippets of amazing news. There is this young girl, maybe my age, in high-heeled shoes and lipstick! She looks so vulgar, I complain. Or maybe this is just some sort of costume? There is also a black man at whom I stare for a while; he's as handsome as Harry Belafonte, the only black man whose face I know from pictures in Polish magazines, except here he is, big as life. Are all black men this handsome, I wonder?

Eventually, a man speaking broken Polish approaches us, takes us 2 to the ticket window, and then helps us board our train. And so begins yet another segment of this longest journey—all the longer because we don't exactly know when it will end, when we'll reach our destination. We only know that Vancouver is very far away.

The people on the train look at us askance, and avoid sitting close 3 to us. This may be because we've brought suitcases full of dried cake, canned sardines, and sausages, which would keep during the long transatlantic journey. We don't know about dining cars, and when we discover that this train has such a thing, we can hardly afford to go there once a day on the few dollars that my father has brought with him. Two dollars could buy a bicycle, or several pairs of shoes in Poland. It seems like a great deal to pay for four bowls of soup.

The train cuts through endless expanses of terrain, most of it flat 4
and monotonous, and it seems to me that the relentless rhythm of the
wheels is like scissors cutting a three-thousand-mile rip through my
life. From now on, my life will be divided into two parts, with the line
drawn by that train. After a while, I subside into a silent indifference,
and I don't want to look at the landscape anymore; these are not the
friendly fields, the farmyards of Polish countryside; this is vast, dull,
and formless. By the time we reach the Rockies, my parents try to pull
me out of my stupor and make me look at the spectacular landscapes
we're passing by. But I don't want to. These peaks and ravines, these
mountain streams and enormous boulders hurt my eyes—they hurt
my soul. They're too big, too forbidding, and I can't imagine feeling
that I'm part of them, that I'm in them. I recede into sleep; I sleep
through the day and the night, and my parents can't shake me out of
it. My sister, perhaps recoiling even more deeply from all this strange-
ness, is in a state of feverish illness and can hardly raise her head.

On the second day, we briefly meet a passenger who speaks Yid- 5
dish. My father enters into an animated conversation with him and
learns some thrilling tales. For example, there's the story of a Polish
Jew who came to Canada and made a fortune—he's now a millionaire!—on producing Polish pickles. Pickles! If one can make a fortune
on that, well—it shouldn't be hard to get rich in this country. My father is energized, excited by this story, but I subside into an even
more determined sullenness. "Millionaire" is one of those fairy-tale
words that has no meaning to me whatsoever—a word like "emigration" or "Canada." In spite of my parents' protestations, I go back to
sleep, and I miss some of the most prized sights on the North American continent.

* * *

By the time we've reached Vancouver, there are very few people 6
left on the train. My mother has dressed my sister and me in our best
outfits—identical navy blue dresses with sailor collars and gray coats
handmade of good gabardine. My parents' faces reflect anticipation
and anxiety. "Get off the train on the right foot," my mother tells us.
"For luck in the new life."

I look out of the train window with a heavy heart. Where have I 7
been brought to? As the train approaches the station, I see what is indeed a bit of nowhere. It's a drizzly day, and the platform is nearly
empty. Everything is the color of slate. From this bleakness, two figures approach us—a nondescript middle-aged man and woman—and
after making sure that we are the right people, the arrivals from the
other side of the world, they hug us; but I don't feel much warmth in
their half-embarrassed embrace. "You should kneel down and kiss the

ground," the man tells my parents. "You're lucky to be here." My parents' faces fill with a kind of naïve hope. Perhaps everything will be well after all. They need signs, portents, at this hour.

Then we all get into an enormous car—yes, this is America—and 8 drive into the city that is to be our home.

The Rosenbergs' house is a matter of utter bafflement to me. This one- 9 story structure surrounded by a large garden surely doesn't belong in a city—but neither can it be imagined in the country. The garden itself is of such pruned and trimmed neatness that I'm half afraid to walk in it. Its lawn is improbably smooth and velvety (Ah, the time and worry spent on the shaving of these lawns! But I will only learn of that later), and the rows of marigolds, the circles of geraniums seem almost artificial in their perfect symmetries, in their subordination to orderliness.

Still, I much prefer sitting out here in the sun to being inside. The 10 house is larger than any apartment I have seen in Poland, with enormous "picture" windows, a separate room for every member of the family and soft pastel-colored rugs covering all the floors. These are all features that, I know, are intended to signify good taste and wealth— but there's an incongruity between the message I'm supposed to get and my secret perceptions of these surroundings. To me, these interiors seem oddly flat, devoid of imagination, ingenuous. The spaces are so plain, low-ceilinged, obvious; there are no curves, niches, odd angles, nooks or crannies—nothing that gathers a house into itself, giving it a sense of privacy, or of depth—of interiority. There's no solid wood here, no accretion either of age or dust. There is only the open sincerity of the simple spaces, open right out to the street (No peering out the window here, to catch glimpses of exchanges on the street; the picture windows are designed to give everyone full view of everyone else, to declare there's no mystery, nothing to hide. Not true, of course, but that's the statement). There is also the disingenuousness of the furniture, all of it whitish with gold trimming. The whole thing is too revealing of an aspiration to good taste, but the unintended effect is thin and insubstantial—as if it was planned and put up just yesterday, and could just as well be dismantled tomorrow. The only rooms that really impress me are the bathroom and the kitchen—both of them so shiny, polished, and full of unfamiliar, fabulously functional appliances that they remind me of interiors which we occasionally glimpsed in French or American movies, and which, in our bedraggled Poland, we couldn't distinguish from fantasy. "Do you think people really live like this?" we would ask after one of these films, neglecting all the drama of the plot for the interest of these incidental features. Here is something worth describing to my friends in Cracow, down to such mind-boggling details as a shaggy rug in the bathroom and toilet paper that comes in different colors.

For the few days we stay at the Rosenbergs', we are relegated to 11 the basement, where there's an extra apartment usually rented out to lodgers. My father looks up to Mr. Rosenberg with the respect, even a touch of awe due to someone who is a certified millionaire. Mr. Rosenberg is a big man in the small Duddy Kravitz community of Polish Jews, most of whom came to Canada shortly after the war, and most of whom have made good in junk peddling and real estate—but none as good as he. Mr. Rosenberg, who is now almost seventy, had the combined chutzpah and good luck to ride on Vancouver's real-estate boom—and now he's the richest of them all. This hardly makes him the most popular, but it automatically makes him the wisest. People from the community come to him for business advice, which he dispenses, in Yiddish, as if it were precious currency given away for free only through his grandiose generosity.

In the uncompromising vehemence of adolescence and injured 12 pride, I begin to see Mr. Rosenberg not as our benefactor but as a Dickensian figure of personal tyranny, and my feeling toward him quickly rises to something that can only be called hate. He has made stinginess into principle; I feel it as a nonhuman hardness, a conversion of flesh and feeling into stone. His face never lights up with humor or affection or wit. But then, he takes himself very seriously; to him too his wealth is the proof of his righteousness. In accordance with his principles, he demands money for our train tickets from Montreal as soon as we arrive. I never forgive him. We've brought gifts we thought handsome, but in addition, my father gives him all the dollars he accumulated in Poland—something that would start us off in Canada, we thought, but is now all gone. We'll have to scratch out our living somehow, starting from zero: my father begins to pinch the flesh of his arms nervously.

Mrs. Rosenberg, a worn-faced, nearly inarticulate, diffident 13 woman, would probably show us more generosity were she not so intimidated by her husband. As it is, she and her daughter, Diane, feed us white bread with sliced cheese and bologna for lunch, and laugh at our incredulity at the mushy textures, the plastic wrapping, the presliced convenience of the various items. Privately, we comment that this is not real food: it has no taste, it smells of plastic. The two women also give us clothing they can no longer use. I can't imagine a state of affairs in which one would want to discard the delicate, transparent bathrobes and the angora sweaters they pass on to us, but luscious though these items seem—beyond anything I ever hoped to own—the show of gratitude required from me on receiving them sours the pleasure of new ownership. "Say thank you," my mother prompts me in preparation for receiving a batch of clothing. "People like to be appreciated." I coo and murmur ingratiatingly; I'm beginning to master the trick of saying thank you with just the right turn of the head, just the right balance between modesty and obsequiousness. In the next few years, this is a skill I'll have to use often. But in my heart I feel no real gratitude at being the recipient of so much mercy.

On about the third night at the Rosenbergs' house, I have a night- 14
mare in which I'm drowning in the ocean while my mother and father swim farther and farther away from me. I know, in this dream, what it is to be cast adrift in incomprehensible space; I know what it is to lose one's mooring. I wake up in the middle of a prolonged scream. The fear is stronger than anything I've ever known. My parents wake up and hush me up quickly; they don't want the Rosenbergs to hear this disturbing sound. I try to calm myself and go back to sleep, but I feel as though I've stepped through a door into a dark place. Psychoana-lysts talk about "mutative insights," through which the patient gains an entirely new perspective and discards some part of a cherished neurosis. The primal scream of my birth into the New World is a mu-tative insight of a negative kind—and I know that I can never lose the knowledge it brings me. The black, bituminous terror of the dream solders itself to the chemical base of my being—and from then on, fragments of the fear lodge themselves in my consciousness, thorns and pinpricks of anxiety, loose electricity floating in a psyche that has been forcibly pried from its structures. Eventually, I become accus-tomed to it; I know that it comes, and that it also goes; but when it hits with full force, in its pure form, I call it the Big Fear.

After about a week of lodging us in his house, Mr. Rosenberg de- 15
cides that he has done enough for us, and, using some acquired Amer-ican wisdom, explains that it isn't good for us to be dependent on his charity; there is of course no question of kindness. There is no ques-tion, either, of Mrs. Rosenberg intervening on our behalf, as she might like to do. We have no place to go, no way to pay for a meal. And so we begin.

"Shut up, shuddup," the children around us are shouting, and it's the 16
first word in English that I understand from its dramatic context. My sister and I stand in the schoolyard clutching each other, while kids all around us are running about, pummeling each other, and screaming like whirling dervishes. Both the boys and girls look sharp and aggres-sive to me—the girls all have bright lipstick on, their hair sticks up and out like witches' fury, and their skirts are held up and out by stiff, wiry crinolines. I can't imagine wanting to talk their harsh-sounding language.

We've been brought to this school by Mr. Rosenberg, who, two 17
days after our arrival, tells us he'll take us to classes that are provided by the government to teach English to newcomers. This morning, in the rinky-dink wooden barracks where the classes are held, we've ac-quired new names. All it takes is a brief conference between Mr. Rosenberg and the teacher, a kindly looking woman who tries to give

us reassuring glances, but who has seen too many people come and go to get sentimental about a name. Mine—"Ewa"—is easy to change into its near equivalent in English, "Eva." My sister's name—"Alina"— poses more of a problem, but after a moment's thought, Mr. Rosenberg and the teacher decide that "Elaine" is close enough. My sister and I hang our heads wordlessly under this careless baptism. The teacher then introduces us to the class, mispronouncing our last name—"Wydra"—in a way we've never heard before. We make our way to a bench at the back of the room; nothing much has happened, except a small, seismic mental shift. The twist in our names takes them a tiny distance from us—but it's a gap into which the infinite hobgoblin of abstraction enters. Our Polish names didn't refer to us; they were as surely us as our eyes or hands. These new appellations, which we ourselves can't yet pronounce, are not us. They are identification tags, disembodied signs pointing to objects that happen to be my sister and myself. We walk to our seats, into a roomful of unknown faces, with names that make us strangers to ourselves.

When the school day is over, the teacher hands us a file card on which she has written, "I'm a newcomer. I'm lost, I live at 1785 Granville Street. Will you kindly show me how to get there? Thank you." We wander the streets for several hours, zigzagging back and forth through seemingly identical suburban avenues, showing this deaf-mute sign to the few people we see, until we eventually recognize the Rosenbergs' house. We're greeted by our quietly hysterical mother and Mrs. Rosenberg, who, in a ritual she has probably learned from television, put out two glasses of milk on her red Formica counter. The milk, homogenized, and too cold from the fridge, bears little resemblance to the liquid we used to drink called by the same name. 18

Every day I learn new words, new expressions. I pick them up from school exercises, from conversations, from the books I take out of Vancouver's well-lit, cheerful public library. There are some turns of phrase to which I develop strange allergies. "You're welcome," for example, strikes me as a gaucherie, and I can hardly bring myself to say it—I suppose because it implies that there's something to be thanked for, which in Polish would be impolite. The very places where language is at its most conventional, where it should be most taken for granted, are the places where I feel the prick of artifice. 19

Then there are words to which I take an equally irrational liking, for their sound, or just become I'm pleased to have deduced their meaning. Mainly they're words I learn from books, like "enigmatic" or "insolent"—words that have only a literary value, that exist only as signs on the page. 20

But mostly, the problem is that the signifier has become severed from the signified. The words I learn now don't stand for things in the 21 same unquestioned way they did in my native tongue. "River" in Polish was a vital sound, energized with the essence of riverhood, of my rivers, of my being immersed in rivers. "River" in English is cold—a word without an aura. It has no accumulated associations for me, and it does not give off the radiating haze of connotation. It does not evoke.

The process, alas, works in reverse as well. When I see a river now, 22 it is not shaped, assimilated by the word that accommodates it to the psyche—a word that makes a body of water a river rather than an un-contained element. The river before me remains a thing, absolutely other, absolutely unbending to the grasp of my mind.

When my friend Penny tells me that she's envious, or happy, or dis- 23 appointed, I try laboriously to translate not from English to Polish but from the word back to its source, to the feeling from which it springs. Already, in that moment of strain, spontaneity of response is lost. And anyway, the translation doesn't work. I don't know how Penny feels when she talks about envy. The word hangs in a Platonic stratosphere, a vague prototype of all envy, so large, so all-encompassing that it might crush me—as might disappointment or happiness.

I am becoming a living avatar of structuralist wisdom; I cannot 24 help knowing that words are just themselves. But it's a terrible knowl-edge, without any of the consolations that wisdom usually brings. It does not mean that I'm free to play with words at my wont; anyway, words in their naked state are surely among the least satisfactory play objects. No, this radical disjoining between word and thing is a desic-cating alchemy, draining the world not only of significance but of its colors, striations, nuances—its very existence. It is the loss of a living connection.

The worst losses come at night. As I lie down in a strange bed in a 25 strange house—my mother is a sort of housekeeper here, to the aging Jewish man who has taken us in in return for her services—I wait for that spontaneous flow of inner language which used to be my night-time talk with myself, my way of informing the ego where the id had been. Nothing comes. Polish, in a short time, has atrophied, shriveled from sheer uselessness. Its words don't apply to my new experiences; they're not coeval with any of the objects, or faces, or the very air I breathe in the daytime. In English, words have not penetrated to those layers of my psyche from which a private conversation could proceed. This interval before sleep used to be the time when my mind became both receptive and alert, when images and words rose up to con-sciousness, reiterating what had happened during the day, adding the day's experiences to those already stored there, spinning out the thread of my personal story.

Now, this picture-and-word show is gone; the thread has been 26 snapped. I have no interior language, and without it, interior images—

those images through which we assimilate the external world, through which we take it in, love it, make it our own—become blurred too. My mother and I met a Canadian family who live down the block today. They were working in their garden and engaged us in a conversation of the "Nice weather we're having, isn't it?" variety, which culminated in their inviting us into their house. They sat stiffly on their couch, smiled in the long pauses between the conversation, and seemed at a loss for what to ask. Now my mind gropes for some description of them, but nothing fits. They're a different species from anyone I've met in Poland, and Polish words slip off of them without sticking. English words don't hook on to anything. I try, deliberately, to come up with a few. Are these people pleasant or dull? Kindly or silly? The words float in an uncertain space. They come up from a part of my brain in which labels my be manufactured but which has no connection to my instincts, quick reactions, knowledge. Even the simplest adjectives sow confusion in my mind; English kindliness has a whole system of morality behind it, a system that makes "kindness" an entirely positive virtue. Polish kindness has the tiniest element of irony. Besides, I'm beginning to feel the tug of prohibition, in English, against uncharitable words. In Polish, you can call someone an idiot without particularly harsh feelings and with the zest of a strong judgment. Yes, in Polish these people might tend toward "silly" and "dull"—but I force myself toward "kindly" and "pleasant." The cultural unconscious is beginning to exercise its subliminal influence.

The verbal blur covers these people's faces, their gestures with a 27 sort of fog. I can't translate them into my mind's eye. The small event, instead of being added to the mosaic of consciousness and memory, falls through some black hole, and I fall with it. What has happened to me in this new world? I don't know. I don't see what I've seen, don't comprehend what's in front of me. I'm not filled with language anymore, and I have only a memory of fullness to anguish me with the knowledge that, in this dark and empty state, I don't really exist.

Working with the Text

1. Hoffman has a dream in which she imagines she discovers a new knowledge: "I know, in this dream, what it is to be cast adrift in incomprehensible space; I know what it is to lose one's mooring." What does she mean? What life experience might she be referring to?
2. Hoffman mentions a psychological concept, "mutative insights." What does this idea mean? How does this idea apply to her own experiences? That is, how did she "mutate" and what were her "insights"?
3. Hoffman describes the experience of losing a known language while learning a new one and the feeling of being caught between the two languages.

How does she explain these sensations? In what specific situations do they become clear to her?

4. Hoffman's narrative is written in the present tense: "We are in Montreal" rather than "We were in Montreal." Why might she have chosen to describe her personal experiences in this way? What is the effect on you as a reader of using present tense rather than past tense?

5. The flow of Hoffman's story is interrupted by spaces on the page—for example, after paragraphs seven, fourteen, eighteen, and so on. Why? What is the function of these spaces? What do they allow Hoffman to do?

Working beyond the Text

1. When Hoffman and her sister go to school for the first time, they are given new first names: Eva instead of Ewa, Elaine instead of Alina. Even their last name is mispronounced. What effect does this have on Hoffman's thoughts and feelings? Have you ever had experiences in which people changed or mispronounced your name? How did you feel?

2. What is the larger social or historical frame of reference for Hoffman's personal experiences? That is, what do you know about the emigration of Eastern European Jews to Canada and the United States after World War II? (You might make a visit to the library.) Is Hoffman's experience typical of others who emigrated to North America?

From Outside, In
Barbara Mellix

Barbara Mellix has a degree in writing and is an administrator at the University of Pittsburgh. In this essay, published in *The Georgia Review* (1988) and later included in the anthology *Writing: The Translation of Memory* (1990), Mellix looks at her writing throughout her life: from short sentences written for her second-grade class in Greeleyville, South Carolina, to papers she wrote for college classes. She sees the evolution of her writing as reflecting changes in her identity.

Two years ago, when I started writing this paper, trying to bring order out of chaos, my ten-year-old daughter was suffering from an acute attack of boredom. She drifted in and out of the room complaining that she had nothing to do, no one to "be with" because none of her friends were at home. Patiently I explained that I was working on something special and needed peace and quiet, and I suggested that she paint, read, or work with her computer. None of these interested her. Finally, she pulled up a chair to my desk and watched me, now and then heaving long, loud sighs. After two or three minutes (nine or ten sighs), I lost my patience. "Looka here, Allie," I said, "you too old for this kinda carryin' on. I done told you this is important. You wronger than dirt to be in here haggin' me like this and you know it. Now git on outta here and leave me off before I put my foot all the way down."

I was at home, alone with my family, and my daughter under- 2 stood that this way of speaking was appropriate in that context. She knew, as a matter of fact, that it was almost inevitable; when I get angry at home, I speak some of finest, most cherished black English. Had I been speaking to my daughter in this manner in certain other environments, she would have been shocked and probably worried that I had taken leave of my sense of propriety.

Like my children, I grew up speaking what I considered two dis- 3 tinctly different languages—black English and standard English (or as I thought of them then, the ordinary everyday speech of "country" coloreds and "proper" English)—and in the process of acquiring these languages, I developed an understanding of when, where, and how to use them. But unlike my children, I grew up in a world that was primarily black. My friends, neighbors, minister, teachers—almost everybody I associated with every day—were black. And we spoke to one another in our own special language: *That sho is a pretty dress you got on. If she don' soon leave me off I'm gon tell her head a mess. I was so mad I could'a pissed a blue nail. He all the time trying to low-rate somebody. Ain't that just about the nastiest thing you ever set ears on?*

Then there were the "others," the "proper" blacks, transplanted 4 relatives and one-time friends who came home from the city for weddings, funerals, and vacations. And the whites. To these we spoke standard English. "Ain't?" my mother would yell at me when I used the term in the presence of "others." "You *know* better than that." And I would hang my head in shame and say the "proper" word.

I remember one summer sitting in my grandmother's house in 5 Greeleyville, South Carolina, when it was full of the chatter of city relatives who were home on vacation. My parents sat quietly, only now and then volunteering a comment or answering a question. My mother's face took on a strained expression when she spoke. I could see that she was being careful to say just the right words in just the right way. Her voice sounded thick, muffled. And when she finished speaking, she would lapse into silence, her proper smile on her face. My father was more articulate, more aggressive. He spoke quickly, his words sharp and clear. But he held his proud head higher, a signal that he, too, was uncomfortable. My sisters and brothers and I stared at our aunts, uncles, and cousins, speaking only when prompted. Even then, we hesitated, formed our sentences in our minds, then spoke softly, shyly.

My parents looked small and anxious during those occasions, and 6 I waited impatiently for our leave-taking when we would mock our relatives the moment we were out of their hearing. "Reeely," we would say to one another, flexing our wrists and rolling our eyes. "how dooo you stan' this heat? Chile, it just too hy*ooo*-mid for words." Our relatives had made us feel "country," and this was our way of regaining pride in ourselves while getting a little revenge in the bargain. The words bubbled in our throats and rolled across our tongues, a balming.

As a child I felt this same doubleness in uptown Greeleyville 7 where the whites lives. "Ain't that a pretty dress you're wearing!" Toby, the town policeman, said to me one day when I was fifteen. "Thank you very much," I replied, my voice barely audible in my own ears. The words felt wrong in my mouth, rigid, foreign. It was not that I had never spoken that phrase before—it was common in black English, too—but I was extremely conscious that this was an occasion for proper English. I had taken out my English and put it on as I did my church clothes, and I felt as if I were wearing my Sunday best in the middle of the week. It did not matter that Toby had not spoken grammatically correct English. He was white and could speak as he wished. I had something to prove. Toby did not.

Speaking standard English to whites was our way of demon- 8 strating that we knew their language and could use it. Speaking it to standard-English-speaking blacks was our way of showing them that we, as well as they, could "put on airs." But when we spoke standard English, we acknowledged (to ourselves and to others—but primarily to ourselves) that our customary way of speaking was inferior. We felt foolish, embarrassed, somehow diminished because we were ashamed to be our real selves. We were reserved, shy in the presence of those who owned and/or spoke *the* language.

My parents never set aside time to drill us in standard English. 9 Their forms of instruction were less formal. When my father was feeling particularly expansive, he would regale us with tales of his exploits in the outside world. In almost flawless English, complete with dialogue and flavored with gestures and embellishment, he told us about his attempt to get a haircut at a white barbershop; his refusal to acknowledge one of the town merchants until the man addressed him as "Mister"; the time he refused to step off the sidewalk uptown to let some whites pass; his airplane trip to New York City (to visit a sick relative) during which the stewardesses and porters—recognizing that he was a "gentleman"—addressed him as "Sir." I did not realize then—nor, I think, did my father—that he was teaching us, among other things, standard English and the relationship between language and power.

My mother's approach was different. Often, when one of us said, 10
"I'm gon wash off my feet," she would say, "And what will you walk
on if you wash them off?" Everyone would laugh at the victim of my
mother's "proper" mood. But it was different when one of us children
was in a proper mood. "You think you are so superior," I said to my
oldest sister one day when we were arguing and she was winning.
"Superior!" my sister mocked. "You mean I'm acting 'biggidy'?" My
sisters and brothers sniggered, then joined in teasing me. Finally, my
mother said, "Leave your sister alone. There's nothing wrong with
using proper English." There was a half-smile on her face. I had gotten
"uppity," had "put on airs" for no good reason. I was at home, alone
with the family, and I hadn't been prompted by one of my mother's
proper moods. But there was also a proud light in my mother's eyes;
her children were learning English very well.

Not until years later, as a college student, did I begin to under- 11
stand our ambivalence toward English, our scorn of it, our need to
master it, to own and be owned by it—an ambivalence that extended
to the public-school classroom. In our school, where there were no
whites, my teachers taught standard English but used black English to
do it. When my grammar-school teachers wanted us to write, for example, they usually said something like, "I want y'all to write five sentences that make a statement. Anybody git done before the rest can
color." It was probably almost those exact words that led me to write
these sentences in 1953 when I was in the second grade:

The white clouds are pretty.
There are only 15 people in our room.
We will go to gym.
We have a new poster.
We may go out doors.

Second grade came after "Little First" and "Big First," so by then I
knew the implied rules that accomplished all writing assignments.
Writing was an occasion for proper English. I was not to write in the
way we spoke to one another: The white clouds pretty; There ain't but
15 people in our room; We going to gym; We got a new poster; We can
go out in the yard. Rather I was to use the language of "other": clouds
are, there *are,* we *will,* we *have,* we *may.*

My sentences were short, rigid, perfunctory, like the letters my 12
mother wrote to relatives:

Dear Papa,

How are you? How is Mattie? Fine I hope. We are fine. We will come
to see you Sunday. Cousin Ned will give us a ride.
                                        Love,
                                        Daughter

The language was not ours. It was something from outside us, something we used for special occasions.

But my coloring on the other side of that second-grade paper is different. I drew three hearts and a sun. The sun has a smiling face that radiates and envelops everything it touches. And although the sun and its world are enclosed in a circle, the colors I used—red, blue, green, purple, orange, yellow, black—indicate that I was less restricted with drawing and coloring than I was with writing standard English. My valentines were not just red. My sun was not just a yellow ball in the sky. 13

By the time I reached the twelfth grade, speaking and writing standard English had taken on new importance. Each year, about half of the newly graduated seniors of our school moved to large cities—particularly in the North—to live with relatives and find work. Our English teacher constantly corrected our grammar: "Not 'ain't,' but 'isn't.'" We seldom wrote papers, and even those few were usually plot summaries of short stories. When our teacher returned the papers, she usually lectured on the importance of using standard English: "I *am*, you *are*, he, she, or it *is*," she would say, writing on the chalkboard as she spoke. "How you gon git a job talking about 'I is,' or 'I isn't' or 'I ain't'?" 14

In Pittsburgh, where I moved after graduation, I watched my aunt and uncle—who had always spoken standard English when in Greeleyville—switch from black English to standard English to a mixture of the two, according to where they were or who they were with. At home and with certain close relatives, friends, and neighbors, they spoke black English. With those less close, they spoke a mixture. In public and with strangers, they generally spoke standard English. 15

In time, I learned to speak standard English with ease and to switch smoothly from black to standard or a mixture, and back again. But no matter where I was, no matter what the situation or occasion, I continued to write as I had in school: 16

Dear Mommie,

How are you? How is everybody else? Fine I hope. I am fine. So are Aunt and Uncle. Tell everyone I said hello. I will write again soon.

Love,
Barbara

At work, at a health insurance company, I learned to write letters to customers. I studied form letters and letters written by co-workers, memorizing the phrases and the ways in which they were used. I dictated:

Thank you for your letter of January 5. We have made the changes in your coverage you requested. Your new premium will be $150 every three months. We are pleased to have been of service to you.

In a sense, I was proud of the letters I wrote for the company: they were proof of my ability to survive in the city, the outside world—an indication of my growing mastery of English. But they also indicated that writing was still mechanical for me, something that didn't require much thought.

Reading also become a more significant part of my life during 17 those early years in Pittsburgh. I had always liked reading, but now I devoted more and more of my spare time to it. I read romances, mysteries, popular novels. Looking back, I realize that the books I liked best were simple, unambiguous: good versus bad and right versus wrong with right rewarded and wrong punished, mysteries unraveled and all set right in the end. It was how I remembered life in Greeleyville.

Of course I was romanticizing. Life in Greeleyville had not been so 18 very uncomplicated. Back there I had been—first as a child, then as a young woman with limited experience in the outside world—living in a relatively closed-in society. But there were implicit and explicit principles that guided our way of life and shaped our relationships with one another and the people outside—principles that a newcomer would find elusive and baffling. In Pittsburgh, I had matured, become more experienced: I had worked at three different jobs, associated with a wider range of people, married, had children. This new environment with different prescripts for living required that I speak standard English much of the time, and slowly, imperceptibly, I had ceased seeing a sharp distinction between myself and "others." Reading romances and mysteries, characterized by dichotomy, was a way of shying away from change, from the person I was becoming.

But that other part of me—that part which took great pride in my 19 ability to hold a job writing business letters—was increasingly drawn to the new developments in my life and the attending possibilities, opportunities for even greater change. If I could write letters for a nationally known business, could I not also do something better, more challenging, more important? Could I not, perhaps, go to college and become a school teacher? For years, afraid and a little embarrassed, I did no more than imagine this different me, this possible me. But sixteen years after coming north, when my youngest daughter entered kindergarten, I found myself unable—or unwilling—to resist the lure of possibility. I enrolled in my first college course: Basic Writing, at the University of Pittsburgh.

For the first time in my life, I was required to write extensively 20 about myself. Using the most formal English at my command, I wrote these sentences near the beginning of the term:

> One of my duties as a homemaker is simply picking up after others.
> A day seldom passes that I don't search for a mislaid toy, book, or
> gym shoe, etc. I change the Ty-D-Bol, fight "ring around the collar,"

and keep our laundry smelling "April fresh." Occasionally, I settle arguments between my children and suggest things to do when they're bored. Taking telephone messages for my oldest daughter is my newest (and sometimes most aggravating) chore. Hanging the toilet paper roll is my most insignificant.

My concern was to use "appropriate" language, to sound as if I belonged in a college classroom. But I felt separated from the language—as if it did not and could not belong to me. I couldn't think and feel genuinely in that language, couldn't make it express what I thought and felt about being a housewife. A part of me resented, among other things, being judged by such things as the appearance of my family's laundry and toilet bowl, but in that language I could only imagine and write about a conventional housewife.

For the most part, the remainder of the term was a period of adjustment, a time of trying to find my bearings as a student in a college composition class, to learn to shut out my black English whenever I composed, and to prevent it from creeping into my formulations; a time for trying to grasp the language of the classroom and reproduce it in my prose; for trying to talk about myself in that language, reach others through it. Each experience of writing was like standing naked and revealing my imperfection, my "otherness." And each new assignment was another chance to make myself over in language, reshape myself, make myself "better" in my rapidly changing image of a student in a college composition class.   21

But writing became increasingly unmanageable as the term progressed, and by the end of the semester, my sentences sounded like this: 22

> My excitement was soon dampened, however, by what seemed like a small voice in the back of my head saying that I should be careful with my long awaited opportunity. I felt frustrated and this seemed to make it difficult to concentrate.

There is a poverty of language in these sentences. By this point, I knew that the clichéd language of my Housewife essay was unacceptable, and I generally recognized trite expressions. At the same time, I hadn't yet mastered the language of the classroom, hadn't yet come to see it as belonging to me. Most notable is the lifelessness of the prose, the apparent absence of a person behind the words. I wanted those sentences—and the rest of the essay—to convey the anguish of yearning to, at once, become something more and yet remain the same. I had the sensation of being split in two, part of me going into a future the other part didn't believe possible. As that person, the student writer at that moment, I was essentially mute. I could not—in the process of composing—use the language of the old me, yet I couldn't imagine myself in the language of "others."

I found this particularly discouraging because at midsemester I had 23 been writing in a much different way. Note the language of this introduction to an essay I had written then, near the middle of the term:

> Pain is a constant companion to the people in "Footwork." Their jobs are physically damaging. Employers are insensitive to their feelings and in many cases add to their problems. The general public wounds them further by treating them with disgrace because of what they do for a living. Although the workers are as diverse as they are similar, there is a definite link between them. They suffer a great deal of abuse.

The voice here is stronger, more confident, appropriating terms like "physically damaging," "wounds them further," "insensitive," "diverse"—terms I couldn't have imagined using when writing about my own experience—and shaping them into sentences like "Although the workers are as diverse as they are similar, there is a definite link between them." And there is the sense of a personality behind the prose, someone who sympathizes with the workers: "The general public wounds them further by treating them with disgrace because of what they do for a living."

What caused these differences? I was, I believed, explaining other 24 people's thoughts and feelings, and I was free to move about in the language of "others" so long as I was speaking *of* others. I was unaware that I was transforming into my best classroom language my own thoughts and feelings about people whose experiences and ways of speaking were in many ways similar to mine.

The following year, unable to turn back or to let go of what had be- 25 come something of an obsession with language (and hoping to catch and hold the sense of control that had eluded me in Basic Writing), I enrolled in a research writing course. I spent most of the term learning how to prepare for and write a research paper. I chose sex education as my subject and spent hours in libraries, searching for information, reading, taking notes. Then (not without messiness and often-demoralizing frustration) I organized my information into categories, wrote a thesis statement, and composed my paper—a series of paraphrases and quotations spaced between carefully constructed transitions. The process and results felt artificial, but as I would later come to realize I was passing through a necessary stage. My sentences sounded like this:

> This reserve becomes understandable with examination of who the abusers are. In an overwhelming number of cases, they are people the victims know and trust. Family members, relatives, neighbors

and close family friends commit seventy-five percent of all reported sex crimes against children, and parents, parent substitutes and relatives are the offenders in thirty to eighty percent of all reported cases. While assault by strangers does occur, it is less common, and is usually a single episode. But abuse by family members, relatives and acquaintances may continue for an extended period of time. In cases of incest, for example, children are abused repeatedly for an average of eight years. In such cases, "the use of physical force is rarely necessary because of the child's trusting, dependent relationship with the offender. The child's cooperation is often facilitated by the adult's position of dominance, an offer of material goods, a threat of physical violence, or a misrepresentation of moral standards.

The completed paper gave me a sense of profound satisfaction, 26 and I read it often after my professor returned it. I know now that what I was pleased with was the language I used and the professional voice it helped me maintain. "Use better words," my teacher had snapped at me one day after reading the notes I'd begun accumulating from my research, and slowly I began taking on the language of my sources. In my next set of notes, I used the word "vacillating"; my professor applauded. And by the time I composed the final draft, I felt at ease with terms like "overwhelming number of cases," "single episode," and "reserve," and I shaped them into sentences similar to those of my "expert" sources.

If I were writing the paper today, I would of course do some 27 things differently. Rather than open with an anecdote—as my teacher suggested—I would begin simply with a quotation that caught my interest as I was researching my paper (and which I scribbled, without its source, in the margin of my notebook): "Truth does not do so much good in the world as the semblance of truth does evil." The quotation felt right because it captured what was for me the central idea of my essay—an idea that emerged gradually during the making of my paper—and expressed it in a way I would like to have said it. The anecdote, a hypothetical situation I invented to conform to the information in the paper, felt forced and insincere because it represented— to a great degree—my teacher's understanding of the essay, *her* idea of what in it was most significant. Improving upon my previous experiences with writing, I was beginning to think and feel in the language I used, to find my own voices in it, to sense that how one speaks influences how one means. But I was not yet secure enough, comfortable enough with the language to trust my intuition.

Now that I know that to seek knowledge, freedom, and autonomy 28 means always to be in the concentrated process of becoming—always to be venturing into new territory, feeling one's way at first, then getting one's balance, negotiating, accommodating, discovering one's self in ways that previously defined "others"—I sometimes get tired. And

I ask myself why I keep on participating in this highbrow form of violence, this slamming against perplexity. But there is no real futility in the question, no hint of that part of the old me who stood outside standard English, hugging to herself a disabling mistrust of a language she thought could not represent a person with her history and experience. Rather, the question represents a person who feels the consequence of her education, the weight of her possibilities as a teacher and writer and human being, a voice in society. And I would not change that person, would not give back the good burden that accompanies my growing expertise, my increasing power to shape myself in language and share that self with "others."

"To speak," say Frantz Fanon, "means to be in a position to use a ²⁹ certain syntax, to grasp the morphology of this or that language, but it means above all to assume a culture, to support the weight of a civilization." ¹ To write means to do the same, but in a more profound sense. However, Fanon also says that to achieve mastery means to "get" in a position of power, to "grasp," to "assume." This, I have learned—both as a student and subsequently as a teacher—can involve tremendous emotional and psychological conflict for those attempting to master academic discourse. Although as a beginning student writer I had a fairly good grasp of ordinary spoken English and was proficient at what Labov calls "code-switching" (and what John Baugh in *Black Street Speech* terms "style shifting"), when I came face to face with the demands of academic writing, I grew increasingly self-conscious, constantly aware of my status as a black and a speaker of one of the many black English vernaculars—a traditional outsider. For the first time, I experienced my sense of doubleness as something menacing, a built-in enemy. Whenever I turned inward for salvation, the balm so available during my childhood, I found instead this new fragmentation which spoke to me in many voices. It was the voice of my desire to prosper, but at the same time it spoke of what I had relinquished and could not regain: a safe way of being, a state of powerlessness which exempted me from responsibility for who I was and might be. And it accused me of betrayal, of turning away from blackness. To recover balance, I had to take on the language of the academy, the language of "others." And to do that, I had to learn to imagine myself a part of the culture of that language, and therefore someone free to manage that language, to take liberties with it. Writing and rewriting, practicing, experimenting, I came to comprehend more fully the generative power of language. I discovered—with the help of some especially sensitive teachers—that through writing one can continually bring new selves into being, each with new responsibilities and difficulties, but also with new possibilities. Remarkable power, indeed. I write and continually give birth to myself.

¹ *Black Skin, White Masks* (1952; rpt. New York: Grove Press, 1967), pp. 17–18.

Working with the Text

1. Mellix experiences a number of pressures to learn standard English and use it in various situations. What are the pressures, and where do they come from? What are the situations in which she learns she should speak standard English? Why does she sometimes feel ambivalent about speaking standard English even when she knows the situation calls for it?

2. Mellix says she realizes at one point that "through writing one can continually bring new selves into being, each with new responsibilities and difficulties, and also with new possibilities." What does she mean? What is the relationship between language and identity? How is it possible for language to create a self?

3. Mellix says that in telling stories to his children, her father was "teaching us . . . the relationship between language and power." What is the relationship, in her father's stories and in Mellix's life experiences, between language and power? What does her own learning of standard English have to do with power?

4. Mellix begins her essay with an anecdote about being interrupted by her daughter while writing the essay. Why, do you suppose? What is the point of the anecdote? What themes does it enable her to introduce?

5. Mellix's essay is basically a personal narrative based on her life experiences. However, in her last paragraph she chooses to quote two scholars. Why? What might be the purpose of quoting these authorities in an essay about her own life?

Working beyond the Text

1. Mellix mentions the work of Frantz Fanon, especially his *Black Skin, White Masks.* Who was Fanon? What ideas was he famous for? (You might make a visit to the library.) How does understanding his ideas give you a better understanding of Mellix's main points?

2. Mellix mentions that trying to use standard English, especially academic English, makes her feel that she cannot be herself or say what she really thinks. Where does she explain this feeling and what examples does she use? Have you ever felt that your writing was limited by being forced to write in a certain academic style, and have you ever wished you could just "be yourself" and write as you please? When?

3. Mellix analyzes her development as a writer by examining her own writing, quoting it, and tracing the changes in her language as she tried to come closer to writing standard English. Can you do the same with your own writing? If you can, locate pieces of your writing from the past several years, written either in or out of school, and try to say in what direction your writing seems to move and why.

Language as Image Maker
Ingrid Mundari

Ingrid Mundari's first educational experiences took place in a convent school in Trinidad, the country of her birth. Later, while studying English literature at the University of Pittsburgh, she contributed this essay to the 1990 anthology *Writing: The Translation of Memory.* Along with her critical work, Mundari writes short fiction, which has appeared in several literary journals. Here Mundari discusses how her experiences with different languages and dialects in Trinidad influenced the person she became.

The West Indies is a multi-lingual, multi-ethnic cluster of islands 1 and Trinidad, my home for the first fifteen years of my life, is a prime example of this "melting pot." It is a melting pot, however, with subtle delineations and demarcations which enforce a class system based upon language. The system of education is based upon traditionally British lines and the common language is English—it is the shared language of public intercourse and the one which defines the island's public life. Patois, the Creole dialect and one of the island's secondary languages, is used mainly in the home and in the marketplace.

As a child, I would accompany my mother on her shopping trips 2 to the big, open-air market which stood at one end of the city. Amidst the cacophony of sounds and the constantly shifting swirls of people and colors—brightly dressed vendors hovering over deep red mangoes, yellow guavas and green coconuts—the farmers would call to each other and to the shoppers in Patois, splicing their dialogues with announcements about their wares, and a sentence or two of English. With my hand tightly clasped in my mother's, I would walk with her from stall to stall, tiptoeing to peer at the array of produce displayed on the slabs of waist-high sandstone. I would stare fascinatedly at the deft movement of the fisherman's knife as he eviscerated a huge mackerel or swordfish, while he kept up a running commentary in Patois to my mother. I was able to understand a phrase or two here and there, but Patois was a language of secrets and great mystery to me, made more so by the fact that is was a language of my elders. None of my friends spoke it, but their parents and grandparents did.

English was spoken everywhere else, but in the marketplace and 3 the home Patois held sway. Of course when visitors dropped by everyone spoke English, and in the commercial districts of the city where the men dressed in suits and the women wore their hair piled on top of their heads, it was the same.

As a child, Patois seemed to me to be a language of exclusion. If 4 the adults were having a conversation and there were children present, they would speak Patois when the topic was something we were not allowed to hear. This was generally the case with my mother and my aunts. They would be having a normal conversation and one of them would suddenly throw a significant look in our direction which would then cause them to switch to "their" language. When, at the market with my mother, I was able to respond in the few sentences of Patois I knew to queries about my age and my preference for either mangoes or guavas, I was petted and praised. However, when I tried to demonstrate this knowledge at home it produced different results. When I would unexpectedly break into one of my mother's Patois conversations, she would look at me as though seeing me for the first time and send me off to the garden to play with my cousins. I couldn't understand this. I felt proud of the fact that I was able to grasp enough of what was being said to participate in the conversation, but conversely, it seemed that my very understanding of their language shut me out even more.

At school it was altogether different. There, I entered another 5 world, the boundaries of which were delineated by English and religion. Apart from Patois, and to a lesser extent, French, Portuguese and Spanish, there were two "types" of English spoken on the island: "the King's English" as the nuns at my school labeled it, and the sing-song dialect spoken by many islanders. This dialect dispensed with the phonemic sounds of many English words so that the "th" and "g" sounds disappeared, and the substitution of the verb "done" for various forms of the verb "to be" comprised a large part of its structure. In response to a query regarding someone's whereabouts the answer might be: "He done gone a long time now." In addition, there were word substitutions and portmanteau words which conveyed entirely different areas of meaning from the original English. Then, too, a shift in the tone or cadence of an islander's voice could do the same.

By the time I was ten, I was quite used to speaking Patois with 6 some degree of fluency at the market, speaking "Island English" with my friends at home, and speaking school English in the classroom. There were several prep schools run by nuns of different orders on the island, and these schools were considered special. They were where young girls went not only to be made into ladies, but to receive a sound education in the process. A convent girl was always immediately recognizable, from the spotless white shirt and neatly pleated skirt of her uniform, to the way in which she carried herself. But the real test of a convent girl, as we were reminded time and again, was the way in which she spoke. "Even if she's out of uniform, from the time a convent girl opens her mouth, you know who she is."

The way in which a convent girl spoke, of course, had everything 7 to do with the way she was taught to speak in school. Throughout my early school years, it seemed that part of each day was given over to a reading and recitation period during which our teacher would read a story, poem, or passage aloud, and we would recite it back to her line by line, while following along in our Readers. She would have us repeat certain words and phrases over and over until she was sure we had mastered the pronunciation. Those of us who allowed the island-lilt to creep into our voices were made to go over each syllable again and again, until she was satisfied with the result. In the beginning we saw it as nothing more than learning to read; curling our tongues around words with a lot of letters and stringing them together.

Our Reader in the second grade was a long, thin book with a red   8 cover which contained rhymes such as:

> There was a naughty boy
> And a naughty boy was he
> He ran away to Scotland
> The people there to see
> And he found that the ground was hard
> That a yard was long
> That a song was merry
> That a cherry was red
> As a berry . . .

We enjoyed reciting these, and the tendency was to run all the words together. They seemed to have a momentum that rushed your tongue along and allowed you to swallow half of the words as you progressed. But that was precisely it—you weren't supposed to swallow any part of the word, or drop any part of its sound. We would be made to repeat the rhyme until the "d" could be clearly heard, and the tendency to say "foun" and "groun" was given over to the desire to enunciate clearly.

There were Speech Days for which the entire school was assem-   9 bled and prizes were given to the best elocutor for her rendition of a poem, or a piece of prose. The accent was on pronunciation, inflection and cadence. You didn't allow your voice to rise at the end of the line unless you were asking a question; you pronounced your "g's" and "th's" clearly, and you certainly 'idn't offer your delivery in a sing-song tone of voice.

I was being initiated into the mysteries of language through these   10 techniques, realizing that if a certain word were said a certain way it could have a whole new meaning. And nowhere was this clearer than at choral rehearsals. Sister Columba, the music mistress, had a habit of walking through our ranks during choir practice and putting her ear to our mouths. Ostensibly, this was to ascertain pitch and make sure we were in the right key, but it was a technique that served other purposes as well. On one occasion as she stood in front of a classmate, she motioned the rest of us into silence and listened intently as the un-happy culprit was made to sing the same line over and over. The line was "As we bathe in your blood, cleanse us O Lord," and the word "bathe" was being sung as "bade." She told us that the entire meaning of the line had been changed, assured us that the two words had noth-ing in common, and assigned us the task of looking up both words in the dictionary and formulating several sentences to demonstrate the correct usage of each word. My days were filled with many such inci-dental lessons, stemming not only from my music teacher, but from anyone in whose presence/hearing we had violated the rules of pro-nunciation.

As I grew older, it became increasingly difficult to shift my use of language as I had been accustomed to doing. The ease with which I had once moved from Patois to "Island English" to school English was rapidly evaporating. At home, when my playmates made verbal mis-takes, I couldn't help correcting them. Of course I was teased for being one of those convent girls, who thought she knew everything. At the same time, my visits to the market were becoming more and more in-frequent, as was my use of Patois. The fascination of Saturday morn-ing trips to the market was beginning to fade, although the fascination with words and the rich and varied levels of meaning they could cre-ate was growing. 11

Interestingly enough, Latin and French were the languages which had begun to replace my interest in Patois. The Mass, as well as many of our school prayers, was said in Latin, and most of us had memo-rized whole sections of the Liturgy long before we fully know what the words meant. It was enough to repeat them phonetically and take pleasure in the heavy, full syllables which rolled off our tongues. 12

"Do-mi-nus For-bis-cum." 13

"E-cum-spi-ri-tuo." 14

By the time we were eleven we had already begun a formal study of Latin, and although the text of the Mass had already begun its changeover into English, the learning of Latin was still stressed. It was the language next to "school English" which quickly came to shape my world. We attended Mass every morning in the school chapel and twice on Holy Feast Days. We were constantly surrounded by or par-ticipating in some form of prayer, and we learned hymns in Latin and English and sang both versions. 15

Latin, like Patois, was also shrouded in a mystery I had difficulty penetrating. The difference, however, was that with Latin I did not seem to mind as much. I didn't feel as shut out as I had in my earlier interactions with Patois. Whatever secrets the priests held as they in-toned the words of the Mass, they gave me a chance to share, and though I could not fully comprehend, I could participate. When I re-sponded during the service, whether in Church or in school, I was in- 16 cluded because my response, my words, and the knowledge I was attaining of the language I was using allowed me entrance into the world which this language had created.

A similar pattern had begun to develop with my study of French. 17 Even though my knowledge of Patois made the transition to French easier, I was conscious of the fact that I was being taught the "proper" words and the "correct" pronunciation, two things which created whole new levels of meaning and opened up entirely new doors for me. The Patois equivalents to the words, phrases, sentences, with which I was becoming daily more familiar, seemed to be different not only in tone and cadence, but in purpose as well. And in the same way I corrected my friends when they spoke "Island English," I now corrected my mother when she spoke Patois, adjuring her to use the "right" French word for its Patois counterpart. Along with the inevitable teasing that this engendered, I was conscious of the fact that my older brother seemed to have little difficulty in moving in and out of the various language systems. He seemed easily able to cross the boundaries between Patois, Island English and "proper English."

For me, however, there existed a gap where none had been. As 18 much as I tried, I couldn't move myself back into a speech pattern with which I had once felt so comfortable. I began to second guess myself, carrying on monologues and pretended snatches of dialogue in my head in my "Island voice" and in my school voice, trying to navigate myself through the differences. The school voice seemed more pronounced, more powerful, and bit by bit, the Island voice seemed to be fading. I found myself listening to people's pronunciation in a way I never had before. This made me even more irritated with myself, not only because I would lose track of what was being said to me during a conversation, but also because of the very intrusiveness of the act in which I was engaged.

At Mass on Sundays when we responded in English, my ears 19 picked up the sounds of swallowed "t's" and bowdlerized "h's," whereas in the school chapel, my voice blended in with a sea of others, all strong, all self-assured. Here, no one faltered at the syllabic stress on the "w" in "hallowed." I imagined our tongues caught firmly between our teeth when we enunciated the "th" sounds, just as I envisioned the sing-song cadences evaporating away when we recited the Pater Noster. We seemed to send forth each word as though they were perfectly round, hard pebbles, making clean arcs through the air before returning to land in the sea of our voices, without eliciting so much as a splash.

The division between who I had been, the person who the combi- 20 nation of "Island English," Patois and school English had shaped, began to separate me from whom I was becoming, the person who had recreated her world in terms of the latter. And, along with this came the realization that the ways in which I used language seemed to have a great bearing on who I was.

On Assembly Days when Mother Superior spoke before the 21 school, her voice stayed with me throughout the rest of my day. What she said seemed as important as the way in which she said it, and one of the things she said repeatedly was "to speak well is to write well." Creating myself through language, through the words I spoke, seemed inextricably meshed with creating myself through the words I wrote. For when I did write I was conscious that sounds like the "wh" in the word "what" had as much significance on the page as when it was pronounced "what" instead of "wat." I was conscious of the fact that the word "witch" had nothing in common with "which" and that the double level of meaning they involved was just as significant on paper as it was when verbalized.

Language and its use came to denote many things for me, not the 22 least of which was the recognition of its shaping power and its ability to structure a world and a world view for its user. The circle of friends and acquaintances with whom I now spent most of my time was comprised of people that made me feel at ease, that didn't shut me out, and didn't tease me about the way I spoke. More importantly, to me at least, I didn't find myself involuntarily correcting anyone's speech, or having to go through a composing process in my head before I spoke. I didn't have to worry about *how* I spoke, because the person I was and the person I had spoken into being were now one and the same.

Working with the Text

1. Mundari says of learning Latin that "the knowledge I was attaining of the language I was using allowed me entrance into the world which this language had created." How does this statement apply to her learning of other languages as well (Patois, Island English, school English)? Into what worlds does her knowledge of other languages "allow her entrance"? In what ways do these languages create different worlds?

2. What happened to Mundari as a result of her experiences with different languages, especially in school? What were the various stages of her development? How does her exposure to different languages make her into the person she is?

3. Of all the languages Mundari knows—Trinidad Patois, the "sing-song dialect" of English spoken in Trinidad, "the King's English," and so on—which language does she choose for writing her essay? How can you tell? Why does she choose that one, do you suppose?

Working beyond the Text

1. Mundari describes Trinidad as a "melting pot." What is your idea of a country described as a melting pot, as the United States often is? Is Trinidad a melting pot in the same sense that the United States is?

2. Mundari is very specific about the features of the various languages she speaks, saying for example that Island English substituted the verb "done" for the verb "to be" in many instances and dropped the "th" and "g" sounds completely. Choose a variety of English that you are familiar with—the language of a subculture or geographical area, for example—and make a list of specific ways in which it differs from "standard" English.

3. Mundari had teachers who paid a great deal of attention to her English, making her repeat words out loud and correcting her pronunciation whenever she made the slightest mistake. Why? Did teachers pay close attention to your language as you went through school? What influence were your teachers trying to have on your language? Why, do you suppose?

UNIT TWO

KEEPING CLOSE TO HOME

Aria: A Memoir of a Bilingual Childhood
Richard Rodriguez

A son of Mexican immigrants, Richard Rodriguez studied at Stanford, Columbia, and the University of California at Berkeley. In his autobiography, *Hunger of Memory*, he describes his assimilation into American culture and takes controversial stands on issues such as affirmative action and bilingual education. In "Aria," later developed into a chapter of *Hunger of Memory* (1982), he describes the feeling of being pulled in two directions by the languages of home and school. Rodriguez's most recent book is *Days of Obligation: An Argument with My Mexican Father* (1994).

I remember, to start with, that day in Sacramento, in a California   1
now nearly thirty years past, when I first entered a classroom—able to understand about fifty stray English words. The third of four children, I had been preceded by my older brother and sister to a neighborhood Roman Catholic school. But neither of them had revealed very much about their classroom experiences. They left each morning and returned each afternoon, always together, speaking Spanish as they climbed the five steps to the porch. And their mysterious books, wrapped in brown shopping-bag paper, remained on the table next to the door, closed firmly behind them.

An accident of geography sent me to a school where all my class-   2
mates were white and many were the children of doctors and lawyers and business executives. On that first day of school, my classmates must certainly have been uneasy to find themselves apart from their families, in the first institution of their lives. But I was astonished. I was fated to be the "problem student" in class.

The nun said, in a friendly but oddly impersonal voice: "Boys and   3
girls, this is Richard Rodriguez." (I heard her sound it out: *Rich-heard Road-ree-guess.*) It was the first time I had heard anyone say my name in English. "Richard," the nun repeated more slowly, writing my name down in her book. Quickly I turned to see my mother's face dissolve in a watery blur behind the pebbled-glass door.

Now, many years later, I hear of something called "bilingual edu- 4
cation"—a scheme proposed in the late 1960s by Hispanic-American
social activists, later endorsed by a congressional vote. It is a program
that seeks to permit non-English-speaking children (many from lower
class homes) to use their "family language" as the language of school.
Such, at least, is the aim its supporters announce. I hear them, and am
forced to say no: It is not possible for a child, any child, ever to use his
family's language in school. Not to understand this is to misunderstand the public uses of schooling and to trivialize the nature of intimate life.

Memory teaches me what I know of these matters. The boy reminds 5
the adult. I was a bilingual child, but of a certain kind: "socially disadvantaged," the son of working-class parents, both Mexican immigrants.

In the early years of my boyhood, my parents coped very well in 6
America. My father had steady work. My mother managed at home.
They were nobody's victims. When we moved to a house many blocks
from the Mexican-American section of town, they were not intimidated by those two or three neighbors who initially tried to make us
unwelcome. ("Keep your brats away from my sidewalk!") But despite
all they achieved, or perhaps because they had so much to achieve,
they lacked any deep feeling of ease, of belonging in public. They regarded the people at work or in crowds as being very distant from us.
Those were the others, *los gringos*. That term was interchangeable in
their speech with another, even more telling: *los americanos*.

I grew up in a house where the only regular guests were my rela- 7
tions. On a certain day, enormous families of relatives would visit us,
and there would be so many people that the noise and the bodies
would spill out to the backyard and onto the front porch. Then for
weeks no one would come. (If the doorbell rang, it was usually a salesman.) Our house stood apart—gaudy yellow in a row of white bunga-
lows. We were the people with the noisy dog, the people who raised
chickens. We were the foreigners on the block. A few neighbors would
smile and wave at us. We waved back. But until I was seven years old,
I did not know the name of the old couple living next door or the
names of the kids living across the street.

In public, my father and mother spoke a hesitant, accented, and 8
not always grammatical English. And then they would have to strain,
their bodies tense, to catch the sense of what was rapidly said by *los
gringos*. At home, they returned to Spanish. The language of their Mexican past sounded in counterpoint to the English spoken in public. The
words would come quickly, with ease. Conveyed through those
sounds was the pleasing, soothing, consoling reminder that one was at
home.

During those years when I was first learning to speak, my mother 9
and father addressed me only in Spanish; in Spanish I learned to reply.

By contrast, English (*inglés*) was the language I came to associate with gringos, rarely heard in the house. I learned my first words of English overhearing my parents speaking to strangers. At six years of age, I knew just enough words for my mother to trust me on errands to stores one block away—but no more.

I was then a listening child, careful to hear the very different sounds of Spanish and English. Wide-eyed with hearing, I'd listen to sounds more than to words. First, there were English (gringo) sounds. So many words still were unknown to me that when the butcher or the lady at the drugstore said something, exotic polysyllabic sounds would bloom in the midst of their sentences. Often the speech of people in public seemed to me very loud, booming with confidence. The man behind the counter would literally ask, "What can I do for you?" But by being so firm and clear, the sound of his voice said that he was a gringo; he belonged in public society. There were also the high, nasal notes of middle-class American speech—which I rarely am conscious of hearing today because I hear them so often, but could not stop hearing when I was a boy. Crowds at Safeway or at bus stops were noisy with the birdlike sounds of *los gringos*. I'd move away from them all— all the chirping chatter above me. [10]

My own sounds I was unable to hear, but I knew that I spoke English poorly. My words could not extend to form complete thoughts. And the words I did speak I didn't know well enough to make distinct sounds. (Listeners would usually lower their heads to hear better what I was trying to say.) But it was one thing for *me* to speak English with difficulty; it was more troubling to hear my parents speaking in public: their high-whining vowels and guttural consonants; their sentences that got stuck with "eh" and "ah" sounds; the confused syntax; the hesitant rhythm of sounds so different from the way gringos spoke. I'd notice, moreover, that my parents' voices were softer than those of gringos we would meet. [11]

I am tempted to say now that none of this mattered. (In adulthood I am embarrassed by childhood fears.) And, in a way, it didn't matter very much that my parents could not speak English with ease. Their linguistic difficulties had no serious consequences. My mother and father made themselves understood at the county hospital clinic and at government offices. And yet, in another way, it mattered very much. It was unsettling to hear my parents struggle with English. Hearing them, I'd grow nervous, and my clutching trust in their protection and power would be weakened. [12]

There were many times like the night at a brightly lit gasoline station (a blaring white memory) when I stood uneasily hearing my father talk to a teenage attendant. I do not recall what they were saying, but I cannot forget the sounds my father made as he spoke. At one point his words slid together to form one long word—sounds as con- [13]

fused as the threads of blue and green oil in the puddle next to my shoes. His voice rushed through what he had left to say. Toward the end, he reached falsetto notes, appealing to his listener's understanding. I looked away at the lights of passing automobiles. I tried not to hear any more. But I heard only too well the attendant's reply, his calm, easy tones. Shortly afterward, headed for home, I shivered when my father put his hand on my shoulder. The very first chance that I got, I evaded his grasp and ran on ahead into the dark, skipping with feigned boyish exuberance.

But then there was Spanish: *español*, the language rarely heard 14 away from the house; *español*, the language which seemed to me therefore a private language, my family's language. To hear its sounds was to feel myself specially recognized as one of the family, apart from *los otros*. A simple remark, an inconsequential comment could convey that assurance. My parents would say something to me and I would feel embraced by the sounds of their words. Those sounds said: *I am speaking with ease in Spanish. I am addressing you in words I never use with los gringos. I recognize you as someone special, close, like no one outside. You belong with us. In the family, Ricardo.*

At the age of six, well past the time when most middle-class chil- 15 dren no longer notice the difference between sounds uttered at home and words spoken in public, I had a different experience. I lived in a world compounded of sounds. I was a child longer than most. I lived in a magical world, surrounded by sounds both pleasing and fearful. I shared with my family a language enchantingly private—different from that used in the city around us.

Just opening or closing the screen door behind me was an impor- 16 tant experience. I'd rarely leave home all alone or without feeling reluctance. Walking down the sidewalk, under the canopy of tall trees, I'd warily notice the (suddenly) silent neighborhood kids who stood warily watching me. Nervously, I'd arrive at the grocery store to hear there the sounds of the gringo, reminding me that in this so-big world I was a foreigner. But if leaving home was never routine, neither was coming back. Walking toward our house, climbing the steps from the sidewalk, in summer when the front door was open, I'd hear voices beyond the screen door talking in Spanish. For a second or two I'd stay, linger there listening. Smiling, I'd hear my mother call out, saying in Spanish, "Is that you, Richard?" Those were her words, but all the while her sounds would assure me: *You are home now. Come closer inside. With us.* "Sí," I'd reply.

Once more inside the house, I would resume my place in the fam- 17 ily. The sounds would grow harder to hear. Once more at home, I would grow less conscious of them. It required, however, no more than the blurt of the doorbell to alert me all over again to listen to sounds. The house would turn instantly quiet while my mother went to the door. I'd hear her hard English sounds. I'd wait to hear her voice turn to soft-sounding Spanish, which assured me, as surely as did the clicking tongue of the lock on the door, that the stranger was gone.

Plainly it is not healthy to hear such sounds so often. It is not 18 healthy to distinguish public from private sounds so easily. I remained cloistered by sounds, timid and shy in public, too dependent on the voices at home. And yet I was a very happy child when I was at home. I remember many nights when my father would come back from work, and I'd hear him call out to my mother in Spanish, sounding relieved. In Spanish, his voice would sound the light and free notes that he never could manage in English. Some nights I'd jump up just hearing his voice. My brother and I would come running into the room where he was with our mother. Our laughing (so deep was the pleasure!) became screaming. Like others who feel the pain of public alienation, we transformed the knowledge of our public separateness into a consoling reminder of our intimacy. Excited, our voices joined in a celebration of sounds. *We are speaking now the way we never speak out in public—we are together*, the sounds told me. Some nights no one seemed willing to loosen the hold that sounds had on us. At dinner we invented new words that sounded Spanish, but made sense only to us. We pieced together new words by taking, say, an English verb and giving it Spanish endings. My mother's instructions at bedtime would be lacquered with mock-urgent tones. Or a word like *sí*, sounded in several notes, would convey added measures of feeling. Tongues lingered around the edges of words, especially fat vowels, and we happily sounded that military drum roll, the twirling roar of the Spanish *r*. Family language, my family's sounds: the voices of my parents and sisters and brother. Their voices insisting: *You belong here. We are family members. Related. Special to one another. Listen!* Voices singing and sighing, rising and straining, then surging, teeming with pleasure which burst syllables into fragments of laughter. At times it seemed there was steady quiet only when, from another room, the rustling whispers of my parents faded and I edged closer to sleep.

Supporters of bilingual education imply today that students like 19 me miss a great deal by not being taught in their family's language. What they seem not to recognize is that, as a socially disadvantaged child, I regarded Spanish as a private language. It was a ghetto language that deepened and strengthened my feeling of public separateness. What I needed to learn in school was that I had the right, and the obligation, to speak the public language. The odd truth is that my first-grade classmates could have become bilingual, in the conventional sense of the word, more easily than I. Had they been taught early (as upper middle-class children often are taught) a "second language" like Spanish or French, they could have regarded it simply as another public language. In my case, such bilingualism could not have been so quickly achieved. What I did not believe was that I could speak a single public language.

Without question, it would have pleased me to have heard my teachers address me in Spanish when I entered the classroom. I would have felt much less afraid. I would have imagined that my instructors were somehow "related" to me; I would indeed have heard their Spanish as my family's language. I would have trusted them and responded with ease. But I would have delayed—postponed for how long?—having to learn the language of public society. I would have evaded—and for how long?—learning the great lesson of school: that I had a public identity.

Fortunately, my teachers were unsentimental about their responsibility. What they understood was that I needed to speak public English. So their voices would search me out, asking me questions. Each time I heard them I'd look up in surprise to see a nun's face frowning at me. I'd mumble, not really meaning to answer. The nun would persist. "Richard, stand up. Don't look at the floor. Speak up. Speak to the entire class, not just to me!" But I couldn't believe English could be my language to use. (In part, I did not want to believe it.) I continued to mumble. I resisted the teacher's demands. (Did I somehow suspect that once I learned this public language my family life would be changed?) Silent, waiting for the bell to sound, I remained dazed, diffident, afraid.

Because I wrongly imagined that English was intrinsically a public language and Spanish was intrinsically private, I easily noted the difference between classroom language and the language at home. At school, words were directed to a general audience of listeners. ("Boys and girls . . .") Words were meaningfully ordered. And the point was not self-expression alone, but to make oneself understood by many others. The teacher quizzed: "Boys and girls, why do we use that word in this sentence? Could we think of a better word to use there? Would the sentence change its meaning if the words were differently arranged? Isn't there a better way of saying much the same thing?" (I couldn't say. I wouldn't try to say.)

Three months passed. Five. A half year. Unsmiling, ever watchful, my teachers noted my silence. They began to connect my behavior with the slow progress my brother and sisters were making. Until, one Saturday morning, three nuns arrived at the house to talk to our parents. Stiffly they sat on the blue living-room sofa. From the doorway of another room, spying on the visitors, I noted the incongruity, the clash of two worlds, the faces and voices of school intruding upon the familiar setting of home. I overheard one voice gently wondering, "Do your children speak only Spanish at home, Mrs. Rodriguez?" While another voice added, "That Richard especially seems so timid and shy."

20

21

22

23

That Rich-heard!   24

With great tact, the visitors continued, "Is it possible for you and   25
your husband to encourage your children to practice their English
when they are home?" Of course my parents complied. What would
they not do for their children's well-being? And how could they question the Church's authority which those women represented? In an instant they agreed to give up the language (the sounds) which had revealed and accentuated our family's closeness. The moment after the
visitors left, the change was observed. *"Ahora,* speak to us only *en inglés,"* my father and mother told us.

At first, it seemed a kind of game. After dinner each night, the   26
family gathered together to practice "our" English. It was still then *inglés,* a language foreign to us, so we felt drawn to it as strangers.
Laughing, we would try to define words we could not pronounce. We
played with strange English sounds, often overanglicizing our pro-
nunciations. And we filled the smiling gaps of our sentences with familiar Spanish sounds. But that was cheating, somebody shouted, and
everyone laughed.

In school, meanwhile, like my brother and sisters, I was required   27
to attend a daily tutoring session. I needed a full year of this special
work. I also needed my teachers to keep my attention from straying in
class by calling out, *"Rich-heard"*—their English voices slowly loosen-
ing the ties to my other name, with its three notes, *Ri-car-do.* Most of
all, I needed to hear my mother and father speak to me in a moment
of seriousness in "broken"—suddenly heartbreaking—English. This
scene was inevitable. One Saturday morning I entered the kitchen
where my parents were talking, but I did not realize that they were
talking in Spanish until, the moment they saw me, their voices
changed and they began speaking English. The gringo sounds they uttered startled me. Pushed me away. In that moment of trivial misunderstanding and profound insight, I felt my throat twisted by un-
sounded grief. I simply turned and left the room. But I had no place to
escape to where I could grieve in Spanish. My brother and sisters were
speaking English in another part of the house.

Again and again in the days following, as I grew increasingly   28
angry, I was obliged to hear my mother and father encouraging me:
"Speak to us *en inglés.*" Only then did I determine to learn classroom
English. Thus, sometime afterward it happened: one day in school, I
raised my hand to volunteer an answer to a question. I spoke out in a
loud voice and I did not think it remarkable when the entire class understood. That day I moved very far from being the disadvantaged
child I had been only days earlier. Taken hold at last was the belief, the
calming assurance, that I *belonged* in public.

Shortly after, I stopped hearing the high, troubling sounds of *los*   29
gringos. A more and more confident speaker of English, I didn't listen

to how strangers sounded when they talked to me. With so many English-speaking people around me, I no longer heard American accents. Conversations quickened. Listening to persons whose voices sounded eccentrically pitched, I might note their sounds for a few seconds, but then I'd concentrate on what they were saying. Now when I heard someone's tone of voice—angry or questioning or sarcastic or happy or sad—I didn't distinguish it from the words it expressed. Sound and word were thus tightly wedded. At the end of each day I was often bemused, and always relieved, to realize how "soundless," though crowded with words, my day in public had been. An eight-year-old boy, I finally came to accept what had been technically true since my birth: I was an American citizen.

But diminished by then was the special feeling of closeness at 30 home. Gone was the desperate, urgent, intense feeling of being at home among those with whom I felt intimate. Our family remained a loving family, but one greatly changed. We were no longer so close, no longer bound tightly together by the knowledge of our separateness from *los gringos*. Neither my older brother nor my sisters rushed home after school any more. Nor did I. When I arrived home, often there would be neighborhood kids in the house. Or the house would be empty of sounds.

Following the dramatic Americanization of their children, even 31 my parents grew more publicly confident—especially my mother. First she learned the names of all the people on the block. Then she decided we needed to have a telephone in our house. My father, for his part, continued to use the word gringo, but it was no longer charged with bitterness or distrust. Stripped of any emotional content, the word simply became a name for those Americans not of Hispanic descent. Hearing him, sometimes, I wasn't sure if he was pronouncing the Spanish word *gringo*, or saying gringo in English.

There was a new silence at home. As we children learned more 32 and more English, we shared fewer and fewer words with our parents. Sentences needed to be spoken slowly when one of us addressed our mother or father. Often the parent wouldn't understand. The child would need to repeat himself. Still the parent misunderstood. The young voice, frustrated, would end up saying, "Never mind"—the subject was closed. Dinners would be noisy with the clinking of knives and forks against dishes. My mother would smile softly between her remarks; my father, at the other end of the table, would chew and chew his food while he stared over the heads of his children.

My mother! My father! After English became my primary lan- 33 guage, I no longer knew what words to use in addressing my parents. The old Spanish words (those tender accents of sound) I had earlier used—*mamá* and *papá*—I couldn't use any more. They would have been all-too-painful reminders of how much had changed in my life.

On the other hand, the words I heard neighborhood kids call their parents seemed equally unsatisfactory. "Mother" and "father," "ma," "papa," "pa," "dad," "pop" (how I hated the all-American sound of that last word)—all these I felt were unsuitable terms of address for *my* parents. As a result, I never used them at home. Whenever I'd speak to my parents, I would try to get their attention by looking at them. In public conversations, I'd refer to them as my "parents" or my "mother" and "father."

My mother and father, for their part, responded differently, as their children spoke to them less. My mother grew restless, seemed troubled and anxious at the scarceness of words exchanged in the house. She would question me about my day when I came home from school. She smiled at my small talk. She pried at the edges of my sentences to get me to say something more. ("What . . . ?") She'd join conversations she overheard, but her intrusions often stopped her children's talking. By contrast, my father seemed to grow reconciled to the new quiet. Though his English somewhat improved, he tended more and more to retire into silence. At dinner he spoke very little. One night his children and even his wife helplessly giggled at his garbled English pronunciation of the Catholic "Grace Before Meals." Thereafter he made his wife recite the prayer at the start of each meal, even on formal occasions when there were guests in the house. 34

Hers became the public voice of the family. On official business it was she, not my father, who would usually talk to strangers on the phone or in stores. We children grew so accustomed to his silence that years later we would routinely refer to his "shyness." (My mother often tried to explain: both of his parents died when he was eight. He was raised by an uncle who treated him as little more than a menial servant. He was never encouraged to speak. He grew up alone—a man of few words.) But I realized my father was not shy whenever I'd watch him speaking Spanish with relatives. Using Spanish, he was quickly effusive. Especially when talking with other men, his voice would spark, flicker, flare alive with varied sounds. In Spanish he expressed ideas and feelings he rarely revealed when speaking English. With firm Spanish sounds he conveyed a confidence and authority that English would never allow him. 35

The silence at home, however, was not simply the result of fewer words passing between parents and children. More profound for me was the silence created by my inattention to sounds. At about the time I no longer bothered to listen with care to the sounds of English in public, I grew careless about listening to the sounds made by the family when they spoke. Most of the time I would hear someone speaking at home and didn't distinguish his sounds from the words people uttered in public. I didn't even pay much attention to my parents' accented and ungrammatical speech—at least not at home. Only when I 36 was with them in public would I become alert to their accents. But even then their sounds caused me less and less concern. For I was growing increasingly confident of my own public identity.

I would have been happier about my public success had I not re- 37 called, sometimes, what it had been like earlier, when my family conveyed its intimacy through a set of conveniently private sounds. Sometimes in public, hearing a stranger, I'd hark back to my lost past. A Mexican farm worker approached me one day downtown. He wanted directions to some place. *"Hijito, . . ."* he said. And his voice stirred old longings. Another time I was standing beside my mother in the visiting room of a Carmelite convent, before the dense screen which rendered the nuns shadowy figures. I heard several of them speaking Spanish in their busy, singsong, overlapping voices, assuring my mother that, yes, yes, we were remembered, all our family was remembered, in their prayers. Those voices echoed faraway family sounds. Another day a dark-faced old woman touched my shoulder lightly to steady herself as she boarded a bus. She murmured something to me I couldn't quite comprehend. Her Spanish voice came near, like the face of a never-before-seen relative in the instant before I was kissed. That voice, like so many of the Spanish voices I'd hear in public, recalled the golden age of my childhood.

Bilingual educators say today that children lose a degree of "indi- 38 viduality" by becoming assimilated into public society. (Bilingual schooling is a program popularized in the seventies, that decade when middle-class "ethnics" began to resist the process of assimilation—the "American melting pot.") But the bilingualists oversimplify when they scorn the value and necessity of assimilation. They do not seem to realize that a person is individualized in two ways. So they do not realize that, while one suffers a diminished sense of *private* individuality by being assimilated into public society, such assimilation makes possible the achievement of *public* individuality.

Simplistically again, the bilingualists insist that a student should 39 be reminded of his difference from others in mass society, of his "heritage." But they equate mere separateness with individuality. The fact is that only in private—with intimates—is separateness from the crowd a prerequisite for individuality; an intimate "tells" me that I am unique, unlike all others, apart from the crowd. In public, by contrast, full individuality is achieved, paradoxically, by those who are able to consider themselves members of the crowd. Thus it happened for me. Only when I was able to think of myself as an American, no longer an alien in gringo society, could I seek the rights and opportunities necessary for full public individuality. The social and political advantages I enjoy as a man began on the day I came to believe that my name is indeed *Rich-heard Road-ree-guess*. It is true that my public society today is often impersonal; in fact, my public society is usually mass society. But despite the anonymity of the crowd, and despite the fact that the individuality I achieve in public is often tenuous—because it depends on my being one in a crowd—I celebrate the day I acquired my new name. Those middle-class ethnics who scorn assimilation seem to me filled with decadent self-pity, obsessed by the burden of public life. Dangerously, they romanticize public separateness and trivialize the dilemma of those who are truly socially disadvantaged.

If I rehearse here the changes in my private life after my Americanization, it is finally to emphasize a public gain. The loss implies the gain. The house I returned to each afternoon was quiet. Intimate sounds no longer greeted me at the door. Inside there were other noises. The telephone rang. Neighborhood kids ran past the door of the bedroom where I was reading my schoolbooks—covered with brown shopping-bag paper. Once I learned the public language, it would never again be easy for me to hear intimate family voices. More and more of my day was spent hearing words, not sounds. But that may only be a way of saying that on the day I raised my hand in class and spoke loudly to an entire roomful of faces, my childhood started to end. 40

Working with the Text

1. Rodriguez discusses certain vocabulary that he associates with entering the broader world outside the home or the immediate community. What words does he say he learned when he entered "the world"? What is the difference between those words and his home language?

2. Trace the changes in Rodriquez's life from the time he enters "the world" outside his home. How does he feel about the changes in his character and personality?

3. Although Rodriguez's focus is on himself, he also discusses changes in his parents' lives and behavior. As he changes, how do his parents change? In what ways are the changes in his parents' behavior related to the changes in his own life?

4. When children receive more education than their parents, it can drive a wedge between parents and children. In what way is this true in Rodriguez's life? What are the symptoms of the widening gulf between Rodriguez and his parents?

5. Rodriguez begins his essay by telling the story of his first moments in school, and includes some very particular images: the sound of his name being pronounced "in English," the face of his mother disappearing through the classroom door. Why do you think Rodriguez places these images at the beginning of the essay?

6. The organization of the essay is loosely "chronological"—that is, it traces the progress of Rodriguez's early life for several years. At the same time,

however, this progression is interrupted by references to events before and after the events of Rodriguez's childhood. Chart the leaps in time, showing where the essay makes sudden movements outside the chronological narrative. Why does Rodriguez use this technique, do you think?

Working beyond the Text

1. Make a list of the passages in "Aria" that relate to leaving the home or community to enter "the world," the relationship between learning new languages and "growing up," and the things we gain and the things we lose by entering the broader world. How does Rodriguez's experience compare to your own?

2. Rodriguez has strong opinions about bilingual education. Do you agree or disagree with his assessment? Why?

3. "Aria" is about leaving one world of language and entering another. Have you ever left a familiar language world and spent time in another? You may have moved to the United States from another country, lived or traveled in a foreign country, or moved from one part of the United States to another. What does it feel like to be a member of a "language minority"?

Whose Voice Is It Anyway?
Rodriguez' Speech in Retrospect
Victor Villanueva, Jr.

Victor Villanueva, Jr. was raised in lower-class, multiracial neighborhoods in New York and Los Angeles. He dropped out of high school, served in Vietnam, came home to receive a GED, and eventually earned a Ph.D. in English from the University of Washington. He is the author of *Bootstraps: From an American Academic of Color* and teaches at Western Washington University. In this essay, which first appeared in *English Journal* (December 1987), Villanueva takes Richard Rodriguez to task for many of the ideas expressed in *Hunger of Memory* and elsewhere.

During the 1986 annual conference of the NCTE (National Council of Teachers of English) I attended a luncheon sponsored by the secondary section. Richard Rodriguez, author of *Hunger of Memory*, was the guest speaker. He spoke of how he came to be an articulate speaker of this standard dialect, and he spoke of the conclusions concerning language learning that his experiences had brought him to. He was impressive. I was taken by his quiet eloquence. His stage presence recalled Olivier's Hamlet. He spoke well. But for all his eloquence and his studied stage presence, I was nevertheless surprised by the audience's response, an enthusiastic, uncritical acceptance, marked by a long, loud standing ovation. I was surprised because he had blurred distinctions between language and culture, between his experiences and those more typical of the minority in America, between the history of the immigrant and that of the minority, in a way that I had thought would raise more than a few eyebrows. Yet all he raised was the audience to its feet.

In retrospect, I think I can understand the rave reception. The message he so softly delivered relieved us all of some anxiety. Classroom teachers' shoulders stoop under the weight of the paper load. They take 150 students through writing and grammar, spelling and punctuation. Within those same forty-five-minute spurts they also work on reading: drama, poetry, literature, the great issues in literature. After that, there's the writers' club or the school paper or the yearbook, coaching volleyball or producing the school play. And throughout it all, they are to remain sensitive to the language of the nonstandard or non-English speaker. They are not really told how—just "be sensitive," while parents, the media, sometimes it seems the whole world, shake their fingers at them for not doing something about America's literacy problems. Richard Rodriguez told the teachers to continue to be sensitive but to forget about doing anything special. The old ways may be painful, but they really are best. There is a kind of violence to the melting pot, he said, but it is necessary. He said that this linguistic assimilation is like alchemy, initially destructive perhaps but magical, creating something new and greater than what was. Do as you have always done. And the teachers sighed.

Richard Rodriguez is the authority, after all: a bilingual child of immigrant parents, a graduate of two of the nation's more prestigious schools, Stanford and Berkeley, an English teacher, the well-published author of numerous articles and a well-received, well-anthologized book. He knows. And he says that the teachers who insisted on a particular linguistic form can be credited with his fame. But what is it, really, that has made him famous? He is a fine writer; of that there can be no doubt. But it is his message that has brought him fame, a message that states that the minority is no different than any other immigrant who came to this country not knowing its culture or its language, leaving much of the old country behind to become part of this new one, and in becoming part of America subtly changing what it means to be American. The American who brought his beef and pudding from England became the American of the frankfurter, the bologna sandwich, pizza. Typically American foods—like typical Americans—partake of the world.

At the luncheon, Richard Rodriguez spoke of a TV ad for Mexican- 4
style Velveeta, "the blandest of American cheeses," he called it, now
speckled with peppers. This cultural contrast, said Rodriguez, demonstrated how Mexico—no less than England or Germany—is part of
America.

But I think it shows how our times face a different kind of assimi- 5
lation. Let's put aside for the moment questions as to why, if Mexicans
really are being assimilated, they have taken so much longer than
other groups, especially since Mexicans were already part of the West
and Southwest when the West and Southwest became part of America.
Let's look, rather, at the hyphen in Mexican-Velveeta. Who speaks of a
German-American sausage, for instance? It's a hot dog. Yet tacos remain ethnic, sold under a mock Spanish mission bell or a sombrero.
You will find refried beans under "ethnic foods" in the supermarket,
not among other canned beans, though items as foreign-sounding as
sauerkraut are simply canned vegetables. Mexican foods, even when
as Americanized as the taco salad or Mexican-Velveeta, remain distinctly Mexican.[1]

And like the ethnic food, some ethnic minorities have not been as- 6
similated in the way the Ellis Islanders were. The fires of the melting
pot have cooled. No more soup. America's more a stew today. The difference is the difference between the immigrant and the minority, a
difference having to do with how each, the immigrant and the minority, came to be Americans, the difference between choice and colonization. Those who emigrated from Europe chose to leave unacceptable
conditions in search of better. Choice, I realize, is a tricky word in this
context: religious persecution, debtor's prison, potato famine, fascism,
foreign takeover, when compared with a chance at prosperity and self-
determination doesn't seem to make for much of a choice; yet most
people apparently remained in their homelands despite the intolerable, while the immigrants did leave, and in leaving chose to sever ties
with friends and families, created a distance between themselves and
their histories, cultures, languages. There is something heroic in this.
It's a heroism shared by the majority of Americans.

But choice hardly entered into most minorities' decisions to be- 7
come American. Most of us recognize this when it comes to Blacks or
American Indians. Slavery, forcible displacement, and genocide are
fairly clear-cut. Yet the circumstances by which most minorities became Americans are no less clear-cut. The minority became an Ameri-

---

[1]Mexican food is not the only ethnic food on the market, of course. Asian and Mediterranean
foods share the shelves. But this too is telling, since Asians alone had had restricted access to the
US before the country ended its Open Door Immigration Policy. When the US closed its doors in
1924, it was to regulate the flow of less desirable "new immigrants"—the Eastern and Southern
Europeans who remain "ethnic" to this day. See Oscar Handlin's *Race in American Life*, New
York: Anchor, 1957.

can almost by default, as part of the goods in big-time real estate deals
or as some of the spoils of war. What is true for the Native American
applies to the Alaska Native, the Pacific Islander (including the Asian),
Mexican-Americans, Puerto Ricans. Puerto Rico was part of Christopher Columbus' great discovery, Arawaks and Boriquens among his
"Indians," a real-estate coup for the Queen of Spain. Then one day in
1898, the Puerto Ricans who had for nearly four hundred years been
made proud to be the offspring of Spain, so much so that their native
Arawak and Boricua languages and ways were virtually gone, found
themselves the property of the United States, property without the
rights and privileges of citizenship until—conveniently—World War I.
But citizenship notwithstanding, Puerto Rico remains essentially a
colony today.[2]

One day in 1845 and in 1848 other descendants of Spain who had 8
all but lost their Indian identities found themselves Americans. These
were the long-time residents and landowners of the Republic of Texas
and the California Republic: the area from Texas to New Mexico, Arizona, Utah, and California. Residents in the newly established US ter-
ritories were given the option to relocate to Mexico or to remain on
their native lands, with the understanding that should they remain
they would be guaranteed American Constitutional rights. Those who
stayed home saw their rights not very scrupulously guarded, falling
victim over time to displacement, dislocation, and forced expatriation.
There is something tragic in losing a long-established birthright, tragic
but not heroic—especially not heroic to those whose ancestors had
fled their homelands rather than acknowledge external rule.

The immigrant gave up much in the name of freedom—and for 9
the sake of dignity. For the Spanish-speaking minority in particular,
the freedom to be American without once again relinquishing one's
ancestry is also a matter of dignity.

This is not to say that Richard Rodriguez forfeited his dignity in 10
choosing not to be Ricardo. The Mexican's status includes not only the
descendants of the West and Southwest, Spanish-speaking natives to
America, but also immigrants and the descendants of immigrants.
Richard Rodriguez is more the immigrant than the minority. His father, he told us, had left his native Mexico for Australia. He fell in love
along the way, eventually settling with wife and family in Sacramento.
America was not his father's first choice for a new home perhaps, but
he did choose to leave his homeland in much the same way European
immigrants had. The Rodriguezes no doubt felt the immigrants' hard-
ships, the drive to assimilate, a drive compounded perhaps by the as-

---

[2]Nor is it a simple matter of Puerto Rico's deciding whether it wants to remain a commonwealth,
gaining statehood, or independence. The interests of US industry, of the US military, and the social and economic ramifications of Puerto Rico's widespread poverty complicate matters.

sociation in their and others' minds between them and the undocumented migrant worker or between them and the minority.

And it is this confusion of immigrant and minority in Richard Rodriguez with which we must contend. His message rings true to the immigrant heritage of his audience because it happens to be the immigrant's story. It is received as if it were a new story because it is confused with this story of the minority. The complexities of the minority are rendered simple—not easy—but easily understood.

Others tell the story of the minority. I think, for instance, of Piri Thomas and Tato Laviera, since theirs are stories of Puerto Ricans. My own parents had immigrated to New York from Puerto Rico, though not in the way of most. My mother, an American, a US citizen like all Puerto Ricans, fair-skinned, and proud of her European descent, had been sold into servitude to a wealthy Chicago family. My father, recently discharged from the US Army, followed my mother, rescued his sweetheart, and together they fled to New York. I was born a year later, 1948.

My mother believed in the traditional idea of assimilation. She and my father would listen to radio shows in English and try to read the American newspapers. They spoke to me in two languages from the start. The local parochial school's tuition was a dollar a month, so I was spared PS 168. Rodriguez tells of nuns coming to his home to suggest that the family speak English at home. For Rodriguez this was something of a turning point in his life; intimacy lost, participation in the public domain gained. A public language would dominate, the painful path to his assimilation, the path to his eventual success. A nun spoke to my parents, too, when I was in kindergarten. I spoke with an accent, they were told. They should speak to me in English. My mother could only laugh: my English was as it was *because* they spoke to me in English. The irony reinforced our intimacy while I continued to learn the "public language."

There is more to assimilating than learning the language. I earned my snacks at the Saturday matinee by reading the credits on the screen. I enjoyed parsing sentences, was good at it too. I was a Merriam-Webster spelling bee champ. I was an "A" student who nevertheless took a special Saturday course on how to do well on the standardized test that would gain me entry to the local Catholic high school. I landed in the public vo-tech high school, slotted for a trade. Jarapolk, whose parents had fled the Ukraine, made the good school; so did Marie Engels, the daughter of German immigrants. Lana Walker, a Black girl whose brains I envied, got as far as the alternate list. I don't recall any of the Black or Puerto Rican kids from my class getting in. I never finished high school, despite my being a bright boy who knew the public language intimately.

I don't like thinking minorities were intentionally excluded from the better school. I would prefer to think minorities didn't do as well because we were less conscious than the immigrants of the cultural distances we had to travel to be truly Americans. We were Americans, after all, not even seeing ourselves as separated by language by the time most of us got to the eighth grade. I spoke Spanglish at home, a hybrid English and Spanish common to New York Puerto Ricans; I spoke the Puerto Rican version of Black English in the streets, and as far as I knew, I spoke something close to the standard dialect in the classroom. We thought ourselves Americans, assimilated. We didn't know about cultural bias in standardized tests. I still don't do well on standardized tests.

A more pointed illustration of the difference between the minority   16 and the immigrant comes by way of a lesson from my father. I was around ten. We went uptown one day, apartment hunting. I don't recall how he chose the place. He asked about an apartment in his best English, the sounds of a Spanish speaker attempting his best English. No vacancies. My father thanked the man, then casually slipped into the customary small talk of the courteous exit. During the talk my father mentioned our coming from Spain. By the end of the chat a unit became available. Maybe my father's pleasing personality had gained us entry. More likely, Puerto Rican stereotypes had kept us out. The immigrant could enter where the minority could not. My father's English hadn't improved in the five minutes it had taken for the situation to change.

Today I sport a doctorate in English from a major university,   17 study and teach rhetoric at another university, do research in and teach composition, continue to enjoy and teach English literature. I live in an all-American city in the heart of America. And I know I am not quite assimilated. In one weekend I was asked if I was Iranian one day and East Indian the next. "No," I said. "You have an accent," I was told. Yet tape recordings and passing comments throughout the years have told me that though there is a "back East" quality to my voice, there isn't much of New York to it anymore, never mind the Black English of my younger years or the Spanish of my youngest. My "accent" was in my not sounding midwestern, which does have a discernable, though not usually a pronounced, regional quality. And my "accent," I would guess, was in my "foreign" features (which pale alongside the brown skin of Richard Rodriguez).

Friends think I make too much of such incidents. Minority hyper-   18 sensitivity, they say. They desensitize me (and display their liberal attitudes) with playful jabs at Puerto Ricans: greasy hair jokes, knife-in-pocket jokes, spicy food jokes (and Puerto Ricans don't even eat hot foods, unless we're eating Mexican or East Indian foods). If language alone were the secret to assimilation, the rate of Puerto Rican and Mexican success would be greater, I would think. So many Mexican-Americans and Puerto Ricans remain in the barrios—even those who are monolingual, who have never known Spanish. If language alone were the secret, wouldn't the secret have gotten out long before Richard Rodriguez recorded his memoirs? In fact, haven't we always worked with the assumption that language learning—oral and written—is the key to parity, even as parity continues to elude so many?

I'm not saying the assumption is wrong. I think teachers are right 19 to believe in the potential power of language. We want our students to be empowered. That's why we read professional journals. That's why we try to accommodate the pronouncements of linguists. That's why we listen to the likes of Richard Rodriguez. But he spoke more of the English teacher's power than the empowerment of the student. "Listen to the sound of my voice," he said. He asked the audience to forget his brown skin and listen to his voice, his "unaccented voice." "This is your voice," he told the teachers. Better that we, teachers at all levels, give students the means to find their own voices, voices that don't have to ask that we ignore what we cannot ignore, voices that speak of their brown or yellow or red or black skin with pride and without need for bravado or hostility, voices that can recognize and exploit the conventions we have agreed to as the standards of written discourse— without necessarily accepting the ideology of those for whom the standard dialect is the language of home as well as commerce, for whom the standard dialect is as private as it is public, to use Rodriguez' terms.

Rodriguez said at the luncheon that he was not speaking of peda- 20 gogy as much as of ideology. He was. It is an ideology which grew out of the memoirs of an immigrant boy confronting contrasts, a child accommodating his circumstances. He remembers a brown boy in a white middle-class school and is forced to say no to bilingual education. His classmates were the descendants of other immigrants, the products of assimilation, leading him to accept the traditional American ideology of a multiculturalism that manifests as one new culture and language, a culture and language which encompasses and transcends any one culture. I remember a brown boy among other brown boys and girls, blacks, and olives, and variations on white, and must agree with Richard that bilingualism in the classroom would have been impractical. But my classmates were in the process of assimilation—Polish, German, Ukrainian, and Irish children, the first of their families to enter American schools; my classmates were also Black and Puerto Rican. It seemed to this boy's eyes that the immigrants would move on but the minority would stay, that the colonized do not melt. Today I do not hear of the problems in educating new immigrants, but the problems of Black literacy continue to make the news. And I hear of an eighty percent dropout rate among Puerto Ricans in Boston, of Mexicans in the Rio Grande Valley, where the dropout rate exceeds seventy percent, of places where English and the education system do not address the majority—Spanish speakers for whom menial labor has been the tradition and is apparently the future. I must ask how *not* bilingual education in such situations. One person's experiences must remain one person's, applicable to many others, perhaps, but not all others. Simple, monolithic, universal solutions simply can't work in a complex society.

When it comes to the nonstandard speaker, for instance, we are 21 torn between the findings of linguists and the demands of the marketplace. Our attempts at preparing students for the marketplace only succeed in alienating nonstandard speakers, we are told. Our attempts at accommodating their nonstandard dialects, we fear, only succeed in their being barred from the marketplace. So we go back to the basics. Or else we try to change their speech without alienating them, in the process perhaps sensing that our relativism might smack of condescension. Limiting the student's language to the playground and home still speaks of who's right and who's wrong, who holds the power. I would rather we left speaking dialects relatively alone (truly demonstrating a belief in the legitimacy of the nonstandard). The relationship between speaking and writing is complex, as the debate sparked by Thomas Farrell has made clear. My own research and studies, as well as my personal experiences, suggest that exposure to writing and reading affects speaking. My accent changes, it seems, with every book I read. We don't have to give voices to students. If we give them pen and paper and have them read the printed page aloud, no matter what their grade, they'll discover their own voices.

And if we let the printed page offer a variety of world views, of 22 ideologies, those voices should gather the power we wish them to have. Booker T. Washington, Martin Luther King, Jr., W. E. B. DuBois all wrote with eloquence. Each presents a different world view. Maxine Hong Kingston's "voice" resounds differently from Frank Chin's. Ernesto Galarza saw a different world than Richard Rodriguez. Rodriguez' is only one view, one voice. Yet it's his voice which seems to resound the loudest. Rodriguez himself provided the reason why this is so. He said at the luncheon that the individual's story, the biography or autobiography, has universal appeal because it strikes at experiences we have in common. The immigrant's story has the most in common with the majority.

Rodriguez implied that he didn't feel much kinship to minority 23 writers. He said he felt a special bond with D. H. Lawrence. It seems appropriate that Rodriguez, who writes of his alienation from family in becoming part of the mainstream, would turn to Lawrence. Lawrence, too, was a teacher turned writer. Lawrence, too, felt alienated from his working-class background. It was Lawrence who argued, in "Reflections on the Death of the Porcupine," that equality is not achievable; Lawrence who co-opted, left the mastered to join the masters. Is this what we want for our minority students? True, Lawrence's mastery of the English language cannot be gainsaid. I would be proud to have a Lawrence credit me with his voice, would appreciate his acknowledging my efforts as a teacher, and would surely applaud his accomplishment. But I would rather share credit in a W. B. Yeats, Anglo and Irish, assimilated but with a well-fed memory of his ancestry, master of the English language, its beauty, its traditions—and voice of the colony.

Working with the Text

1. Villanueva says, "If language alone were the secret to assimilation, the rate of Puerto Rican and Mexican success would be greater, I would think." What does he mean?
2. Villanueva tells a story of going apartment hunting with his father. What is the significance of the story? What point does it help Villanueva illustrate?
3. How does Villanueva explain Rodriguez's popularity? How is Villanueva's explanation of this popularity a criticism both of Rodriguez and his audience?
4. Villanueva's essay mixes his personal narrative (as a New Yorker of Puerto Rican descent) and history (especially the history of Hispanics in the United States). What is the connection between these two aspects of the essay? How does one reinforce the meaning of the other? Try to connect specific passages.

Working beyond the Text

1. Villanueva's final paragraph draws a distinction between the English writer D. H. Lawrence and the Irish writer William Butler Yeats. What is the distinction? Why does Villanueva prefer the example of Yeats to that of Lawrence? You might visit the library to learn more about each writer and use what you learn to help you explain your answers.
2. Villanueva draws a distinction between the immigrant and the minority in America. What is the difference? Would you characterize your family as immigrant or minority according to Villanueva's definition? Does his definition fit your family and its experiences?
3. Villanueva speaks of the requirement in many schools that students leave their home languages at the door: "Limiting the student's language to the playground and home still speaks of who's right and who's wrong, who holds the power." What does he mean? Have you ever felt you were the "wrong" kind of person because of the language you used in a classroom?
4. If you have read the Richard Rodriguez piece in this chapter, what do you make of Villanueva's criticism of his ideas? Do you understand Rodriguez the same way Villanueva does? Or do you object to Villanueva's criticism?

Keeping Close to Home: Class and Education
bell hooks

bell hooks is the pen name of Gloria Watkins, a writer, teacher, feminist, and black activist. In her many collections of essays, including *Talking Back, Thinking Black, Feminist Theory: from margin to center,* and, most recently, *Teaching to Transgress,* hooks is often critical of mainstream theories of racial activism, feminism, and teaching. Raised in rural Kentucky and educated at Stanford University, hooks explains in this essay—a chapter from *Talking Back* (1989)—how she attempts to keep the two worlds connected and how her views contradict those of Richard Rodriguez on the same topic.

We are both awake in the almost dark of 5 a.m. Everyone else is   1
sound asleep. Mama asks the usual questions. Telling me to look around, make sure I have everything, scolding me because I am uncertain about the actual time the bus arrives. By 5:30 we are waiting outside the closed station. Alone together, we have a chance to really talk. Mama begins. Angry with her children, especially the ones who whisper behind her back, she says bitterly, "Your childhood could not have been that bad. You were fed and clothed. You did not have to do without—that's more than a lot of folks have and I just can't stand the way y'all go on." The hurt in her voice saddens me. I have always wanted to protect mama from hurt, to ease her burdens. Now I am part of what troubles. Confronting me, she says accusingly, "It's not just the other children. You talk too much about the past. You don't just listen." And I do talk. Worse, I write about it.

Mama has always come to each of her children seeking different   2
responses. With me she expresses the disappointment, hurt, and anger of betrayal: anger that her children are so critical, that we can't even have the sense to like the presents she sends. She says, "From now on there will be no presents. I'll just stick some money in a little envelope the way the rest of you do. Nobody wants criticism. Everybody can criticize me but I am supposed to say nothing." When I try to talk, my voice sounds like a twelve year old. When I try to talk, she speaks louder, interrupting me, even though she has said repeatedly, "Explain it to me, this talk about the past." I struggle to return to my thirty-five year old self so that she will know by the sound of my voice that we are two women talking together. It is only when I state firmly in my very adult voice, "Mama, you are not listening," that she becomes quiet. She waits. Now that I have her attention, I fear that my explanations will be lame, inadequate. "Mama," I begin, "people usually go to therapy because they feel hurt inside, because they have pain that will not stop, like a wound that continually breaks open, that

does not heal. And often these hurts, that pain has to do with things that have happened in the past, sometimes in childhood, often in childhood, or things that we believe happened." She wants to know, "What hurts, what hurts are you talking about?" "Mom, I can't answer that. I can't speak for all of us, the hurts are different for everybody. But the point is you try to make the hurt feel better, to heal it, by understanding how it came to be. And I know you feel mad when we say something happened or hurt that you don't remember being that way, but the past isn't like that, we don't have the same memory of it. We remember things differently. You know that. And sometimes folk feel hurt about stuff and you just don't know or didn't realize it, and they need to talk about it. Surely you understand the need to talk about it."

Our conversation is interrupted by the sight of my uncle walking 3 across the park toward us. We stop to watch him. He is on his way to work dressed in a familiar blue suit. They look alike, these two who rarely discuss the past. This interruption makes me think about life in a small town. You always see someone you know. Interruptions, intrusions are part of daily life. Privacy is difficult to maintain. We leave our private space in the car to greet him. After the hug and kiss he has given me every year since I was born, they talk about the day's funerals. In the distance the bus approaches. He walks away knowing that they will see each other later. Just before I board the bus I turn, staring into my mother's face. I am momentarily back in time, seeing myself eighteen years ago, at this same bus stop, staring into my mother's face, continually turning back, waving farewell as I returned to college—that experience which first took me away from our town, from family. Departing was as painful then as it is now. Each movement away makes return harder. Each separation intensifies distance, both physical and emotional.

To a southern black girl from a working-class background who 4 had never been on a city bus, who had never stepped on an escalator, who had never travelled by plane, leaving the comfortable confines of a small town Kentucky life to attend Stanford University was not just frightening; it was utterly painful. My parents had not been delighted that I had been accepted and adamantly opposed my going so far from home. At the time, I did not see their opposition as an expression of their fear that they would lose me forever. Like many working-class folks, they feared what college education might do to their children's minds even as they unenthusiastically acknowledged its importance. They did not understand why I could not attend a college nearby, an all-black college. To them, any college would do. I would graduate, become a school teacher, make a decent living and a good marriage. And even though they reluctantly and skeptically supported my educational endeavors, they also subjected them to constant harsh and bitter critique. It is difficult for me to talk about my parents and their impact on me because they have always felt wary, ambivalent, mistrusting of my intellectual aspirations even as they have been caring and supportive. I want to speak about these contradictions because sorting through them, seeking resolution and reconciliation has been important to me both as it affects my development as a writer, my effort to be fully self-realized, and my longing to remain close to the family and community that provided the groundwork for much of my thinking, writing, and being.

Studying at Stanford, I began to think seriously about class differences. To be materially underprivileged at a university where most folks (with the exception of workers) are materially privileged provokes such thought. Class differences were boundaries no one wanted to face or talk about. It was easier to downplay them, to act as though we were all from privileged backgrounds, to work around them, to confront them privately in the solitude of one's room, or to pretend that just being chosen to study at such an institution meant that those of us who did not come from privilege were already in transition toward privilege. To not long for such transition marked one as rebellious, as unlikely to succeed. It was a kind of treason not to believe that it was better to be identified with the world of material privilege than with the world of the working class, the poor. No wonder our working-class parents from poor backgrounds feared our entry into such a world, intuiting perhaps that we might learn to be ashamed of where we had come from, that we might never return home, or come back only to lord it over them.

Though I hung with students who were supposedly radical and chic, we did not discuss class. I talked to no one about the sources of my shame, how it hurt me to witness the contempt shown the brown-skinned Filipina maids who cleaned our rooms, or later my concern about the $100 a month I paid for a room off-campus which was more than half of what my parents paid for rent. I talked to no one about my efforts to save money, to send a little something home. Yet these class realities separated me from fellow students. We were moving in different directions. I did not intend to forget my class background or alter my class allegiance. And even though I received an education designed to provide me with a bourgeois sensibility, passive acquiescence was not my only option. I knew that I could resist. I could rebel. I could shape the direction and focus of the various forms of knowledge available to me. Even though I sometimes envied and longed for greater material advantages (particularly at vacation times when I would be one of few if any students remaining in the dormitory because there was no money for travel), I did not share the sensibility and values of my peers. That was important—class was not just about money; it was about values which showed and determined behavior. While I often needed more money, I never needed a new set of beliefs and values. For example, I was profoundly shocked and disturbed when peers would talk about their parents without respect, or would even say that they hated their parents. This was especially troubling to me when it seemed that these parents were caring and concerned. It was often explained to me that such hatred was "healthy and normal." To my white, middle-class California roommate, I explained the way we were taught to value our parents and their care, to understand that they were not obligated to give us care. She would always shake her head, laughing all the while, and say, "Missy, you will learn that it's different here, that we think differently." She was right. Soon, I lived alone, like the one Mormon student who kept to himself as he made a concentrated effort to remain true to his religious beliefs and values. Later in graduate school I found that classmates believed "lower class" people had no beliefs and values. I was silent in such discussions, disgusted by their ignorance.

Carol Stack's anthropological study, *All Our Kin*, was one of the 7 first books I read which confirmed my experiential understanding that within black culture (especially among the working class and poor, particularly in southern states), a value system emerged that was counter-hegemonic, that challenged notions of individualism and private property so important to the maintenance of white-supremacist, capitalist patriarchy. Black folk created in marginal spaces a world of community and collectivity where resources were shared. In the preface to *Feminist Theory: from margin to center*, I talked about how the point of difference, this marginality can be the space for the formation of an oppositional world view. That world view must be articulated, named if it is to provide a sustained blueprint for change. Unfortunately, there has existed no consistent framework for such naming. Consequently both the experience of this difference and documentation of it (when it occurs) gradually loses presence and meaning.

Much of what Stack documented about the "culture of poverty," 8 for example, would not describe interactions among most black poor today irrespective of geographical setting. Since the black people she described did not acknowledge (if they recognized it in theoretical terms) the oppositional value of their world view, apparently seeing it more as a survival strategy determined less by conscious efforts to oppose oppressive race and class biases than by circumstance, they did not attempt to establish a framework to transmit their beliefs and values from generation to generation. When circumstances changed, values altered. Efforts to assimilate the values and beliefs of privileged white people, presented through media like television, undermine and destroy potential structures of opposition.

Increasingly, young black people are encouraged by the dominant 9 culture (and by those black people who internalize the values of this hegemony) to believe that assimilation is the only possible way to survive, to succeed. Without the framework of an organized civil rights or black resistance struggle, individual and collective efforts at black liberation that focus on the primacy of self-definition and self-determination often go unrecognized. It is crucial that those among us who resist and rebel, who survive and succeed, speak openly and honestly about our lives and the nature of our personal struggles, the means by which we resolve and reconcile contradictions. This is no easy task. Within the educational institutions where we learn to develop and strengthen our writing and analytical skills, we also learn to think, write, and talk in a manner that shifts attention away from personal experience. Yet if we are to reach our people and all people, if we are to remain connected (especially those of us whose familial backgrounds are poor and working-class), we must understand that the telling of one's personal story provides a meaningful example, a way for folks to identify and connect.

Combining personal with critical analysis and theoretical perspec- 10 tives can engage listeners who might otherwise feel estranged, alienated. To speak simply with language that is accessible to as many folks as possible is also important. Speaking about one's personal experience or speaking with simple language is often considered by academics and/or intellectuals (irrespective of their political inclinations) to be a sign of intellectual weakness or oven anti-intellectualism. Lately, when I speak, I do not stand in place—reading my paper, making little or no eye contact with audiences—but instead make eye contact, talk extemporaneously, digress, and address the audience directly. I have been told that people assume I am not prepared, that I am anti-intellectual, unprofessional (a concept that has everything to do with class as it determines actions and behavior), or that I am reinforcing the stereotype of black people as non-theoretical and gutsy.

Such criticism was raised recently by fellow feminist scholars after 11 a talk I gave at Northwestern University at a conference on "Gender, Culture, Politics" to an audience that was mainly students and academics. I deliberately chose to speak in a very basic way, thinking especially about the few community folks who had come to hear me. Weeks later, KumKum Sangari, a fellow participant who shared with me what was said when I was no longer present, and I engaged in quite rigorous critical dialogue about the way my presentation had been perceived primarily by privileged white female academics. She was concerned that I not mask my knowledge of theory, that I not appear anti-intellectual. Her critique compelled me to articulate concerns that I am often silent about with colleagues. I spoke about class allegiance and revolutionary commitments, explaining that it was disturbing to me that intellectual radicals who speak about transforming society, ending the domination of race, sex, class, cannot break with behavior patterns that reinforce and perpetuate domination, or continue to use as their sole reference point how we might be or are per-

ceived by those who dominate, whether or not we gain their acceptance and approval.

This is a primary contradiction which raises the issue of whether   12
or not the academic setting is a place where one can be truly radical or
subversive. Concurrently, the use of a language and style of presentation that alienates most folks who are not also academically trained reinforces the notion that the academic world is separate from real life,
that everyday world where we constantly adjust our language and behavior to meet diverse needs. The academic setting is separate only
when we work to make it so. It is a false dichotomy which suggests
that academics and/or intellectuals can only speak to one another, that
we cannot hope to speak with the masses. What is true is that we make
choices, that we choose our audiences, that we choose voices to hear
and voices to silence. If I do not speak in a language that can be understood, then there is little chance for dialogue. This issue of language
and behavior is a central contradiction all radical intellectuals, particularly those who are members of oppressed groups, must continually
confront and work to resolve. One of the clear and present dangers
that exists when we move outside our class of origin, our collective
ethnic experience, and enter hierarchical institutions which daily reinforce domination by race, sex, and class, is that we gradually assume a
mindset similar to those who dominate and oppress, that we lose critical consciousness because it is not reinforced or affirmed by the environment. We must be ever vigilant. It is important that we know who
we are speaking to, who we most want to hear us, who we most long
to move, motivate, and touch with our words.

When I first came to New Haven to teach at Yale, I was truly sur-   13
prised by the marked class divisions between black folks—students
and professors—who identify with Yale and those black folks who
work at Yale or in surrounding communities. Style of dress and self-
presentation are most often the central markers of one's position. I
soon learned that the black folks who spoke on the street were likely to
be part of the black community and those who carefully shifted their
glance were likely to be associated with Yale. Walking with a black female colleague one day, I spoke to practically every black person in
sight (a gesture which reflects my upbringing), an action which disturbed my companion. Since I addressed black folk who were clearly
not associated with Yale, she wanted to know whether or not I knew
them. That was funny to me. "Of course not," I answered. Yet when I
thought about it seriously, I realized that in a deep way, I knew them
for they, and not my companion or most of my colleagues at Yale, re-
semble my family. Later that year, in a black women's support group I
started for undergraduates, students from poor backgrounds spoke
about the shame they sometimes feel when faced with the reality of
their connection to working-class and poor black people. One student

confessed that her father is a street person, addicted to drugs, someone who begs from passersby. She, like other Yale students, turns away from street people often, sometimes showing anger or contempt; she hasn't wanted anyone to know that she was related to this kind of person. She struggles with this, wanting to find a way to acknowledge and affirm this reality, to claim this connection. The group asked me and one another what we do to remain connected, to honor the bonds we have with working-class and poor people even as our class experience alters.

Maintaining connections with family and community across class 14 boundaries demands more than just summary recall of where one's roots are, where one comes from. It requires knowing, naming, and being ever-mindful of those aspects of one's past that have enabled and do enable one's self-development in the present, that sustain and support, that enrich. One must also honestly confront barriers that do exist, aspects of that past that do diminish. My parents' ambivalence about my love for reading led to intense conflict. They (especially my mother) would work to ensure that I had access to books, but would threaten to burn the books or throw them away if I did not conform to other expectations. Or they would insist that reading too much would drive me insane. Their ambivalence nurtured in me a like uncertainty about the value and significance of intellectual endeavor which took years for me to unlearn. While this aspect of our class reality was one that wounded and diminished, their vigilant insistence that being smart did not make me a "better" or "superior" person (which often got on my nerves because I think I wanted to have that sense that it did indeed set me apart, make me better) made a profound impression. From them I learned to value and respect various skills and talents folk might have, not just to value people who read books and talk about ideas. They and my grandparents might say about somebody, "Now he don't read nor write a lick, but he can tell a story," or as my grandmother would say, "call out the hell in words."

Empty romanticization of poor or working-class backgrounds un- 15 dermines the possibility of true connection. Such connection is based on understanding difference in experience and perspective and working to mediate and negotiate these terrains. Language is a crucial issue for folk whose movement outside the boundaries of poor and working-class backgrounds changes the nature and direction of their speech. Coming to Stanford with my own version of a Kentucky accent, which I think of always as a strong sound quite different from Tennessee or Georgia speech, I learned to speak differently while maintaining the speech of my region, the sound of my family and community. This was of course much easier to keep up when I returned home to stay often. In recent years, I have endeavored to use various speaking styles in the classroom as a teacher and find it disconcerts those who feel that the use of a particular patois excludes them as listeners, even if there is translation into the usual, acceptable mode of speech. Learning to listen to different voices, hearing different speech challenges the notion that we must all assimilate—share a single, similar talk—in educational institutions. Language reflects the culture from which we emerge. To deny ourselves daily use of speech patterns that are common and familiar, that embody the unique and distinctive aspect of our self is one of the ways we become estranged and alienated from our past. It is important for us to have as many languages on hand as we can know or learn. It is important for those of us who are black, who speak in particular patois as well as standard English to express ourselves in both ways.

Often I tell students from poor and working-class backgrounds 16 that if you believe what you have learned and are learning in schools and universities separates you from your past, this is precisely what will happen. It is important to stand firm in the conviction that nothing can truly separate us from our pasts when we nurture and cherish that connection. An important strategy for maintaining contact is ongoing acknowledgment of the primacy of one's past, of one's background, affirming the reality that such bonds are not severed automatically solely because one enters a new environment or moves toward a different class experience.

Again, I do not wish to romanticize this effort, to dismiss the reality of conflict and contradiction. During my time at Stanford, I did go 17 through a period of more than a year when I did not return home. That period was one where I felt that it was simply too difficult to mesh my profoundly disparate realities. Critical reflection about the choice I was making, particularly about why I felt a choice had to be made, pulled me through this difficult time. Luckily I recognized that the insistence on choosing between the world of family and community and the new world of privileged white people and privileged ways of knowing was imposed upon me by the outside. It is as though a mythical contract had been signed somewhere which demanded of us black folks that once we entered these spheres we would immediately give up all vestiges of our underprivileged past. It was my responsibility to formulate a way of being that would allow me to participate fully in my new environment while integrating and maintaining aspects of the old.

One of the most tragic manifestations of the pressure black people 18 feel to assimilate is expressed in the internalization of racist perspectives. I was shocked and saddened when I first heard black professors at Stanford downgrade and express contempt for black students, expecting us to do poorly, refusing to establish nurturing bonds. At every university I have attended as a student or worked at as a teacher, I have heard similar attitudes expressed with little or no understanding of factors that might prevent brilliant black students from performing to their full capability. Within universities, there are few educational and social spaces where students who wish to affirm positive ties to ethnicity—to blackness, to working-class backgrounds— can receive affirmation and support. Ideologically, the message is clear—assimilation is the way to gain acceptance and approval from those in power.

Many white people enthusiastically supported Richard Rodriguez's vehement contention in his autobiography, *Hunger of Memory*, that attempts to maintain ties with his Chicano background impeded his progress, that he had to sever ties with community and kin to succeed at Stanford and in the larger world, that family language, in his case Spanish, had to be made secondary or discarded. If the terms of success as defined by the standards of ruling groups within white-supremacist, capitalist patriarchy are the only standards that exist, then assimilation is indeed necessary. But they are not. Even in the face of powerful structures of domination, it remains possible for each of us, especially those of us who are members of oppressed and/or exploited groups as well as those radical visionaries who may have race, class, and sex privilege, to define and determine alternative standards, to decide on the nature and extent of compromise. Standards by which one's success is measured, whether student or professor, are quite different for those of us who wish to resist reinforcing the domination of race, sex, and class, who work to maintain and strengthen our ties with the oppressed, with those who lack material privilege, with our families who are poor and working-class.

When I wrote my first book, *Ain't I A Woman: black women and feminism*, the issue of class and its relationship to who one's reading audience might be came up for me around my decision not to use footnotes, for which I have been sharply criticized. I told people that my concern was that footnotes set class boundaries for readers, determining who a book is for. I was shocked that many academic folks scoffed at this idea. I shared that I went into working-class black communities as well as talked with family and friends to survey whether or not they ever read books with footnotes and found that they did not. A few did not know what they were, but most folks saw them as indicating that a book was for college-educated people. These responses influenced my decision. When some of my more radical, college-educated friends freaked out about the absence of footnotes, I seriously questioned how we could ever imagine revolutionary transformation of society if such a small shift in direction could be viewed as threatening. Of course, many folks warned that the absence of footnotes would make the work less credible in academic circles. This information also highlighted the way in which class informs our choices. Certainly I did feel that choosing to use simple language, absence of footnotes, etc. would mean I was jeopardizing the possibility of being taken seriously in academic circles but then this was a political matter and a political decision. It utterly delights me that this has proven not to be the case and that the book is read by many academics as well as by people who are not college-educated.

Always our first response when we are motivated to conform or 21 compromise within structures that reinforce domination must be to engage in critical reflection. Only by challenging ourselves to push against oppressive boundaries do we make the radical alternative possible, expanding the realm and scope of critical inquiry. Unless we share radical strategies, ways of rethinking and revisioning with students, with kin and community, with a larger audience, we risk perpetuating the stereotype that we succeed because we are the exception, different from the rest of our people. Since I left home and entered college, I am often asked, usually by white people, if my sisters and brothers are also high achievers. At the root of this question is the longing for reinforcement of the belief in "the exception" which enables race, sex, and class biases to remain intact. I am careful to separate what it means to be exceptional from a notion of "the exception."

Frequently I hear smart black folks, from poor and working-class 22 backgrounds, stressing their frustration that at times family and community do not recognize that they are exceptional. Absence of positive affirmation clearly diminishes the longing to excel in academic endeavors. Yet it is important to distinguish between the absence of basic positive affirmation and the longing for continued reinforcement that we are special. Usually liberal white folks will willingly offer continual reinforcement of us as exceptions—as special. This can be both patronizing and very seductive. Since we often work in situations where we are isolated from other black folks, we can easily begin to feel that encouragement from white people is the primary or only source of support and recognition. Given the internalization of racism, it is easy to view this support as more validating and legitimizing than similar support from black people. Still, nothing takes the place of being valued and appreciated by one's own, by one's family and community. We share a mutual and reciprocal responsibility for affirming one another's successes. Sometimes we have to talk to our folks about the fact that we need their ongoing support and affirmation, that it is unique and special to us. In some cases we may never receive desired recognition and acknowledgment of specific achievements from kin. Rather than seeing this as a basis for estrangement, for severing connection, it is useful to explore other sources of nourishment and support.

I do not know that my mother's mother ever acknowledged my 23 college education except to ask me once, "How can you live so far away from your people?" Yet she gave me sources of affirmation and nourishment, sharing the legacy of her quilt-making, of family history, of her incredible way with words. Recently, when our father retired after more than thirty years of work as a janitor, I wanted to pay tribute to this experience, to identify links between his work and my own as writer and teacher. Reflecting on our family past, I recalled ways he had been an impressive example of diligence and hard work, approaching tasks with a seriousness of concentration I work to mirror and develop, with a discipline I struggle to maintain. Sharing these thoughts with him keeps us connected, nurtures our respect for each other, maintaining a space, however large or small, where we can talk.

Open, honest communication is the most important way we main- 24
tain relationships with kin and community as our class experience and backgrounds change. It is as vital as the sharing of resources. Often financial assistance is given in circumstances where there is no meaningful contact. However helpful, this can also be an expression of estrangement and alienation. Communication between black folks from various experiences of material privilege was much easier when we were all in segregated communities sharing common experiences in relation to social institutions. Without this grounding, we must work to maintain ties, connection. We must assume greater responsibility for making and maintaining contact, connections that can shape our intellectual visions and inform our radical commitments.

The most powerful resource any of us can have as we study and 25
teach in university settings is full understanding and appreciation of the richness, beauty, and primacy of our familial and community backgrounds. Maintaining awareness of class differences, nurturing ties with the poor and working-class people who are our most intimate kin, our comrades in struggle, transforms and enriches our intellectual experience. Education as the practice of freedom becomes not a force which fragments or separates, but one that brings us closer, expanding our definitions of home and community.

Working with the Text

1. hooks discusses the reasons that some parents might fear sending their children to college. What kind of parents does she mean? What do they fear will happen to their children?
2. What does hooks mean when she says that "class was not just about money; it was about values which showed and determined behavior"? What are her examples to show that "class" and "values" and "behavior" are linked?
3. According to hooks, in what ways does "movement outside the boundaries of poor and working-class backgrounds" affect the language people from those backgrounds speak? In hooks' view, why is this a "crucial issue"?

4. hooks mixes simple "everyday" language ("Mama asks the usual questions") with very complicated "academic" language ("If the terms of success as defined by the standards of ruling groups within white-supremacist, capitalist patriarchy are the only standards that exist . . ."). Find other examples of both kinds of language. Why do you think hooks mixes the two kinds of language?

Working beyond the Text

1. hooks uses vocabulary that might be unfamiliar to some of her readers: counter-hegemonic, individualism, private property, white-supremacist, capitalist, and so on. Make a list of all the words hooks uses that you do not understand but know are important to her meaning and define them. How does knowing the definitions enhance your understanding of hooks' meaning?

2. According to hooks, what are the difficulties and rewards of trying to keep close to home? Do you think there's a danger of your not being able to keep close to your own home? If not, why not? If so, what can you do to keep close to home in your own life?

3. In several places in the essay, hooks characterizes her writing style as accessible to people who are not highly educated academics. Do you find her style as accessible as she claims it is? Why or why not?

4. If you have read the Richard Rodriguez piece in this chapter, how do you understand hooks' criticism of his ideas in paragraph nineteen of her essay? Does she offer a satisfactory answer to his dilemma about "severing ties" with family?

3

LANGUAGES OF

ACADEMIC DISCOURSE

INTRODUCTION

Why should students have to learn "academic discourse," with its strange vocabulary, stilted grammar, footnotes, bibliographies, and all the rest? Some people, including many teachers, feel there's no need for students to learn such a difficult, alienating, elitist kind of language. Others feel that since academic discourse is a language of power and prestige, students who don't learn it are cheated out of opportunities for success in school and beyond.

The writers represented in this chapter discuss these issues from many different perspectives, take many different stands, offer many different solutions. But what *is* academic discourse? Some people deny that it can be defined at all, since, for example, the language of physics is completely different from the language of philosophy and the language of anthropology is completely different from the language of physiology. Others, however, do find certain common properties in all (or at least most) academic discourse and claim that students can learn to write using these basic features.

First, academic discourse is a *conversation* among scholars. Students can learn to listen in on the conversation and begin to add their own comments to it; they can, in Mike Rose's famous phrase, "join the conversation." When students try to read difficult academic discourse, they may feel excluded at first, but if teachers don't teach academic discourse, then students will remain excluded forever rather than becoming gradually included in the conversation (Rose 329–30).

Second, techniques and strategies common to all (or most) academic discourse can be categorized and learned. If academic discourse is a conversation, but, at the same time, is the product of a single writer, then writers of academic discourse must take pains to include other voices in the conversation as they write. Therefore, they read other parts of the conversation (essays by other scholars) and quote them in their work. Then they respond to them, agreeing or disagreeing, modifying or expanding, adding something new to the conversation.

Along the way, scholars may speak as "insiders" to other insiders, making students feel like "outsiders." Cathy Popkin sarcastically complains about what she calls the "of course" statements of a lot of academic discourse: a teacher may say, "'You have, of course, read Skovoroda,'" when students have never even heard of someone named Skovoroda (Popkin 174). The third paragraph of this introduction has an "of course" statement: "in Mike Rose's famous phrase." Have the readers of this introduction ever heard of Mike Rose or his supposedly "famous phrase"? Possibly not. However, having read that statement, readers may learn that Mike Rose is a common name in a conversation they may want to join, and that "joining the conversation" is an important idea to know if they want to understand that conversation and contribute ideas to it.e

This strategy can backfire. In an episode of *M*A*S*H*, Radar O'Reilly tries to impress a nurse he wants to date by trying to seem more cultured than he is. A friend teaches him that when she says a name he doesn't know, such as Bach, he should respond knowingly, "Ah! Bach!" The nurse easily sees through this trick; Radar clearly is not a member of the community that regularly discusses Bach. Learning academic discourse isn't as easy as learning a few simple tricks ("Ah! Mike Rose!"). It takes longer than a few minutes or even a few sentences. Can it be done? Is it worth doing? These are the questions addressed in this chapter.

WORKS CITED

Popkin, Cathy. "A Plea to the Wielders of Academic Dis(of)course." *College English* 54 (1992): 173–81.

Rose, Mike. "Remedial Writing Courses: A Critique and a Proposal." *The Writing Teacher's Sourcebook.* 2nd ed. Eds. Gary Tate and Edward P.J. Corbett. New York: Oxford UP, 1988. 318–37.

—————————— Before You Read ——————————

Before you read any combination of essays in this chapter, you might prepare by doing any of the activities below as either class or small group discussions, or as formal or informal writing assignments. They are designed to help you find out what you already know about the issues discussed by the authors in the chapter, so you have some background for understanding what the authors say.

1. Everywhere in popular culture—in movies, television shows, popular music—we see representations of students and teachers, schools and colleges. How is the language of the university characterized in the popular media? What's the stereotype of "scholarly" language? Explain with reference to specific movies, shows, or songs.

2. Make a catalogue of all the writing you do in college, from class

notes to lab reports, from homework to formal essays. How are the requirements of different assignments from different classes different from each other? That is, how do the requirements for an English literature paper differ from those of a physics lab report?

3. What is "academic discourse"? How is the language you read and are expected to write in school (especially college) different from the everyday language you speak in other situations? Using a passage from one of your textbooks, explain features that identify it unmistakably as academic discourse.

4. Some people have more trouble than others in learning academic discourse. Why? What in a person's personality or background could lead him or her to have trouble learning how to read and write at the college level for college audiences?

5. A lot of people, especially new college students, hate academic discourse; they find it boring, confusing, and needlessly wordy. If this is your opinion, take a moment to consider why academic discourse is still being produced. If it is so difficult to read and write, what good is it? What would the people who want you to learn it say in its defense? What can it do that other kinds of language can not?

After You Read

After you read any combination of essays in this chapter, you might follow up by doing any of the activities below as either class or small group discussions, or as formal or informal writing assignments. They are designed to help you extend what you have learned from the authors in the chapter by discovering new perspectives on the chapter's themes on your own.

1. Some of the writers in this chapter may have given you new insights that made you think about scholarly language in a different way than you did before. What preconceived ideas or stereotypes did you have about professors and their language that were thrown into question by the essays in this chapter? In what ways?

2. We often hear that there is a "literacy crisis" in our country. Several of the writers in this chapter touch upon issues related to the growing difficulties students have in producing "literate" texts according to college standards. What are the various views presented? Supplement your explanation by going to the library and discovering what various other critics have said about the "literacy crisis."

3. What major views are presented in this chapter about the idea of teaching a "standard" form of academic language to college students? Which writers advocate it and why? Which writers oppose it

and why? Which writers seem to have a more complicated view than simple advocacy or opposition?

4. Interview your composition instructor, and perhaps other composition instructors at your school, about the reasons that they teach as they do. What are their goals for the kind of language you will learn to produce? What techniques do they use to teach you to read and write that kind of language? How do their ideas relate to any of the ideas expressed by writers in this chapter?

5. Which reading in which class is giving you the most trouble this semester? Why? Take a close look at a specific text from the class. Use everything you've learned from this chapter about how and why academic discourse is difficult for many students to explain your own difficulty in understanding that specific text. Which essays from this chapter give you the most help in understanding your difficulties?

UNIT ONE

USES OF ACADEMIC DISCOURSE

The Politics of Remediation

Mike Rose

Mike Rose was raised in a working-class neighborhood in Los Angeles, where he attended working-class schools and was routed early
onto a "vo-tech" track. He managed to overcome these obstacles to
attend UCLA and become a professor of English. As a writer, his special focus is on students who share his background and on how the
education establishment must change in order to help them succeed.
In this excerpt from his book *Lives on the Boundary* (1989), he shows
how alienating academic language can be for students who are new
to it.

The students are taking their seats in the large auditorium, moving in   1
two streams down the main aisles, entering from a side exit to capture seats
in the front. You're a few minutes late and find a seat somewhere in the
middle. There are a couple of hundred students around you and in front of
you, a hundred or so behind. A youngish man walks onto the stage and lays
a folder and a book on the podium. There are track lights above him, and in
back of him there's a system of huge blackboards that rise and descend on
rollers in the wall. The man begins talking. He raises his voice and taps the
podium and sweeps his hand through the air. Occasionally, he'll turn to the
moving boards and write out a phrase or someone's name or a reference to a
section of the textbook. You begin writing these things down. He has a
beard and smiles now and then and seems wrapped up in what he's talking
about.

This is Introductory Sociology. It's one of the courses students can elect to   2
fulfill their general education requirements. The catalogue said that Introduc-
tory Sociology would deal with "the characteristics of social life" and "the
processes of Social interaction." It also said that the course would cover the
"tools of sociological investigation," but that came last and was kind of general
and didn't seem too important. You're curious about what it is that makes peo-
ple tick and curious, as well, about the causes of social problems, so a course on
social interaction sounded interesting. You filled Sociology 1 in on some cards

and sent them out and eventually got other cards back that told you you were enrolled.

"These are the social facts that are reflected in the interpretations we 3 *make of them," says the man on the stage and then extends his open hand toward the audience. "Now, this is not the place to rehearse the arguments between Kantian idealists and Lockean realists, but . . ." You're still writing down, ". . . reflected in the interpretations we make of them. . . ." and he continues: "But let us stop for a moment and consider what it means to say 'social fact.' What is a fact? And in considering this question, we are drawn into hermeneutics." He turns to write that last word on the board, and as he writes you copy it down in your notes. He refers the class to the textbook, to a "controlling metaphor" and to "microanalyses"—and as you're writing this down, you hear him stressing "constructivist interpretations" and reading a quotation from somebody and concluding that "in the ambiguity lies the richness."*

People are taking notes and you are taking notes. You are taking notes on 4 *a lecture you don't understand. You get a phrase, a sentence, then the next loses you. It's as though you're hearing a conversation in a crowd or from another room—out of phase, muted. The man on the stage concludes his lecture and everyone rustles and you close your notebook and prepare to leave. You feel a little strange. Maybe tomorrow this stuff will clear up. Maybe by tomorrow this will be easier. But by the time you're in the hallway, you don't think it will be easier at all.*

Some of the students I worked with were admitted to college, as I 5 had been, under a special policy, or they had transferred in from a community college. But many, actually most, of the freshmen who visited the Tutorial Center had high school records that were different from mine; they were not somnambulant and did not have spotty transcripts. They were the kids who held class offices and saw their names on the honor roll; they went out for sports and were involved in drama and music and a variety of civic and religious clubs. If they had trouble with mathematics or English or science, they could depend on the fairness of a system that rewarded effort and involvement: They participated in class discussions, got their work in on time, helped the teacher out, did extra-credit projects. In short, they were good academic citizens, and in some high schools—especially beleaguered ones—that was enough to assure them a B. So though some of them came to UCLA aware that math or English or science was hard for them, they figured they'd do okay if they put in the time, if they read the textbook carefully and did all their homework. They saw themselves as academic successes.

These were the first students I'd worked with who did not have 6 histories of failure. Their placement in a course designated "remedial" or the receipt of a D or an F on a midterm examination—even being encouraged by counselors to sign up for tutorial support—was strange and unsettling. They simply had little experience of being on the academic fringe. Thus it was not uncommon for visitors to the Tutorial Center at first to deny what was happening to them. People whose placement tests had indicated a need for English-as-a-second-language courses would often ask us to try to get that judgment reversed. They considered themselves to be assimilated, achieving Americans. Their names had shifted from Keiko to Kay, from Cheung to Chuck. They did not want to be marked as different. Students who were placed in Remedial English would ask us to go look at their tests, hoping there had been a mistake. Tutors often had to spend their first session working through the various emotions this labeling produced. You knew when that student walked through the door; you could sense the feeling of injustice he brought with him as he sat down alongside you. "Something's wrong," Tony blurted out soon after he introduced himself. "This class is way below my level." The tutor assured him that the class was a tough one and would soon get harder. "Well, I hope so," he said, "cause I took Advanced English in high school. I feel kind of silly doing this stuff."

But others among these young people knew or had long suspected 7 that their math or English needed improvement. Their placement in a remedial course confirmed their suspicions. The danger here was that they might not be able to separate out their particular problems with calculus or critical writing from their own image of themselves as thinkers, from their intellectual self-worth. The ugly truth was exposed. The remedial designation or the botched essay or the disastrous midterm ripped through their protective medals. "I'm just no good at this," said one young woman, holding her smudged essay. "I'm so stupid." Imagine, then, how they felt as they found themselves in a four-hundred-acre aggregation of libraries and institutes and lecture halls, where they could circle the campus and not be greeted by anyone who knew anything about them, where a professor who had no idea who they were used a microphone to inform them that social facts are reflected in the interpretations we make of them.

"It was so weird," said Kathy. "I was walking down the hall in the 8 Engineering building and suddenly I felt really strange. I felt I was completely alone here. Do you know what I mean? Like I go for days and don't see anybody I know." The huge lecture halls, the distance from the professor, the streams of students you don't know. One of the tasks facing all freshmen is to figure out ways to counter this loneliness. Some will eventually feel the loneliness as passage, as the rending of the familiar that is part of coming of age. The solitude of vast libraries and unfamiliar corridors will transform into college folklore, the bittersweet tales told about leaving home, about the crises of becoming adult. But a much deeper sense of isolation comes if the loneliness you feel is rooted in the books and lectures that surround you, in the very language of the place. You are finally sitting in the lecture hall you have been preparing to sit in for years. You have been the good student, perhaps even the star—you are to be the engineer, the lawyer, the doctor. Your parents have knocked themselves out for you. And you can't get what some man is saying in an *introductory* course. You're not what you thought you were. The alien voice of the lecturer is telling you that something central to your being is, after all, a wish spun in the night, a ruse, the mist and vapor of sleep.

I had seen Andrea before, but this time she was limping. Her back- 9 pack was stretched with books. Her collar and pleats were pressed, and there was a perfect white ribbon in her hair. She had been secretary of her high school and a gymnast, belonged to the Biology Club, and worked on the annual. Her father was a bell captain at a hotel in Beverly Hills; her mother a seamstress. They immigrated when Andrea was five, and when they were alone at home, they spoke Japanese. Andrea was fluently bilingual. She graduated fifteenth in a class of five hundred. She came to UCLA with good grades, strong letters, and an interest in science. She had not been eating well since she'd been here. The doctors told her she was making herself anemic. A week before she had passed out while she was driving and hit a tree on a sidewalk near her home. Her backpack must have weighed twenty pounds.

All colleges have their killer courses, courses meant to screen stu- 10 dents from science or engineering or those departments in arts and humanities that aren't desperate for enrollments. At UCLA the most infamous killer course is Chemistry 11-A, General Chemistry. The course is difficult for lots of reasons, but the primary one is that it requires students not just to understand and remember individual facts, formulas, and operations but to use them to solve problems, to recognize what kind of problem a particular teaser is and to combine and recombine facts, formulas, and operations to solve it. Andrea failed the midterm. Her tutor explained that she didn't seem to have much experience solving chemistry problems. Andrea would sit before her book for hours evening after evening, highlighting long stretches of text with a yellow marker, sketching the structure of benzene and butadiene, writing down Avogadro's law and Dalton's law, repeating to herself the differences between ionic and covalent bonds. The midterm exam hit her like a blind punch. It didn't require her to dump her memory. It gave her a short list of problems and asked her to solve them.

Andrea felt tremendous pressure to succeed, to continue to be all 11 things to all people. She was speaking so softly I had to lean toward her. She said she was scared. Her cheek was still bruised from the accident. She missed a week of school then, and as she spoke, I had the sudden, chilling recognition that further injuries could save her, that deliverance could come in the form of another crash. I began talking to her about counseling, how helpful it can be to have someone to talk to, how I'd done it myself, how hard the sciences are for so many of us, how we all need someone to lean on. She looked up at me, and said in a voice drifting back somewhere toward childhood, "You know, I wish you had known me in high school."

James had a different reaction to failure.   12

He sat in my office and repeated that he was doing okay, that he'd   13 been studying hard and would pull his grades up on his finals. "I've got my study skills perfected, and I am punctual about visiting the library." He paused and looked at his legs, placed his two hands palms down on his thighs, and then he pressed. "I will make it. My confidence was down before." James was on academic probation; he needed to pass all his courses or he would be what they called STD: subject to dismissal. "I've got the right attitude now. I took a motivation course over the break, and that helped me improve my study skills and get my priorities straight." He was looking right at me as he said all this: handsome, muscular, preppy. Dressed for success. Mechanical successfulness. I'm okay, you're okay. Jay Gatsby would have noted his poise and elocution. I sat there quietly listening, trying to decide what to do with his forced jock talk. I drifted a little, trying to conjure up the leader of James' "motivation seminar," the person delivering to him a few techniques and big promises: a way to skim a page or manage his time. James listened desperately and paid his money and went off with a positive attitude and his study skills perfected, emboldened with a set of gimmicks, holding a dream together with gum and string.

James's tutor suggested that he come see me because he was get-   14 ting somewhere between a C and a D in his composition course and seemed increasingly unable to concentrate. His responses to the tutor's questions were getting vague and distracted. I asked James for his paper and could quickly see that he had spent time on it; it was typed and had been proofread. I read further and understood the C–; his essay missed the mark of the assignment, which required James to critically analyze a passage from John Berger's *Ways of Seeing*. What he did instead was summarize. This was something I had seen with students who lacked experience writing papers that required them to take an idea carefully apart. They approach the task in terms they can handle, retell the material to you, summarize it, demonstrate that, yes, they can understand the stuff, and here it is. Sometimes it is very hard to get them to see that summary is not adequate, for it had been adequate so many times before. What you have to do, then, is model step by step the kind of critical approach the paper requires. And that was what I started to do with James.

I asked him what he thought Berger's reason was for writing *Ways* 15
of Seeing, and he gave me a pretty good answer. I asked another question, and for a brief while it seemed that he was with me. But then he
stopped and said, "I should have gotten better than a C–. I think I deserve way higher than that." There it was. A brand. I said that I knew
the grade was a disappointment, but if he'd stick with me he'd do better. He didn't say much more. He looked away. I had tacitly agreed
with his teacher, so we were past discussing the paper: We were discussing his identity and his future. I work hard, he's really saying to
me. I go to class. I read the book. I write the paper. Can't you see. I'm
not a C–. Don't tell me I'm a C–. He was looking straight ahead past
me at the wall. His hands were still on his legs.

The counselor's office was always dusky, the sun blocked by thick 16
trees outside the windows. There was an oversize easy chair by his
desk. In it sat Marita, thin, head down, hands in her lap, her shiny hair
covering her face. The counselor spoke her name, and she looked up,
her eyes red in the half-light. The counselor explained that the graduate student who taught her English had accused Marita of plagiarism
and had turned her paper over to the director of Freshman English. He
asked her to continue, to tell me the story herself.

Marita had been at UCLA for about three weeks. This was her first 17
writing assignment. The class had read a discussion of creativity by
Jacob Bronowski and were supposed to write papers agreeing or disagreeing with his discussion. What, Marita wondered, would she say?
"What is the insight with which the scientist tries to see into nature?"
asked Bronowski. Marita wasn't a scientist, and she didn't consider
herself to be a particularly creative person, like an artist or an actress.
Her father had always been absolute about the expression of opinion,
especially with his daughters: "Don't talk unless you know." "All science is the search for unity in hidden likenesses," asserted Bronowski.
"The world is full of fools who speak in ignorance," Marita's father
would say, and Marita grew up cautious and reticent. Her thoughts on
creativity seemed obvious or, worse yet, silly next to this man
Bronowski. What did it mean anyway when he said: "We remake nature by the act of discovery, in the poem or in the theorem"?[1] She
wanted to do well on the assignment, so she went to the little library
by her house and looked in the encyclopedia. She found an entry on
creativity and used some selections from it that had to do with mathe-
maticians and scientists. On the bottom of the last page of her paper,
she listed the encyclopedia and her English composition textbook as

---

[1]Jacob Bronowski, "The Creative Mind," in *The Norton Reader, Shorter Edition*, ed. Arthur M. East-
man et al. (New York: Norton, 1965), pp. 123–134.

her references. What had she done wrong? "They're saying I cheated. I didn't cheat." She paused and thought. "You're supposed to use other people, and I did, and I put the name of the book I used on the back of my paper."

The counselor handed me the paper. It was clear by the third sen- 18
tence that the writing was not all hers. She had incorporated stretches of old encyclopedia prose into her paper and had quoted only some of it. I couldn't know if she had lifted directly or paraphrased the rest, but it was formal and dated and sprinkled with high-cultural refer-ences, just not what you'd find in freshman writing. I imagined that it had pleased her previous teachers that she cared enough about her work to go find sources, to rely on experts. Marita had come from a tough school in Compton—an area to the southeast of where I'd grown up—and her conscientiousness and diligence, her commitment to the academic way, must have been a great joy to those who taught her. She shifted, hoisting herself back up from the recesses of the coun-selor's chair. "Are they going to dismiss me? Are they going to kick me out of school?"

Marita was adrift in a set of conventions she didn't fully under- 19
stand; she offended without knowing why. Virtually all the writing academics do is built on the writing of others. Every argument pro-cedes from the texts of others. Marita was only partially initiated to how this works: She was still unsure as to how to weave quotations in with her own prose, how to mark the difference, how to cite whom she used, how to strike the proper balance between her writing and some-one else's—how, in short, to position herself in an academic discus-sion.

I told Marita that I would talk with her teacher and that I was sure 20
we could work something out, maybe another chance to write the paper. I excused myself and walked slowly back to my office, half lost in thought, reading here and there in the Bronowski excerpt. It was typical fare for Freshman English anthologies, the sort of essay you'd originally find in places like *The New Yorker*. Bronowski, the eminent scientist, looking back on his career, weaving poetry in with cybernet-ics, quoting *Faust* in German, allusive, learned, reflective.

The people who put together those freshman anthologies are 21
drawn to this sort of thing: It's in the tradition of the English essay and reflects rich learning and polished style. But it's easy to forget how dif-ficult these essays can be and how developed a taste they require. When I was at Loyola, someone recommended I buy Jacques Barzun's *The Energies of Art,* a collection of "fifteen striking essays on art and culture." I remember starting one essay and stopping, adrift, two or three pages later. Then another, but no go. The words arose from a depth of knowledge and a developed perception and a wealth of re-ceived ways to talk about art and a seemingly endless reserve of allu-

sions. I felt like a janitor at a gallery opening, silent, intimidated, little flecks of knowledge—Bagehot, Stendhal, baroque ideology—sticking to the fiber of my broom.

Marita's assignment assumed a number of things: an ability to slip 22 into Bronowski's discussion, a reserve of personal experiences that the writer herself would perceive as creative, a knowledge of and facility with—confidence with, really—the kinds of stylistic moves you'd find in those *New Yorker* essays. And it did *not* assume that someone, by family culture, by gender, would be reluctant to engage the reading on its own terms. Marita was being asked to write in a cognitive and social vacuum. I'm sure the other students in her class had a rough time of it as well. Many competent adult writers would too. But the solution Marita used marked her as an outsider and almost tripped the legal switches of the university.

At twenty-eight, Lucia was beginning her second quarter at 23 UCLA. There weren't many people here like her. She was older, had a family, had transferred in from a community college. She represented a population that historically hadn't gained much entrance to places like this: the returning student, the single, working mother. She had a network of neighbors and relatives that provided child care. On this day, though, the cousin on tap had an appointment at Immigration, so Lucia brought her baby with her to her psychology tutorial. Her tutor had taken ill that morning, so rather than turn her away, the receptionist brought her in to me, for I had spoken with her before. Lucia held her baby through most of our session, the baby facing her, Lucia's leg moving rhythmically, continually—a soothing movement that rocked him into sleep.

Upon entrance to UCLA, Lucia declared a psychology major. She 24 had completed all her preliminary requirements at her community college and now faced that same series of upper-division courses that I took when I abandoned graduate study in English some years before: Physiological Psychology, Learning, Perception . . . all that. She was currently enrolled in Abnormal Psychology, "the study of the dynamics and prevention of abnormal behavior." Her professor had begun the course with an intellectual curve ball. He required the class to read excerpts from Thomas Szasz's controversial *The Myth of Mental Illness,* a book that debunks the very notions underlying the traditional psychological study of abnormal behavior, a book that was proving very difficult for Lucia.

My previous encounter with Lucia had convinced me that she was 25 an able student. She was conscientious about her studies—recopied notes, visited professors—and she enjoyed writing: she wrote poems in an old copy book and read popular novels, both in Spanish and English. But Szasz—Szasz was throwing her. She couldn't get through the twelve-and-a-half pages of introduction. I asked her to read some passages out loud and explain them to me as best she could. And as Lucia read and talked, it became clear to me that while she could, with some doing, pick her way through Szasz's sophisticated prose, certain elements of his argument, particular assumptions and allusions, were foreign to her—or, more precisely, a frame of mind or tradition or set of assumptions that was represented by a single word, phrase, or allusion was either unknown to her or clashed dramatically with frames of mind and traditions of her own.

Here are the first few lines of Szasz's introduction: 26

> Psychiatry is conventionally defined as a medical specialty concerned with the diagnosis and treatment of mental diseases. I submit that this definition, which is still widely accepted, places psychiatry in the company of alchemy and astrology and commits it to the category of pseudoscience. The reason for this is that there is no such thing as "mental illness."

One powerful reason Lucia had decided to major in psychology was that she wanted to help people like her brother, who had a psychotic break in his teens and had been in and out of hospitals since. She had lived with mental illness, had seen that look in her brother's eyes, felt drawn to help people whose mind had betrayed them. The assertion that there was no such thing as mental illness, that it was a myth, seemed incomprehensible to her. She had trouble even entertaining it as a hypothesis, and thus couldn't play out its resonances and implications in the pages that followed. Szasz's bold claim was a bone sticking in her assumptive craw.

Here's another passage alongside which she had placed a question 27 mark:

> The conceptual scaffolding of medicine, however, rests on the principles of physics and chemistry, as indeed it should, for it has been, and continues to be, the task of medicine to study and if necessary to alter, the physiochemical structure and function of the human body. Yet the fact remains that human sign-using behavior does not lend itself to exploration and understanding in these terms. We thus remain shackled to the wrong conceptual framework and terminology.

To understand this passage, you need to have some orientation to the "semiotic" tenet that every human action potentially carries some kind of message, that everything we do can be read as a sign of more than itself. This has become an accepted notion in high-powered liberal studies, an inclination to see every action and object as a kind of language that requires interpretation. The notion and its implications—

the conversation within which the phrase "sign-using" situates you—was foreign to Lucia. So it was difficult for her to see why Szasz was claiming that medicine was the "wrong conceptual framework" with which to study abnormal behavior.

Here's a third passage: 28

> Man thus creates a heavenly father and an imaginary replica of the protected childhood situation to replace the real or longed-for father and family. The differences between traditional religious doctrine, modern political historicism, and psychoanalytic orthodoxy thus lie mainly in the character of the "protectors": they are, respectively, God and the priests, the totalitarian leader and his apologists, and Freud and the psychoanalysts.
>
> While Freud criticized revealed religion for the patent infantilism that it is, he ignored the social characteristics of closed societies and the psychological characteristics of their loyal supporters. He thus failed to see the religious character of the movement he himself was creating.[2]

Lucia's working-class Catholicism made it difficult for her to go   29
along with, to intellectually toy with, the comparison of Freud to God, but there was another problem here too, not unlike the problem she had with the "sign-using" passage. It is a standard move in liberal studies to find religious analogues to nonreligious behaviors, structures, and institutions. Lucia could certainly "decode" and rephrase a sentence like: "He thus failed to see the religious character of the movement he himself was creating," but she didn't have the background to appreciate what happens to Freud and psychoanalysis the moment Szasz makes his comparison, wasn't familiar with the wealth of conclusions that would follow from the analogy.

And so it went with other key passages. Students like Lucia are   30
often thought to be poor readers or to have impoverished vocabularies (though Lucia speaks two languages); I've even heard students like her referred to as culturally illiterate (though she has absorbed two cultural heritages). It's true there were words Lucia didn't know (*alchemy, orthodoxy*) and sentences that took us two or three passes to untangle. But it seemed more fruitful to see Lucia's difficulties in understanding Szasz as having to do with her belief system and with her lack of familiarity with certain ongoing discussions in humanities and social science—with frames of mind, predispositions, and background knowledge. To help Lucia with her reading, then, I explained five or six central discussions that go on in liberal studies: the semiotic discussion, the sacred-profane discussion, the medical vs. social model

---

[2]Thomas S. Szasz, *The Myth of Mental Illness* (New York: Harper & Row, 1974), pp. 1, 4, 7.

discussion. While I did this, I was encouraging her to talk through opinions of her own that ran counter to these discussions. That was how she improved her reading of Szasz. The material the professor assigned that followed the introduction built systematically off it, so once Lucia was situated in that introduction, she had a framework to guide her through the long passages that followed, all of which elaborated those first twelve pages.

The baby pulled his face out of his mother's chest, yawned, squirmed, and turned to fix on me, wide-eyed. Lucia started packing up her books with a free hand. I had missed lunch. "Let's go," I said. "I'll walk out with you." Her movement distressed the baby, so Lucia soothed him with soft coos and clicks, stood up, and shifted him to her hip. We left Campbell Hall and headed southeast, me toward a sandwich, Lucia toward the buses that ran up and down Hilgard on UCLA's east boundary. It was a beautiful California day, and the jacarandas were in full purple bloom. Lucia talked about her baby's little discoveries, about a cousin who worried her, about her growing familiarity with this sprawling campus. "I'm beginning to know where things are," she said, pursing her lips. "You know, the other day some guy stopped me and asked *me* where Murphy Hall was . . . and I could tell him." She looked straight at me: "It felt pretty good!" We walked on like this, her dress hiked up where the baby rode her hip, her books in a bag slung over her shoulder, and I began to think about how many pieces had to fall into place each day in order for her to be a student: The baby couldn't wake up sick, no colic or rashes, the cousin or a neighbor had to be available to watch him, the three buses she took from East L.A. had to be on time—no accidents or breakdowns or strikes—for travel alone took up almost three hours of her school day. Only if all these pieces dropped in smooth alignment could her full attention shift to the complex and allusive prose of Thomas Szasz. "Man thus creates a heavenly father and an imaginary replica of the protected childhood situation to replace the real or longed-for father and family." 31

Students were coming to college with limited exposure to certain kinds of writing and reading and with conceptions and beliefs that were dissonant with those in the lower-division curriculum they encountered. And that curriculum wasn't doing a lot to address their weaknesses or nurture their strengths. They needed practice writing academic essays; they needed opportunities to talk about their writing—and their reading; they needed people who could quickly determine what necessary background knowledge they lacked and supply it in comprehensible ways. What began troubling me about the policy documents and the crisis reports was that they focused too narrowly on test scores and tallies of error and other such measures. They lacked careful analysis of the students' histories and lacked, as well, 32

analysis of the cognitive and social demands of the academic culture
the students now faced. The work I was doing in the Tutorial Center,
in the Writing Research Project, and in the Summer Program was
guiding me toward a richer understanding of what it meant to be underprepared in the American research university. It seemed to me
there were five overlapping problem areas—both cognitive and social—that could be used to explain the difficulties experienced by students like Marita and James and Lucia. These by no means applied
equally to all the students whom I came to know, but taken together
they represent, better than pie charts and histograms, what it means to
be underprepared at a place like UCLA.

    Many young people come to the university able to summarize the 33
events in a news story or write a personal response to a play or a
movie or give back what a teacher said in a straightforward lecture.
But they have considerable trouble with what has come to be called
critical literacy: framing an argument or taking someone else's argument apart, systematically inspecting a document, an issue, or an
event, synthesizing different points of view, applying a theory to disparate phenomena, and so on. The authors of the crisis reports got
tremendously distressed about students' difficulty with such tasks,
but it's important to remember that, traditionally, such abilities have
only been developed in an elite: in priests, scholars, or a leisure class.
Ours is the first society in history to expect so many of its people to
be able to perform these very sophisticated literacy activities. And
we fail to keep in mind how extraordinary it is to ask *all* our schools
to conduct this kind of education—not just those schools with lots of
money and exceptional teachers and small classes—but massive,
sprawling schools, beleaguered schools, inner-city schools, overcrowded schools. It is a charge most of them simply are not equipped
to fulfill, for our educational ideals far outstrip our economic and political priorities.
    We forget, then, that by most historical—and current—standards, 34
the vast majority of a research university's underprepared students
would be considered competently literate. Though they fail to meet
the demands made of them in their classes, they fail from a literate
base. They are literate people straining at the boundaries of their ability, trying to move into the unfamiliar, to approximate a kind of writing they can't yet command. And as they try, they'll make all the blunders in word choice and sentence structure and discourse strategy that
regularly get held up for ridicule, that I made when I was trying to
write for my teachers at Loyola. There's a related phenomenon, and
we have research evidence of this: As writers move further away from
familiar ways of expressing themselves, the strains on their cognitive

and linguistic resources increase, and the number of mechanical and grammatical errors they make shoots up.[3] Before we shake our heads at these errors, we should also consider the possibility that many such linguistic bungles are signs of growth, a stretching beyond what college freshmen can comfortably do with written language. In fact, we should *welcome* certain kinds of errors, make allowance for them in the curricula we develop, analyze rather than simply criticize them. Error marks the place where education begins.

Associated with these difficulties with critical literacy are students' 35 diverse orientations toward inquiry. It is a source of exasperation to many freshmen that the university is so predisposed to question past solutions, to seek counterexplanations—to continually turn something nice and clean and clear into a problem. English professor David Bartholomae recalls a teacher of his suggesting that, when stuck, student writers should try the following "machine": "While most readers of ____ have said ____, a close and careful reading shows that ____." The teacher's machine perfectly expresses the ethos of the university, a fundamental orientation toward inquiry. University professors have for so long been socialized into this critical stance, that they don't realize how unsettling it can be to students who don't share their unusual background. There is Scott sitting in an Astronomy tutorial, his jaw set, re- 36 sponding to another student's question about a finite versus an infinite universe: "This is the kind of question," he says, "that you'll argue and argue about. It's stupid. No one wins. So why do it?" And there is Rene who can't get beyond the first few sentences of her essay for Speech. She has to write a critical response to an address of Ronald Reagan's. "You can't criticize the president," she explains. "You've gotta support your president even if you don't agree with him." When students come from other cultures, this discordance can be even more pronounced. Our tutors continually encouraged their students to read actively, to ask why authors say what they say, what their claims are, what assumptions they make, where you, the reader, agree or disagree. Hun's tutor is explaining this to him, then has him try it, has him read aloud so she can guide him. He reads a few lines and stops short. After two more abortive trials, she pulls out of Hun the explanation that what gets written in books is set in tradition, and he is not learned enough to question the authority of the book.

The discourse of academics is marked by terms and expressions 37 that represent an elaborate set of shared concepts and orientations: alienation, authoritarian personality, the social construction of the self,

---

[3]See, for example, Brooke Nielson, "Writing as a Second Language: Psycholinguistic Processes in Composing" (Ph. D. diss., University of California at San Diego, 1979).

determinism, hegemony, equilibrium, intentionality, recursion, reinforcement, and so on. This language weaves through so many lectures and textbooks, is integral to so many learned discussions, that it's easy to forget what a foreign language it can be. Freshmen are often puzzled by the talk they hear in their classrooms, but what's important to note here is that their problem is not simply one of limited vocabulary. If we see the problem as knowing or not knowing a list of words, as some quick-fix remedies suggest, then we'll force glossaries on students and miss the complexity of the issue. Take, for example, *authoritarian personality*. The average university freshman will know what *personality* means and can figure out *authoritarian*; the difficulty will come from a lack of familiarity with the conceptual resonances that *authoritarian personality* has acquired in the discussions of sociologists and psychologists and political scientists. Discussion ... you could almost define a university education as an initiation into a variety of powerful ongoing discussions, an initiation that can occur only through the repeated use of a new language in the company of others. More than anything, this was the opportunity people like Father Albertson, my Shakespeare teacher at Loyola, provided to me. The more comfortable and skillful students become with this kind of influential talk, the more they will be included in further conversations and given access to further conceptual tools and resources—the acquisition of which virtually defines them as members of an intellectual community.

All students require such an opportunity. But those coming to the 38 university with less-than-privileged educations, especially those from the lower classes, are particularly in need. They are less likely to have participated, in any extended way, in such discussions in the past. They won't have the confidence or the moves to enter it, and can begin to feel excluded, out of place, put off by a language they can't command. Their social marginality, then, is reinforced by discourse and, as happened to me during my first year at Loyola, they might well withdraw, retreat to silence.

This sense of linguistic exclusion can be complicated by various 39 cultural differences. When I was growing up, I absorbed an entire belief system—with its own characteristic terms and expressions—from the worried conversations of my parents, from the things I heard and saw on South Vermont, from the priest's fiery tales. I thought that what happened to people was preordained, that ability was a fixed thing, that there was one true religion. I had rigid notions about social roles, about the structure of society, about gender, about politics. There used to be a rickety vending machine at Manchester and Vermont that held a Socialist Workers newspaper. I'd walk by it and feel something alive and injurious: The paper was malevolent and should be destroyed. Imagine, then, the difficulty I had when, at the beginning of my senior year at Mercy High, Jack MacFarland tried to explain Marxism to us. How could I absorb the language of atheistic materialism and class struggle when it seemed so strange and pernicious? It wasn't just that Marxist terms-of-art were unfamiliar; they felt assaultive. What I did was revert to definitions of the social order more familiar to me, and Mr. MacFarland had to draw them out of me and have me talk about them and consider them alongside Marx's vision and terminology, examining points of conflict and points of possible convergence. It was only then that I could appropriate Marx's strange idiom.

Once you start to think about underprepared students in terms 40 of these overlapping problem areas, all sorts of solutions present themselves. Students need more opportunities to write about what they're learning and guidance in the techniques and conventions of that writing—what I got from my mentors at Loyola. They need more opportunities to develop the writing strategies that are an intimate part of academic inquiry and what has come to be called critical literacy—comparing, synthesizing, analyzing—the sort of thing I gave the veterans. They need opportunities to talk about what they're learning: to test their ideas, reveal their assumptions, talk through the places where new knowledge clashes with ingrained belief. They need a chance, too, to talk about the ways they may have felt excluded from all this in the past and may feel threatened by it in the present. They need the occasion to rise above the fragmented learning the lower-division curriculum encourages, a place within a course or outside it to hear about and reflect on the way a particular discipline conducts its inquiry: Why, for example, *do* so many psychologists who study thinking rely on computer modeling? Why is mathematics so much a part of economics? And they need to be let in on the secret talk, on the shared concepts and catchphrases of Western liberal learning.

There is nothing magical about this list of solutions. In fact, in 41 many ways, it reflects the kind of education a privileged small number of American students have received for some time. The basic question our society must ask, then, is: How many or how few do we want to have this education? If students didn't get it before coming to college—and most have not—then what are we willing to do it give it to them now? Chip and I used to talk about our special programs as attempts to create an Honors College for the underprepared. People would smile as we spoke, but, as our students would have said, we were serious as a heart attack. The remedial programs we knew about did a disservice to their students by thinking of them as *remedial*. We wanted to try out another perspective and see what kind of program it would yield. What would happen if we thought of our students' needs and goals in light of the comprehensive and ambitious program structures more often reserved for the elite?

Working with the Text

1. What sorts of problems do the students who come to Rose to be tutored have? What are their attitudes toward themselves and their schoolwork? How does Rose try to help them? How do some students resist his efforts to help them? What are Rose's suggestions for improving these students' education?

2. Rose says that students are coming to college "with limited exposure to certain kinds of writing and reading"—the kinds of reading and writing, that is, that they are required to do in college. Is this true in your case? What are some general differences between college reading and writing and other reading and writing?

3. Rose begins the essay with a passage in the second person ("You're a few minutes late . . ."). Why, do you suppose? What effect is he hoping to have on you, his reader?

4. Why do you think Rose includes specific stories about specific students: Andrea, James, Marita, Lucia? Why doesn't he talk about students in general and offer statistics about big groups of students?

Working beyond the Text

1. The opening of the essay describes a typical lecture in a class called Introductory Sociology. Do you have any classes like this one: big, crowded, impersonal lecture classes? In what ways did Rose's description seem familiar?

2. Did you see any of your own background or character traits in any of the students Rose describes? Which ones?

3. Rose does a close reading of a passage from Thomas Szasz's *The Myth of Mental Illness* (pp. 182–85). Pick a difficult passage from a book you're reading for one of your classes and do a similar reading, identifying all the special vocabulary and background knowledge necessary for an understanding of the text. What about your background, either social or educational, has prepared you (or failed to prepare you) to read the text?

Other Voices, Other Rooms

Gerald Graff

Gerald Graff teaches literature at the University of Chicago and writes about higher education in popular books such as *Beyond the Culture Wars: How Teaching the Conflicts Can Revitalize American Edu-*

cation (1992). Graff advocates showing students the ways scholars within a field disagree about the fundamental questions in the field, and also showing them how knowledge from various fields is related by these fundamental disagreements. In this essay, from *Beyond the Culture Wars,* he explains how students may become lost in academic language and suggests some solutions to this problem.

An undergraduate tells of an art history course in which the instructor observed one day, "As we now know, the idea that knowledge can be objective is a positivist myth that has been exploded by postmodern thought." It so happens the student is concurrently enrolled in a political science course in which the instructor speaks confidently about the objectivity of his discipline as if it had not been "exploded" at all. What do you do? the student is asked. "What else can I do?" he says. "I trash objectivity in art history, and I presuppose it in political science." 1

A second undergraduate describes a history teacher who makes a point of stressing the superiority of Western culture in developing the ideas of freedom, democracy, and free market capitalism that the rest of the world is now rushing to imitate. She also has a literature teacher who describes such claims of Western supremacy as an example of the hegemonic ideology by which the United States arrogates the right to police the world. When asked which course she prefers, she replies, "Well, I'm getting an A in both." 2

To some of us these days, the moral of these stories would be that students have become cynical relativists who care less about convictions than about grades and careers. In fact, if anything is surprising, it is that more students do not behave in this cynical fashion, for the established curriculum encourages it. The disjunction of the curriculum is a far more powerful source of relativism than any doctrine preached by the faculty. 3

One of the oddest things about the university is that it calls itself a community of scholars yet organizes its curriculum in a way that conceals the links of the community from those who are not already aware of them. The courses being given at any moment on a campus represent any number of rich potential conversations within and across the disciplines. But since students experience these conversations only as a series of monologues, the conversations become actual only for the minority who can reconstruct them on their own. No self-respecting educator would deliberately design a system guaranteed to keep students dependent on the whim of the individual instructor. Yet this is precisely the effect of a curriculum composed of courses that are not in dialogue with one another. 4

The problem deepens when teachers are further apart. A student ⁵
today can go from a course in which the universality of Western culture is taken for granted (and therefore not articulated) to a course in
which it is taken for granted (and therefore not articulated) that such
claims of universality are fallacious and deceptive. True, for the best
students the resulting cognitive dissonance is no great problem. The
chance to try on a variety of clashing ideas, to see what they feel like, is
one of the most exciting opportunities an education can provide; it can
be especially rewarding for students who come to the university with
already developed skills at summarizing and weighing arguments
and synthesizing conflicting positions on their own. Many students,
however, become confused or indifferent and react as the above two
students did by giving their teachers whatever they seem to want even
though it is contradictory.

Then, too, when their teachers' conflicting perspectives do not ⁶
enter into a common discussion, students may not even be able to
infer what is wanted. Like everyone else, teachers tend to betray their
crucial assumptions as much in what they do *not* say, what they take
to go without saying, as in what they say explicitly. To students who
are not at home in the academic intellectual community, the significance of these silences and exclusions is likely to be intimidating, if it
does not elude them entirely.

Furthermore, in an academic environment in which there is in- ⁷
creasingly less unspoken common ground, it may not even be clear to
students that their teachers are in conflict, for different words may be
used by several teachers for the same concepts or the same words for
different concepts. If students do not know that "positivism" has in
some quarters become a derogatory buzzword for any belief in objectivity, they may not become aware that the art history and political science teachers in the above example are in disagreement. A student
who goes from one humanist who speaks of "traditional moral
themes" to another who speaks of "patriarchal discursive practices"
may not become aware that the two teachers are actually referring to
the same thing. Students in such cases are being exposed to some of
the major cultural debates of their time, but in a way that makes it difficult to recognize them *as* debates.

Note, too, that the instructors in these situations are protected by ⁸
the insularity of their classrooms, which makes it unnecessary, if not impossible, for them to confront the challenges to their assumptions that
would be represented by their colleagues. Professors do not expect such
immunity from peer criticism when they publish their work or appear
at professional conferences. It is only in the classroom that such immunity is taken for granted as if it were a form of academic freedom. Since
students enjoy no such protection, one can hardly blame them if they,
too, protect themselves by compartmentalizing the contradictions to

which they are exposed, as my first student did when he became an objectivist in one course and an antiobjectivist in the other.

I recall a semester late in college when I took a course in modern 9 poetry taught by a New Critic, a follower of T. S. Eliot, and a course in seventeenth-century English literature taught by an older scholar who resented Eliot and the New Critics, who had attacked John Milton for his grandiloquence and lack of irony. Three days a week between ten and eleven I listened with dutiful respect to the New Critic's theories of irony and paradox, and between eleven and twelve I listened with dutiful respect to the argument that these New Critical theories had no application whatsoever to Milton, Dryden, and their contemporaries. What was really odd, however, is that I hardly focused at the time on the fact that my two teachers were in disagreement.

Was I just ridiculously slow to comprehend the critical issues that 10 were at stake? Perhaps so, but since no one was asking me to think about the relationship between the two courses, I did not. If my teachers disagreed, this was their business—a professional dispute that did not concern me. Each course was challenging enough on its own terms, and to have raised the question of how they related would have only risked needlessly multiplying difficulties for myself. Then, too, for me to ask my teachers about their differences might have seemed impertinent and ill mannered—who was I to impugn their authority? Only later did it dawn on me that studying different centuries and clashing theories without having them brought together had made things much *harder* since it removed the element of contrast.

Contrast is fundamental to understanding, for no subject, idea, or 11 text is an island. In order to become intelligible "in itself," it needs to be seen in its relation to other subjects, ideas, and texts. When this relation of interdependence is obscured because different courses do not communicate, subjects, ideas, and texts become harder to comprehend, if not unintelligible. We think we are making things simpler for students by abstracting periods, texts, and authors from their relationships with other periods, texts, and authors so that we can study them closely in a purified space. But the very act of isolating an object from its contrasting background and relations makes it hard to grasp. Since we cannot talk about everything all at once, subjects do have to be distinguished and to that extent isolated from one another. But this isolation does not have to preclude connections and relations. It is hard to grasp the modernity of modern literature unless one can compare it with something that is not modern.

A rhetoric scholar, Gregory Colomb, has studied the disorientation 12 experienced by a bright high school graduate who, after doing well in a humanities course as a freshman at the University of Chicago, tried to apply her mastery to a social science course, only to come up with a grade of C.[1] Imagine trying to write an academic paper when you sense that almost anything you say can be used against you and that the intellectual moves that got you an A in existentialist philosophy may get you a C minus and a dirty look in Skinnerian behaviorism.

Consider the fact that the passive voice that is so standard in sociology writing ("it will be contended in this paper . . .") has been perennially rebuked in English courses.[2] Or consider something so apparently trivial as the convention of using the present tense to describe actions in literature and philosophy and the past tense to describe them in history. Plato *says* things in literary and philosophical accounts while in historical accounts he *said* them. Experienced writers become so accustomed to such tense shifting that it seems a simple matter, but it reflects deep-rooted and potentially controversial differences between disciplines. Presumably, Plato speaks in the present in literary and philosophical contexts because ideas there are considered timeless; only when we move over to history does it start to matter that the writer is dead.[3] We English teachers write "tense shift" in the margin when student writers betray uncertainty about this convention, but how do we expect them to "get" it when they pass from the very different time zones of history and philosophy/English with no engagement of the underlying issues?

One of the most frequent comments teachers make on student papers is "What's your evidence?" But nobody would ever finish a piece of writing if it were necessary to supply evidence for everything being said, so in order to write, one must acquire a sense of which statements have to be supported by evidence (or further argument) and which ones a writer can get away with because they are already taken for granted by the imagined audience. What happens, then, when a writer has no way of knowing whether an assumption that he or she got away with with audience A will also be conceded by audience B? It is no wonder that students protect themselves from the insecurity of such a situation by "psyching out" each course as it comes—and then forgetting about it as soon as possible after the final exam in order to clear their minds for the seemingly unrelated demands of the next set of courses.

It is not only ideas and reasoning processes but the recall of basic information as well that figure to be impaired by *disjunctive curricular organization*. To use the jargon of information theory, an information system that is experienced as an unrelated series of signals will be weak in the kind of redundancy that is needed for information to be

---

[1]Gregory Colomb, *Disciplinary "Secrets" and the Apprentice Writer: The Lessons for Critical Thinking* (Upper Montclair, N.J.: Montclair State College, Institute for Critical Thinking, 1988), pp. 2–3.

[2]For this point I am indebted to an unpublished talk by Susan Lowry.

[3]I am indebted for this point to Susan H. McLeod, "Writing across the Curriculum: An Introduction," in *Writing across the Curriculum: A Guide to Developing Programs*, eds. McLeod and Margot Soven (Newberry Park, Calif.: Sage, 1992).

retained. Faced with a curriculum overloaded with data and weak in redundancy, students may find it difficult to know which items of information they are supposed to remember. Then, too, a student may be exposed to the same information in several courses while failing to recognize it as "the same," since it is contextualized differently in each course. When students fail to identify a cultural literacy item on a test, the problem may be not that they don't know the information but that they don't know they know it; they may have learned it in a context whose relevance to the test question they don't recognize. What is learned seems so specific to a particular course that it is difficult for students to see its application beyond.

The critic Kenneth Burke once compared the intellectual life of a 16 culture to a parlor in which different guests are forever dropping in and out. As the standard curriculum represents the intellectual life, however, there is no parlor; the hosts congregate in separate rooms with their acolytes and keep their differences and agreements to themselves. Making one's way through the standard curriculum is rather like trying to comprehend a phone conversation by listening at only one end.[4] You can manage it up to a point, but this is hardly the ideal way to do it.

To venture a final comparison, it is as if you were to try to learn 17 the game of baseball by being shown a series of rooms in which you see each component of the game separately: pitchers going through their windups in one room; hitters swinging their bats in the next; then infielders, outfielders, umpires, fans, field announcers, ticket scalpers, broadcasters, hot dog vendors, and so on. You see them all in their different roles, but since you see them separately you get no clear idea of what the game actually looks like or why the players do what they do. No doubt you would come away with a very imperfect understanding of baseball under these conditions. Yet it does not seem farfetched to compare these circumstances with the ones students face when they are exposed to a series of disparate courses, subjects, and perspectives and expected not only to infer the rules of the academic-intellectual game but to play it competently themselves.

Working with the Text

1. Graff uses the term "cognitive dissonance" to characterize the relation between different classrooms teaching the same subject (for example, literature) and different classrooms teaching different subjects (for example, history and biology). What does he mean?

---

[4]I adapt an observation made in a somewhat different context by Mary Louise Pratt, "Humanities for the Future: Reflections on the Western Culture Debate at Stanford," in *Politics of Liberal Education,* p. 19.

2. Graff's essay ends with two paragraphs that present two different metaphors for scholarly life. Graff says that Kenneth Burke's idea of a "parlor in which guests are forever dropping in and out" does not describe the average college student's experience. Instead, he offers a metaphor based on learning to play baseball. What does his metaphor imply about a college education?

3. Graff uses several specific examples of student experiences in paragraphs one, two, nine, and twelve. What points do these experiences help him make? Why did he decide to use specific student experiences to make these points?

Working beyond the Text

1. Graff discusses the idea of unspoken, underlying, "unarticulated" assumptions that a scholar in a field may have. Do you ever have the feeling that your teachers assume you know more than you do? Describe the experience.

2. Approach one or more of your instructors this semester and ask about the major conflicts in the instructor's field. You might ask a psychology teacher about the conflict between those who believe in a psychoanalytic approach to human psychology and a behavioralist approach, or you might ask a physics teacher about different explanations for the behavior of matter at the quantum level. Go on to ask your instructors how these conflicts relate to the course material you are learning from them this semester.

3. Graff discusses the different expectations of different teachers a college student may have. Teachers in different disciplines and even two teachers teaching within the same department may have very different rules for writing essays and ways of grading them. Have you experienced this in your college classes?

From Silence to Words: Writing as Struggle
Min-zhan Lu

Min-zhan Lu was born in China, and grew up speaking English along with several Chinese dialects. She now teaches composition, autobiography, and literary and cultural criticism at Drake University. She has written a number of articles about issues in composition for journals such as *College English,* as well as stories about her early life in China. In this selection, published in 1987, Lu relates how her life experiences in China and the United States have affected her conceptions of language, writing, and teaching.

Imagine that you enter a parlor. You come late. When you arrive, others have long preceded you, and they are engaged in a heated discussion. . . . You listen for a while, until you decide that you have caught the tenor of the argument; then you put in your oar. Someone answers; you answer him; another comes to your defense; another aligns himself against you, to either the embarrassment or gratification of your opponent, depending upon the quality of your ally's assistance. However, the discussion is interminable. The hour grows late, you must depart. And you do depart, with the discussion still vigorously in progress.

—Kenneth Burke, The Philosophy of Literary Form

Men are not built in silence, but in word, in work, in action-reflection.

—Paulo Freire, Pedagogy of the Oppressed

My mother withdrew into silence two months before she died. A few nights before she fell silent, she told me she regretted the way she had raised me and my sisters. I knew she was referring to the way we had been brought up in the midst of two conflicting worlds—the world of home, dominated by the ideology of the Western humanistic tradition, and the world of a society dominated by Mao Tse-tung's Marxism. My mother had devoted her life to our education, an education she knew had made us suffer political persecution during the Cultural Revolution. I wanted to find a way to convince her that, in spite of the persecution, I had benefited from the education she had worked so hard to give me. But I was silent. My understanding of my education was so dominated by memories of confusion and frustration that I was unable to reflect on what I could have gained from it.

This paper is my attempt to fill up that silence with words, words I didn't have then, words that I have since come to by reflecting on my earlier experience as a student in China and on my recent experience as a composition teacher in the United States. For in spite of the frustration and confusion I experienced growing up caught between two conflicting worlds, the conflict ultimately helped me to grow as a reader and writer. Constantly having to switch back and forth between the discourse of home and that of school made me sensitive and self-conscious about the struggle I experienced every time I tried to read, write, or think in either discourse. Eventually, it led me to search for constructive uses for such struggle.

From early childhood, I had identified the differences between home and the outside world by the different languages I used in each. My parents had wanted my sisters and me to get the best education they could conceive of—Cambridge. They had hired a live-in tutor, a Scot, to make us bilingual. I learned to speak English with my parents, my tutor, and my sisters. I was allowed to speak Shanghai dialect only with the servants. When I was four (the year after the Communist Revolution of 1949), my parents sent me to a local private school where I learned to speak, read, and write in a new language—Standard Chinese, the official written language of New China.

In those days I moved from home to school, from English to Standard Chinese to Shanghai dialect, with no apparent friction. I spoke each language with those who spoke the language. All seemed quite "natural"—servants spoke only Shanghai dialect because they were servants; teachers spoke Standard Chinese because they were teachers; languages had different words because they were different languages. I thought of English as my family language, comparable to the many strange dialects I didn't speak but had often heard some of my classmates speak with their families. While I was happy to have a special family language, until second grade I didn't feel that my family language was any different than some of my classmates' family dialects.

My second grade homeroom teacher was a young graduate from a missionary school. When she found out I spoke English, she began to practice her English on me. One day she used English when asking me to run an errand for her. As I turned to close the door behind me, I noticed the puzzled faces of my classmates. I had the same sensation I had often experienced when some stranger in a crowd would turn on hearing me speak English. I was more intensely pleased on this occasion, however, because suddenly I felt that my family language had been singled out from the family languages of my classmates. Since we were not allowed to speak any dialect other than Standard Chinese in the classroom, having my teacher speak English to me in class made English an official language of the classroom. I began to take pride in my ability to speak it.

This incident confirmed in my mind what my parents had always told me about the importance of English to one's life. Time and again they had told me of how my paternal grandfather, who was well versed in classic Chinese, kept losing good-paying jobs because he couldn't speak English. My grandmother reminisced constantly about how she had slaved and saved to send my father to a first-rate missionary school. And we were made to understand that it was my father's fluent English that had opened the door to his success. Even though my family had always stressed the importance of English for my future, I used to complain bitterly about the extra English lessons we had to take after school. It was only after my homeroom teacher had "sanctified" English that I began to connect English with my education. I became a much more eager student in my tutorials.

What I learned from my tutorials seemed to enhance and reinforce what I was learning in my classroom. In those days each word had one meaning. One day I would be making a sentence at school: "The national flag of China is red." The next day I would recite at home, "My love is like a red, red rose." There seemed to be an agreement between the Chinese "red" and the English "red," and both corresponded to the patch of color printed next to the word. "Love" was my love for my mother at home and my love for my "motherland" at school; both "loves" meant how I felt about my mother. Having two loads of homework forced me to develop a quick memory for words and a sensitivity to form and style. What I learned in one language carried over to the other. I made sentences such as, "I saw a red, red rose among the green leaves," with both the English lyric and the classic Chinese lyric—red flower among green leaves—running through my mind, and I was praised by both teacher and tutor for being a good student.

Although my elementary schooling took place during the fifties, I   8 was almost oblivious to the great political and social changes happening around me. Years later, I read in my history and political philosophy textbooks that the fifties were a time when "China was making a transition from a semi-feudal, semi-capitalist, and semi-colonial country into a socialist country," a period in which "the Proletarians were breaking into the educational territory dominated by Bourgeois Intellectuals." While people all over the country were being officially classified into Proletarians, Petty-bourgeois, National-bourgeois, Poor-peasants, and Intellectuals, and were trying to adjust to their new social identities, my parents were allowed to continue the upper middle-class life they had established before the 1949 Revolution because of my father's affiliation with British firms. I had always felt that my family was different from the families of my classmates, but I didn't perceive society's view of my family until the summer vacation before I entered high school.

First, my aunt was caught by her colleagues talking to her husband   9 over the phone in English. Because of it, she was criticized and almost labeled a Rightist. (This was the year of the Anti-Rightist movement, a movement in which the Intellectuals became the target of the "socialist class-struggle.") I had heard others telling my mother that she was foolish to teach us English when Russian had replaced English as the "official" foreign language. I had also learned at school that the American and British Imperialists were the arch-enemies of New China. Yet I had made no connection between the arch-enemies and the English our family spoke. What happened to my aunt forced the connection on me. I began to see my parents' choice of a family language as an anti-Revolutionary act and was alarmed that I had participated in such an act. From then on, I took care not to use English outside home and to conceal my knowledge of English from my new classmates.

Certain words began to play important roles in my new life at the   10 junior high. On the first day of school, we were handed forms to fill out with our parents' class, job, and income. Being one of the few people not employed by the government, my father had never been officially classified. Since he was a medical doctor, he told me to put him down as an Intellectual. My homeroom teacher called me into the office a couple of days afterwards and told me that my father couldn't be an Intellectual if his income far exceeded that of a Capitalist. He also told me that since my father worked for Foreign Imperialists, my father should be classified as an Imperialist Lackey. The teacher looked nonplussed when I told him that my father couldn't be an Imperialist Lackey because he was a medical doctor. But I could tell from the way he took notes on my form that my father's job had put me in an unfavorable position in his eyes.

The Standard Chinese term "class" was not a new word for me. 11 Since first grade, I had been taught sentences such as, "The Working class are the masters of New China." I had always known that it was good to be a worker, but until then, I had never felt threatened for not being one. That fall, "class" began to take on a new meaning for me. I noticed a group of Working-class students and teachers at school. I was made to understand that because of my class background, I was excluded from that group.

Another word that became important was "consciousness." One 12 of the slogans posted in the school building read, "Turn our students into future Proletarians with socialist consciousness and education!" For several weeks we studied this slogan in our political philosophy course, a subject I had never had in elementary school. I still remember the definition of "socialist consciousness" that we were repeatedly tested on through the years: "Socialist consciousness is a person's political soul. It is the consciousness of the Proletarians represented by Marxist Mao Tse-tung thought. It takes expression in one's action, language, and lifestyle. It is the task of every Chinese student to grow up into a Proletarian with a socialist consciousness so that he can serve the people and the motherland." To make the abstract concept accessible to us, our teacher pointed out that the immediate task for students from Working-class families was to strengthen their socialist consciousnesses. For those of us who were from other class backgrounds, the task was to turn ourselves into Workers with socialist consciousnesses. The teacher never explained exactly how we were supposed to "turn" into Workers. Instead, we were given samples of the ritualistic annual plans we had to write at the beginning of each term. In these plans, we performed "self-criticism" on our consciousnesses and made vows to turn ourselves into Workers with socialist consciousnesses. The teacher's division between those who did and those who didn't have a socialist consciousness led me to reify the notion of "consciousness" into a thing one possesses. I equated this intangible "thing" with a concrete way of dressing, speaking, and writing. For instance, I never doubted that my political philosophy teacher had a socialist consciousness because she was from a steelworker's family (she announced this the first day of class) and was a party member who wore grey cadre suits and talked like a philosophy textbook. I noticed other things about her. She had beautiful eyes and spoke Standard Chinese with such a pure accent that I thought she should be a film star. But I was embarrassed that I had noticed things that ought not to have been associated with her. I blamed my observation on my Bourgeois consciousness.

At the same time, the way reading and writing were taught 13 through memorization and imitation also encouraged me to reduce concepts and ideas to simple definitions. In literature and political philosophy classes, we were taught a large number of quotations from Marx, Lenin, and Mao Tse-tung. Each concept that appeared in these quotations came with a definition. We were required to memorize the definitions of the words along with the quotations. Every time I memorized a definition, I felt I had learned a word: "The national red flag symbolizes the blood shed by Revolutionary ancestors for our socialist cause"; "New China rises like a red sun over the eastern horizon." As I memorized these sentences, I reduced their metaphors to dictionary meanings: "red" meant "Revolution" and "red sun" meant "New China" in the "language" of the Working class. I learned mechanically but eagerly. I soon became quite fluent in this new language.

As school began to define me as a political subject, my parents 14 tried to build up my resistance to the "communist poisoning" by exposing me to the "great books"—novels by Charles Dickens, Nathaniel Hawthorne, Emily Brontë, Jane Austen, and writers from around the turn of the century. My parents implied that these writers represented how I, their child, should read and write. My parents replaced the word "Bourgeois" with the word "cultured." They reminded me that I was in school only to learn math and science. I needed to pass the other courses to stay in school, but I was not to let the "Red doctrines" corrupt my mind. Gone were the days when I could innocently write, "I saw the red, red rose among the green leaves," collapsing, as I did, English and Chinese cultural traditions. "Red" came to mean Revolution at school, "the Commies" at home, and adultery in *The Scarlet Letter*. Since I took these symbols and metaphors as meanings natural to people of the same class, I abandoned my earlier definitions of English and Standard Chinese as the language of home and the language of school. I now defined English as the language of the Bourgeois and Standard Chinese as the language of the Working class. I thought of the language of the Working class as someone else's language and the language of the Bourgeois as my language. But I also believed that, although the language of the Bourgeois was my real language, I could and would adopt the language of the Working class when I was at school. I began to put on and take off my Working class language in the same way I put on and took off my school clothes to avoid being criticized for wearing Bourgeois clothes.

In my literature classes, I learned the Working-class formula for 15 reading. Each work in the textbook had a short "Author's Biography": "X X X, born in 19—in the province of X X, is from a Worker's family. He joined the Revolution in 19—. He is a Revolutionary realist with a passionate love for the Party and Chinese Revolution. His work expresses the thoughts and emotions of the masses and sings praise to the prosperous socialist construction on all fronts of China." The teacher used the "Author's Biography" as a yardstick to measure the texts. We were taught to locate details in the texts that illustrated these summaries, such as words that expressed Workers' thoughts and emotions or events that illustrated the Workers' lives.

I learned a formula for Working-class writing in the composition 16 classes. We were given sample essays and told to imitate them. The theme was always about how the collective taught the individual a lesson. I would write papers about labor-learning experiences or school-cleaning days, depending on the occasion of the collective activity closest to the assignment. To make each paper look different, I dressed it up with details about the date, the weather, the environment, or the appearance of the Master-worker who had taught me "the lesson." But as I became more and more fluent in the generic voice of the Working-class Student, I also became more and more self-conscious about the language we used at home.

For instance, in senior high we began to have English classes ("to 17 study English for the Revolution," as the slogan on the cover of the textbook said), and I was given my first Chinese-English dictionary. There I discovered the English version of the term "class-struggle." (The Chinese characters for a school "class" and for a social "class" are different.) I had often used the English word "class" at home in sentences such as, "So and so has class," but I had not connected this sense of "class" with "class-struggle." Once the connection was made, I heard a second layer of meaning every time someone at home said a person had "class." The expression began to mean the person had the style and sophistication characteristic of the bourgeoisie. The word lost its innocence. I was uneasy about hearing that second layer of meaning because I was sure my parents did not hear the word that way. I felt that therefore I should not be hearing it that way either. Hearing the second layer of meaning made me wonder if I was losing my English.

My suspicion deepened when I noticed myself unconsciously 18 merging and switching between the "reading" of home and the "reading" of school. Once I had to write a report on *The Revolutionary Family,* a book about an illiterate woman's awakening and growth as a Revolutionary through the deaths of her husband and all her children for the cause of the Revolution. In one scene the woman deliberated over whether or not she should encourage her youngest son to join the Revolution. Her memory of her husband's death made her afraid to encourage her son. Yet she also remembered her earlier married life and the first time her husband tried to explain the meaning of the Revolution to her. These memories made her feel she should encourage her son to continue the cause his father had begun.

I was moved by this scene. "Moved" was a word my mother and 19 sisters used a lot when we discussed books. Our favorite moments in novels were moments of what I would now call internal conflict, moments which we said "moved" us. I remember that we were "moved" by Jane Eyre when she was torn between her sense of ethics, which compelled her to leave the man she loved, and her impulse to stay with the only man who had ever loved her. We were also moved by Agnes in *David Copperfield* because of the way she restrained her love for David so that he could live happily with the woman he loved. My standard method of doing a book report was to model it on the review by the Publishing Bureau and to dress it up with detailed quotations from the book. The review of *The Revolutionary Family* emphasized the woman's Revolutionary spirit. I decided to use the scene that had moved me to illustrate this point. I wrote the report the night before it was due. When I had finished, I realized I couldn't possibly hand it in. Instead of illustrating her Revolutionary spirit, I had dwelled on her internal conflict, which could be seen as a moment of weak sentimentality that I should never have emphasized in a Revolutionary heroine. I wrote another report, taking care to illustrate the grandeur of her Revolutionary spirit by expanding on a quotation in which she decided that if the life of her son could change the lives of millions of sons, she should not begrudge his life for the cause of Revolution. I handed in my second version but kept the first in my desk.

I never showed it to anyone. I could never show it to people out- 20 side my family, because it had deviated so much from the reading enacted by the jacket review. Neither could I show it to my mother or sisters, because I was ashamed to have been so moved by such a "Revolutionary" book. My parents would have been shocked to learn that I could like such a book in the same way they liked Dickens. Writing this book report increased my fear that I was losing the command over both the "language of home" and the "language of school" that I had worked so hard to gain. I tried to remind myself that, if I could still tell when my reading or writing sounded incorrect, then I had retained my command over both languages. Yet I could no longer be confident of my command over either language because I had discovered that when I was not careful—or even when I was—my reading and writing often surprised me with its impurity. To prevent such impurity, I became very suspicious of my thoughts when I read or wrote.

I was always asking myself why I was using this word, how I was using it, always afraid that I wasn't reading or writing correctly. What confused and frustrated me most was that I could not figure out why I was no longer able to read or write correctly without such painful deliberation.

I continued to read only because reading allowed me to keep my 21 thoughts and confusion private. I hoped that somehow, if I watched myself carefully, I would figure out from the way I read whether I had really mastered the "languages." But writing became a dreadful chore. When I tried to keep a diary, I was so afraid that the voice of school might slip in that I could only list my daily activities. When I wrote for school, I worried that my Bourgeois sensibilities would betray me.

The more suspicious I became about the way I read and wrote, the 22 more guilty I felt for losing the spontaneity with which I had learned to "use" these "languages." Writing the book report made me feel that my reading and writing in the "language" of either home or school could not be free of the interference of the other. But I was unable to acknowledge, grasp, or grapple with what I was experiencing, for both my parents and my teachers had suggested that, if I were a good student, such interference would and should not take place. I assumed that once I had "acquired" a discourse, I could simply switch it on and off every time I read and wrote as I would some electronic tool. Furthermore, I expected my readings and writings to come out in their correct forms whenever I switched the proper discourse on. I still regarded the discourse of home as natural and the discourse of school as alien, but I never had doubted before that I could acquire both and switch them on and off according to the occasion.

When my experience in writing conflicted with what I thought 23 should happen when I used each discourse, I rejected my experience because it contradicted what my parents and teachers had taught me. I shied away from writing to avoid what I assumed I should not experience. But trying to avoid what should not happen did not keep it from recurring whenever I had to write. Eventually my confusion and frustration over these recurring experiences compelled me to search for an explanation: how and why had I failed to learn what my parents and teachers had worked so hard to teach me?

I now think of the internal scene for my reading and writing about 24 *The Revolutionary Family* as a heated discussion between myself, the voices of home, and those of school. The review on the back of the book, the sample student papers I came across in my composition classes, my philosophy teacher—these I heard as voices of one group. My parents and my home readings were the voices of an opposing group. But the conversation between these opposing voices in the internal scene of my writing was not as polite and respectful as the parlor scene Kenneth Burke has portrayed (see epigraph). Rather, these voices struggled to dominate the discussion, constantly incorporating, dismissing, or suppressing the arguments of each other, like the battles between the hegemonic and counter-hegemonic forces described in Raymond Williams' *Marxism and Literature* (108–14).

When I read *The Revolutionary Family* and wrote the first version of   25 my report, I began with a quotation from the review. The voices of both home and school answered, clamoring to be heard. I tried to listen to one group and turn a deaf ear to the other. Both persisted. I negotiated my way through these conflicting voices, now agreeing with one, now agreeing with the other. I formed a reading out of my interaction with both. Yet I was afraid to have done so because both home and school had implied that I should speak in unison with only one of these groups and stand away from the discussion rather than participate in it.

My teachers and parents had persistently called my attention to   26 the intensity of the discussion taking place on the external social scene. The story of my grandfather's failure and my father's success had from my early childhood made me aware of the conflict between Western and traditional Chinese cultures. My political education at school added another dimension to the conflict; the war of Marxist-Maoism against them both. Yet when my parents and teachers called my attention to the conflict, they stressed the anxiety of having to live through China's transformation from a semi-feudal, semi-capitalist, and semi-colonial society to a socialist one. Acquiring the discourse of the dominant group was, to them, a means of seeking alliance with that group and thus of surviving the whirlpool of cultural currents around them. As a result, they modeled their pedagogical practices on this utilitarian view of language. Being the eager student, I adopted this view of language as a tool for survival. It came to dominate my understanding of the discussion on the social and historical scene and to restrict my ability to participate in that discussion.

To begin with, the metaphor of language as a tool for survival led   27 me to be passive in my use of discourse, to be a bystander in the discussion. In Burke's "parlor," everyone is involved in the discussion. As it goes on through history, what we call "communal discourses"— arguments specific to particular political, social, economic, ethnic, sexual, and family groups—form, re-form and transform. To use a discourse in such a scene is to participate in the argument and to contribute to the formation of the discourse. But when I was growing up, I could not take on the burden of such an active role in the discussion. For both home and school presented the existent conventions of the discourse each taught me as absolute laws for my action. They turned verbal action into a tool, a set of conventions produced and shaped prior to and outside of my own verbal acts. Because I saw language as a tool, I separated the process of producing the tool from the process of using it. The tool was made by someone else and was then acquired and used by me. How the others made it before I acquired it determined and guaranteed what it produced when I used it. I imagined that the more experienced and powerful members of the community were the ones responsible for making the tool. They were the ones who participated in the discussion and fought with opponents. When I used what they made, their labor and accomplishments would ensure the quality of my reading and writing. By using it, I could survive the heated discussion. When my immediate experience in writing the book report suggested that knowing the conventions of school did not guarantee the form and content of my report, when it suggested that I had to write the report with the work and responsibility I had assigned to those who wrote book reviews in the Publishing bureau, I thought I had lost the tool I had earlier acquired.

Another reason I could not take up an active role in the argument 28 was that my parents and teachers contrived to provide a scene free of conflict for practicing my various languages. It was as if their experience had made them aware of the conflict between their discourse and other discourses and of the struggle involved in reproducing the conventions of any discourse on a scene where more than one discourse exists. They seemed convinced that such conflict and struggle would overwhelm someone still learning the discourse. Home and school each contrived a purified space where only one discourse was spoken and heard. In their choice of textbooks, in the way they spoke, and in the way they required me to speak, each jealously silenced any voice that threatened to break the unison of the scene. The homogeneity of home and of school implied that only one discourse could and should be relevant in each place. It led me to believe I should leave behind, turn a deaf ear to, or forget the discourse of the other when I crossed the boundary dividing them. I expected myself to set down one discourse whenever I took up another just as I would take off or put on a particular set of clothes for school or home.

Despite my parents' and teachers' attempts to keep home and 29 school discrete, the internal conflict between the two discourses continued whenever I read or wrote. Although I tried to suppress the voice of one discourse in the name of the other, having to speak aloud in the voice I had just silenced each time I crossed the boundary kept both voices active in my mind. Every "I think . . ." from the voice of home or school brought forth a "However . . ." or a "But . . ." from the voice of the opponents. To identify with the voice of home or school, I had to negotiate through the conflicting voices of both by restating, taking back, qualifying my thoughts. I was unconsciously doing so when I did my book report. But I could not use the interaction comfortably and constructively. Both my parents and my teachers had implied that my job was to prevent that interaction from happening.

My sense of having failed to accomplish what they had taught silenced me.

To use the interaction between the discourses of home and school 30 constructively, I would have to have seen reading or writing as a process in which I worked my way towards a stance through a dialectical process of identification and division. To identify with an ally, I would have to have grasped the distance between where he or she stood and where I was positioning myself. In taking a stance against an opponent, I would have to have grasped where my stance identified with the stance of my allies. Teetering along the "wavering line of pressure and counter-pressure" from both allies and opponents, I might have worked my way towards a stance of my own (Burke, *A Rhetoric of Motives*, 23). Moreover, I would have to have understood that the voices in my mind, like the participants in the parlor scene, were in constant flux. As I came into contact with new and different groups of people or read different books, voices entered and left. Each time I read or wrote, the stance I negotiated out of these voices would always be at some distance from the stances I worked out in my previous and my later readings or writings.

I could not conceive such a form of action for myself because I saw 31 reading and writing as an expression of an established stance. In delineating the conventions of a discourse, my parents and teachers had synthesized the stance they saw as typical for a representative member of the community. Burke calls this the stance of a "god" or the "prototype"; Williams calls it the "official" or "possible" stance of the community. Through the metaphor of the survival tool, my parents and teachers had led me to assume I could automatically reproduce the official stance of the discourse I used. Therefore, when I did my book report on *The Revolutionary Family*, I expected my knowledge of the official stance set by the book review to ensure the actual stance of my report. As it happened, I began by trying to take the official stance of the review. Other voices interrupted. I answered back. In the process, I worked out a stance approximate but not identical to the official stance I began with. Yet the experience of having to labor to realize my knowledge of the official stance or to prevent myself from wandering away from it frustrated and confused me. For even though I had been actually reading and writing in a Burkean scene, I was afraid to participate actively in the discussion. I assumed it was my role to survive by staying out of it.

Not long ago, my daughter told me that it bothered her to hear her 32 friend "talk wrong." Having come to the United States from China with little English, my daughter has become sensitive to the way English, as spoken by her teachers, operates. As a result, she has amazed her teachers with her success in picking up the language and in adapting to life at school. Her concern to speak the English taught in the classroom "correctly" makes her uncomfortable when she hears people using "ain't" or double negatives, which her teacher considers "improper." I see in her the me that had eagerly learned and used the discourse of the Working class at school. Yet while I was torn between the two conflicting worlds of school and home, she moves with seeming ease from the conversations she hears over the dinner table to her teacher's words in the classroom. My husband and I are proud of the good work she does at school. We are glad she is spared the kinds of conflict between home and school I experienced at her age. Yet as we watch her becoming more and more fluent in the language of the classroom, we wonder if, by enabling her to "survive" school, her very fluency will silence her when the scene of her reading and writing expands beyond that of the composition classroom.

For when I listen to my daughter, to students, and to some composition teachers talking about the teaching and learning of writing, I am often alarmed by the degree to which the metaphor of a survival tool dominates their understanding of language as it once dominated my own. I am especially concerned with the way some composition classes focus on turning the classroom into a monological scene for the students' reading and writing. Most of our students live in a world similar to my daughter's, somewhere between the purified world of the classroom and the complex world of my adolescence. When composition classes encourage these students to ignore those voices that seem irrelevant to the purified world of the classroom, most students are often able to do so without much struggle. Some of them are so adept at doing it that the whole process has for them become automatic. 33

However, beyond the classroom and beyond the limited range of these students' immediate lives lies a much more complex and dynamic social and historical scene. To help these students become actors in such a scene, perhaps we need to call their attention to voices that may seem irrelevant to the discourse we teach rather than encourage them to shut them out. For example, we might intentionally complicate the classroom scene by bringing into it discourses that stand at varying distances from the one we teach. We might encourage students to explore ways of practicing the conventions of the discourse they are learning by negotiating through these conflicting voices. We could also encourage them to see themselves as responsible for forming or transforming as well as preserving the discourse they are learning. 34

As I think about what we might do to complicate the external and internal scenes of our students' writing, I hear my parents and teachers saying: "Not now. Keep them from the wrangle of the marketplace until they have acquired the discourse and are skilled at using it." And 35

I answer: "Don't teach them to 'survive' the whirlpool of crosscurrents by avoiding it. Use the classroom to moderate the currents. Moderate the currents, but teach them from the beginning to struggle." When I think of the ways in which the teaching of reading and writing as classroom activities can frustrate the development of students, I am almost grateful for the overwhelming complexity of the circumstances in which I grew up. For it was this complexity that kept me from losing sight of the effort and choice involved in reading or writing with and through a discourse.

REFERENCES

Burke, Kenneth. *The Philosophy of Literary Form: Studies in Symbolic Action.* 2nd ed. Baton Rouge: Louisiana State UP, 1967.

——. *A Rhetoric of Motives.* Berkeley: U of California P, 1969.

Freire, Paulo. *Pedagogy of the Oppressed.* Trans. M. B. Ramos. New York: Continuum, 1970.

Williams, Raymond. *Marxism and Literature.* New York: Oxford UP, 1977.

Working with the Text

1. What is the split for Lu as a child between the language of home and the language of school? Why is there so much tension between the two languages? How is her situation similar to and different from that of her daughter?

2. In her second paragraph, Lu says she searched for "constructive uses" for "the struggle I experienced every time I tried to read, write, or think" in the two discourses of home and school. What "constructive uses" for her personal struggle does she hint at in the essay?

3. Lu says that she came to understand language as a "tool" that someone else made and she acquired, a tool that "determined and guaranteed what it produced when I used it." If the languages of home and school were two different "tools," how did those two languages "determine" what she was able to say? Point to specific explanations of the limits the two languages impose on her thinking.

4. Lu begins her essay with two epigraphs. Why? What is the purpose of beginning in this way, with quotations from other authors, even before introducing the subject of the essay to the reader?

Working beyond the Text

1. The background of Lu's essay is the Chinese Revolution of 1949 and the so-called Cultural Revolution of the 1960s. What do you know about these events? Find out as much as you can by doing research in the library, and

relate what you learn to the events of Lu's life. How does what you learn about politics in China help explain the gap between her family life and her school life?

2. Who was Kenneth Burke? What are his ideas of "identification" and "division"? Try investigating them in a dictionary of philosophy or an encyclopedia of rhetorical terms. How does understanding these concepts help you understand the points Lu makes near the end of her essay?

3. Lu summarizes the formula that is used in her textbooks for the "author's biography": "X X X, born in 19—in the province of X X, is from a Worker's family," and so on. Why do you suppose the books used author's biographies in that format? What formula is used for the author's biographies in *Living Languages?* How and why are the two formats different, do you think?

4. Explain how Lu's personal experience relates to ideas from the essays by Mike Rose and Gerald Graff that appear earlier in this chapter. What might Rose or Graff say about Lu's struggle between different worlds of language and the "constructive uses" to which she puts her struggle?

UNIT TWO

MISUSES OF ACADEMIC DISCOURSE

How to Sound Erudite

Paul Pacentrilli

Paul Pacentrilli teaches English literature to high school students in Calgary, Alberta. In this satirical essay, which was originally published in the magazine *World Press Review* (August 1993), he makes fun of erudite language and presents twelve tongue-in-cheek "rules" for sounding intelligent and powerful.

We live in a society where image holds sway over substance, and that should be kept in mind when investigating the current controversy over language usage and its teaching. Why should anyone learn to use the language "properly"? For success, power, prestige, admiration. Allow me to outline 12 rules that are guaranteed to lead you to be considered a master of our tongue. Toss out your grammar texts and dusty workbooks; all the material you need is here, small enough to be carried around in your wallet.

- Never use the word "me." Decades of conditioning by pointer-wielding grammarians has resulted in a generation of "me-ophobics." Even if "me" is the correct choice for the sentence you intend to utter, join with most others in the butchering of the word "myself." Never before has this word been used and abused so often. Do not forget—it's not what you know that counts, it's what they think you know.
- Use the suffixes "-esque" and "-ian." Rather than saying "Gee, that gal looks just like Oprah!" you can elevate your diction—and perhaps compensate for your taste in television programs—by saying, "My, she is Oprahesque."
- Speaking of television, there are a few guidelines you should follow when discussing popular culture: Never refer to a television "show"—call it a "program." Never say "movie," always "film." Never say "book"—call it a "read," as in "His latest is a great read." Connotation is everything.

- Make references to highbrow magazines. Start a thought with, "I was reading . . . in *The New Yorker.* . . ." Don't worry about what you say next—the hook has been set.
- Although some listeners may be catching on to this one, using the word "basically" at the beginning of many of your sentences may still give the impression that what you have to say has been carefully thought out and refined. Gauge your audience carefully, then go ahead—use it.
- Never use a short word when you can replace it with a polysyllabic tongue buster. There are endless examples of this: For training, listen to William F. Buckley.
- Similarly, never use simple sentence construction when you can substitute a convoluted mess. Rather than saying, "Last night, I almost forgot to feed the hogs," offer the more lyrical, "To feed the hogs . . . last night—I almost forgot." Note the tone of *angst* in the latter.
- Have a half-dozen obscure quotations from Shakespeare in your oral repertoire. These need not be carefully selected, because, in most cases, when you use them, you will get knowing smiles and nods all around even if what you have said is nonsense. Do not concern yourself with remembering which play or sonnet they come from—you will not be asked.
- Make references to Greek or Roman myths. Again, you need only a half dozen or so at your disposal. Compare "Wow, he's a strong guy," with "His powers are truly Herculean." Marvelous.
- Memorize a short list of foreign terms commonly—or even uncommonly—used in English. Throwing in a "sine qua non" or a "persona non grata" here and there at a cocktail party is certain to raise your linguistic stock.
- Use the word "existential" at least once in any conversation. This word is a godsend to the superficial. It can be used to refer to just about anything in any context. It makes a great impression, and no one is sure what it means.
- I've left the most important rule for last, because if you can manage this one, it allows you to dispense with all the others. Develop or affect a British accent. Even if the content of your speech resembles compost, this strategy will insure your place in the pantheon of English usage.

Above all, never forget the guiding principle as spoken by the archetype of the image conscious, Willy Loman: "It's not what you say but how you say it." Take a good look around you and see how many successful people have already discovered these rules. You probably need look no farther than your boss's office.

Working with the Text

1. Pacentrilli's article is clearly a satire, but what or whom is he satirizing? What is his implied criticism?
2. Pacentrilli makes a tongue-in-cheek connection between learning to "use the language 'properly'" and obtaining "success, power, prestige, admiration." On a more serious note, is there a connection? What is it?
3. Why does Pacentrilli choose satire, do you think, to get across what might be a serious point about the misuse of academic language?

Working beyond the Text

1. Though Pacentrilli's list is supposed to be satirical, some of the rules he lists are similar to rules that teachers actually give students. Make a list of rules for writing you have been given that you consider ridiculous.
2. Pacentrilli lists a dozen rules "guaranteed to lead you to be considered a master of our tongue." Add to the list with a few (or a lot) more rules that clearly ridicule the kind of "erudite" language people use when they want to sound educated. Remember to give examples, as Pacentrilli does.
3. Pacentrilli describes "how to sound erudite" with his list of a dozen rules. Make a list of your own describing "how to sound" a particular way. You might describe how to sound sensitive, for example, or "politically correct," or knowledgeable in an area such as art, sports, or computer technology.
4. Who is Willy Loman? What ideas does he represent? How does knowing who he is help you understand the ironic meaning of Pacentrilli's last paragraph? (Hint: look for the works of Arthur Miller in your library's drama section.)

This Pen for Hire: On Grinding Out Papers for College Students
Abigail Witherspoon

According to the original author biography for this article, which first appeared in *Harper's* (June 1995), "Abigail Witherspoon is, of necessity, a pseudonym. Were the writer to be identified, she could be fired or deported." "Abigail Witherspoon" is in the illegal business of writing term papers for college students, and in the article she also changes the names of her company, her employer, and her fellow workers. She sketches the details of what she and her colleagues do for a living, and along the way delivers a harsh criticism of an educational system that makes such a business possible.

I am an academic call girl. I write college kids' papers for a living. 1
Term papers, book reports, senior theses, take-home exams. My "spe-
cialties": art history and sociology, international relations and compar-
ative literature, English, psychology, "communications," western philosophy (ancient and contemporary), structural anthropology, film
history, evolutionary biology, waste management and disposal, media
studies, and pre-Confederation Canadian history. I throw around allusions to Caspar Weinberger and Alger Hiss, Sacco and Vanzetti,
Haldeman and Ehrlichman, Joel Steinberg and Baby M. The teaching
assistants eat it up. I can do simple English or advanced jargon. Like
other types of prostitutes, I am, professionally, very accommodating.

I used to tell myself I'd do this work only for a month or two, until 2
I found something else. But the official unemployment rate in this
large Canadian city where I live is almost 10 percent, and even if it
were easy to find a job, I'm American, and therefore legally prohibited
from receiving a paycheck. So each day I walk up the stairs of a rotting
old industrial building to an office with a sign on the window: TAI-
LORMADE ESSAYS, WRITING AND RESEARCH. The owner, whom
I'll call Matthew, claims that he started the business for ghostwriters,
speechwriters, and closet biographers, and only gradually moved into
academic work as a sideline. But even Grace, the oldest surviving
writer on Tailormade's staff, can't remember anybody ever writing
much other than homework for students at one university or another.

This is a good city for Tailormade. Next door is the city's univer- 3
sity and its tens of thousands of students, a school that was once somewhat better when not all of its computer-registered classes numbered
in the hundreds. Orders come in from Vancouver, Calgary, Winnipeg.
There are plenty of essay services in the States, of course; they advertise in campus newspapers and the back pages of music magazines.
Some of the big ones have toll-free phone numbers. They're sprinkled
all over: California, Florida, New Jersey. But we still get American
business too. Orders come in here from Michigan, Vermont, Pennsylvania; from Illinois, Wisconsin, upstate New York, sometimes California; from Harvard, Cornell, and Brown. They come in from teachers'
colleges, from people calling themselves "gifted students" (usually
teenagers at boarding schools), and, once in a while, from the snazzy
places some of our customers apparently vacation with their divorced
dads, like Paris.

Matthew runs the business with his wife, Sylvia. Or maybe she is 4
his ex-wife, nobody's exactly sure. When you call Tailormade—it's
now in the phone book—you hear Sylvia say that Tailormade is
Canada's foremost essay service; that our very qualified writers handle most academic subjects; and that we are fast, efficient, and completely confidential. Sylvia speaks loudly and slowly and clearly, especially to Asian customers. She is convinced that everyone who phones

the office will be Asian, just as she's convinced that all Asians drive white Mercedes, or black BMWs with cellular phones in them. From my personal experience, I find the Asian customers at least more likely to have done the assigned reading. Matthew and Sylvia are oddly complementary. Matthew, gentle and fumbly, calls out mechanically, "Thank you, sir, ma'am, come again" after each departing back slinking down the hall. Sylvia asks the Chinese customers loudly, "SIMPLE ENGLISH?" She tells the uncertain, "Well, don't show up here till you know what you want," and demands of the dissatisfied, "Whaddya mean you didn't like it? You ordered it, din'cha?"

This afternoon, October 10, I'm here to hand in a paper and fight it 5 out with the other writers for more assignments. Some of us are legal, some aren't. Some have mortgages and cars, some don't. All of us are hungry. The office is jammed, since it's almost time for midterms. Tailormade does a brisk business from October to May, except for January. The chairs are full of customers studiously filling out order forms. You can always tell who is a student and who is a writer. The students are dressed elegantly and with precision; the writers wear ripped concert T-shirts or stained denim jackets with white undershirts peeking out. The students wear mousse and hair gel and nail polish and Tony Lama western boots and Tourneau watches and just the right amount of makeup. They smell of Escape, Polo for men, and gum. The writers smell of sweat, house pets, and crushed cigarettes. Four of the other writers are lolling in their chairs and fidgeting; work usually isn't assigned until all the order forms have been filled out, unless somebody requests a topic difficult to fill. Then Matthew will call out like an auctioneer: "Root Causes of the Ukrainian Famine? Second year? Anyone? Grace?" or "J. S. Mill's Brand of Humane Utilitarianism? Third year? Henry, that for you?" as some customer hovers in front of the desk, eyes straight ahead. Someone else in the room might idly remark that he or she took that course back in freshman year and it was a "gut" or a "real bird."

I suspect that each of us in the Tailormade stable of hacks sorts out 6 the customers differently: into liberal-arts students and business students; into those that at least do the reading and those that don't bother; into those that have trouble writing academic English and those that just don't care about school; into those that do their assignments in other subjects and those that farm every last one of them out to us; into the struggling and inept versus the rich, lazy, and stupid. But for Matthew and Sylvia, the clientele are divisible, even before cash versus credit card, or paid-up versus owing, into Asian customers and non-Asian ones. There's been an influx of wealthy immigrants from Hong Kong in recent years, fleeing annexation. Matthew and Sylvia seem to resent their presence and, particularly, their money. Yet they know that it's precisely this pool of customers—who

have limited written English language skills but possess education, sophistication, ambition, cash, and parents leaning hard on them for
good grades—that keeps the business going.

When I hand in my twelve pages on "The Role of Market Factors 7
in the Development of the Eighteenth-Century Fur Trade," Matthew
tells me, "This lady's been patiently waiting without complaining." I
must be very late. Turning to the client, he picks up one of my sheets
and waves it. "At least it's a nice bib," he points out to her. "Look at
that." Although I wasn't provided with any books for this essay, I
managed to supply an extensive bibliography. I can't remember what
I put on it.

I'm still waiting for an assignment. In fact, all the writers are still 8
waiting. We often wait at the bar around the corner; Tailormade has its
own table there, permanently reserved. But we all have to get ourselves to the office eventually to pick up assignments. Grace, the oldest writer and by now, probably the best, sits sorrowfully by the window, her long gray hair falling into her lap and her head jammed into
her turtleneck, on her thin face a look of permanent tragedy. Grace
gets up at three in the morning to work; she never forgets a name, a
fact, or an assignment; she has a deep, strange love for Japanese history and in ten years here has probably hatched enough pages and research for several doctoral dissertations in that field. Elliott, another
writer, reclines near the door, his little dog asleep under his chair. He
uses the dog as an icebreaker with the clients, especially young
women. He is six and a half feet tall and from somewhere far up in the
lunar landscape of northern Ontario. He has a huge head of blond hair
down to his eyes and pants as tight as a rock star's. Elliott is the business writer. He specializes in finance, investment, management, and
economics. He lives out of a suitcase; he and the little dog, perhaps
practicing fiscal restraint, seem to stay with one of a series of girl-
friends. When the relationship comes to an end, Elliott and the little
dog wind up back in the office, where they sleep in the fax room and
Elliott cranks out essays on his laptop. Henry and Russell, two other
writers, twist around, changing position, the way travelers do when
they're trying to nap on airport lounge chairs. They both look a little
like El Greco saints, although perhaps it just seems that way to me because lately I've been doing a lot of art history papers. They both have
long skinny legs, long thin white nervous twiddling hands, long thin
faces with two weeks' worth of unintentional beard. Henry points out
how good Russell looks, and we all agree. Russell is forty. He has a
new girlfriend half his age who has, he says, provided a spiritual
reawakening. Before he met her, Russell drank so much and held it so
badly that he had the distinction of being the only staff member to be
banned from the bar around the corner for life. Henry, by contrast,
looks terrible. He's always sick, emaciated, coughing, but he invari-

ably manages to meet his deadlines, to make his page quotas, and to show up on time. We used to have another writer on staff, older even than Russell or Grace, who smoked a pipe, nodded a lot, and never said anything. He was a professor who'd been fired from some school, we were never really sure where. Eventually, he went AWOL and started an essay-writing service of his own. He's now Tailormade's main competition. The only other competitors, apparently, worked out of a hot-dog stand parked next to a campus bookstore. Nobody knows whether they're open anymore.

In general, there is a furtiveness about the way we writers talk to 9 one another, the way we socialize. In the office, we're a little like people who know each other from A.A. meetings or rough trade bars encountering each other on a Monday morning at the photocopy machine. It's not because we're competing for work. It's not even because some of us are illegal and everyone else knows it. It is, if anything, collective embarrassment. We know a lot more than Matthew and Sylvia do. They sit dumbly as we bullshit with the clients about their subjects and assignments ("Ah, introductory psychology! The evolution of psychotherapy is a fascinating topic . . . ever read a guy called Russel Jacoby?") in order to impress them and get them to ask for us. This must be the equivalent of the harlots' competitive bordello promenade. But we work for Matthew and Sylvia. They have the sense to pit us against each other, and it works. We can correct their pronunciation of "Goethe" and they don't care. They know it makes no difference. I suspect they have never been farther away than Niagara Falls; neither of them may have even finished high school. It doesn't matter. The laugh's on us, of course: they own the business.

OCTOBER 12, 1994. A tall gangly kid comes in for a twenty-page 10 senior history essay about the ancient local jail. It involves research among primary sources in the provincial archives, and I spend a week there, going page by page through the faded brown script of the warden's prison logbooks of the 1830s. Agitators are being executed for "high treason" or "banished from the realm," which, I assume, means being deported. Once in a while there's a seductive joy to a project. You forget that you've undertaken it for money, that it isn't yours.

Most of the time, though, all I think about is the number of pages 11 done, the number to go. Tailormade charges twenty dollars Canadian a page for first- and second-year course assignments, twenty-two a page for third- and fourth-year assignments, twenty-four for "technical, scientific, and advanced" topics. "Technical, scientific, and advanced" can mean nuclear physics, as it does in September when there is no business. Or it can mean anything Matthew and Sylvia want it to, as it does in March. Most major spring-term essays are due when final exams begin, in April, and so in March kids are practically lined up in the office taking numbers and spilling out into the hall. The writers get half, in cash: ten and eleven bucks a page; twelve for the technical, scientific, and advanced.

There's one other charge: if the client doesn't bring in her or his 12 own books, except in September and January, she or he is "dinged," charged an extra two dollars a page for research. When the writers get an assignment, we ask if there are books. If there are, it saves us time, but we have to lug them home, and often they're the wrong books. If there are no books, we have to go to the libraries and research the paper ourselves. "Client wants twelve pages on clinical social work intervention," Matthew and Sylvia might tell us. "She has a reading list but no books. I think we can ding her." "He wants a book report on something called *Gravity's Rainbow?* Doesn't have the book, though. I'm gonna ding him."

NOVEMBER 8. I will not go into any of the university's libraries. I 13 will not risk running into anyone I know, anyone who might think I'm one of those perpetual graduate students who never finished their dissertations and drift pathetically around university libraries like the undead, frightening the undergraduates. It would be as bad to be thought one of these lifelong grad students as to be suspected of being what I am. So I use the public libraries, usually the one closest to my apartment, on my street corner. It's a community library, with three wonderful librarians, three daily newspapers, and remarkably few books. If I haven't been given the books already, if the client has been dinged and I have to do research on my own, I come here. I have my favorite chair. The librarians assume I am a "mature" and "continuing" community college student, and make kind chitchat with me.

Sometimes, when I can't find any of the sources listed in the li- 14 brary's computer and don't have time to go to a real library, I use books barely appropriate for the essay: books for "young adults," which means twelve-year-olds, or books I have lying around my apartment—like Jane Jacobs's *The Death and Life of Great American Cities,* H.D.F. Kitto's *The Greeks,* Eduardo Galeano's *Open Veins of Latin America,* Roy Medvedev's book on Stalin or T.H. White's on John Kennedy, books by J.K. Galbraith, Lewis Mumford, Christopher Lasch, Erich Fromm. Books somewhere between the classic and the old chestnut; terrific books, yet with no relation to the topic at hand. But they're good for the odd quote and name-drop, and they can pad a bibliography. Sometimes I can't get away with this, though, and then I have no choice but to go back to an actual place of research, like the archives.

NOVEMBER 18. Things are picking up for Christmas vacation; 15 everything, it seems, is due December 5 or December 15. The essay

order form asks, "Subject & Level," "Topic," "No. of Pages," "Footnotes," "Bibliography," and then a couple of lines marked "Additional
Information," by far the most common of which is "Simple English."
As the year rolls on, we hacks will all, out of annoyance, laziness, or
just boredom, start unsimplifying this simple English; by April it will
approach the mega-watt vocabulary and tortured syntax of the Frank-
furt School. But people hand these papers in and don't get caught,
people who have difficulty speaking complete sentences in English;
perhaps this is because classes and even tutorials are so big they never
have to speak. But in December we're all still on pretty good behavior,
simple instead of spiteful. I've just handed in an assignment in "Simple English," a paper titled "Mozart's Friendship with Joseph and Jo-
hann Michael Haydn and Its Impact on Mozart's Chamber Music." It
reads, in part:

> Mozart was undeniably original. He was never derivative. That
> was part of his genius. So were the Haydn brothers. All of them were
> totally unique.

The little library on my corner didn't have much on Mozart or the   16
Haydn brothers. As a result, one of the items in my bibliography is a
child's book with a cardboard pop-up of a doughy-looking little
Mozart, in a funky pigtail and knee breeches, standing proudly beside
a harpsichord.

DECEMBER 5. A bad assignment: unnecessarily obscure, pedan-   17
tic, pointless. Certain courses seem to consist of teaching kids the use
of jargon as though it were a substitute for writing or thinking well.
Often there is an implied pressure to agree with the assigned book.
And many are simply impossible to understand; I often take home a
textbook or a sheaf of photocopies for an assignment and see, next to a
phrase such as "responsible acceptance of the control dimension,"
long strings of tiny Chinese characters in ballpoint pen. No wonder
the students find the assignments incomprehensible; they are incomprehensible to me.

JANUARY 10, 1995. School has been back in session for a week   18
now. The only work that is in are essays from the education students. I hate these assignments. I have trouble manipulating the self-
encapsulated second language in which teaching students seem compelled to write. But it's after Christmas, and I'm broke. Education
assignments all involve writing up our customers' encounters in their
"practicum." Teaching students work several times a week as assistant
teachers in grade school classrooms; instead of getting paid for this
work, they pay tuition for it. Unfortunately, these expensive practice

sessions don't seem to go well. My first such assignment was to write "reflections" on a "lesson plan" for a seventh-grade English class. The teaching student had given me some notes, and I had to translate these into the pedagogical jargon used in her textbooks. The idea seems to be that you have to say, as obscurely as possible, what you did with your seventh-grade kids and what you think about what you did:

> Preliminary Lesson Formulations: My objectives were to integrate lesson content with methodology to expand students' receptiveness and responsiveness to the material and to one another by teaching them how to disagree with one another in a constructive way. The class will draw up a T-chart covering "Disagreeing in an Agreeable Way," roughly in the manner of Bennett et al. Check for understanding. When the students discuss this, they are encouraged to listen to one another's language carefully and "correct" it if the wording is unhelpful, negative, or destructive. I shared my objectives with the class by asking them to read a fable and then divide into pairs and decide together what the moral was. Clearly, this is the "Think-Pair-Share" technique, as detailed in Bennett et al. The three strategies in use, then, are: 1) pair and sharing; 2) group discussion of the fable with mind-mapping; 3) group discussion of ways of disagreement. The teacher, modeling, divides the board in two with a line.

"Pair and share" seemed to mean "find a partner." I had no idea 19 what "mind-mapping" or a "T-chart" was supposed to be. And come to think of it, after reading the fable, I had no idea what the moral was.

JANUARY 20. When I first started this work, friends of mine 20 would try to comfort me by telling me it would teach me to write better. Actually, academic prostitution, just like any other kind, seems to bring with it diseases, afflictions, vices, and bad habits. There is, for instance, the art of pretending you've read a book you haven't. It's just like every speed-reading course ever offered by the Learning Annex: read the introduction, where the writer outlines what he's going to say, and the conclusion, where he repeats what he's said.

> In his book *The Technological Society*, Jacques Ellul begins by defining the technical simply as the search for efficiency. He claims, however, that technique itself is subdivided into three categories: the social, the organizational, and the economic.

This is all on the book's *first four pages*. Sometimes—often—I find 21 myself eating up as much space as possible. There are several ways to do this. One is to reproduce lengthy, paragraph-long quotes in full; another is to ramble on about your own apparently passionate opinion on something. Or you start talking about the United States and what a handbasket it's going to hell in. This is equally useful, for different reasons, on either side of the border. You can ask rhetorical questions to obsessive excess. ("Can Ellul present the technical in such a reductionist way? Can he really define technique in such a way? And is it really valid to distinguish between the social and the organizational?" etc.) And there's always the art of name-dropping as a way to fill pages and convince the teaching assistant that your client has read *something*, even if it wasn't what was on the syllabus.

> Certainly, as writers from Eduardo Galeano to Andre Gunder Frank to Noam Chomsky to Philip Agee to Allan Frankovich to Ernesto Laclau document, the CIA has long propped up the United Fruit Company.

At least you can make the client feel stupid. It's the third week of January, my apartment is cold, and I am bitter.

MARCH 26. One day I'm given five pages on the Treaty of Versailles. Last year at the same time, I was assigned a paper on the same topic. A memorable paper. Two days after I turned it in, there was a camera crew outside. It turned out to be the local cable station for kids, doing an "exposé" on cheating. We taped it when it came on. It featured kids sitting in shadow, faces obscured, *60 Minutes* style.

"There she is, the little rat," Sylvia glowered at the time. The pretty young fake client handed my paper to some professor sitting behind a desk and asked, "What do you think about this? Is it better or worse than what you would normally get? Would you assume that it was a real paper or one that had been bought?"

"Well . . . it's a *credible* paper," said the professor. "I mean, one wouldn't think it was . . . *synthetic* unless one had reason to."

"What kind of grade would you give it?"

"Oh, I'd give it . . . a B minus."

"*Please.*" I was really offended. Elliott comforted me. "Well, he has to say that. Now that he knows it's ours, he can't admit it's an A paper even if he wants to."

We all sat tight and waited for every professor within fifty miles to call us, threatening death. But professors don't watch cable shows for teenagers; neither do ambitious young teaching assistants. Instead, the show turned out to be a free advertising bonanza. Soon the phone rang off the hook with kids calling up and asking, "You mean, like, you can write my term paper for me if I pay you?"

APRIL 16. Today, working on a paper, I was reminded that there 29 *are* good professors. They're the ones who either convince the kids the course content is inherently interesting and get them to work hard on the assignments or who figure out ways to make the assignments, at least, creative events to enjoy. But students with shaky language skills falter at surprises, even good ones; lazy students farm the assignments out no matter what they are. Such assignments are oddly comforting for me: I can almost pretend the two of us are talking over the clients' heads. When I'm alone in my room, in front of the computer and between the headphones, it's hard not to want to write something good for myself and maybe even for the imaginary absentee professor or appreciative T.A., something that will last. But when I'm standing in the crowded Tailormade office, next to someone elegant and young and in eight hundred bucks' worth of calfskin leather, someone who not only has never heard of John Stuart Mill and never read *Othello* but doesn't even know he hasn't, doesn't even mind that he hasn't, and doesn't even care that he hasn't, the urge to make something that will last somehow vanishes.

APRIL 28. The semester is almost at an end. Exams have started; 30 the essays have all been handed in. Elliott and Russell begin their summer jobs as bike couriers. Henry, like me, is illegal; but he confides to me that he's had enough. "You can only do so much of this," he says. I know, I tell him. I know.

Working with the Text

1. Witherspoon's first sentence might strike you as shocking: "I am an academic call girl." What does she mean? How does the meaning of this first sentence relate to other specific passages in the essay? Where else does she use the same metaphor to express similar feelings?

2. Witherspoon describes the different appearances of the students (customers) and the writers (workers) at the office where she works: "You can always tell who is a student and who is a writer." What does her description communicate about the differences between the two groups of people?

3. According to Witherspoon, what are all the reasons students might use a term-paper service? Which reasons does she seem to understand, and which reasons does she seem to condemn?

4. The author of this essay uses a pseudonym, or a fake name, and also changes the names of other people. Why? What is the effect of using false names?

5. The essay takes the form of a diary. When does it begin and end? Why do you think the author chose this form?

Working beyond the Text

1. Would you agree or disagree with Witherspoon's assertion that "Certain courses seem to consist of teaching kids the use of jargon as though it were a substitute for writing or thinking well"? In what ways? Use your own experiences in specific classes to support your opinion.
2. Witherspoon says that "people hand these papers in and don't get caught." Why not? Could people get away with handing in such papers at your school and not get caught? Why or why not?
3. Are there any term-papers services available in your area? Where can you find out about them? What kinds of papers do they offer, how much do they charge, and how much time do they take to deliver? If you find a telephone number for a service, try doing a little research about it. How does the one you call compare to the one where Witherspoon works?

The Grooves of Academe
Robin Tolmach Lakoff

Robin Lakoff was born in 1942, and teaches linguistics at the University of California at Berkeley. Her writing often focuses on connections between language use and gender; her books have titles such as *Face Value: The Politics of Beauty* (written with Raquel L. Sherr) and *Language and Woman's Place*. In this excerpt from a chapter in her book *Talking Power: The Politics of Language in Our Lives* (1990), Lakoff examines the way unwritten rules about language use reflect power structures in academia, from undergraduates to tenured professors.

My department is at it again.   1

Every five years or so we go through it, only to undo our work,   2
like Penelope, with perfect regularity some five years later. We are fighting about revamping the department's graduate program: how many courses, and which, and in what order, are to be required for the Ph.D. It always turns out to be a long-drawn-out process, entailing almost as much internecine acrimony as our all-time favorite fighting issue—hiring of new colleagues. And the real conflicts, the things that fill a simple process with dissension, are never brought out into the light of day: they remain covert, while we debate superficialities.

The Curriculum Committee (and academics do love committees,   3
almost as much as we love subcommittees! they allow us to postpone the inevitable moment of climax, the decision) has proposed a new

course, to be required of all graduate students in their first semester of residence, for one unit (most courses are three or four), meeting for one and a half hours, once a week—a very small commitment.

Ordinarily, such small fish don't attract a great deal of discussion, 4 pro or con. We reserve our verbal ammunition for the bigger stuff. But the proposed course is largely concerned with the underpinnings of the field, its ineffable mystique. It would cover, for instance, how to get articles published; how to write abstracts; where to look for bibliography; which journals are geared toward which subfields; the professional interests of the various faculty members of the department.

And more, and worse: how power is allocated in the field of lin- 5 guistics; who has it, why, and how to get it. And why linguists are such a contentious group, why we can't listen to one another across theoretical boundaries, why scholarly arguments too often turn into personal vendettas.

Everyone agrees that, to receive a Ph.D. in linguistics from the 6 University of California at Berkeley, a student must demonstrate knowledge in a variety of topics: sounds and sound-systems; word-formation and lexical semantics; syntax and sentence-level semantics; processes of historical change; methodology of various types; the claims of competing theories; and, of course, much much more. All this is the explicit and overt knowledge of the field, our public culture, as it were—what we transmit openly to the young and expect them to demonstrate proof of mastering. But that knowledge alone, however broad and deep, does not a competent professional linguist make.

To be one, you not only have to know facts, theories, and methods, 7 you have to know how to be a linguist, how to play by the rules. You have to know how to cite sources and which sources to cite; how to talk and how to write, in terms of style; how to talk and how to write, in terms of which questions may legitimately be raised and which (apparently equally attractive) may not, and what constitutes an "answer." You have to know something about the history of the field, which in turn explains the politics of the field: who likes who and who hates who, who invites contributions from who in the volume who is editing, who is not invited (though working in the same area) and why. You must master the forms, in terms of length, topic, and style: the *abstract*, the *paper* (or *article*), the *monograph*, the *book*, in writing; the *talk*, the *job talk*, the *lecture*, the *panel contribution*, among oral forms. These requirements exist in all academic fields, but each field does them differently and values them differently. In determining tenurability, some departments rank a single book higher than several articles with about the same number of pages; others, the reverse. It's useful to know these things—in fact, often vital for survival in an increasingly competitive business. But no one will tell you this—certainly not spontaneously. Some students know how to pick up a lot of

underground stuff by judicious looking and listening; others are sophisticated and brash enough to frame the questions and insist on answers from diffident mentors. But many are not, and it takes them
years of agonizing in pre-tenure positions before they understand—
too often, too late.

We would be scandalized at a department that refused to tell its   8
students about sentence-construction or typological differences among
languages. But we are, some of us, equally scandalized at a proposal to
provide the second kind of information openly to all, in the guise of
formal course work. When the Curriculum Committee had submitted
its lengthy proposal, the first and bitterest fight erupted over this pe-
ripheral one-unit course: whether, as "non-intellectual subject matter"
it should be taught at all.

We are, in fact, fighting about something much bigger than a pro-   9
posed Linguistics-200 requirement, but no one says so: that would be
vulgar. We are fighting about mystique. We are elders in the tribal
sweathouse, discussing the rites of initiation the next generation is to
undergo. We went through them once, that's how we achieved our
present esteemed status. They must, too, in their turn. We all agree on
that, and we also agree pretty much that there are certain explicit skills
the youth must know before they are deemed ready to take their place
in adult society. But someone has raised an unheard-of question:
Should they be told the secrets—what happens during the ordeal,
what is done and why it is done? It would make it easier for them; the
suffering (which we all agree is essential) would make sense; it would
be coherent, all the fasting, mutilation, deprivation. Why not enlighten
them?

But the oldest of the elders demurs indignantly. Don't we under-   10
stand *anything?* The whole point is in the mystery. The very senseless-
ness gives the experience a special meaning, a curious depth, makes
tribal membership of greater value. If they have to figure it out themselves, by vague hints and overheard whispers, through trial and
error, with pain and suffering, they will prize full membership, when
it is conferred, all the more. The elders of the tribe must keep its mysteries holy.

Any anthropologically sophisticated Westerner can understand   11
that reasoning in a primitive tribe. But it's a little disconcerting to encounter ourselves at it—ourselves, not only sophisticated Westerners,
but intellectuals to boot and, more, intellectuals in an institution which
claims as its territory the pursuit of knowledge by reason alone. Mystique has a place, but it is not the stuff of which scholarship is made.
But reason alone cannot explain the passions of the argument over
Linguistics 200.

Like any other institution, the university has a complex mission,   12
only some of which is supposed to be overtly visible, even to insiders.

Therefore, its power relations are complex, and its communications—to outsiders, and to and among its members—are more often than not obscure and ambiguous. In fact, the discourse of academe seems (and not only to non-initiates) especially designed for incomprehensibility. This is demonstrably true. But many of its ambiguities and eccentricities are intentional and intrinsic to the institution, not (as sometimes argued) mere side effects of the university's main communicative purpose.

Truth in Language: Mission Impossible?

Every institution has a public mission, its reason for being, generally couched in benign and even lofty language. The mission of psychotherapy is *change* or *understanding;* of the law, *justice;* of the military, *protection* or *defense;* of government, *order.* In this semantic of noble purpose, we can define the university's mission as the production of *truth,* or *knowledge,* a virtuous enterprise if ever there was one. Unlike the others, it would seem to have no dark side, no hidden risk to anyone. There would seem to be nothing to hide or dissemble. 13

But for all its virtuousness, the university is an institution, like the others. As such, it must ensure its own survival and the enhancement of the status of itself and its members. It must appear to the outside world, and to its own personnel, as benevolent and useful: it must have something the outside world needs enough to pay for, to support the institution and guarantee its survival. It must be awesome, to convince others of its value; and more, it must seem *good.* 14

This is a lot to ask of anyone, individual or institution. It is hard to require both love and respect, to retain power and yet radiate benevolence, to get from outsiders scarce resources against strong competition—even more for an institution whose product is abstract, often inscrutable, of no immediate use. We can see why we have to support the government and the military (well, some of us can, some of the time); if we are in pain, we can justify giving money to the medical or psychotherapeutic establishments; if we are legally entangled, we appreciate the necessity of supporting the representatives of the law. But the university has to persuade society that knowledge per se is worthy of support. 15

Institutions, then, like individuals, have interests at stake; they must compete for resources. But at the same time, to succeed in getting their needs met, they must convince others of their benevolence and disinterestedness. We know what individuals do in such a quandary: they lie. Institutions are no different. Unless the lies become too outrageous or harmful, we mostly accept them. Watergate was intolerable, but Iran-Contragate was within bounds. We know Freud lied, or at least engaged in self-deception, about "infantile seduction," but psy- 16 choanalysis retains society's respect. The university, as an institution, can be expected to lie to protect its power and authority.

Cases are not hard to come by. For example, universities are 17 known to reinvent their history when convenient. In 1964, the University of California at Berkeley was shaken by the Free Speech Movement. Popular among students, it was anathema to the administration and many of the faculty, who did everything they could to stamp it out and remove its ringleaders from influence. But life goes on, times change, and what was once a dire threat to institutional business as usual is seen nostalgically, twenty years later, as the shot heard 'round the world, the opening statement of the sixties. It was *important*, it was *historic*, it put the university on the cultural map.

Therefore, in 1984, it seemed appropriate to the university admin- 18 istration—heirs to the men who had called armed deputies in to their rescue—to celebrate the twentieth anniversary of the Free Speech Movement with a plethora of university-sponsored activities stressing the Movement's historic role and the university's participation therein. There were speeches by the powerful and influential, publications, retrospective photography shows, colloquia, everything that can be trotted out to say, This was history and we were a part of it—we made it happen. Lost in the hoopla is the fact that the university was involved, all right—against its will and as a force in opposition. The administration never (that I am aware of) said in so many words: We supported the FSM. But the inviting of celebrities, the holding of public festivities, said as much and, by saying it implicitly, said it more potently, as the message could not easily be contradicted. Nowadays we see the willful distortion of history as evil when it is done by a government or the media. Should it be viewed any differently as an act of the benevolent university?

In fact, it's more troubling. Since it is an institution, it might seem 19 unfair to hold the university to a standard of truthfulness higher than we demand of others. But there is a reason we must. The success of an institution is linked to its efficacy in turning out a well-functioning product. Any institution-internal uncertainty about that product, any hesitation or self-contradiction in the institution, will vitiate the product and, ultimately, eviscerate the institution itself. It may live on (institutions are survivors), but its influence will be much diminished.

Imagine if the military proved unable to protect the people, or if a 20 government allowed rioting to go on unchecked. Those institutions would become objects of ridicule, and be either overthrown or ineffectual, because they were not fulfilling their mission, not producing the goods that they were created and supported in order to produce. Even a partial falling off, a single instance of failure of mission, will weaken an institution's legitimacy, though it probably takes either an egregious example or repeated lesser abuses to actually bring it down.

To catch any institution in a lie is disconcerting, but seldom deeply   21
damaging. The member who lied may be punished, and the institution
close over the injury, essentially untouched. Its mission is not compromised. But the mission of the university *is* truth, or knowledge: so
when the university lies, it is precisely as if the government dissolved
in chaos. To lie is to contravene the mission of the university directly.
Therefore, when the university lies (or rather, is lied for by its representatives), it necessarily contributes in a serious way to its loss of legitimacy as an institution.

Unlike other institutions, then, the university has discourse of a   22
particular sort as its mission and its sole product. Some institutions
use language just peripherally: the military gets its job done via the
giving of orders; but it is weapons that actually do the job, and the job
is not intrinsically communicative in nature. The courts and psychotherapy are somewhat different, in that they use particular forms
of language specifically to create specific real-world situations; the
choice of language influences their result, so that communicative efficacy is crucial for their members, more than in less linguistically oriented institutions.

But the university alone trades only in language, discourse, com-   23
munication. The university's only acts are speech acts, in Austin's
sense.[1] Truth and knowledge are linguistic entities, existing only
through and in language. Only for the university is language an end in
itself. Therefore (one might argue) the members of the university
ought to be especially skillful communicators, since that is all they
have to offer, and that is solely how they achieve their effects.

Well, but. . . .   24

Surely the members of the university community produce a lot of   25
language, in a lot of forms, oral and written, public and private, formal
and informal. But by any stylistic standards, the university's prose is
inelegant. Indeed, some would call it abysmal—turgid, pompous, in-
flated, impenetrable, closing off understanding rather than furthering
it. The conventional view is that this is a by-product of our mission.
We are here to educate and inform not to entertain. Therefore there is
no need for the product to be delightful, amusing, or pleasurable. But
"no need" does not begin to express the prevailing attitude toward
stylistic amenity. Those who write relatively accessibly are often the
recipients of barely veiled hostility, in the form of scholarly disdain:
"Just a popular piece." The idea is, if more than three people can understand it, it can't be worth much. In fact, the distress clarity arouses
is oddly reminiscent of the discomfiture, at the faculty meeting described earlier at the breaching of the mystique. It's not that there's no
need to be intelligible. It's that there is a need not to. Our power, our

---

[1]Compare J. L. Austin 1962.

authority, is intertwined with our ability to maintain secrets even as we seem to dispense them. We write and speak, but we do not communicate. That is our art.

Horizontal Communication

The university and its members must speak with many voices to 26 fit their many functions—no easy task. First, the university as an institution communicates with the outside world, to show that it is doing a valuable job well. Most universities have public relations offices to send out items to the media on the accomplishments of the university and its members: awards won, public works performed, research completed. It arranges interviews with the media—if a reporter needs a semanticist in a hurry, it will provide one. The university also puts out informational pamphlets: how to apply for admission, the availability of financial aid, and so on. There are publications produced by and about the university intended for the outside world, often alumni, to solicit financial contributions. In all of these contacts, the university presents itself as "the University," a faceless monolith rather than the assortment of diverse interests that it is.

Individuals within the university sometimes communicate, in 27 their identities as university personnel, with the world at large or at least non-academic institutions. They carry from the university, as part of the presuppositions underlying their discourse, the intellectual legitimacy that comes of being a member of that community: expertise is implicitly, if not always legitimately, transferable. In these roles, members consult for industry and government, serve on the panels of government and private granting agencies, serve as expert witnesses in the courtroom. In these roles almost uniquely, professors are addressed and referred to as "Professor" and "Doctor." Within the university, these titles are dispensed with; their use is a mark of naïveté, outsidership (and so is mostly reserved for undergraduates, who are neither members nor even potential members).

More often, and more significantly, members of the university 28 community, especially faculty, communicate as individuals to individuals. Faculty status brings with it membership in several constituencies. First, one is a member of a discipline, a relatively egalitarian relationship. At the same time, one is a member of a department, entailing some hierarchical distinctions; and of one's university's cross-disciplinary community, entailing status distinctions of a different kind. A linguist keeps in contact with other linguists, through publication, professional society meetings, and other conferences, as well as letters and visits. We exchange letters of recommendation for our students and junior colleagues; we review one another's grant applications and submissions for publication.

Within disciplines, we develop special languages. Like any lin- 29
guistic code, these play two roles. Toward the outside world, they are
élitist: we know, you cannot understand, you may not enter. But for
insiders they are a secret handshake. When I encounter my profession's terms of art in a piece of writing or a talk, I am obscurely comforted: I am at home among friends. True, "ethnomethodology" and
"equi-noun-phrase deletion" are not the friends everyone would
choose, but when I find them, I know I am welcome. An article submitted for publication in a professional journal may contain useful and
significant information; but if it has been submitted (as occasionally
happens) by someone outside the field who does not know the communicative conventions, the reviewer will immediately sense that
something is amiss from the absence of the secret wink. In all probability the paper will be rejected. It isn't just that we are being snobbish
(we are, of course); but over time we become attuned to our special
form of discourse, and literally become unable to understand anything
labeled "linguistics" that is not expressed as "linguistics" is supposed
to be. The form must match the context, or understanding fails.

A significant part of a graduate student's education consists of 30
learning this language. Part of becoming worthy of the Ph.D., the certificate of membership, is the demonstration that one knows and can
use the language.

There are recognizable power ploys in academic discourse, often 31
lost on outsiders. In intradisciplinary prose, the footnote is wielded as
cavemen wielded clubs, a blunt but effective weapon. The footnote
(nowadays, to save printing expenses, more often the end note) says: I
know everything about this topic. I could go on forever. Maybe I will.
In any case, don't think you can overwhelm me with obscure information. I said it first, here. I control the scholarship, I've read everything,
this is my turf. The conscientious reader of academic prose must break
concentration to read the footnote, another secret signal between
writer and reader: We are serious professionals. This communication
is not for entertainment. It is *supposed* to be obnoxious.[2]

How to Write Like a Professor

The written style of the university, too, has its own separate for- 32
mats, each justified by function. This is especially true of intradisciplinary scholarly writing. A significant part of a student's training involves learning these procedures, learning how to sound right as well
as how to make valid contributions. I spoke earlier of the relation between the traditional convoluted style of academia and the academic's

[2]See what I mean?

need for signals of solidarity and acceptance by peers. But turgidity does not come naturally. It must be acquired by slow degrees. Deviation in any direction is punishable.

Neophytes must learn both correct surface form and deeper matters 33 of style and content. They must, first and most obviously, learn how to juggle the technical terminology of their field: the secret handshake *par excellence*. They must learn what each special term means, who introduced it, and therefore its political significance. (While *scenario, frame,* and *schema* may, in discourse semantics and pragmatics, be mutually interchangeable, students who study with the scholars responsible for each term will use that term rather than the others in their own writing.) They will learn what ideas justify the postulation of special terminology: how revolutionary, how important they must be. They will read enough of the literature to know, when they have thought of an idea, whether a term already exists for it, to avoid duplication. They will also learn that creating a term, and offering it to the world, is an act of power best left to the established members of the field. It takes some gall for graduate students to propose terms for their own ideas; for an undergraduate to attempt this borders on the treasonable. And of course, to propose a term when one already exists exposes one to ridicule; and to misuse someone else's terminology, worse.

Undergraduates (and beginning graduate students) are not en- 34 couraged to play the same game as their betters. It does not become an undergraduate to sound like a professor. Moreover, since the undergraduate does not have sufficient experience or knowledge, the attempt is apt to be risible. As students progress through graduate school, they are expected to acquire academic style, a little in course papers, more in qualifying papers. But the usage must grow gradually, sparingly, avoiding the appearance of presumptuousness, the accusations of usurpation of territory that belongs to the elders. The pinnacle is reached with the dissertation, wherein a student demonstrates worthiness to become a full-fledged member of the society, having passed all the ordeals the elders have to provide. The dissertation shows not only that the student has mastered the knowledge of the field and its methods; not only that the student has something original to add to that store of knowledge; but that the student knows the rules, knows how to behave like a member of the culture. So the dissertation must be couched in the finest and most etiolated of academese, redolent of footnotes, stylistically impenetrable, bristling with jargon. Only thus can proper deportment be demonstrated.

Indeed, never again is it expected to this extent. For the next sev- 35 eral years, through the assistant professorship and until tenure, caution is recommended: style should be academic, though a little relaxation is permissible. The dissertation showed one could take direction: now one must show an ability to be on one's own. Tenure decisions involve the assessment of "collegiality": practically speaking, that means, Do nothing that might offend the thinnest-skinned colleague. Only after the granting of tenure is it safe to abandon the style for something snappier; and even then, obloquy is a probable outcome. But tenure smiles at obloquy.

If academic style were merely the result of carelessness or uncon- 36 cern for the graces, it would increase as its user advanced in the field, in a straight upward direction; and if undergraduates were capable of using the style, it would be deemed an unmixed sign of competence, not a little off-color. But we find instead the parabolic curve . . . [in the figure below], which suggests that the style is connected to notions of privilege and power. You are *allowed* to use academese when you have convinced the elders that you are a serious apprentice, no longer an outsider (who is not allowed knowledge of the mysteries). You *must* use academese to prove your worthiness of acceptance and your ability to submit to discipline. You *may* abandon academese, wholly or more likely in part, when you are the gatekeeper and need no longer worry about being excluded from the society.

Privilege and Power in Academia

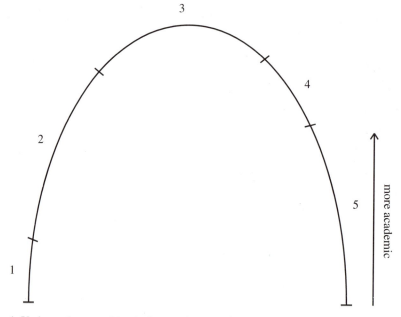

1. Undergraduates and beginning graduate students
2. Advanced graduate students
3. Students writing dissertations
4. Nontenured faculty
5. Tenured faculty

Over the course of an academic career, writing gradually becomes   37
more overtly territorial, assumes more power for its producer, by
achieving more length and broader topical scope. Undergraduate and
early graduate course papers are unseemly if they exceed twenty
pages or so. They deal with small and concrete topics: no total solutions, no metatheoretical debate. Later, through qualifying papers and
other predissertation work, length increases to a maximum of fifty to
one hundred pages, and topics become more abstract, more cutting-
edge, and of broader scope, as the student demonstrates the desire to
achieve full maturity and the ability to understand what the territorial
battles are about. The dissertation stakes a claim. The writer takes a
theoretical stance, either adapting a mentor's theory or inventing a
modest theoretical innovation; applies it to a fairly broad swath of language; and tests it against the best that the field has to offer, engaging
in conflict with established members of the group (but always respectfully). A dissertation is longer, too, around three hundred pages.
Much more than that, though, or too grandiose a proposal, marks the
writer as hubristic. The assistant professor is allowed a larger swath of
territory. But because of the pressure to publish, the tendency is to
stick to only mildly controversial topics that can be handled in a relatively short space, in a relatively short time. Later, with tenure, the
sky's the limit—on length, breadth, and self-assurance, as well as in-
terpersonal obnoxiousness.

The discourse style of academia turns out not to be solely a by-   38
product of the knowledge factory. It is also the language of a society
with complex and covert power and territorial assumptions, often in
conflict with its express mission. As an institution, the university is relatively but not totally benign. As a society it is hierarchical and authoritarian, yet necessarily egalitarian and collaborative in its creation of a
product. That it does so often produce products of value, that it protects its members from evaluation by the crass standards of the outside, make it an unusually benevolent institution. But that fact should
not blind observers to its shortcomings, or cause them to overlook the
ways in which those who have power in the university, as in any other
institution, misuse it and abuse its weaker members.

Working with the Text

1. Lakoff asserts that when professors in her Linguistics Department bicker,
   "the real conflicts . . . are never brought out into the light of day; they remain covert, while we debate superficialities." What does Lakoff consider
   "the superficialities"? What are "the real conflicts"? Why, in her opinion,
   do the professors avoid discussing "the real conflicts"?

2. According to Lakoff, what does a person with a Ph.D. in linguistics need in order to succeed as a professor in addition to knowing the principles of linguistics? Why?

3. What does Lakoff mean when she says that "the university alone trades only in language, discourse, communication"? How does this impose special responsibilities on a university?

4. What role does language play in the development of a professor throughout his or her career, according to Lakoff? What kind of language must be used at each stage, and why?

5. Even as Lakoff criticizes certain "misuses" and "abuses" of academic discourse, she also employs it herself, sometimes satirically. Where does she use it for serious purposes and where for comical purposes?

Working beyond the Text

1. Near the beginning of her essay, Lakoff asserts that a successful linguist will "not only have to know facts, theories, and methods," but also "how to play by the rules." Choose another field or career (medicine, engineering, art, and so on) and describe what a successful person will know in addition to knowledge of "facts, theories, and methods."

2. Lakoff says, "Within disciplines, we develop special languages. Like any linguistic code, these play two roles. Toward the outside world, they are élitist; we know, you cannot understand, you may not enter. But for insiders they are a secret handshake." Explain her meaning by referring to some experience of your own in college as either an "outsider" or an "insider."

3. Interview one or more of your teachers about the stages of their career in their field. What specific steps did they have to take, what hurdles did they have to clear, to get where they are? And where are they in the process? How does what you learn compare to Lakoff's description?

"Nobody Mean More to Me than You[1] and the Future Life of Willie Jordan"
June Jordan

Born in 1936, June Jordan is a prominent African-American writer of poems, essays, novels, and children's books who also teaches English at the State University of New York at Stony Brook. Her books in-

---

[1]Black English aphorism crafted by Monica Morris, a Junior at S.U.N.Y. at Stony Brook, October, 1984.

clude *Who Look at Me* and *Things That I Do in the Dark: Selected Poetry.* Much of Jordan's writing focuses on personal and political struggles faced by African Americans. In this essay, from her 1989 book *On Call: Political Essays,* she recounts a college class's exploration of black English, and its real-world experience with issues of language and power as students reacted to the killing of a class member's brother at the hands of the police.

Black English is not exactly a linguistic buffalo; as children, most 1 of the thirty-five million Afro-Americans living here depend on this language for our discovery of the world. But then we approach our maturity inside a larger social body that will not support our efforts to become anything other than the clones of those who are neither our mothers nor our fathers. We begin to grow up in a house where every true mirror shows us the face of somebody who does not belong there, whose walk and whose talk will never look or sound "right," because that house was meant to shelter a family that is alien and hostile to us. As we learn our way around this environment, either we hide our original word habits, or we completely surrender our own voice, hoping to please those who will never respect anyone different from themselves: Black English is not exactly a linguistic buffalo, but we should understand its status as an endangered species, as a perishing, irreplaceable system of community intelligence, or we should expect its extinction, and, along with that, the extinguishing of much that constitutes our own proud, and singular identity.

What we casually call "English" less and less defers to England 2 and its "gentlemen." "English" is no longer a specific matter of geography or an element of class privilege; more than thirty-three countries use this tool as a means of "intranational communication."[2] Countries as disparate as Zimbabwe and Malaysia, or Israel and Uganda, use it as their non-native currency of convenience. Obviously, this tool, this "English," cannot function inside thirty-three discrete societies on the basis of rules and values absolutely determined somewhere else, in a thirty-fourth other country, for example.

In addition to that staggering congeries of non-native users of 3 English, there are five countries, or 333,746,000 people, for whom this thing called "English" serves as a native tongue.[3] Approximately ten percent of these native speakers of "English" are Afro-American citizens of the U.S.A. I cite these numbers and varieties of human beings dependent on "English" in order, quickly, to suggest how strange and how tenuous is any concept of "Standard English." Obviously, numer-

---

[2]*English Is Speaking, But What Is English?* A presentation by Professor S. N. Sridahr, Dept. of Linguistics, S.U.N.Y. at Stony Brook, April 9, 1985: Dean's Conversation Among the Disciplines.
[3]Ibid.

ous forms of English now operate inside a natural, an uncontrollable, continuum of development. I would suppose "the standard" for English in Malaysia is not the same as "the standard" in Zimbabwe. I know that standard forms of English for Black people in this country do not copy that of whites. And, in fact, the structural differences between these two kinds of English have intensified, becoming more Black, or less white, despite the expected homogenizing effects of television[4] and other mass media.

Nonetheless, white standards of English persist, supreme and un- 4
questioned, in these United States. Despite our multilingual population, and despite the deepening Black and white cleavage within that conglomerate, white standards control our official and popular judgments of verbal proficiency and correct, or incorrect, language skills, including speech. In contrast to India, where at least fourteen languages co-exist as legitimate Indian languages, in contrast to Nicaragua, where all citizens are legally entitled to formal school instruction in their regional or tribal languages, compulsory education in America compels accommodation to exclusively white forms of "English." White English, in America, is "Standard English."

This story begins two years ago. I was teaching a new course, "In 5
Search of the Invisible Black Woman," and my rather large class seemed evenly divided between young Black women and men. Five or six white students also sat in attendance. With unexpected speed and enthusiasm we had moved through historical narratives of the 19th century to literature by and about Black women, in the 20th. I had assigned the first forty pages of Alice Walker's *The Color Purple,* and I came, eagerly, to class that morning:

"So!" I exclaimed, aloud. "What did you think? How did you 6
like it?"

The students studied their hands, or the floor. There was no re- 7
sponse. The tense, resistant feeling in the room fairly astounded me.

At last, one student, a young woman still not meeting my eyes, 8
muttered something in my direction:

"What did you say?" I prompted her.   9

"Why she have them talk so funny. It don't sound right."   10

"You mean the language?"   11

Another student lifted his head: "It don't look right, neither. I 12
couldn't hardly read it."

At this, several students dumped on the book. Just about unani- 13
mously, their criticisms targeted the language. I listened to what they

[4]*New York Times,* March 15, 1985, Section One, p. 14: Report on study by linguists at the University of Pennsylvania.

wanted to say and silently marvelled at the similarities between their casual speech patterns and Alice Walker's written version of Black English.

But I decided against pointing to these identical traits of syntax; 14 I wanted not to make them self-conscious about their own spoken language—not while they clearly felt it was "wrong." Instead I decided to swallow my astonishment. Here was a negative Black reaction to a prize winning accomplishment of Black literature that white readers across the country had selected as a best seller. Black rejection was aimed at the one irreducibly Black element of Walker's work: the language—Celie's Black English. I wrote the opening lines of *The Color Purple* on the blackboard and asked the students to help me translate these sentences into Standard English:

> *You better not never tell nobody but God. It'd kill your mammy.*
> Dear God,
>   I am fourteen years old. I have always been a good girl. Maybe you can give me a sign letting me know what is happening to me.
>   Last spring after Little Lucious come I heard them fussing. He was pulling on her arm. She say it too soon, Fonso. I aint well. Finally he leave her alone. A week go by, he pulling on her arm again. She say, Naw, I ain't gonna. Can't you see I'm already half dead, an all of the children.[5]

Our process of translation exploded with hilarity and even hyster- 15 ical, shocked laughter: The Black writer, Alice Walker, knew what she was doing! If rudimentary criteria for good fiction includes the manipulation of language so that the syntax and diction of sentences will tell you the identity of speakers, the probable age and sex and class of speakers, and even the locale—urban/rural/southern/western—then Walker had written, perfectly. This is the translation into Standard English that our class produced:

> *Absolutely, one should never confide in anybody besides God. Your se-crets could prove devastating to your mother.*
> Dear God,
>   I am fourteen years old. I have always been good. But now, could you help me to understand what is happening to me?
>   Last spring, after my little brother, Lucious, was born, I heard my parents fighting. My father kept pulling at my mother's arm. But she told him, "It's too soon for sex, Alfonso. I am still not feeling well." Finally, my father left her alone. A week went by, and then he began bothering my mother, again: Pulling her arm. She told him,

---

[5] Alice Walker, *The Color Purple*, p. 11, Harcourt Brace, N.Y.

"No, I won't! Can't you see I'm already exhausted from all of these children?"

(Our favorite line was "It's too soon for sex, Alphonso.")

Once we could stop laughing, once we could stop our exponen-   16
tially wild improvisations on the theme of Translated Black English, the students pushed me to explain their own negative first reactions to their spoken language on the printed page. I thought it was probably akin to the shock of seeing yourself in a photograph for the first time. Most of the students had never before seen a written facsimile of the way they talk. None of the students had ever learned how to read and write their own verbal system of communication: Black English. Alternatively, this fact began to baffle or else bemuse and then infuriate my students. Why not? Was it too late? Could they learn how to do it, now? And, ultimately, the final test question, the one testing my sincerity: Could I teach them? Because I had never taught anyone Black English and, as far as I knew, no one, anywhere in the United States, had ever offered such a course, the best I could say was "I'll try."

He looked like a wrestler.   17

He sat dead center in the packed room and, every time our eyes   18
met, he quickly nodded his head as though anxious to reassure, and encourage, me.

Short, with strikingly broad shoulders and long arms, he spoke   19
with a surprisingly high, soft voice that matched the soft bright movement of his eyes. His name was Willie Jordan. He would have seemed even more unlikely in the context of Contemporary Women's Poetry, except that ten or twelve other Black men were taking the course, as well. Still, Willie was conspicuous. His extreme fitness, the muscular density of his presence underscored the riveted, gentle attention that he gave to anything anyone said. Generally, he did not join the loud and rowdy dialogue flying back and forth, but there could be no doubt about his interest in our discussions. And, when he stood to present an argument he'd prepared, overnight, that nervous smile of his vanished and an irregular stammering replaced it, as he spoke with visceral sincerity, word by word.

That was how I met Willie Jordan. It was in between "In Search of   20
the Invisible Black Woman" and "The Art of Black English." I was waiting for departmental approval and I supposed that Willie might be, so to speak, killing time until he, too, could study Black English. But Willie really did want to explore Contemporary Women's poetry and, to that end, volunteered for extra research and never missed a class.

Towards the end of that semester, Willie approached me for an in-   21
dependent study project on South Africa. It would commence the next

semester. I thought Willie's writing needed the kind of improvement only intense practice will yield. I knew his intelligence was outstanding. But he'd wholeheartedly opted for "Standard English" at a rather late age, and the results were stilted and frequently polysyllabic, simply for the sake of having more syllables. Willie's unnatural formality of language seemed to me consistent with the formality of his research into South African apartheid. As he projected his studies, he would have little time, indeed, for newspapers. Instead, more than 90 percent of his research would mean saturation in strictly historical, if not archival, material. I was certainly interested. It would be tricky to guide him into a more confident and spontaneous relationship both with language and apartheid. It was going to be wonderful to see what happened when he could catch up with himself, entirely, and talk back to the world.

September, 1984: Breezy fall weather and much excitement! My 22 class, "The Art of Black English," was full to the limit of the fire laws. And, in Independent Study, Willie Jordan showed up, weekly, fifteen minutes early for each of our sessions. I was pretty happy to be teaching, altogether!

I remember an early class when a young brother, replete with his 23 ever present pork-pie hat, raised his hand and then told us that most of what he'd heard was "all right" except it was "too clean." "The brothers on the street," he continued, "they mix it up more. Like 'fuck' and 'motherfuck.' Or like 'shit.'" He waited. I waited. Then all of us laughed a good while, and we got into a brawl about "correct" and "realistic" Black English that led to Rule 1.

Rule 1: *Black English is about a whole lot more than mothafuckin.*   24

As a criterion, we decided, "realistic" could take you anywhere 25 you want to go. Artful places. Angry places. Eloquent and sweetalkin places. Polemical places. Church. And the local Bar & Grill. We were checking out a language, not a mood or a scene or one guy's forgettable mouthing off.

It was hard. For most of the students, learning Black English re- 26 quired a fallback to patterns and rhythms of speech that many of their parents had beaten out of them. I mean *beaten.* And, in a majority of cases, correct Black English could be achieved only by striving for *incorrect* Standard English, something they were still pushing at, quite uncertainly. This state of affairs led to Rule 2.

Rule 2: *If it's wrong in Standard English it's probably right in Black* 27 *English, or, at least, you're hot.*

It was hard. Roommates and family members ridiculed their stud- 28 ies, or remained incredulous, "You *studying* that shit? At school?" But we were beginning to feel the companionship of pioneers. And we decided that we needed another rule that would establish each one of us as equally important to our success. This was Rule 3.

Rule 3: *If it don't sound like something that come out somebody mouth* ₂₉ *then it don't sound right. If it don't sound right then it ain't hardly right. Period.*

This rule produced two weeks of compositions in which the stu- ₃₀ dents agonizingly tried to spell the sound of the Black English sentence they wanted to convey. But Black English is, preeminently, an oral spoken means of communication. *And spelling don't talk.* So we needed Rule 4.

Rule 4: *Forget about the spelling. Let the syntax carry you.* ₃₁

Once we arrived at Rule 4 we started to fly because syntax, the ₃₂ structure of an idea, leads you to the world view of the speaker and reveals her values. The syntax of a sentence equals the structure of your consciousness. If we insisted that the language of Black English adheres to a distinctive Black syntax, then we were postulating a profound difference between white and Black people, *per se.* Was it a difference to prize or to obliterate?

There are three qualities of Black English—the presence of life, ₃₃ voice, and clarity—that testify to a distinctive Black value system that we became excited about and self-consciously tried to maintain.

1. Black English has been produced by a pre-technocratic, if not ₃₄ anti-technological, culture. More, our culture has been constantly threatened by annihilation or, at least, the swallowed blurring of assimilation. Therefore, our language is a system constructed by people constantly needing to insist that we exist, that we are present. Our language devolves from a culture that abhors all abstraction, or anything tending to obscure or delete the fact of the human being who is here and now/the truth of the person who is speaking or listening. Consequently, *there is no passive voice construction possible in Black English.* For example, you cannot say, "Black English is being eliminated." You must say, instead, "White people eliminating Black English." The assumption of the presence of life governs all of Black English. Therefore, overwhelmingly, *all action takes place in the language of the present indicative.* And every sentence assumes the living and active participation of at least two human beings, the speaker and the listener.

2. A primary consequence of the person-centered values of Black ₃₅ English is the delivery of voice. If you speak or write Black English, your ideas will necessarily possess that otherwise elusive attribute, *voice.*

3. One main benefit following from the person-centered values of ₃₆ Black English is that of *clarity.* If your idea, your sentence, assumes the presence of at least two living and active people, you will make it understandable because the motivation behind every sentence is the wish to say something real to somebody real.

As the weeks piled up, translation from Standard English 37
into Black English or vice versa occupied a hefty part of our course
work.

> Standard English (hereafter S.E.): "In considering the idea of
> studying Black English those questioned suggested—"
> (What's the subject? Where's the person? Is anybody alive in
> there, in that idea?)
> Black English (hereafter B.E.): "I been asking people what you
> think about somebody studying Black English and they answer me
> like this."

But there were interesting limits. You cannot "translate" instances of
Standard English preoccupied with abstraction or with nothing/no-
body evidently alive, into Black English. That would warp the language into uses antithetical to the guiding perspective of its community of users. Rather you must first change those Standard English
sentences, themselves, into ideas consistent with the person-centered
assumptions of Black English.

Guidelines for Black English

1. Minimal number of words for every idea: This is the source for 38
the aphoristic and/or poetic force of the language; eliminate every
possible word.

2. Clarity: If the sentence is not clear it's not Black English.   39

3. Eliminate use of the verb *to be* whenever possible. This leads to 40
the deployment of more descriptive and therefore, more precise verbs.

4. Use *be* or *been* only when you want to describe a chronic, ongo- 41
ing state of things.

> He *be* at the office, by 9. (He is always at the office by 9.)
> He *been* with her since forever.

5. Zero copula: Always eliminate the verb *to be* whenever it would 42
combine with another verb, in Standard English.

> S.E. : She is going out with him.
> B.E. : She going out with him.

6. Eliminate *do* as in: 43

> S.E. : What do you think? What do you want?
> B.E. : What you think? What you want?

Rules number 3, 4, 5, and 6 provide for the use of the minimal 44
number of verbs per idea and, therefore, greater accuracy in the choice
of verb.

7. In general, if you wish to say something really positive, try to 45
formulate the idea using emphatic negative structure.

S.E. : He's fabulous.
B.E. : He bad.

8. Use double or triple negatives for dramatic emphasis.   46

S.E. : Tina Turner sings out of this world.
B.E. : Ain nobody sing like Tina.

9. Never use the -ed suffix to indicate the past tense of a verb.   47

S.E. : She closed the door.
B.E. : She close the door. Or, she have close the door.

10. Regardless of intentional verb time, only use the third person 48
singular, present indicative, for use of the verb to have, as an auxiliary.

S.E. : He had his wallet then he lost it.
B.E. : He have him wallet then he lose it.
S.E. : He had seen that movie.
B.E. : We seen that movie. Or, we have see that movie.

11. Observe a minimal inflection of verbs. Particularly, never 49
change from the first person singular forms to the third person
singular.

S.E. : Present Tense Forms: He goes to the store.
B.E. : He go to the store.
S.E. : Past Tense Forms: He went to the store.
B.E. : He go to the store. Or, he gone to the store. Or, he been to the
       store.

12. The possessive case scarcely ever appears in Black English. 50
Never use an apostrophe ('s) construction. If you wander into a possessive case component of an idea, then keep logically consistent:
ours, his, theirs, mines. But, most likely, if you bump into such a component, you have wandered outside the underlying world-view of
Black English.

S.E. : He will take their car tomorrow.
B.E. : He taking they car tomorrow.

13. Plurality: Logical consistency, continued: If the modifier indi- 51
cates plurality then the noun remains in the singular case.

S.E. : He ate twelve doughnuts.
B.E. : He eat twelve doughnut.
S.E. : She has many books.
B.E. : She have many book.

14. Listen for, or invent, special Black English forms of the past 52
tense, such as: "He losted it. That what she felted." If they are clear
and readily understood, then use them.

15. Do not hesitate to play with words, sometimes inventing them: 53.
e.g. "astropotomous" means huge like a hippo plus astronomical and,
therefore, signifies real big.

16. In Black English, unless you keenly want to underscore the 54
past tense nature of an action, stay in the present tense and rely on the
overall context of your ideas for the conveyance of time and sequence.

17. Never use the suffix-*ly* form of an adverb in Black English.   55

S.E. : The rain came down rather quickly.
B.E. : The rain come down pretty quick.

18. Never use the indefinite article *an* in Black English.   56

S.E. : He wanted to ride an elephant.
B.E. : He wanted to ride him a elephant.

19. Invariant syntax: in correct Black English it is possible to for- 57
mulate an imperative, an interrogative, and a simple declarative idea
with the same syntax:

B.E. : You going to the store?
       You going to the store.
       You going to the store!

Where was Willie Jordan? We'd reached the mid-term of the se- 58
mester. Students had formulated Black English guidelines, by consensus, and they were now writing with remarkable beauty, purpose, and
enjoyment:

I ain hardly speakin for everybody but myself so understan that.

—Kim Parks

Samples from student writings:

Janie have a great big ole hole inside her. Tea Cake the only thing that fit that hole. . . .

That pear tree beautiful to Janie, especial when bees fiddlin with the blossomin pear there growin large and lovely. But personal speakin, the love she get from starin at that tree ain the love what starin back at her in them relationship. (Monica Morris)

Love is a big theme in, *They Eye Was Watching God.* Love show people new corners inside theyself. It pull out good stuff and stuff back bad stuff . . . Joe worship the doing uh his own hand and need other people to worship him too. But he ain't think about Janie that she a person and ought to live like anybody common do. Queen life not for Janie. (Monica Morris)

In both life and writin, black womens have varietous experience of love that be cold like a iceberg or fiery like a inferno. Passion got for the other partner involve, man or woman, seem as shallow, ankle-deep water or the most profoundest abyss. (Constance Evans)

Family love another bond that ain't never break under no pressure. (Constance Evans)

You know it really cold / When the friend you / Always get out the fire / Act like they don't know you / When you in the heat. (Constance Evans)

Big classroom discussion bout love at this time. I never take no class where us have any long arguin for and against for two or three day. New to me and great. I find the class time talkin a million time more interestin than detail bout the book. (Kathy Esseks)

As these examples suggest, Black English no longer limited the students, in any way. In fact, one of them, Philip Garfield, would shortly "translate" a pivotal scene from Ibsen's *Doll House*, as his final term paper. [59]

NORA : I didn't gived no shit. I thinked you a asshole back then, too, you make it so hard for me save mines husband life.
KROGSTAD : Girl, it clear you ain't any idea what you done. You done exact what once done, and I losed my reputation over it.
NORA : You asks me believe you once act brave save you wife life?

KROGSTAD : Law care less why you done it.

NORA : Law must suck.

KROGSTAD : Suck or no, if I wants, judge screw you wid dis paper.

NORA : No way, man. (Philip Garfield)

But where was Willie? Compulsively punctual, and always thor-   60
oughly prepared with neatly typed compositions, he had disappeared.
He failed to show up for our regularly scheduled conference, and I received neither a note nor a phone call of explanation. A whole week
went by. I wondered if Willie had finally been captured by the extremely current happenings in South Africa: passage of a new constitution that did not enfranchise the Black majority, and militant Black
South African reaction to that affront. I wondered if he'd been hurt,
somewhere. I wondered if the serious workload of weekly readings
and writings had overwhelmed him and changed his mind about independent study. Where was Willie Jordan?

One week after the first conference that Willie missed, he called: 61
"Hello, Professor Jordan? This is Willie. I'm sorry I wasn't there last
week. But something has come up and I'm pretty upset. I'm sorry but I
really can't deal right now."

I asked Willie to drop by my office and just let me see that he was   62
okay. He agreed to do that. When I saw him I knew something hideous
had happened. Something had hurt him and scared him to the marrow.
He was all agitated and stammering and terse and incoherent. At last,
his sadly jumbled account let me surmise, as follows: Brooklyn police
had murdered his unarmed, twenty-five-year-old brother, Reggie Jordan. Neither Willie nor his elderly parents knew what to do about it.
Nobody from the press was interested. His folks had no money. Police
ran his family around and around, to no point. And Reggie was really
dead. And Willie wanted to fight, but he felt helpless.

With Willie's permission I began to try to secure legal counsel for   63
the Jordan family. Unfortunately Black victims of police violence are
truly numerous while the resources available to prosecute their killers
are truly scarce. A friend of mine at the Center for Constitutional
Rights estimated that just the preparatory costs for bringing the cops
into court normally approaches $180,000. Unless the execution of
Reggie Jordan became a major community cause for organizing, and
protest, his murder would simply become a statistical item.

Again, with Willie's permission, I contacted every newspaper and   64
media person I could think of. But the William Bastone feature article
in *The Village Voice* was the only result from that canvassing.

Again, with Willie's permission, I presented the case to my class in   65
Black English. We had talked about the politics of language. We had

talked about love and sex and child abuse and men and women. But the murder of Reggie Jordan broke like a hurricane across the room.

There are few "issues" as endemic to Black life as police violence. 66 Most of the students knew and respected and liked Jordan. Many of them came from the very neighborhood where the murder had occurred. All of the students had known somebody close to them who had been killed by police, or had known frightening moments of gratuitous confrontation with the cops. They wanted to do everything at once to avenge death. Number One: They decided to compose personal statements of condolence to Willie Jordan and his family written in Black English. Number Two: They decided to compose individual messages to the police, in Black English. These should be prefaced by an explanatory paragraph composed by the entire group. Number Three: These individual messages, with their lead paragraph, should be sent to *Newsday*.

The morning after we agreed on these objectives, one of the young 67 women students appeared with an unidentified visitor, who sat through the class, smiling in a peculiar, comfortable way.

Now we had to make more tactical decisions. Because we wanted 68 the messages published, and because we thought it imperative that our outrage be known by the police, the tactical question was this: Should the opening, group paragraph be written in Black English or Standard English?

I have seldom been privy to a discussion with so much heart at the 69 dead heat of it. I will never forget the eloquence, the sudden haltings of speech, the fierce struggle against tears, the furious throwaway, and useless explosions that this question elicited.

That one question contained several others, each of them extraor- 70 dinarily painful to even contemplate. How best to serve the memory of Reggie Jordan? Should we use the language of the killers—Standard English—in order to make our ideas acceptable to those controlling the killers? But wouldn't what we had to say be rejected, summarily, if we said it in our own language, the language of the victim, Reggie Jordan? But if we sought to express ourselves by abandoning our language wouldn't that mean our suicide on top of Reggie's murder? But if we expressed ourselves in our own language wouldn't that be suicidal to the wish to communicate with those who, evidently, did not give a damn about us/Reggie/police violence in the Black community?

At the end of one of the longest, most difficult hours of my own 71 life, the students voted, unanimously, to preface their individual messages with a paragraph composed in the language of Reggie Jordan. *"At least we don't give up nothing else. At least we stick to the truth: Be who we been. And stay all the way with Reggie."*

It was heartbreaking to proceed, from that point. Everyone in the 72 room realized that our decision in favor of Black English had doomed our writings, even as the distinctive reality of our Black lives always has doomed our efforts to "be who we been" in this country.

I went to the blackboard and took down this paragraph, dictated 73 by the class:

> . . . YOU COPS!
> WE THE BROTHER AND SISTER OF WILLIE JORDAN, A FEL-
> LOW STONY BROOK STUDENT WHO THE BROTHER OF THE
> DEAD REGGIE JORDAN. REGGIE, LIKE MANY BROTHER AND
> SISTER, HE A VICTIM OF BRUTAL RACIST POLICE, OCTOBER 25,
> 1984. US APPAL, FED UP, BECAUSE THAT ANOTHER SENSELESS
> DEATH WHAT OCCUR IN OUR COMMUNITY. THIS WHAT WE
> FEEL, THIS, FROM OUR HEART, FOR WE AIN'T STAYIN' SILENT
> NO MORE:

With the completion of this introduction, nobody said anything. I 74 asked for comments. At this invitation, the unidentified visitor, a young Black man, ceaselessly smiling, raised his hand. He was, it so happens, a rookie cop. He had just joined the force in September and, he said, he thought he should clarify a few things. So he came forward and sprawled easily into a posture of barroom, or fireside, nostalgia:

"See," Officer Charles enlightened us, "most times when you out 75 on the street and something come down you do one of two things. Over-react or under-react. Now, if you under-react then you can get yourself kilt. And if you over-react then maybe you kill somebody. Fortunately it's about nine times out of ten and you will over-react. So the brother got kilt. And I'm sorry about that, believe me. But what you have to understand is what kilt him: Over-reaction. That's all. Now you talk about Black people and white police but see, now, I'm a cop myself. And (big smile) I'm Black. And just a couple months ago I was on the other side. But see it's the same for me. You a cop, you the ultimate authority: the Ultimate Authority. And you on the street, most of the time you can only do one of two things: over-react or under-react. That's all it is with the brother. Over-reaction. Didn't have nothing to do with race."

That morning Officer Charles had the good fortune to escape 76 without being boiled alive. But barely. And I remember the pride of his smile when I read about the fate of Black policemen and other col-laborators, in South Africa. I remember him, and I remember the shock and palpable feeling of shame that filled the room. It was as though that foolish, and deadly, young man had just relieved himself of his foolish, and deadly, explanation, face to face with the grief of Reggie Jordan's father and Reggie Jordan's mother. Class ended quietly. I copied the paragraph from the blackboard, collected the individual messages and left to type them up.

Newsday rejected the piece.   77

The Village Voice could not find room in their "Letters" section to 78
print the individual messages from the students to the police.

None of the tv news reporters picked up the story.   79

Nobody raised $180,000 to prosecute the murder of Reggie Jordan. 80

Reggie Jordan is really dead.   81

I asked Willie Jordan to write an essay pulling together everything 82
important to him from that semester. He was still deeply beside himself with frustration and amazement and loss. This is what he wrote,
unedited, and in its entirety:

> Throughout the course of this semester I have been researching
> the effects of oppression and exploitation along racial lines in South
> Africa and its neighboring countries. I have become aware of South
> African police brutalization of native Africans beyond the extent of
> the law, even though the laws themselves are catalyst affliction upon
> Black men, women and children. Many Africans die each year as a re-
> sult of the deliberate use of police force to protect the white power
> structure.
>
> Social control agents in South Africa, such as policemen, are also
> used to force compliance among citizens through both overt and
> covert tactics. It is not uncommon to find bold-faced coercion and
> cold-blooded killings of Blacks by South African police for undeter-
> mined and/or inadequate reasons. Perhaps the truth is that the only
> reasons for this heinous treatment of Blacks rests in racial differences.
> We should also understand that what is conveyed through the media
> is not always accurate and may sometimes be construed as the tip of
> the iceberg at best.
>
> I recently received a painful reminder that racism, poverty, and
> the abuse of power are global problems which are by no means
> unique to South Africa. On October 25, 1984 at approximately 3:00
> p.m. my brother, Mr. Reginald Jordan, was shot and killed by two
> New York City policemen from the 75th precinct in the East New
> York section of Brooklyn. His life ended at the age of twenty-five.
> Even up to this current point in time the Police Department has failed
> to provide my family, which consists of five brothers, eight sisters,
> and two parents, with a plausible reason for Reggie's death. Out of
> the many stories that were given to my family by the Police Depart-
> ment, not one of them seems to hold water. In fact, I honestly believe
> that the Police Department's assessment of my brother's murder is
> nothing short of ABSOLUTE BULLSHIT, and thus far no evidence
> had been produced to alter perception of the situation.
>
> Furthermore, I believe that one of three cases may have occurred
> in this incident. First, Reggie's death may have been the desired out-
> come of the police officer's action, in which case the killing was pre-
> meditated. Or, it was a case of mistaken identity, which clarifies the
> fact that the two officers who killed my brother and their command-
> ing parties are all grossly incompetent. Or, both of the above cases

are correct, i.e., Reggie's murderers intended to kill him and the Police Department behaved insubordinately.

Part of the argument of the officers who shot Reggie was that he had attacked one of them and took his gun. This was their major claim. They also said that only one of them had actually shot Reggie. The facts, however, speak for themselves. According to the Death Certificate and autopsy report, Reggie was shot eight times from point-blank range. The Doctor who performed the autopsy told me himself that two bullets entered the side of my brother's head, four bullets were sprayed into his back, and two bullets struck him in the back of his legs. It is obvious that unnecessary force was used by the police and that it is extremely difficult to shoot someone in his back when he is attacking or approaching you.

After experiencing a situation like this and researching South Africa I believe that to a large degree, justice may only exist as rhetoric. I find it difficult to talk of true justice when the oppression of my people both at home and abroad attests to the fact that inequality and injustice are serious problems whereby Blacks and Third World people are perpetually short-changed by society. Something has to be done about the way in which this world is set up. Although it is a difficult task, we do have the power to make a change.

—Willie J. Jordan, Jr.

EGL 487, Section 58, November 14, 1984

It is my privilege to dedicate this book to the future life of Willie J. [83] Jordan, Jr.   *August 8, 1985*

Working with the Text

1. What does Jordan mean in her first sentence when she asserts that "Black English is not exactly a linguistic buffalo"? Why is it important to establish this idea immediately in the essay? How does it relate to the rest of the essay?

2. What is the relation between Jordan's students' home language and their school language: What is the basis of the conflict? Why does Jordan decide to try to bring the students' home language into the classroom?

3. At the end of Jordan's essay, her students choose to write in a style that they know will make their message less powerful in the world: may make it unpublishable, may turn off some potential readers. Why do they choose to do this?

4. In what ways is Jordan taught by her own students? How do they surprise her? What does she learn through her teaching?

5. Jordan ties the story of teaching a course in "The Art of Black English" to the story of Willie Jordan and his family. Why, do you think? How does it help her make her points about Black English, Standard English, and the relation between them?

Working beyond the Text

1. A common phenomenon discussed in the field of sociolinguistics is "code switching." Code switching is alternating back and forth between two different languages or dialects or styles. When do you use code switching in your own life? What languages or dialects or styles do you use?

2. If you are familiar with a dialect or style of English other than Standard English, imitate Jordan's students by writing formal rules for it. You may know some regional dialect, for example (Deep South or big city Northeast), or some style of slang used by musicians, athletes, or a social group in your school.

3. Jordan discusses a situation in which classroom life gets connected to social and political issues outside the classroom. Other people feel that the educational process should be kept separate from life outside the classroom, especially politics. Do you think that the classroom should be made to relate to "the outside world" or kept separate from it? Why?

4

LANGUAGES OF
PROFESSIONAL LIFE

INTRODUCTION

If you have a job now, whether it's at a fast-food restaurant, on a golf course, or in an office, you probably speak a specific kind of on-the-job language when you're at work. You and your coworkers probably use a certain vocabulary to help you communicate efficiently and clearly about your work: "run twelve," "grill one," and "grill up," or "par five," "dog leg," and "slice." When you've completed your college education, you probably plan to enter some type of professional field. You may plan to be a lab technician, a lawyer, a journalist, or a computer programmer. Each of these fields has its own specialized language, made up of specific words ("MRI," "res judicata," "graph," "GIGO"), but also its own rules: unwritten conventions about *what* and *how* to communicate.

While professionals within a certain field often understand and share vocabulary, knowledge, and conventions, people outside that field are often mystified by how they communicate. Just as in academic discourse, outsiders may find a certain professional language confusing and intimidating. Sometimes this may not seem important; it may not matter to you whether you comprehend the details of a marketing strategy for a product you don't buy anyway. But sometimes it *is* important to understand professional language: when an accountant gives you financial advice, a doctor explains an illness you have, or when you're involved in a legal dispute, for example. In these cases, if you misunderstand what the other person is saying you might suffer personal consequences.

Several selections in this chapter talk about trying to understand an unfamiliar professional language. They discuss the features of the languages of different professions—law, statistics, biology, computer programming—and explain the reasons behind these features. While professional language is in many ways different from other types of language, it is still part of the "real world," and has some of the same conflicts about issues such as race, class, and gender that face the rest of our culture. Some writers represented in this chapter discuss these conflicts, especially the misunderstandings professional languages can cause when people outside the profession encounter them, and the consequences of these misunderstandings.

Whatever field you end up working in, you will find yourself using some kind of professional language, and the course of your life will no doubt bring you into contact with other professions and other specialized languages. A little understanding about the languages of professional life—not just their special vocabularies but also the reasons they're used and the problems that sometimes accompany them—will go a long way toward your success in your field and in other areas of your life.

Before You Read

Before you read any combination of essays in this chapter, you might prepare by doing any of the activities below as either class or small group discussions, or as formal or informal writing assignments. They are designed to help you find out what you already know about the issues discussed by the authors in the chapter, so you have some background for understanding what the authors say.

1. Many popular movies and television shows are based on people practicing a particular profession: doctors, lawyers, professors, scientists. Choose one profession and discuss how it is portrayed in popular culture, with special attention to the way these fictional professionals use language. How do doctors in doctor movies and on doctor shows talk? Lawyers? Professors? Scientists?

2. Thinking about some specific job you've had, discuss the language that was spoken or written on the job. What new and specialized terms did you have to learn to perform the job? What was the purpose of using such specialized terms? How might an "outsider" have misunderstood some of the terms?

3. You may have heard some of the debates about "sexist" language. What are they? How can language be sexist? What are some examples of sexist language? Why do some people feel that recognizing and eliminating sexist language, especially in the workplace, is so important? How do you feel about it?

4. The language you use to describe an event or tell a story has a lot to do with the meaning your listener will get from you. Describe some simple event—a natural phenomenon, an interaction between two people—in two completely different ways, using different words but changing none of the basic events. Try to give the two versions completely different meanings.

5. We often hear that mathematics, statistics, charts and graphs—the description of facts through numbers—are all "languages" in their own right. In what ways? How do numbers communicate meaning

about human life? How can numbers, like other languages, mislead us about meaning?

After You Read

After you read any combination of essays in this chapter, you might follow up by doing any of the activities below as either class or small group discussions, or as formal or informal writing assignments. They are designed to help you extend what you have learned from the authors in the chapter by discovering new perspectives on the chapter's themes on your own.

1. In reading the selections from this chapter written by lawyers, scientists, and professors, have you learned anything that makes you question the stereotypes we have about being a lawyer, a scientist, or a professor? What new understandings do you have about these professions, especially in terms of the way professionals use language?

2. Most of the selections in this chapter address, in some form, the relation between "language" and "reality": how language portrays reality and the gap that may exist between what language *says* and what actually *is*. Choose several of the writers and explain what they say about these issues. What common reasons do they offer for the gap that can occur between language and reality? How and why do people sometimes exploit that gap for their own benefit?

3. Several essays in this chapter explore controversial language issues in specific fields and contexts: science, statistics, the law. Pick a field not mentioned in this chapter and investigate what people in that field are saying about controversies concerning language: literature, for example, or politics, computer science, journalism, psychology, or history.

4. In what ways can language be "political"? Using the essays in the chapter as a start, explore how it is possible to take a "political" view of language use in the workplace or other public places.

5. The selections in this chapter all focus in one way or another on the idea that what we understand through language depends on who we are, our background, our perspective on the world. A lawyer or scientist will hear the language of the law or science in a different way than an average layperson; a poor person or a member of an ethnic minority will hear the language of discrimination differently from other people. What "discourses" in the world has your background prepared you to understand? What "discourses" in the world might you misunderstand?

UNIT ONE

"TALKING ON THE JOB"

Vocation

Gail Griffin

Gail Griffin teaches English and Women's Studies at Kalamazoo College in Michigan. She has published many articles and essays on the topic of gender issues in education, some of which were collected in her book *Calling: Essays on Teaching in the Mother Tongue* (1992). She has also published poetry in journals such as *Calyx* and *New Delta Review*. In this excerpt from a chapter in *Calling*, Griffin reflects on the issues of power, language, and gender that emerged during her first months and years on the job as a new professor.

In an ultimate sense, I don't know what I do in this place.

Dr. Martin Dysart, Equus

Vocabulary

"Job"—a piece of work.   1

"occupation"—from Latin, *occupare*, to seize. That which seizes or takes over one's time.

"profession"—that which one professes to the world. A job for which extensive formal academic training is required. Formerly, one "made a profession"—of faith in something.

"career"—from Latin, *carraria*, a road, which became, in French, *carriere*, a racecourse. A rapid course or swift progression; a charge at full tilt.

"vocation"—from "vox," a voice. A voicing; a calling.

Job Description

profess: **1.** to affirm openly; declare or claim.

2. to make a pretense of.

3. to claim skill or knowledge in.

4. to affirm belief in.

5. to receive into a religious order. (from the Latin: to declare publicly *pro*, forth, in public; + *faleri*, to acknowledge, confess.)

professor: a teacher of the highest rank in an institution of higher learning.

teach: **1.** to impart knowledge or skill to; to give instruction to.

2. to provide knowledge of; to instruct in.

3. to cause to learn by example or experience.

4. to advocate; preach. (from Middle English: *techen,* tahte.)

teacher: one who teaches; especially, a person hired by a school to teach.

Affirm, declare, claim, make a pretense of. Versus impart, provide, 2 cause, example, experience. Austere old Latin versus grubby old Anglo-Saxon. Two verbs, the one taking an intellectual object (to profess some*thing*), the other, primarily, a human one (to teach some*one*). A friend of mine, a middle-school teacher, when asked what she teaches, responds, "I teach kids."

Poor Professor, standing up there in the highest rank in an institu- 3 tion of higher learning, affirming and declaring and claiming and making a pretense, before the entire world, or, for all we know, the empty air. One somehow feels he has something to defend.

Teacher, on the other hand, is very much of this earth, "hired by a 4 school." To profess is to speak; to teach is to speak to and with someone. To profess is an act; to teach, a relationship.

Once I tried an experiment with a freshman composition class. 5 Under the guise of a "comparison/contrast" assignment, I asked them to make two lists of connotative qualities they associated with the terms "professor" and "teacher." There was remarkable homogeneity in the lists. The images corresponded pretty closely to those offered by Webster, though the students described them slightly differently. The teacher, they told me, was someone who worked really hard, long hours and wasn't paid very well. Also, the teacher was likely to be female.

Called Out of Your Name

At Kalamazoo, they use "Doctor." Coming from institutions 6 where "Professor" or "Mr./Miss/Mrs./Ms." is the norm, you are repeatedly jolted when you hear yourself called "Doctor." Maybe it's a delightful shock: You've made it. Maybe it's a disconcerting or downright uncomfortable shock: Who do they think you are? If you're female, it's probably the latter.

You haven't thought much about what you will be called by your   7
students, but this suddenly becomes a real and pressing issue. Perhaps you think "Doctor" hopelessly pretentious. Will you go to Professor? But that's not the coin of the realm here, and it feels itchy. What did you call Them when you were student? You called most of Them "Mr." until, as a senior major, you crossed that wonderful threshold where one of the junior faculty said, "Hey, call me Tom."

You notice that some of them are making the decision for them-   8
selves and calling you "Miss" or "Mrs." These commonalities suddenly sound strange, even absurd to you. The sheer irrelevance of your marital status strikes you as worth making a small deal about. But you notice that when they ask if it's one or the other and you respond, "It's Ms.," they either are embarrassed or start drawing conclusions about you, looking scared, or hostile, or mocking. "Oh, *Ms. Excuse* me." You see bras burning wildly behind their eyes.

You also notice that they do not make this distinction with your   9
colleague Dennis, who is unfailingly "Dr. Vaughan." You and he are introduced by a student to her father one Parents' Weekend as follows: "Dad, this is Dr. Vaughan. And this is Gail." This really pisses you off. And then you realize with a jolt that you're getting awfully concerned with superficialities, aren't you, and you've never known yourself to fret so about hierarchies and authority and titles. What's happening to you?

Toughen up, you tell yourself. Insist on Doctor. Yet when you say   10
the word to yourself, you see a clear image: beard, jacket with elbow patches, pipe, rumpled shirt, wool tie. No way in your wildest dreams are you ever going to wake up looking like Him.

After a while you give up and go back to basics: "Please call me   11
Gail." Some of the kids love it, instantly loosen and warm up. Others are nervous for a while. Some few, still enjoying the high school mindset whereby the object of the game is to shore up whatever power you can against the Teacher, take it as license. Regardless, you decide you will have to draw your authority from something other than your title.

The Voice of Authority

If their voices surprise and confuse you, no less does your own.   12

Half the time, in those first months, you feel like a foreigner, you   13
do not speak the language. You become intensely aware of vocal blunders—the moments when your voice sounds terribly high amongst a chorus of baritones and tenors; when you have laughed too loudly, too freely; when you have sounded suddenly shrill, emotional in a committee meeting; when you mentally replay a meeting with the provost and it sounds like a little girl talking to her father; when you have con-

fessed your classroom anxieties to the department chair and subsequently realize how patronizing he sounded as you left, how delighted to learn that you were struggling.

You find yourself listening intently as an immigrant does to learn 14 the lingua franca: High Father Tongue. Your gift for mimicry deepens in those first years, and you learn which voice goes with which setting. In particular, you learn to do Blasé, Disinterested Intellectual, Cynical Questioner, and Rational Proponent to perfection. Rational Adversary you still struggle with; when you're fighting, your vocal cords tend still to tighten, so that you sound, god help you, Emotional.

You become vocally nimble beyond your wildest dreams: You can 15 switch instantly from the Classroom Voice to the Office Voice to the Committee Voice to the Faculty Meeting Voice; from the Motherly to the Sisterly to the Collegial—that is, the Brotherly. You speak to the smart-ass from the comp class in one tone, to the sweetheart from the novel class in entirely another. And you're surprised by your own relief when you are in a roomful of female voices.

Some voices you decide not to master. You walk into a depart- 16 ment office and hear a colleague speaking to the secretary as if she were a favorite dog. You recall that just yesterday, when you called this number and identified yourself, her voice took on shades of deference and eagerness to please that made you squirm in your chair. In such conversations, you sometimes call upon the old female modes of speech—the interrogatory endings, the apologies, the underscoring of your own ignorance and ineptness—in order to demote yourself, to assure her that you're female too.

One of the first shocks of the new is the power of the professorial 17 voice, including even your own. Suddenly, in the space of a month or two, you seem to have come to own the voice toward which you have been striving for seventeen years. It is yours. When you speak in class, forty heads dip, forty hands go for the pen, especially if you have uttered the word "exam" or "assignment." One negative word turns out to have haunted a young soul for weeks. One positive word redeems that same soul, at least for a few days. One word from you and a student's proposed Senior Project is certified Legitimate and funded. A letter from you is at least one significant factor in whether he will attend law school or not. One sentence of support and her Senior Project is granted Honors and she thus has Honors in English at graduation. One private word to the registrar and he is admitted to an overbooked course. On your word she is exempt from the writing requirement.

It is not nearly as much fun as you assumed it was as a student, 18 this vocal power. In fact, it is somewhat frightening. No, it is very frightening. You begin to see what havoc you could wreak. Remember Mr. Margolis, who wrote at the end of one of your papers that your writing was "clear as a bell"? Remember how you heard that very bell in your head for months afterward? What if he had said you really ought to consider another major?

The campus paper comes out one Thursday and you are chagrined   19
to see the women's basketball team termed the "Lady Hornets." You consider a letter to the editor and decide against it; faculty letters of complaint send the whole beleaguered staff into nervous collapse. So you write a private letter to the editor, who is a friend of yours, and you make sure the tone is gentle and jesting. She rushes in to assure you that it was a mistake on the part of a new sports editor rather than policy. You laugh about it together. Next edition: an editorial by someone on the staff, attacking faculty censorship of the paper. It appears that the sports editor has sworn to abandon journalism for good as a result of a letter of complaint from an unnamed "feminist in the English Department." You find out who this person is whose career you have just torpedoed, and you realize you have never laid eyes on him.

You become highly attuned to the power of voices. A woman stu-   20
dent comes to see you, distraught. Dr. X has said her idea for a Senior Project is "not really very serious." You, in fact, find her idea rather intriguing, and you spend half an hour convincing her that it is, and another half suggesting how she might go about exploring it further. When she leaves, smiling, full of thanks, you know that you have exerted considerable power. You are amazed that you can do it. You are disturbed that you have had to do it.

Another woman creeps in and closes the door. Dr. Y has said she   21
might have problems in her chosen field because she "exudes a sexuality" that will be troublesome for male co-workers. Is it true? Should she think about other options?

Does your voice stand a chance against those of X and Y?   22

The phone rings at eleven one night, and it is a student who grad-   23
uated two years earlier. "Remember me?" she asks, tentatively. She is about to start applying to graduate schools in philosophy. You talk with her aimlessly about this for fifteen minutes or so, in a fog as to why she has called you. Finally she unwraps the real problem: She finds herself unaccountably interested in finding out which programs have women's studies emphases, and how many women there are on the faculty. She cannot even articulate why this is suddenly important to her; she knows only that it is important. Her boyfriend thinks she's nuts. Clearly, part of her is in agreement. Forty-five minutes later, she signs off: "Oh, thanks so much. I'm really sorry to have bothered you with this, but I just didn't know who else to call. I just wanted to hear you say that. I just needed to hear it from somebody, I guess."

You are surprised to discover how often this is the case, how often   24
all they need and want from you is to hear you say it. What that means is that something in them is saying it, and they need the close harmony of another, external, more authoritative voice.

You are even more surprised to discover that it is yours, that voice 25 that they need. You, who have never felt like you had much authority or even the right to much, hear yourself speaking in that voice, firmly and easily. Because they need it, you have it.

And finally, you are amazed to hear yourself saying, with perfect 26 confidence, things you yourself have needed to believe all your life.

When one true voice calls and another responds, that is a vocation. 27

Working with the Text

1. Griffin contrasts two ways of looking at her job, using two nouns (professor, teacher) and two verbs (to profess, to teach). What are the differences? Which way of looking at her job does she prefer, and why?
2. What power does Griffin say there is in a professor's "voice," by which she means all the language a professor uses on the job, either oral or written? What influence on people can her "voice" have, both destructive and constructive?
3. What does Griffin's gender have to do with her "voice"? That is, how does being a woman influence her use of language on the job?
4. Griffin's use of the second person ("you") in the essay may be confusing at first, since it refers mostly to herself, sometimes as a student and sometimes as a professor. Where in the essay is "you" used, and what does it mean in each place? Why do you think Griffin risks confusion in this way? What idea might she be trying to communicate?
5. Griffin begins her essay in an unusual way: she introduces her topic with a series of definitions. Why do you think she chose to present a bare list of definitions rather than use a more conventional introduction? How do the definitions help introduce the themes of the essay?

Working beyond the Text

1. What do you call your various college teachers, from among the choices Griffin offers: Doctor? Professor? "Mr./Miss/Mrs./Ms."? A first name? How did you learn to call them by those names or titles? Which titles do you prefer using and why? What are the different connotations involved in the various titles used for college teachers?
2. Griffin describes a stereotypical college professor: "beard, jacket with elbow patches, pipe, rumpled shirt, wool tie." In reality, few college teachers fit this description. Describe yours. What, if anything, do they share, in their variety?

3. Has it occurred to you that some of your college teachers might have the problems Griffin describes in asserting authority over you? What problems does she have? Interview one or more of your teachers about the topic.

4. Find the source of Griffin's epigraph, the drama *Equus*. Where in the play does the quotation appear, and what does it mean there? How does this meaning apply to Griffin's themes in her essay?

The Death of the Profane

Patricia J. Williams

Patricia Williams has taught law at the University of Wisconsin and Columbia University. Her works include *The Alchemy of Race and Rights* (1991), a book about the interaction of race and law in U.S. society and in her personal life. In the following chapter from that book, Williams tells of a personal encounter with "race and rights," in which her efforts to publish an account of being barred from a store because she was African American were discouraged by a law journal and misinterpreted by the local newspaper.

Buzzers are big in New York City. Favored particularly by smaller stores and boutiques, merchants throughout the city have installed them as screening devices to reduce the incidence of robbery: if the face at the door looks desirable, the buzzer is pressed and the door is unlocked. If the face is that of an undesirable, the door stays locked. Predictably, the issue of undesirability has revealed itself to be a racial determination. While controversial enough at first, even civil-rights organizations backed down eventually in the face of arguments that the buzzer system is a "necessary evil," that it is a "mere inconvenience" in comparison to the risks of being murdered, that suffering discrimination is not as bad as being assaulted, and that in any event it is not all blacks who are barred, just "17-year-old black males wearing running shoes and hooded sweatshirts."[1]

The installation of these buzzers happened swiftly in New York; stores that had always had their doors wide open suddenly became exclusive or received people by appointment only. I discovered them and their meaning one Saturday in 1986. I was shopping in Soho and saw in a store window a sweater that I wanted to buy for my mother. I pressed my round brown face to the window and my finger to the

---

[1]"When 'By Appointment' Means Keep Out," *New York Times*, December 17, 1986, p. B1. Letter to the Editor from Michael Levin and Marguerita Levin, *New York Times*, January 11, 1987, p. E32.

buzzer, seeking admittance. A narrow-eyed, white teenager wearing running shoes and feasting on bubble gum glared out, evaluating me for signs that would pit me against the limits of his social understanding. After about five seconds, he mouthed "We're closed," and blew pink rubber at me. It was two Saturdays before Christmas, at one o'clock in the afternoon; there were several white people in the store who appeared to be shopping for things for *their* mothers.

I was enraged. At that moment I literally wanted to break all the 3 windows of the store and *take* lots of sweaters for my mother. In the flicker of his judgmental gray eyes, that saleschild had transformed my brightly sentimental, joy-to-the-world, pre-Christmas spree to a shambles. He snuffed my sense of humanitarian catholicity, and there was nothing I could do to snuff his, without making a spectacle of myself.

I am still struck by the structure of power that drove me into such 4 a blizzard of rage. There was almost nothing I could do, short of physically intruding upon him, that would humiliate him the way he humiliated me. No words, no gestures, no prejudices of my own would make a bit of difference to him; his refusal to let me into the store—it was Benetton's, whose colorfully punnish ad campaign is premised on wrapping every one of the world's peoples in its cottons and woolens—was an outward manifestation of his never having let someone like me into the realm of his reality. He had no compassion, no remorse, no reference to me; and no desire to acknowledge me even at the estranged level of arm's-length transactor. He saw me only as one who would take his money and therefore could not conceive that I was there to give him money.

In this weird ontological imbalance, I realized that buying some- 5 thing in that store was like bestowing a gift, the gift of my commerce, the lucre of my patronage. In the wake of my outrage, I wanted to take back the gift of appreciation that my peering in the window must have appeared to be. I wanted to take it back in the form of unappreciation, disrespect, defilement. I wanted to work so hard at wishing he could feel what I felt that he would never again mistake my hatred for some sort of plaintive wish to be included. I was quite willing to disenfranchise myself, in the heat of my need to revoke the flattery of my purchasing power. I was willing to boycott Benetton's, random white-owned businesses, and anyone who ever blew bubble gum in my face again.

My rage was admittedly diffuse, even self-destructive, but it was 6 symmetrical. The perhaps loose-ended but utter propriety of that rage is no doubt lost not just to the young man who actually barred me, but to those who would appreciate my being barred only as an abstract precaution, who approve of those who would bar even as they deny that they would bar *me*.

The violence of my desire to burst into Benetton's is probably quite 7 apparent. I often wonder if the violence, the exclusionary hatred, is equally apparent in the repeated public urgings that blacks understand the buzzer system by putting themselves in the shoes of white storeowners—that, in effect, blacks look into the mirror of frightened white faces for the reality of their undesirability; and that then blacks would "just as surely conclude that [they] would not let [themselves] in under similar circumstances."[2] (That some blacks might agree merely shows that some of us have learned too well the lessons of privatized intimacies of self-hatred and rationalized away the fullness of our public, participatory selves.)

On the same day I was barred from Benetton's, I went home and 8 wrote the above impassioned account in my journal. On the day after that, I found I was still brooding, so I turned to a form of catharsis I have always found healing. I typed up as much of the story as I have just told, made a big poster of it, put a nice colorful border around it, and, after Benetton's was truly closed, stuck it to their big sweater-filled window. I exercised my first-amendment right to place my business with them right out in the street.

So that was the first telling of this story. The second telling came a 9 few months later, for a symposium on Excluded Voices sponsored by a law review. I wrote an essay summing up my feelings about being excluded from Benetton's and analyzing "how the rhetoric of increased privatization, in response to racial issues, functions as the rationalizing agent of public unaccountability and, ultimately, irresponsibility." Weeks later, I received the first edit. From the first page to the last, my fury had been carefully cut out. My rushing, run-on-rage had been reduced to simple declarative sentences. The active personal had been inverted in favor of the passive impersonal. My words were different; they spoke to me upsidedown. I was afraid to read too much of it at a time—meanings rose up at me oddly, stolen and strange.

A week and a half later, I received the second edit. All reference to 10 Benetton's had been deleted because, according to the editors and the faculty adviser, it was defamatory; they feared harassment and liability; they said printing it would be irresponsible. I called them and offered to supply a footnote attesting to this as my personal experience at one particular location and of a buzzer system not limited to Benetton's; the editors told me that they were not in the habit of publishing things that were unverifiable. I could not but wonder, in this refusal even to let me file an affidavit, what it would take to make my experience verifiable. The testimony of an independent white bystander? (a

---

[2]*New York Times,* January 11, 1987, p. E32.

requirement in fact imposed in U.S. Supreme Court holdings through the first part of the century[3]).

Two days *after* the piece was sent to press, I received copies of the 11
final page proofs. All reference to my race had been eliminated because it was against "editorial policy" to permit descriptions of physiognomy. "I realize," wrote one editor, "that this was a very personal experience, but any reader will know what you must have looked like when standing at that window." In a telephone conversation to them, I ranted wildly about the significance of such an omission. "It's irrelevant," another editor explained in a voice gummy with soothing and patience; "It's nice and poetic," but it doesn't "advance the discussion of any principle. . . . This is a law review, after all." Frustrated, I accused him of censorship; calmly he assured me it was not. "This is just a matter of style," he said with firmness and finality.

Ultimately I did convince the editors that mention of my race was 12
central to the whole sense of the subsequent text; that my story became one of extreme paranoia without the information that I am black; or that it became one in which the reader had to fill in the gap by assumption, presumption, prejudgment, or prejudice. What was most interesting to me in this experience was how the blind application of principles of neutrality, through the device of omission, acted either to make me look crazy or to make the reader participate in old habits of cultural bias.

That was the second telling of my story. The third telling came last 13
April, when I was invited to participate in a law-school conference on Equality and Difference. I retold my sad tale of exclusion from Soho's most glitzy boutique, focusing in this version on the law-review editing process as a consequence of an ideology of style rooted in a social text of neutrality. I opined:

> Law and legal writing aspire to formalized, color-blind, liberal ideals. Neutrality is the standard for assuring these ideals; yet the adherence to it is often determined by reference to an aesthetic of uniformity, in which difference is simply omitted. For example, when segregation was eradicated from the American lexicon, its omission led many to actually believe that racism therefore no longer existed. Race-neutrality in law has become the presumed antidote for race bias in real life. With the entrenchment of the notion of race-neutrality came attacks on the concept of affirmative action and the rise of reverse discrimination suits. Blacks, for so many generations deprived of jobs based on the color of our skin, are now told that we ought to

---

[3]See generally *Blyew v. U.S.,* 80 U.S. 581 (1871), upholding a state's right to forbid blacks to testify against whites.

find it demeaning to be hired based on the color of our skin. Such is the silliness of simplistic either-or inversions as remedies to complex problems.

What is truly demeaning in this era of double-speak-no-evil is going on interviews and not getting hired because someone doesn't think we'll be comfortable. It is demeaning not to get promoted because we're judged "too weak," then putting in a lot of energy the next time and getting fired because we're "too strong." It is demeaning to be told what we find demeaning. It is very demeaning to stand on street corners unemployed and begging. It is downright demeaning to have to explain why we haven't been employed for months and then watch the job go to someone who is "more experienced." It is outrageously demeaning that none of this can be called racism, even if it happens only to, or to large numbers of, black people; as long as it's done with a smile, a handshake and a shrug; as long as the phantom-word "race" is never used.

The image of race as a phantom-word came to me after I moved into my late godmother's home. In an attempt to make it my own, I cleared the bedroom for painting. The following morning the room asserted itself, came rushing and raging at me through the emptiness, exactly as it had been for twenty-five years. One day filled with profuse and overwhelming complexity, the next day filled with persistently recurring memories. The shape of the past came to haunt me, the shape of the emptiness confronted me each time I was about to enter the room. The force of its spirit still drifts like an odor throughout the house.

The power of that room, I have thought since, is very like the power of racism as status quo: it is deep, angry, eradicated from view, but strong enough to make everyone who enters the room walk around the bed that isn't there, avoiding the phantom as they did the substance, for fear of bodily harm. They do not even know they are avoiding; they defer to the unseen shapes of things with subtle responsiveness, guided by an impulsive awareness of nothingness, and the deep knowledge and denial of witchcraft at work.

The phantom room is to me symbolic of the emptiness of formal equal opportunity, particularly as propounded by President Reagan, the Reagan Civil Rights Commission and the Reagan Supreme Court. Blindly formalized constructions of equal opportunity are the creation of a space that is filled in by a meandering stream of unguided hopes, dreams, fantasies, fears, recollections. They are the presence of the past in imaginary, imagistic form—the phantom-roomed exile of our longing.

It is thus that I strongly believe in the efficacy of programs and paradigms like affirmative action. Blacks are the objects of a constitutional omission which has been incorporated into a theory of neutrality. It is thus that omission is really a form of expression, as oxymoronic as that sounds: racial omission is a literal part of original intent; it is the fixed, reiterated prophecy of the Founding Fathers. It is thus that affirmative action is an affirmation; the affirmative act of hiring—or hearing—blacks is a recognition of individuality that re-places blacks as a social statistic, that is profoundly interconnective to the fate of blacks and whites either as sub-groups or as one group. In this sense, affirmative action is as mystical and beyond-the-self as an initiation ceremony. It is an act of verification and of vision. It is an act of social as well as professional responsibility.

The following morning I opened the local newspaper, to find that 14 the event of my speech had commanded two columns on the front page of the Metro section. I quote only the opening lines: "Affirmative action promotes prejudice by denying the status of women and blacks, instead of affirming them as its name suggests. So said New York City attorney Patricia Williams to an audience Wednesday."[4]

I clipped out the article and put it in my journal. In the margin 15 there is a note to myself; eventually, it says, I should try to pull all these threads together into yet another law-review article. The problem, of course, will be that in the hierarchy of law-review citation, the article in the newspaper will have more authoritative weight about me, as a so-called "primary resource," than I will have; it will take precedence over my own citation of the unverifiable testimony of my speech.

I have used the Benetton's story a lot, in speaking engagements at 16 various schools. I tell it whenever I am too tired to whip up an original speech from scratch. Here are some of the questions I have been asked in the wake of its telling:

Am I not privileging a racial perspective, by considering only the 17 black point of view? Don't I have an obligation to include the "sales-man's side" of the story?

Am I not putting the salesman on trial and finding him guilty of 18 racism without giving him a chance to respond to or cross-examine me?

Am I not using the store window as a "metaphorical fence" 19 against the potential of his explanation in order to represent my side as "authentic"?

How can I be sure I'm right? 20

What makes my experience the real black one anyway? 21

Isn't it possible that another black person would disagree with my 22 experience? If so, doesn't that render my story too unempirical and subjective to pay any attention to?

Always a major objection is to my having put the poster on Benet- 23 ton's window. As one law professor put it: "It's one thing to publish this in a law review, where no one can take it personally, but it's an-

---

[4]"Attorney Says Affirmative Action Denies Racism, Sexism," *Dominion Post,* (Morgantown, West Virginia), April 8, 1988, p. B1.

other thing altogether to put your own interpretation right out there, just like that, uncontested, I mean, with nothing to counter it."[5]

Working with the Text

1. What does Williams mean when she says of the "saleschild" that he had "snuffed my sense of humanitarian catholicity, and there was nothing I could do to snuff his"? Why does she feel powerless?

2. Williams is clearly critical of "the blind application of principles of neutrality" in the law to her experience at Benetton's. In what ways? How do the editors of the law review for which she is writing attempt to use legal language to change the meaning of her experience?

3. Williams tells not one but two personal stories in this essay: the first is about her attempt to shop at Benetton's, the second is about her attempt to publicize the first story. How do these two personal stories relate to her broader themes? What general truths beyond her personal life do they help her express?

---

[5]These questions put me on trial—an imaginary trial where it is I who have the burden of proof—and proof being nothing less than the testimony of the salesman actually confessing yes yes I am a racist. These questions question my own ability to know, to assess, to be objective. And of course, since anything that happens to me is inherently subjective, they take away my power to know what happens to me in the world. Others, by this standard, will always know better than I. And my insistence on recounting stories from my own perspective will be treated as presumption, slander, paranoid hallucination, or just plain lies.

Recently I got an urgent call from Thomas Grey of Stanford Law School. He had used this piece in his jurisprudence class, and a rumor got started that the Benetton's story wasn't true, that I had made it up, that it was a fantasy, a lie that was probably the product of a diseased mind trying to make all white people feel guilty. At this point I realized it almost didn't make any difference whether I was telling the truth or not—that the greater issue I had to face was the overwhelming weight of a disbelief that goes beyond my disinclination to believe and becomes active suppression of anything I might have to say. The greater problem is a powerfully oppressive mechanism for denial of black self-knowledge and expression. And this denial cannot be separated from the simultaneously pathological willingness to believe certain things about blacks—not to believe them, but things about them.

When students in Grey's class believed and then claimed that I had made it all up, they put me in a position like that of Tawana Brawley. I mean that specifically: the social consequence of concluding that we are liars operates as a kind of public absolution of racism—the conclusion is not merely that we are troubled or that I am eccentric, but that we, as liars, are the norm. Therefore, the nonbelievers can believe, things of this sort really don't happen (even in the face of statistics to the contrary). Racism or rape is all a big fantasy concocted by troublesome minorities and women. It is interesting to recall the outcry in every national medium, from the *New York Post* to the *Times* to the major networks, in the wake of the Brawley case: who will ever again believe a black woman who cries rape by a white man? . . . Now shift the frame a bit, and imagine a white male facing a consensus that he lied. Would there be a difference? Consider Charles Stuart, for example, the white Bostonian who accused a black man of murdering his pregnant wife and whose brother later alleged that in fact the brothers had conspired to murder her. Most people and the media not only did not claim but actively resisted believing that Stuart represented any kind of "white male" norm. Instead he was written off as a troubled weirdo, a deviant—again even in the face of spousal-abuse statistics to the contrary. There was not a story I could find that carried on about "who will ever believe" the next white man who cries murder.

4. Williams ends her essay with a series of questions that she is asked by listeners when she tells her Benetton story, but she doesn't say how she answers them. How do you suppose she responds to these questions, based on the ideas she presents in the essay?

5. The last item in Williams' essay is a very long footnote. What is its main idea? Why does Williams choose to put this information in a footnote rather than in the main text of the essay?

Working beyond the Text

1. Have you ever been a victim of discrimination similar to Williams' experience? If so, what did you do about it? If not, can you imagine what you might do? Would you have the ability or opportunity to "fight back" as Williams does? In what ways?

2. Williams describes the recent phenomenon of buzzers on shop doors, which make it possible to allow some people in while keeping others out. How has this issue been discussed in the popular press? Using Williams' footnotes as a starting point, find materials in the library to help you explain the various arguments attacking and defending the practice.

3. Williams describes the process of writing something very important to her, and her response to the changes various readers and editors made to her writing. What is her reaction? Have you ever shown a piece of writing to several readers and incorporated their suggestions? Was your process and reaction similar to Williams'?

Men and Women Talking on the Job

Deborah Tannen

Deborah Tannen, born in 1945, is a professor of linguistics at Georgetown University. Her scholarly writing focuses on language issues such as conversational styles or gender and language. Her books include *That's Not What I Meant!: How Conversational Style Makes or Breaks Your Relations with Others* and *You Just Don't Understand: Women and Men in Conversation*. In the following essay from her book *Talking from 9 to 5: How Women's and Men's Conversational Styles Affect Who Gets Heard, Who Gets Credit, and What Gets Done at Work* (1994), Tannen asserts that male and female workers express themselves differently on the job and offers suggestions about how to create more understanding between men and women in the workplace.

Amy was a manager with a problem: She had just read a final re- 1
port written by Donald, and she felt it was woefully inadequate. She
faced the unsavory task of telling him to do it over. When she met
with Donald, she made sure to soften the blow by beginning with
praise, telling him everything about his report that was good. Then
she went on to explain what was lacking and what needed to be done
to make it acceptable. She was pleased with the diplomatic way she
had managed to deliver the bad news. Thanks to her thoughtfulness in
starting with praise, Donald was able to listen to the criticism and
seemed to understand what was needed. But when the revised report
appeared on her desk, Amy was shocked. Donald had made only
minor, superficial changes, and none of the necessary ones. The next
meeting with him did not go well. He was incensed that she was now
telling him his report was not acceptable and accused her of having
misled him. "You told me before it was fine," he protested.

Amy thought she had been diplomatic; Donald thought she had 2
been dishonest. The praise she intended to soften the message "This is
unacceptable" sounded to him like the message itself: "This is fine." So
what she regarded as the main point—the needed changes—came
across to him as optional suggestions, because he had already registered her praise as the main point. She felt he hadn't listened to her.
He thought she had changed her mind and was making him pay the
price.

Work days are filled with conversations about getting the job 3
done. Most of these conversations succeed, but too many end in im-
passes like this. It could be that Amy is a capricious boss whose wishes
are whims, and it could be that Donald is a temperamental employee
who can't hear criticism no matter how it is phrased. But I don't think
either was the case in this instance. I believe this was one of innumerable misunderstandings caused by differences in conversational style.
Amy delivered the criticism in a way that seemed to her self-evidently
considerate, a way she would have preferred to receive criticism herself: taking into account the other person's feelings, making sure he
knew that her ultimate negative assessment of his report didn't mean
she had no appreciation of his abilities. She offered the praise as a
sweetener to help the nasty-tasting news go down. But Donald didn't
expect criticism to be delivered in that way, so he mistook the praise as
her overall assessment rather than a preamble to it.

This conversation could have taken place between two women or 4
two men. But I do not think it is a coincidence that it occurred between
a man and a woman. This book will explain why. First, it gives a view
of the role played by talk in our work lives. To do this, I show the
workings of conversational style, explaining the ritual nature of conversation[1] and the confusion that arises when rituals are not shared
and therefore not recognized as such. I take into account the many in-

fluences on conversational style, but I focus in particular on the differing rituals that typify women and men (although, of course, not all individual men and women behave in ways that are typical). Conversational rituals common among men often involve using opposition such as banter, joking, teasing, and playful put-downs, and expending effort to avoid the one-down position in the interaction. Conversational rituals common among women are often ways of maintaining an appearance of equality, taking into account the effect of the exchange on the other person, and expending effort to downplay the speakers' authority so they can get the job done without flexing their muscles in an obvious way.

When everyone present is familiar with these conventions, they 5 work well. But when ways of speaking are not recognized as conventions, they are taken literally, with negative results on both sides. Men whose oppositional strategies are interpreted literally may be seen as hostile when they are not, and their efforts to ensure that they avoid appearing one-down may be taken as arrogance. When women use conversational strategies designed to avoid appearing boastful and to take the other person's feelings into account, they may be seen as less confident and competent than they really are. As a result, both women and men often feel they are not getting sufficient credit for what they have done, are not being listened to, are not getting ahead as fast as they should.

When I talk about women's and men's characteristic ways of speak- 6 ing, I always emphasize that both styles make sense and are equally valid in themselves, though the difference in styles may cause trouble in interaction. In a sense, when two people form a private relationship of love or friendship, the bubble of their interaction is a world unto itself, even though they both come with the prior experience of their families, their community, and a lifetime of conversations. But someone who takes a job is entering a world that is already functioning, with its own characteristic style already in place. Although there are many influences such as regional background, the type of industry involved, whether it is a family business or a large corporation, in general, workplaces that have previously had men in positions of power have already established male-style interaction as the norm. In that sense, women, and others whose styles are different, are not starting out equal, but are at a

---

[1]*"... the ritual nature of conversation ..."* As my colleague Rom Harré pointed out to me, it would be useful to note, for readers interested in finer distinctions, that I am using the term "ritual" rather loosely to capture the automatic, nonliteral, conventionalized nature of conversational language. There are, of course, a number of different levels on which this operates. Technically, a "ritual" per se is a symbolic means of accomplishing a social act. Other ways in which talk is not meant literally include what scholars refer to as "phatic speech," which refers to relatively "empty" verbiage whose main purpose is the maintenance of social relations, or recognizing the other as a person.

disadvantage. Though talking at work is quite similar to talking in private, it is a very different enterprise in many ways.

Negotiating from the Inside Out or the Outside In

Two co-workers who were on very friendly terms with each other 7 were assigned to do a marketing survey together. When they got the assignment, the man began by saying, "I'll do the airline and automobile industry, and you can do the housewares and direct-mail market." The woman was taken aback. "Hey," she said. "It sounds like you've got it all figured out. As a matter of fact, *I'd* like to do airlines and autos. I've already got a lot of contacts in those areas." "Oh," he said, a little chagrined and a lot surprised. She continued, "I wish you wouldn't come on so strong." "Well, how would you have started?" he asked. She said, "I wouldn't have just said what I wanted to do. I would have asked, 'What parts do you want to do?'" This made no sense to him. "Then what are you complaining about? If you had asked me what parts I wanted to do, I would have said, 'I'll do the airlines and autos.' We would have ended up in the same place anyway."

The woman saw his point. But if the conversation had gone that 8 way, she still would have been frustrated. To her, the question "What parts of the survey would you like to do?" is not an invitation to grab the parts he wants and run away with them. It's an invitation to talk about the various parts—which ones interest him, which he has experience in, which he would like to learn more about. Then he would ask, "What do you want to do?" and she would say what interests her, where her experience lies, and where she'd like to get more experience. Finally, they would divvy up the parts in a way that gave them both some of what they wanted, while taking advantage of both their expertise.

Making decisions is a crucial part of any workday. Daily, weekly, 9 monthly, decisions must be made with never enough information and never enough time. People have very different ways of reaching decisions, and none is clearly better than others. But when two people with different styles have to make decisions together, both styles may have worse results than either would have if their styles were shared, unless the differences are understood and accommodated.

Beginning by stating what you will do is a style of negotiating that 10 starts inside and works its way out. If others have different ideas, you expect them to say so, and you'll negotiate. Opening with a question like "What would you like to do?" or "What do you think?" is a style that begins by being vague and works its way in. It specifically invites others to express their perspective. Either style can work well. What makes the machine go TILT! is the difference in styles. Someone who expects negotiation to proceed from the inside and work its way out hears a vague question as an invitation to decide; someone who tends to negotiate from the outside in hears a specific claim as a nonnegotiable demand. In this sense, both styles are indirect—they depend on an unspoken understanding of how the subsequent conversation is expected to go. This is a sense in which conversation is ritualized: It follows a preset sequencing scheme that seems self-evidently appropriate.

More on Negotiating Styles

The managers of a medium-size company got the go-ahead to hire 11
a human-resources coordinator, and two managers who worked well together were assigned to make the choice. As it turned out, Maureen and Harold favored different applicants, and both felt strongly about their preferences. Maureen argued with assurance and vigor that the person she wanted to hire was the most creative and innovative, and that he had the most appropriate experience. Harold argued with equal conviction that the applicant he favored had a vision of management that fit with the company's, whereas her candidate might be a thorn in their side. They traded arguments for some time, neither convincing the other. Then Harold said that hiring the applicant Maureen wanted would make him so uncomfortable that he would have to consider resigning. Maureen respected Harold. What's more, she liked him and considered him a friend. So she felt that his admission of such strong feelings had to be taken into account. She said what seemed to her the only thing she could say under the circumstances: "Well, I certainly don't want you to feel uncomfortable here; you're one of the pillars of the place. If you feel that strongly about it, I can't argue with that." Harold's choice was hired.

In this case, the decision-making power went not to the manager 12
who had the highest rank in the firm (their positions were parallel) and not necessarily to the one whose judgment was best, but to the one whose arguing strategies were most effective in the negotiation. Maureen was an ardent and persuasive advocate for her view, but she assumed that she and Harold would have to come to an agreement in order to make a decision, and that she had to take his feelings into account. Since Harold would not back down, she did. Most important, when he argued that he would have to quit if she got her way, she felt she had no option but to yield.

What was crucial was not Maureen's and Harold's individual 13
styles in isolation but how their styles interacted—how they played in concert with the other's style. Harold's threat to quit ensured his triumph—when used with someone who would not call his bluff. If he had been arguing with someone who regarded this threat as simply another move in the negotiation rather than as a nonnegotiable expression of deep feelings that had to be respected, the result might have

been different. For example, had she said, "That's ridiculous; of course you're not going to quit!" or "If that's how shallow your commitment to this firm is, then we'd be better off without you," the decision might well have gone the other way.

When you talk to someone whose style is similar to yours, you can 14 fairly well predict the response you are going to get. But when you talk to someone whose style is different, you can't predict, and often can't make sense of, the response. Hearing the reaction you get, if it's not the one you expected, often makes you regret what you said. Harold later told Maureen that he was sorry he had used the argument he did. In retrospect he was embarrassed, even a bit ashamed of himself. His retrospective chagrin was like what you feel if you slam down something in anger and are surprised and regretful to see that it breaks. You wanted to make a gesture, but you didn't expect it to come out with such force. Harold regretted what he said precisely because it caused Maureen to back down so completely. He'd known he was upping the ante—he felt he had to do something to get them out of the loop of recycling arguments they were in—but he had not expected it to end the negotiation summarily; he expected Maureen to meet his move with a balancing move of her own. He did not predict the impact that personalizing his argument would have on her. For her part, Maureen did not think of Harold's threat as just another move in a negotiable argument; she heard it as a personal plea that she could not reject. Their different approaches to negotiation put her at a disadvantage in negotiating with him.

"How Certain Are You of That?"

Negotiating is only one kind of activity that is accomplished 15 through talk at work. Other kinds of decision-making are also based as much on ways of talking as on the content of the arguments. The CEO of a corporation explained to me that he regularly has to make decisions based on insufficient information—and making decisions is a large part of his work life. Much of his day is spent hearing brief presentations following which he must either approve or reject a course of action. He has to make a judgment in five minutes about issues the presenters have worked on for months. "I decide," he explained, "based on how confident they seem. If they seem very confident, I call it a go. If they seem unsure, I figure it's too risky and nix it."

Here is where the rule of competence and the role of communica- 16 tion go hand in hand. Confidence, after all, is an internal feeling. How can you judge others' confidence? The only evidence you have to go on is circumstantial—how they talk about what they know. You judge by a range of signs, including facial expression and body posture, but most of all, speech. Do they hesitate? Do they speak up or swallow half their words? Is their tone of voice declamatory or halting? Do they make bald statements ("This is a winner! We've got to go for it!") or hedge ("Um . . . from what I can tell, I think it'll work, but we'll never know for sure until we try")? This seems simple enough. Surely, you can tell how confident people are by paying attention to how they speak, just as you can tell when someone is lying.

Well, maybe not. Psychologist Paul Ekman has spent years study- 17 ing lying, and he has found that most people are very sure they can tell when others are lying. The only trouble is, most can't. With a few thus-far inexplicable exceptions, people who tell him they are absolutely sure they can tell if someone is lying are as likely to be wrong as to be right—and he has found this to be as true for judges as for the rest of us.

In the same way, our ability to determine how confident others are 18 is probably quite limited. The CEO who does not take into account the individual styles of the people who make presentations to him will find it difficult, if not impossible, to make the best judgment. Different people will talk very differently, not because of the absolute level of their confidence or lack of it, but because of their habitual ways of speaking. There are those who sound sure of themselves even when inside they're not sure at all, and others who sound tentative even when they're very sure indeed. So being aware of differences in ways of speaking is a prerequisite for making good decisions as well as good presentations.

Feasting on Humble Pie

Although these factors affecting decision-making are the same for 19 men and women, and every individual has his or her own style, it seems that women are more likely to downplay their certainty, men more likely to downplay their doubts. From childhood, girls learn to temper what they say so as not to sound too aggressive—which means too certain. From the time they are little, most girls learn that sounding too sure of themselves will make them unpopular with their peers. Groups of girls, as researchers who have studied girls at play have found, will penalize and even ostracize a girl who seems too sure she's right. Anthropologist Marjorie Harness Goodwin found that girls criticize other girls who stand out by saying, "She thinks she's cute," or "She thinks she's something." Talking in ways that display self-confidence is not approved for girls.[2]

---

[2]"*girls criticize other girls who stand out . . .*" Marjorie Harness Goodwin spent a year and a half observing the girls and boys in her inner-city black Philadelphia neighborhood and found the girls sanctioning other girls who seemed to stand out by saying, in the dialect of their community, "She thinks she cute." Goodwin found, for example, that girls criticized a girl who dressed too well and did too well in school.

It is not only peers who disapprove of girls talking in ways that [20] call attention to their accomplishments. Adults too can be critical of such behavior in girls, as was a woman who wrote a letter that was published in a magazine. The letter-writer was responding to an article about a ten-year-old girl named Heather DeLoach who became a child celebrity by tap-dancing in a bee costume on a rock video.[3] Heather was portrayed in the magazine as still being awed by others' fame ("I got to meet Pauly Shore and Janet Jackson, and I got Madonna's autograph, but I wasn't allowed to take pictures") and unawed by her own ("I see myself so much on TV that when the Bee Girl comes on, I just click right through the channel"). Sounding very much like other girls, she hedged when mentioning her good grades ("sort of like straight-A"). But she was also quoted as saying, "I'm extremely talented. I guess when the director first set eyes on me, he liked me. I try my best to be an actress, and I'm just great. I'm the one and only Bee Girl."

Although the article did not explain what question the interviewer [21] asked to elicit Heather's truthful description of herself, the disapproving reader zeroed in on those words and admonished, "Heather De-Loach, the Bee Girl, describes herself as 'extremely talented' and 'just great.' Perhaps 10-year-old Heather should stop being a *bumble*bee and start being a *humble* bee." Not only did this reader tell the child star to start being more humble, but she also told her to stop being a bumblebee—that is, doing what she's so good at that it's bringing her attention, reward, and too much—or too obvious—self-confidence.

Reactions like these teach girls how they are expected to talk in [22] order to be liked. It is not surprising that when she spoke in this guileless way, Heather DeLoach was ten. By the time she gets through junior high school and puberty, chances are she will have learned to talk differently, a transformation—and loss of confidence—that white middle-class American girls experience at that stage of their lives, according to a great deal of current research.[4] But it is crucial to bear in mind that ways of talking are not literal representations of mental states, and refraining from boasting may not reveal a true lack of confidence. A pair of studies by a team of psychologists makes this clear.

---

[3]The article about ten-year-old Heather DeLoach appeared in *People* magazine, November 29, 1993, p. 102. The letter criticizing her for not being humble was published in the same magazine, December 20, 1993, p. 8.

[4]The crisis of confidence that girls undergo during adolescence was first brought to public attention by psychologist Carol Gilligan and her colleagues (see the essays in *Making Connections,* edited by Gilligan, Lyons, and Hanmer). Journalist Judy Mann discusses the evidence for and causes of this troubling phenomenon in *The Difference,* and provides an eloquent personal expansion on it with reference to her own daughter. Psychotherapist Mary Pipher tells the stories of adolescent girls she has seen in psychotherapy in *Reviving Ophelia.*

Laurie Heatherington and her colleagues had student experi- 23
menters ask hundreds of incoming college students to predict how
they thought their first year at college would go by forecasting the
grades they expected to get. In some cases, the predictions were made
anonymously: They were put in writing and placed in an envelope. In
others, they were made publicly, either orally to the experimenter or
by writing on a paper that the experimenter promptly read. The researchers found that women predicted lower grades for themselves
than men did—but only when they made their predictions publicly.
The predictions the women students made in private did not differ
from the men's, just as the grades they actually earned as the year progressed did not differ from the men's. In other words, their lower predictions evidenced not lack of confidence but reluctance to reveal the
level of confidence they felt.

The same researchers conducted a second study that captured 24
women's characteristic balancing act between their own interests and
those of the person they are talking to. In half the cases, the experi-
menters told their own grade-point averages to the students they in-
terviewed, and the grades they claimed to have gotten were compara-
tively low. Lo and behold, when women students thought they were
talking to someone who had gotten low grades, they lowered their
predictions of what they expected their own grades to be. Whether or
not the experimenter claimed to have gotten low grades did not affect
the predictions made by men students.

The first of these ingenious experiments dramatizes that the social 25
inhibition against seeming to boast can make women appear less confident than they really are. And the second study shows that part of
the reason many women censor themselves from proclaiming their
confidence is that they are balancing their own interests with those of
the person they are talking to. In other words, they modify their
speech to take into account the impact of what they say on the other
person's feelings.

There may be something peculiarly white middle class and Ameri- 26
can about the cultural constraint against women boasting. Those who
have studied the remarkable change in how girls talk about their own
talents and prospects during the crucial junior high school years have
noted that the pattern is not necessarily found, or is not as strong,
among black American teenage girls.[5] And anthropologist Thomas
Kochman notes that talking about one's own accomplishments can be
a highly valued source of humor for members of the cultural group he

---

[5]"... *have noted that the pattern is not necessarily found, or is not as strong among black American
teenage girls.*" See, for example, The AAUW Report, *How Schools Shortchange Girls*, p. 13.

calls "community blacks," as illustrated by the widely publicized self-congratulatory verbal performances of the African-American prize-fighter Muhammad Ali. But every culture makes distinctions that outsiders may miss. Kochman contrasts acceptable African-American "boasting" to the kind of self-aggrandizement that is negatively sanctioned by the same community as "bragging."

To emphasize the cultural relativity of attitudes toward boasting, I 27 should mention, too, the reaction of a British man who was certain that in his country, a boy who spoke like Heather DeLoach would be as likely as a girl to be chastised. Indeed, this Briton remarked, the British often find Americans annoyingly boastful.

For middle-class American women, though, the constraint is clear: 28 Talking about your own accomplishments in a way that calls attention to yourself is not acceptable. This social constraint became both a source of criticism and a dodge for figure-skater Nancy Kerrigan when an inordinate amount of media attention was focused on her during the 1994 winter Olympics. *Newsweek* magazine called her "ungracious" for saying of her own performance, "I was flawless," and of her competitor's, "Oksana wasn't clean." But when a microphone picked up what Kerrigan thought was private grumbling about how "corny" and "dumb" it was to parade through Disney World with life-size cartoon characters, her "handlers" issued a statement that "she was referring merely to her mom's insistence that she wear her silver medal. She feared it would 'look like bragging.'"[6]

The expectation that women should not display their own accom- 29 plishments brings us back to the matter of negotiating that is so important in the workplace. A man who owned a medium-sized company remarked that women who came to ask him for raises often supported their requests by pointing to a fellow worker on the same level who earned more. He considered this a weak bargaining strategy because he could always identify a different coworker at that level who earned less. They would do better, he felt, to argue for a raise on the basis of how valuable their own work is to the company. Yet it is likely that many women would be less comfortable "blowing their own horn" than making a claim based on fairness.

Follow the Leader

Similar expectations constrain how girls express leadership. Being 30 a leader often involves giving directions to others, but girls who tell other girls what to do are called "bossy." It is not that girls do not exert

---

[6] *"She feared it would 'look like bragging.'" Newsweek*, March 14, 1994, p. 79.

influence on their group—of course they do—but, as anthropologists like Marjorie Harness Goodwin have found, many girls discover they get better results if they phrase their ideas as suggestions rather than orders, and if they give reasons for their suggestions in terms of the good of the group. But while these ways of talking make girls—and, later, women—more likable, they make women seem less competent and self-assured in the world of work. And women who do seem competent and self-assured are as much in danger of being negatively labeled as are girls. After her retirement, Margaret Thatcher was described in the press as "bossy." Whereas girls are ready to stick this label on each other because they don't think any girl should boss the others around, it seems odd to apply it to Thatcher, who, after all, was the boss. And this is the rub: Standards of behavior applied to women are based on roles that do not include being boss.

Boys are expected to play by different rules, since the social organization of boys is different. Boys' groups tend to be more obviously hierarchical: Someone is one-up, and someone is one-down. Boys don't typically accuse each other of being "bossy" because the high-status boys are expected to give orders and push the low-status boys around. Daniel Maltz and Ruth Borker summarize research by many scholars showing that boys tend to jockey for center stage, challenge those who get it, and deflect challenges. Giving orders and telling the others what to do are ways of getting and keeping the high-status role. Another way of getting high status is taking center stage by telling stories, jokes, and information. Along with this, many boys learn to state their opinions in the strongest possible terms and find out if they're wrong by seeing if others challenge them. These ways of talking translate into an impression of confidence. 31

The styles typical of women and men both make sense given the context in which they were learned, but they have very different consequences in the workplace. In order to avoid being put in the one-down position, many men have developed strategies for making sure they get the one-up position instead, and this results in ways of talking that serve them well when it comes to hiring and promotion. In relation to the examples I have given, women are more likely to speak in the styles that are less effective in getting recognized and promoted. But if they speak in the styles that are effective when used by men— being assertive, sounding sure of themselves, talking up what they have done to make sure they get credit for it—they run the risk that everyone runs if they do not fit their culture's expectations for appropriate behavior: They will not be liked and may even be seen as having psychological problems. 32

Both women and men pay a price if they do not behave in ways expected of their gender: Men who are not very aggressive are called "wimps," whereas women who are not very aggressive are called 33 "feminine." Men who are aggressive are called "go-getters," though if they go too far, from the point of view of the viewer, they may be called "arrogant." This can hurt them, but not nearly as much as the innumerable labels for women who are thought to be too aggressive—starting with the most hurtful one: bitch.

Even the compliments that we receive are revealing. One woman [34] who had designed and implemented a number of innovative programs was praised by someone who said, "You have such a gentle way of bringing about radical change that people don't realize what's happening—or don't get threatened by it." This was a compliment, but it also hinted at the downside of the woman's gentle touch: Although it made it possible for her to be effective in instituting the changes she envisioned, her unobtrusive style ensured a lack of recognition. If people don't realize what's happening, they won't give her credit for what she has accomplished.

Not only advancement and recognition, but hiring is affected by [35] ways of speaking. A woman who supervised three computer programmers mentioned that her best employee was another woman whom she had hired over the objections of her own boss. Her boss had preferred a male candidate, because he felt the man would be better able to step into her supervisory role if needed. But she had taken a dislike to the male candidate. For one thing, she had felt he was inappropriately flirtatious with her. But most important, she had found him arrogant, because he spoke as if he already had the job, using the pronoun "we" to refer to the group that had not yet hired him.

I have no way of knowing whether the woman hired was indeed [36] the better of these two candidates, or whether either she or the man was well suited to assume the supervisory role, but I am intrigued that the male boss was impressed with the male candidate's take-charge self-presentation, while the woman supervisor was put off by it. And it seems quite likely that whatever it was about his way of talking that struck her as arrogant was exactly what led her boss to conclude that this man would be better able to take over her job if needed.

This example brings to mind a small item in an unusual mem- [37] oire: the autobiography of an Australian woman with autism. In her remarkable memoir *Somebody Somewhere*, Donna Williams explains that although her autism made it difficult for her to process language, she managed to function in the world by mimicking the speech she heard around her. However, she regarded her successful performances not as her own doing but as the work of two imaginary personas, Carol and Willie. Although there is no evidence that Williams herself thought of these two "characters" (as she called them) as female and male, when reading her account of the kinds of things they could say and do, I repeatedly noticed that Carol performed stereotypically female behavior (she cocked her head, filled the air with social chatter, and, above all, smiled), while Willie played the stereotypically male part (he was strong, detached, and accumulated facts to impress people). So it struck me as amusing, but also troubling, when I read in Williams's memoir that it was Willie who went for interviews but Carol who held down jobs. This is not to imply that men do not deserve the jobs they get, but that ways of talking typically associated with men are more likely to impress many job interviewers as well as those making decisions about promotions to managerial levels.

I believe these patterns explain why it is common to hear that a 38 particular woman lacks confidence or that a particular man is arrogant. Though we think of these as individual weaknesses, underconfidence and arrogance are disproportionately observed in women and men respectively, because they result from an overabundance of ways of speaking that are expected of females and males. Boys are expected to put themselves forward, emphasize the qualities that make them look good, and deemphasize those that would show them in a less favorable light. Too much of this is called arrogance. Girls are expected to be "humble"—not try to take the spotlight, emphasize the ways they are just like everyone else, and deemphasize ways they are special. A woman who does this really well comes off as lacking in confidence. Ironically, those who learn the lessons best are most in danger of falling into traps laid by conversational conventions.

Working with the Text

1. According to Tannen, what are the major differences between "male-style" uses of language and "female-style" uses? How do these differences lead to misunderstandings on the job?

2. What researchers does Tannen cite? What specific work by those researchers does she use to develop her points? What point does each researcher help her make?

3. Tannen acknowledges that there may be limits to her theories about men's and women's styles of communicating. What are they?

4. Tannen uses many "hypothetical" cases that may or may not be based on fact: Amy and Donald, Maureen and Harold, two unnamed co-workers trying to divide the duties of a marketing survey, a supervisor of computer programmers. Why does she use examples like these? Do you find them effective? Why or why not?

5. How would you characterize Tannen's style of language compared to some of the other essays in this chapter, especially those by Patricia Williams, Stephen Jay Gould, and Emily Martin?

Working beyond the Text

1. Tannen asserts that "workplaces that have previously had men in positions of power have already established male-style interaction as the norm." Using her definitions, characterize the language style of any place where you've worked as "male-style" or "female-style." Give concrete examples of interactions.

2. Would you agree with Tannen that when it comes to speaking with confidence, "women are more likely to downplay their certainty, men more likely to downplay their doubts"? Explain your answer with examples from your own experience.

3. Tannen says that "women are more likely to speak in the styles that are less effective in getting recognized and promoted," or even hired in the first place. If this is true, what solutions can you suggest?

4. Tannen explains differences in communication styles in terms of gender: "male-style" and "female-style." Can you think of other ways to explain possible differences in communication styles, and possible conflicts or miscommunications arising from those different styles?

Getting Close to the Machine

Ellen Ullman

Ellen Ullman is a software engineer, consultant, and editor who lives in San Francisco. She has published articles and essays about computers in magazines such as *Byte* and *PC World*. This essay, which appeared in *Harper's* (June 1995), is an excerpt from "Out of Time: Reflections on the Programming Life." The longer version is a chapter in an anthology entitled *Resisting the Virtual Life* (1995). Ullman reflects on her experience as a computer programmer, wondering if the cold, mechanical, asocial nature of computer programming is becoming a model for social behavior in our country.

People imagine that computer programming is logical, a process 1 like fixing a clock. Nothing could be further from the truth. Programming is more like an illness, a fever, an obsession. It's like riding a train and never being able to get off.

The problem with programming is not that the computer is illogi- 2 cal—the computer is terribly logical, relentlessly literal. It demands that the programmer explain the world on its terms; that is, as an algorithm that must be written down in order, in a specific syntax, in a strange language that is only partially readable by regular human beings. To program is to translate between the chaos of human life and the rational, line-by-line world of computer language.

When you program, reality presents itself as thousands of details, 3 millions of bits of knowledge. This knowledge comes at you from one perspective and then another, then comes a random thought, then you remember something else important, then you reconsider that idea with a what-if attached. For example, try to think of everything you know about something as simple as an invoice. Now try to tell an idiot how to prepare one. That is programming.

I used to have dreams in which I was overhearing conversations I 4 had to program. Once I dreamed I had to program two people making love. In my dream they sweated and tumbled while I sat looking for the algorithm. The couple went from gentle caresses to ever-deepening passion, and I tried desperately to find a way to express the act of love in the C computer language.

When you are programming, you must not let your mind wander. 5 As the human-world knowledge tumbles about in your head, you must keep typing, typing. You must not be interrupted. Any break in your concentration causes you to lose a line here or there. Some bit comes, then—oh no, it's leaving, please come back. But it may not come back. You may lose it. You will create a bug and there's nothing you can do about it.

People imagine that programmers don't like to talk because they 6 prefer machines to people. This is not completely true. Programmers don't talk because they must not be interrupted.

This need to be uninterrupted leads to a life that is strangely 7 asynchronous to the one lived by other human beings. It's better to send e-mail to a programmer than to call. It's better to leave a note on the chair than to expect the programmer to come to a meeting. This is because the programmer must work in mind time while the phone rings and the meetings happen in real time. It's not just ego that prevents programmers from working in groups—it's the synchronicity problem. Synchronizing with other people (or their representations in telephones, buzzers, and doorbells) can only mean interrupting the thought train. Interruptions mean bugs. You must not get off the train.

I once had a job in which I didn't talk to anyone for two years. 8 Here was the arrangement: I was the first engineer to be hired by a start-up software company. In exchange for large quantities of stock that might be worth something someday, I was supposed to give up my life.

I sat in a large room with two other engineers and three worksta- 9 tions. The fans in the machines whirred, the keys on the keyboards clicked. Occasionally one of us would grunt or mutter. Otherwise we did not speak. Now and then I would have an outburst in which I pounded the keyboard with my fists, setting off a barrage of beeps. My colleagues might have looked up, but they never said anything.

Real time was no longer compelling to me. Days, weeks, months, 10 and years came and went without much change in my surroundings. Surely I was aging. My hair must have grown, I must have cut it, it must have slowly become grayer. Gravity must have been working on my late-thirties body, but I didn't pay attention.

What was compelling was the software. I was making something 11 out of nothing, I thought, and I admit that the software had more life for me during those years than a brief love affair, my friends, my cat, my house, or my neighbor who was stabbed and nearly killed by her husband. One day I sat in a room by myself, surrounded by computer monitors. I remember looking at the screens and saying, "Speak to me."

I was creating something called a device-independent interface li- 12 brary. ("Creating"—that is the word we used, each of us a genius in the attic.) I completed the library in two years and left the company. Five years later, the company's stock went public, and the original arrangement was made good: the engineers who stayed—the ones who had given seven years of their lives to the machine—became very, very wealthy.

If you want money and prestige, you need to write code that only 13 machines or other programmers understand. Such code is called "low." In regular life, "low" usually signifies something bad. In programming, "low" is good. Low means that you are close to the machine.

If the code creates programs that do useful work for regular 14 human beings, it is called "high." Higher-level programs are called "applications." Applications are things that people use. Although it would seem that usefulness is a good thing, direct people-use is bad from a programmer's point of view. If regular people, called "users," can understand the task accomplished by your program, you will be paid less and held in lower esteem.

A real programmer wants to stay close to the machine. The ma- 15 chine means midnight dinners of Diet Coke. It means unwashed clothes and bare feet on the desk. It means anxious rides through mind time that have nothing to do with the clock. To work on things used only by machines or other programmers—that's the key. Programmers and machines don't care how you live. They don't care when you live. You can stay, come, go, sleep—or not. At the end of the project looms a deadline, the terrible place where you must get off the train. But in between, for years at a stretch, you are free: free from the obligations of time.

I once designed a graphical user interface with a man who wouldn't 16 speak to me. My boss hired him without letting anyone else sit in on the interview. My boss lived to regret it.

I was asked to brief my new colleague with the help of the third 17
member of our team. We went into a conference room, where my coworker and I filled two white boards with lines, boxes, circles, and ar-
rows while the new hire watched. After about a half hour, I noticed
that he had become very agitated.

"Are we going too fast?" I asked him.   18

"Too much for the first day?" asked my colleague.   19

"No," said our new man, "I just can't do it like this."   20

"Do what?" I asked. "Like what?"   21

His hands were deep in his pockets. He gestured with his elbows. 22
"Like this," he said.

"You mean design?" I asked.   23

"You mean in a meeting?" asked my colleague.   24

No answer from the new guy. A shrug. Another elbow motion.   25

Something terrible was beginning to occur to me. "You mean talk- 26
ing?" I asked.

"Yeah, talking," he said. "I can't do it by talking."   27

By this time in my career, I had met many strange software engi- 28
neers. But here was the first one who wouldn't talk at all. We had a lot
of design work to do. No talking was certainly going to make things
difficult.

"So how *can* you do it?" I asked.   29

"Mail," he said. "Send me e-mail."   30

Given no choice, we designed a graphical user interface by e-mail. 31
Corporations across North America and Europe are still using a system designed by three people in the same office who communicated
via computer, one of whom barely spoke at all.

Pretty graphical interfaces are commonly called "user-friendly." 32
But they are not really your friends. Underlying every user-friendly
interface is terrific contempt for the humans who will use it.

The basic idea of a graphical interface is that it will not allow any- 33
thing alarming to happen. You can pound on the mouse button, your
cat can run across it, your baby can punch it, but the system should
not crash.

To build a crash-proof system, the designer must be able to imag- 34
ine—and disallow—the dumbest action possible. He or she has to
think of every single stupid thing a human being could do. Gradually,
over months and years, the designer's mind creates a construct of the
user as an imbecile. This image is necessary. No crash-proof system
can be built unless it is made for an idiot.

The designer's contempt for your intelligence is mostly hidden 35
deep in the code. But now and then the disdain surfaces. Here's a
small example: You're trying to do something simple such as copying
files onto a diskette on your Mac. The program proceeds for a while,
then encounters an error. Your disk is defective, says a message, and

below the message is a single button. You absolutely must click this button. If you don't click it, the program will hang there indefinitely. Your disk is defective, your files may be bollixed up, but the designer leaves you only one possible reply. You must say, "OK."

The prettier the user interface, and the fewer replies the system al- 36 lows you to make, the dumber you once appeared in the mind of the designer. Soon, everywhere we look, we will see pretty, idiot-proof interfaces designed to make us say, "OK." Telephones, televisions, sales kiosks will all be wired for "interactive," on-demand services. What power—demand! See a movie, order seats to a basketball game, make hotel reservations, send a card to mother—all of these services will be waiting for us on our televisions or computers whenever we want them, midnight, dawn, or day. Sleep or order a pizza: it no longer matters exactly what we do when. We don't need to involve anyone else in the satisfaction of our needs. We don't even have to talk. We get our services when we want them, free from the obligations of regularly scheduled time. We can all live, like programmers, close to the machine. "Interactivity" is misnamed. It should be called "asynchrony": the engineering culture come to everyday life.

The very word "interactivity" implies something good and wonder- 37 ful. Surely a response, a reply, an answer is a positive thing. Surely it signifies an advance over something else, something bad, something that doesn't respond. There is only one problem: what we will be interacting with is a machine. We will be "talking" to programs that are beginning to look surprisingly alike; each has little animated pictures we are supposed to choose from, like push buttons on a toddler's toy. The toy is meant to please us. Somehow it is supposed to replace the rewards of fumbling for meaning with a mature human being, in the confusion of a natural language, together, in a room, within touching distance.

As the computer's pretty, helpful face (and contemptuous under- 38 lying code) penetrates deeper into daily life, the cult of the engineer comes with it. The engineer's assumptions and presumptions are in the code. That's the purpose of the program, after all: to sum up the intelligence and intentions of all the engineers who worked on the system over time—tens and hundreds of people who have learned an odd and highly specific way of doing things. The system reproduces and re-enacts life as engineers know it: alone, out of time, disdainful of anyone far from the machine.

Working with the Text

1. Ullman explores a very specific "on-the-job" language: the "code" used in computer programming. According to Ullman, how does this type of language differ from everyday human languages?

2. What is the point of the dreams Ullman describes in her fourth paragraph? What point is she making about computers, computer language, and human life?

3. According to Ullman, what does "getting close to the machine" do to a human being's sense of time?

4. Ullman tells specific anecdotes from her life as a programmer. What are they? How do they help her make her points clear?

5. Ullman teaches her readers several special jargon words from her profession, such as "low" and "high" code, "user" and "user-friendly," and "interactive." Why do you suppose she feels the need to use these words in order to get her point across? What is the point she gets across with these words?

Working beyond the Text

1. What part do computers play in your everyday life? Where do you encounter them in school, on the job, in the world? Do you ever worry, as Ullman does in her last three paragraphs, about the effects of computers on human life?

2. Have you ever spent hours on end in front of a computer with no human contact, as Ullman says she and other computer programmers do? What were you working on? Did you notice any of the antisocial effects that Ullman mentions are common among programmers? What are the possible costs of "getting close to the machine"?

3. Are you "computer literate," or are you the kind of person Ullman and her fellow programmers label as "idiots"? If you have ever written any computer programming, show the lines of code you wrote and explain what they mean to a complete novice. If you have never written any programming, locate lines of code (in a programming textbook, for example) and reflect on their difference from written lines of everyday human language.

UNIT TWO

PROFESSIONAL LANGUAGE AND THE PUBLIC

The Invisible Discourse of Law

James Boyd White

James Boyd White was born in 1938, and has worked as a lawyer and professor of law since 1965. He now teaches at the University of Michigan in Ann Arbor. His books, including *The Legal Imagination* and *When Words Lose Their Meaning*, reflect his interest in language, meaning, and law. This selection is from White's book entitled *Heracles' Bow: Essays on the Rhetoric and Poetics of the Law* (1985). He explains how legal language is like and (more importantly) unlike everyday language and warns that the differences can lead to misunderstandings and legal trouble for nonlawyers.

My subject today is "legal literacy," but to put it that way requires 1 immediate clarification, for that phrase has a wide range of possible meanings, with many of which we shall have nothing to do. At one end of its spectrum of significance, for example, "legal literacy" means full competence in legal discourse, both as reader and as writer. This kind of literacy is the object of a professional education, and it requires not only a period of formal schooling but years of practice as well. Indeed, as is also the case with other real languages, the ideal of perfect competence in legal language can never be attained. The practitioner is always learning about his or her language and about the world, is in a sense always remaking both, and these processes never come to an end. What this sort of professional literacy entails, and how it is to be talked about, are matters of interest to lawyers and law teachers, but are not my subject here. The other end of the spectrum of "legal literacy" is the capacity to recognize legal words and locutions as foreign to oneself, as part of the World of Law. A person literate in this minimal sense would know that there was a world of language and action called "law," but little more about it: certainly not enough to have any real access to it.

Between these extremes is another possible meaning of "legal literacy": that degree of competence in legal discourse required for 2 meaningful and active life in our increasingly legalistic and litigious culture. The citizen who was ideally literate in this sense would not be expected to know how to draft deeds and wills or to try cases or to manage the bureaucratic maze, but would know when and how to call upon the specialists who can do these things. More important, in the rest of life such a person would be able to protect and advance his or her own interests: for example in dealing with a landlord or a tenant, or in interactions with the police, with the zoning commission, or with the Social Security Administration. He or she would be able not only to follow but to evaluate news reports and periodical literature dealing with legal matters, from Supreme Court decisions to House Committee Reports; and to function effectively in positions of responsibility and leadership (say as an elected member of a school board, or as chair of a neighborhood association, or as a member of a zoning board or police commission). The ideal is that of a fully competent and engaged citizen, and it is a wholly proper one to keep before us.

But this ideal is for our purposes far too inclusive, for however 3 one defines "legal literacy," such a figure possesses a great deal in addition to that: he or she has a complete set of social, intellectual, and political relations and capacities. But perhaps we can meaningfully ask: what is the "legal literacy" that such an ideal figure would have? How could this sort of competence be taught? What seem to be the natural barriers to its acquisition? In the first part of this essay I deal with these questions, but in reverse order: I began by identifying those features of legal discourse that make it peculiarly difficult for the nonlawyer to understand and to speak; I then suggest some ways in which those features might be made comprehensible and manageable, and their value and function appreciated.

It is a common experience for a nonlawyer to feel that legal lan- 4 guage is in a deep sense foreign: not only are its terms incomprehensible, but its speakers seem to have available to them a repertoire of moves that are denied the rest of us. We neither understand the force of their arguments nor know how to answer them. But the language is, if possible, worse than merely foreign: it is an unpredictable, exasperating, and shifting mixture of the foreign and the familiar. Much of what lawyers say and write is after all intelligible to the nonlawyer, who can sometimes speak in legally competent ways. But at any moment things can change without notice: the language slides into the incomprehensible, and the nonlawyer has no idea how or why the shift occurred. This is powerfully frustrating, to say the least.

But it is more than frustrating, for it entails an increasingly impor- 5 tant disability, almost a disenfranchisement. At one time in our history it could perhaps have been assumed that a citizen did not need to have any specialized knowledge of law, for our law was a common law that reflected the customs and expectations of the people to such a degree that ordinary social competence was normally enough for effectiveness in the ordinary enterprises of life. No special legal training was required. But in our increasingly bureaucratic and legalistic world, this seems less and less the case: frustrated citizens are likely to feel that their lives are governed by language—in leases, in form contracts, or in federal or state regulations—that they cannot understand. Who, for example, can read and understand an insurance contract, or a pension plan? An OSHA or IRS regulation? Yet these govern our lives, and are even said in some sense to have the standing of our own acts: either directly, as in the case of contracts we sign, or indirectly, as in the case of laws promulgated by officials who represent us. In a democracy this unintelligibility is doubly intolerable, for "We the people" are supposed to be competent both as voters to elect the lawmakers, and as jurors to apply the laws, and we cannot do these things if we cannot understand the law.

What can explain this flickering pattern of intelligibility and unintelligibility, the stroboscopic alternation of the familiar with the strange? The most visible and frequently denounced culprits are the arcane vocabulary of the law and the complicated structure of its sentences and paragraphs. This leads some to ask: why can lawyers not be made to speak in words we recognize and in sentences we can understand? This would enable the ordinary citizen to become competent as a reader of law, and even as a legal speaker. Our political method of democracy and its moral premise of equality demand no less. It may be, indeed, that the only actual effect of this obfuscating legal jargon is to maintain the mystique of the legal profession, and if that mystique is destroyed so much better. 6

Impulses such as these have given rise to what is known as the Plain English Movement, which aims at a translation of legal language into comprehensible English. This movement has had practical effects. At the federal level, for example, one of President Carter's first actions was to order that all regulations be cast in language intelligible to the ordinary citizen, and New York and other states have passed laws requiring that state regulations and form contracts meet a similar standard. 7

If such directives were seriously regarded, they might indeed reduce needless verbosity and obscurity, and streamline unwieldy legal sentences. But even if they succeeded in these desirable goals, they would not solve the general problem they address, for, as I will try to show, the most serious obstacles to comprehensibility are not the vocabulary and sentence structure employed in the law, but the unstated conventions by which the language operates: what I call the "invisible discourse" of the law. Behind the words, that is, are expectations about the ways in which they will be used, expectations that do not find explicit expression anywhere but are part of the legal culture that the 8 surface language simply assumes. These expectations are constantly at work, directing argument, shaping responses, determining the next move, and so on. Their effects are everywhere, but they themselves are invisible. It is these conventions, not the diction, that primarily determine the mysterious character of legal speech and literature—not the "vocabulary" of the law, but what might be called its "cultural syntax."

In what follows I will first identify those features of what I call the "cultural syntax" of legal language that seem most radically to differentiate it from ordinary speech. I will then outline some methods by which I think students can be taught to become at least somewhat literate in a language that works in these ways.

Many of the special difficulties of legal language derive from the fact that at the center of most legal conversations will be found a form we call the legal rule. Not so general as to be a mere maxim or platitude (though we have those in the law, too), nor so specific as to be a mere order or command (though there are legal versions of these), the legal rule is a directive of intermediate generality. It establishes relations among classes of objects, persons, and events: "All A are [or: shall be] B"; or, "If A, then B." Examples would include the following:

> Burglary consists of breaking and entering a dwelling house in the nighttime with intent to commit a felony therein. A person convicted of burglary shall be punished by imprisonment not to exceed 5 years.

> Unless otherwise ordered by the court or agreed by the parties, a former husband's obligation to pay alimony terminates upon the remarriage of his former wife.

Legal conversations about rules such as these have three characteristics that tend to mystify and confuse the nonlawyer. The first of these is that the form of the legal rule misleads the ordinary reader into expecting that once it is understood, its application will be very simple. The rules presented above, for example, have a plain and authoritative air and seem to contemplate no difficulty whatever in their application. (Notice that with the possible exception of the word "felony," there is nothing legalistic in their diction.) One will simply look at the facts and determine whether or not the specified conditions exist: If so, the consequence declared by the rule will follow; if not, it will not. "Did she remarry? Then the alimony stops." Nothing to it, the rule seems to say: just look at the world and do what we tell you. It calls for nothing more than a glance to check the name against the reality, followed by obedience to a plain directive.

In practice of course the rule does not work so simply, or not always. Is it "breaking and entering" if the person pushes open a screen door but has not yet entered the premises? Is a garage with a loft used as an apartment a "dwelling house"? Is dusk "nighttime"? Is a remarriage that is later annulled a "remarriage" for the purpose of terminating prior alimony? Or what if there is no formal remarriage but the ex-wife has a live-in boyfriend? These questions do not answer themselves but require thought and conversation of a complex kind, of which no hint is expressed in the rule itself.

Of course there will be some cases so clear that no one could reasonably argue about the meaning of the words, and in these cases the rule will work in a fairly simple and direct fashion. This is in fact our experience of making most rules work: we can find out what to do to get a passport, we know what the rules of the road require, we can figure out when we need a building permit, and so on. But these are occasions of rules-obedience for which no special social or intellectual competence is required.

One way to identify what is misleading about the form of a legal rule might be to say that it appears to be a language of description, which works by a simple process of comparison, but in cases of any difficulty it is actually a language of judgment, which works in ways that find no expression in the rule itself. In such cases the meaning of its terms is not obvious, as the rule seems to assume, but must be determined by a process of interpretation and judgment to which the rule gives no guidance whatever. The discourse by which it works is in this sense invisible.

The second mystifying feature of the legal rule is that its form is likely to mislead the reader into thinking that the kind of reasoning it requires (and makes possible) is deductive in character. A legal rule looks rather like a rule of geometry, and we naturally expect it to work like one. For example, when the meaning of a term in a rule is unclear—say "dwelling house" or "nighttime" in the burglary statute—we expect to find a stipulative definition somewhere else (perhaps in a special section of the statute) that will define it for us, just as Euclid tells us the meaning of his essential terms. Or if there is no explicit definition, we expect there to be some other rule, general in form, which when considered in connection with our rule will tell us what it must mean. But we look for such definitions and such rules often in vain, and when we find them they often prove to be of little help.

Suppose for example the question is whether a person who is caught breaking into a garage that has a small apartment in the loft can be convicted of burglary: does a statutory definition of "dwelling house" as "any residential premises" solve the problem? Or suppose one finds in the law dealing with mortgages a definition of "dwelling house" that plainly does (or does not) cover the garage with the loft: does that help? Upon reflection about the purpose of the burglary statute, which is to punish a certain kind of wrongdoing, perhaps "dwelling house" will suddenly be seen to have a subjective or moral dimension, and properly mean: "place where the actor knows that people are living" or, if that be thought too lenient, "place where he has reason to believe that people are living."

Or consider the annulment example. Suppose one finds a statu- 17 tory statement that "an annulled marriage is a nullity at law." Does that mean that the duty to make alimony payments revives upon the annulment of the wife's second marriage? Even if the annulment takes place fifteen years after her second wedding? Or suppose that there is another statute, providing that "alimony may be awarded in an annulment proceeding to the same extent as in a divorce proceeding"? This would mean that the wife could get alimony from her second husband, and if the question is seen in terms of fairness among the parties, this opportunity would be highly relevant to whether or not her earlier right to alimony has expired.

The typical form of the legal rule thus seems to invite us to think 18 that in reading it our main concern will be with the relations among propositions, as one rule is related to others by the logical rules of non-contradiction and the like, and that the end result of every intellectual operation will be determined by the rules of deduction.

In fact the situation could hardly be more different. Instead of each 19 term having a meaning of the sort necessary for deductive operations to go on, each term in a legal rule has a range of possible meanings, among which choices will have to be made. There is no one right answer to the question whether this structure is a "dwelling house," or that relationship a "remarriage"; there are several linguistically and logically tolerable possibilities, and the intellectual process of law is one of arguing and reasoning about which of them is to be preferred. Of course the desirability of internal consistency is a factor (though we shall soon see that the law tolerates a remarkable degree of internal contradiction), and of course in some cases some issues will be too plain for argument. But the operations that lawyers and judges engage in with respect to legal rules are very different from what we might expect from the form of the rule itself: they derive their substance and their shape from the whole world of legal culture, and draw upon the most diverse materials, ranging from general maxims to particular cases and regulations. The discourse of the law is far less technical, far more purposive and sensible, than the nonlawyer is likely to think. Argument about the meaning of words in the burglary statute, for example, would include argument about the reasons for having such a statute, about the kind of harm it is meant to prevent or redress, and about the degree and kind of blameworthiness it should therefore require. Legal discourse is continuous at some points with moral or philosophic discourse, at others with history or anthropology or sociology; and in its tension between the particular and the general, in its essentially metaphorical character, it has much in common with poetry itself.

These characteristics of legal language convert what looks like a 20
discourse connected with the world by the easy process of naming,
and rendered internally coherent by the process of deduction, into a
much more complex linguistic and cultural system. The legal rule
seems to foreclose certain questions of fact and value, and of course in
the clear cases it does so. But in the uncertain cases, which are those
that cause trouble, it can better be said to open than to close a set of
questions: it gives them definition, connection with other questions,
and a place in a rhetorical universe, and this permits their elaboration
and resolution in a far more rich and complex way than could otherwise be the case. Except in the plainest cases the function of the ordinary meanings of the terms used in legal rules is not to determine a
necessary result but to establish the uncertain boundaries of permissible decision; the function of logic is not to require a particular result by
deductive force, but to limit the range of possibilities by prohibiting
(or making difficult) contradictory uses of the same terms in the same
sentences.

But you have perhaps noticed an odd evasion in that last sentence, 21
and may be wondering: does not the law prohibit inconsistent uses of
the same terms in the same rules? Indeed it does not, or not always,
and this is the last of the three mystifying features of legal discourse
about which I wish to speak.

I have thus far suggested that while the legal rule appears to oper- 22
ate by a very simple process of looking at the world to see whether a
named object can be found (the "dwelling house" or the "remarriage"), this appearance is highly misleading, for in fact the world
often does not present events in packages that are plainly within the
meaning of a legal label. Behind the application of the label is a complex world of reasoning which is in fact the real life of the law, but to
which the rule makes no overt allusion, and for which it gives no guidance, or, more precisely, gives guidance that is misleading. For the
form of the rule often suggests that it should be interpreted and applied by the use of deductive reasoning, an expectation that is seriously incomplete. The real discourse of the law is invisible.

This may seem bad enough, but in practice things are even worse, 23
and for two reasons. First, however sophisticated and complex one's
reasoning may in fact be, at the end of the process the legal speaker is
required after all to express his or her judgment in the most simple binary terms: either the label in the rule fits or it does not. No third possibility is admitted. All the richness and complexity of legal life seems
to be denied by the kind of act in which the law requires it to be expressed. For example, while we do not know precisely how the
"dwelling house" or "remarriage" questions would in fact be argued
out, we can see that the process would be complex and challenging,
with room both for uncertainty and for invention. But at the end of the

process the judge or jury will have to make a choice between two alter-
natives, and express it by the application (or nonapplication) of the
label in question: this is, or is not, a "dwelling house." In this way the
legal actors are required to act as if the legal world really were as simple as the rule misleadingly pretends it is. Everything is reduced to a
binary choice after all.

Second, it seems that the force of this extreme reductionism cannot 24
be evaded by giving the terms of legal rules slightly different meanings in different contexts, for the rudiments of logic and fairness alike
require that the term be given the same meaning each time it is used,
or the system collapses into incoherence and injustice. The most
basic rule of logic (the rule of noncontradiction) and the most basic
rule of justice (like results in like cases) both require consistency of
meaning.

A familiar example demonstrating the requirement of internal 25
consistency in systematic talk about the world is this: "However you
define 'raining,' the term must be used for the purposes of your system such that it is always true that it either is or is not 'raining.'" Any
other principle would lead to internal incoherence and would destroy
the regularity of the discourse as a way of talking about the world. To
put the principle in terms of the legal example we have been using:
however one defines "dwelling house" for purposes of the burglary
statute, it must be used in such a manner that everything in the world
either is or is not a "dwelling house"; and because the law is a system
for organizing experience coherently across time and space, it must be
given the same meaning every time it is used. Logic and fairness alike
require no less.

You will notice that these principles of discourse are very different 26
from those employed in ordinary conversation. Who in real life would
ever take the view that it must be the case that it either is or is not
"raining"? Suppose it is just foggy and wet? If someone in ordinary
life asked you whether it was raining out, you would not expect that
person to insist upon an answer cast in categorical terms, let alone in
categorical terms that were consistent over a set of conversations. The
answer to the question would depend upon the reason it was asked:
does your questioner want to know whether to wear a raincoat?
Whether to water the garden? To call off a picnic? To take a sunbath?
In each case the answer will be different, and the speaker will in no
case feel required to limit his or her response to an affirmation or
negation of the condition "raining." One will speak to the situation as
a whole, employing all of one's resources. And one will not worry
much about how the word "raining" has been used in other conversations, on other occasions, for the convention of ordinary speech is that
critical terms are defined anew each time for the purposes of a particular conversation, not as part of a larger system.

What is distinctive about conversations about the meaning of rules 27
is thus their systematic character: terms are defined not for the purposes of a particular conversation, but for a class of conversations, and
the principle of consistency applies across the class. And this class of
conversations has a peculiar form. In the operation of the rule all experience is reduced to a single set of questions—say whether the elements of burglary exist in this case—each of which must be answered
yes or no. We are denied what would be the most common response in
our ordinary life, which would be to say that the label fits in this way
and not in that, or that it depends on why you ask. The complex
process of argument and judgment that is involved in understanding a
legal rule and relating it to the facts of a particular case is at the end
forced into a simple statement of "application" or "nonapplication" of
a label.

But there is another layer to the difficulty. We may talk about the 28
requirement of consistency as a matter of logic or justice, but how is it
to be achieved? Can we, for example, ensure that "dwelling house"
will be used exactly the same way in every burglary case? Obviously
we cannot, for a number of reasons. We know that different triers of
fact will resolve conflicts of testimony in different ways—one judge or
jury would believe one side, a second the other—and this builds inconsistency into the process at the most basic level, that of descriptive
fact. Also, while the judge may be required to give the same instruction to the jury in every case, the statement of that instruction will be
cast in general terms and to some extent admit a fair variation of interpretation, even where the historical facts are settled. (For example, a
definition of "dwelling house" as "premises employed as a regular
residence by those entitled to possession thereof.") And if the instruction includes, as well it might, a subjective element (such as something
to the effect that the important question is whether the defendant *knew*
he or she was breaking into a place where people were living), there
will be an even larger variation in the application of what is on the surface the same language.

In short, the very generality of legal language, which constitutes 29
for us an important part of its character as rational and as fair, means
that some real variation in application must be tolerated. As the language becomes more general, the delegation of authority to the applier
of the language, and hence the toleration of inconsistency in result, becomes greater. As the language becomes more specific, this delegation
is reduced, and with it the potential inconsistency. But increasing
specificity has its costs, and they too can be stated in terms of consistency. Consider a sentencing statute, for example, that authorizes the
punishment of burglars by sentences ranging from probation to five
years in prison. This delegation of sentencing authority (usually to a
judge) seems to tolerate a wide variation in result. But it depends upon

how the variation is measured. For to insist that all burglars receive the same sentence, say three years in jail, is to treat the hardened repeater and the impressionable novice as if they were identical. That treatment is "consistent" on one measure (burglars treated alike), "inconsistent" on another (an obvious difference among offenders not recognized).

For our purposes the point is this: the two requirements (1) that $_{30}$ terms be defined not for a single conversation but for the class of conversation established by the rule in question, and (2) that the meaning given words be consistent through the system, are in practice seriously undercut by a wide toleration of inconsistency in result and in meaning. I do not mean to suggest, however, that either the requirement of consistency or its qualifications are inappropriate. Quite the reverse: it seems to me that we have here a dilemma central to the life of any discourse that purports to be systematic, rational, and just. My purpose has simply been to identify a structural tension in legal discourse that differentiates it sharply from most ordinary speech.

Legal literature is radically distinguished from ordinary language in $_{31}$ another way: by its procedural character. That is, in working with a rule as a lawyer one must not only articulate the substantive questions it is the purpose of the legal rule to define—is dusk "nighttime"? is a bicycle a "vehicle"? etc—but one must also ask a set of related procedural questions, of which very little recognition is usually to be found in the rule itself. For every question of interpretation necessarily involves these procedural questions as well: who shall decide what this language means? Under what conditions or circumstances, and subject to what limits or controls? Why? In what body of discourse are these procedural questions themselves to be thought about, argued out, and decided?

Suppose for example the question is what the word "nighttime" $_{32}$ should mean in the burglary statute; or, to begin not with a rule but with a difficulty in ordinary life, whether the development of a shopping center should be permitted on Brown's farm. It is the professional habit of the lawyer to think not only about the substantive merits of the question, and how he or she would argue it, but also about (1) the person or agency who ought to decide it, and (2) the procedure by which it ought to be decided. Is the shopping center question a proper one for the zoning commission, for the neighbors, for the city as a whole, or for the county court? Is the "nighttime" question one for the judge to decide, for the jury, or—if you think what matters is the defendant's intent in that respect—in part for the defendant himself or herself? Every legal rule, however purely substantive in form, is also by implication a procedural and institutional statement as well, and the lawyers who read it will realize this and start to argue about its meaning in this dimension too. The function of the rule is thus to define not only substantive topics but procedures of argument and debate, questions about the definition and allocation of competencies to act. The rule does this either expressly or by implication, but in either event it calls upon a discourse that is largely invisible to the ordinary reader.

To sum up my point in a phrase, what characterizes legal dis- 33 course is that it is in a double sense (both substantively and procedurally) constitutive in nature: it creates a set of questions that reciprocally define and depend upon a world of thought and action; it creates a set of roles and voices by which meanings will be established and shared. In creating both a set of topics and a set of occasions and methods for public speech it does much to constitute us as a community and as a polity. In all of this it has its own ways of working, which are to be found not in the rules that seem to be at the center of the structure, but in the culture that determines how these rules are to be read and talked about.

I have identified some of the special ways of thinking and talking 34 that characterize legal discourse. Far more than any technical vocabulary, it is these conventions that are responsible for the foreignness of legal speech. To put it slightly differently, there is a sense in which one creates technical vocabulary whenever one creates a rule of the legal kind, for the operation of the rule in a procedural system itself necessarily involves an artificial way of giving meaning both to words and to events. These characteristics of legal discourse mean that the success of any movement to translate legal speech into Plain English will be severely limited. For if one replaces a Legal Word with an Ordinary English Word, the sense of increased normalcy will be momentary at best: the legal culture will go immediately to work, and the Ordinary Word will begin to lose its shape, its resiliency, and its familiarity, and become, despite all the efforts of the writer, a Legal Word after all. The reason for this is that the word will work as part of the legal language, and it is the way this language works that determines the meaning of its terms. This is what I meant when I said that it is not the vocabulary of the legal language that is responsible for its obscurity and mysteriousness, but its "cultural syntax," the invisible expectations governing the way the words are to be used.

Working with the Text

1. In the first two paragraphs, White offers three definitions of "legal literacy." What are they? How do they differ? Which one is the focus of the essay?

2. White uses two actual "legal rules" (one defining burglary, the other pertaining to alimony). What points does White make about legal language with these two examples?

3. What does White mean by the "invisible discourse" of the law or the "cultural syntax" of the law? What about legal language is "invisible" to the av-

erage nonlawyer? How does the language of the law help define a "culture" that is "foreign" to nonlawyers?

4. How can you tell that White's audience is not a group of lawyers, but a group of nonlawyers? Point to specific passages in which White acknowledges the identity of his audience and their lack of knowledge of legal language.

Working beyond the Text

1. At one point White says, "Legal discourse is continuous at some points with moral or philosophic discourse, at others with history or anthropology or sociology; and in its tension between the particular and the general, in its essentially metaphorical character, it has much in common with poetry itself." Using White's own explanations, pick just one of the other "discourses" he mentions (philosophy, history, poetry, etc.) and describe what legal language might have in common with it.

2. As a nonlawyer, what did you learn from White's essay that might help you with any legal encounters you may have in the future? What situations do you envision finding yourself in where knowing what you learned from White about legal language might be useful?

3. White asserts that our ability to be good citizens in a democracy is becoming more difficult "in our increasingly bureaucratic and legalistic world" where "frustrated citizens are likely to feel that their lives are governed by language" that they can't understand, such as leases, contracts, and government regulations. Would you agree or disagree? In what ways?

The Median Isn't the Message

Stephen Jay Gould

Stephen Jay Gould is a paleontologist and professor of geology at Harvard University. His well-known columns in *Natural History* magazine deal with a variety of scientific issues, especially evolution and the misuse of scientific methods. Collections of his monthly columns appear in several books, including *Ever Since Darwin, The Panda's Thumb* and *The Mismeasure of Man*. In this essay, from his book *Bully for Brontosaurus* (1980), Gould demonstrates how statistics can be misinterpreted by telling about his discoveries while researching a rare form of cancer with which he had just been diagnosed.

My life has recently intersected, in a most personal way, two of   1
Mark Twain's famous quips. One I shall defer to the end of this essay.
The other (sometimes attributed to Disraeli) identified three species of

mendacity, each worse than the one before—lies, damned lies, and statistics.

Consider the standard example of stretching truth with numbers—a case quite relevant to my story. Statistics recognizes different measures of an "average," or central tendency. The *mean* represents our usual concept of an overall average—add up the items and divide them by the number of sharers (100 candy bars collected for five kids next Halloween will yield 20 for each in a fair world). The *median,* a different measure of central tendency, is the halfway point. If I line up five kids by height, the median child is shorter than two and taller than the other two (who might have trouble getting their mean share of the candy). A politician in power might say with pride, "The mean income of our citizens is $15,000 per year." The leader of the opposition might retort, "But half our citizens make less than $10,000 per year." Both are right, but neither cites a statistic with impassive objectivity. The first invokes a mean, the second a median. (Means are higher than medians in such cases because one millionaire may outweigh hundreds of poor people in setting a mean, but can balance only one mendicant in calculating a median.)

The larger issue that creates a common distrust or contempt for statistics is more troubling. Many people make an unfortunate and invalid separation between heart and mind, or feeling and intellect. In some contemporary traditions, abetted by attitudes stereotypically centered upon Southern California, feelings are exalted as more "real" and the only proper basis for action, while intellect gets short shrift as a hang-up of outmoded elitism. Statistics, in this absurd dichotomy, often becomes the symbol of the enemy. As Hilaire Belloc wrote, "Statistics are the triumph of the quantitative method, and the quantitative method is the victory of sterility and death."

This is a personal story of statistics, properly interpreted, as profoundly nurturant and life-giving. It declares holy war on the downgrading of intellect by telling a small story to illustrate the utility of dry, academic knowledge about science. Heart and head are focal points of one body, one personality.

In July 1982, I learned that I was suffering from abdominal mesothelioma, a rare and serious cancer usually associated with exposure to asbestos. When I revived after surgery, I asked my first question of my doctor and chemotherapist: "What is the best technical literature about mesothelioma?" She replied, with a touch of diplomacy (the only departure she has ever made from direct frankness), that the medical literature contained nothing really worth reading.

Of course, trying to keep an intellectual away from literature works about as well as recommending chastity to *Homo sapiens,* the sexiest primate of all. As soon as I could walk, I made a beeline for Harvard's Countway medical library and punched mesothelioma into the computer's bibliographic search program. An hour later, surrounded by the latest literature on abdominal mesothelioma, I realized with a gulp why my doctor had offered that humane advice. The literature couldn't have been more brutally clear: Mesothelioma is incurable, with a median mortality of only eight months after discovery. I sat stunned for about fifteen minutes, then smiled and said to myself: So that's why they didn't give me anything to read. Then my mind started to work again, thank goodness.

If a little learning could ever be a dangerous thing, I had encountered a classic example. Attitude clearly matters in fighting cancer. We don't know why (from my old-style materialistic perspective, I suspect that mental states feed back upon the immune system). But match people with the same cancer for age, class, health, and socioeconomic status, and, in general, those with positive attitudes, with a strong will and purpose for living, with commitment to struggle, and with an active response to aiding their own treatment and not just a passive acceptance of anything doctors say, tend to live longer. A few months later I asked Sir Peter Medawar, my personal scientific guru and a Nobelist in immunology, what the best prescription for success against cancer might be. "A sanguine personality," he replied. Fortunately (since one can't reconstruct oneself at short notice and for a definite purpose), I am, if anything, even-tempered and confident in just this manner.

Hence the dilemma for humane doctors: Since attitude matters so ₈ critically, should such a somber conclusion be advertised, especially since few people have sufficient understanding of statistics to evaluate what the statements really mean? From years of experience with the

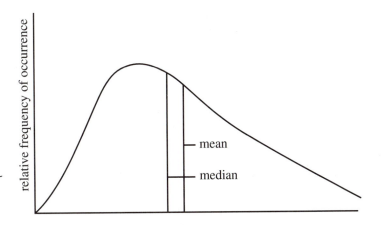

A RIGHT-SKEWED distribution showing that means must be higher than medians, and that the right side of the distribution extends out into a long tail.

small-scale evolution of Bahamian land snails treated quantitatively, I have developed this technical knowledge—and I am convinced that it played a major role in saving my life. Knowledge is indeed power, as Francis Bacon proclaimed.

The problem may be briefly stated: What does "median mortality 9 of eight months" signify in our vernacular? I suspect that most people, without training in statistics, would read such a statement as "I will probably be dead in eight months"—the very conclusion that must be avoided, both because this formulation is false, and because attitude matters so much.

I was not, of course, overjoyed, but I didn't read the statement in 10 this vernacular way either. My technical training enjoined a different perspective on "eight months median mortality." The point may seem subtle, but the consequences can be profound. Moreover, this perspective embodies the distinctive way of thinking in my own field of evolutionary biology and natural history.

We still carry the historical baggage of a Platonic heritage that 11 seeks sharp essences and definite boundaries. (Thus we hope to find an unambiguous "beginning of life" or "definition of death," although nature often comes to us as irreducible continua.) This Platonic heritage, with its emphasis on clear distinctions and separated immutable entities, leads us to view statistical measures of central tendency wrongly, indeed opposite to the appropriate interpretation in our actual world of variation, shadings, and continua. In short, we view means and medians as hard "realities," and the variation that permits their calculation as a set of transient and imperfect measurements of this hidden essence. If the median is the reality and variation around the median just a device for calculation, then "I will probably be dead in eight months" may pass as a reasonable interpretation.

But all evolutionary biologists know that variation itself is nature's 12 only irreducible essence. Variation is the hard reality, not a set of imperfect measures for a central tendency. Means and medians are the abstractions. Therefore, I looked at the mesothelioma statistics quite differently—and not only because I am an optimist who tends to see the doughnut instead of the hole, but primarily because I know that variation itself is the reality. I had to place myself amidst the variation.

When I learned about the eight-month median, my first intellec- 13 tual reaction was: Fine, half the people will live longer; now what are my chances of being in that half. I read for a furious and nervous hour and concluded, with relief: damned good. I possessed every one of the characteristics conferring a probability of longer life: I was young; my disease had been recognized in a relatively early state; I would receive the nation's best medical treatment; I had the world to live for; I knew how to read the data properly and not despair.

Another technical point then added ever more solace. I immedi- 14
ately recognized that the distribution of variation about the eight-
month median would almost surely be what statisticians call "right
skewed." (In a symmetrical distribution, the profile of variation to the
left of the central tendency is a mirror image of variation to the right.
Skewed distributions are asymmetrical, with variation stretching out
more in one direction than the other—left skewed if extended to the
left, right skewed if stretched out to the right.) The distribution of variation had to be right skewed, I reasoned. After all, the left of the distribution contains an irrevocable lower boundary of zero (since mesothelioma can only be identified at death or before). Thus, little space exists
for the distribution's lower (or left) half—it must be scrunched up between zero and eight months. But the upper (or right) half can extend
out for years and years, even if nobody ultimately survives. The distribution must be right skewed, and I needed to know how long the extended tail ran—for I had already concluded that my favorable profile
made me a good candidate for the right half of the curve.

The distribution was, indeed, strongly right skewed, with a long 15
tail (however small) that extended for several years above the eight-
month median. I saw no reason why I shouldn't be in that small tail,
and I breathed a very long sigh of relief. My technical knowledge had
helped. I had read the graph correctly. I had asked the right question
and found the answers. I had obtained, in all probability, that most
precious of all possible gifts in the circumstances—substantial time. I
didn't have to stop and immediately follow Isaiah's injunction to
Hezekiah—set thine house in order: for thou shalt die, and not live. I
would have time to think, to plan, and to fight.

One final point about statistical distributions. They apply only to a 16
prescribed set of circumstances—in this case to survival with mesothelioma under conventional modes of treatment. If circumstances
change, the distribution may alter. I was placed on an experimental
protocol of treatment and, if fortune holds, will be in the first cohort of
a new distribution with a high median and a right tail extending to
death by natural causes at advanced old age.*

It has become, in my view, a bit too trendy to regard the accep- 17
tance of death as something tantamount to intrinsic dignity. Of course
I agree with the preacher of Ecclesiastes that there is a time to love and
a time to die—and when my skein runs out I hope to face the end
calmly and in my own way. For most situations, however, I prefer the
more martial view that death is the ultimate enemy—and I find nothing reproachable in those who rage mightily against the dying of the
light.

*So far so good.

The swords of battle are numerous, and none more effective than 18 humor. My death was announced at a meeting of my colleagues in Scotland, and I almost experienced the delicious pleasure of reading my obituary penned by one of my best friends (the so-and-so got suspicious and checked; he too is a statistician, and didn't expect to find me so far out on the left tail). Still, the incident provided my first good laugh after the diagnosis. Just think, I almost got to repeat Mark Twain's most famous line of all: The reports of my death are greatly exaggerated.**

Working with the Text

1. What is the difference, according to Gould's explanation, between the "mean" and the "median" in statistics? Why is the distinction so important to Gould's argument?

2. Gould offers a graph to explain what he means by the distribution of death by mesothelioma being "right-skewed." Why are the median and the mean in different places on that graph?

3. How does Gould try to make the fine points of statistics clear to his reader? What techniques does he use?

4. We might say that this is an essay about statistics that also incorporates personal material, or a personal essay that includes material about statistics. Which is it, do you think? Which description best fits the overall meaning of the essay?

Working beyond the Text

1. Gould quotes Mark Twain's famous joke about "three species of mendacity" and gives an example of how two politicians might use statistics based on the same facts to create two different meanings. Can you write several other examples of how statistics might lie even more than Twain's "damned lies"?

2. Draw a left-skewed graph and explain its meaning in terms of the number of years a person might survive some disease. Where will the median and the mean appear on that graph and why?

3. Have you ever solved a serious personal problem through reading, as Gould does when he conducts research on his disease? Or could you ever imagine doing it? What would the situation be?

**Since writing this, my death has actually been reported in two European magazines, five years apart. *Fama volat* (and lasts a long time). I squawked very loudly both times and demanded a retraction; guess I just don't have Mr. Clemens's *savoir faire*.

The Egg and the Sperm: How Science Has Constructed a Romance Based on Stereotypical Male-Female Roles

Emily Martin

Emily Martin, born in 1944, teaches anthropology at Johns Hopkins University. Her research and writing often involve both anthropology and biological sciences; she is the author of *The Woman in the Body: A Cultural Analysis of Reproduction.* In the following essay, which appeared in the feminist journal *Signs: Journal of Women in Culture and Society* in 1991, Martin shows how gender stereotypes influence the way scientists describe human reproduction.

The theory of the human body is always a part of a world-picture . . . .The theory of the human body is always a part of a fantasy.[1]

As an anthropologist, I am intrigued by the possibility that culture 1 shapes how biological scientists describe what they discover about the natural world. If this were so, we would be learning about more than the natural world in high school biology class; we would be learning about cultural beliefs and practices as if they were part of nature. In the course of my research I realized that the picture of egg and sperm drawn in popular as well as scientific accounts of reproductive biology relies on stereotypes central to our cultural definitions of male and female. The stereotypes imply not only that female biological processes are less worthy than their male counterparts but also that women are less worthy than men. Part of my goal in writing this article is to shine a bright light on the gender stereotypes hidden within the scientific language of biology. Exposed in such a light, I hope they will lose much of their power to harm us.

Egg and Sperm: A Scientific Fairy Tale

At a fundamental level, all major scientific textbooks depict male 2 and female reproductive organs as systems for the production of valuable substances, such as eggs and sperm.[2] In the case of women, the monthly cycle is described as being designed to produce eggs and pre-

---

[1]James Hillman, *The Myth of Analysis* (Evanston, Ill.: Northwestern University Press, 1972), 220.

[2]The textbooks I consulted are the main ones used in classes for undergraduate premedical students or medical students (or those held on reserve in the library for these classes) during the past few years at Johns Hopkins University. These texts are widely used at other universities in the country as well.

pare a suitable place for them to be fertilized and grown—all to the end of making babies. But the enthusiasm ends there. By extolling the female cycle as a productive enterprise, menstruation must necessarily be viewed as a failure. Medical texts describe menstruation as the "debris" of the uterine lining, the result of necrosis, or death of tissue. The descriptions imply that a system has gone awry, making products of no use, not to specification, unsalable, wasted, scrap. An illustration in a widely used medical text shows menstruation as a chaotic disintegration of form, complementing the many texts that describe it as "ceasing," "dying," "losing," "denuding," "expelling."[3]

Male reproductive physiology is evaluated quite differently. One of the texts that sees menstruation as failed production employs a sort of breathless prose when it describes the maturation of sperm: "The mechanisms which guide the remarkable cellular transformation from spermatid to mature sperm remain uncertain. . . . Perhaps the most amazing characteristic of spermatogenesis is its sheer magnitude: the normal human male may manufacture several hundred million sperm per day."[4] In the classic text *Medical Physiology*, edited by Vernon Mountcastle, the male/female, productive/destructive comparison is more explicit: "Whereas the female *sheds* only a single gamete each month, the seminiferous tubules *produce* hundreds of millions of sperm each day" (emphasis mine).[5] The female author of another text marvels at the length of the microscopic seminiferous tubules, which, if uncoiled and placed end to end, "would span almost one-third of a mile!" She writes, "In an adult male these structures produce millions of sperm cells each day." Later she asks, "How is this feat accomplished?"[6] None of these texts expresses such intense enthusiasm for any female processes. It is surely no accident that the "remarkable" process of making sperm involves precisely what, in the medical view, menstruation does not: production of something deemed valuable.[7]

One could argue that menstruation and spermatogenesis are not analogous processes and, therefore, should not be expected to elicit the same kind of response. The proper female analogy to spermatogenesis, biologically, is ovulation. Yet ovulation does not merit enthusiasm in these texts either. Textbook descriptions stress that all of the ovarian follicles containing ova are already present at birth. Far from being

[3] Arthur C. Guyton, *Physiology of the Human Body*, 6th ed. (Philadelphia: Saunders College Publishing, 1984), 624.

[4] Arthur J. Vander, James H. Sherman, and Dorothy S. Luciano, *Human Physiology: The Mechanisms of Body Function*, 3rd ed. (New York: McGraw Hill, 1980), 483–84.

[5] Vernon B. Mountcastle, *Medical Physiology*, 14th ed. (London: Mosby, 1980), 2:1624.

[6] Eldra Pearl Solomon, *Human Anatomy and Physiology* (New York: CBS College Publishing, 1983), 678.

[7] For elaboration, see Emily Martin, *The Woman in the Body: A Cultural Analysis of Reproduction* (Boston: Beacon, 1987), 27–53.

produced, as sperm are, they merely sit on the shelf, slowly degenerating and aging like overstocked inventory: "At birth, normal human ovaries contain an estimated one million follicles [each], and no new ones appear after birth. Thus, in marked contrast to the male, the newborn female already has all the germ cells she will ever have. Only a few, perhaps 400, are destined to reach full maturity during her active productive life. All the others degenerate at some point in their development so that few, if any, remain by the time she reaches menopause at approximately 50 years of age."[8] Note the "marked contrast" that this description sets up between male and female: the male, who continuously produces fresh germ cells, and the female, who has stockpiled germ cells by birth and is faced with their degeneration.

Nor are the female organs spared such vivid descriptions. One scientist writes in a newspaper article that a woman's ovaries become old and worn out from ripening eggs every month, even though the woman herself is still relatively young: "When you look through a laparoscope . . . at an ovary that has been through hundreds of cycles, even in a superbly healthy American female, you see a scarred, battered organ."[9]

To avoid the negative connotations that some people associate with the female reproductive system, scientists could begin to describe male and female processes as homologous. They might credit females with "producing" mature ova one at a time, as they're needed each month, and describe males as having to face problems of degenerating germ cells. This degeneration would occur throughout life among spermatogonia, the undifferentiated germ cells in the testes that are the long-lived, dormant precursors of sperm.

But the texts have an almost dogged insistence on casting female processes in a negative light. The texts celebrate sperm production because it is continuous from puberty to senescence, while they portray egg production as inferior because it is finished at birth. This makes the female seem unproductive, but some texts will also insist that it is she who is wasteful.[10] In a section heading for *Molecular Biology of the Cell,* a best-selling text, we are told that "Oogenesis is wasteful." The text goes on to emphasize that of the seven million oogonia, or egg

---

[8]Vander, Sherman, and Luciano, 568.

[9]Melvin Konner, "Childbearing and Age," *New York Times Magazine* (December 27, 1987), 22–23, esp. 22.

[10]I have found but one exception to the opinion that the female is wasteful: "Smallpox being the nasty disease it is, one might expect nature to have designed antibody molecules with combining sites that specifically recognize the epitopes on smallpox virus. Nature differs from technology, however: it thinks nothing of wastefulness. (For example, rather than improving the chance that a spermatozoan will meet an egg cell, nature finds it easier to produce millions of spermatozoa.)" (Niels Kaj Jerne, "The Immune System," *Scientific American* 229, no. 1 [July 1973]: 53). Thanks to a *Signs* reviewer for bringing this reference to my attention.

germ cells, in the female embryo, most degenerate in the ovary. Of those that do go on to become oocytes, or eggs, many also degenerate, so that at birth only two million eggs remain in the ovaries. Degeneration continues throughout a woman's life: by puberty 300,000 eggs remain, and only a few are present by menopause. "During the 40 or so years of a woman's reproductive life, only 400 to 500 eggs will have been released," the authors write. "All the rest will have degenerated. It is still a mystery why so many eggs are formed only to die in the ovaries."[11]

The real mystery is why the male's vast production of sperm is not 8 seen as wasteful.[12] Assuming that a man "produces" 100 million (10^8) sperm per day (a conservative estimate) during an average reproductive life of sixty years, he would produce well over two trillion sperm in his lifetime. Assuming that a woman "ripens" one egg per lunar month, or thirteen per year, over the course of her forty-year reproductive life, she would total five hundred eggs in her lifetime. But the word "waste" implies an excess, too much produced. Assuming two or three offspring, for every baby a woman produces, she wastes only around two hundred eggs. For every baby a man produces, he wastes more than one trillion (10^{12}) sperm.

How is it that positive images are denied to the bodies of women? 9 A look at language—in this case, scientific language—provides the first clue. Take the egg and the sperm.[13] It is remarkable how "femininely" the egg behaves and how "masculinely" the sperm.[14] The egg is seen as large and passive.[15] It does not *move* or *journey*, but passively

[11]Bruce Alberts et al., *Molecular Biology of the Cell* (New York: Garland, 1983), 795.

[12]In her essay "Have Only Men Evolved?" (in *Discovering Reality: Feminist Perspectives on Epistemology, Metaphysics, Methodology, and Philosophy of Science*, ed. Sandra Harding and Merrill B. Hintikka [Dordrecht, The Netherlands: Reidel, 1983], 45–69, esp. 60–61), Ruth Hubbard points out that sociobiologists have said the female invests more energy than the male in the production of her large gametes, claiming that this explains why the female provides parental care. Hubbard questions whether it "really takes more 'energy' to generate the one or relatively few eggs than the large excess of sperms required to achieve fertilization." For further critique of how the greater size of eggs is interpreted in sociobiology, see Donna Haraway, "Investment Strategies for the Evolving Portfolio of Primate Females," in *Body/Politics*, ed. Mary Jacobus, Evelyn Fox Keller, and Sally Shuttleworth (New York: Routledge, 1990), 155–56.

[13]The sources I used for this article provide compelling information on interactions among sperm. Lack of space prevents me from taking up this theme here, but the elements include competition, hierarchy, and sacrifice. For a newspaper report, see Malcolm W. Browne, "Some Thoughts on Self Sacrifice," *New York Times* (July 5, 1988), C6. For a literary rendition, see John Barth, "Night-Sea Journey," in his *Lost in the Funhouse* (Garden City, N.Y.: Doubleday, 1968), 3–13.

[14]See Carol Delaney, "The Meaning of Paternity and the Virgin Birth Debate," *Man* 21, no. 3 (September 1986): 494–513. She discusses the difference between this scientific view that women contribute genetic material to the fetus and the claim of long-standing Western folk theories that the origin and identity of the fetus comes from the male, as in the metaphor of planting a seed in soil.

[15]For a suggested direct link between human behavior and purportedly passive eggs and active sperm, see Erik H. Erikson, "Inner and Outer Space: Reflections on Womanhood," *Daedalus* 93, no. 2 (Spring 1964): 582–606, esp. 591.

"is transported," "is swept,"[16] or even "drifts"[17] along the fallopian tube. In utter contrast, sperm are small, "streamlined,"[18] and invariably active. They "deliver" their genes to the egg, "activate the developmental program of the egg,"[19] and have a "velocity" that is often remarked upon.[20] Their tails are "strong" and efficiently powered.[21] Together with the forces of ejaculation, they can "propel the semen into the deepest recesses of the vagina."[22] For this they need "energy," "fuel,"[23] so that with a "whiplash-like motion and strong lurches"[24] they can "burrow through the egg coat"[25] and "penetrate" it.[26]

At its extreme, the age-old relationship of the egg and the sperm   10 takes on a royal or religious patina. The egg coat, its protective barrier, is sometimes called its "vestments," a term usually reserved for sacred, religious dress. The egg is said to have a "corona,"[27] a crown, and to be accompanied by "attendant cells."[28] It is holy, set apart and above, the queen to the sperm's king. The egg is also passive, which means it must depend on sperm for rescue. Gerald Schatten and Helen Schatten liken the egg's role to that of Sleeping Beauty: "a dormant bride awaiting her mate's magic kiss, which instills the spirit that brings her to life."[29] Sperm, by contrast, have a "mission,"[30] which is to "move through the female genital tract in quest of the ovum."[31] One popular account has it that the sperm carry out a "perilous journey" into the "warm darkness," where some fall away "exhausted." "Survivors" "assault" the egg, the successful candidates "surrounding the prize."[32] Part of the urgency of this journey, in more scientific terms, is that "once released from the supportive environment of the ovary, an

---

[16]Guyton (n. 3), 619; and Mountcastle (n. 5), 1609.

[17]Jonathan Miller and David Pelham, *The Facts of Life* (New York: Viking Penguin, 1984), 5.

[18]Alberts et al., 796.

[19]Ibid., 796.

[20]See, e.g., William F. Ganong, *Review of Medical Physiology*, 7th ed. (Los Altos, Calif.: Lange Medical Publications, 1975), 322.

[21]Albets et al. (n. 11), 796.

[22]Guyton, 615.

[23]Solomon (n. 6), 683.

[24]Vander, Sherman, and Luciano (n. 4), 4th ed. (1985), 580.

[25]Alberts et al., 796.

[26]All biology texts quoted use the word "penetrate."

[27]Solomon, 700.

[28]A. Beldecos et al., "The Importance of Feminist Critique for Contemporary Cell Biology," *Hypatia* 3, no. 1 (Spring 1988): 61–76.

[29]Gerald Schatten and Helen Schatten, "The Energetic Egg," *Medical World News* 23 (January 23, 1984): 51–53, esp. 51.

[30]Alberts et al., 796.

[31]Guyton (n. 3), 613.

[32]Miller and Pelham (n. 17), 7.

egg will die within hours unless rescued by a sperm."[33] The wording stresses the fragility and dependency of the egg, even though the same text acknowledges elsewhere that sperm also live for only a few hours.[34]

In 1948, in a book remarkable for its early insights into these mat- 11 ters, Ruth Herschberger argued that female reproductive organs are seen as biologically interdependent, while male organs are viewed as autonomous, operating independently and in isolation:

> At present the functional is stressed only in connection with women: it is in them that ovaries, tubes, uterus, and vagina have endless interdependence. In the male, reproduction would seem to involve "organs" only.
>
> Yet the sperm, just as much as the egg, is dependent on a great many related processes. There are secretions which mitigate the urine in the urethra before ejaculation, to protect the sperm. There is the reflex shutting off of the bladder connection, the provision of prostatic secretions, and various types of muscular propulsion. The sperm is no more independent of its milieu than the egg, and yet from a wish that it were, biologists have lent their support to the notion that the human female, beginning with the egg, is congenitally more dependent than the male.[35]

Bringing out another aspect of the sperm's autonomy, an article in 12 the journal *Cell* had the sperm making an "existential decision" to penetrate the egg: "Sperm are cells with a limited behavioral repertoire, one that is directed toward fertilizing eggs. To execute the decision to abandon the haploid state, sperm swim to an egg and there acquire the ability to effect membrane fusion."[36] Is this a corporate manager's version of the sperm's activities—"executing decisions" while fraught with dismay over difficult options that bring with them very high risk?

There is another way the sperm, despite their small size, can be 13 made to loom in importance over the egg. In a collection of scientific papers, an electron micrograph of an enormous egg and tiny sperm is titled "A Portrait of the Sperm."[37] This is a little like showing a photo of a dog and calling it a picture of the fleas. Granted, microscopic sperm are harder to photograph than eggs, which are just large enough to see with the naked eye. But surely the use of the term "por-

---

[33]Alberts et al. (n. 11), 804.

[34]Ibid., 801.

[35]Ruth Herschberger, *Adam's Rib* (New York: Pelligrini & Cudaby, 1948), esp. 84. I am indebted to Ruth Hubbard for telling me about Herschberger's work, although at a point when this paper was already in draft form.

[36]Bennett M. Shapiro. "The Existential Decision of a Sperm," *Cell* 49, no. 3 (May 1987): 293–94, esp. 293.

[37]Lennart Nilsson, "A Portrait of the Sperm," in *The Functional Anatomy of the Spermatozoan*, ed. Bjorn A. Afzelius (New York: Pergamon, 1975), 79–82.

trait," a word associated with the powerful and wealthy, is significant. Eggs have only micrographs or pictures, not portraits.

One depiction of sperm as weak and timid, instead of strong and 14 powerful—the only such representation in western civilization, so far as I know—occurs in Woody Allen's movie *Everything You Always Wanted to Know About Sex** But Were Afraid to Ask*. Allen, playing the part of an apprehensive sperm inside a man's testicles, is scared of the man's approaching orgasm. He is reluctant to launch himself into the darkness, afraid of contraceptive devices, afraid of winding up on the ceiling if the man masturbates.

The more common picture—egg as damsel in distress, shielded 15 only by her sacred garments; sperm as heroic warrior to the rescue— cannot be proved to be dictated by the biology of these events. While the "facts" of biology may not *always* be constructed in cultural terms, I would argue that in this case they are. The degree of metaphorical content in these descriptions, the extent to which differences between egg and sperm are emphasized, and the parallels between cultural stereotypes of male and female behavior and the character of egg and sperm all point to this conclusion.

New Research, Old Imagery

As new understandings of egg and sperm emerge, textbook gen- 16 der imagery is being revised. But the new research, far from escaping the stereotypical representations of egg and sperm, simply replicates elements of textbook gender imagery in a different form. The persistence of this imagery calls to mind what Ludwik Fleck termed "the self-contained" nature of scientific thought. As he described it, "the interaction between what is already known, what remains to be learned, and those who are to apprehend it, go to ensure harmony within the system. But at the same time they also preserve the harmony of illusions, which is quite secure within the confines of a given thought style."[38] We need to understand the way in which the cultural content in scientific descriptions changes as biological discoveries unfold, and whether that cultural content is solidly entrenched or easily changed.

In all of the texts quoted above, sperm are described as penetrat- 17 ing the egg, and specific substances on a sperm's head are described as binding to the egg. Recently, this description of events was rewritten in a biophysics lab at Johns Hopkins University—transforming the egg from the passive to the active party.[39]

---

[38]Ludwik Fleck, *Genesis and Development of a Scientific Fact*, ed. Thaddeus J. Trenn and Robert K. Merton (Chicago: University of Chicago Press, 1979), 38.

[39]Jay M. Baltz carried out the research I describe when he was a graduate student in the Thomas C. Jenkins Department of Biophysics at Johns Hopkins University.

Prior to this research, it was thought that the zona, the inner vest- 18
ments of the egg, formed an impenetrable barrier. Sperm overcame the
barrier by mechanically burrowing through, thrashing their tails and
slowly working their way along. Later research showed that the sperm
released digestive enzymes that chemically broke down the zona;
thus, scientists presumed that the sperm used mechanical *and* chemical means to get through to the egg.

In this recent investigation, the researchers began to ask questions 19
about the mechanical force of the sperm's tail. (The lab's goal was to
develop a contraceptive that worked topically on sperm.) They discovered, to their great surprise, that the forward thrust of sperm is extremely weak, which contradicts the assumption that sperm are forceful penetrators.[40] Rather than thrusting forward, the sperm's head was
now seen to move mostly back and forth. The sideways motion of the
sperm's tail makes the head move sideways with a force that is ten
times stronger than its forward movement. So even if the overall force
of the sperm were strong enough to mechanically break the zona, most
of its force would be directed sideways rather than forward. In fact, its
strongest tendency, by tenfold, is to escape by attempting to pry itself
off the egg. Sperm, then, must be exceptionally efficient at *escaping*
from any cell surface they contact. And the surface of the egg must be
designed to trap the sperm and prevent their escape. Otherwise, few if
any sperm would reach the egg.

The researchers at Johns Hopkins concluded that the sperm and 20
egg stick together because of adhesive molecules on the surfaces of
each. The egg traps the sperm and adheres to it so tightly that the
sperm's head is forced to lie flat against the surface of the zona, a little
bit, they told me, "like Br'er Rabbit getting more and more stuck to tar
baby the more he wriggles." The trapped sperm continues to wiggle
ineffectually side to side. The mechanical force of its tail is so weak
that a sperm cannot break even one chemical bond. This is where the
digestive enzymes released by the sperm come in. If they start to
soften the zona just at the tip of the sperm and the sides remain stuck,
then the weak, flailing sperm can get oriented in the right direction
and make it through the zona—provided that its bonds to the zona
dissolve as it moves in.

Although this new version of the saga of the egg and the sperm 21
broke through cultural expectations, the researchers who made the
discovery continued to write papers and abstracts as if the sperm were

---

[40]Far less is known about the physiology of sperm than comparable female substances, which
some feminists claim is no accident. Greater scientific scrutiny of female reproduction has long
enabled the burden of birth control to be placed on women. In this case, the researchers' discovery did not depend on development of any new technology. The experiments made use of glass
pipettes, a manometer, and a simple microscope, all of which have been available for more than
one hundred years.

the active party who attacks, binds, penetrates, and enters the egg. The only difference was that sperm were now seen as performing these actions weakly.[41] Not until August 1987, more than three years after the findings described above, did these researchers reconceptualize the process to give the egg a more active role. They began to describe the zona as an aggressive sperm catcher, covered with adhesive molecules that can capture a sperm with a single bond and clasp it to the zona's surface.[42] In the words of their published account: "The innermost vestment, the *zona pellucida,* is a glyco-protein shell, which captures and tethers the sperm before they penetrate it. . . . The sperm is captured at the initial contact between the sperm tip and the *zona.* . . . Since the thrust [of the sperm] is much smaller than the force needed to break a single affinity bond, the first bond made upon the tip-first meeting of the sperm and *zona* can result in the capture of the sperm."[43]

Experiments in another lab reveal similar patterns of data interpretation. Gerald Schatten and Helen Schatten set out to show that, contrary to conventional wisdom, the "egg is not merely a large, yolk-filled sphere into which the sperm burrows to endow new life. Rather, recent research suggests the almost heretical view that sperm and egg are mutually active partners."[44] This sounds like a departure from the stereotypical textbook view, but further reading reveals Schatten and Schatten's conformity to the aggressive-sperm metaphor. They describe how "the sperm and egg first touch when, from the tip of the sperm's triangular head, a long, thin filament shoots out and harpoons the egg." Then we learn that "remarkably, the harpoon is not so much fired as assembled at great speed, molecule by molecule, from a pool of protein stored in a specialized region called the acrosome. The filament may grow as much as twenty times longer than the sperm head itself before its tip reaches the egg and sticks."[45] Why not call this "making a bridge" or "throwing out a line" rather than firing a har-

22

[41]Jay Baltz and Richard A. Cone, "What Force Is Needed to Tether a Sperm?" (abstract for Society for the Study of Reproduction, 1985), and "Flagellar Torque on the Head Determines the Force Needed to Tether a Sperm" (abstract for Biophysical Society, 1986).

[42]Jay M. Baltz, David F. Katz, and Richard A. Cone, "The Mechanics of the Sperm-Egg Interaction at the Zona Pellucida," *Biophysical Journal* 54, no. 4 (October 1988): 643–54. Lab members were somewhat familiar with work on metaphors in the biology of female reproduction. Richard Cone, who runs the lab, is my husband, and he talked with them about my earlier research on the subject from time to time. Even though my current research focuses on biological imagery and I heard about the lab's work from my husband every day, I myself did not recognize the role of imagery in the sperm research until many weeks after the period of research and writing I describe. Therefore, I assume that any awareness the lab members may have had about how underlying metaphors might be guiding this particular research was fairly inchoate.

[43]Ibid., 643, 650.

[44]Schatten and Schatten (n. 29), 51.

[45]Ibid., 52.

poon? Harpoons pierce prey and injure or kill them, while this filament only sticks. And why not focus, as the Hopkins lab did, on the stickiness of the egg, rather than the stickiness of the sperm?[46] Later in the article, the Schattens replicate the common view of the sperm's perilous journey into the warm darkness of the vagina, this time for the purpose of explaining its journey into the egg itself: "[The sperm] still has an arduous journey ahead. It must penetrate farther into the egg's huge sphere of cytoplasm and somehow locate the nucleus, so that the two cells' chromosomes can fuse. The sperm dives down into the cytoplasm, its tail beating. But it is soon interrupted by the sudden and swift migration of the egg nucleus, which rushes toward the sperm with a velocity triple that of the movement of chromosomes during cell division, crossing the entire egg in about a minute."[47]

Like Schatten and Schatten and the biophysicists at Johns Hopkins, another researcher has recently made discoveries that seem to point to a more interactive view of the relationship of egg and sperm. This work, which Paul Wassarman conducted on the sperm and eggs of mice, focuses on identifying the specific molecules in the egg coat (the zona pellucida) that are involved in egg-sperm interaction. At first glance, his descriptions seem to fit the model of an egalitarian relationship. Male and female gametes "recognize one another," and "interactions . . . take place between sperm and egg."[48] But the article in *Scientific American* in which those descriptions appear begins with a vignette that presages the dominant motif of their presentation: "It has been more than a century since Hermann Fol, a Swiss zoologist, peered into his microscope and became the first person to see a sperm penetrate an egg, fertilize it and form the first cell of a new embryo."[49] This portrayal of the sperm as the active party—the one that *penetrates* and *fertilizes* the egg and *produces* the embryo—is not cited as an example of an earlier, now outmoded view. In fact, the author reiterates the point later in the article: "Many sperm can bind to and penetrate the zona pellucida, or outer coat, of an unfertilized mouse egg, but only one sperm will eventually fuse with the thin plasma membrane surrounding the egg proper (*inner sphere*), fertilizing the egg and giving rise to a new embryo."[50]

The imagery of sperm as aggressor is particularly startling in this case: the main discovery being reported is isolation of a particular molecule *on the egg coat* that plays an important role in fertilization!

---

[46]Surprisingly, in an article intended for a general audience, the authors do not point out that these are sea urchin sperm and note that human sperm do not shoot out filaments at all.

[47]Schatten and Schatten, 53.

[48]Paul M. Wassarman, "Fertilization in Mammals," *Scientific American* 259, no. 6 (December 1988): 78–84, esp. 78, 84.

[49]Ibid., 78.

[50]Ibid., 79.

Wassarman's choice of language sustains the picture. He calls the molecule that has been isolated, ZP3, a "sperm receptor." By allocating the passive, waiting role to the egg, Wassarman can continue to describe the sperm as the actor, the one that makes it all happen: "The basic process begins when many sperm first attach loosely and then bind tenaciously to receptors on the surface of the egg's thick outer coat, the zona pellucida. Each sperm, which has a large number of egg-binding proteins on its surface, binds to many sperm receptors on the egg. More specifically, a site on each of the egg-binding proteins fits a complementary site on a sperm receptor, much as a key fits a lock."[51] With the sperm designated as the "key" and the egg the "lock," it is obvious which one acts and which one is acted upon. Could this imagery not be reversed, letting the sperm (the lock) wait until the egg produces the key? Or could we speak of two halves of a locket matching, and regard the matching itself as the action that initiates the fertilization?

It is as if Wassarman were determined to make the egg the receiving partner. Usually in biological research, the *protein* member of the pair of binding molecules is called the receptor, and physically it has a pocket in it rather like a lock. As the diagrams that illustrate Wassarman's article show, the molecules on the sperm are proteins and have "pockets." The small, mobile molecules that fit into these pockets are called ligands. As shown in the diagrams, ZP3 on the egg is a polymer of "keys"; many small knobs stick out. Typically, molecules on the sperm would be called receptors and molecules on the egg would be called ligands. But Wassarman chose to name ZP3 on the egg the receptor and to create a new term, "the egg-binding protein," for the molecule on the sperm that otherwise would have been called the receptor.[52]

Wassarman does credit the egg coat with having more functions than those of a sperm receptor. While he notes that "the zona pellucida has at times been viewed by investigators as a nuisance, a barrier to sperm and hence an impediment to fertilization," his new research reveals that the egg coat "serves as a sophisticated biological security system that screens incoming sperm, selects only those compatible with fertilization and development, prepares sperm for fusion with the egg and later protects the resulting embryo from polyspermy [a lethal condition caused by fusion of more than one sperm with a single egg]."[53] Although this description gives the egg an active role, that

[51]Ibid., 78.

[52]Since receptor molecules are relatively *immotile* and the ligands that bind to them relatively *motile,* one might imagine the egg being called the receptor and the sperm the ligand. But the molecules in question on egg and sperm are immotile molecules. It is the sperm as a *cell* that has motility, and the egg as a cell that has relative immotility.

[53]Wassarman, 78–79.

role is drawn in stereotypically feminine terms. The egg *selects* an appropriate mate, *prepares* him for fusion, and then *protects* the resulting offspring from harm. This is courtship and mating behavior as seen through the eyes of a sociobiologist: woman as the hard-to-get prize, who, following union with the chosen one, becomes woman as servant and mother.

And Wassarman does not quit there. In a review article for *Science,* 27 he outlines the "chronology of fertilization."[54] Near the end of the article are two subject headings. One is "Sperm Penetration," in which Wassarman describes how the chemical dissolving of the zona pellucida combines with the "substantial propulsive force generated by sperm." The next heading is "Sperm-Egg Fusion." This section details what happens inside the zona after a sperm "penetrates" it. Sperm "can make contact with, adhere to, and fuse with (that is, fertilize) an egg."[55] Wassarman's word choice, again, is astonishingly skewed in favor of the sperm's activity, for in the next breath he says that sperm *lose* all motility upon fusion with the egg's surface. In mouse and sea urchin eggs, the sperm enters at the *egg's* volition, according to Wasserman's description: "Once fused with egg plasma membrane [the surface of the egg], how does a sperm enter the egg? The surface of both mouse and sea urchin eggs is covered with thousands of plasma membrane-bound projections, called microvilli [tiny "hairs"]. Evidence in sea urchins suggests that, after membrane fusion, a group of elongated microvilli cluster tightly around and interdigitate over the sperm head. As these microvilli are resorbed, the sperm is drawn into the egg. Therefore, sperm motility, which ceases at the time of fusion in both sea urchins and mice, is not required for sperm entry."[56] The section called "Sperm Penetration" more logically would be followed by a section called "The Egg Envelops," rather than "Sperm-Egg Fusion." This would give a parallel—and more accurate—sense that both the egg and the sperm initiate action.

Another way that Wassarman makes less of the egg's activity is by 28 describing components of the egg but referring to the sperm as a whole entity. Deborah Gordon has described such an approach as "atomism" ("the part is independent of and primordial to the whole") and identified it as one of the "tenacious assumptions" of Western science and medicine.[57] Wassarman employs atomism to his advantage. When he refers to processing going on within sperm, he consistently

---

[54]Paul M. Wassarman, "The Biology and Chemistry of Fertilization," *Science* 235, no. 4788 (January 30, 1987): 553–60, esp. 554.

[55]Ibid., 557.

[56]Ibid., 557–58. This finding throws into question Schatten and Schatten's description (n. 29 above) of the sperm, its tail beating, diving down into the egg.

[57]Deborah R. Gordon, "Tenacious Assumptions in Western Medicine," in *Biomedicine Examined*, ed. Margaret Lock and Deborah Gordon (Dordrecht, The Netherlands: Kluwer, 1988), 19–56, esp. 26.

returns to descriptions that remind us from whence these activities came: they are part of sperm that penetrate an egg or generate propulsive force. When he refers to processes going on within eggs, he stops there. As a result, any active role he grants them appears to be assigned to the parts of the egg, and not to the egg itself. In the quote above, it is the microvilli that actively cluster around the sperm. In another example, "the driving force for engulfment of a fused sperm comes from a region of cytoplasm just beneath an egg's plasma membrane."[58]

Social Implications: Thinking Beyond

All three of these revisionist accounts of egg and sperm cannot seem to escape the hierarchical imagery of older accounts. Even though each new account gives the egg a larger and more active role, taken together they bring into play another cultural stereotype: woman as a dangerous and aggressive threat. In the Johns Hopkins lab's revised model, the egg ends up as the female aggressor who "captures and tethers" the sperm with her sticky zona, rather like a spider lying in wait in her web.[59] The Schatten lab has the egg's nucleus "interrupt" the sperm's dive with a "sudden and swift" rush by which she "clasps the sperm and guides its nucleus to the center."[60] Wassarman's description of the surface of the egg "covered with thousands of plasma membrane-bound projections, called microvilli" that reach out and clasp the sperm adds to the spiderlike imagery.[61]

These images grant the egg an active role but at the cost of appearing disturbingly aggressive. Images of woman as dangerous and aggressive, the femme fatale who victimizes men, are widespread in Western literature and culture.[62] More specific is the connection of spider imagery with the idea of an engulfing, devouring mother.[63] New data did not lead scientists to eliminate gender stereotypes in their descriptions of egg and sperm. Instead, scientists simply began to describe egg and sperm in different, but no less damaging, terms. 30

Can we envision a less stereotypical view? Biology itself provides 31 another model that could be applied to the egg and the sperm. The cybernetic model—with its feedback loops, flexible adaptation to change, coordination of the parts within a whole, evolution over time,

[58]Wassarman, "The Biology and Chemistry of Fertilization," 558.

[59]Baltz, Katz, and Cone (n. 42 above), 643, 650.

[60]Schatten and Schatten, 53.

[61]Wassarman, "The Biology and Chemistry of Fertilization," 557.

[62]Mary Ellman, *Thinking about Women* (New York: Harcourt Brace Jovanovich, 1968), 140; Nina Auerbach, *Woman and the Demon* (Cambridge, Mass.: Harvard University Press, 1982), esp. 186.

[63]Kenneth Alan Adams, "Arachnophobia: Love American Style," *Journal of Psychoanalytic Anthropology* 4, no. 2 (1981): 157–97.

and changing response to the environment—is common in genetics, endocrinology, and ecology and has a growing influence in medicine in general.[64] This model has the potential to shift our imagery from the negative, in which the female reproductive system is castigated both for not producing eggs after birth and for producing (and thus wasting) too many eggs overall, to something more positive. The female reproductive system could be seen as responding to the environment (pregnancy or menopause), adjusting to monthly changes (menstruation), and flexibly changing from reproductivity after puberty to nonreproductivity later in life. The sperm and egg's interaction could also be described in cybernetic terms. J. F. Hartman's research in reproductive biology demonstrated fifteen years ago that if an egg is killed by being pricked with a needle, live sperm cannot get through the zona.[65] Clearly, this evidence shows that the egg and sperm *do* interact on more mutual terms, making biology's refusal to portray them that way all the more disturbing.

We would do well to be aware, however, that cybernetic imagery 32 is hardly neutral. In the past, cybernetic models have played an important part in the imposition of social control. These models inherently provide a way of thinking about a "field" of interacting components. Once the field can be seen, it can become the object of new forms of knowledge, which in turn can allow new forms of social control to be exerted over the components of the field. During the 1950s, for example, medicine began to recognize the psychosocial *environment* of the patient: the patient's family and it psychodynamics. Professions such as social work began to focus on this new environment, and the resulting knowledge became one way to further control the patient. Patients began to be seen not as isolated, individual bodies, but as psychosocial entities located in an "ecological" system: management of "the patient's psychology was a new entrée to patient control."[66]

The models that biologists use to describe their data can have im- 33 portant social effects. During the nineteenth century, the social and natural sciences strongly influenced each other: the social ideas of Malthus about how to avoid the natural increase of the poor inspired Darwin's *Origin of Species*.[67] Once the *Origin* stood as a description of the natural world, complete with competition and market struggles, it could be reimported into social science as social Darwinism, in order to justify the social order of the time. What we are seeing now is simi-

---

[64]William Ray Arney and Bernard Bergen, *Medicine and the Management of Living* (Chicago: University of Chicago Press, 1984).

[65]J. F. Hartman, R. B. Gwatkin, and C. F. Hutchison, "Early Contact Interactions between Mammalian Gametes *In Vitro*," *Proceedings of the National Academy of Sciences* (U.S.) 69, no. 10 (1972): 2767–69.

[66]Arney and Bergen, 68.

[67]Ruth Hubbard, "Have Only Men Evolved?" (n. 12 above), 51–52.

lar: the importation of cultural ideas about passive females and heroic males into the "personalities" of gametes. This amounts to the "implanting of social imagery on representations of nature so as to lay a firm basis for reimporting exactly that same imagery as natural explanations of social phenomena."[68]

Further research would show us exactly what social effects are being wrought from the biological imagery of egg and sperm. At the very least, the imagery keeps alive some of the hoariest old stereotypes about weak damsels in distress and their strong male rescuers. That these stereotypes are now being written in at the level of the *cell* constitutes a powerful move to make them seem so natural as to be beyond alteration.

The stereotypical imagery might also encourage people to imagine that what results from the interaction of egg and sperm—a fertilized egg—is the result of deliberate "human" action at the cellular level. Whatever the intentions of the human couple, in this microscope "culture" a cellular "bride" (or femme fatale) and a cellular "groom" (her victim) make a cellular baby. Rosalind Petchesky points out that through visual representations such as sonograms, we are given *"images of younger and younger, and tinier and tinier, fetuses being 'saved.'"* This leads to "the point of viability being 'pushed back' *indefinitely."*[69] Endowing egg and sperm with intentional action, a key aspect of personhood in our culture, lays the foundation for the point of viability being pushed back to the moment of fertilization. This will likely lead to greater acceptance of technological developments and new forms of scrutiny and manipulation, for the benefit of these inner "persons": court-ordered restrictions on a pregnant woman's activities in order to protect her fetus, fetal surgery, amniocentesis, and rescinding of abortion rights, to name but a few examples.[70]

Even if we succeed in substituting more egalitarian, interactive metaphors to describe the activities of egg and sperm, and manage to avoid the pitfalls of cybernetic models, we would still be guilty of endowing cellular entities with personhood. More crucial, then, than what *kinds* of personalities we bestow on cells is the very fact that we are doing it at all. This process could ultimately have the most disturbing social consequences.

One clear feminist challenge is to wake up sleeping metaphors in science, particularly those involved in descriptions of the egg and the

---

[68]David Harvey, personal communication, November 1989.

[69]Rosiland Petchesky, "Fetal Images: The Power of Visual Culture in the Politics of Reproduction," *Feminist Studies* 13, no. 2 (Summer 1987): 263–92, esp. 272.

[70]Rita Arditti, Renate Klein, and Shelley Minden, *Test-Tube Women* (London: Pandora, 1984); Ellen Goodman, "Whose Right to Live?" *Baltimore Sun* (November 17, 1987); Tamar Lewin, "Courts Acting to Force Care of the Unborn," *New York Times* (November 23, 1987), A1 and B10; Susan Irwin and Brigitte Jordan, "Knowledge, Practice, and Power: Court Ordered Cesarean Sections," *Medical Anthropology Quarterly* 1, no. 3 (September 1987): 319–34.

sperm. Although the literary convention is to call such metaphors "dead," they are not so much dead as sleeping, hidden within the scientific content of texts—and all the more powerful for it.[71] Waking up such metaphors, by becoming aware of when we are projecting cultural imagery onto what we study, will improve our ability to investigate and understand nature. Waking up such metaphors, by becoming aware of their implications, will rob them of their power to naturalize our social conventions about gender.

Working with the Text

1. Which "stereotypes central to our cultural definitions of male and female" help shape "how biological scientists describe what they discover about the natural world"? In other words, how can science be sexist? Point to specific examples from Martin's essay.
2. What does Martin mean when she says that sexist metaphors in science help to "naturalize our social conventions about gender"? In other words, how does science define what is "natural" not just biologically but also culturally?
3. How does the epigraph from James Hillman that Martin uses help introduce the main idea of her essay? What does she explain that relates to the idea that "The theory of the human body is always part of a fantasy"?
4. Martin's fairly short article has 71 footnotes. Why, do you think? What is her purpose in offering so many citations? What different kinds of works does she cite? How do the different groups of citations help her make her points?

Working beyond the Text

1. Before you read this essay, were you familiar with the familiar "love story" of the sperm and the egg? Where did you learn it? Have you believed its features (active sperm and passive egg, for example) as "fact"? After reading Martin's essay, do you still believe them?
2. Here and there in her essay, Martin gives hints of an alternate "story" to account for the phenomenon of conception. Picking up on these hints and using what you learned about biology from the essay, can you write a description of conception at the cellular level that has none of the sexist implications to which Martin objects?
3. Martin asserts that there are many other sexist "sleeping metaphors" in science in addition to the active sperm/passive egg cultural metaphor. Can you think of any?

[71]Thanks to Elizabeth Fee and David Spain, who in February 1989 and April 1989, respectively, made points related to these.

5

LANGUAGES OF

CULTURAL CRITICISM

INTRODUCTION

As you may have seen in readings from previous chapters, different kinds of language come to us from many sources: from our families and communities, from our early experiences with school, from academic fields we encounter in college, from our jobs. But there is another important source of language in our lives: the culture around us. Each day we are exposed to hundreds of messages from television, radio, newspapers, junk mail, our friends—it's almost impossible to avoid receiving messages from the world around us. Some of the language of what we call "popular culture," especially advertisements that we see or hear over and over, can even become part of our own language: "Just do it." "Just say no." "You've come a long way, baby." "Be all that you can be."

Because it plays such an important role in our lives, some scholars and journalists are beginning to pay serious attention to our everyday culture, including popular culture, creating a field called cultural criticism. Cultural criticism defines and uses language in special ways. It views virtually everything in a culture as a "text" that has its own "language" or way of communicating with us. Cultural critics may look at the language of written texts like catalogs and advertisements, oral or visual texts like songs and television shows, and even objects such as toys and sports. Cultural critics "read" or analyze these kinds of texts to understand what they say about us, in order to understand our culture and ourselves. Why are catalogs from businesses such as J. Crew, Victoria's Secret, the Body Shop, and the Pottery Barn so popular—what kinds of messages are they sending that so many people respond to by buying their clothes and lingerie, their cosmetics and furniture? Or what does a Barbie doll, with her long, silky blond hair, her long, thin legs and curvy body, tell us about our culture's attitude towards women? What does professional wrestling reveal about our culture's feelings about violence and aggression?

Essays in this chapter focus on language in a variety of "texts" from American culture: the language of the self-help movement, the language we use to talk about AIDS, and the language of "hate radio." Other writers in this chapter focus on the language of commercials, clothing catalogs, and popular music. Although the essays talk about different aspects of our culture, they share an interest in language used in everyday life and culture, and an interest in what these types of language tell us about our culture and ourselves. The essays draw conclusions about the effects of these texts on the people that watch, read, and listen to them, and they give insight into the hopes and fears of the people that create them.

―――――――――― **Before You Read** ――――――――――

Before you read any combination of essays in this chapter, you might prepare by doing any of the activities below as either class or small group discussions, or as formal or informal writing assignments. They are designed to help you find out what you already know about the issues discussed by the authors in the chapter, so you have some background for understanding what the authors say.

1. What is "culture"? How many different definitions of the word can you find or create? Which definitions make the most sense in relation to the ideas of "commentary" and "criticism"? That is, how is it possible to "criticize" a "culture"? What would be the purpose of doing so?

2. What is "pop culture"? What aspects of "pop culture" do you know well or participate in? Make a list and compare it with your friends' and classmates' lists. What aspects of pop culture do you share with which people? Are you surprised, for example, at who else listens to rap music or who else watches horror movies?

3. Is there some aspect of culture or pop culture that you take seriously though other people might make fun of it? Examples might be sports, fashion, pop music, romance novels, or comic books. Why do you take it seriously? What "meaning" do you find there that others might not?

4. In addition to the languages we would all recognize as "languages" (English, Spanish, Chinese, etc.), what other "languages" are there? That is, how else do we communicate with each other using systems of organized signs and signals? What other "languages" do you "speak"? After brainstorming a list, choose one "language" and explain it in more detail. Perhaps you can write a "vocabulary" or "grammar" for this "language."

5. Some people say that popular culture is in conflict with high culture, especially school culture and academic languages such as those discussed in Chapter 3. They may complain, for example, that students spend more time watching television than doing homework, and in this way popular culture is linked to a decline in edu-

cation. Do you agree or disagree with this idea? In what ways? How do you balance popular culture and school culture in your own life?

—————————— **After You Read** ——————————

After you read any combination of essays in this chapter, you might follow up by doing any of the activities below as either class or small group discussions, or as formal or informal writing assignments. They are designed to help you extend what you have learned from the authors in the chapter by discovering new perspectives on the chapter's themes on your own.

1. One feature of the "languages of cultural commentary and criticism" that can be observed in the essays in this chapter is a focus on popular culture as being worthy of serious attention. The writers analyze self-help bestsellers, radio talk shows, pop music, even clothing catalogs. Choose an aspect of popular culture yourself, perhaps one you know something about already. Taking it very seriously, try to account for the existence or popularity of the phenomenon. Who is the audience? What do they like about it? What meaning (that they may not recognize themselves) does it hold for them?

2. The writers in this chapter are "cultural critics" in the sense that each examines some small aspect of our culture in order to criticize the culture as a whole. Use two or three of the essays to show how this is possible.

3. The writers in this chapter might call themselves "cultural critics." We often use the word "critic" in a different sense to refer to critics of movies, television, or music. If you have read or heard the work of this second group of critics, usually in the form of movie or music "reviews" from newspapers, magazines, or television, try to say how that kind of "criticism" differs from "cultural criticism." For example, how does Siskel and Ebert's attitude toward movies differ from Miller's attitude toward television or Light's attitude toward rap music?

4. The essays in this chapter suggest that popular culture is not simply entertainment, but is also a powerful shaper of cultural beliefs and values. If we take the essays seriously, it is difficult to "consume" popular culture uncritically. How has your reading of the essays affected your perspective on popular culture? Apply what you learn from one of the essays to a specific aspect of popular culture, such as country music, cop shows, or music videos.

UNIT ONE

THE LANGUAGE OF "DIS-EASE"

Needed: A Radical Recovery

Elayne Rapping

Elayne Rapping is a professor of communications at Adelphi University. Her work often focuses on women, addiction, and the recovery movement. In the following essay, which was originally published in the news commentary magazine *The Progressive* (January 1993), she asserts that the language of the current recovery movement diverts our attention from the real sources (and, therefore, possible solutions) of the rash of psychological problems plaguing the nation.

A recent issue of *Time* magazine ran a piece on Al Gore's frequent   1
use of "recovery talk"—the now widely spoken language of the
Twelve Step/Addiction/Self-Help movement—in his campaign appearances. *The New York Times,* a few weeks earlier, ran a similar piece
about Bill Clinton's frequent references to his experience with family
"dysfunction," drug and alcohol abuse, and therapy.

To which Bush aide Torie Clarke responded—invoking the days   2
when a candidate could easily be defeated by the mere disclosure that
he had sought treatment for emotional problems (Thomas Eagleton) or
by allowing the cameras to see a single tear-filled eye (Edmund
Muskie)—that "real men don't lie on couches."

But, as the Republicans found out, "the times they are a-changin'."   3
"Codependency," wounded "inner children," "adult children" of various kinds of "dysfunctional" parents, are the cultural and, increasingly, the *real* currency of today's marketplace of ideas and things.
Melody Beattie's *Beyond Codependency* and *Codependent No More* were
on *The Times* bestseller list for many months. So were Robin Norwood's *Women Who Love Too Much* and the continuous tumble of John
Bradshaw treatises on every calamity that might befall a person growing up in a dysfunctional family.

Bradshaw offers books, tapes, seminars, and even vacation "recov-   4
ery" cruises for those fortunate enough to have "survived" family dysfunction and also prospered. And the Hazelden addiction empire, famous for leading such notables as Liz Taylor, Kitty Dukakis, and Liza

Minnelli to "recovery"—to name just one of many treatment-centers-turned-million-dollar corporations—also markets everything from greeting cards to key chains, necklaces and bracelets, from coffee mugs (decaf only) to "daily meditation" books, all inscribed with uplifting slogans from the gurus of the movement.

And then there are the electronic media. You can hardly watch a 5 day of daytime talk (and that's a lot of talk these days, what with all the cable clones of Oprah and Phil) without coming up against at least one problem for which the solution turns out to be a twelve-step recovery program. A random sample of freeze frames on any channel-surfing excursion will almost surely hit on one or two talking heads with identification tags like "drug-addicted transsexual prostitute" or "compulsive blinker." And in every case, there will be an "expert" hawking another self-help book with information on how to find the appropriate Anonymous group for this "addiction."

In the last ten years or so, more than seventy made-for-TV movies 6 have dealt with addictive disorders and their family-destroying aftermaths. Lately, more and more of them end with the sufferers attending group meetings where they are seen to weep with relief at having found the "solution" to their "problem."

Just last month, I saw two starring Connie Sellecca. In the first, 7 made in the 1980s, she suffers from bulimia. In the second, brand new, she plays a successful career woman in a "codependent" relationship with a man who is a "sexaholic." In the end, she goes to Codependents Anonymous (CODA) while he, terminally "in denial," goes from bad to worse.

If any of this makes sense to you, if you recognize the language 8 and the gestalt it refers to, you know that this recovery stuff represents a major cultural phenomenon in American life. Nor is it obviously, as too many critics blithely assume, a politically "conservative" (as opposed to "liberal" or "progressive") movement. Not with such left-feminists as Gloria Steinem writing bestsellers on the need for "healing" one's "inner child" and developing the "self-esteem" destroyed by "dysfunctional" family dynamics.

No, traditional political terminology is not so easily applied to this 9 brave New Age world of recovery. Like all totalizing discourses, "recovery thought" reflects a world view that explains and addresses everything, in its own terms. Any troublesome behavior pattern, from shopping "too much" to sleeping "too much" to worrying "too much," can be made to fit the loose definition of "addiction." Any objection or doubt can be answered with the all-purpose dismissal that one must be "in denial."

Do you worry that such self-absorption takes people away from 10 political matters? You are using political activity "addictively" as a way of avoiding "your problem." I have been told so many times, "You can't change the world until you heal yourself" that I don't raise the issue any more. Do you insist that your own moderate, but regular, use of alcohol is a pleasure rather than a problem? You are, so far, "controlling" your addiction, but it will soon "progress" and "become unmanageable." Just wait.

It is this totalizing, politically reductive aspect of the movement 11 that critics—most notably Wendy Kaminer in *I'm Dysfunctional, You're Dysfunctional* and David Rieff in "Victims, All? Recovery, Codependency, and the Art of Blaming Somebody Else," in the October 1991 issue of *Harper's*—most oppose.

Movement people call everyone a "victim" of a "dysfunctional," 12 "abusive" family system: Bradshaw and friends use a widely quoted figure of 96 per cent as their official statistic on dysfunctional families, and most agree with Robin Norwood that virtually everyone in therapy "could use" a twelve-step program. Their critics argue, however, that to do so is to trivialize the idea of "victimization" and "oppression."

"A quick way of seeing just how specific the recovery idea is to 13 prosperous Americans," says Rieff, "is to think how preposterous it would seem . . . to a man whose daughter had just been killed by a terrorist bomb, to someone who was hungry, to someone, anyone, in Croatia, the Soviet Union, or South Africa." And Kaminer agrees. "The recovery movement's cult of victimization mocks the notion of social justice by denying that there are degrees of injustice," she says. "It equalizes all levels of abuse. . . . The personal subsumes the political."

While I agree with much of this argument, I am deeply offended 14 by its tone. Kaminer and Rieff, progressives both, actually ape the smugness and cold-bloodedness of such right-wing Republicans as William F. Buckley Jr. and Pat Buchanan when they dismiss the suffering of everyday people in this vicious world as so much whining and whimpering and suggest that they simply pull themselves up by their Bruno Magli bootstraps and get on with the dirty business of being grownups in a tough world.

"Imagine everyone grappling with their problems and forging 15 their identities, using their own intuitions and powers of analysis," says the tough-minded, I-did-it-my-way Kaminer. That, agrees Rieff, would be facing "the splendor and misery of being an adult."

But this kind of Emersonian self-reliance misses the political point. 16 It assumes that the pain for which so many seek help in the recovery movement is wholly "personal," which it certainly is not. That people drink, eat, take drugs, shop, and spend themselves into oblivion or the poor house; that they starve themselves into fashionability; that they endlessly and compulsively seek sexual conquest and novelty—these are not merely "personal" matters. They have everything to do with capitalism and its effects on daily life and social relations.

The fact is that much of the thinking found in recovery books 17 makes perfect sense, as far as it goes. Bradshaw's analysis of dysfunctional family dynamics actually says a lot of things feminists and leftists have been saying for twenty years. The family isn't working. Patriarchal power relations breed abuses of power, both emotional and physical. They encourage women to feel they can't function without men and to bond with (typically patriarchal) men who won't communicate emotionally and who use the cultural capital they were born with to dominate, manipulate, and exploit those who are less powerful.

The workplace is just as bad. Now that men have gotten into the 18 recovery thing—via Robert Bly and pals—there are almost as many books that use New Left and feminist ideas to decry the emotional toll taken by life in corporate and bureaucratic settings as in the family. Ann Wilson Schaef has built her own empire of books, conferences, consulting gigs, and recovery retreats and hotels to go along with her many bestselling treatises on the "addictive" nature of American society as a whole. Using feminist and New Left ideas, she explains how the stresses of work and politics grow from institutional "male-style" power "addictions" which can only be ended by putting "success" and "work" addicts into their own recovery groups.

Most of the self-help stuff about addiction, unhealthy sexual and 19 child-parent relationships, and self-destructive, compulsive habits uses this kind of Left/feminist model. Much of it reads like a 1972 issue of *Ms.* or *Liberation* magazine.

Except for the political conclusions. There aren't any.   20

Instead, we are given a complete ideological system of explaining 21 human suffering which replaces political and economic forces with biologically determined genetic causes. It offers prayer, group conformity, and the giving up of one's personal and political agency to a "higher power" as an ultimate "cure" for everything.

Since, according to this model, the "disease" of addiction is not 22 only inborn but incurable, there is no help for it but to put oneself—permanently—in the hands of the movement and religiously attend meetings and work one's programs. Once in the movement, one always discovers more addictive tendencies; how could it be otherwise? These are the feelings and behaviors of people trying to live up to the *common* demands of advanced capitalism and to avoid the *common*, socially caused kinds of stress, misery, and loneliness this social system breeds. Lest one be accused of a lingering case of "denial," however, one must forget about trying to change institutions and power relations until one is "healed."

The recovery rhetoric works because it manages to shift attention 23
away from social reality and redefine *actual* political, social, and personal ills and miseries in ways that work to contain and control impulses toward realistic social solutions. In fact, the rhetoric of addiction and recovery has become a subtle form of social control in a world
in which more and more of us are at the ends of our ropes, our wits,
and our emotional resources. Just as the managed-media Gulf war
thwarted Vietnam-style protest by redefining reality in terms of images which masked the actual situation, the recovery movement
works to thwart protest against domestic madness by redefining *that*
reality in ways which keep us from seeing the real situation.

In fact, the discourse of addiction and recovery, now circulated so 24
effectively and ubiquitously through the mass media, can be seen as a
subtler version of the War on Drugs aimed at inner-city, mostly male,
African-Americans. Hard drugs like crack and heroin, it is argued,
lead to street crime and violence, and so we must put users in jail. This
is a form of social control widely accepted as necessary, even though
theorists of the Left and Right agree, more and more, that it is erro-
neous, costly, and ineffective. The real causes of crime and violence
are, after all, the same as the real causes of drug use—poverty and despair. The law-and-order solutions, then, are public-relations smoke-
screens for a society that has never had any intention of ending drug
abuse, only of "controlling" and demonizing it, making it a scapegoat
for systemic-bred social crises.

This PR strategy of keeping us confused and agitated over the 25
mysteriously intractable "drug problem" can be seen—if you look
carefully—in the media's approach to the "softer," middle-class "addictions" so in vogue these days. To watch a talk show about any of
the compulsive disorders is to see a very clever kind of social control
mechanism at work, only this time the socially dangerous "abusers"
being "controlled" are not violent, dark-skinned young criminals but
white middle-class men, women, and teenagers whose inability to
function in the world they find themselves in has become socially
problematic.

These people don't rob banks, of course, but they do get out of 26
control personally. And that leads to problems in the professional
work force, in family stability (which women are depended upon to
maintain), and in the socialization of middle-class youth into productive work habits.

The real "solution" would be to go back to the original Left/femi- 27
nist analyses of these problems and take another look at the ideas
about changing institutions and power relations they laid out. But that
has never been television's way of doing things.

Better to sell Excedrin than find a cure for headaches, after all. So 28
television keeps things up close and personal, within the family unit,

where it seems as though we cause and can therefore solve our own problems, with the help, at most, of (free) self-help groups, private therapy, and mass-market paperbacks. It offers us Nytol, Calgon bubble baths, an occasional trip to Disney World, and now the recovery movement.

On *Oprah* in recent months there have been many examples of 29 how this works, but I'll use just one. A group of people who, as children, were subjected to emotionally painful teasing and ridicule because of the way they dressed were the guests. In the audience were some of the very people who had persecuted them. During the opening segments—when the problematic experiences were recalled—the emotional distress felt by these "adult children" was extreme. After the passage of decades, after their lives had gone in different, adult directions, they still could not recall these incidents without tearing up and stifling sobs.

Oprah's method of handling the situation was, typically, to force a 30 therapeutic confrontation between abusers and victims, in which the persecutors came to acknowledge the effects of their behavior, accept responsibility, and ask forgiveness. This technique, quite moving and useful as far as it goes, was also used recently in Oprah's exemplary prime-time special about sexually abusive fathers and their daughters/victims. It is no small thing to get a grown man to cry on television, acknowledge his sexual abuse of power, and beg his victim not to blame herself even if she can never forgive him.

Nonetheless, here, as in the segment on childhood teasing, the real 31 political issues are not only avoided; they are ideologically reformulated to fit a nonpolitical world view. The children who had been tormented were working-class and poor. Among the hurtful labels used against them—which still pained them to the point of tears—was "white trash." But when the "expert" came on to give closure to the matter, she ignored the entire class basis upon which children shame each other in this materialist, consumer culture for failing to own the right "things." Instead, she advised the victims to find a group (Bad Dressers Anonymous? People Who Cry Too Much?) and "heal your inner child." Given time, I'm sure she would have offered the same advice to the middle-class tormentors who were, by now—judging by their fashionable and expensive clothing—surely in the grip of their own inner-child problems with addictive shopping, workaholism, or credit-card debt.

TV movies about such issues do much the same thing. The co- 32 dependency/sexaholism movie, for example, was actually—in its first half—a good portrayal of the dynamics of a destructive marriage between a successful woman and her insecure, competitive, subtly hostile husband. In the 1970s—when movies like *Alice Doesn't Live Here Anymore* and *An Unmarried Woman* were popular—a woman in this kind of marriage would have gone to a consciousness-raising group, or at least gotten support from friends in leaving the marriage. Today, she is sent to a group where she gets support in "recovering" from a problem that is defined as "hers," not his—and not sexism's.

Or take the case of the prize-winning *Shattered Spirits*, in which 33 Martin Sheen played an alcoholic who abused his children and wife emotionally and jeopardized them economically, until he finally "hit bottom" and agreed to family therapy. There they learned that they were all "sick" members of a "dysfunctional family system." No mention of the economic and power relations that kept the woman and children captive and emotionally complicit in this "sick" system. No mention of the economic and power relations of the demeaning Willy Loman-esque job the man had.

The usefulness of this kind of "help" model in keeping people 34 functioning, just barely, in intolerable, unjust circumstances is obvious. The ideas of these experts and therapists aren't wrong. They do address one level of socially induced suffering and failure. Nor, I am eager to explain, do I underestimate the value and efficacy of therapy, support, and self-help groups in helping us negotiate the treacherous terrain of daily life. These kinds of things are often lifesavers and godsends for people experiencing *any* level of emotional distress.

I am concerned, however, politically and theoretically, with the 35 broader social implications of their theories, taken out of their proper therapeutic context and used, as the media now use them, as panaceas for socially induced troubles.

To suggest, as the media do, that nothing more is needed to keep 36 us happy and at peace is—implicitly—to ensure that nothing changes in the broader structure that causes this suffering and injustice. These groups and experts and dramas turn things upside down logically and insist that our problems are internal and the solutions personal. As the critics say, they do dissolve the political into the personal, but that's only because they deny the political nature of personal problems, as do Kaminer and Rieff themselves.

Instead of simply attacking the recovery movement and alienating 37 millions who have experienced it as a lifesaver, we need to reclaim its ideas as our own and reformulate them in our own politically oriented terms. The social movements of the 1960s did not "fail," as Gloria Steinem suggests, because we were too emotionally damaged to be politically effective. It was never "us" that was the problem. It was the "damaged," "dysfunctional" society itself, and it still is.

In fact, we were too politically effective for comfort. So much so 38 that our ideas and analyses have had to be incorporated and redirected into "self-help" directions in order to contain their very dangerous—still very dangerous—implications. Nor are the many problems addressed by the recovery movement just the whimperings of a bunch of rich, spoiled babies. As Bradshaw and others rightly suggest, they are experienced by the vast majority of Americans these days. The pain and anxiety are real enough. It's the "Higher Power," Savior solutions that are phony.

Working with the Text

1. In her eighth paragraph, Rapping observes, "If any of this makes sense to you . . . you know that this recovery stuff represents a major cultural phenomenon in American life." Before this paragraph, had "any of this stuff" made sense to you? Did you recognize the terms ("codependent," "dysfunctional") and the cultural references ("Oprah and Phil," "made-for-TV movies" about addiction and recovery)? Do you agree that the language of "recovery thought" is widely known and understood?

2. Rapping presents the objections of critics like Wendy Kaminer and David Rieff to the "recovery movement." What are their objections? What does Rapping find lacking in them and why?

3. Rappings' own criticisms of the recovery movement have to do with its "political conclusions. There aren't any." What does she mean? What, ultimately, is wrong with the movement, according to Rapping?

4. Rapping's style in the essay is flippant, even sarcastic: she says that Republicans found out that "the times they are a-changin'" and says that afternoon talk shows may feature a "drug-addicted transsexual prostitute" or a "compulsive blinker." Find other examples of her sarcasm. Why do you think she chooses to be sarcastic in her criticism of the recovery movement?

Working beyond the Text

1. Have you ever participated in a twelve-step program or known anyone who did? In the light of your knowledge of such programs, do you think that Rapping's criticism is justified?

2. Examples of the language of "recovery thought" fill Rapping's essay. Even if you've never participated in a twelve-step program or taken part in a "recovery group," you may use the language of "recovery thought" to describe events in your life. If so, how do you use that language?

3. If you are not familiar with the titles Rapping mentions, such as the best-selling books of Melody Beattie, John Bradshaw, Ann Wilson Schaef, or Robin Norwood, locate one and read it. Do you think it represents the ideas Rapping attributes to the "recovery movement"? Relate passages from Rapping's essay to passages from the book. If you disagree with Rapping's assessment, use the book to show how she might be wrong.

On AIDS

Susan Sontag

Born in 1933, Susan Sontag is a well-known writer of essays, plays, and novels. Much of her writing centers on the way language influences how we look at issues and events. A survivor of breast cancer, Sontag explores the language of disease and illness in her books *Illness as Metaphor* and *AIDS and Its Metaphors* (1987). In this essay, from *AIDS and Its Metaphors*, Sontag examines the way in which the language we use to talk about AIDS shapes our perceptions of the disease and its victims.

"Plague" is the principal metaphor by which the AIDS epidemic is 1 understood. And because of AIDS, the popular misidentification of cancer as an epidemic, even a plague, seems to be receding: AIDS has banalized cancer.

Plague, from the Latin *plaga* (stroke, wound), has long been used 2 metaphorically as the highest standard of collective calamity, evil, scourge—Procopius, in his masterpiece of calumny, *The Secret History*, called the Emperor Justinian worse than the plague ("fewer escaped")—as well as being a general name for many frightening diseases. Although the disease to which the word is permanently affixed produced the most lethal of recorded epidemics, being experienced as a pitiless slayer is not necessary for a disease to be regarded as plaguelike. Leprosy, very rarely fatal now, was not much more so when at its greatest epidemic strength, between about 1050 and 1350. And syphilis has been regarded as a plague—Blake speaks of "the youthful Harlot's curse" that "blights with plagues the Marriage hearse"—not because it killed often, but because it was disgracing, disempowering, disgusting.

It is usually epidemics that are thought of as plagues. And these 3 mass incidences of illness are understood as inflicted, not just endured. Considering illness as a punishment is the oldest idea of what causes illness, and an idea opposed by all attention to the ill that deserves the noble name of medicine. Hippocrates, who wrote several treatises on epidemics, specifically ruled out "the wrath of God" as a cause of bubonic plague. But the illnesses interpreted in antiquity as punishments, like the plague in *Oedipus*, were not thought to be shameful, as leprosy and subsequently syphilis were to be. Diseases, insofar as they acquired meaning, were collective calamities, and judgments on a community. Only injuries and disabilities, not diseases, were thought of as individually merited. For an analogy in the literature of antiquity to the modern sense of a shaming, isolating disease, one would have to turn to Philoctetes and his stinking wound.

The most feared diseases, those that are not simply fatal but trans- 4
form the body into something alienating, like leprosy and syphilis and
cholera and (in the imagination of many) cancer, are the ones that
seem particularly susceptible to promotion to "plague." Leprosy and
syphilis were the first illnesses to be consistently described as repulsive. It was syphilis that, in the earliest descriptions by doctors at the
end of the fifteenth century, generated a version of the metaphors that
flourish around AIDS: of a disease that was not only repulsive and retributive but collectively invasive. Although Erasmus, the most influential European pedagogue of the early sixteenth century, described
syphilis as "nothing but a kind of leprosy" (by 1529 he called it "something worse than leprosy"), it had already been understood as something different, because sexually transmitted. Paracelsus speaks (in
Donne's paraphrase) of "that foule contagious disease which then had
invaded mankind in a few places, and since overflowes in all, that for
punishment of generall licentiousnes God first inflicted that disease."
Thinking of syphilis as a punishment for an individual's transgression
was for a long time, virtually until the disease became easily curable,
not really distinct from regarding it as retribution for the licentious-
ness of a community—as with AIDS now, in the rich industrial countries. In contrast to cancer, understood in a modern way as a disease
incurred by (and revealing of) individuals, AIDS is understood in a
premodern way, as a disease incurred by people both as individuals
and as members of a "risk group"—that neutral-sounding, bureaucratic category which also revives the archaic idea of a tainted community that illness has judged.

Not every account of plague or plague-like diseases, of course, is a 5
vehicle for lurid stereotypes about illness and the ill. The effort to
think critically, historically, about illness (about disaster generally)
was attempted throughout the eighteenth century: say, from Defoe's *A
Journal of the Plague Year* (1722) to Alessandro Manzoni's *The Betrothed*
(1827). Defoe's historical fiction, purporting to be an eyewitness account of bubonic plague in London in 1665, does not further any understanding of the plague as punishment or, a later part of the script,
as a transforming experience. And Manzoni, in his lengthy account of
the passage of plague through the duchy of Milan in 1630, is avowedly
committed to presenting a more accurate, less reductive view than his
historical sources. But even these two complex narratives reinforce
some of the perennial, simplifying ideas about plague.

One feature of the usual script for plague: the disease invariably 6
comes from somewhere else. The names for syphilis, when it began its
epidemic sweep through Europe in the last decade of the fifteenth century, are an exemplary illustration of the need to make a dreaded disease foreign. It was the "French pox" to the English, *morbus Germani-
cus* to the Parisians, the Naples sickness to the Florentines, the Chinese

disease to the Japanese. But what may seem like a joke about the inevitability of chauvinism reveals a more important truth: that there is a link between imagining disease and imagining foreignness. It lies perhaps in the very concept of wrong, which is archaically identical with the non-us, the alien. A polluting person is always wrong, as Mary Douglas has observed. The inverse is also true: a person judged to be wrong is regarded as, at least potentially, a source of pollution.

The foreign place of origin of important illnesses, as of drastic 7 changes in the weather, may be no more remote than a neighboring country. Illness is a species of invasion, and indeed is often carried by soldiers. Manzoni's account of the plague of 1630 begins:

> The plague which the Tribunal of Health had feared might enter the Milanese provinces with the German troops had in fact entered, as is well known; and it is also well known that it did not stop there, but went on to invade and depopulate a large part of Italy.

Defoe's chronicle of the plague of 1665 begins similarly, with a 8 flurry of ostentatiously scrupulous speculation about its foreign origin:

> It was about the beginning of September, 1664, that I, among the rest of my neighbours, heard in ordinary discourse that the plague was returned again in Holland; for it had been very violent there, and particularly at Amsterdam and Rotterdam, in the year 1663, whither, they say, it was brought, some said from Italy, others from the Levant, among some goods which were brought home by their Turkey fleet; others said it was brought from Candia; others from Cyprus. It mattered not from where it came; but all agreed it was come into Holland again.

The bubonic plague that reappeared in London in the 1720s had 9 arrived from Marseilles, which was where plague in the eighteenth century was usually thought to enter Western Europe; brought by seamen, then transported by soldiers and merchants. By the nineteenth century the foreign origin was usually more exotic, the means of transport less specifically imagined, and the illness itself had become phantasmagorical, symbolic.

At the end of *Crime and Punishment* Raskolnikov dreams of plague: 10 "He dreamt that the whole world was condemned to a terrible new strange plague that had come to Europe from the depths of Asia." At the beginning of the sentence it is "the whole world," which turns out by the end of the sentence to be "Europe," afflicted by a lethal visitation from Asia. Dostoevsky's model is undoubtedly cholera, called Asiatic cholera, long endemic in Bengal, which had rapidly become and remained through most of the nineteenth century a worldwide epidemic disease. Part of the centuries-old conception of Europe as a privileged cultural entity is that it is a place which is colonized by lethal diseases coming from elsewhere. Europe is assumed to be by rights free of disease. (And Europeans have been astoundingly callous about the far more devastating extent to which they—as invaders, as colonists—have introduced *their* lethal diseases to the exotic, "primitive" world: think of the ravages of smallpox, influenza, and cholera on the aboriginal populations of the Americas and Australia.) The tenacity of the connection of exotic origin with dreaded disease is one reason why cholera, of which there were four great outbreaks in Europe in the nineteenth century, each with a lower death toll than the preceding one, has continued to be more memorable than smallpox, whose ravages increased as the century went on (half a million died in the European smallpox pandemic of the early 1870s) but which could not be construed as, plague-like, a disease with a non-European origin.

Plagues are no longer "sent," as in Biblical and Greek antiquity, 11 for the question of agency has blurred. Instead, peoples are "visited" by plagues. And the visitations recur, as is taken for granted in the subtitle of Defoe's narrative, which explains that it is about that "which happened in London during the Last Great Visitation in 1665." Even for non-Europeans, lethal disease may be called a visitation. But a visitation on "them" is invariably described as different from one on "us." "I believe that about one half of the whole people was carried off by this visitation," wrote the English traveler Alexander Kinglake, reaching Cairo at a time of the bubonic plague (sometimes called "oriental plague"). "The Orientals, however, have more quiet fortitude than Europeans under afflictions of this sort." Kinglake's influential book *Eothen* (1844)—suggestively subtitled "Traces of Travel Brought Home from the East"—illustrates many of the enduring Eurocentric presumptions about others, starting from the fantasy that peoples with little reason to expect exemption from misfortune have a lessened capacity to *feel* misfortune. Thus it is believed that Asians (or the poor, or blacks, or Africans, or Muslims) don't suffer or don't grieve as Europeans (or whites) do. The fact that illness is associated with the poor— who are, from the perspective of the privileged, aliens in one's midst— reinforces the association of illness with the foreign: with an exotic, often primitive place.

Thus, illustrating the classic script for plague, AIDS is thought to 12 have started in the "dark continent," then spread to Haiti, then to the United States and to Europe, then. . . . It is understood as a tropical disease: another infestation from the so-called Third World, which is after all where most people in the world live, as well as a scourge of the *tristes tropiques*. Africans who detect racist stereotypes in much of the speculation about the geographical origin of AIDS are not wrong.

(Nor are they wrong in thinking that depictions of Africa as the cradle of AIDS must feed anti-African prejudices in Europe and Asia.) The subliminal connection made to notions about a primitive past and the many hypotheses that have been fielded about possible transmission from animals (a disease of green monkeys? African swine fever?) cannot help but activate a familiar set of stereotypes about animality, sexual license, and blacks. In Zaire and other countries in Central Africa where AIDS is killing tens of thousands, the counterreaction has begun. Many doctors, academics, journalists, government officials, and other educated people believe that the virus was sent to Africa from the United States, an act of bacteriological warfare (whose aim was to decrease the African birth rate) which got out of hand and has returned to afflict its perpetrators. A common African version of this belief about the disease's provenance has the virus fabricated in a CIA-Army laboratory in Maryland, sent from there to Africa, and brought back to its country of origin by American homosexual missionaries returning from Africa to Maryland.

At first it was assumed that AIDS must become widespread else- 13 where in the same catastrophic form in which it has emerged in Africa, and those who still think this will eventually happen invariably invoke the Black Death. The plague metaphor is an essential vehicle of the most pessimistic reading of the epidemiological prospects. From classic fiction to the latest journalism, the standard plague story is of inexorability, inescapability. The unprepared are taken by surprise; those observing the recommended precautions are struck down as well. *All* succumb when the story is told by an omniscient narrator, as in Poe's parable "The Masque of the Red Death" (1842), inspired by an account of a ball held in Paris during the cholera epidemic of 1832. Almost all—if the story is told from the point of view of a traumatized witness, who will be a benumbed survivor, as in Jean Giono's Stendhalian novel *Horseman on the Roof* (1951), in which a young Italian nobleman in exile wanders through cholera-stricken southern France in the 1830s.

Plagues are invariably regarded as judgments on society, and the 14 metaphoric inflation of AIDS into such a judgment also accustoms people to the inevitability of global spread. This is a traditional use of sexually transmitted diseases: to be described as punishments not just of individuals but of a group ("generall licentiousnes"). Not only venereal diseases have been used in this way, to identify transgressing or vicious populations. Interpreting any catastrophic epidemic as a sign of moral laxity or political decline was as common until the later part of the last century as associating dreaded diseases with foreignness. (Or with despised and feared minorities.) And the assignment of fault is not contradicted by cases that do not fit. The Methodist preachers in England who connected the cholera epidemic of 1832 with drunkenness (the temperance movement was just starting) were not understood to be claiming that *everybody* who got cholera was a drunkard: there is always room for "innocent victims" (children, young women). Tuberculosis, in its identity as a disease of the poor (rather than of the "sensitive"), was also linked by late-nineteenth-century reformers to alcoholism. Responses to illnesses associated with sinners and the poor invariably recommended the adoption of middle-class values: the regular habits, productivity, and emotional self-control to which drunkenness was thought the chief impediment. Health itself was eventually identified with these values, which were religious as well as mercantile, health being evidence of virtue as disease was of depravity. The dictum that cleanliness is next to godliness is to be taken quite literally. The succession of cholera epidemics in the nineteenth century shows a steady waning of religious interpretations of the disease; more precisely, these increasingly coexisted with other explanations. Although, by the time of the epidemic of 1866, cholera was commonly understood not simply as a divine punishment but as the consequence of remediable defects of sanitation, it was still regarded as the scourge of the sinful. A writer in *The New York Times* declared (April 22, 1866): "Cholera is especially the punishment of neglect of sanitary laws; it is the curse of the dirty, the intemperate, and the degraded."

That it now seems unimaginable for cholera or a similar disease to 15 be regarded in this way signifies not a lessened capacity to moralize about diseases but only a change in the kind of illnesses that are used didactically. Cholera was perhaps the last major epidemic disease fully qualifying for plague status for almost a century. (I mean cholera as a European and American, therefore a nineteenth-century, disease; until 1817 there had never been a cholera epidemic outside the Far East.) Influenza, which would seem more plague-like than any other epidemic in this century if loss of life were the main criterion, and which struck as suddenly as cholera and killed as quickly, usually in a few days, was never viewed metaphorically as a plague. Nor was a more recent epidemic, polio. One reason why plague notions were not invoked is that these epidemics did not have enough of the attributes perennially ascribed to plagues. (For instance, polio was construed as typically a disease of children—of the innocent.) The more important reason is that there has been a shift in the focus of the moralistic exploitation of illness. This shift, to diseases that can be interpreted as judgments on the individual, makes it harder to use epidemic disease as such. For a long time cancer was the illness that best fitted this secular culture's need to blame and punish and censor through the imagery of disease. Cancer was a disease of an individual, and understood as the result not of an action but rather of a failure to act (to be prudent, to exert proper self-control, or to be properly expressive). In the twentieth century, it has become almost impossible to moralize about epidemics—except those which are transmitted sexually.

The persistence of the belief that illness reveals, and is a punish- 16 ment for, moral laxity or turpitude can be seen in another way, by noting the persistence of descriptions of disorder or corruption as a disease. So indispensable has been the plague metaphor in bringing summary judgments about social crisis that its use hardly abated during the era when collective diseases were no longer treated so moralistically—the time between the influenza and encephalitis pandemics of the early and mid-1920s and the acknowledgment of a new, mysterious epidemic illness in the early 1980s—and when great infectious epidemics were so often and confidently proclaimed a thing of the past. The plague metaphor was common in the 1930s as a synonym for social and psychic catastrophe. Evocations of plague of this type usually go with rant, with antiliberal attitudes: think of Artaud on theatre and plague, of Wilhelm Reich on "emotional plague." And such a generic "diagnosis" necessarily promotes antihistorical thinking. A theodicy as well as a demonology, it not only stipulates something emblematic of evil but makes this the bearer of a rough, terrible justice. In Karel Čapek's *The White Plague* (1937), the loathsome pestilence that has appeared in a state where fascism has come to power afflicts only those over the age of forty, those who could be held morally responsible.

Written on the eve of the Nazi takeover of Czechoslovakia, 17 Čapek's allegorical play is something of an anomaly—the use of the plague metaphor to convey the menace of what is defined as barbaric by a mainstream European liberal. The play's mysterious, grisly malady is something like leprosy, a rapid, invariably fatal leprosy that is supposed to have come, of course, from Asia. But Čapek is not interested in identifying political evil with the incursion of the foreign. He scores his didactic points by focusing not on the disease itself but on the management of information about it by scientists, journalists, and politicians. The most famous specialist in the disease harangues a reporter ("The disease of the hour, you might say. A good five million have died of it to date, twenty million have it and at least three times as many are going about their business, blithely unaware of the marble-like, marble-sized spots on their bodies"); chides a fellow doctor for using the popular terms, "the white plague" and "Peking leprosy," instead of the scientific name, "the Cheng Syndrome"; fantasizes about how his clinic's work on identifying the new virus and finding a cure ("every clinic in the world has an intensive research program") will add to the prestige of science and win a Nobel Prize for its discoverer; revels in hyperbole when it is thought a cure has been found ("it was the most dangerous disease in all history, worse than the bubonic plague"); and outlines plans for sending those with symptoms to well-guarded detention camps ("Given that every carrier of the disease is a potential spreader of the disease, we *must* protect the uncontaminated from the contaminated. All sentimentality in this regard is fatal and therefore criminal"). However cartoonish Čapek's ironies may seem, they are a not improbable sketch of catastrophe (medical, ecological) as a managed public event in modern mass society. And however conventionally he deploys the plague metaphor, as an agency of retribution (in the end the plague strikes down the dictator himself), Čapek's feel for public relations leads him to make explicit in the play the understanding of disease *as* a metaphor. The eminent doctor declares the accomplishments of science to be as nothing compared with the merits of the dictator, about to launch a war, "who has averted a far worse scourge: the scourge of anarchy, the leprosy of corruption, the epidemic of barbaric liberty, the plague of social disintegration fatally sapping the organism of our nation."

Camus's *The Plague*, which appeared a decade later, is a far less literal use of plague by another great European liberal, as subtle as Čapek's *The White Plague* is schematic. Camus's novel is not, as is sometimes said, a political allegory in which the outbreak of bubonic plague in a Mediterranean port city represents the Nazi occupation. This plague is not retributive. Camus is not protesting anything, not corruption or tyranny, not even morality. The plague is no more or less than an exemplary event, the irruption of death that gives life its seriousness. His use of plague, more epitome than metaphor, is detached, stoic, aware—it is not about bringing judgment. But, as in Čapek's play, characters in Camus's novel declare how unthinkable it is to have a plague in the twentieth century . . . as if the belief that such a calamity could not happen, could not happen *anymore*, means that it must. 18

Working with the Text

1. Were you surprised, after reading Sontag's title, to see that her essay isn't about AIDS, as such, at all? That is, you learned nothing new about AIDS as a disease, its symptoms, its possible causes, its possible cures. Instead, what *is* the essay about?

2. What does Sontag mean when she says that, by contrast with cancer, "AIDS is understood in a premodern way"?

3. Sontag says that Čapek's portrayal of a plague in his drama *The White Plague* is "a not improbable sketch of catastrophe (medical, ecological) as a managed public event in modern mass society." What does she mean? What recent national or international catastrophes have been "managed public events"? In what ways?

4. Sontag is considered a leading American intellectual. What in the tone of her essay is different from that of some of the other essays in this chapter,

such as the journalism of Elayne Rapping and the popular essay of Patricia Williams? What about her language shows that her style is more academic? Point to specific passages. How does this style help define her attitude toward her subject?

Working beyond the Text

1. The word "plague" is often associated with the Black Death of the Middle Ages. What was the Black Death? When did it occur, how many people did it kill, and where? What did people think caused it, and what actually caused it? What did religious leaders of the time have to say about it? Do you see any connections between that historical event and today's AIDS?

2. In the library, follow up on any of the references to writers that Sontag makes: Procopius, Blake, Erasmus, Donne, Defoe, Alessandro Manzoni, Dostoevsky, Alexander Kinglake, Poe, Jean Giono, Artaud, Karel Čapek, Camus. What could be her purpose for including so many literary references in an essay about AIDS as a modern plague?

3. At a 1995 political rally at Independence Hall in Philadelphia, one demonstrator held a sign that said, "Thank God for AIDS." How does that man's opinion of AIDS and those who have it relate to Sontag's ideas about plagues as a "judgment" and a "punishment"?

4. We hear references to AIDS practically everywhere, practically every day. For a few days, keep a list of all the references to AIDS you notice in conversations with friends, on the television, in the newspaper. How do people talk about AIDS? How do the ways in which people talk about AIDS compare to the ways discussed by Sontag?

Hate Radio

Patricia J. Williams

Patricia Williams has taught law at the University of Wisconsin and Columbia University. Her works include *The Alchemy of Race and Rights,* a book about the interaction of race and law in U.S. society and in her personal life. In this article, published in *Ms.* magazine (March/April 1994), Williams argues that the language of talk radio shows with hosts like Rush Limbaugh and Howard Stern creates an atmosphere of hatred against minorities and women.

Three years ago I stood at my sink, washing the dishes and listen- 1
ing to the radio. I was tuned to rock and roll so I could avoid thinking about the big news from the day before—George Bush had just nomi-

nated Clarence Thomas to replace Thurgood Marshall on the Supreme Court. I was squeezing a dot of lemon Joy into each of the wineglasses when I realized that two smoothly radio-cultured voices, a man's and a woman's, had replaced the music.

"I think it's a stroke of genius on the president's part," said the female voice.   2

"Yeah," said the male voice. "Then those blacks, those African Americans, those Negroes—hey 'Negro' is good enough for Thurgood Marshall—whatever, they can't make up their minds [what] they want to be called. I'm gonna call them Blafricans. Black Africans. Yeah, I like it. Blafricans. Then they can get all upset because now the president appointed a Blafrican."   3

"Yeah, well, that's the way those liberals think. It's just crazy."   4

"And then after they turn down his nomination the president can say he tried to please 'em, and then he can appoint someone with some intelligence."   5

Back then, this conversation seemed so horrendously unusual, so singularly hateful, that I picked up a pencil and wrote it down. I was certain that a firestorm of protest was going to engulf the station and purge those foul radio mouths with the good clean soap of social outrage.   6

I am so naive. When I finally turned on the radio and rolled my dial to where everyone else had been tuned while I was busy watching Cosby reruns, it took me a while to understand that there's a firestorm all right, but not of protest. In the two and a half years since Thomas has assumed his post on the Supreme Court, the underlying assumptions of the conversation I heard as uniquely outrageous have become commonplace, popularly expressed, and louder in volume. I hear the style of that snide polemicism everywhere, among acquaintances, on the street, on television in toned-down versions. It is a crude demagoguery that makes me heartsick. I feel more and more surrounded by that point of view, the assumptions of being without intelligence, the coded epithets, the "Blafrican"-like stand-ins for "nigger," the mocking angry glee, the endless tirades filled with nonspecific, nonempirically based slurs against "these people" or "those minorities" or "feminazis" or "liberals" or "scumbags" or "pansies" or "jerks" or "sleazeballs" or "loonies" or "animals" or "foreigners."   7

At the same time I am not so naive as to suppose that this is something new. In clearheaded moments I realize I am not listening to the radio anymore, I am listening to a large segment of white America think aloud in ever louder resurgent thoughts that have generations of historical precedent. It's as though the radio has split open like an egg, Morton Downey, Jr.'s clones and Joe McCarthy's ghost spilling out, broken yolks, a great collective of sometimes clever, sometimes small, but uniformly threatened brains—they have all come gushing out. Just   8 as they were about to pass into oblivion, Jack Benny and his humble black sidekick Rochester get resurrected in the ungainly bodies of Howard Stern and his faithful black henchwoman, Robin Quivers. The culture of Amos and Andy has been revived and reassembled in Bob Grant's radio minstrelry and radio newcomer Daryl Gates's sanctimonious imprecations on behalf of decent white people. And in striking imitation of Jesse Helms's nearly forgotten days as a radio host, the far Right has found its undisputed king in the personage of Rush Limbaugh—a polished demagogue with a weekly radio audience of at least twenty million, a television show that vies for ratings with the likes of Jay Leno, a newsletter with a circulation of 380,000, and two best-selling books whose combined sales are closing in on six million copies.

From Churchill to Hitler to the old Soviet Union, it's clear that 9 radio and television have the power to change the course of history, to proselytize, and to coalesce not merely the good and the noble, but the very worst in human nature as well. Likewise, when Orson Welles made his famous radio broadcast "witnessing" the landing of a spaceship full of hostile Martians, the United States ought to have learned a lesson about the power of radio to appeal to mass instincts and incite mass hysteria. Radio remains a peculiarly powerful medium even today, its visual emptiness in a world of six trillion flashing images allowing one of the few remaining playgrounds for the aural subconscious. Perhaps its power is attributable to our need for an oral tradition after all, some conveying of stories, feelings, myths of ancestors, epics of alienation, and the need to rejoin ancestral roots, even ignorant bigoted roots. Perhaps the visual quiescence of radio is related to the popularity of E-mail or electronic networking. Only the voice is made manifest, unmasking worlds that cannot—or dare not?—be seen. Just yet. Nostalgia crystallizing into a dangerous future. The preconscious voice erupting into the expressed, the prime time.

What comes out of the modern radio mouth could be the *Iliad*, the 10 *Rubaiyat*, the griot's song of our times. If indeed radio is a vessel for the American "Song of Songs," then what does it mean that a manic, adolescent Howard Stern is so popular among radio listeners, that Rush Limbaugh's wittily smooth sadism has gone the way of prime-time television, and that both vie for the number one slot on all the best-selling book lists? What to make of the stories being told by our modern radio evangelists and their tragic unloved chorus of callers? Is it really just a collapsing economy that spawns this drama of grown people sitting around scaring themselves to death with fantasies of black feminist Mexican able-bodied gay soldiers earning $100,000 a year on welfare who are so criminally depraved that Hillary Clinton or the Antichrist-of-the-moment had no choice but to invite them onto the government payroll so they can run the country? The panicky exaggeration reminds me of a child's fear. . . . *And then, and then, a huge lion jumped out of the shadows and was about to gobble me up, and I can't ever sleep again for a whole week.*

As I spin the dial on my radio, I can't help thinking that this stuff 11 must be related to that most poignant of fiber-optic phenomena, phone sex. Aural Sex. Radio Racism and a touch of S & M. High-priest hosts with the power and run-amok ego to discipline listeners, to smack with the verbal back of the hand, to smash the button that shuts you up once and for all. "Idiot!" shouts New York City radio demagogue Bob Grant and then the sound of droning telephone emptiness, the voice of dissent dumped out some trapdoor in aural space.

As I listened to a range of such programs what struck me as the 12 most unifying theme was not merely the specific intolerance on such hot topics as race and gender, but a much more general contempt for the world, a verbal stoning of anything different. It is like some unusually violent game of "Simon Says," this mockery and shouting down of callers, this roar of incantations, the insistence on agreement.

But, ah, if you *will* but only agree, what sweet and safe reward, 13 what soft enfolding by a stern and angry radio god. And as an added bonus, the invisible shield of an AM community, a family of fans who are Exactly Like You, to whom you can express, in anonymity, all the filthy stuff you imagine "them" doing to you. The comfort and relief of being able to ejaculate, to those who understand, about the dark imagined excess overtaking, robbing, needing to be held down and taught a good lesson, needing to put it in its place before the ravenous demon enervates all that is true and good and pure in this life.

The audience for this genre of radio flagellation is mostly young, 14 white, and male. Two thirds of Rush Limbaugh's audience is male. According to *Time* magazine, 75 percent of Howard Stern's listeners are white men. Most of the callers have spent their lives walling themselves off from any real experience with blacks, feminists, lesbians, or gays. In this regard, it is probably true, as former Secretary of Education William Bennett says, that Rush Limbaugh "tells his audience that what you believe inside, you can talk about in the marketplace." Unfortunately, what's "inside" is then mistaken for what's outside, treated as empirical and political reality. The *National Review* extols Limbaugh's conservative leadership as no less than that of Ronald Reagan, and the Republican party provides Limbaugh with books to discuss, stories, angles, and public support. "People were afraid of censure by gay activists, feminists, environmentalists—now they are not because Rush takes them on," says Bennett.

U.S. history has been marked by cycles in which brands of this or 15 that hatred come into fashion and go out, are unleashed and then restrained. If racism, homophobia, jingoism, and woman-hating have been features of national life in pretty much all of modern history, it rather begs the question to spend a lot of time wondering if right-wing radio is a symptom or a cause. For at least 400 years, prevailing attitudes in the West have considered African Americans less intelligent. Recent statistics show that 53 percent of people in the United States agree that blacks and Latinos are less intelligent than whites, and a majority believe that blacks are lazy, violent, welfare-dependent, and unpatriotic.

I think that what has made life more or less tolerable for "out" 16 groups have been those moments in history when those "inside" feelings were relatively restrained. In fact, if I could believe that right-wing radio were only about idiosyncratic, singular, rough-hewn individuals thinking those inside thoughts, I'd be much more inclined to agree with Columbia University media expert Everette Dennis, who says that Stern's and Limbaugh's popularity represents the "triumph of the individual" or with *Time* magazine's bottom line that "the fact that either is seriously considered a threat . . . is more worrisome than Stern or Limbaugh will ever be." If what I were hearing had even a tad more to do with real oppressions, with real white *and* black levels of joblessness and homelessness, or with the real problems of real white men, then I wouldn't have bothered to slog my way through hours of Howard Stern's miserable obsessions.

Yet at the heart of my anxiety is the worry that Stern, Limbaugh, 17 Grant, et al. represent the very antithesis of individualism's triumph. As the *National Review* said of Limbaugh's ascent, "It was a feat not only of the loudest voice but also of a keen political brain to round up, as Rush did, the media herd and drive them into the conservative corral." When asked about his political aspirations, Bob Grant gloated to the *Washington Post,* "I think I would make rather a good dictator."

The polemics of right-wing radio are putting nothing less than 18 hate onto the airwaves, into the marketplace, electing it to office, teaching it in schools, and exalting it as freedom. What worries me is the increasing-to-constant commerce of retribution, control, and lashing out, fed not by fact but fantasy. What worries me is the re-emergence, more powerfully than at any time since the institution of Jim Crow, of a socio-centered self that excludes "the likes of," well, me for example, from the civic circle, and that would rob me of my worth and claim and identity as a citizen. As the *Economist* rightly observes, "Mr. Limbaugh takes a mass market—white, mainly male, middle-class, ordinary America—and talks to it as an endangered minority."

I worry about this identity whose external reference is a set of be- 19 liefs, ethics, and practices that excludes, restricts, and acts in the world on me, or mine, as the perceived if not real enemy. I am acutely aware of losing *my* mythic individualism to the surface shapes of my mythic group fearsomeness as black, as female, as left wing. "I" merge not fluidly but irretrievably into a category of "them." I become a suspect self, a moving target of loathsome properties, not merely different but dangerous. And that worries me a lot.

What happens in my life with all this translated license, this per- 20 mission to be uncivil? What happens to the social space that was supposedly at the sweet mountaintop of the civil rights movement's trail? Can I get a seat on the bus without having to be reminded that I *should* be standing? Did the civil rights movement guarantee us nothing more than to use public accommodations while surrounded by raving lunatic bigots? "They didn't beat this idiot [Rodney King] enough," says Howard Stern.

Not long ago I had the misfortune to hail a taxicab in which the 21 driver was listening to Howard Stern undress some woman. After some blocks, I had to get out. I was, frankly, afraid to ask the driver to turn it off—not because I was afraid of "censoring" him, which seems to be the only thing people will talk about anymore, but because the driver was stripping me too, as he leered through the rearview mirror. "Something the matter?" he demanded, as I asked him to pull over and let me out well short of my destination. (I'll spare you the full story of what happened from there—trying to get another cab, as the cabbies stopped for all the white businessmen who so much as scratched their heads near the curb; a nice young white man, seeing my plight, giving me his cab, having to thank him, he hero, me saved-but-humiliated, cabdriver pissed and surly. I fight my way to my destination, finally arriving in bad mood, militant black woman, cranky feminazi.)

When Yeltsin blared rock music at his opponents holed up in the 22 parliament building in Moscow, in imitation of the U.S. Marines trying to torture Manuel Noriega in Panama, all I could think of was that it must be like being trapped in a crowded subway car when all the portable stereos are tuned to Bob Grant or Howard Stern. With Howard Stern's voice a tinny, screeching backdrop, with all the faces growing dreamily mean as though some soporifically evil hallucinogen were gushing into their bloodstreams, I'd start begging to surrender.

Surrender to what? Surrender to the laissez-faire resegregation 23 that is the metaphoric significance of the hundreds of "Rush rooms" that have cropped up in restaurants around the country; rooms broadcasting Limbaugh's words, rooms for your listening pleasure, rooms where bigots can capture the purity of a Rush-only lunch counter, rooms where all those unpleasant others just "choose" not to eat? Surrender to the naughty luxury of a room in which a Ku Klux Klan meeting could take place in orderly, First Amendment fashion? Everyone's "free" to come in (and a few of you outsiders do), but mostly the undesirable nonconformists are gently repulsed away. It's a high-tech world of enhanced choice. Whites choose mostly to sit in the Rush room. Feminists, blacks, lesbians, and gays "choose" to sit elsewhere. No need to buy black votes, you just pay them not to vote; no need to insist on white-only schools, you just sell the desirability of black-only schools. Just sit back and watch it work, like those invisible shock shields that keep dogs cowering in their own backyards.

How real is the driving perception behind all the Sturm und 24 Drang of this genre of radio-harangue—the perception that white men are an oppressed minority, with no power and no opportunity in the land that they made great? While it is true that power and opportunity are shrinking for all but the very wealthy in this country (and would that Limbaugh would take that issue on), the fact remains that white men are still this country's most privileged citizens and market actors. To give just a small example, according to the *Wall Street Journal*, blacks were the only racial group to suffer a net job loss during the 1990–91 economic downturn at the companies reporting to the Equal Employment Opportunity Commission. Whites, Latinos, and Asians, meanwhile, gained thousands of jobs. While whites gained 71,144 jobs at these companies, Latinos gained 60,040, Asians gained 55,104, and blacks lost 59,479. If every black were hired in the United States tomorrow, the numbers would not be sufficient to account for white men's expanding balloon of fear that they have been specifically dispossessed by African Americans.

Given deep patterns of social segregation and general ignorance of 25 history, particularly racial history, media remain the principal source of most Americans' knowledge of each other. Media can provoke violence or induce passivity. In San Francisco, for example, a radio show on KMEL called "Street Soldiers" has taken this power as a responsibility with great consequence: "Unquestionably," writes Ken Auletta in *The New Yorker*, "the show has helped avert violence. When a Samoan teenager was slain, apparently by Filipino gang members, in a drive-by shooting, the phones lit up with calls from Samoans wanting to tell [the hosts] they would not rest until they had exacted revenge. Threats filled the air for a couple of weeks. Then the dead Samoan's father called in, and, in a poignant exchange, the father said he couldn't tolerate the thought of more young men senselessly slaughtered. There would be no retaliation, he vowed. And there was none." In contrast, we must wonder at the phenomenon of the very powerful leadership of the Republican party, from Ronald Reagan to Robert Dole to William Bennett, giving advice, counsel, and friendship to Rush Limbaugh's passionate divisiveness.

The outright denial of the material crisis at every level of U.S. soci- 26 ety, most urgently in black inner-city neighborhoods but facing us all, is a kind of political circus, dissembling as it feeds the frustrations of the moment. We as a nation can no longer afford to deal with such crises by *imagining* an excess of bodies, of babies, of job-stealers, of welfare mothers, of overreaching immigrants, of too-powerful (Jewish, in whispers) liberal Hollywood, of lesbians and gays, of gang members ("gangsters" remain white, and no matter what the atrocity, less vilified than "gang members," who are black), of Arab terrorists, and uppity women. The reality of our social poverty far exceeds these scapegoats. This right-wing backlash resembles, in form if not substance, phenomena like anti-Semitism in Poland: there aren't but a handful of Jews left in that whole country, but the giant balloon of heated anti-Semitism flourishes apace, Jews blamed for the world's evils.

The overwhelming response to right-wing excesses in the United 27 States has been to seek an odd sort of comfort in the fact that the First Amendment is working so well that you can't suppress this sort of thing. Look what's happened in Eastern Europe. Granted. So let's not talk about censorship or the First Amendment for the next ten minutes. But in Western Europe, where fascism is rising at an appalling rate, suppression is hardly the problem. In Eastern and Western Europe as well as the United States, we must begin to think just a little bit about the fiercely coalescing power of media to spark mistrust, to fan it into forest fires of fear and revenge. We must begin to think about the levels of national and social complacence in the face of such resolute ignorance. We must ask ourselves what the expected result is, not of censorship or suppression, but of so much encouragement, so much support, so much investment in the fashionability of hate. What future is it that we are designing with the devotion of such tremendous resources to the disgraceful propaganda of bigotry?

Working with the Text

1. Williams traces what she calls the racist, sexist, antiforeigner, and homophobic tendencies of much talk radio today to older tendencies in American history. Which ones? Why, in her opinion, is "hate radio" gaining in popularity?

2. What is Williams' criticism of the idea that "hate radio" is free speech, and that if people don't like it then they're free to turn it off and not listen? How does she feel that talk radio infringes upon her freedom?

3. What is Williams' opinion of the general intelligence and emotional state of the hosts and listeners of "hate radio" programs? Point to specific passages where her idea is clear.

4. In contrast to other writers, for example Elayne Rapping and Susan Sontag in this unit, Williams writes in a very personal way about her subject, including personal narratives about listening to hate radio shows. Why does she do this, do you think? How does this help her communicate her message about hate radio?

Working beyond the Text

1. What do you think of Williams' description of listening to "hate radio" as "listening to a large segment of white America think aloud"? Do you agree that hate radio expresses what many white Americans "believe inside"? Why have so many opinions, formerly characterized as racist or sexist, suddenly become so acceptable in public?

2. Have you ever listened to any of the programs that Williams characterizes as "hate radio"? Which ones? If you have ever listened to one with a group or discussed it with other listeners, would you agree that the audience, as Williams asserts, is "mostly young, white, and male"? Why did you listen?

3. Williams mentions a few "hate radio" celebrities, such as Howard Stern, Bob Grant, and Rush Limbaugh. How many more "hate radio" programs are there? Using the library and the listings for radio stations in your area, try to catalog all the programs and characterize the personalities and styles of the "hosts."

4. If you have never or rarely heard the "hate radio" programs Williams discusses, test her assertions about their style and content by listening to one. Take notes about the topics discussed, the language used, the general manner of the host, and so on. Compare what you hear to Williams' account.

5. "Hate radio" may be one part of a general trend in our country toward less "civility" in the public language of the media, including entertainment. Why has public language become increasingly aggressive and crude? What are the consequences of such public language? To support your point of view, point to examples as concrete as the ones Williams uses in her essay.

UNIT TWO

LANGUAGE IN THE MARKETPLACE

Deride and Conquer

Mark Crispin Miller

Mark Crispin Miller teaches writing and film studies at Johns Hopkins University. Much of his writing, collected for example in *Boxed In* (1988), focuses on popular culture, particularly film, television, rock music, and advertising. This essay is an excerpt from a longer version, which appeared in an anthology of essays about television and culture entitled *Watching Television* (1986). In it, Miller analyzes television commercials and programs, arguing that their sarcastic, derisive attitude encourages viewers to be contemptuous and passive.

Nobody could watch it all—and that's the point. There is a choice. Your choice. American television and you.

> Jim Duffy, President of Communications, ABC, in one of a series of
> ads promoting network television (1986)

Every evening, TV makes a promise, and seems at once to keep it. 1
TV's nightly promise is something like the grand old promise of America herself. Night after night, TV recalls the promise that was first extended through America's peerless landscape, with its great mountains, cliffs, and canyons, tumbling falls, gigantic woodlands, intricate bayous, lakes the size of seas, heavenly valleys, broiling deserts, and a network of massive rivers hurrying in all directions, through a north thick with trees, through interminable plains, through multicolored tropics, through miles and miles of grass or corn or granite, clay or wheat, until those rushing waters ultimately cascade into the surrounding ocean. And throughout this astonishing land mass lie a multitude of huge and spreading cities, each distinctive and yet each itself diverse, bustling with the restless efforts of a population no less heroically varied than the land itself—white and black and brown and yellow, bespeaking the peculiarities of every creed and culture in the world, and yet all now living here, savoring the many freedoms that

distinguish the United States so clearly from those other places where our citizens, or their ancestors, came from.

Here all enjoy the promise of that very opportunity, that very dif-   2
ferentiation which they, and this great land mass, represent: the promise of unending *choice*. Here they are not ground down by party rule, church dictate, authoritarian tyranny, or the daily dangers of fanatical vendetta; and in this atmosphere of peace and plenty, they are free to work and play, have families, and contemplate, if not yet actually enjoy, the bounty of our unprecedented system.

Such is the promise of America; and TV, every evening, makes a   3
similar sort of promise. Each night (and every day, all day), TV offers and provides us with an endless range of choices. Indeed, TV can be said to have itself incorporated the American dream of peaceful choice. This development was poignantly invoked by one of the hostages taken, in June of 1985, by the Shiite gunmen who hijacked TWA Flight 847. Back home after his captivity in Lebanon, Clint Suggs observed that "when you go to Beirut, you live war, you hear it, you smell it and it's real. It made me appreciate my freedom, the things we take for granted."[1] In America, such freedom is available to any viewer: "When we sit here in our living room, with the sun setting, the baby sleeping, we can watch television, change channels. We have choices."

TV's promise of eternal choice arises from the whole tempting   4
spectacle that is prime time: the full breasts, the gleaming cars, the glistening peaks of ice cream, mounds of candy, long clean highways, colossal frosted drinks, endless laughter, bands of dedicated friends, majestic houses, and cheeseburgers. The inexhaustible multitude of TV's images, sounds, and rhythms, like the dense catalog on every page of *TV Guide*, reassures us again and again that TV points to everything we might ever want or need. Nor is this promise merely implicit. The commercials, perhaps the quintessential components of TV's nonstop display, not only reconfirm our sense of privilege with millions of alluring images, but refer explicitly and often to this extensive "choice" of ours: AT&T offers us "The Right Choice," electricity, we are told, grants us "The Power of Choice," Wendy's reminds us that "There Is No Better Choice," McDonald's is "America's Choice," Coke is "The Real Choice" "In copiers, the choice is Canon," Taster's Choice is "The Choice for Taste"—all such assurances, and the delicious images that bolster them, combining to enhance even further TV's rich, ongoing paean to its own unimaginable abundances. And yet, consider carefully just one of those innumerable commercials that seem to celebrate "choice."

[1]Quoted in the *New York Times*, July 7, 1985.

A white van parks on a hot beach crowded with young people. ₅ Unnoticed by these joggers and sunbathers, the driver jumps from the front seat and quickly hoists himself inside the van's rear compartment—a complete broadcasting facility. Seated at the console, with a sly look on his boyish face, he puts on a pair of headphones and flips a switch. Two white speakers rise out of the van's roof. He then picks up a cold bottle of Pepsi-Cola, tilts it toward the microphone before him, and opens it. The enticing *pop* and *whoosh* reverberate across the beach. A young woman, lying as if unconscious on a beach chair, suddenly comes to, turning her face automatically toward the speakers. The hubbub starts to die down.

Grinning now, the driver pours the Pepsi into a tall Styrofoam ₆ cup, so that everyone can hear the plash, the fizz, the wet ascending arpeggio of liquid decanted from a bottle. Inside the van, the full cup sighs and sparkles at the microphone. Outside, the air is filled with the dense crackle of carbonation. Intrigued by the sound, a dog—with a white kite draped raffishly across its head—looks to its right, toward the speakers. Intrigued, a young man shifts his gaze in exactly the same way, taking off his glasses as he does so.

Now the driver leans toward his microphone and drinks the Pepsi ₇ noisily. At the sound of his parched gulping, the crowd falls completely still. One girl reflexively smacks her lips. His cup emptied, the driver sits back and delivers a long, convincing "aaaaaaahhh!"

The crowd snaps out of its collective daze. There is an atmosphere ₈ of stampede. Now ringed by customers, the driver stands behind his van, its rear doors opened wide, revealing a solid wall of fresh six-packs, each bearing the familiar Pepsi logo. He puts on a Pepsi vendor's cap and chirps, "Okay! Who's first?" Each customer immediately raises one arm high, and all clamor for a Pepsi, as the camera zooms far back to show that the driver's victory is total. All those beach-goers have suddenly converged on the white van like houseflies descending on a fallen Popsicle. Except for that tight throng of consumers in the distance, the beach is a wide wasteland of deserted towels. In this de-populated space, a single figure wanders, the only one who has not (yet) succumbed to Pepsi—a man equipped with a metal detector, presumably searching for loose change, and so protected, by his earphones, from the driver's irresistible sound effects. Finally, there is this signature, printed over the final image and solemnly intoned by Martin Sheen: "Pepsi. The Choice of a New Generation."

Thus, this ad leaves us with the same vague conviction that all ad- ₉ vertising, and TV in general, continually reconfirm: that we are bold, experienced, fully self-aware, and therefore able to pick out what's best from the enormous range of new sensations now available. Like most ads, then, this one seems to salute its viewers for their powers of discrimination, their advanced ability to choose; and yet, like most ads, this one contradicts its own celebration of "choice" by making choice itself seem inconceivable.

Within the little beach universe devised for Pepsico by BBDO, 10 "choice" is nothing but a quaint illusion. The members of this "new generation" succumb at once to the driver's expert Pavlovian technique, like so many rats responding to any systematic stimulus. This easy mass surrender is no "choice," nor are these Pepsi drinkers capable of exercising "choice," since they are the mere tanned particles of a summer mob—transient, pretty, easygoing and interchangeable. To belong to such a "generation" is not to derive one's own identity from that multitude of peers, but to give up all identity, to dissolve into a single reactive mass, and become a thing lightweight and indefinite, like so much flotsam. In such a primal group, dog and man are indeed equals, the dog trying, just like a man, to beat the heat by covering its head, the man removing his glasses, as if to be more like a dog, the two of them responding identically to the sound of Pepsi streaming from a bottle.

In place of those capacities that might distinguish man from dog, 11 here it is merely Pepsi that fills up every heart and mind, just as it fills that Styrofoam cup. No one thus saturated could make choices. Although not, it seems, as malleable as his customers, the driver himself is no less driven by Pepsi, blitzing his territory on behalf of himself and the company combined. And even the sole survivor of the pitch, temporarily deaf to those delicious noises, escapes only by cutting himself off. His solitary project, moreover, does not really distinguish him from all the rest, since there is apparently nothing he can do, having scrounged those dimes and pennies from the sand, but spend his income on a Pepsi.

So it cannot matter, in this beach universe, that there is no one ca- 12 pable of choosing, because there isn't anything to choose. Here there is nothing but Pepsi, and the mass compulsion to absorb it. As soon as the sound of Pepsi fills the air, all the pleasures of the afternoon evaporate, so that this full beach, with its sunny fraternizing, its soporific heat, its quiet surf returning and returning, becomes, in an instant, nothing more than a sandy area where you crave a certain beverage. Despite the ad's salute to "choice," what triumphs over all the free and various possibilities of that summer day is an eternal monad: Pepsi, whose taste, sound, and logo you will always recognize, and always "choose," whether you want to or not.

It is not "choice," then, that this ad is celebrating, but the total 13 negation of choice and choices. Indeed, the product itself is finally incidental to the pitch. The ad does not so much extol Pepsi per se as recommend it by implying that a lot of people have been fooled into buying it. In other words, the point of this successful bit of advertising is that Pepsi has been advertised successfully. The ad's hero is himself an adman, a fictitious downscale version of the dozens of professionals who collaborated to produce him. He, like them, moves fast, works too hard (there are faint dark circles under his eyes), and gets his kicks by manipulating others en masse for the sake of a corporate entity. It is his power—the power of advertising—that is the subject of this powerful advertisement, whose crucial image reveals the driver surrounded by his sudden customers, who face him eagerly, each raising one arm high, as if to hail the salesman who has so skillfully distracted them.

This ad, in short, is perfectly self-referential; and that self-reflection serves to immunize the ad against the sort of easy charges often leveled against advertising. This commercial cannot, for example, be said to tell a lie, since it works precisely by acknowledging the truth about itself: it is a clever ad meant to sell Pepsi, which people buy because it's advertised so cleverly. It would be equally pointless to complain that this ad manipulates its viewers, since the ad wittily exults in its own process of manipulation. To object to the ad at all, in fact, is to sound priggish, because the ad not only admits everything, but also seems to take itself so lightly, offering up its mininarrative of mass capitulation in a spirit of sophisticated humor, as if to say, "Sure, this is what we do. Funny, huh?"

In the purity of its self-reference, this ad is entirely modern. Before the eighties, an ad for Pepsi, or for some comparable item, would have worked differently—by enticing its viewers toward a paradise radiating from the product, thereby offering an illusory escape from the market and its unrelenting pressures. In such an ad, the Pepsi would (presumably) admit its drinker to some pastoral retreat, which would not then—like that beach—lose all of its delightfulness to the product, but would retain its otherworldly charms. In this way, advertising, until fairly recently, proffered some sort of transcendence over the world of work, trying to conceal the hard economic character of its suasive project with various "human" appeals—to family feeling, hunger, romantic fantasy, patriotism, envy, fear of ostracism, the urge to travel, and dozens of other "noncommercial" longings and anxieties. Of course, there are ads out now that attempt to make this dated offer, but nowhere near as often, or as convincingly, as the advertising of the past. Like this Pepsi commercial, more and more of today's mass advertisements offer no alternative to or respite from the marketplace but the marketplace itself, which (in the world as advertising represents it) appears at last to have permeated every one of the erstwhile havens in its midst. Now products are presented as desirable not because they offer to release you from the daily grind, but because they'll pull you under, take you in.

Like the Pepsi ad, with its cool and knowing tone, TV is perva- 16
sively ironic, forever flattering the viewer with a sense of his/her own
enlightenment. Even at its most self-important, TV is also charged
with this seductive irony. On the news, for instance, the anchorman or
correspondent is often simultaneously pompous and smirky, as if to
let us know that he, like us, cannot be taken in. When covering politicians or world leaders, newsmen like Chris Wallace, David Brinkley,
Harry Reasoner, Roger Mudd, and Sam Donaldson seem to jeer at the
very news they report, evincing an iconoclastic savvy that makes them
seem like dissidents despite their ever-readiness to fall in line. The object of the telejournalistic smirk is usually an easy target like "Congress" or "the Democrats," or a foreign leader backed by the Soviets,
or an allied dictator who is about to lose his grip. Seldom does the
newsman raise a serious question about the policies or values of the
multinationals, the CIA, the State Department, or the president.
Rather, the TV news tends to "raise doubts" about the administration
by playing up the PR problems of its members (PR problems which
the TV news thereby creates): Can David Stockman be muzzled? Can
Pat Buchanan get along with Donald Regan? Can George Bush alter
the perception that he doesn't know what he's saying? Through such
trivialities, the TV news actually conceals what goes on at the top and
in the world, enhancing its own authority while preserving the authority of those in power, their ideology, their institutions.

Nevertheless, the telejournalists' subversive air can often seem like 17
the exertion of a mighty democratic force. Certainly, TV's newsmen
like to think that a jaundiced view is somehow expressive of a populist
sympathy with all the rest of us; and, of course, if we glance back
through TV's history since the sixties, we will recall a number of
thrilling confrontations between some potentate and a reporter bold
enough to question him: Frank Reynolds putting it to Richard Nixon,
Dan Rather talking back to Richard Nixon, Sam Donaldson hectoring
Jimmy Carter or Ronald Reagan. Each time Ted Koppel sits before
someone like Ferdinand Marcos, each time Mike Wallace interrogates
some well-dressed hireling whose desk cannot protect him from that
cool scrutiny, we sense a moment of modern heroism, as the newsman, with his level gaze and no-nonsense queries, seems about to top-
ple one more bad authority for the sake of a vast, diverse, and right-
eous public—or republic, for there is something in this routine
televisual agon that seems quintessentially American. We are, the TV
news seems always to be telling us, a young and truth-loving nation,
founded upon the vigorous rejection of the old European priests and
kings, and still distrustful of all pompous father figures; and so those
boyish skeptics who face down the aging crook or tyrant thereby act
out a venerable ideal of American innocence.

TV's reflection on the knowing viewer is a cynical appeal not only 18 to the weakest part of each of us, but to the weakest and least experienced among us. It is therefore not surprising that this reflection has transformed the children's shows along with the rest of TV. Today the slow and beaming parent figures of the past—Fran Allison, Captain Kangaroo, Miss Frances, Mr. Wizard—recur to us like lame old jokes; and the only current survivor of the type, the very easygoing Mr. Rogers, has been the object of hip satire by, among others, Eddie Murphy on *Saturday Night Live,* and J. Walter Thompson for Burger King. The old children's shows were hardly free from commercialism; often the parent figure would engage in shameless huckstering, advising his "boys and girls" to "ask" for the sponsor's latest item. Although often disingenuous, however, the parental guise of the early hosts comprised a subtle barrier to the corporate exploitation of the very young, because that guise was based on the assumption that the child should be regarded as an innocent—fanciful and trusting, in need of some protection from the world that would absorb him all too soon. Such a child would, if respected, be off-limits to the market forces. That child's capacity for play and make-believe also might impede the corporate project, since his or her delight in such free pleasures would, if universally indulged, make trouble for Mattel, Hasbro, Coleco Industries, and other giant manufacturers of games and toys.

In order to prevent this hardship, TV now urges its youngest 19 viewers to adopt the same contemptuous and passive attitude that TV recommends to grown-ups. The child who sits awed by He-Man, the GoBots, the Thundercats, or G.I. Joe is not encouraged to pretend or sing or make experiments, but is merely hypnotized by those speedy images; and in this trance he learns only how to jeer. The superheroes wage interminable war, and yet it is not belligerence per se that these shows celebrate, but the particular belligerence that TV incites toward all that seems nontelevisual. The villains are always frenzied and extremely ugly, whereas the good guys are well built, smooth, and faceless, like the computers that are programmed to animate them. Empowered by this contrast, they attack their freaky enemies not just with swords and guns, but with an endless stream of witless personal insults—"bonehead," "fur-face," "long-legged creep," and on and on. Like TV's ads, these shows suggest that nothing could be worse than seeming different; but TV now teaches the same smug derisiveness even on those children's shows without commercials. For example, *Sesame Street*—despite its long-standing reputation as a pedagogical triumph—has become, in the eighties, merely one more exhibition of contagious jeering. The puppets often come across as manic little fools, while the hosting grown-ups come across as wise and cool—a marked superiority which they express through the usual bewildered or exasperated looks. Thus, the program's little viewers learn how to behave themselves—i.e., as viewers only. They are invited not to share the puppet's crazed exuberance, but only to look down on it; and so they practice that ironic posture which the show advises just as unrelentingly as it repeats the primary numbers and the letters of the alphabet.

As this flattery of the viewer now nearly unifies TV, so has it, necessarily, all but unified the culture which TV has pervaded. The movies now repeat the formulaic subversions that have served TV, debunking the heroics of the past through parodies of the Western, the Saturday matinee, the spy thriller, and yet preserving and intensifying the most hostile impulses of that defunct heroism: sadism, xenophobia, misogyny, paranoid anticommunism, each enacted graphically, and yet with a wink that tells us not to take it too seriously, however much we might like it. Even the less overtly bellicose films are, more often than not, merely televisual, despite the greater cost and scope of their images: *Ghostbusters, Beverly Hills Cop,* and *Back to the Future,* to pick just a few exemplary blockbusters, are each little more than a series of broadly subversive confrontations between some ludicrous butt and the cool young star(s). From TV, American film has now absorbed a stream of ironists—Chevy Chase, Bill Murray, Martin Mull, Michael Keaton, Tom Hanks, Steve Martin, Michael J. Fox, and others, some brilliant, some mediocre, but all used to make a smirking audience feel powerful. This archetype of boyish irony has spread beyond the silver screen, having become, in the eighties, through TV, the very paradigm of national leadership. Ronald Reagan, that low-key and aged lad, deftly quoting movie dialogue, and otherwise half jesting at his own theatricality, is yet another sly pseudoinsurgent, forever seeming to stand off, on our behalf, against those grand, archaic entities that menace him and all the rest of us—the "evil empire" based in Moscow, "the bureaucrats" and "special interests" here at home.

Increasingly, TV is nothing but a series of assurances that it can never put one over on us. Those on TV collaborate with those who sit before it, in order to reconfirm forever our collective immunity to TV as it used to be, back when its stars and viewers were not as cool as all of us are now. Pat Sajak, the MC on *Wheel of Fortune,* distinguishes himself from the sort of overheated game show host that was once common on TV: "'You've just won TEN THOUSAND DOLLARS!'" Sajak jabbers in unctuous parody, then adds, in his own more laid-back manner, "I just can't do that." Ruben Blades, schmoozing with Johnny Carson after a hot salsa number, complains of "the stereotypes" that TV has imposed on Hispanics: "Lootsie! I'm home!" he shouts in mimicry of Desi Arnaz, then pleads suavely, "Hey, gimme a break!", and the audience laughs, breaking into applause. And Susan Saint James, hosting *Friday Night Videos* with the two teenage girls who perform with her on *Kate & Allie,* has them giggling at her imitation of the heavy-handed acting she used to do on *Name of the Game.*

Such knowingness sustains the widespread illusion that we have 22 all somehow recovered from a bout of vast and paralyzing gullibility; and yet we cannot be confirmed in this illusion unless we keep on watching, or half watching. Thus, the most derisive viewer is also the most dependent: "Students do not take *General Hospital* seriously," writes Mark Harris in *TV Guide.* "They know it's not life; they say it's a 'soporific'; they feel superior to it. But *General Hospital* is also necessary, indispensable." In short, our jeering hurts TV's commercial project not at all. Everybody knows that TV is mostly false and stupid, that almost no one pays that much attention to it—and yet it's on for over seven hours a day in the average household, and it sells innumerable products. In other words, TV manages to do its job even as it only yammers in the background, despised by those who keep it going.

And it certainly is despised. Everybody watches it, but no one re- 23 ally likes it. This is the open secret of TV today. Its only champions are its own executives, the advertisers who exploit it, and a compromised network of academic boosters. Otherwise, TV has no spontaneous defenders, because there is almost nothing in it to defend. In many ways at once, TV negates the very "choices" that it now promotes with rising desperation. It promises an unimpeded vision of the whole known universe, and yet it shows us nothing but the laughable reflection of our own unhappy faces. It seems to offer us a fresh, "irreverent" view of the oppressive past, and yet that very gesture of rebelliousness turns out to be a ploy by those in power. Night after night, TV displays a bright infinitude of goods, employs a multitude of shocks and teases; and the only purpose of that spectacle is to promote the habit of spectatorship. It celebrates unending "choice" while trying to keep a jeering audience all strung out. TV begins by offering us a beautiful hallucination of diversity, but it is finally like a drug whose high is only the conviction that its user is too cool to be addicted.

Working with the Text

1. What is the relation of the first two paragraphs to the rest of the essay? Why does Miller open his essay with a long celebration of freedom in America? What does that message have to do with what he says about television commercials?

2. What does Miller mean when he says about the Pepsi commercial he analyzes, and by extension all television commercials, that "'choice' is nothing but a quaint illusion"?

3. Miller's title, "Deride and Conquer," is a play on the well-known phrase

"divide and conquer." What does the original phrase mean? What is the significance of Miller's use of it? What does he mean, that is, when he says that television "teaches . . . smug derisiveness" from its commercials to its new programs to its children's shows?

4. Why does Miller begin his essay with a quotation from a network television executive? How does the meaning of the quotation about "choice" relate to Miller's thesis in the essay as a whole?

5. Catalog all the references Miller makes to specific commercials and television shows. Why does he use so many, do you think?

Working beyond the Text

1. Choose a television commercial that seems to you to be extremely well made, clever, or efficient in selling its product. Imitate Miller's analysis of the Pepsi commercial by narrating the commercial in detail and by accounting for its appeal. Does the commercial obey Miller's rule for modern commercials by making fun of itself, inviting you to laugh at its purpose, drawing attention to itself selling you something as it sells you something?

2. Miller points to television as one example of "the illusion of choice" in the United States. Can you point to others? Where else are we offered "choices" that are not choices at all?

3. What children's shows were you raised on? Do you recognize Miller's references to Captain Kangaroo, Mr. Wizard, Mr. Rogers, He-Man, and the Thundercats? Would you agree that the newer children's shows encourage children to "adopt the same contemptuous and passive attitude that TV recommends to grown-ups"?

The Imagined Nostalgic Consumer Utopia
Ian Johnson

Ian Johnson was a first-year student at the University of Arizona in 1993 when he wrote this essay for an accelerated English composition class. It appeared subsequently in the 1994–95 edition of the University of Arizona's *A Student's Guide to First-Year Composition*. His instructor asked students to analyze a text from a popular source in terms of its wider social context. Johnson shows how J. Peterman's *Owner's Manual*, a popular clothing catalog, creates a sense of mystique and nostalgia that has more to do with the fantasy life of the potential buyer than with any real quality of the product.

It might have been like this.

It might have been, if you'd been born a half century earlier. The era of ocean voyages, well-to-do families summering in Tuscany.

A girl 17-½ years old, not yet aware of the effect she had on men. Not entirely.

He sketched her, drifting on the pond. They exchanged secrets. So incredibly serious. A lifetime in a month.

She would never be able to explain any of it to her friends in Rochester. The sketch he gave her would have to do.

(The sketch, in fact, froze the moment, and her, very nicely. Later, in fact, he became quite a famous painter. Of course, by then nobody would be able to understand his paintings at all.)

Ten-Button Skirt. (The one she wore in the sketch.) Pure linen. . . . (Peterman 15)

This is one of many brief vignettes and micro-short stories that showed up on my doorstep last week—not in a literary magazine or even an artsy weekly publication. It was in the J. Peterman Company's *Owner's Manual*, a quarterly clothing catalog for the over-educated, over-worked, and nostalgic credit-card-carrying middle class. This catalog, the high-browed literary equivalent of Budweiser billboards, is also the merchant's version of E.M. Forster's stories: the same impulses that drove Americans to see *A Room with a View* make this catalog a marketing success. J. Peterman's *Owner's Manual* is an extreme example of a trend evident in almost every field of advertising and popular culture: the romantic trend away from practical description towards the marketing of aura. The nature of the aura varies from notions of personal potency and sexual attractiveness to connotations of wealth and class, most often—but not always—dependent upon the product marketed. The rather pretentious sales pitches of J. Peterman's *Owner's Manual* remain just that: sales pitches.

The *raison d'être* of a catalog is to hawk its wares, regardless of its target market or its marketing strategy. In reading J. Peterman's *Owner's Manual*, one must be constantly aware of both what is being sold and to whom. At least eighty-five per cent of the text in this catalog is devoted not to product description, but instead to short anecdotes like the one above linking products (presumably cheap, presumably made in Taiwan) not only to history, but to wealth, the elite, the aristocracy, and old money. The product itself becomes incidental in the medium of this catalog: what is sold here is the psychological satisfaction of being linked to all of these entirely mental concepts. To be given a shirt from this catalog for Christmas, without ever having seen the catalog (and read the stories), is an entirely different experience from ordering it yourself.

My mother did exactly that: she gave me a linen shirt with loose, even billowy, sleeves, tight cuffs, and huge, hand-crafted button. I opened it; she watched me, beaming expectantly. I examined this odd shirt, uncomprehending and somewhat disbelieving: why would my mother give me a shirt out of a Gilbert and Sullivan musical? Apparently, however, she had foreseen this dilemma and had thoughtfully included a copy of J. Peterman's *Owner's Manual* to explain exactly what she had bought me. She had not bought me simply an odd shirt; no, she had given me a shirt like Thomas Jefferson's. But even this is not clear, actually: the shirt she gave me, I think, has something to do with Jefferson, but I'm not entirely sure what:

> Jefferson disliked stuffy people, stuffy houses, stuffy societies. So he changed a few things. Law. Gardening. Government. Architecture.
> Of the thousand castles, mansions, chateaux you can walk through today, only Monticello, only Jefferson's own mansion, makes you feel so comfortable that you want to live in it.
> I think you will feel the same about his 18th century shirt. (Peterman 83)

I have worn this shirt once, around the house; I would feel too 4 flamboyant and theatrical to be seen wearing it in a public place. But I don't get rid of it because it continues, amazingly, to mystify me. It hangs even now in my closet, and I often gaze upon it reverently. Democracy. Self-made man. Wealthy intellectual. Hmmm. Someday I'll wear it.

It becomes clear even in this example that what J. Peterman is sell- 5 ing is not so much the shirt, but the mystique or aura. The illustrations of the products are impressionistic sketches; the products themselves are secondary, mere signifiers for the concepts that Peterman bluntly associates them with. But Peterman is not alone in this association: it is only appropriate that in this society raised and nurtured on costume-drama cinema that there should be a catalog devoted—essentially—to selling the costumes of that drama. By buying the "Gatsby Shirt" you are transported not to the jazz age, but to Hollywood's representation of the Jazz age. Peterman's does not sell clothes from eras that are likely to be actually remembered by any of the buyers; the clothes would then become actual signifiers of individual and real memories. Instead the dating cut-off lies around 1930 or so; anyone with actual and real (i.e. non-Hollywood) memories of that era would be in their late 70's and 80's—definitely not J. Peterman's target market. (Interestingly, there are exceptions to this era bracketing: the few items that are presumably in active manufacture and use today are all of exotic origin and usually made with preindustrial methods in preindustrial communities, though usually not in "third-world" communities which would smack unsavorably as exploitation).

By closely sticking to the more elusive and consensual Hollywood 6 nostalgia, J. Peterman avoids half the work of mental association. Film nouveau presents life in a realistic manner; Hollywood certainly does not. Hollywood's history is a series of clearly linked and rapidly succeeding climactic moments and significant pauses. It is the life we are trained to desire, but which of course is inaccessible except through memory and cinema. We are perpetually dissatisfied with reality and the moment precisely because it is *not* Hollywood. Herein lies the lure of J. Peterman: he sells the hope that upon purchasing the product you will find some of that elusive cinema world, or hyper-reality.

In this way J. Peterman's marketing strategy becomes transparent. 7 He is selling to people who live in "stuffy houses" with "stuffy people" in "stuffy society." He is selling to the struggling middle and upper-middle class in America which is for the most part very hard at work and without history. Middle-class America does not have the luxury of the landed aristocracy that Peterman describes (or alludes to) so frequently. The middle class is essentially rootless and forced to move to where money can be made: they do not have estates and land to support them. Moreover, unlike more traditional nomadic societies, America's middle class does not have an oral tradition to maintain its cohesiveness. (Though it is a charming thought: a group of half-naked accountants smeared with mud and pigments, chanting around a fire and recounting family histories. Perhaps this is the attraction of Robert Bly's men's movement.) Hollywood has obligingly stepped in to fill this void with collective memories for us all (with hefty commercial backing). Unfortunately, few of us are so misled as to be able to accept these collective memories without physical proof. In the absence of family heirlooms, J. Peterman's *Owner's Manual* has given us just that. But Peterman's surrogates are better than family heirlooms: they are collective heirlooms, and all the larger for it. Moreover, by donning the costume of the Hollywood characters, one essentially assumes their position as spectacle: one becomes the adored and admired event of conspicuous consumption.

J. Peterman's persistent references to his own world-skipping and 8 cosmopolitan lifestyle (more than likely imagined from a florescent-lit office in Hoboken) eventually prove irritating to most readers. Most readers are intelligent enough to quickly see Peterman's ploy and grow annoyed at his presumption of the consumer's susceptibility. Peterman waxes poetic about the memories and experiences of the English elite, the gossip of the wealthy, and the social habits of Isak Dinesen-derived characters—all events and subjects inaccessible to your average salesman in Iowa except through the intermediary media of cinema and novels. Peterman makes constant references to secrets, as if he himself were next to you (in an elegant tea room) telling you about his own experiences, initiating you into the crowd that "knows."

References to history and art are abundant: the products become 9 grounded in the tradition of the landed gentry with prices to match. One blurb describes the thoughts of an admiring spectator upon seeing the consumer dressed in a certain sweater: "he probably has a gull-wing Mercedes. . ." (Peterman 121). Another describes mountains of "saddles and hats" obscuring a certain desirable leather bag and a woman who "owns three homes" (Peterman 121, 129). This is not a world in which you can imagine anyone doing taxes or buying milk in plastic jugs: this is the preindustrial world of the privileged elite. It is absurd upon examination to imagine anyone being impelled to purchase based on this strategy, yet apparently it is successful.

But J. Peterman's *Owner's Manual* is only a small example of a   10 much larger phenomenon. Like "Lifestyles of the Rich and Famous" (which J. Peterman's *Owner's Manual* could be the accessory catalog for), J. Peterman's *Owner's Manual* exploits the middle-class need for history and escape. But instead of presenting the past as history, both venues present the past as a role model for consumption. The sixties and seventies have made simple greed a somewhat unacceptable reason for consumption; by presenting a transcendent world of wealth and preindustrial exoticism, both venues provide a mental rationalization for the same exploitative and wasteful consumption that has been the hallmark of American society since the turn of the century.

J. Peterman's *Owner's Manual* functions as the accessory peddler to   11 the imagined communities created by Hollywood and our own memories. The worlds presented in movies and novels are necessarily products of memory and records which cannot be actual transcriptions of experience. If they were they would be like a map on a one-to-one scale: pointless. The abbreviation of memory and of records is not random; the abbreviator chooses climactic moments and often neglects the less satisfying details. This results in a hyperclimactic representation of reality, or a sort of "best of" collection. It disregards the very crap that makes human experience human. No one could ever live in these imagined communities: I think most of us would get tired very quickly. (Margaret Atwood related one of her primary rules in fiction writing: "I always feed my characters." This attention to realistic detail is just the sort of thing that most Hollywood dramas somehow neglect.) But even if we could not live in them, we are still tempted by the possibility. Tempted enough, anyway, to buy Thomas Jefferson's pirate shirt.

Working with the Text

1. What does Johnson mean when he calls the J. Peterman catalog "the high-browed literary equivalent of Budweiser billboards"? In what ways does he imply that the catalog and the billboards are similar?

2. According to Johnson, if the readers of the J. Peterman catalog can see the nature of its sales pitch, become irritated by it, even make fun of it, why is the pitch successful anyway?

3. How does Johnson's tone suggest that he is immune to J. Peterman's advertising ploys? Point to specific passages that illustrate Johnson's detached, ironic distance from the text he analyzes.

Working beyond the Text

1. Which catalogs are you familiar with? Analyze one of them as Johnson analyzes the J. Peterman catalog. How are products presented? What style of photography is used, and what kind of language is used to describe the products? What audience is being targeted? How can you tell?

2. A lot of modern advertising tries not so much to sell a product as an image, implying that if you buy the product you'll fit the image. In what ways does the J. Peterman catalog do this? In what other advertising do you see this operation at work?

3. Johnson claims to see a "romantic trend" in some popular culture, a shift of attention away from the concrete everyday world and toward a vague romantic past (the past of Thomas Jefferson, or of the fictional character Jay Gatsby). Do you see this trend at work in any other aspects of popular culture? Where? Why might Americans be so interested in such visions of life?

About a Salary or Reality? Rap's Recurrent Conflict

Alan Light

Alan Light writes for *Rolling Stone* magazine. For years Light has followed the growth of the hip-hop movement, profiling its major trends and pacesetters. His senior thesis at Yale University, where he earned a degree in American Studies, focused on the rap group the Beastie Boys. The following article appeared in an issue of the *South Atlantic Quarterly* (a journal of literary and cultural studies) devoted to "Rock & Roll and Culture." Light discusses tensions in the rap music industry between the social or political content of the music and the need to sell records.

In 1990, rap dominated headlines and the pop charts as never before. Large segments of the American public were introduced to rap— or at least forced to confront its existence for the first time—through a

pack of unlikely and sometimes unseemly performers. The year
started with the January release of Public Enemy's single "Welcome to
the Terrordome," which prompted widespread accusations (in the
wake of remarks made by Professor Griff, the group's "Minister of Information," that Jews are responsible for "the majority of wickedness
that goes on across the globe") that rap's most politically outspoken
and widely respected group was anti-Semitic. The obscenity arrest of
2 Live Crew in June filled news, talk shows, and editorial pages for
weeks. The concurrent rise of graphic, violent "Gangster Rap" from
such artists as Ice Cube and the Geto Boys stoked these fires, even if
their brutal streetscapes often made for complex, visceral, and challenging records.

It's easy to vilify any or all of these artists. *Newsweek* lumped sev- 2
eral of them together and ran a cover story (19 March 1990) entitled
"Rap Rage," which proved to be a savage attack on the form (including, by some curious extension, the heavy-metal band Guns n' Roses)
as "ugly macho boasting and joking about anyone who hangs out on a
different block," and as having taken "sex out of teenage culture, substituting brutal fantasies of penetration and destruction." Certainly,
Luther Campbell and 2 Live Crew aren't exactly the First Amendment
martyrs of the ACLU's dreams; their music consists of junior high-
school locker-room fantasies set to monotonous, mighty uninspired
beats. The "horror rap" of the Geto Boys is deliberately shocking, and
songs such as "Mind of a Lunatic," in which the narrator slashes a
woman's throat and has sex with her corpse, raise issues that are a
long way from the Crew's doo-doo jokes. Public Enemy, for all of its
musical innovation and political insight, has an uncanny knack for
talking its way deeper into trouble, and leader Chuck D.'s incomprehensible waffling during the Griff incident, first dismissing Griff, then
breaking up the group, then reforming and announcing a "boycott of
the music industry," was maddening and painful to watch.

But there was also a different side to the rap story that was at least 3
as prominent in 1990. M.C. Hammer's harmless dance-pop *Please Hammer Don't Hurt 'Em* became the year's best-selling album and rap's
biggest hit ever. It was finally displaced from the top of the charts by
white superhunk Vanilla Ice's *To the Extreme*, which sold five million
copies in twelve weeks, making it the fastest-moving record in any
style in five years.

Hammer has been defended by the likes of Chuck D. for being 4
rap's first real performer, a dancer/showman/business tycoon of the
first order, but his simplistic regurgitation of hooks from familiar hits
quickly wears thin. Vanilla Ice not only lacks Hammer's passable
delivery, he also manufactured a none-too-convincing false autobiography to validate his appropriation of black culture and subsequent unprecedented commercial success. Both are given to a self-

aggrandizement so far beyond their talents that the biggest problem is simply how annoying they are.

There's nothing criminal about bad music or even simple- 5 mindedness. And it's nothing new for the most one-dimensional, reductive purveyors of a style to be the ones who cash in commercially. But the most unfortunate result of the year of Hammer, Ice, and the Crew is that it may have determined a perception of rap for the majority of America. Any definitions of rap formed by the millions of Americans introduced to it in the last year would probably (and, sad to say, reasonably) center on a simplified analysis of the genre's basest cultural and sociological components and the most uninspired uses of its musical innovation.

If, in 1990, people new to rap gave it any thought at all, they 6 would have concentrated on the crudeness of 2 Live Crew—who may have a constitutional right to be nasty, but there is no way around the ugliness of their lyrics. Newcomers might (understandably, given much of the mainstream press coverage) have dismissed Public Enemy, self-styled "prophets of rage," as mere traffickers in hate. Whatever one thinks of the controversial sampling process, in which pieces of existing records are isolated and digitally stored and then reconstructed as a kind of montage to form a new musical track, the derivative, obvious samples of Hammer and Ice represented the triumph of the technology at its worst. And rap diehards and novices all had to contend with the cheers of "go, white boy, go" as Vanilla Ice became the biggest star yet to emerge from this black-created style.

This has made for a lot of sociocultural analysis and interpreta- 7 tion, which is perfectly appropriate; rap is unarguably the most culturally significant style in pop, the genre that speaks most directly to and for its audience, full of complications, contradictions, and confusion. But what gets lost in this discussion, tragically, is that rap is also the single most creative, revolutionary approach to music and to music making that this generation has constructed.

The distance between M.C. Hammer and the Geto Boys seems to 8 be the final flowering of a contradiction built into rap from its very beginning. Though the polarity may seem inexplicable—is it progress now that we hear not just "how can both be called music?" but "how can both be called rap?"—it is actually a fairly inevitable progression that has been building for years. We can be sure that rap artists are more aware than anyone of the current condition; a press release touting the new group Downtown Science quotes rapper Bosco Money's definitive statement of purpose for 1990: "Our crusade is to fuse street credibility with a song that's accessible to the mainstream."

Rap, however, has seen problematic moments before, times when 9 people were sure it was dead or played out or irrelevant. It has, with relatively alarming frequency for such a young art form, repeatedly found itself at seemingly impassable stylistic crossroads. Off and on for years, it has been torn between the apparently irreconcilable agendas inherent in such a radical pop creation. Throughout the decade of its recorded existence, though, rap has always emerged stronger due to its openness to musical and technological innovation and diversification.

Hip-hop is first and foremost a pop form, seeking to make people 10 dance and laugh and think, to make them listen and feel, and to sell records by doing so. From its early days, even before it became a recorded commodity, it was successful at these things—Russell Simmons recalls promoting rap parties with DJ Hollywood and drawing thousands of devoted New Yorkers years before rap made it to vinyl. "It's not about a salary/It's all about reality," rap N.W.A; even if they didn't claim that life "ain't nothing but bitches and money" on the same album, the fallacy would be clear. On a recent PBS rap special, San Francisco rapper Paris said that "[e]verybody gets into rap just to get the dollars or to get the fame."

At the same time, rap by definition has a political content; even 11 when not explicitly issues-oriented, rap is about giving voice to a black community otherwise underrepresented, if not silent, in the mass media. It has always been and remains (despite the curse of pop potential) directly connected to the streets from which it came. It is still a basic assumption among the hip-hop community that rap speaks to real people in a real language about real things. As *Newsweek* and the 2 Live Crew arrest prove, rap still has the ability to provoke and infuriate. If there is an up side to this hostile response, it is that it verifies rap's credibility for the insider audience. If it's ultimately about a salary, it's still about reality as well. Asked why hip-hop continues to thrive, Run-D.M.C.'s DJ Jam Master Jay replied, "because for all those other musics you had to change or put on something to get into them. You don't have to do that for hip-hop."

At a certain level, these differences are irreconcilable. Since Run- 12 D.M.C. and the Beastie Boys established rap's crossover potential, and Public Enemy demonstrated that pop sales didn't have to result from concessions to more conventional pop structures, the two strains have been forced to move further apart and to work, in many ways, at cross-purposes. It is a scenario familiar in the progression of rock & roll from renegade teen threat to TV commercial music. Perhaps more relevant, the situation is reminiscent of punk's inability to survive the trip from England, where it was a basic component of a radical life, to America, where it was the sound track to a fashionable lifestyle.

If this conflict is fundamental to all pop that is the product of 13 youth culture, it is heightened immeasurably by rap's legitimately radical origins and intentions. But success with a wide, white audience need not be fatal to the genre. The rage directed by much of the rap community at Hammer and Vanilla Ice is ultimately unwarranted—if they make bad records, they're hardly the first, and if that's what hits, it's not going to take the more sophisticated listeners away.

Rap has thus far proven that it can retain a strong sense of where it   14 comes from and how central those origins are to its purpose. If this has sometimes meant shock value for its own sake—which often seems the norm for recent Gangster records, such as N.W.A's *100 Miles and Run-nin'*—and if that is as much a dead end as Hammer's boring pop, the legacy of De La Soul is that there are other ways to work out rap's possibilities. Some of the best new groups, such as Main Source and Gang Starr, may have disappeared by the time this article appears, but they have been integrating melody, live instruments, and samples from less familiar sources into their tracks, learning from De La Soul and Digital Underground and company that hip-hop has other roads still left untrodden.

The paradigmatic hip-hop figure of 1990 would have to be Ice   15 Cube, formerly N.W.A's main lyricist. He recorded *AmeriKKKa's Most Wanted* with Public Enemy's production team, the first real collaboration between the two coasts, and it ruled the streets for most of the year. The album's layered, crunching, impossibly dense sound set a new standard for rap production, the progression we've been waiting for since *It Takes a Nation of Millions to Hold Us Back*. Ice Cube's technical verbal prowess is astonishing: his razor-sharp imagery is cut up into complicated internal rhymes, then bounced over and across the beat, fluid but never predictable, like a topflight bebop soloist.

The content, though, is somewhat more troublesome. When   16 rhyming about the harsh realities of ghetto life, Ice Cube is profane, powerful, and insightful. When writing about women—make that bitches, since he uses that word a full sixty times on the album—things get more disturbing. He has defended "You Can't Fade Me," a first-person account of contemplating murderous revenge on a woman who falsely accuses him of fathering her expected child, by saying that he's just telling a story and illustrating that people really do think that way. It's a fair enough defense, but it's hard to believe that many listeners won't hear it as Ice Cube's own attitude. If part of rap's appeal is the "reality" of the rappers, their lack of constructed stage personae and distance from the audience, Ice Cube simply doesn't establish the constructedness sufficiently to make the song's "objective" narrative effective.

But here's the surprise. At a press conference late in 1990, Ice Cube   17 said that "a lot of people took mixed messages from my album, so I'm just going to have to try to make my writing clearer in the future." It's something rappers have always had a hard time doing—when a performance style is so rooted in boasting and competition, admitting that you might be wrong or even just imperfect is a risky matter. If Public Enemy had been willing to take such an attitude, of course, they could have handled the Griff affair much more gracefully. But if Ice Cube is sincere about improving his expression without compromising it (and his moving, somber antiviolence track "Dead Homiez" bodes well), he may have shown us the future. Like De La Soul's radical rewriting of sampling and hip-hop personae, gangster rap that moves beyond gore and shock is evidence that rap is not trapped in a dead-end dichotomy.

Writing about rap always has a certain dispatches-from-the-front- 18 lines quality; sounds and style change so fast that by the time any generalizations or predictions appear, they have often already been proven false. At any moment, a new rapper or a new attitude or a new technology may appear and the troubled times hip-hop faced in 1990 will be nothing but ancient history. This may be its first real struggle with middle age, but rap has never failed to reinvent itself whenever the need's been there.

Working with the Text

1. What is "rap's recurrent conflict," according to Light? What examples does he use to explain the idea?
2. Light clearly prefers some kinds of rap, and some rap artists, to others. What qualities does Light say make for good rap, and what qualities make for poor rap?
3. Light asserts that "rap is unarguably the most cultural significant style in pop" and "the single most creative revolutionary approach to music and to music making that this generation has constructed." What does he mean? What evidence does he offer?
4. One choice Light makes is not to quote many lyrics from rap songs. Why, do you think? Where in the essay might he have quoted lyrics, and what is the effect of not doing it?

Working beyond the Text

1. Are you interested in rap? If not, what is your impression of it? Where have you heard it and what does it sound like to you? If so, who are your favorite artists and why? Do you see it as pop or dance music, or do you see it as a more serious form of music, as Light seems to?
2. Light discusses the way rap originated as a marginal art form in urban black ghettos and then was absorbed by mainstream pop culture, including

white culture. What other musical forms have followed a similar progression? What other art forms?

3. Rap has been controversial because of the offensive or obscene lyrics of some rap musicians. What have been the arguments against allowing rap artists to record such lyrics? Should "art," including popular art forms such as rap, be censored? If so, under what conditions? If not, why not?

6

LANGUAGES OF PERSONAL

EXPLORATION

The unexamined life is not worth living.

—*Socrates*

INTRODUCTION

Students and teachers may disagree about the purpose of writing about personal experience. Students may feel that a good personal essay tells a story of an important event in their lives, and that if the event is momentous enough, the meaning should be clear. Teachers, on the other hand, may expect students to be more introspective and analytical about their experiences. Instructors sometimes give students the advice from Socrates quoted above, and often counsel students to write about less dramatic, more mundane events from their lives. Why?

English novelist E. M. Forster writes in *Aspects of the Novel* that a "story" can be reduced to a simple chain of events: "and then and then and then." We listen to such stories out of simple curiosity about what will happen next. A "plot," by contrast to a simple story, links the events in the chain with causes and effects, telling not just *what* happened but also *why* it happened. Teachers who ask students to write essays that explore events in their personal lives are usually asking for more than just a story ("and then and then and then"); they are asking for a plot, a procession of moments that, upon examination, reveals patterns—motivations and consequences, plans and accidents, choices and failures to choose. Life, thus examined, becomes worth writing about and reading about.

Why do teachers sometimes advise students not to write about the most traumatic events in their lives? Serious accidents, deaths, rites of passage involving sex, drugs, or drunkenness are the staples of young people's "personal narratives" in popular culture. Why can't students write their own versions of these stories so familiar from TV movies of the week? In many cases, familiarity works against real examination of our lives. Our minds are full of stereotypical, greeting card responses to traumatic events. Rather than analyze our lives, we may simply repeat the ways we have already been taught to think and feel about things. Therefore, the smaller, less momentous event may make a better topic choice. Such events linger in our minds, unattended by the usual, conventional ways of thinking about them, waiting for us to examine and understand them in new ways.

The writers in this chapter reflect on events in their lives, some large and some small, dramatizing specific moments from memory, linking these moments to other moments, creating meaning from the connections. In particular, they explain the importance language has had in their lives, and they use language to shape narratives out of the confusion of experience and memory. In examining their lives in this way, through the analytical lens of language, these writers generate the stories (and plots) that become the ways they understand their lives.

Before You Read

Before you read any combination of essays in this chapter, you might prepare by doing any of the activities below as either class or small group discussions, or as formal or informal writing assignments. They are designed to help you find out what you already know about the issues discussed by the authors in this chapter, so you have some background for understanding what the authors say.

1. Write an account of one of your most vivid childhood memories. Use details that will make the story clear to your reader. As soon as you've finished, write an account of the problems you had in writing down the memory. For example, was it difficult to remember things "just as they happened"? Were you able to write down as many details as you wanted to? How did you solve these problems? As a final step, you might try to combine both the memory and the story about writing down the memory into one narrative.

2. What is "personal writing"? What personal writing have you read? What personal writing have you done yourself? What is personal writing for? In what ways is it "better," truer, or more meaningful than other kinds of writing? What does it lack that other kinds of writing have?

3. One view of personal writing is that it is free of the rules that apply to other writing, especially academic writing. In what ways is it free? What is it not obligated to do that more scholarly forms of writing must do? On the other hand, what "rules" might there be for personal writing? What should or must it do?

4. Keep a diary of the steps you go through to complete a piece of writing in this or another class. Where does the idea for the essay come from? What is your original idea, and how does the idea

change as you write the essay? What problems do you have to solve, and what difficulties do you have to overcome? What advice and help do you get along the way? How satisfied are you with the final result?

After You Read

After you read any combination of essays in this chapter, you might follow up by doing any of the activities below as either class or small group discussions, or as formal or informal writing assignments. They are designed to help you extend what you have learned from the authors in the chapter by discovering new perspectives on the chapter's themes on your own.

1. All of the essays in this chapter deal with the struggle to put "life" into "words." What are the problems and complications of this struggle for each of the writers you read? What are the joys and rewards? Why does each writer feel compelled to keep trying in spite of the complexities involved?

2. All the writers in this chapter are known as writers of essays, poetry, and fiction. Choose a writer whose essay you enjoyed and locate more of his or her work. How does the work you find elsewhere compare with what you read in the essay? Is it clear that the essay and the other work are written by the same person, or are you surprised by differences?

3. Three of the writers in this chapter (Mosle, Rich, and Chávez) describe their diaries and even include excerpts from them. How does each writer use her diary? What is the relation between a diary and life, between a diary and other writing, for each writer? How are the uses of the diary similar and different among the writers?

4. The writers in this chapter describe very personal sources for their writing, tracing their urge to write to aspects of their personal lives. What seems to compel these writers to write? What personal sources for writing are there in your life?

5. Many of the writers in this chapter describe the influence of teachers on students' writing and some are teachers of writing themselves. Has a teacher ever inspired you to write as the contributors to this chapter describe? Do you wish you had met a writing teacher like some of those described?

UNIT ONE

THE EDUCATION OF THE POET

Writing Down Secrets

Sara Mosle

Sara Mosle is a journalist who has published many articles, mostly on education, in such prominent magazines as *The New Yorker* and *The New Republic.* In this essay from *The New Yorker* (September 1995), Mosle explores the problems her inner-city students encounter in their lives and schoolwork, and, in the process of working with them on their daily journals, finds connections between their experiences and hers.

One morning, in the third-grade class where I taught public 1 school, Shameka was sulking. She had arrived late and empty-handed, in what seemed at first like a defiant mood. "Where's your book bag?" I called from the back of the room. (No book bag meant no books, no pencils, no paper.) She flashed me a bored look, gave an exaggerated shrug, and plopped into her seat. I had more than thirty students in my class and had just got them settled in their morning reading groups when Shameka showed up; I was fenced into a corner by a circle of kids sitting cross-legged on the rug. Then Andrew shouted out, "Hey, Miss Mosle! Shameka's crying!" All heads turned so eyes could look her way. I hated to disrupt the lesson, but what to do? Shameka usually returned such unwelcome attention with a feisty "Shut up!"; her silence made me think her tears weren't trivial. I gave out an impromptu assignment and stepped over the kids' heads to investigate. I crouched down next to her and asked, "Shameka, what's wrong?" But she couldn't, or wouldn't, say. As I tried to coax an answer from her, I kept an eye on the kids in the back of the room. Huey had just punched Frederico in the arm. My class was in danger of unravelling.

I was in my third—and, for now, last—year of teaching public 2 school, in Washington Heights, a predominantly Dominican and African-American community that extends some forty-five blocks from Harlem, which ends at about West 155th Street, to Dyckman Street, near the northern tip of Manhattan. The public schools in the neighborhood have some of the most overcrowded classes in the city, and it wasn't until later that day, when I had a free period, that I had a chance to talk to Shameka alone. (Her name, like the names of the other children mentioned here, has been changed.) I took her to an empty lunchroom, the only private spot I could find in the school. She still couldn't talk, but she began to nod or shake her head in response to my questions; this was progress. I tried to pare down the possible causes of her unhappiness, a method that often worked with my students. (By admitting what the problem wasn't, a kid could often acknowledge what it was.) "Is it something that happened at school?" *No.* "Is it something that someone said?" *No.* "Are you in physical pain?" *No.* "Does it have something to do with your family?" Shameka began to cry again: I was getting close. Finally, I asked, "Do you think you could write to me about what is wrong?" She nodded. I ran and got her some paper and a pencil and left her alone for a few minutes.

When I returned, her head lay on the long linoleum-topped table; 3 she had placed the paper and pencil carefully to one side. A single sentence sloped precariously down the page: "I had I DO not have a home but my sister Best frnded home and sha DO not like me."

Huh? Shameka lived a few blocks away, with her mother and sev- 4 eral brothers and sisters; I'd walked her home just a few days before.

With the help of the school's social worker, I decoded the note's 5 meaning. Unbeknownst to Shameka, her family had been evicted from its apartment. Her mother, not wanting to take the kids to a shelter, which she regarded as dangerous, had farmed them out among her friends. She hadn't told Shameka what was happening, because she didn't want to upset her until she had found another place for all of them to live. As I talked to Shameka, I realized that, in the absence of an explanation, her imagination had conjured up a far worse reason for the family's sudden dissolution: she assumed that her mother had died.

I used to tell my students, "I can't help you unless you tell me 6 what's wrong." But they weren't accustomed to asking for help, because in their lives help wasn't always forthcoming. Lost toys were often lost forever. A pair of prescription glasses broken in a playground pratfall and worth a third of the rent might remain broken for months. One kid in my class wept when a button fell off his shirt. (He owned very few clothes, and this shirt was brand-new.) When I produced a needle and thread and sewed the button back on, he grinned at me as though I'd performed a miracle. I suspected that his mother could have performed the same magic, and I turned the incident into a parable: "See? All you have to do is ask for help." But I knew things weren't always that simple. Unlike adults, who have more perspective on their lives, my students often had little idea that the world could be other than what it was for them.

In fact, Shameka's fear about her mother was perfectly plausible. 7
From 1990 to 1992, Washington Heights had more homicides than any
other neighborhood in New York. Partly because of the area's proxim-
ity to the George Washington Bridge, it has an active—and deadly—
drug trade. Suburbanites cross the bridge to buy marijuana, cocaine,
and heroin (the current hot drug among the middle class). I've been
approached several times by dealers on the street who seemed to assume that because I'm white I must be in the neighborhood to buy
drugs. Despite these problems, the neighborhood has a friendly feel.
People congregate and socialize on stoops. Milk jugs with the bottoms
knocked out are pinned on fences and fire escapes to form basketball
hoops. When one boy was murdered, a crossing guard at the school
collected more than a hundred dollars from passers-by, in less than an
hour, to help his family pay for the burial. Recently, the area has become something of an artists' community: opera singers, actors, and
painters have moved in, attracted by low rents and the bohemian atmosphere. Tens of thousands of Dominican immigrants have also
poured into this tiny patch of real estate over the last decade, making
the neighborhood one of the most densely populated in the city, and
creating tensions between Latinos and African-Americans, who have
been there longer. The neighborhood has its share of "welfare mothers," but many of my students' parents worked twelve-hour days,
often at more than one job. They were usually lucky if they earned the
minimum wage. Some labored in what sounded like sweatshops, and
their children often went unsupervised while they worked. (Fifteen
thousand people are currently on the waiting list for child-care programs in the area.) Nearly ninety per cent of the kids at the school
qualified for free lunches. My students were poor.

Had Shameka not been able to write to me, I might never have dis- 8
covered what was wrong with her that day. We'd been working on
first-person narratives—my students kept daily journals in class. But
at first they didn't know how to write about themselves. The skill
doesn't necessarily come naturally, as I learned during my first year in
the classroom. I would put a topic on the board—"What is your favorite movie?" or "What did you dream last night?"—and my students would invariably groan, "I don't want to write about that!" And
who could blame them? Adults don't write in such a void. The purpose of writing—a business letter, a poem, even a bit of graffiti—is to
communicate. But in my early, contrived lessons my students weren't
writing to anyone.

I asked a friend, Gillian Williams, who was also a first-year 9
teacher, for advice. She told me, "Instead of putting topics on the
board, I've started writing back to each kid individually in his or her
own notebook." Every morning, students wrote in their journals, and
every afternoon, Gillian responded to what they had written with a

few lines of her own, asking questions, remarking on their entries, answering questions that her students put to her. The next day, the kids would reply. She had a different dialogue going with each student. She didn't correct spelling or punctuation—she wanted to encourage her students to write freely in this forum, and work on grammar in other lessons. I later learned that this looser method of teaching writing is part of a larger trend in early-childhood education known as "whole language," but Gillian, in the trial-and-error fashion of teachers, had simply devised the approach on her own. I decided to try it in my classroom.

I've never been able to keep a journal. When I start one, the entries 10 usually peter out in a matter of days. Once, when I was in the fifth grade, I did keep a diary for several months, but after my older brother found it and teased me about its contents I threw it away. In Dallas, Texas, where I grew up, in the late sixties and early seventies, reticence was a virtue. In those days, the heartland was, in the words of one writer, a "vast non-Freudian America." I learned to read with "Dick and Jane." Rote exercises constituted most of the writing that I did at the public school I attended. The only time I can remember crying in class was when I sat on a tack in the third grade, and I recall the ordeal mainly because of the injustice involved: the teacher unfairly blamed me for the incident.

Another emotion, however, snakes around this memory: unhappi- 11 ness. Even then, I knew I was crying because of it; the tack had simply provided an alibi for my tears. I seriously doubt whether I could have articulated why I was unhappy then. I don't think it even occurred to me that my unhappiness had a source, although in retrospect it seems obvious: my older sister had died of cancer the year before. The effects of this, however, were so all-encompassing that I thought of her death as simply a fact of life.

I have one sample of my own writing from that period—an ac- 12 count of a trip our family took to Chicago by train over Easter break one year. I was in the third grade—the same age as many of my future students. Here's a typical passage:

> I looked out the window. It was fun. Then I went to the room.
> We were almost to Chicago. Then we went to the lounge. And we
> looked out the window. Then I sang. Then I looked out the window.
> Then we were in Chicago.

And so it goes: then, then, then—up to the top of the John Han- 13 cock building, through the Museum of Science and Industry, and down to the shores of Lake Michigan. What I recall most vividly about that trip now is the giant Seurat painting at the Art Institute of Chicago; back at the hotel, I tried unsuccessfully to mimic his Pointillist style with crayons. But I didn't have the wit, or the knowhow, to write about that. And we certainly didn't discuss the recent death in the family, although I was aware that the trip was our family's first since my sister died, and that we were all trying very hard to have fun. I can no longer recall what I thought about my sister's death then, only that I thought about it a lot. I think that in the isolation of our family's silence I regarded her death somewhat selfishly, as something that had happened to me, and to me alone.

My sister's belongings were stored in a closet in the now spare   14
bedroom of our house. It was a kind of shrine. I used to stand in there and stare at the contents: her jewelry box; her clothing; a large get-well card painted by a family friend who was an artist; her sixth-grade notebook, which still contained her schoolwork and smelled of new plastic. Once, while rummaging through her stuff, I came across a small white vinyl diary with a blue heart on the cover and a tiny silver-and-green padlock that held it shut. I asked my mom if I could read it. She said "No" in a way that communicated anguish. I immediately assumed that she must have read it herself and discovered something upsetting inside. A few years later, when my brother uncovered my diary, he threatened to reveal some childish remarks I had made about being mad at my mom. I threw the diary away rather than risk her finding it. I can still remember what I was thinking: What if *I* died? And my mother read *my* diary? I didn't want to upset her, too.

I became fascinated with my students' journals. As my friend had   15
advised, I encouraged the kids not to worry about spelling or grammar but to get their thoughts down, the way they spoke, in "rough draft." I replied to what they wrote. Although my grammar had been better, they were far more expressive than I had been at their age. And I wondered why. It occurred to me as I read their journals that when I was a kid grownups seldom asked me about my life. Children and adults remained strange to one another. I know that I regarded my own elementary-school teachers as creatures from another planet— ageless and not human. My students, however, seemed to view me as far less mysterious. The journals were what bridged the gap. They operated a little like an apartment-house air shaft, providing a common area where we could communicate. Like neighbors leaning out of windows, we exchanged gossip, inquired after family, caught glimpses of one another's lives. They wrote freely, I think, partly because they were also writing to themselves:

I'm feeling smart today Ms. Mosle yo! and one more thing Ms. Mosle I still want more homework.

They sought advice: 16

Ms. Mosle you said you was going to tell me what to do to help my friend because her mother throw's her out of the house.

They took me to task for perceived injustices: 17

Why don't you put [me as] the office monetor why did you chang my seat. Just because Marla says that I wana change seats with Colleen doesn't mean that you have to change my seat and your the teacher not Marla or me and anyway I want to go back to the dolphins [table] and my freinds too.

They described events in their lives: 18

My firends boyfirend died. And she was sad. I herd in the phone tha she was sad. . . . She lives in New Jersey he was selling drugs for 100 dollars and a man came with 50 dollars and sede if he could take a pack and he sede no. So he had a gun and shot him three times in the chest. then he died. I did not go to the funirow.

When one boy's uncle died, I made the mistake of asking, "Are 19 you sad?" He replied:

Why would you aske a question like that? You make me feel sader because my uncle is Dead. I'll get over it Don't remind me any more please? I loves him so much.

Because many of my students were recent immigrants, they some- 20 times had trouble with idiomatic English. (Certain spelling and syntax errors—for instance, their use of double negatives—consistently reminded me that Spanish was their first language.) Before school one day, I noticed Valentino's mother hovering near her son, and I asked him about it in his journal: "I see your mother every morning. Are you and she close?" Valentino took the question literally, and replied:

Yes becuse sometimes she is cold and I got to grab her a little so she could be a little hot and so she cannot get sick from the wind.

But he went on to answer my question: 21

My mother allways tells me if I'm cold and [I] and [just] a little becuse I got a coat. Sometimes my mother where's a jacket cuse she don't have no coat that's why she holds me and my hands too. . . . In winter she holds me real tied [tight] cuse she is cold. Someday she is gonna buy herself a coat so she cannot be cold too much. My mother she gots to hold me cuse she dosen't have a coat. She gonna buy a big hot coat for herself.

Valentino's entries were always these little prose poems, full of repetitions, which crescendoed and then culminated in a sly last line. Once, when I asked him about his weekend plans, he wrote:

> I'm going to rent a tape of supernintendo tomorrow afternoon. I'm going to my cusun's house to ride a bike a little bit and its gonna be fun in my cusin's house plus my other friend too. All of them are gonna play with me in the house supernintendo. It's gonna be fun tomorrow. Tomorrow thier gonna give me $25 doller and Im gonna have $40 dollers tomorrow. I am gonna have a lot of fun. Tomorrow it is my birthday.

I often asked my students about their earliest memories; I had to 22 struggle to recall my own life at their age. I asked Valentino, "Do you remember being a baby? What's the first thing in your life that you remember? How far back does your memory go?" He gave an uncanny description of infancy:

> A long time ago I used to cry alot. . . . I used to do things that is too dangurous. My mother always had to give me milk cause I was always hungry. . . . When I was a baby I used to make a lot of noice and cry real hard cause I wanted milk. I used to jump in the bed a lot too. Sometimes I used to hit somebody by mistake. . . . Sometimes I use glue and knife and stiked it into my nose but my mother took it out. I hide under the furniture and under my mother's bed. . . . I used to take toys and throw it in the floor.

Most of my students had no books at home. (Many of them didn't 23 even own crayons.) One day, Colleen began her journal entry this way:

> This is a spell:
>
> Double, double toil and trouble,
> fire burn and caldron bubble
>
> Eye of newt and toe of frog
> wool of bat and toung of dog
> Adder's for blindworm sting
> Lizzard's legs and owelts wing
> for acharm in powerfull trouble
> Ike a hell broth boil and bubble
>
> By Me Colleen Acevedo

She had apparently written out the passage from memory. I asked her in her journal where the spell had come from. The next day, she replied:

It is from this dictionary and then is Shakespear is all I know.
What is the story of Thy Romeo and Juliat?

I wrote back: "The spell is from Shakespeare. He was a man who
wrote plays many years ago. The spell is from a play called 'Macbeth.'
It's named for an evil king." This knowledge only excited her further:

I'm right? he did? Where did the name Macbeth [come from]? I
do no[t] know nithing about Romeo and Juliet.

I replied: "'Romeo and Juliet' is a love story. They love each other, but
their parents hate each other and won't let their kids marry. One commits suicide and then so does the other. It's a sad story. Can you tell
me a love story?" She responded:

yes I can.
Well is not exactly a love story is my sister who misses the guy
she likes and he live in Dykeman [Street] his is 14 years old and my
sister is only 12 but still she never forgets him. One day she asked
him that she want to go to the movies but she did not know that [the
movie was rated R] but she did not care and she went with him. He
was kind. . . . he did not did anything bad to her then when my sister
came home my mother gave a rusult to my sister that she is grouned
for 2 weeks no phone, no raido, and no going outside.

We had been studying cause and effect in class and had been talking
about the "results" of characters' actions. Colleen continued:

from that day she was sad and she promised my mother tha she
will never Do it again that's my sister love story. Did you like the
story? Answer yes or no on the bottom
yes or no

I circled "Yes."
Not all my students were as enterprising as Colleen. It's hard to be 24
resourceful without any resources. Cooped up in their tiny apart-
ments, the kids complained most of being bored. Accounts of some
weekends read like the movie listings in *TV Guide*. Daniel described
his weekend: "On Satuerday I saw two movies about Keratie First it
was (The Last Dragon) then it was kickboxer and Sunday I saw Hower
the Duck and then Pee Wee Hermen after that I saw teneg mutie
ningja trunle and at ten o'clock I saw Houes partys 2." Daniel's parents weren't supervising their son, because they were working twelve-
hour days; his mother also attended school. "She is smart," Daniel
wrote. "She goes to school she allways pass the Test it is good haveing
a mother that knows lots of stoff." But for some parents, particularly

working mothers, television was the only available child-care option. Daniel often did the babysitting himself; he was responsible for looking after his bedridden grandmother, a task he actually enjoyed. He explained:

> She is sick that's why I went to her houes but my little brother made it wrost he was jumping all arounded the houes. I'm going to her house until she gets better but with out my little brother. . . . on Thursday I'm going to buy her medison For she could get better and a presnt to cheer her up. We are close but we are closer than that is like glue we are stick.

My students weren't always sweet and nice. Gloria spent several entries impishly describing her skirmishes with her brother: "I hit him in the face so he started to cry." I asked, "Was there any way you could have gotten him to stop hitting you without hitting back?" Gloria replied:

> I hit any way becouse he is a brat. I fight with him a lot becous it get's him mad Pluse I like fighting him it's a lot of fun. . . . he is too much of a crybaby haha. babycryer

I persisted somewhat earnestly:
"How would you like to have a sister who hits you? . . . Is there anything that you like to do with your brother?" She wrote back:

> the only relashanship I have withe my brother is rollerskating me and him is good rollershaking but he always crys because me and him always have races and he always loses to much Pluse in the other letter I told you that he is a brat. That little brat.

I had a feeling that I was being baited. I tried a different tactic: "Are you ever bratty? What would your brother say about you if he were writing to me?" Gloria responded:

> Well I am sometimes bratty but at least I don't cry when they take something away from me.

I gave up: "What do you want to be for Halloween?" Gloria wrote:

> I want to be a devil but [my brother] keeps [bugging] me he could be one. So it look like I have to be a angle. But what I realy want to be is a wich and one more thing why did you chang the subject?

She was onto me.

Like the kids of more affluent working families, my students jeal- 26
ously monitored their parents' attention to them. Colleen wrote:

> I hated Sunday because when I went to my mother's work and
> then when this baby named Michael came he got me so jelous tha he
> climbed on my mother knees. Of course I missed school.

Indeed, the neighborhood where I taught was not so different from far
wealthier communities. There were good parents and bad parents.
Penelope's mom made up spelling quizzes and offered her daughter
incentives to learn:

> I studey words when I already studied the words my mother
> then she gives me a test and if I get all 40 words right she gives me
> $5.00 . . . I studyed foolish-big-large-gocery-detective and many hard
> words.

Some kids went to work with their parents. Renaldo helped his fa- 27
ther on weekends and after school at what sounded like a bodega:

> Today, I worked with my father waching people if there stealing,
> and opening boxes. being the cashier and giving chang

Denny appreciated his father's cameo one weekend: 28

> On Saturday I had a basketball game. they blew us out the score
> was 7–32 My father was there. This is his first time coming to see me
> he said I can play [well] . . . Saturday I saw the duncking and shotout
> [contest]. . . . a rookie won they call him baby Jordan! I can't believe
> that he won because he played agisnst pros.

When one girl's father reneged on his promise to buy her a new 29
coat, she surmised:

> I am a little bit angry with him because he said he was going to
> buy a new coat and dint he always comes up with a lie story he said
> he had a headace that was just that he dosen't want to spend money.

And a few kids' parents were dead or in jail. These facts would 30
trickle out over time. One kid, William, had transferred to my class
several weeks into the year. He was smart, but he never did his homework, and he often picked on other kids in class. I hadn't had much
success in talking to him about his difficulties. I asked him what he
had done over his Thanksgiving vacation. He replied:

> I had a nice Thanksgiving. I ate turkey and rice and ham. I
> played with my friends I went to see home alone!!! I had a nice
> thanksgiving. I went to see my father in jail. I am happy to see him in
> thanksgiveing.

Beneath what he wrote he drew a picture of a building with a man
standing in a window at the top. I asked, "Is this the picture of the jail?
How long has your father been there? . . . Will he be there long? Have
you visited him before?" He wrote back:

> Yes I visited him before a long tie ago and he geting fat and big
> he look nice. I see my bother and my father I saw my bother on
> thanksgiveing and we had fun we want to see my father in jail.

Sometimes I wasn't sure how to respond. I tried not to be judg- 31
mental: "I bet you miss your father. If you could write him a letter,
what would you say?" William wrote, "Dear Dad, I LOVE you. I miss
you a lot and I wish you could come out of jail today. I love you, me,
mom, brother, and sister." I asked William if he wanted to send his father a real letter, and he said yes. He stayed after school one day, and
we made it together, out of construction paper, markers, and glue. He
brought his father's address to school the next day, and we mailed his
creation. From that moment on, William's behavior changed; he
started doing his work and stopped picking fights. He often stayed
after school to do homework or just hang out in my classroom while I
graded papers or prepared the next day's lessons. And William's father had begun to write to him. William sent his father a valentine and
described his father's reply in his journal:

> He wrote me a ltter saiding he like it he said to write him alot he
> said he love me and my mother.

During that last year of teaching, I had one student, Drew, who in- 32
dicated just before Christmas that his mother was ill. Encouraged by
my success with William, I asked him if he wanted to make her a get-
well card. He nodded, and stayed after school that same afternoon.
Drew was a good artist; he decorated his card with a cut-out Christmas tree and freehand drawings of cartoon characters. In his best
handwriting, he wrote: "Dear Mom, I hope you feel better. I miss you
lots and lots. I hope to see you soon. xxx ooo love, Drew." Below this
letter he sketched a picture of a woman lying in a hospital bed, surrounded by doctors. When I asked him if he wanted to mail it, he gave
me a bewildered look and shook his head. I assumed that his mother
was at home and that he would take the card to her there. A couple of

months later, another teacher revealed that Drew's mother had died two years earlier; she'd been burned to death by drug dealers.

To this day, I'm not sure why Drew fabricated that story, but I 33 know that there can be shame for a kid in having a dead mother. I occasionally lied as a kid about my sister; friends would come over and ask me who the girl was in all the family photographs and I'd say a cousin, or, incredibly, myself at a younger age; it was easier than trying to explain. At the end of the year, I found the card Drew had made in his desk. Drew, who tore the covers off his workbooks, wadded up assignments, and once scribbled in a brand-new library book, had preserved for more than six months the card that he'd made to comfort himself.

Over time, I began to realize how often even young children can 34 feel as responsible as adults do for the people around them. My students wanted to protect their families; they wanted to protect *me*. "You don't have to walk me home, Ms. Mosle. My block is dangerous," one nine-year-old insisted. It was too dangerous for me but not for him. Another student, Roberto, described the sense of responsibility he felt when his mother fell and broke her leg:

> She was trying to walk on her foot with a walker and sometimes I help her walk but sometimes she don't want help. . . . she try to go to the bathroom and try to take a bath. Witch is the hard part so I help her to cary the chiar that's so heavy so [I ask] my father to hlep me and I help him sometimes, and [sometimes] he don't want no help so I said ok dad.

He gave me periodic updates on her recovery in his journal:

> She's walking a littile now and I help mom to walk and I give her water oh! . . . and I help her take a bath bursh her teeth help get dressed and help her cook and help her do breakfast put on her shoes and sock's and help put on her shirt and puts me to sleep at 8:00.

I wrote, "She is lucky to have such a nice son as you." At one point, he confessed:

> I was afraid that mother is going to die but she did'nt die and I was happy and proud of myself and when she came home it was her birthday and I speprail [surprise] her and give her gifts then she went to sleep. thank you for listen.

A few years ago, I finally pried open my sister's diary; I was in my 35 late twenties. I had always assumed that my mother had forbidden me to read it because it contained some revelation that she feared would upset me: a dreadful description by my sister of her cancer or her fear of death—or even, perhaps, some damning remark about me. But these, it turned out, were childhood fantasies. My imagination, like Shameka's, had conjured up something far worse than the reality, and after reading the diary I concluded that my mom had never read it herself. I then set to wondering what she might have been afraid of finding inside: Criticism? Descriptions of an illness and suffering that she couldn't prevent or cure? Or just a glimpse of her dauther's lost personality—a loss that she didn't need or want to relive? Maybe my mother, unlike me, didn't need to go searching for clues to who my sister was. (As it happened, I was wrong: I recently learned that of course she had read it, too.)

The diary is, in fact, almost completely empty. The entries begin 36 on September 14, 1969; my sister was ten years old and had just begun the fourth grade. For several months, her entries continue in this vein:

> Sept. 19th, 1969 forgot.
>
> _____
>
> Sept. 20th 1969 forgot.
>
> _____
>
> September 21, 1969 Go to 9:00 church, then 10:50 church (choir). Come home from church. Play Kickball & Soccer with Brian and Jon (Sara, too) Try on clothes. Help mom.
>
> _____
>
> Sept. 22nd, 1969 School (Test) Music Dinner Bed.
>
> _____
>
> Sept. 23rd, 1969 School (Test) (orchestra) choir Dinner Bed.
>
> _____
>
> Sept. 24, 1969 School (Test) play bed.

I had to laugh: my sister's prose style was not unlike my own as a 37 kid. Then, near the end of November, the entries abruptly stop. A few weeks before Christmas of that year, my sister woke up with a sharp pain in her abdomen, and my parents took her to the hospital. She had a malignant tumor on her liver, an almost unheard-of diagnosis in a child her age. On December 21st, she had the first of several operations; I can remember the date because it was the day after my sixth birthday. Entries don't appear again until the spring, and then there are only three, much like those above; another week's worth arrive when my sister attended summer camp; then there is nothing more until the following June.

I was grateful to learn that my sister's illness hadn't transformed 38 her completely. (At the back of her diary is this list: "BOYS I LIKE: CHRIS B., DALE M., JEFF B.") Only in her last few entries is there any indication that she was ill:

> June 16, 1971. Wed. Went to have plasmapharesis blood test.
> Went have regular blood. Checked in at Methodist Hospital in Hous-
> ton. Visited with David Mumford. Dr. Crawford and Dr. Eiband
> dropped by. Granny and Grandpa and Dad came by. Watch TV.
> Went to bed.

My sister's handwriting reveals a struggle over the spelling of
"plasmapheresis." She had obviously encountered something that she
didn't want or know how to explain. Does that mean, though, that she
didn't understand what was happening to her? I don't know.
Nowhere does she mention the chemotherapy, the needles, the
catheters, the wig. Reading what she wrote, I understood the desire to
back away from these things. (Our family's reticence finally made
sense to me.) My sister made her last entry three months before she
died:

> June 17, 1971. Went and have liver scan. Had biopsy. Laid on my
> side for four hours.

One afternoon, after my sister's death—I must have been eight or 39
nine years old—I was sitting at my mother's dressing table, trying on
her makeup and perfume. Grownups, I think, misunderstand the purpose of playing dress-up. I wasn't pretending to be my mother; I was
trying to understand her. In my mind, those bottles and jars contained
the secrets of adulthood. As I rummaged through her things, I came
across a small cardboard box and opened it. I immediately recognized
the contents and their import, and closed the box and put it away. I'd
found what I was looking for; I never mentioned the discovery to my
mom. Although I'm not sure how, I knew that the lock of blond hair
was my sister's, and that it bespoke an enormous and unmentionable
grief.

I had forgotten this incident until I began to teach. In education 40
classes, I was constantly taught to be sensitive to the obvious differences between my students' backgrounds and my own. But by empha-
sizing the differences, I think, we sometimes forget that other people's
children are like our own. As I read my students' journals, I came to appreciate our unexpected similarities. My students, like my sister, were
recognizably children. They, like me, had a secret life that they were
yearning to share. Roberto's mother did get well, but some weeks after
her accident I asked him in his journal how she was doing. He wrote:

> I like to be a doctor and How about she dies before I grow up,
> and I will tell you when [she] dies. it a secret . . . it just between us,
> when my mother dies, am going to take a sissor and cut my mother
> hair for I won't forget her when she dies. P.S. don't tell nobody. See
> you soon.

Working with the Text

1. Mosle begins her essay with an anecdote about a troubled student named Shameka. What is the story she tells about Shameka? What is the point of beginning the essay with it? How does that story relate to any overall point of the essay?

2. Why do Mosle's students have trouble responding to her early writing assignments, such as, "What is your favorite movie?" and "What did you dream last night?" Why does the idea of journal writing that she learns from her friend, Gillian Williams, work better?

3. In an essay about her students' journal writing, Mosle includes material about her own journal writing, about her sister's journal, about reading her sister's journal, and so on. Why? What is the connection between her students' experiences and her own? What point does the connection help her make?

4. Mosle writes a long description of the neighborhood where she works and ends it with a simple sentence: "My students were poor." Why does she save this sentence for the end of the paragraph? Why is it so short and simple? How does the style of the sentence contribute to the meaning of the paragraph?

5. Mosle reproduces her students' writing without correcting their spelling or grammar. Why, do you think?

Working beyond the Text

1. Mosle says that personal writing is a skill that "doesn't necessarily come naturally." Would you agree? What is hard about writing a personal narrative? Why is it more difficult than writing in a more academic style, for example? How can you solve the problems of writing personal narratives? If you have recently done a piece of personal writing or are currently working on one, you might refer to it to explain the problems you had and how you solved them.

2. Mosle mentions the "whole language" approach to language teaching. What is the "whole language" approach? Use the library to define it for yourself. Is Mosle's approach a good example of "whole language"? Were you taught with a "whole language" approach in elementary school? Describe how you were taught to write.

3. Do you think that the method Mosle used with her third-graders is appropriate for adults? Try the method for a while, either with your teacher or with friends or classmates. Write journal entries about any topic that interests you, and then trade journals. Write comments on the journals of others similar to Mosle's comments to her students, asking for opinions or more information. Respond in your journal to the questions of others.

How I Started Writing Poetry

Reginald Lockett

Reginald Lockett, born in 1947, writes poetry and teaches creative writing in Northern California. His works include *Good Times & No Bread*. He grew up in Oakland, California, and refers to himself as having been a "thug" in those days. This essay was published in an anthology called *California Childhood: Recollections and Stories of the Golden State* (1988). In it, Lockett recounts his experiences in a junior high school creative writing class, where he wrote poetry for the first time and discovered a creative alternative to being a "thug."

At the age of fourteen I was what Richard Pryor over a decade 1 later would call "going for bad," or what my southern-bred folks said was "smellin' your pee." That is, I had cultivated a facade of daring-do, hip, cool, con man bravado so prevalent among adolescent males in West Oakland. I "talked that talk and walked that walk" most parents found downright despicable. In their minds these were dress rehearsals of fantasies that were Popsicles that would melt and evaporate under the heat of blazing hot realities. And there I was doing the pimp limp and talking about nothing profound or sustaining. All I wanted to do was project that image of being forever cool like Billy Boo, who used to wear three T-shirts, two slipover sweaters and a thick Pendleton shirt tucked neatly in his khaki or black Ben Davidsons to give everybody the impression that he was buffed (muscle bound) and definitely not to be messed with. Cool. Real cool. Standing in front of the liquor store on 35th and San Pablo sipping white port and lemon juice, talking smack by the boatloads until some real hoodlum from Campbell Village (or was it Harbor Homes?) with the *real* biceps, the shonuff triceps and sledgehammer fists beat the shirt, both sweaters, the T-shirts and pants right off of Billy Boo's weak, bony body.

Herbert Hoover Junior High, the school I attended, was consid- 2 ered one of three toughest in Oakland at that time. It was a dirty, gray, forbidding looking place where several fights would break out every day. There was a joke going around that a mother, new to the city, mistook it for the Juvenile Detention Center that was further down in West Oakland on 18th and Poplar, right across the street from DeFremery Park.

During my seventh-grade year there were constant referrals to the 3 principal's office for any number of infractions committed either in Miss Okamura's third-period music class or Mrs. George's sixth-period math class in the basement where those of us with behavioral problems and assumed learning disabilities were sent. It was also around this time that Harvey Hendricks, my main running buddy, took it upon himself to hip me to everything he thought I needed to know about sex while we were doing a week's detention in Mrs. Balasco's art class for capping on "them steamer trunks" or "suitcases" under her eyes. As we sat there, supposedly writing "I will not insult the teacher" one hundred times, Harvey would draw pictures of huge tits and vaginas, while telling me how to rap, kiss and jump off in some twanks and stroke. Told me that the pimples on my face were "pussy bumps," and that I'd better start getting some trim or end up just like Crater Face Jerome with the big, nasty-looking quarter-size pus bumps all over his face.

Though my behavior left a lot to be desired, I managed to earn 4 some fairly decent grades. I loved history, art and English, and somehow managed to work my way up from special education classes to college prep courses by the time I reached ninth grade, my last year at Hoover. But by then I had become a full-fledged, little thug, and had been suspended—and damn near expelled—quite a few times for going to knuckle city at the drop of a hat for any real or imagined reason. And what an efficient thief I'd become. This was something I'd picked up from my cousins, R.C. and Danny, when I started hanging out with them on weekends in San Francisco's Haight-Ashbury. We'd steal clothes, records, liquor, jewelry—anything for the sake of magnifying to the umpteenth degree that image of death-defying manhood and to prove I was indeed a budding Slick Draw McGraw. Luckily, I was never caught, arrested and hauled off to Juvenile Hall or the California Youth Authority like so many of the guys I ran with.

Probably through pressure from my parents and encouragement 5 from my teachers and counselors, I forced myself to start thinking about pursuing a career after graduation from high school, which was three years away. Reaching into the grab bag of professional choices, I decided I wanted to become a physician, since doctors were held in such high esteem, particularly in an Afro-American community like West Oakland. I'd gotten it in my head that I wanted to be a plastic surgeon, no less, because I liked working with my hands and found science intriguing. Then something strange happened.

Maybe it was the continuous violence, delinquency and early preg- 6 nancies that made those Oakland Unified School District administrators (more than likely after some consultation with psychologists) decide to put a little Freudian theory to practical use. Just as I was grooving, really getting into this fantastic project in fourth-period art class, I was called up to the teacher's desk and handed a note and told to report to a classroom downstairs on the first floor. What had I done this time? Was it because I snatched Gregory Jones' milkshake during lunch a couple of days ago and gulped it down, savoring every drop like an old loathsome suck-egg dog, and feeling no pain as the chump, big as he was, stood there and cried? And Mr. Foltz, the principal, was known to hand out mass suspensions. Sometimes fifteen, twenty, twenty-five people at a time. But when I entered the classroom, there sat this tall, gangly, goofy-looking white woman who wore her hair unusually long for that time, had thick glasses and buckteeth like the beaver on the Ipana Toothpaste commercials. Some of the roughest, toughest kids that went to Hoover were in there. Especially big old mean, ugly Martha Dupree who was known to knock out boys, girls, and teachers when she got the urge. If Big Martha asked you for a last-day-of-school kiss, you'd better give it up or make an appointment with your dentist.

When Miss Nettelbeck finally got our attention, she announced 7 that this was a creative writing class that would meet twice a week. Creative writing? What the hell is creative writing a couple of us asked. She explained that it was a way to express what was on your mind, and a better way of getting something off of your chest instead of beating up your fellow students. Then she read a few poems to us and passed out some of that coarse school-issue lined paper and told us to write about something we liked, disliked, or really wanted. What I wanted to know was, did it have to be one of "them pomes." "If that's how you want to express yourself, Reginald," she said. So I started racking my brain, trying to think about what I liked, didn't like and what I really wanted. Well, I liked football, track and Gayle Johnson, who would turn her cute little "high yella" nose up in total disgust everytime I tried to say something to her.

I couldn't stand the sight—not even the thought—of old monkey- 8 face Martha. And what I really wanted was either a '57 Buick Roadmaster or a '56 Chevy with mag wheels and tuck 'n' roll seats that was dropped in the front like the ones I'd seen older dudes like Mack's brother, Skippy, riding around in. Naw, I told herself, I couldn't get away with writing about things like that. I might get into some more trouble, and Big Martha would give me a thorough asskicking for writing something about mashing her face in some dough and baking me some gorilla cookies. Who'd ever heard of a poem about cars? One thing I really liked was the ocean. I guess that was in my blood because my father was then a Master Chief Steward in the Navy, and, when I was younger, would take me aboard ships docked at Hunter's Point and Alameda. I loved the sea so much that I would sometimes walk from my house on Market and W. MacArthur all the way to the Berkeley Pier or take a bus to Ocean Beach in San Francisco whenever I wasn't up to no good. So I wrote:

> I sit on a rock
> watching
> the evening tide
> come in.

The green waves travel
  with the wind.
They seem to carry
  a message of
warning, of plea
  from the dimensions
of time and distance.

When I gave it to Miss Nettelbeck, she read it and told me it was 9
good for a first attempt at writing poetry, and since there was still
some time left in the period, I should go back to my seat and write
something else. Damn! These teachers never gave you any kind of
slack, no matter what you did and how well you did it. Now, what
else could I think of to write about? How about a tribute to Miss
Bobby, the neighborhood drag queen, who'd been found carved up
like a Christmas turkey a week ago? Though me, Harvey and Mack
used to crack jokes about "her" giving up the boodie, we still liked and
respected "her" because she would give you five or six dollars to run
an errand to the cleaners or the store, never tried to hit on you, and
would get any of the other "girls" straight real quick if they even said
you were cute or something. So I wrote:

Bring on the hustlers
In Continental suits
And alligator shoes.
Let ladies of the night
In short, tight dresses
And spiked heels enter.
We are gathered here
To pay tribute to
The Queen of Drag.

What colorful curtains
And rugs!
Look at the stereo set
And the clothes in the closet.
On the bed, entangled
In a bloody sheet,
Is that elegant one
Of ill repute
But good carriage
Oh yes! There
Was none like her.
The Queen of Drag.

When she read that one, I just knew Miss Nettelbeck would imme- 10
diately write a referral and have me sent back upstairs. But she liked it

and said I was precocious for someone at such an innocent age. Innocent! When was I ever innocent? I was guilty of just about everything I was accused of doing. Like, get your eyes checked, baby. And what was precocious? Was it something weird? Did it mean I was queer like Miss Bobby? Was I about to go to snap city like poor Donny Moore had a year ago when he suddenly got up and started jacking off in front of Mr. Lee's history class? What did this woman, who looked and dressed like one of them beatniks I'd seen one night on *East Side, West Side*, mean? My Aunt Audry's boyfriend, Joe, told me beatniks were smart and used a lot of big words like precocious so nobody could understand what they were talking about. Had to be something bad. This would mess with me for the rest of the week if I didn't ask her what she meant. So I did, and she told me it meant that I knew about things somebody my age didn't usually know about. Wow! That could only mean that I was "hip to the lip." But I already knew that.

For some reason I wasn't running up and down the streets with the fellas much anymore. Harvey would get bent out of shape everytime I'd tell him I had something else to do. I had to, turning punkish or seeing some broad I was too chinchy to introduce him to. This also bothered my mother because she kept telling me I was going to ruin my eyes if I didn't stop reading so much; and what was that I spent all my spare time writing in a manila notebook? Was I keeping a diary or something? Only girls kept diaries, and people may start thinking I was one of "them sissy mens" if I didn't stop. Even getting good grades in citizenship and making the honor roll didn't keep her off my case. But I kept right on reading and writing, looking forward to Miss Nettelbeck's class twice a week. I stopped fighting, too. But I was still roguish as ever. Instead of raiding Roger's Men's Shop, Smith's and Flagg Brothers' Shoes, I was stealing books by just about every poet and writer Miss Nettelbeck read to the class. That's how I started writing poetry.

Working with the Text

1. What does Lockett mean when he says that the school district administrators decided to "put a little Freudian theory to practical use"? Why did the school decide to give the "roughest, toughest kids" a poetry class?

2. What is the difference between the two poems that Lockett writes during the first class period with Miss Nettelbeck? Why does he decide against writing about cars? What does he think she will think of the poem about Miss Bobby? Why do you think she likes it?

3. What kind of teacher is Miss Nettelbeck, based on Lockett's narrative about her creative writing class? What are her goals for her students? What methods does she use? Is her teaching effective?

4. Lockett begins with a sketch of his rough neighborhood and calls himself a "full-fledged little thug." He ends by talking about "stealing books by just about every poet and writer Miss Nettelbeck read to the class." Why might Lockett give the reader these images at the strategic beginning and end of the essay?

Working beyond the Text

1. What is your image of a "poet"? What kind of people write poetry, and what kinds of things do they write about? What poems have you read, and by whom? How does Lockett defy the stereotype of a "poet," and how are the two poems in the essay different from the stereotypical "poem"?

2. Have you ever written poems? If so, what were they like? Why did you write them, and who did you show them to? If not, why not? Did it never occur to you to try to "express yourself" in poetry, as Miss Nettelbeck puts it, or were there other reasons?

3. Locate some poems by Lockett by finding his books or using a guide to periodicals in your library. How do the poems compare to the first two poems he ever wrote, during the first day of poetry class with Miss Nettelbeck?

The Education of the Poet

Louise Glück

Louise Glück, a poet and English professor, was born in New York City. Like much contemporary poetry, Glück's writing often experiments with language; her books of poetry include *Firstborn*, *The House on Marshland*, and *Ararat*. In this essay, included in an anthology entitled *The Confidence Woman*, Glück examines the events of her personal life that influence her poetry, including her family life, her anorexia and subsequent psychotherapy, and her apprenticeship with older poets.

The fundamental experience of the writer is helplessness. This 1 does not mean to distinguish writing from being alive: it means to correct the fantasy that creative work is an ongoing record of the triumph of volition, that the writer is someone who has the good luck to be able to do what he or she wishes to do: to confidently and regularly imprint his being on a sheet of paper. But writing is not decanting of personality. And most writers spend much of their time in various kinds of torment: wanting to write, being unable to write; wanting to write differently, being unable to write differently. In a whole lifetime, years are spent waiting to be claimed by an idea. The only real exercise of will is negative: we have toward what we write the power of veto.

It is a life dignified, I think, by yearning, not made serene by sen- 2 sations of achievement. In the actual work, a discipline, a service. Or, to utilize the metaphor of childbirth which seems never to die: the writer is the one who attends, who facilitates: the doctor, the midwife, not the mother.

I use the word *writer* deliberately. *Poet* must be used cautiously; it 3 names an aspiration, not an occupation. In other words: not a noun for a passport.

It is very strange to want so badly what cannot be achieved in life. 4 The high jumper knows, at the instant after performance, how high he has been; his achievement can be measured both immediately and with precision. But for those of us attempting dialogue with the great dead, it isn't a matter of waiting: the judgment we wait for is made not by the dead but by the unborn; we can never, in our lifetimes, know it.

The profundity of our ignorance concerning the merit of what we 5 do creates despair; it also fuels hope. Meanwhile contemporary opinion rushes to present itself as the intelligent alternative to ignorance: our task is somehow to insulate ourselves from opinion in its terminal forms: verdict and directive, while still retaining alert receptiveness to useful criticism.

If it is improper to speak as a poet, it is equally difficult to speak 6 on the subject of education. The point, I think, would be to speak of what has left indelible impressions. But I discover such impressions slowly, often long after the fact. And I like to think they are still being made, and the old ones still being revised.

The axiom is that the mark of poetic intelligence or vocation is pas- 7 sion for language, which is thought to mean delirious response to language's smallest communicative unit: to the word. The poet is supposed to be the person who can't get enough of words like *incarnadine*. This was not my experience. From the very beginning, from the time, at four or five or six, I first started reading poems, first thought of the poets I read as my companions, my predecessors, from the beginning I preferred the simplest vocabulary. What fascinated me were the possibilities of context. What I responded to, on the page, was the way a poem could liberate, by means of a word's setting, through subtleties of timing, of pacing, that word's full and surprising range of meaning. It seemed to me that simple language best suited this enterprise; such language, in being generic, is likely to contain the greatest and most dramatic variety of meaning within individual words. I liked scale, but I liked it invisible: I loved those poems that seemed so small on the page but that swelled in the mind; I didn't like the windy, dwindling kind. Not surprisingly, the sort of sentence I was drawn to, which reflected these tastes and native habit of mind, was paradox. Which has the added advantage of nicely rescuing the dogmatic nature from a too-moralizing rhetoric.

I was born into the worst possible family, given this bias. I was 8 born into an environment in which the right of any family member to complete the sentence of another was assumed. Like most of the people in that family, I had a strong desire to speak, but that desire was regularly frustrated: my sentences were, in being cut off, radically changed—transformed, not paraphrased. The sweetness of paradox is that its outcome cannot be anticipated: this ought to ensure the attention of the audience. But in my family all discussion was carried on in that single cooperative voice.

I had, early on, a very strong sense that there was no point to 9 speech if speech did not precisely articulate perception. To my mother, speech was the socially acceptable form of murmur: its function was to fill a room with ongoing, consoling human sound. And to my father it was performance and disguise. My response was silence. Sulky silence, since I never stopped wanting deferential attention. I was bent on personal distinction, which was linked, in my mind, to the making of sentences.

In other ways, my family was remarkable. Both my parents ad- 10 mired intellectual accomplishment; my mother, in particular, revered creative gifts. At a time when women were not, commonly, especially well educated, my mother fought to go to college; she went to Wellesley. My father was the first and only son among five daughters, the first child born here. His parents had come from Hungary; my grandfather was a better dreamer than administrator of the family land: when the crops failed and the cattle died, he came to America, opened a grocery store. By family legend, a just man, less forceful than his wife and daughters. Before he died, his little store was the last piece of real estate on a block being bought up by one of the Rockefellers. This was generally deemed remarkable good fortune, in that my grandfather could ask, now, any price at all. For which behavior my grandfather had complete contempt. He would ask, he said, the fair price: by definition, the same for Mr. Rockefeller as for anyone else.

I didn't know my father's parents; I knew his sisters. Fierce 11 women, in the main dogmatic, who put themselves through college and had, in the remote past, dramatic and colorful love lives. My father refused to compete, which, in his family, meant he refused to go to school. In a family strong on political conscience but generally deficient in imagination, my father wanted to be a writer. But he lacked certain qualities: lacked the adamant need which makes it possible to endure every form of failure: the humiliation of being overlooked, the humiliation of being found moderately interesting, the unanswerable fear of doing work that, in the end, really isn't more than moderately interesting, the discrepancy, which even the great writers live with (unless, possibly, they attain great age) between the dream and the evidence. Had my father's need been more acute, he probably would have found a means to overcome his emotional timidity; in the absence of acute need, he lacked motive to fight that battle. Instead, he went into business with his brother-in-law, made a notable success and lived, by most criteria, a full and fortunate life.

All this time, I pitied him his decision. I think now that, in regard 12 to my father, I'm blind, because I see in him my own weaknesses. But what my father needed to survive was not writing, it was belief in his potential—that he chose not to test that potential may have been good judgment, not, wholly, want of courage.

My mother was the sort of maid-of-all-work moral leader, the 13 maker of policy. She considered my father the inspired thinker. She was dogged; he had that quality of mind my mother lacked, which she equated with imaginative capacity: he had lightness, wit. My mother was the judge. It was she who read my poems and stories and, later, the essays I wrote for school; it was her approval I lived on. It wasn't easy to get, since what we did, my sister and I, was invariably weighed against what, in my mother's view, we had the ability to do. I used to make regularly the mistake of asking her what she thought. This was intended as a cue for praise, but my mother responded to the letter, not the spirit: always, and in detail, she told me exactly what she thought.

Despite these critiques, my sister and I were encouraged in every 14 gift. If we hummed, we got music lessons. If we skipped, dance. And so on. My mother read to us, then taught us to read very early. Before I was three, I was well grounded in the Greek myths, and the figures of those stories, together with certain images from the illustrations, became fundamental referents. My father didn't read; he told stories. Sometimes these were wholly invented, like the adventures of a pair of bugs, and sometimes they were revised history, his particular favorite being the tale of Saint Joan, with the final burning deleted.

My sister and I were being raised, if not to save France, to recog- 15 nize and honor and aspire to glorious achievement. We were never given to believe that such achievement was impossible, either to our sex or our historical period. I'm puzzled, not emotionally, but logically, by the contemporary determination of women to write as women. Puzzled because this seems an ambition limited by the existing conception of what, exactly, differentiates the sexes. If there are such differences, it seems to me reasonable to suppose that literature reveals them, and that it will do so more interestingly, more subtly, in the absence of intention. In a similar way, all art is historical: in both its confrontations and evasions, it speaks of its period. The dream of art is not to assert what is already known but to illuminate what has been hidden, and the path to the hidden world is not inscribed by will.

I read early, and wanted, from a very early age, to speak in return. 16 When, as a child, I read Shakespeare's songs or, later, Blake and Yeats and Keats and Eliot, I did not feel exiled, marginal. I felt, rather, that this was the tradition of my language: *my* tradition, as English was my language. My inheritance. My wealth. Even before they've been lived through, a child can sense the great human subjects: time which breeds loss, desire, the world's beauty.

Meanwhile, writing answered all sorts of needs. I wanted to make 17 something. I wanted to finish my own sentences. And I was sufficiently addicted to my mother's approval to want to shine at something she held in high esteem. When I wrote, our wishes coincided. And this was essential: hungry as I was for praise, I was also proud and could not bear to ask for it, to seem to need it.

Because I remember, verbatim, most of what I've written in the 18 course of my life, I remember certain of my early poems; where written records exist, they confirm these memories. Here's one of the earliest, written around the time I was five:

> If kitty cats liked roastbeef bones
> And doggies sipped up milk;
> If elephants walked round the town
> All dressed in purest silk;
> If robins went out coasting,
> They slid down, crying *whee;*
> If all this happened to be true,
> Then where would people be?

Plainly, I loved the sentence, as a unit: the beginning of a preoccu- 19 pation with syntax. Those who love syntax less find in it the stultifying air of the academy: it is, after all, a language of rules, of order. Its opposite is music, pure sound, that quality of language which is felt to persist in the absence of rule. One possible idea behind such preferences is the fantasy of the poet as renegade, as the lawless outsider. It seems to me that the idea of lawlessness is a romance, and romance is what I most struggle to be free of.

I experimented with other mediums. For awhile I thought of 20 painting, for which I had a small gift. Small, but, like my other aptitudes, relentlessly developed. At some point in my late teens, I realized I was at the end of what I could imagine on canvas, but I think that, had my gift been larger, or more compelling, I would still have found the visual arts a less congenial language. Writing suits the conservative temperament. What is edited can be preserved. Whereas the painter who recognizes that, in the interest of the whole, a part must be sacrificed, loses that part forever: it ceases to exist, except insofar as memory, or photographs, reproduce it. I couldn't bear the endless forfeits this involved; or perhaps I lack sufficient confidence in my immediate judgments.

In other ways as well, my preferences have not much changed. I 21 experience, as a reader, two primary modes of poetic speech. One, to the reader, feels like confidence; one seems intercepted meditation. My preference, from the beginning, has been the poetry that requests or craves a listener. This is Blake's little black boy, Keats's living hand, Eliot's Prufrock, as opposed, say, to Stevens's astonishments. I don't intend, in this, to set up any sort of hierarchy, simply to say that I read to feel addressed; the complement, I suppose, to speaking in order to be heeded. There are exceptions, but the general preference remains intact.

The preference for intimacy, of course, makes of the single reader 22 an elite. A practical advantage to this innate preference is that one cares less about the size of an audience. Or maybe the point here is that the writer's audience is chronological. The actor and dancer perform in the present; if their work exists in the future, it exists as memory, as legend. Whereas the canvas, the bronze, and, more durably because they exist in multiple, the poem, the sonata, exist not as memory but as fact; the artists who work in these forms scorned or overlooked in their own time can still find an audience.

There are other profound divisions in literary work as well as that 23 between speech which craves a listener and speech that permits itself to be overheard. There's much talk recently about closure, about any openended form, the idea being that such form is distinctly feminine. More interesting to me is a larger difference of which this is an example, the difference between symmetry and asymmetry, harmony and assonance.

I have always preferred irregularity. I remember an argument I 24 had with someone's mother when I was eight or nine; it was her day for carpool duty and our assignment in school had involved composition. I'd written a poem and was asked to recite it, which I readily did. My special triumph, with this poem, had involved a metrical reversal in the last line (not that I called it that), an omission of the final rhyme: to my ear it was exhilarating, a kind of explosion of form. The form, of course, was doggerel. In any case, our driver congratulated me: a very good poem, she said, right till the last line. Which she then proceeded to rearrange aloud into the order I had explicitly intended to violate. You see, she told me, all that was missing was that last rhyme. I was furious, and especially furious in that I knew my objections would read as defensive response to obvious failure.

It seems sometimes very strange to me, that image of a child so   25
wholly bent on a vocation. So ambitious. The nature of that ambition,
of literary ambition, seems to me a profound subject, too large for this
occasion. Like most people hungry for praise and ashamed of that, of
any, hunger, I alternated between contempt for the world that judged
me and lacerating self-hatred. To my mind, to be wrong in any smallest particular was to be wrong utterly. On the surface, I was poised,
cool, indifferent, given to laconic exhibitions of disdain. A description,
I suppose, of any adolescent.

The discrepancy, in my life, between what I would show the   26
world and the chaos I felt grew steadily more intense. I wrote and
painted, but these activities were hardly the famous release of such
pressure they are contended to be. I cared too much about the quality
of what I made; the context in which I judged what I made was not the
schoolroom, but the history of art. In mid-adolescence, I developed a
symptom perfectly congenial to the demands of my spirit. I had great
resources of will and no self. Then, as now, my thought tended to define itself in opposition; in those days, what remains characteristic was
the single characteristic. I couldn't say what I was, what I wanted, in
any day-to-day, practical way. What I could say was *no:* the way I saw
to separate myself, to establish a self with clear boundaries, was to oppose myself to the declared desire of others, utilizing their wills to give
shape to my own. This conflict played itself out most fiercely with my
mother. And, insofar as I could tell, my mother only wavered when I
began to refuse food, when I claimed, through implicit threat, ownership of my body, which was her great accomplishment. My mother
loved her children, but the only sign of love I was equipped to recognize was terror.

The tragedy of anorexia seems to me that its intent is not self-   27
destructive, though its outcome so often is. Its intent is to construct, in
the only way possible when means are so limited, a plausible self. But
the sustained act, the repudiation, designed to distinguish the self
from the other also separates self and body. And, as well, frustrates
disdain for flesh, since the spectre of death demonstrates not the soul's
superiority but its dependence on flesh.

By the time I was sixteen, a number of things were clear to me. It   28
was clear that what I had thought of as an act of will, an act I was perfectly capable of controlling, of terminating, was not that; I realized
that I had no control over this behavior at all. And I realized, logically,
that to be eighty-five, then eighty, then seventy-five pounds was to be
thin; I understood that at some point I was going to die. What I knew
more vividly, more viscerally, was that I didn't want to die. Even then,
dying seemed a pathetic metaphor for establishing a separation between myself and my mother. I knew, at the time, very little about
psychoanalysis; certainly, in those days, it was less common than now;

there were not so many proliferating therapies. Less common, even in the affluent surburbs.

My parents, during these months, were wise enough to recognize that any suggestion they made I'd be committed to rejecting; therefore, they made no suggestions. And finally, one day, I told my mother I thought perhaps I should see a psychoanalyst. This was nearly thirty years ago—I have no idea where the idea, the word, came from. Nor was there, in those days, any literature about anorexia—at least, I knew of none. If there had been, I'd have been stymied; to have a disease so common, so typical, would have obliged me to devise some entirely different gestures to prove my uniqueness. 29

I was immensely fortunate in the analyst my parents found. I began seeing him in the fall of my senior year of high school; a few months later, I was taken out of school. For the next seven years, analysis was what I did with my time, and with my mind; it would be impossible for me to speak of education without speaking of this process. 30

I was afraid of psychoanalysis in conventional ways. I thought what kept me alive, in that it gave me hope, was my ambition, my sense of vocation; I was afraid to tamper with the mechanism. But a certain rudimentary pragmatism told me that I had not as yet accomplished a body of work likely to endure; therefore I couldn't afford to die. In any case, I felt I had no choice, which was, for me, a piece of luck. Because at seventeen I was not wild, not volcanic; I was rigid and self-protective; the form my self-protectiveness took was exclusion: that which I feared, I ignored; what I ignored, most of my central feelings, was not present in my poems. Which is to say: the poems I was writing were narrow, mannered, static; they were also other-worldly, mystical. These qualities were entirely defining. What was worse: by the time I began analysis, I'd stopped writing. So there was nothing, really, to protect. 31

But periodically, in the course of those seven years, I'd turn to my doctor with the old accusation: he'd make me so well, so whole, I'd never write again. Finally, he silenced me; the world, he told me, will give you sorrow enough. I think he waited to say that because, at the outset, the fact that the world existed at all was beyond me, as it is beyond all egoists. 32

Analysis taught me to think. Taught me to use my tendency to object to articulated ideas on my own ideas, taught me to use doubt, to examine my own speech for its evasions and excisions. It gave me an intellectual task capable of transforming paralysis—which is the extreme form of self-doubt—into insight. I was learning to use native detachment to make contact with my self, which is the point, I suppose, of dream analysis: what's utilized are objective images. I cultivated a capacity to study images and patterns of speech, to see, as objectively 33 as possible, what ideas they embodied. Insofar as I was, obviously, the source of those dreams, those images, I could infer these ideas were mine, the embodied conflicts, mine. The longer I withheld conclusions, the more I saw. I was learning, I believe, how to write, as well: not to have a self which, in writing, is projected into images. And not, simply, to permit the production of images, a production unencumbered by mind. But to use the mind to explore the resonances of such images, to separate the shallow from the deep, and to choose the deep.

It is fortunate that that discipline gave me a place to use my mind 34 because my emotional condition, my extreme rigidity of behavior and frantic dependence on ritual, made other forms of education impossible. In fact, for many years every form of social interaction seemed impossible, so acute was my shame. But there was, after the first year, one other form open to me, or one need more powerful than shame. At eighteen, instead of going to college as I had always assumed I would, I enrolled in Leonie Adams's poetry workshop at the school of General Studies at Columbia.

I've written elsewhere about the years that followed, about the 35 two spent studying with Dr. Adams, and the many years with Stanley Kunitz. Here's a poem, written long afterward, which simply records a few of the dreams in which Kunitz figures:

Four Dreams Concerning the Master

1. The supplicant

S. is standing in a small room, reading to himself.
It is a privilege to see S.
alone in this serene environment.
Only his hand moves, thoughtfully turning the pages.
Then, from under the closed door, a single hazelnut
rolls into the room, coming to rest, at length,
at S.'s foot. With a sigh, S. closes the heavy volume
and stares down wearily at the round nut. "Well," he
    says,
"what do you want now, Stevens?"

2. Conversation with M.

"Have you ever noticed," he remarked,
"that when women sleep
they're really looking at you?"

3. Noah's Dream

Where were you in the dream?
    The North Pole.

Were you alone?
  No. My friend was with me.

Which friend was that?
  My old friend. My friend the poet.

What were you doing?
  We were crossing a river. But the clumps of ice
  were far apart, we had to jump.

Were you afraid?
  Just cold. Our eyes filled up with snow.

And did you get across?
  It took a long time. Then we got across.

What did you do then, on the other side?
  We walked a long time.

And was the walk the end?
  No. The end was the morning.

4. Conversation with X.

"You," he said, "you're just like Eliot.
You think you know everything in the world
but you don't believe anything."

Much is said of what a teacher in a creative enterprise cannot do. 36
Whatever they can't do, what they can do, the whole experience of apprenticeship, seems to me beyond value. I was working, of course,
with extraordinary minds. And I was being exposed to images of dedication, not of the kind I knew, which I was not wholly prepared to
comprehend. The poetic vocation is felt to be dramatic, glamorous;
this is in part because consecration, which is dynamic, is so often mistaken for dedication. My notions of persistence were necessarily limited by youth. I was being shown, though, what it looked like, a steady
upward labor; I was in the presence of that stamina I would find necessary. And I was privileged in feeling the steady application of
scrutiny—from outside, from the world, from another human being.
One of the rare, irreplaceable gifts of such apprenticeships is this
scrutiny; seldom, afterward, is any poem taken with such high seriousness. Those of us trained in this environment have felt, I think,
deeply motivated to provide for one another a comparable readership,
and that need, founded so long ago, helps fend off the animosities, the
jealousies, to which most of us are prone.

I was writing, in those years, with the inspiration of that teacher, 37
that reader, the poems that were collected in my first book.

And if I had, as yet, no idea what kind of patience would be called 38
for in my life, I had, by that time, already ample experience of what is

called writer's block. Though I hated the condition, a sense that the world had gone gray and flat and dull, I came to mistrust the premise behind the term. To be more precise: I can make sense of that premise in only two ways. It makes sense to presume fluency when the basis of the work is some intuition about language profound enough to be explored over a lifetime. Or when the work is anecdotal in nature. Even for the writer whose creative work arises out of the act of bearing witness—even for such a writer—a subject, a focus, must present itself, or be found. The artist who bears witness begins with a judgment, though it is moral, not aesthetic. But the artist whose gift is the sketch, the anecdote: that artist makes, as far as I can tell, no such judgment; nothing impedes the setting down of detail, because there is no investment in the idea of importance. When the aim of the work is spiritual insight, it seems absurd to expect fluency. A metaphor for such work is the oracle, which needed to be fed questions.

In practical terms, this means that the writer who means to outlive 39 the useful rages and despairs of youth must somehow learn to endure the desert.

I have wished, since I was in my early teens, to be a poet; over a 40 period of more than thirty years, I have had to get through extended silences. By silences, I mean periods, sometimes two years in duration, during which I have written nothing. Not written badly, written nothing. Nor do such periods feel like fruitful dormancy.

It seems to me that the desire to make art produces an ongoing ex- 41 perience of longing, a restlessness sometimes, but not inevitably, played out romantically, or sexually. Always there seems something ahead, the next poem or story, visible, at least, apprehensible, but unreachable. To perceive it at all is to be haunted by it; some sound, some tone, becomes a torment—the poem embodying that sound seems to exist somewhere already finished. It's like a lighthouse, except that, as one swims toward it, it backs away.

That's my sense of the poem's beginning. What follows is a period 42 of more concentrated work, so called because as long as one is working the thing itself is wrong or unfinished: a failure. Still, this engagement is absorbing as nothing else I have ever in my life known. And then the poem is finished and, at that moment, instantly detached; it becomes what it was first perceived to be, a thing always in existence. No record exists of the poet's agency. And the poet, from that point, isn't a poet anymore: simply someone who wishes to be one.

In practical terms, this has meant having a good deal of unused 43 time, and one of the crucial decisions of my life has been the decision, made almost accidentally, to teach.

My experience as a student taught me a profound gratitude, a 44 sense of indebtedness. In the days when teaching jobs began to be possible to me, when, to support myself, I worked as a secretary in various offices, I feared teaching. I feared that, in the presence of a poem that seemed nearly remarkable, my competitiveness would seek to suppress the remarkable, not draw it out. What I saw, when, during one of my most difficult silences, I finally began to teach, was that at such moments authorship matters not at all; I realized that I felt compelled to serve others' poems in the same way, with the same ferocity, as I felt compelled to serve my own. It mattered to get the poem right, to get it memorable, toward which end nothing was held back. In this act, all the forces in my nature I least approve, the competitiveness, the envy, were temporarily checked. Whatever benefits accrued to individual poems through this activity, the benefits to myself proved enormous. That I found an activity in which to feel myself benign, empowering—that, obviously. But also I had discovered that I need not myself be writing to feel my mind work. Teaching became, for me, the prescription for lassitude. It doesn't always work, of course, but it has worked often enough, and steadily enough. On that first occasion, it worked miraculously quickly.

I'd moved to Vermont, taken a three-month job at Goddard. I'd 45 written one book, and nothing else in the last two years. I began teaching in September; in September, I began writing again, writing poems entirely different from those in *Firstborn*.

This difference was intended, at least hoped for. What you learn 46 organizing a book, making of a pile of poems an arc, a shaped utterance, is both exhilarating and depressing: as you discern the book's themes, its fundamental perceptions, you see as well the poems' habitual gestures, those habits of syntax and vocabulary, the rhythmic signatures which, ideally, give the volume at hand its character but which it would be death to repeat.

Each book I've written has culminated in a conscious diagnostic 47 act, a swearing off. After *Firstborn*, the task was to make Latinate suspended sentences, and to figure out a way to end a poem without sealing it shut. Since the last poems of *The House on Marshland* were written concurrently with the earliest poems in *Descending Figure*, the second book becomes more difficult to speak of singly. I wanted to learn a longer breath. And to write without the nouns central to that second book; I had done about as much as I could with *moon* and *pond*. What I wanted, after *Descending Figure*, was a poem less perfect, less stately; I wanted a present tense that referred to something more fluent than the archetypal present. And then, obviously, the task was to write something less overtly heroic, something devoid of mythic reference.

This is far too compressed a synopsis to be accurate, but it will 48 give a sense, I hope, of some compulsion to change, a compulsion not, perhaps, actually chosen. I see in this gesture the child I was, unwilling to speak if to speak meant to repeat myself.

Working with the Text

1. In her opening paragraph Glück mentions wanting "to correct the fantasy that creative work is an ongoing record of the triumph of volition." Where in the rest of the essay does she show that writing is not a matter of "volition," or willpower, or control?

2. Also in the first paragraph and elsewhere in the essay, Glück uses the word "torment" to describe writing. In her opinion, what is "tormenting" about writing? Why does she do it anyway?

3. Make a list of all the influences on what Glück calls her "education" as a writer, from family to teachers to her own personality. What is the role of each influence?

4. Glück says that through psychoanalysis she learned to "use native detachment to make contact with myself." What does she mean? How does this statement apply to her writing?

5. Glück includes two of her own poems in the essay. Why, do you think? What function do they perform? What point does each one help to make? Why did she use poetry, rather than ordinary language, to make those points?

Working beyond the Text

1. Glück mentions the titles of several of her books of poetry. What else has she written? What has been written about her work? Use the library to find out more about her, her writing, and her reputation among the critics. How does what you find out help you understand her essay?

2. Glück mentions several poets who have influenced her from childhood to the present, including Shakespeare, Blake, Yeats, Keats, T. S. Eliot, and Wallace Stevens. Investigate the names of any writers you don't recognize. Who were they? When did they live? What are they famous for?

3. It is clear that from very early childhood Glück loved books and poetry, and that these early experiences helped shape her life as an adult. What did you love doing as a child? Have these early experiences continued to exert an influence on your adult life?

4. Writers in other chapters in this book (especially Chapters 1, 3, and 4) have discussed the differences between men's language and women's language and the struggle of women writers to find a language of their own. Glück comments that she is "puzzled . . . by the contemporary determination of women to write as women." What does she mean? How do you feel about this issue?

Books and Silence

Jonathan Strong

Jonathan Strong teaches English at Tufts University. His novels include *Offspring, An Untold Tale,* and *Secret Words.* In this essay, which
appeared in the journal *American Literature* (March 1996), Strong
traces his urge to write to elements in his family background as well
as more personal, private sources. In this essay, he documents his effort to "speak" from the "silence" of writing.

1   I spent the early months of life, at the end of the war, in the room
where my grandfather died. It was a small room next to my grandmother's bedroom. With her sons away in the war, she had brought
their wives to live in the house with her. My aunt had two kids, so she
was down the hall. My mother and I had the smaller room, but it
meant keeping me as quiet as she could, not to disturb Granny. My
mother has told me she'd wake me up before I could let out a cry, and
she'd get herself and me in and out of the bathroom before Granny
needed it. I was to be the unobtrusive grandchild, in the quiet room, in
the room of sad memory, at a time when all the young fathers were far
away and in danger.

2   I don't remember any of this. I remember the room from later visits to my grandmother's, from slow Sunday afternoons sitting there at
her writing desk, doodling and drawing. Above me was a shelf of
books, novels written by my great uncle Harry, my grandmother's eldest brother, who had died before I could have known him. I used to
pick these fat books off the shelf, hold them, feel their weight, investigate their spines, their typefaces, their chapter titles and frontispieces;
I never read more than a hard-to-read long sentence here or there. But
they were my most personal idea of a book, of a book written by a person, by a person I might have known, a person I might even be like.

3   Henry Kitchell Webster's novels had been rather popular in the
early decades of the century. *The Real Adventure,* about a suburban
midwestern Nora fleeing her doll's house, was a big bestseller in 1915.
By now I have read almost all of his books and find them stylishly
written, of considerable period interest, politically progressive, but
somewhat disappointing in the neatness of their resolutions. They
have joined thousands of similarly well-made novels from eras past, to
be found now only in used-book barns or small-town library sales,
where most of us novelists will end up some day.

4   I discovered Uncle Harry's books in silence. No one in the family
seemed to have read them in years, and none of my teachers had
heard of my great uncle's books, so I couldn't boast of him to my
friends. And when I sought out my own collection of the complete

H. K. Webster and began, as an adult, to read through them, there was no one to discuss them with. He was an author all my own, my personal literary heritage.

I learned three big things from him: that it must take an awful lot of work to write over thirty books; that writing is somehow connected to privacy and quiet, and maybe even secrecy; and that you shouldn't tie up your story too neatly—you shouldn't leave your readers feeling quite so sure about all the things they already know or have decided on.

In my family, my mother was the novel reader. She spent many a fifties suburban hour reading in her favorite chair. She was also the school librarian. Somewhat nervously, as I recall, she added *On the Road* and *Lolita* to the high school collection but never got in trouble for it. She loved her quiet library, and I saw there how books and silence belonged together—even dangerous books. But her nervous admiration of Kerouac and Nabokov (an odd pair) gave me a notion of how a book, conceived in deep impassioned silence and read by a silent submissive imagination, could shout aloud. Then I, too, the unobtrusive grandchild, could begin to shout now in my own quiet way. It was possible to unsettle people, to disturb their early morning rest perhaps, by something as flat and silent as a page of prose. I wanted to do that. It was the only polite and admirable way I could think of to throw a tantrum.

After my grandmother's death, when my first book was published, I overhead my great aunt Anne saying to my great aunt Virginia, "I'm so glad Josephine isn't alive to read this!" And when I caught her eye, she stammered apologetically, "But, Jonny, I just didn't know you *knew* about all these things!" Later, my great uncle Maurice, the artistic one, came up to me and asked if I knew where he could buy some pot. I had benefited, I admit, from being twenty-four when publishers were looking for writers who spoke for the "new generation." But what did I know, yet, about being young? In 1969 I was in the middle of the mess of it. I wasn't even much of a hippie, and so I had nothing to offer my uncle Maurice.

I conceived this essay by asking myself why I write. Then I read George Orwell on the subject, and to me his four reasons seem to hold remarkably true: sheer egoism, aesthetic enthusiasm, historical impulse, and political purpose—in varying proportions. To say what you feel about how things should be, about how things are and have been, about the sounds and shapes of language itself, and to display your very own singular self—only such deep needs can keep you toiling away at a task likely to offer scant rewards.

Are things so much worse now than they have always been? The current impediments are obvious, but at the risk of seeming to whine,

I'll run through some of them: oil companies own publishing houses; superstore chains stock a title in high stacks or hardly at all; a good shelf life is two months; novelists scratch the backs of fellow novelists in the *New York Times Book Review;* graduate writing programs churn out (shall we say) adequate writers; contemporary literature is categorized by cultural identity; certain academics don't even believe authors exist; aesthetics is an obsolete word; television has zombified us; only a movie can make a book famous (we can immediately discuss a movie with *all* our friends); the computer screen outshines the printed page; the spell checker has replaced the spelling bee. . . .

But I suspect that a similarly dire set of circumstances might be 10 compiled for any time or place (no one knows how to read; the censor has banned everything; black people ought not write books . . .). Finally, all these factors are irrelevant because most writers have no choice, and those who find they do move on to something more encouraging and are the better for it. Did Emily Dickinson have a choice? Did Franz Kafka? Or could the aging Sinclair Lewis, reputation plummeting, have brought himself to a stop?

I'm not patting myself on the back. There's no special merit in 11 finding writing a psychological necessity. I wasn't always sure it was. I've had two four-year stretches with no real writing at all and assumed it was over; one novel got some forty-five rejections (including one from an English-language Soviet press where I'd sent my uncapitalistic manuscript in a traitorous fit of pique), but it finally found its way to an independent house called Zoland Books, now my safe haven and cheering squad. Zoland, with another institution, Tufts University, has allowed me to feel I really am (in the loud world, out there) who I think I am, even if the order of composition and relative merits of my books bear little resemblance to the way they have been received by that world. I'm lucky. I could never have supported myself the way savvy, industrious Uncle Harry managed to do. But, like him, I have discovered that I can't stop writing for long.

Of Orwell's reasons, I'd like to think I put aesthetic enthusiasm 12 first, but he was bold enough to set egoism at the head of his list, and I suspect that is more honest. Maybe what I want to add is that the tension between the ego and artistry is what each of us must continually struggle with. Don't write what you already know but from what you know toward something you must discover beyond yourself. But this is where we come up against the critical strictures of our day: You're trapped in your identity! Outrageous to think you can transcend it! No such bird as objectivity!

One of the stories in my first book that must have troubled my 13 great aunt was, I imagine, the one about a nineteen-year-old hustler. Before Stonewall there were no shelves of "gay lit"; I had written the story in shy innocence, happy ending and all, never imagining it would get published. In my second book, the novel *Ourselves*, I consciously steered away from the homoerotic undercurrents I'd explored in my earliest work, and it was only in the final draft of the novella *Doing and Undoing* that I returned to that particular theme. My novel *Elsewhere* appeared when "gay writers" were beginning to be noticed as such, but, explicit as the book was, I didn't like to think of it defined by the label "gay novel." The narrator of *Secret Words* shared no "identity" with me at all: she was straight, Italian-American, Catholic, urban, working class, unschooled, and quite chubby (well, I'd been chubby myself once). *Offspring*'s narrator is a straight dad of three; *An Untold Tale*'s is a seventy-year-old who's lived for many years with a much younger man. What does all this say—about *me?* That I'm uncommitted? That I'm evasive? That I'm a crank? Where does my "identity" end?

I find myself thinking back to that quiet room and that shelf of 14
Uncle Harry's books, which represents, to me, the long haul. I also find myself turning to Oscar Wilde's famous phrases: "There is no such thing as a moral or immoral book. Books are well written, or badly written. That is all." And: "All art is quite useless." Why do these words now give me a quietly warm feeling when some decades ago I heard only arch posturing?

Because, having completed eight books of my own and having 15
watched them be both noticed and ignored, I know that as sheer egoism fails me art is still there, the sought-for, unreachable ideal of art, bigger than me. Death means a good deal more to me now than it could have three decades ago. The driving egoism that aspires to end up on shelves where Austen and Beckett and Chekhov abide, rather than in the dreaded book barn, is still operating—for all I know, it's even stronger now with my new sense of life's finitude. But what is also stronger is a sense that it does not matter now if I should be seen as a marketable "gay" writer or dismissed as unrepresentative, if I should be seen as speaking for our culture or against it. In the sixties, when no one could dispute my publisher's claim that I was young, my youth guaranteed nothing about my work, neither its politics nor its aesthetics. Now, in my thirtieth year as a published writer, I do not care to be swept along by someone else's idea of loudness. I want to keep experiencing how hard it is to write; I want to delve deep, in privacy, quiet, and maybe even secrecy; I don't want to know anything quite for sure, to reassure myself or anyone else.

They may be subjective innocent fools, but writers seem to come 16
upon necessary moments when the living thing begins to write itself. Only a far away, unknown reader can say with any confidence at all, on some future day, if that ancient thing called inspiration has struck, if those silent words still speak aloud.

Working with the Text

1. Beginning with his title, Strong plays throughout the essay with the various meanings of the word "silence" in relation to books, including both the reading and the writing of books. What are the various relationships Strong discusses between silence (and its opposites—speaking and shouting) and the written word?

2. Strong's great aunt Anne clearly finds something shocking in his first book, saying that she "didn't know you *knew* about these things." To what "things" might she be referring, as far as you can tell from the context of the essay?

3. Strong provides a long list of "current impediments" to writing and publishing. Explain what he might mean by each item in the list, as well as you can.

4. The style of Strong's essay seems loose and informal, with information presented in what seems to be a random order. Try outlining the essay and explaining the system of organization Strong might be using.

Working beyond the Text

1. Strong alludes to George Orwell's essay, "Why I Write," and the four reasons Orwell gives for writing. Locate the essay and read it. Is Strong's summary of the four reasons accurate? What else does Orwell have to say about writing? How do Orwell's (and Strong's) reasons for writing compare to yours? (You might also locate and read Joan Didion's essay "Why I Write," which also begins with an allusion to Orwell.)

2. Strong says that his mother was nervous about adding Kerouac's *On the Road* and Nabokov's *Lolita* to his school library. Why were these "dangerous" books? What do you know about them? What other "dangerous" books do you know about that you would be surprised to find in a high school library? Why might Strong find that these books make him able to "begin to shout . . . in my own quiet way"?

3. Strong's advice is: "Don't write what you already know but from what you know toward something you must discover beyond yourself." What attitude about writing does he seem to be criticizing? How would you feel about following this advice in your own writing? Or have you followed it already? If so, describe the experience.

4. Strong alludes to "Stonewall" in the context of being categorized as a "gay" writer. What is "Stonewall" in the history of the struggle for gay rights in the United States? What is Strong's objection to being categorized as a "gay" writer?

UNIT TWO:

SOURCES OF PERSONAL WRITING

I Stand Here Writing

Nancy Sommers

Nancy Sommers teaches writing at Harvard University. She is co-author, with Linda Simon, of *The HarperCollins Guide to Writing* and has published influential articles in the fields of rhetoric and composition. In the following essay, originally published in the professional journal *College English* (April 1993), Sommers discusses the dynamic relationships among her experiences of reading, researching, writing, and living, examining in particular the effort to render lived experience in language.

I stand in my kitchen, wiping the cardamom, coriander, and 1 cayenne off my fingers. My head is abuzz with words, with bits and pieces of conversation. I hear a phrase I have read recently, something about "a radical loss of certainty." But, I wonder, how did the sentence begin? I search the air for the rest of the sentence, can't find it, shake some more cardamom, and a bit of coriander. Then, by some play of mind, I am back home again in Indiana with my family, sitting around the kitchen table. Two people are talking, and there are three opinions; three people are talking, and there are six opinions. Opinions grow exponentially. I fight my way back to that sentence. Writing, that's how it begins: "Writing is a radical loss of certainty." (Or is it uncertainty?) It isn't so great for the chicken when all these voices start showing up, with all these sentences hanging in mid-air, but the voices keep me company. I am a writer, not a cook, and the truth is I don't care much about the chicken. Stories beget stories. Writing emerges from writing.

The truth. Has truth anything to do with the facts? All I know is 2 that no matter how many facts I might clutter my life with, I am as bound to the primordial drama of my family as the earth is to the sun. This year my father, the son of a severe Prussian matriarch, watched me indulge my daughters, and announced to me that he wished I had been his mother. This year, my thirty-ninth, my last year to be thirty-something, my mother—who has a touch of magic, who can walk into the middle of a field of millions of clovers and find the *one* with four leaves—has begun to think I need help. She sends me cards monthly with four-leaf clovers taped inside. Two words neatly printed in capital letters—GOOD LUCK! I look at these clovers and hear Reynolds Price's words: "Nobody under forty can believe how nearly everything's inherited." I wonder what my mother knows, what she is trying to tell me about the facts of my life.

When I was in high school studying French, laboring to conjugate 3 verbs, the numerous four-leaf clovers my mother had carefully pressed inside her French dictionary made me imagine her in a field of clovers lyrically conjugating verbs of love. This is the only romantic image I have of my mother, a shy and conservative woman whose own mother died when she was five, whose grandparents were killed by the Nazis, who fled Germany at age thirteen with her father and sister. Despite the sheer facts of her life, despite the accumulation of grim knowable data, the truth is my mother is an optimistic person. She has the curious capacity always to be looking for luck, putting her faith in four-leaf clovers, ladybugs, pennies, and other amulets of fortune. She has a vision different from mine, one the facts alone can't explain. I, her daughter, was left, for a long time, seeing only the ironies; they were my defense against the facts of my life.

In this world of my inheritance in which daughters can become 4 their fathers' mothers and mothers know their daughters are entering into a world where only sheer good luck will guide them, I hear from my own daughters that I am not in tune with their worlds, that I am just like a 50s mom, that they are 90s children, and I should stop acting so primitive. My children laugh uproariously at my autograph book, a 1959 artifact they unearthed in the basement of my parents' home. "Never kiss by the garden gate. Love is blind, but the neighbors aint," wrote one friend. And my best friend, who introduced herself to me on the first day of first grade, looking me straight in the eye—and whispering through her crooked little teeth "the Jews killed Jesus"—wrote in this autograph book: "Mary had a little lamb. Her father shot it dead. Now she carries it to school between two slices of bread."

My ten-year-old daughter, Rachel, writes notes to me in hiero- 5 glyphics and tapes signs on the refrigerator in Urdu. "Salaam Namma Man Rachaal Ast" reads one sign. Simply translated it means "Hello, my name is Rachel." Alex, my seven-year-old daughter, writes me lists, new lists each month, visibly reminding me of the many things I need to buy or do for her. This month's list includes a little refrigerator filled with Coke and candy; ears pierced; a new toilet; neon nail polish and *real* adult make-up.

How do I look at these facts? How do I embrace these experiences, 6 these texts of my life, and translate them into ideas? How do I make sense of them and the conversations they engender in my head? I look at Alex's list and wonder what kind of feminist daughter I am raising whose deepest desires include neon nail polish and *real* adult makeup. Looking at her lists a different way, I wonder if this second child of mine is asking me for something larger, something more permanent and real than adult make-up. Maybe I got that sentence wrong. Maybe it is that "Love (as well as writing) involves a radical loss of certainty."

Love is blind, but the neighbors ain't. Mary's father shot her little 7 lamb dead, and now she carries it to school between two slices of bread. I hear these rhymes today, and they don't say to me what they say to my daughters. They don't seem so innocent. I hear them and think about the ways in which my neighbors in Indiana could only see my family as Jews from Germany, exotic strangers who ate tongue, outsiders who didn't celebrate Christmas. I wonder if my daughter Rachel needs to tell me her name in Urdu because she thinks we don't share a common language. These sources change meaning when I ask the questions in a different way. They introduce new ironies, new questions.

I want to understand these living, breathing, primary sources all 8 around me. I want to be, in Henry James's words, "a person upon whom nothing is lost." These sources speak to me of love and loss, of memory and desire, of the ways in which we come to understand something through difference and opposition. Two years ago I learned the word *segue* from one of my students. At first the word seemed peculiar. Segue sounded like something you did only on the Los Angeles freeway. Now I hear that word everywhere, and I have begun using it. I want to know how to segue from one idea to the next, from one thought to the fragment lying beside it. But the connections don't always come with four-leaf clovers and the words GOOD LUCK neatly printed beside them.

My academic need to find connections sends me to the library. 9 There are eleven million books in my University's libraries. Certainly these sanctioned voices, these authorities, these published sources can help me find the connections. Someone, probably some three thousand someones, has studied what it is like to be the child of survivors. Someone has written a manual on how the granddaughter of a severe Prussian matriarch and the daughter of a collector of amulets ought to raise feminist daughters. I want to walk into the fields of writing, into those eleven million books, and find the one book that will explain it all. But I've learned to expect less from such sources. They seldom have the answers. And the answers they do have reveal themselves to me at the most unexpected times. I have been led astray more than once while searching books for the truth.

Once I learned a lesson about borrowing someone else's words 10 and losing my own.

I was fourteen, light years away from thirty-something. High 11 school debate teams across the nation were arguing the pros and cons of the United States Military Aid Policy. It all came back to me as I listened to the news of the Persian Gulf War, as I listened to Stormin' Norman giving his morning briefings, an eerie resonance, all our arguments, the millions of combative words—sorties—fired back and forth. In my first practice debate, not having had enough time to assemble my own sources, I borrowed quote cards from my teammates. I attempted to bolster my position that the U.S. should limit its military aid by reading a quote in my best debate style: "W.W. Rostow says: 'We should not give military aid to India because it will exacerbate endemic rivalries.'"

Under cross-examination, my nemesis, Bobby Rosenfeld, the 12 neighbor kid, who always knew the right answers, began firing a series of questions at me without stopping to let me answer:

"Nancy, can you tell me who W.W. Rostow is? And can you tell 13 me why he might say this? Nancy, can you tell me what 'exacerbate' means? Can you tell me what 'endemic rivalries' are? And exactly what does it mean to 'exacerbate endemic rivalries'?"

I didn't know. I simply did not know who W.W. Rostow was, why 14 he might have said that, what "exacerbate" meant, or what an "endemic rivalry" was. Millions of four-leaf clovers couldn't have helped me. I might as well have been speaking Urdu. I didn't know who my source was, the context of the source, nor the literal meaning of the words I had read. Borrowing words from authorities had left me without any words of my own.

My debate partner and I went on that year to win the Indiana state 15 championship and to place third in the nationals. Bobby Rosenfeld never cross-examined me again, but for twenty years he has appeared in my dreams. I am not certain why I would dream so frequently about this scrawny kid whom I despised. I think, though, that he became for me what the Sea Dyak tribe of Borneo calls a *ngarong*, a dream guide, someone guiding me to understanding. In this case, Bobby guided me to understand the endemic rivalries within myself. The last time Bobby appeared in a dream he had become a woman.

I learned a more valuable lesson about sources as a college senior. 16 I was the kind of student who loved words, words out of context, words that swirled around inside my mouth, words like *exacerbate, undulating, lugubrious,* and *zeugma.* "She stained her honour or her new brocade," wrote Alexander Pope. I would try to write zeugmas whenever I could, exacerbating my already lugubrious prose. Within the English department, I was known more for my long hair, untamed and untranslatable, and for my long distance bicycle rides than for my scholarship.

For my senior thesis, I picked Emerson's essay "Eloquence." Har- 17 rison Hayford, my advisor, suggested that I might just get off my bicycle, get lost in the library, and read all of Emerson's essays, journals, letters. I had picked one of Emerson's least distinguished essays, an essay that the critics mentioned only in passing, and if I were not entirely on my own, I had at least carved out new territory for myself.

I spent weeks in the library reading Emerson's journals, reading 18 newspaper accounts from Rockford and Peoria, Illinois, where he had first delivered "Eloquence" as a speech. Emerson stood at the podium, the wind blowing his papers hither and yon, calmly picking them up, and proceeding to read page 8 followed by page 3, followed by page 6, followed by page 2. No one seemed to know the difference. Emerson's Midwestern audience was overwhelmed by this strange man from Concord, Massachusetts, this eloquent stranger whose unit of expression was the sentence.

As I sat in the library, wearing my QUESTION AUTHORITY 19 T-shirt, I could admire this man who delivered his Divinity School Address in 1838, speaking words so repugnant to the genteel people of Cambridge that it was almost thirty years before Harvard felt safe having him around again. I could understand the Midwestern audience's awe and adulation as they listened but didn't quite comprehend Emerson's stunning oratory. I had joined the debate team not to argue the U.S. Military Aid Policy, but to learn how to be an orator who could stun audiences, to learn a personal eloquence I could never learn at home. Perhaps only children of immigrant parents can understand the embarrassing moments of inarticulateness, the missed connections that come from learning to speak a language from parents who claim a different mother tongue.

As an undergraduate, I wanted to free myself from that mother 20 tongue. Four-leaf clovers and amulets of oppression weighed heavy on my mind, and I could see no connection whatsoever between those facts of my life and the untranslatable side of myself that set me in opposition to authority. And then along came Emerson. Like his Midwest audience, I didn't care about having him whole. I liked the promise and the rhapsodic freedom I found in his sentences, in his invitation to seize life as our dictionary, to believe that "Life was not something to be learned but to be lived." I loved his insistence that "the one thing of value is the active soul." I read that "Books are for the scholar's idle time," and I knew that he had given me permission to explore the world. Going into Emerson was like walking into a revelation; it was the first time I had gone into the texts not looking for a specific answer, and it was the first time the texts gave me the answers I needed. Never mind that I got only part of what Emerson was telling me. I got inspiration, I got insight, and I began to care deeply about my work.

Today I reread the man who set me off on a new road, and I find a 21 different kind of wisdom. Today I reread "The American Scholar," and I don't underline the sentence "Books are for the scholar's idle time." I continue to the next paragraph, underlining the sentence "One must be an inventor to read well." The second sentence doesn't contradict the one I read twenty years ago, but it means more today. I bring more to it, and I know that I can walk into text after text, source after source, and they will give me insight, but not answers. I have learned too that my sources can surprise me. Like my mother, I find myself sometimes surrounded by a field of four-leaf clovers, there for the picking, waiting to see what I can make of them. But I must be an inventor if I am to read those sources well, if I am to imagine the connections.

As I stand in my kitchen, the voices that come to me come by way 22 of a lifetime of reading, they come on the waves of life, and they seem to be helping me translate the untranslatable. They come, not at my bidding, but when I least expect them, when I am receptive enough to listen to their voices. They come when I am open.

I say to myself that I don't believe in luck. And yet. Not too long 23 ago Rachel came home speaking with some anxiety about an achievement test that she had to take at school. Wanting to comfort her, I urged her to take my rabbit's foot to school the next day. Always alert to life's ironies, Rachel said, "Sure, Mom, a rabbit's foot will really help me find the answers. And even if it did, how would I know the answer the next time when I didn't have that furry little claw?" The next day, proud of her ease in taking the test, she remained perplexed by the one question that seized her and wouldn't let go. She tried it on me: "Here's the question," she said. "Can you figure out which of these sentences cannot be true?"

(a) We warmed our hands by the fire.
(b) The rain poured in and around the windows.
(c) The wind beckoned us to open the door.

Only in the mind of someone who writes achievement tests, and wants to close the door on the imagination, could the one false sentence be "The wind beckoned us to open the door." Probably to this kind of mind, Emerson's sentence "Life is our dictionary" is also not a true sentence.

But life *is* our dictionary, and that's how we know that the wind 24 can beckon us to open the door. Like Emerson, we let the wind blow our pages hither and yon, forcing us to start in the middle, moving from page 8 to page 2, forward to page 7, moving back and forth in time, losing our certainty.

Like Emerson, I love basic units, the words themselves, words like 25 cardamom, coriander, words that play around in my head, swirl

around in my mouth. The challenge, of course, is not to be a ventrilo-
quist—not to be a mouther of words—but to be open to other voices,
untranslatable as they might be. Being open to the unexpected, we can
embrace complexities: canaries and lemons, amulets and autograph
books, fathers who want their daughters to be their mothers, and
daughters who write notes in Urdu—all those odd, unusual conjunc-
tions can come together and speak through us.

The other day, I called my mother and told her about this essay,   26
told her that I had been thinking about the gold bracelet she took with
her as one of her few possessions from Germany—a thin gold chain
with three amulets: a mushroom, a lady bug, and, of course, a four-leaf
clover. Two other charms fell off years ago—she lost one, I the other. I
used to worry over the missing links, thinking only of the loss, of what
we could never retrieve. When I look at the bracelet now, I think about
the Prussian matriarch, my grandmother, and my whole primordial
family drama. I think too of Emerson and the pages that blew in the
wind and the gaps that seemed not to matter. The bracelet is but one of
many sources that intrigues me. Considering them in whatever order
they appear, with whatever gaps, I want to see where they will lead
me, what they tell me.

With writing and with teaching, as well as with love, we don't   27
know how the sentence will begin and, rarely ever, how it will end.
Having the courage to live with uncertainty, ambiguity, even doubt,
we can walk into all of those fields of writing, knowing that we will
find volumes upon volumes bidding *us* enter. We need only be inven-
tors, we need only give freely and abundantly to the texts, imagining
even as we write that we too will be a source from which other readers
can draw sustenance.

Working with the Text

1. This entire essay seems to occur in Sommers' mind as she prepares a
   chicken for cooking, and yet the title is "I Stand Here Writing." Why? In
   what way can Sommers be said to be "writing" as she cooks? Why did
   Sommers choose to write the essay in this form, do you think? What idea
   does it help her get across?

2. Sommers tells two stories about using written sources: borrowing someone
   else's notecards for a debate and reading Emerson for a senior thesis. What
   is the difference between the two experiences? What meaning does Sommers find in the contrast?

3. What does Sommers mean when she says (paraphrasing Emerson), "I must
   be an inventor if I am to read those sources well." In what ways is "reading" "inventing"? What are her examples?

4. Individual words stand for a lot in Sommers' essay. What individual words

seem important in her thinking? What connections does she make between memories of individual words and the ideas they stand for?

Working beyond the Text

1. In her opening paragraph and throughout the essay, Sommers tries to capture the movements of her mind (memories, judgments, emotions) as she performs a simple task. Try to write an imitation of this style by describing the movements of your mind skipping from topic to topic as you perform a simple everyday task.

2. Sommers talks about the experience of reading a text (Emerson's "The American Scholar") as a college student and then rereading it later in life. She finds a particular sentence that "means more today" since "I bring more to it." What does she mean? How could a sentence "mean more" at one time than another? Have you ever had a similar experience? If so, describe it.

3. Sommers sketches a complicated relationship between reading, writing, and life. Using her examples, explain what connections she sees. Then imitate her by looking for similar connections in your own experience between reading, writing, and the everyday flow of life. When have you had the experience of writing something that combined the reading you've done with your personal life?

Anger and Tenderness
Adrienne Rich

Adrienne Rich, born in 1929, is a prominent poet, essayist, and English professor whose books include *Diving Into the Wreck, The Dream of a Common Language,* and *Of Woman Born: Motherhood as Experience and Institution.* Her poems and essays often explore issues such as gender, motherhood, sexuality, and other social issues such as black power and American involvement in Vietnam. In this chapter from *Of Woman Born* (1976), Rich looks back at her journal entries from the early 1960s to reflect on her life at a time when she was an established author trying to raise three small children, torn between her career and family.

> *. . . to understand is always an ascending movement; that is why comprehension ought always to be concrete. (one is never got out of the cave, one comes out of it.)*
>
> —Simone Weil, *First and Last Notebooks*

Entry from my journal, November 1960

My children cause me the most exquisite suffering of which I have any experience. It is the suffering of ambivalence: the murderous alternation between bitter resentment and raw-edged nerves, and blissful gratification and tenderness. Sometimes I seem to myself, in my feelings toward these tiny guiltless beings, a monster of selfishness and intolerance. Their voices wear away at my nerves, their constant needs, above all their need for simplicity and patience, fill me with despair at my own failures, despair too at my fate, which is to serve a function for which I was not fitted. And I am weak sometimes from held-in rage. There are times when I feel only death will free us from one another, when I envy the barren woman who has the luxury of her regrets but lives a life of privacy and freedom.*

And yet at other times I am melted with the sense of their helpless, charming and quite irresistible beauty—their ability to go on loving and trusting—their staunchness and decency and unselfconsciousness. *I love them.* But it's in the enormity and inevitability of this love that the sufferings lie.

April 1961

A blissful love for my children engulfs me from time to time and seems almost to suffice—the aesthetic pleasure I have in these little, changing creatures, the sense of being loved, however dependently, the sense too that I'm not an utterly unnatural and shrewish mother—much though I am!

May 1965

To suffer with and for and against a child—maternally, egotistically, neurotically, sometimes with a sense of helplessness, sometimes with the illusion of learning wisdom—but always, everywhere, in body and soul, *with* that child—because that child is a piece of oneself.

To be caught up in waves of love and hate, jealousy even of the child's childhood; hope and fear for its maturity; longing to be free of responsibility, tied by every fibre of one's being.

That curious primitive reaction of protectiveness, the beast defending her cub, when anyone attacks or criticizes him—And yet no one more hard on him than I!

---

*The term "barren woman" was easy for me to use, unexamined, fifteen years ago. As should be clear throughout this book, it seems to me now a term both tendentious and meaningless, based on a view of women which sees motherhood as our only positive definition.

September 1965
Degradation of anger. Anger at a child. How shall I learn to absorb the violence and make explicit only the caring? Exhaustion of anger. Victory of will, too dearly bought—far too dearly!

March 1966
Perhaps one is a monster—an anti-woman—something driven and without recourse to the normal and appealing consolations of love, motherhood, joy in others . . .

Unexamined assumptions: First, that a "natural" mother is a person without further identity, one who can find her chief gratification in being all day with small children, living at a pace tuned to theirs; that the isolation of mothers and children together in the home must be taken for granted; that maternal love is, and should be, quite literally selfless; that children and mothers are the "causes" of each others' suffering. I was haunted by the stereotype of the mother whose love is "unconditional"; and by the visual and literary images of motherhood as a single-minded identity. If I knew parts of myself existed that would never cohere to those images, weren't those parts then abnormal, monstrous? And—as my eldest son, now aged twenty-one, remarked on reading the above passages: "You seemed to feel you ought to love us all the time. But there *is* no human relationship where you love the other person at every moment." Yes, I tried to explain to him, but women—above all, mothers—have been supposed to love that way.

From the fifties and early sixties, I remember a cycle. It began when I had picked up a book or began trying to write a letter, or even found myself on the telephone with someone toward whom my voice betrayed eagerness, a rush of sympathetic energy. The child (or children) might be absorbed in busyness, in his own dreamworld; but as soon as he felt me gliding into a world which did not include him, he would come to pull at my hand, ask for help, punch at the typewriter keys. And I would feel his wants at such a moment as fraudulent, as an attempt moreover to defraud me of living even for fifteen minutes as myself. My anger would rise; I would feel the futility of any attempt to salvage myself, and also the inequality between us: my needs always balanced against those of a child, and always losing. I could love so much better, I told myself, after even a quarter-hour of selfishness, of peace, of detachment from my children. A few minutes! But it was as if an invisible thread would pull taut between us and break, to the child's sense of inconsolable abandonment, if I moved—not even physically, but in spirit—into a realm beyond our tightly circumscribed life together. It was as if my placenta had begun to refuse him oxygen. Like so many women, I waited with impatience for the moment when their father would return from work, when for an hour or two at least the circle drawn around mother and children would grow looser, the intensity between us slacken, because there was another adult in the house.

I did not understand that this circle, this magnetic field in which 3 we lived, was not a natural phenomenon.

Intellectually, I must have known it. But the emotion-charged, 4 tradition-heavy form in which I found myself cast as the Mother seemed, then, as ineluctable as the tides. And, because of this form— this microcosm in which my children and I formed a tiny, private emotional cluster, and in which (in bad weather or when someone was ill) we sometimes passed days at a time without seeing another adult except for their father—there *was* authentic need underlying my child's invented claims upon me when I seemed to be wandering away from him. He was reassuring himself that warmth, tenderness, continuity, solidity were still there for him, in my person. My singularity, my uniqueness in the world as his *mother*—perhaps more dimly also as Woman—evoked a need vaster than any single human being could satisfy, except by loving continuously, unconditionally, from dawn to dark, and often in the middle of the night.

In a living room in 1975, I spent an evening with a group of 5 women poets, some of whom had children. One had brought hers along, and they slept or played in adjoining rooms. We talked of poetry, and also of infanticide, of the case of a local woman, the mother of eight, who had been in severe depression since the birth of her third child, and who had recently murdered and decapitated her two youngest, on her suburban front lawn. Several women in the group, feeling a direct connection with her desperation, had signed a letter to the local newspaper protesting the way her act was perceived by the press and handled by the community mental health system. Every woman in that room who had children, every poet, could identify with her. We spoke of the wells of anger that her story cleft open in us. We spoke of our own moments of murderous anger at our children, because there was no one and nothing else on which to discharge anger. We spoke in the sometimes tentative, sometimes rising, sometimes bitterly witty, unrhetorical tones and language of women who had met together over our common work, poetry, and who found another common ground in an unacceptable, but undeniable anger. The words are being spoken now, are being written down; the taboos are being broken, the masks of motherhood are cracking through.

For centuries no one talked of these feelings. I became a mother in 6 the family-centered, consumer-oriented, Freudian-American world of the 1950s. My husband spoke eagerly of the children we would have; my parents-in-law awaited the birth of their grandchild. I had no idea of what *I* wanted, what *I* could or could not choose. I only knew that to have a child was to assume adult womanhood to the full, to prove myself, to be "like other women."

To be "like other women" had been a problem for me. From the 7 age of thirteen or fourteen, I had felt I was only acting the part of a feminine creature. At the age of sixteen my fingers were almost constantly ink-stained. The lipstick and high heels of the era were difficult-to-manage disguises. In 1945 I was writing poetry seriously, and had a fantasy of going to postwar Europe as a journalist, sleeping among the ruins in bombed cities, recording the rebirth of civilization after the fall of the Nazis. But also, like every other girl I knew, I spent hours trying to apply lipstick more adroitly, straightening the wandering seams of stockings, talking about "boys." There were two different compartments, already, to my life. But writing poetry, and my fantasies of travel and self-sufficiency, seemed more real to me; I felt that as an incipient "real woman" I was a fake. Particularly was I paralyzed when I encountered young children. I think I felt men could be— wished to be—conned into thinking I was truly "feminine"; a child, I suspected, could see through me like a shot. This sense of acting a part created a curious sense of guilt, even though it was a part demanded for survival.

I have a very clear, keen memory of myself the day after I was 8 married: I was sweeping a floor. Probably the floor did not really need to be swept; probably I simply did not know what else to do with myself. But as I swept that floor I thought: "Now I am a woman. This is an age-old action, this is what women have always done." I felt I was bending to some ancient form, too ancient to question. *This is what women have always done.*

As soon as I was visibly and clearly pregnant, I felt, for the first 9 time in my adolescent and adult life, not-guilty. The atmosphere of approval in which I was bathed—even by strangers on the street, it seemed—was like an aura I carried with me, in which doubts, fears, misgivings, met with absolute denial. *This is what women have always done.*

Two days before my first son was born, I broke out in a rash which 10 was tentatively diagnosed as measles, and was admitted to a hospital for contagious diseases to await the onset of labor. I felt for the first time a great deal of conscious fear, and guilt toward my unborn child, for having "failed" him with my body in this way. In rooms near mine were patients with polio; no one was allowed to enter my room except in a hospital gown and mask. If during pregnancy I had felt in any vague command of my situation, I felt now totally dependent on my obstetrician, a huge, vigorous, paternal man, abounding with optimism and assurance, and given to pinching my cheek. I had gone through a healthy pregnancy, but as if tranquilized or sleep-walking. I had taken a sewing class in which I produced an unsightly and ill-cut maternity jacket which I never wore; I had made curtains for the baby's room, collected baby clothes, blotted out as much as possible the woman I had been a few months earlier. My second book of poems was in press, but I had stopped writing poetry, and read little except household magazines and books on child-care. I felt myself perceived by the world simply as a pregnant woman, and it seemed easier, less disturbing, to perceive myself so. After my child was born the "measles" were diagnosed as an allergic reaction to pregnancy.

Within two years, I was pregnant again, and writing in a note-   11
book:

> *November 1956*
> Whether it's the extreme lassitude of early pregnancy or some-thing more fundamental, I don't know; but of late I've felt, toward poetry,—both reading and writing it—nothing but boredom and in-difference. Especially toward my own and that of my immediate con-temporaries. When I receive a letter soliciting mss., or someone al-ludes to my "career," I have a strong sense of wanting to deny all responsibility for and interest in that person who writes—or who wrote.

> If there is going to be a real break in my writing life, this is as good a time for it as any. I have been dissatisfied with myself, my work, for a long time.

My husband was a sensitive, affectionate man who wanted chil-   12
dren and who—unusual in the professional, academic world of the fifties—was willing to "help." But it was clearly understood that this "help" was an act of generosity; that *his* work, *his* professional life, was the real work in the family; in fact, this was for years not even an issue between us. I understood that my struggles as a writer were a kind of luxury, a peculiarity of mine; my work brought in almost no money: it even cost money, when I hired a household helper to allow me a few hours a week to write. "Whatever I ask he tries to give me," I wrote in March 1958, "but always the initiative has to be mine." I experienced my depressions, bursts of anger, sense of entrapment, as burdens my husband was forced to bear because he loved me; I felt grateful to be loved in spite of bringing him those burdens.

But I was struggling to bring my life into focus. I had never really   13
given up on poetry, nor on gaining some control over my existence. The life of a Cambridge tenement backyard swarming with children, the repetitive cycles of laundry, the night-wakings, the interrupted moments of peace or of engagement with ideas, the ludicrous dinner parties at which young wives, some with advanced degrees, all seri-

ously and intelligently dedicated to their children's welfare and their husbands' careers, attempted to reproduce the amenities of Brahmin Boston, amid French recipes and the pretense of effortlessness—above all, the ultimate lack of seriousness with which women were regarded in that world—all of this defied analysis at that time, but I *knew* I had to remake my own life. I did not then understand that we—the women of that academic community—as in so many middle-class communities of the period—were expected to fill both the part of the Victorian Lady of Leisure, the Angel in the House, and also of the Victorian cook, scullery maid, laundress, governess, and nurse. I only sensed that there were false distractions sucking at me, and I wanted desperately to strip my life down to what was essential.

> *June 1958*
> These months I've been all a tangle of irritations deepening to anger: bitterness, disillusion with society and with myself; beating out at the world, rejecting out of hand. What, if anything, has been positive? Perhaps the attempt to remake my life, to save it from mere drift and the passage of time . . .
>
> The work that is before me is serious and difficult and not at all clear even as to plan. Discipline of mind and spirit, uniqueness of expression, ordering of daily existence, the most effective functioning of the human self—these are the chief things I wish to achieve. So far the only beginning I've been able to make is to waste less time. That is what some of the rejection has been all about.

By July of 1958 I was again pregnant. The new life of my third— 14 and, as I determined, my last—child, was a kind of turning for me. I had learned that my body was not under my control; I had not intended to bear a third child. I knew now better than I had ever known what another pregnancy, another new infant, meant for my body and spirit. Yet, I did not think of having an abortion. In a sense, my third son was more actively chosen than either of his brothers; by the time I knew I was pregnant with him, I was not sleepwalking any more.

> *August 1958 (Vermont)*
> I write this as the early rays of the sun light up our hillside and eastern windows. Rose with [the baby] at 5:30 A.M. and have fed him and breakfasted. This is one of the few mornings on which I haven't felt terrible mental depression and physical exhaustion.
>
> . . . I have to acknowledge to myself that I would not have chosen to have more children, that I was beginning to look to a time, not too far off, when I should again be free, no longer so physically tired, pursuing a more or less intellectual and creative life. . . . The *only* way

I can develop now is through much harder, more continuous, connected work than my present life makes possible. Another child means postponing this for some years longer—and years at my age are significant, not to be tossed lightly away.

And yet, somehow, something, call it Nature or that affirming fatalism of the human creature, makes me aware of the inevitable as already part of me, not to be contended against so much as brought to bear as an additional weapon against drift, stagnation and spiritual death. (For it is really death that I have been fearing—the crumbling to death of that scarcely-born physiognomy which my whole life has been a battle to give birth to—a recognizable, autonomous self, a creation in poetry and in life.)

If more effort has to be made then I will make it. If more despair has to be lived through, I think I can anticipate it correctly and live through it.

Meanwhile, in a curious and unanticipated way, we really do welcome the birth of our child.

There was, of course, an economic as well as a spiritual margin 15 which allowed me to think of a third child's birth not as my own death-warrant but as an "additional weapon against death." My body, despite recurrent flares of arthritis, was a healthy one; I had good prenatal care; we were not living on the edge of malnutrition; I knew that all my children would be fed, clothed, breathe fresh air; in fact it did not occur to me that it could be otherwise. But, in another sense, beyond that physical margin, I knew I was fighting for my life through, against, and with the lives of my children, though very little else was clear to me. I had been trying to give birth to myself; and in some grim, dim way I was determined to use even pregnancy and parturition in that process.

Before my third child was born I decided to have no more chil- 16 dren, to be sterilized. (Nothing is removed from a woman's body during this operation; ovulation and menstruation continue. Yet the language suggests a cutting- or burning-away of her essential womanhood, just as the old word "barren" suggests a woman eternally empty and lacking.) My husband, although he supported my decision, asked whether I was sure it would not leave me feeling "less feminine." In order to have the operation at all, I had to present a letter, countersigned by my husband, assuring the committee of physicians who approved such operations that I had already produced three children, and stating my reasons for having no more. Since I had had rheumatoid arthritis for some years, I could give a reason acceptable to the male panel who sat on my case; my own judgment would not have been acceptable. When I awoke from the operation, twenty-four hours after my child's birth, a young nurse looked at my chart and remarked coldly: "Had yourself spayed, did you?"

The first great birth-control crusader, Margaret Sanger, remarks 17 that of the hundreds of women who wrote to her pleading for contraceptive information in the early part of the twentieth century, all spoke of wanting the health and strength to be better mothers to the children they already had; or of wanting to be physically affectionate to their husbands without dread of conceiving. None was refusing motherhood altogether, or asking for an easy life. These women—mostly poor, many still in their teens, all with several children—simply felt they could no longer do "right" by their families, whom they expected to go on serving and rearing. Yet there always has been, and there remains, intense fear of the suggestion that women shall have the final say as to how our bodies are to be used. It is as if the suffering of the mother, the primary identification of woman *as* the mother—were so necessary to the emotional grounding of human society that the mitigation, or removal, of that suffering, that identification, must be fought at every level, including the level of refusing to question it at all.

Working with the Text

1. What is the significance of beginning the essay with a quotation from Simone Weil? Who was Weil? What could Rich mean by agreeing with Weil that "comprehension ought always to be concrete"? What is the meaning of "the cave" and coming out of it? How do these ideas relate to Rich's overall thesis in the essay?

2. What is the relation in the essay between writing and the rest of life, especially Rich's life as a mother? What are the conflicts? How does Rich struggle to resolve them?

3. What is the function of all the entries from Rich's diary in this essay? What purpose do they serve? How would the essay have been different without them? Why do you think she decided to include them?

4. How does Rich structure the essay to balance her personal experiences with her broader social criticism? Make an outline of the essay, charting her shifts in focus from the purely personal to the public or social, trying to understand the pattern she might be using.

Working beyond the Text

1. Rich describes the pressures of living up to a cultural image or expectation, and the guilt and depression that may result from not doing a good enough

job of it. What cultural expectations apply to you? Which ones are hard to fulfill? Do you have similar feelings of guilt?

2. Rich speaks of exchanging "taboo" words with a group of women poets. What are the taboo words and ideas that they dare to speak? Why are they taboo? What are the taboo words or ideas that you will speak only among a particular group of friends? Why?

3. The pressures on women that Rich describes are sometimes called "the feminine mystique" after a famous book of that name by Betty Friedan. When was the book published? What is its basic argument? You can answer these questions either by skimming the book or by reading reviews and essays about the book from your library.

4. The pressures to be a perfect mother that Rich describes are often associated with the time in which she lived: the 1950s and 1960s. How much have things changed? Are the pressures the same some 40 to 50 years later? Or have they evolved? Is it easier or harder to be a mother in the late 1990s?

Heat and Rain

Denise Chávez

Denise Chávez, born in New Mexico in 1948, began keeping a diary at the age of eight. She writes poems, stories, and plays about life in her home state. Her works include *Life Is a Two-Way Street, The Last of the Menu Girls,* and *Face of an Angel.* This essay was published in an anthology entitled *Breaking Boundaries: Writing and Critical Readings* (1989). In it, Chávez shares portions of her diaries in order to talk about the relationship between her writing and her life as a Hispanic woman.

My first childhood recollection is of heat. Perhaps because I was 1 born in the middle of August in Southern New Mexico, I have always felt the burningly beautiful intensity of my dry, impenetrable land. Land not often relieved by the rain—that wet, cleansing, and blessed catharsis. I remember as a little girl sitting waist-deep in the cool, grassy water that had been channeled from the irrigation ditch behind our house. The heat, then the rain, and the water were my first friends.

My other friend was my imagination that invented an extended 2 family of loving, congenial spirits who wandered with me nighttimes in my dreams—into the other worlds I inhabited as vividly and completely as I did my own waking existence as middle daughter in a family of three girls, one mother, Delfina Rede Faver Chávez, a teacher divorced by my father, E.E. "Chano" Chávez, one lawyer, long gone.

These friendships with spirits were real to me, and still are. The spirits were voices of people, people I'd known and not known, feelings I felt and couldn't at that time conceive of feeling. I had no way to explain my creative world to anyone, could not even explain it to myself. All I know is that my life was rich and deep and full of wonder. 3

I always felt advanced for my age, somehow different. I always thought I *thought* more than people my own age. My imagination was a friend at first, and later a lover, a guide, a spirit teacher. 4

I grew up in a house of women. That is why I often write about women, women who are without men. My father divorced us early on; he was a brilliant lawyer, but an alcoholic. My mother was incredibly intelligent, with a keen curiosity and love of life and people. Their minds were compatible, their spirits and hearts were not. I grew up knowing separation as a quality of life—and this sorrow went hand in hand with extensions—for despite the fact my parents were apart, both families were an everpresent part of my life. So I grew up solitary in the midst of noise, a quality I didn't know then was essential to my work as a writer. 5

People always ask me how and when I started writing. The answer never varies. From an early age I kept diaries, some with locks, locks I kept losing or misplacing, others with no locks. I'm sure my mother read my diary. I'm positive my younger sister did. 6

DIARY
A Page a Day for 1958
New Year's Day, Wednesday January 1, 1958
1st Day—364 Days to Follow
Dear Diary,
    Today is New Year and the old year is gone and the new one here. Today school starts. I can't wait to go.

Sunday June 15, 1958
166th Day—199 Days to Follow
Dear Diary,
    Today I didn't go to Mass, I must tell the priest my sin. I'm not to happy about it.

Friday, August 15, 1958
227th Day—138 Days to Follow
Dear Diary,
    Today is my birthday. I am ten in a few years I'll be twenty. Boy oh boy ten years old

Tuesday, November 11, 1958

315 Day—50 Days to Follow
Dear Diary,
    School was fun, But I forgot to do my homework. I'm praying for daddy to come home, I hope so. He did. Thank god. Bless us all.

Thursday, November 20, 1958

324th Day—41 Days to Follow
Dear Diary,
    I did not go to school today because we stayed home with Mama. She is heart sick (broken heart) She feels bad, I hope she gets well. I missed school but I loved to stay home. You know why! Don't You?
    All wrong. I did go to school. drat.

Somehow, looking back on myself in these diary entries, I am aware of myself, even then, as an observer of life. Without my diaries, I don't think I'd ever have become a writer. I now see that 1958 was a hard year, the breakup of my parents' marriage, a devastating time for all of us. I see the order I began to put into my life, the need to account for, evaluate, assess. Time was of significance, my life of value. Religion was important then as spirituality is to me now. I wanted to grow up so badly, to be an adult, to understand. My life was rich then, I see that too, with much experience that was to feed me for years to come.

    I see that I was not a good student, ever. I rarely did homework. I 7 would study in bed, usually lying down, waking up the next morning, the light on, in my clothes, very hot and clammy, dry mouthed, Mother yelling for me to wake up, to find the History or Math book mashed into my face. I would race to school, then fly back to enter the latest news into my diary. Painful accounts were entered, then torn. Did *I* tear them, and if not me, who? My mother, my sister? Or that other girl, the me who wanted to be happy? I note with interest my early stream of consciousness technique (not a technique then), my disinterest in chronological time (critics take note), I see the roots of my still poor grammar and spelling, and observe the time I begin to sign my writing—Denise. The writing had become a statement for someone other than me. What I had to say, suddenly, to me "mattered."

    I see also the many gaps between entries, and that too is of signifi- 8 cance. I see that I wrote on sad, happy, elated, and depressed days. The regular days were entry-less. Writing was a gauge of my personal life. It was a record of my physical, spiritual, and emotional ups and downs. I enjoyed writing, always have, the actual physical movement of pen or pencil across a piece of paper. I enjoyed/enjoy the mind-eye-to-hand-acting-out-delineation of internalness. I practiced my handwriting constantly:

I see now that I was training myself unconsciously to "write" effi- 9
ciently, quickly. A sort of "scales" for the writing self/hand. Rolling
letters, moving them through space, limbering up mechanically so that
later I could use my hand like a tool, limbered, unrestrained. I still find
myself practicing the alphabet on random sheets of paper, testing letter style, still looking for a more effective fluid line. Much flight time
on the white canvas of my constantly emerging movement toward my
work as a writer. I didn't know it then. I didn't know it when I got a
notebook and started copying other people's poems, songs. But this
was later, because first there were books, books, and more books to
read, like my favorite childhood book called *Poems of Childhood* by Eu-
gene Field, with scary-wonderful poems like "Seein' Things."

I was a voracious reader. Anything. Everything. I went on binges. 10
My mother would hide our books in the summertime so we would
help her with the housework. My sister would lock herself in the bathroom with a book, heedless of my mother's cries. It never occurred to
me to do that. Everyday my book would be missing, I'd find it, read
awhile, then find it missing. It went on like that. I read fairy tales. Mysteries. Nancy Drew. You name it. Later on it was Ian Fleming's James
Bond, D. H. Lawrence, Thomas Mann, Thomas Wolfe, Chekhov, Eu-
gene O'Neill, Samuel Beckett. Now it's the *Enquirer*. I love the scandal
sheets and movie mags and bowling and soap operas in the middle of
the day, and so much of what everyone else considers pedestrian, sub-
mainstream culture. Director John Waters calls Baltimore the Hairdo
capital of the world. New Mexico/Texas was and is Character Capital
of the Universe. Unbelievable stories, lives. I have always been a
talker, friendly to strangers, and so invariably people tell me about
their lives. It's a gift to listen to so many of these stories. The *Enquirer*
has nothing over New Mexico/Texas or the world I see every day!

But this sense of wonder came early. I began to copy my favorite 11
passages, poems. One of the earliest was a cowboy song. I loved the
rhythm. Sang it to myself. Later on I copied Gibran and the Black
poets, wrote angry poems to the nuns at Madonna High School, where
I attended school for four years, poems they refused to publish in the
Mantle, the school newspaper. Once, as a joke, I invented a quote for
the "Quote of the Day" for World Literature class: "Christmas is the
flowing of honey on a mound of cold, white snow." Mrs. Baker,
lovely, frail, intelligent, and wispy-haired, loved it. I didn't know what
the hell it meant. I was playing the rebellious know-it-all, making up

my own poems and quotes. I didn't know writing was becoming a facile thing. Then it was just a joke. The other day I heard a writer say, "All those lies, writing all those lies—I love it!" I didn't say anything. For me, writing is no longer a facile joke, a prank to be played on a well-meaning and unsuspecting reader, nor is it a lie. I have said to writers I have taught: Don't lie. And to myself: You may lie in other things, but never in this. It's a sacred covenant I have with myself. Honesty. And no meanness. Sometimes it's been hard. Lies always surface, don't you know?

I never thought of lying in my writing. It would have been like 12 hiding in the bathroom to read.

I could never lie to those voices, to those spirits, to those voices I 13 hear clearly. Voices like my mother, who always spoke in Spanish, or my father, who mostly spoke in English. Mother grew up in West Texas, moved to New Mexico as a widow and met and married my father. My father, as a child, was punished for speaking Spanish in the school yard. He decided to beat the Anglos at their game. He went and got a law degree from Georgetown during the Depression. And he became, in his mind, more Anglo than those Anglos who had punished him. I remember my mother saying, "I never think of your father as Mexican." My mother was, though, in her heart and soul. She studied in Mexico for thirteen summers, was a student of Diego Rivera. She'd been widowed for nine years, all that time wearing black, when she met my father, just returned from the Big City. Both my parents were very intelligent, perceptive, sensitive people. My mother's grandparents were the first Spanish-speaking graduates of Sul Ross State College in West Texas. All of them became teachers. Both my grandfathers were miners, all-around men, carpenters, teamsters, fixeruppers, workers with their hands. They used their brains and their hands to support their large families. The women were independent, creative, and did most of the child-rearing, alone. The Chávez men are painters now, artists with canvas and paint, or architects, builders of some kind. The Rede Family (my mother's clan) are educators, fighters for human rights, communicators, and believers in the equality of all people.

I grew up between and in the middle of two languages, Spanish 14 and English, speaking my own as a defense. My mother always said I "made up words." Speaking Spanish to the Redes or English to the get-ahead Chávezes and Spanish to the traditional Chávezes and English to my Rede cousins was all taken in stride. We went back and forth, back and forth. My mother taught Spanish and she was always correcting, in any language. When I asked how to spell a word, she would tell me to sound out the syllables, and to find a dictionary. "There she goes again," I'd think, "teacher-ing me." I was lazy, still am. My English needs work and so does my Spanish. I can't spell, punctuate or understand the possessive. My multiplication is a mess and I can't tell time. I was absent the day we kids learned the 7, 8, and 9 multiplication tables. I have gaps—huge ones. But I've taught myself what little grammar I know, what math I know, and how to type. I can take any vacuum cleaner apart and fix it and my pen hand is very fast at the draw. I really write according to what I hear—sometimes English, sometimes Spanish, sometimes both. As a writer, I have tried to capture as clearly as I am able *voices*, intonation, inflection, mood, timbre, pitch. I write about characters, not treatises, about life, not make-believe worlds. If my characters don't work, I will go back and make them work. Without them, robust and in the living flesh, there is no story for me. Readers should stop looking for traditional stories, ABC. Writing, to me, is an assemblage of parts, a phrase here, an image there, part of a dialogue.

Suddenly it occurs to me that Jesusita Real, the not-so-mousy spin- 15 ster in my play, *Novena Narrativas*, should wear green tennis shoes, and so I add them to the script. When she finally does walk, it will be in comfort, with support from the ground up. I work with my characters in the way an actress or actor assumes a role, slowly, carefully, with attention to physical, emotional, and spiritual detail. I may read the material out loud, speak it into a tape recorder, play it back, rewrite it, and then tape it again. My years as a theatre person have helped me immensely. I have acted, directed, and written for the theatre. I have done props, hung lights, performed for all types of audiences, young, old, handicapped, drunk, aging, for prisoners, in Spanish and English. My work has always been for alternative groups, the people who never get much, for the poor, the forgotten. My writing as well is about the off-off Main street type of characters. My short stories are really scenes and I come from the tradition of the traveling *cuentista*. I believe stories should captivate, delight, move, inspire, and be downright funny, in a way. The "in a way" is what I try to do with all my heart. But always, I go back to the characters and their voices. I see them: flat feet, lagañas, lonjas, lumps, spider veins, and all. From the feet up and back down and around the other side. And I love them. Dearly. But I don't excuse them nor will I lie for them.

I write for you. And me. And Jesusita with the green tennies, spin- 16 ster owner of Rael's Tiendita de Abarrotes, active member of the Third Order of St. Francis, and for the people: Anglo, Hispanic, Black, you name it: anybody out there who doesn't know Jesusita is alive, inside her little store, swatting flies, and wondering aloud about Prudencio Sifuentes, the only man who asked her to marry him.

I write for the viejitas at the Save-And-Gain in black scarves, for 17 the tall blond man testing tomatoes, for the Vietnamese cashier, and for the hot dog man outside the electric door. For me, it is a joy to carry my bag full of stories.

Naturally I write about what I know, who I am. New Mexico. 18
Texas. Chicanismo. Latinismo. Americanismo. Womanismo. Mujero-
tismo. Peopleismo. Worldismo. Peaceismo. Loveismo.

Writing has been my heat, my accounting, my trying to under- 19
stand; and rain has been my prayer for peace, for love, and mercy. August in Southern New Mexico is very hot, for many, unbearable. It has
been my blessing in this life of mine to share that heat. And to remember the rain.

Las Cruces, New Mexico
Summer 1987

Working with the Text

1. Why does Chávez tell details from her life (where she is from, what kinds
   of people her parents are, why they were divorced) in an essay about writing? How do these things relate to her life as a writer?
2. After Chávez hears a writer say that he loves "writing all those lies," she
   thinks, "I have said to writers I have taught: Don't lie. And to myself: You
   may lie in other things, but never in this." What did the first writer mean
   that writing is "all lies"? What does Chávez mean when she says that writing must not lie?
3. Chávez describes her perception that she "*thought* more than people my
   own age," and also that she "grew up solitary in the midst of noise." How
   do these details about her temperament connect to her development as a
   writer?
4. The style Chávez uses in this essay might seem "choppy": she sometimes
   skips from one topic to another without a transition at the beginning of the
   paragraph. Examine the places where she does this. Assuming that there
   are connections of some kind in those places, what might they be? What are
   the "missing transitions"? Why do you think Chávez chooses to leave them
   out?

Working beyond the Text

1. Chávez says she was a "voracious reader. Anything. Everything." Were
   you? Try to remember your earliest experiences with reading and writing.
   How did you learn? From whom? Did you like it, hate it, or fall somewhere
   in between? How can you explain the attitudes toward reading you have
   today?
2. In the end of her essay, Chávez makes a list of the people she writes for:
   "you," "me," Jesusita (one of her characters), "the people: Anglo, Hispanic,
   Black," and so on. What does she mean by each of the people or groups on

her list? In what way does she write "for" them? Who do you write for, and why?

3. Look up some of Chávez's other work in the library. Can you see in her stories and plays the range of influences that she outlines in "Heat and Rain"? Make connections between her writing and what she explains as the sources of her writing.

7

LANGUAGES OF LITERARY EXPRESSION

INTRODUCTION

Stories are stories. Anybody can write them. We tell them all the time, after all. Poems are easy, too. Just make sure the words rhyme at the end of every line. Anybody who writes pop songs can do it.

Because we are surrounded in our everyday lives by stories and poems and other examples of "literary" language, it is easy to forget what literature is made of: language. Nouns, verbs, adjectives. Metaphors, similes, figures of speech. Writers are builders, using language as the raw material of literature. When we shift our focus from everyday examples of stories and poems to literature as such, we also shift our emphasis from the information and feelings conveyed by the writer to the language used to convey the writer's knowledge and feelings.

And there are rules for making literature out of language. We may have a romantic image of a writer as someone who gushes feelings onto the page, more interested in self-expression than anything else. However, John Gardner, a novelist known as a great teacher of writers, claims, "The writer's primary unit of thought is genre." What he means is that writers write best when they obey the conventions of the genre in which they are writing: story, novel, poem, or drama; realism, fantasy, or thriller; sonnet, ballad, or villanelle; tragedy, comedy, or history. Self-expression will come about naturally in the creation of literature through the writer's handling of the conventions.

Gardner's view is not the only one, of course. Avant-garde art may rebel against the conventional rules of art and proclaim the freedom of the artist to create as he or she wishes. Experimental literature may ignore the rules of plot and character, for example. Punk rock used barely competent musicianship and obscure, shouted lyrics to rebel against the conventions of overproduced pop songs. Some writers feel at ease with traditional rules, while others insist that true creativity cannot come out of obeying tradition, but only from refusing tradition.

A related debate centers on the appropriate uses of art. How should the makers of art and literature function in social and political worlds of human decision making? Many artists are inspired by strong impulses to create art for the improvement of society, to create art for the promotion of social change. Others say that "politics" has no business in art, or they believe in "art for art's sake," or they simply take pleasure in fulfilling the potential of an artistic form.

The selections in this chapter address both of these complicated issues: the formal qualities of various literary forms, including how much variation an artist should be allowed or is entitled to, and the writer's relationship to the social, political, and cultural contexts in which he or she works.

———————— Before You Read ————————

Before you read any combination of essays in this chapter, you might prepare by doing any of the activities below as either class or small group discussions, or as formal or informal writing assignments. They are designed to help you find out what you already know about the issues discussed by the authors in the chapter, so you have some background for understanding what the authors say.

1. How does "artistic" or "literary" language differ from any other kind of language, such as scientific language, journalistic language, or everyday conversational language? How do you know literary language when you see it? Try comparing a passage of literary language (from a poem or novel, for example) with several other kinds of language in order to give examples of the differences.

2. What literature have you read? What do you remember about it? What pieces have you liked the most? Why? What do they "mean" to you in your life?

3. Why do people write literature? Few do it for money or success in the conventional sense, since few works of literature become bestsellers. What other purposes could there be? Have you ever read or heard about any writer's stated purpose for writing literature? If you wrote literature, what purposes might motivate you?

4. What is the stereotypical image of a writer of literature? How do writers look, act, and speak? Where do they live, and who are their friends? How do they spend their spare time?

5. What are the limits of literature? That is, if the novels of Jane Austen and Henry James are examples of literature, how about those of Anne Rice and Robert Ludlum? If the poems of Emily Dickinson and Robert Frost are literature, how about the songs of

Stephen Foster and the Beatles? How about urban graffiti? Navajo ritual chants? Television commercial jingles?

_____ **After You Read** _____

After you read any combination of essays in this chapter, you might follow up by doing any of the activities below as either class or small group discussions, or as formal or informal writing assignments. They are designed to help you extend what you have learned from the authors in the chapter by discovering new perspectives on the chapter's themes on your own.

1. When Silko says "it is the _story_ and the feeling of the story which matters more than the language it's told in," she seems to contradict some of the other writers in this chapter, including O'Connor, Huddle, and Bohannan. What do some of the other writers say about the importance of language in writing literature? What does Silko mean when she denies this importance? How do you explain the difference in opinion? What different assumptions might Silko have toward literature than the other writers?

2. All the writers in this chapter discuss the society and specific social settings in which writers find themselves. What effect do a writer's social surroundings have on his or her writing? Trace this idea through the essays in the chapter, and then try to apply it to your own writing.

3. Most of the essays in this chapter, particularly those written by O'Connor, Huddle, and Hammerstein, offer advice to writers, some of it simple "how-to" advice, some of it more profound. What advice do the writers offer? How do they agree and disagree with each other? As a writer yourself, what advice based on your experiences would you offer to other writers?

4. Did any of the essays in this chapter challenge your idea of who literary writers are, how they live and work, and how they think about their writing? Which ones, and in what ways? What new understandings do you think you have about the process of writing literature?

UNIT ONE

LITERARY LANGUAGE AND "THE RULES"

What's the Matter With Poetry?

F. D. Reeve

F. D. Reeve, born in 1928, teaches Russian at Wesleyan University; writes poetry, novels, history, and literary criticism; and translates Russian literature into English. His collections of poetry include *The Blue Cat* and *Concrete Music*. In the following essay, which appeared in the news commentary magazine *The Nation* (May 1993), Reeve explains why poetry is still important in our culture.

Writer A and poet B were talking about poet C: "C has one of the strongest lyric gifts of our time," said B. "He now denies it," said A. "He wants to speak in the people's voice, directly, without emotional flourishes. He wants everybody to understand him. In his new book he has gotten rid of all his lyricism." B shook his head. "Crazy. Impossible. He's mad." A week later, A got a postcard: "I've just finished C's new book. You're right. Incredibly, there's not a lyric note." 1

Victim of the notion that poetry doesn't matter, C supposed that The People speak through best-seller lists and look for their poets, like movie actors, in tabloid gossip columns. If he flattened his lyric voice, he guessed, people would take him up, he'd become popular. But he missed and lost his audience because, in fact, the audience for poetry is stable and faithful. The composer George Walker has said, "Only a small percentage of any group is interested in classical music"; but the percentage interested in poetry is large; it's noncommercial; it reaches across the nation; it discriminates against no one; and it persists despite government hostility, academic manipulation, economic censorship and attacks in the middlebrow press. To be sure, among the Milkens and the Babbitts, it's secondary. For everyone else, poets as different as William Heyen, William Mundell, Mary TallMountain, Jean Valentine, Jay Meek, William Stafford, Ishmael Reed, Julio Marzán, Philip Booth and Stanley Burnshaw matter greatly. 2

In a junk-bond, celluloid world in which a President can say he didn't read the briefing book for the 1983 economic summit because 3

The Sound of Music was on that evening, *nothing* may seem real. But that this world represents *us* is an illusion: The politicians we elect and the news we get may be what we deserve, but they're not what we want.

In this commercial fairyland, we're not told the truth about poetry, 4 either. Not even by poets. Newspapers ignore it; book reviews skip over it; TV and radio avoid it; and even poet Dana Gioia proclaimed in his recent book *Can Poetry Matter?* (the title essay of which appeared in *The Atlantic*) that poetry has vanished as a cultural force in America. "None of it matters very much to readers, publishers, or advertisers."

Not true. Advertisers have always cared about effect, and their 5 hard-sell, subliminal means of marketing have undermined the sense of humor that created the zippy Burma Shave signs. Publishers who are part of conglomerates care primarily about profits—witness the sad case of Pantheon and André Schiffrin's forced resignation three years ago—but small, independent presses are bringing out more poetry than ever. Indeed, some people say there's too much; they can't read it all. Yet readers are avidly reading, poets are offering workshops in schools, and the *American Book Review* and the *American Poetry Review* are keeping as many people abreast as they can. A glance at the Bay Area's *Poetry Flash* or at the *Poetry Calendar* for the New York metropolitan area will astound you by how much poetry is in the air and how many people it is bringing together. Disregard complaints about "lookalike verse" turned out by poetry workshops. Even if bad poetry obscures the good, it serves a good purpose: It binds people together in their culture. In our country today, culture itself threatens to vanish.

Insofar as there is a cultural force in America, poetry is at its base. 6 Because poetry can't easily be made into a commodity like science fiction, murder mystery or Gothic romance and, like even Shakespeare's plays, is not easily made into motion pictures, there's no money in it, as an editor might say. Thanks to the fact that books are marketed like shampoos and to the censorship imposed by the economic policies of publishers with the money to advertise, most American readers never see the poetry that's suppressed, just as voters never hear of the qualified men and women who can't afford to run for public office. And just as incumbents refuse to change the rules, the journals that ignore poetry say it doesn't matter and shed crocodile tears.

A poem need not be on a greeting card to be a greeting, a way of 7 thinking in which people recognize one another. A hundred years ago Celia Thaxter and John Greenleaf Whittier corresponded by poem across the water between Amesbury, Massachusetts, and the Isles of Shoals. Nowadays, many unduly modest people prefer a commercial card, as if their own expressions were inadequate. Such modesty is a result of the cultural repression imposed by our teachers and directly parallels the political conformism inculcated in school and reinforced by the media. Any poet who has taught children and any politician who has organized at the local level knows how deeply a product-oriented, color-based ideology has been worked into the American bone. Poetry is one way of working it out. The poetic imagination protests being herded, thwarted and coerced. It seeks freedom of expression and liberty of thought. It declares human values superior to technological ones, asserts the benefits of peace over the losses of war and opposes the state as an instrument of violence. It can't fill an empty stomach, but it does nourish a hungry mind.

Poetry is a way of taking the world, a way of being taken that allows a clear but impersonal intimacy and demands a clear and personal commitment. Politicians fudge, lie and get re-elected; poets are driven always closer to explaining and praising what matters. People mistrust politicians as cynical opportunists hungry for power and indifferent to their constituents' needs. In this totalitarian democracy, people not only love poets, they want to *be* poets. They want to think critically, to act openly and to write significantly. Because poetry has been thoroughly democratized, there's a lot of poetry around. The country is jumping with poetry, with lots of little magazines like *Free Lunch* and *Waterways* and *CrazyQuilt* and *Mississippi Mud.* TV fills the satellite dishes, but the CB bands are alive with home talk, and the air is crisscrossed with literary messages from citizen to citizen, messages not to be judged or immortalized but to be taken as delivered and responded to. Poetry, like the need for beauty, is insuppressible. 8

Our most intense feelings—our "immortal longings"—persuade us of our uniqueness and awaken our poetic sensibilities. Perhaps poet C's problem was that he stopped being concerned with the visual truth of his poetry—with each word as an image expressing a physical reality—and began to worry about the authority of his image on a literary stage. His mistake, to take a phrase from James Fenton's "Some Mistakes People Make About Poetry" in a recent *New York Review of Books,* "was to think of poetry as a career." He wasn't worried about The People, he wanted to appear in *People.* 9

Pure and corrupt political poetries have been part of our modern culture from the German *Tendenzpoesie* of the mid-nineteenth century to the latest Socialist Realism. Long before that, the great Parian poet of the early seventh century B.C., Archilochus, who perfected, if he didn't invent, the iamb as a verse of debate and invective, composed a poem so effectively attacking Lycambes for reneging on the promise of Neobule in marriage that all Lycambes' daughters, the ancients reported, hanged themselves in shame. In cultures where truth out- 10 weighs falsehood and holds firm against fads, poetry is still effective, and the poetic aspects of even crassly sensationalist fiction, like Salman Rushdie's *The Satanic Verses*, cut to the cultural heart. The best public poetry of our time, like W.H. Auden's and Kenneth Fearing's in the thirties, Tom McGrath's in the fifties and James Scully's in the sixties, is both lyric and dramatic, coming from a profound social, even religious, consciousness. Like Whitman's, it is political in the deepest, most affectionate sense. It is a responsible poetry sung to an audience defined by the social implications of the language. Sometimes it's harsh; sometimes sad; sometimes mocking, silly, lighthearted. Whatever fits into life, said Salvadoran poet Roque Dalton, fits into poetry.

Poetry and life are aspects of one continuum, like time and dis- 11
tance. There is resonance in the work of poets who acknowledge an explicit political frame. "Politically conscious poets tend to be *more* profound, not less," says Scully in *Line Break,* adding that Nazim Hikmet has written "the most credible, full, *caring* love poetry" of our time precisely because he writes of the *other.* The diffractions and diffidences among our poetries and criticisms now, Scully says, reflect the institutional instabilities of our hegemonic political terms.

Our political and commercial languages not only distract from but 12
even seem to deny the existence of our poetic language, but it remains alive among people in their intimate ways and not infrequently reaches the public, noncommercial media. For example, the language of poetry stretches from Berkeley's KPFA to Terry Gross's *Fresh Air* from WHYY in Philadelphia and WNYC's *Spoken Word,* includes old programs like David and Judy Ray's *New Letters on the Air* and Charles Rossiter's *Poetry Motel* on Channel 31 in Albany, New York, and crops up on National Public Radio's weekend news programs. The poems range widely, are treated respectfully. In a society destroying its environment and wasting its resources, they express a large and not-so-secret, fully conscious cultural force pointing out things as they are and striving for nonviolent regeneration. Indeed, given our nationwide political and commercial failures, only through the language of poetry and the politics of consensus can we rebuild our culture.

The atomic bombs dropped on Hiroshima and Nagasaki funda- 13
mentally altered our self-esteem. We, who were so big, who had the power endlessly to transform nature, discovered that we could destroy everything, including ourselves. As the universe expanded around us, we became smaller and insignificant, little clowns waiting for an imaginary Godot. For the past three decades, from Vietnam and Watergate to the banking bailout and the Gulf War, our country has been so publicly corrupt, our government so deceitful and cruel and the media so complicit, that satire has lost its edge. We've lost the community of reasonableness on which to offer a *Dunciad,* a "Modest

Proposal," a *We,* a *Brave New World* or a *1984.* More through our poetry—which keeps our language—than through anything else can we keep in close touch with our past and with one another.

A successfully self-conscious person preserves neat borders, [14] aware that relations spiral in and out, overlie and undercut but demand integrity. It doesn't ultimately matter whether poems are "formal" or "free" because either way the words create a rhythm—an expectation of return and some sort of satisfaction—and the rhythm makes a pattern. Couched in patterns, poetry expresses the heart of the matter because the essence of poetry is metaphor, and metaphor is analogy, an assertion of discreetness by the act of compounding:

> A noiseless patient spider,
> I marked where on a little promontory
>   it stood isolated,
> Marked how to explore the vacant vast
>   surrounding,
> It launched forth filament, filament,
>   filament, out of itself,
> Ever unreeling them, ever tirelessly
>   speeding them.
>
> And you O my soul where you stand,
> Surrounded, detached, in measureless
>   oceans of space,
> Ceaselessly musing, venturing, throwing,
>   seeking the spheres to connect
>   them,
> Till the bridge you will need be formed,
>   till the ductile anchor hold,
> Till the gossamer thread you fling
>   catch somewhere, O my soul
>   (Walt Whitman,
>   "A Noiseless Patient Spider")

These days, one telescope after another is lofted into space to measure those oceans, but who more subtly and more profoundly than our poets measures us?

Society comes down on each of us like Goliath on David. It senti- [15] mentalizes our deepest feelings, sensationalizes our habits, suppresses our differences and reduces our work and our bodies to market value. Must poets also become prostitutes? Must they flex their biceps to market their sonnets? Do we really prefer to be entertained by the so-called war between the sexes rather than to achieve a just and lasting peace in the war between the rich and the poor? Today, most objects of cultural exchange are debased, good poetry is hoarded and bad slogans proliferate.

Poetry's importance is an old issue, reflecting changes in literary 16
taste from age to age. It was raised in Edmund Wilson's 1934 article
"Is Verse a Dying Technique?" and as in a mediocre tennis match, the
cutting and slicing go on. Wilson foresaw prose as the avenue of major
literary expression, but he neither felt nor understood poetry and,
rather like an anthropologist studying a primitive religion, measured
what he thought were its social consequences. In part because of the
anti-intellectualism that followed the failed 1968 rebellions and in part
because of the increasing commercial manipulation of our lives, the ro-
botization of work, the incursions on privacy and the destruction of
community, the issue is with us more depressingly than ever. Had the
spirit of '68 prevailed, had institutional hegemony passed into local
hands, public scandals like Watergate might have been contained and
invasions of Grenada and Panama prevented. There's no rewriting
history, of course, but by putting human relations and human welfare
at the center of social purpose, the spirit of '68 promised an unprecedented transformation. In reaction, society became more narrow-
minded than before, reimposing many orthodoxies that made no
sense. By judicial decree and legislative action, free inquiry has been
hindered and dissent restricted—think of the purity oath for grantees
floated by the National Endowment for the Arts, or photographer Jock
Sturges being arrested for photographing families in the nude.

Dana Gioia asserts that poetry doesn't much matter now and that 17
poets have betrayed the art and brought irrelevance on themselves. "A
poetry industry has been created to serve the interests of the produc-
ers and not the consumers," he writes in *Can Poetry Matter?* Like Fenton, he faults those "teaching others how to write poetry," although he
himself, formerly a business executive, is a veteran leader of writers'
conference workshops and has taught writing as a college instructor.
In the chapter "Notes on the New Formalism," he praises William Carlos Williams's "The Red Wheelbarrow" for challenging the reader vi-
sually and imaginatively but calls it a trick: "The element of surprise
makes this type of poem a difficult trick to repeat and may explain
why so much of the minimalist poetry written in the Williams tradition is so dull." In the forthcoming *Strange Courage: The Spanish-
American Roots of William Carlos Williams,* Julio Marzán gives the Spanish gloss on crucial words in that poem, showing how Williams, the
putative free-verser, like every genuine poet used his poetry not as a
trick or a confessional but as an imaginative means of overcoming his
limitations and the inadequacies of his biography.

For poetry, the deaths in the sixties and seventies of poet-critics 18
such as R.P. Blackmur and John Crowe Ransom, Mark Van Doren and
Randall Jarrell, who made thinking poetically and writing intellectually a way of life—and who, along with people like Wallace Stegner
and Robert Penn Warren, introduced imaginative writing as an educa-

tional tool into the university curriculum—left the academies open to a French invasion, and the journals and reviews open to ax-grinding and backbiting. Except for two or three venerable firms, publishing houses in the so-called free market cost-accounted their poetry lists virtually out of existence. One independent after another was swallowed up; profitability took precedence over prestige; chain stores and large distributors took over the market; and poetry and its criticism all but disappeared from the shelves. Oh, you can still find it, the few "name" volumes in any good bookstore and a great many more in places from Powell's in Portland to The Grolier in Cambridge. Like the small, slim volumes in which it appears and the presses that bring it out, it may seem marginal to American life. My point is that it isn't.

Classical music, legitimate theater, painting and sculpture, ballet 19 and modern dance—performance and visual arts that enjoy some of the general allure of film and, like ball games and sports competitions, often are shown on TV—seem marginal, too, compared with their variety and accessibility fifty years ago. Such apparent marginality in a population that has doubled comes not from people but from money—from twenty years of greed and a tripled national debt and control of culture by profit-minded entrepreneurs. Our general cultural affairs are in good measure dependent on unartistic committees and foundations, much as the making of a Steinway (the family company sold to CBS and resold to Steinway Musical Properties) is now supervised by a former nuclear engineer. Some days only our poetry keeps us from thinking we've already gone to hell in a handbasket.

Poetry hasn't been ruined. Poetry remains what John Berryman 20 said:

> I consider a song will be as
> humming-bird
> swift, down-light, missile-metal-hard,
> & strange
> as the world of anti-matter
> where they are wondering: does time
> run backward—
> which the poet thought was true. . . .

In bookstore corners, upstairs cafes, reading rooms, clubs, schools, churches and public radio programs, it's alive and well, singing, like Jay Meek's young musicians, "songs for men who cannot die."

What's the matter with poetry? Nothing. In some places there's 21 lots of it, like the white-tailed deer; in other places it's as endangered as the spotted owl. But the matter *of* poetry is a broad social concern, the resolution of which will show what we make of ourselves as a society. For years, a fundamental dispute has been between those who would exploit the earth and those who would preserve it. Same with culture: Fools and crooks will exploit us for profit; people serious about poetry will preserve cultural integrity and individual freedom of expression. To say that poetry doesn't matter is to say that people don't matter.

Working with the Text

1.. What does Reeve mean when he talks about "censorship imposed by the economic policies of publishers with the money to advertise"? What is "censorship"? How can "economic policies" censor writing?

2. What is poetry good for? Reeve makes great claims for it: "only through the language of poetry . . . can we rebuild our culture." How does he define poetry so that he can make such a claim?

3. What does Reeve mean when he says, "These days, one telescope after another is lofted into space to measure those oceans, but who more subtly and more profoundly than our poets measures us"? What knowledge does poetry have that science doesn't?

4. Reeve opens the essay with an anecdote about "poet C" and the way he "flattens his lyric voice." What is the point of the story? How does it relate to the message of the rest of the essay?

5. How does Reeve support his bold claim that poetry is important to many Americans? What evidence does he provide? Does this evidence convince you as an audience? Why or why not?

Working beyond the Text

1. Make a list of all the poets that Reeve mentions. Choose one name from the list and prepare a report on the poet. Find out when and where the poet lived, what kind of poetry he or she is famous for, and so on. Read several poems by the writer and discuss his or her style, form, and the possible meanings of the poetry.

2. Reeve insists that poetry "matters." What are his reasons? Why does poetry matter so much to some people? Why do you think poetry doesn't matter to many people? Does poetry "matter" to you? If so, why? If not, why not?

3. Reeve writes, "Our political and commercial languages not only distract from but even seem to deny the existence of our poetic language." What is the difference between poetic language and other types of language, such as commercial and political languages? How do those other types of language "distract from" and "deny" poetic language? Can you provide examples of "commercial" and "political" languages that "deny" poetic language?

Writing Short Stories

Flannery O'Connor

Flannery O'Connor (1925–1964) was a novelist and essayist who suffered from the debilitating disease lupus and died at age thirty-nine, but not before producing two influential novels, *Wise Blood* and *The Violent Bear It Away,* and a body of short stories. In this essay, from her book of essays entitled *Mystery and Manners* (1961), O'Connor exercises her famous sharp wit to tell a group of amateur writers what to do and, more important, what not to do.

I have heard people say that the short story was one of the most 1
difficult literary forms, and I've always tried to decide why people feel
this way about what seems to me to be one of the most natural and
fundamental ways of human expression. After all, you begin to hear
and tell stories when you're a child, and there doesn't seem to be anything very complicated about it. I suspect that most of you have been
telling stories all your lives, and yet here you sit—come to find out
how to do it.

Then last week, after I had written down some of these serene 2
thoughts to use here today, my calm was shattered when I was sent
seven of your manuscripts to read.

After this experience, I found myself ready to admit, if not that the 3
short story is one of the most difficult literary forms, at least that it is
more difficult for some than for others.

I still suspect that most people start out with some kind of ability 4
to tell a story but that it gets lost along the way. Of course, the ability
to create life with words is essentially a gift. If you have it in the first
place, you can develop it; if you don't have it, you might as well forget it.

But I have found that the people who don't have it are frequently 5
the ones hell-bent on writing stories. I'm sure anyway that they are the
ones who write the books and the magazine articles on how-to-write-
short-stories. I have a friend who is taking a correspondence course in
this subject, and she has passed a few of the chapter headings on to
me—such as, "The Story Formula for Writers," "How to Create Characters," "Let's Plot!" This form of corruption is costing her twenty-
seven dollars.

I feel that discussing story-writing in terms of plot, character, and 6
theme is like trying to describe the expression on a face by saying
where the eyes, nose, and mouth are. I've heard students say, "I'm
very good with plot, but I can't do a thing with character," or, "I have
this theme but I don't have a plot for it," and once I heard one say,
"I've got the story but I don't have any technique."

Technique is a word they all trot out. I talked to a writers' club 7 once, and during the question time, one good soul said, "Will you give me the technique for the frame-within-a-frame short story?" I had to admit I was so ignorant I didn't even know what that was, but she assured me there was such a thing because she had entered a contest to write one and the prize was fifty dollars.

But setting aside the people who have no talent for it, there are 8 others who do have the talent but who flounder around because they don't really know what a story is.

I suppose that obvious things are the hardest to define. Everybody 9 thinks he knows what a story is. But if you ask a beginning student to write a story, you're liable to get almost anything—a reminiscence, an episode, an opinion, an anecdote, anything under the sun but a story. A story is a complete dramatic action—and in good stories, the characters are shown through the action and the action is controlled through the characters, and the result of this is meaning that derives from the whole presented experience. I myself prefer to say that a story is a dramatic event that involves a person because he is a person, and a particular person—that is, because he shares in the general human condition and in some specific human situation. A story always involves, in a dramatic way, the mystery of personality. I lent some stories to a country lady who lives down the road from me, and when she returned them, she said, "Well, them stories just gone and shown you how some folks *would* do," and I thought to myself that that was right; when you write stories, you have to be content to start exactly there— showing how some specific folks *will* do, *will* do in spite of everything.

Now this is a very humble level to have to begin on, and most peo- 10 ple who think they want to write stories are not willing to start there. They want to write about problems, not people; or about abstract issues, not concrete situations. They have an idea, or a feeling, or an overflowing ego, or they want to Be A Writer, or they want to give their wisdom to the world in a simple-enough way for the world to be able to absorb it. In any case, they don't have a story and they wouldn't be willing to write it if they did; and in the absence of a story, they set out to find a theory or a formula or a technique.

Now none of this is to say that when you write a story, you are 11 supposed to forget or give up any moral position that you hold. Your beliefs will be the light by which you see, but they will not be what you see and they will not be a substitute for seeing. For the writer of fiction, everything has its testing point in the eye, and the eye is an organ that eventually involves the whole personality, and as much of the world as can be got into it. It involves judgment. Judgment is something that begins in the act of vision, and when it does not, or when it becomes separated from vision, then a confusion exists in the mind which transfers itself to the story.

Fiction operates through the senses, and I think one reason that 12 people find it so difficult to write stories is that they forget how much time and patience is required to convince through the senses. No reader who doesn't actually experience, who isn't made to feel, the story is going to believe anything the fiction writer merely tells him. The first and most obvious characteristic of fiction is that it deals with reality through what can be seen, heard, smelt, tasted, and touched.

Now this is something that can't be learned only in the head; it has 13 to be learned in the habits. It has to become a way that you habitually look at things. The fiction writer has to realize that he can't create compassion with compassion, or emotion with emotion, or thought with thought. He has to provide all these things with a body; he has to create a world with weight and extension.

I have found that the stories of beginning writers usually bristle 14 with emotion, but *whose* emotion is often very hard to determine. Dialogue frequently proceeds without the assistance of any characters that you can actually see, and uncontained thought leaks out of every corner of the story. The reason is usually that the student is wholly interested in his thoughts and his emotions and not in his dramatic action, and that he is too lazy or highfalutin to descend to the concrete where fiction operates. He thinks that judgment exists in one place and sense-impression in another. But for the fiction writer, judgment begins in the details he sees and how he sees them.

Fiction writers who are not concerned with these concrete details 15 are guilty of what Henry James called "weak specification." The eye will glide over their words while the attention goes to sleep. Ford Madox Ford taught that you couldn't have a man appear long enough to sell a newspaper in a story unless you put him there with enough detail to make the reader see him.

I have a friend who is taking acting classes in New York from a 16 Russian lady who is supposed to be very good at teaching actors. My friend wrote me that the first month they didn't speak a line, they only learned to see. Now learning to see is the basis for learning all the arts except music. I know a good many fiction writers who paint, not because they're any good at painting, but because it helps their writing. It forces them to look at things. Fiction writing is very seldom a matter of saying things; it is a matter of showing things.

However, to say that fiction proceeds by the use of detail does not 17 mean the simple, mechanical piling-up of detail. Detail has to be controlled by some overall purpose, and every detail has to be put to work for you. Art is selective. What is there is essential and creates movement.

Now all this requires time. A good short story should not have 18 less meaning than a novel, nor should its action be less complete. Nothing essential to the main experience can be left out of a short story. All the action has to be satisfactorily accounted for in terms of motivation, and there has to be a beginning, a middle, and an end, though not necessarily in that order. I think many people decide that they want to write short stories because they're short, and by short, they mean short in every way. They think that a short story is an incomplete action in which a very little is shown and a great deal suggested, and they think you suggest something by leaving it out. It's very hard to disabuse a student of this notion, because he thinks that when he leaves something out, he's being subtle; and when you tell him that he has to put something in before anything can be there, he thinks you're an insensitive idiot.

Perhaps the central question to be considered in any discussion of 19 the short story is what do we mean by short. Being short does not mean being slight. A short story should be long in depth and should give us an experience of meaning. I have an aunt who thinks that nothing happens in a story unless somebody gets married or shot at the end of it. I wrote a story about a tramp who marries an old woman's idiot daughter in order to acquire the old woman's automobile. After the marriage, he takes the daughter off on a wedding trip in the automobile and abandons her in an eating place and drives on by himself. Now that is a complete story. There is nothing more relating to the mystery of that man's personality that could be shown through that particular dramatization. But I've never been able to convince my aunt that it's a complete story. She wants to know what happened to the idiot daughter after that.

Not long ago that story was adapted for a television play, and the 20 adapter, knowing his business, had the tramp have a change of heart and go back and pick up the idiot daughter and the two of them ride away, grinning madly. My aunt believes that the story is complete at last, but I have other sentiments about it—which are not suitable for public utterance. When you write a story, you only have to write one story, but there will always be people who will refuse to read the story you have written.

And this naturally brings up the awful question of what kind of a 21 reader you are writing for when you write fiction. Perhaps we each think we have a personal solution for this problem. For my own part, I have a very high opinion of the art of fiction and a very low opinion of what is called the "average" reader. I tell myself that I can't escape him, that this is the personality I am supposed to keep awake, but that at the same time, I am also supposed to provide the intelligent reader with the deeper experience that he looks for in fiction. Now actually, both of these readers are just aspects of the writer's own personality, and in the last analysis, the only reader he can know anything about is himself. We all write at our own level of understanding, but it is the peculiar characteristic of fiction that its literal surface can be made to yield entertainment on an obvious physical plane to one sort of reader while the selfsame surface can be made to yield meaning to the person equipped to experience it there.

Meaning is what keeps the short story from being short. I prefer to 22 talk about the meaning in a story rather than the theme of a story. People talk about the theme of a story as if the theme were like the string that a sack of chicken feed is tied with. They think that if you can pick out the theme, the way you pick the right thread in the chicken-feed sack, you can rip the story open and feed the chickens. But this is not the way meaning works in fiction.

When you can state the theme of a story, when you can separate it 23 from the story itself, then you can be sure the story is not a very good one. The meaning of a story has to be embodied in it, has to be made concrete in it. A story is a way to say something that can't be said any other way, and it takes every word in the story to say what the meaning is. You tell a story because a statement would be inadequate. When anybody asks what a story is about, the only proper thing is to tell him to read the story. The meaning of fiction is not abstract meaning but experienced meaning, and the purpose of making statements about the meaning of a story is only to help you to experience that meaning more fully.

Fiction is an art that calls for the strictest attention to the real— 24 whether the writer is writing a naturalistic story or a fantasy. I mean that we always begin with what is or with what has an eminent possibility of truth about it. Even when one writes a fantasy, reality is the proper basis of it. A thing is fantastic because it is so real, so real that it is fantastic. Graham Greene has said that he can't write, "I stood over a bottomless pit," because that couldn't be true, or "Running down the stairs I jumped into a taxi," because that couldn't be true either. But Elizabeth Bowen can write about one of her characters that "she snatched at her hair as if she heard something in it," because that is eminently possible.

I would even go so far as to say that the person writing a fantasy 25 has to be even more strictly attentive to the concrete detail than someone writing in a naturalistic vein—because the greater the story's strain on the credulity, the more convincing the properties in it have to be.

A good example of this is a story called "The Metamorphosis" by 26 Frank Kafka. This is a story about a man who wakes up one morning to find that he has turned into a cockroach overnight, while not discarding his human nature. The rest of the story concerns his life and feelings and eventual death as an insect with human nature, and this situation is accepted by the reader because the concrete detail of the story is absolutely convincing. The fact is that this story describes the dual nature of man in such a realistic fashion that it is almost unbearable. The truth is not distorted here, but rather, a certain distortion is used to get at the truth. If we admit, as we must, that appearance is not the same thing as reality, then we must give the artist the liberty to make certain rearrangements of nature if these will lead to greater depths of vision. The artist himself always has to remember that what he is rearranging *is* nature, and that he has to know it and be able to describe it accurately in order to have the authority to rearrange it at all.

The peculiar problem of the short-story writer is how to make the 27 action he describes reveal as much of the mystery of existence as possible. He has only a short space to do it in and he can't do it by statement. He has to do it by showing, not by saying, and by showing the concrete—so that his problem is really how to make the concrete work double time for him.

In good fiction, certain of the details will tend to accumulate 28 meaning from the action of the story itself, and when this happens they become symbolic in the way they work. I once wrote a story called "Good Country People," in which a lady Ph.D. has her wooden leg stolen by a Bible salesman whom she has tried to seduce. Now I'll admit that, paraphrased in this way, the situation is simply a low joke. The average reader is pleased to observe anybody's wooden leg being stolen. But without ceasing to appeal to him and without making any statements of high intention, this story does manage to operate at another level of experience, by letting the wooden leg accumulate meaning. Early in the story, we're presented with the fact that the Ph.D. is spiritually as well as physically crippled. She believes in nothing but her own belief in nothing, and we perceive that there is a wooden part of her soul that corresponds to her wooden leg. Now of course this is never stated. The fiction writer states as little as possible. The reader makes this connection from things he is shown. He may not even know that he makes the connection, but the connection is there nevertheless and it has its effect on him. As the story goes on, the wooden leg continues to accumulate meaning. The reader learns how the girl feels about her leg, how her mother feels about it, and how the country woman on the place feels about it; and finally, by the time the Bible salesman comes along, the leg has accumulated so much meaning that it is, as the saying goes, loaded. And when the Bible salesman steals it, the reader realizes that he has taken away part of the girl's personality and has revealed her deeper affliction to her for the first time.

If you want to say that wooden leg is a symbol, you can say that. 29 But it is a wooden leg first, and as a wooden leg it is absolutely necessary to the story. It has its place on the literal level of the story, but it operates in depth as well as on the surface. It increases the story in every direction, and this is essentially the way a story escapes being short.

Now a little might be said about the way in which this happens. I 30
wouldn't want you to think that in that story I sat down and said, "I
am now going to write a story about a Ph.D. with a wooden leg, using
the wooden leg as a symbol for another kind of affliction." I doubt myself if many writers know what they are going to do when they start
out. When I started writing that story, I didn't know there was going
to be a Ph.D. with a wooden leg in it. I merely found myself one morning writing a description of two women that I knew something about,
and before I realized it, I had equipped one of them with a daughter
with a wooden leg. As the story progressed, I brought in the Bible
salesman, but I had no idea what I was going to do with him. I didn't
know he was going to steal that wooden leg until ten or twelve lines
before he did it, but when I found out that this was what was going to
happen, I realized that it was inevitable. This is a story that produces a
shock for the reader, and I think one reason for this is that it produced
a shock for the writer.

Now despite the fact that this story came about in this seemingly 31
mindless fashion, it is a story that almost no rewriting was done on. It
is a story that was under control throughout the writing of it, and it
might be asked how this kind of control comes about, since it is not entirely conscious.

I think the answer to this is what Maritain calls "the habit of art." 32
It is a fact that fiction writing is something in which the whole personality takes part—the conscious as well as the unconscious mind. Art is
the habit of the artist; and habits have to be rooted deep in the whole
personality. They have to be cultivated like any other habit, over a
long period of time, by experience; and teaching any kind of writing is
largely a matter of helping the student develop the habit of art. I think
this is more than just a discipline, although it is that; I think it is a way
of looking at the created world and of using the senses so as to make
them find as much meaning as possible in things.

Now I am not so naïve as to suppose that most people come to 33
writers' conferences in order to hear what kind of vision is necessary
to write stories that will become a permanent part of our literature.
Even if you do wish to hear this, your greatest concerns are immediately practical. You want to know how you can actually write a good
story, and further, how you can tell when you've done it; and so you
want to know what the form of a short story is, as if the form were
something that existed outside of each story and could be applied or
imposed on the material. Of course, the more you write, the more you
will realize that the form is organic, that it is something that grows out
of the material, that the form of each story is unique. A story that is
any good can't be reduced, it can only be expanded. A story is good
when you continue to see more and more in it, and when it continues
to escape you. In fiction two and two is always more than four.

The only way, I think, to learn to write short stories is to write 34 them, and then to try to discover what you have done. The time to think of technique is when you've actually got the story in front of you. The teacher can help the student by looking at his individual work and trying to help him decide if he has written a complete story, one in which the action fully illuminates the meaning.

Perhaps the most profitable thing I can do is to tell you about 35 some of the general observations I made about these seven stories I read of yours. All of these observations will not fit any one of the stories exactly, but they are points nevertheless that it won't hurt anyone interested in writing to think about.

The first thing that any professional writer is conscious of in read- 36 ing anything is, naturally, the use of language. Now the use of language in these stories was such that, with one exception, it would be difficult to distinguish one story from another. While I can recall running into several clichés, I can't remember one image or one metaphor from the seven stories. I don't mean there weren't images in them; I just mean that there weren't any that were effective enough to take away with you.

In connection with this, I made another observation that startled 37 me considerably. With the exception of one story, there was practically no use made of the local idiom. Now this is a Southern Writers' Conference. All the addresses on these stories were from Georgia or Tennessee, yet there was no distinctive sense of Southern life in them. A few place-names were dropped, Savannah or Atlanta or Jacksonville, but these could just as easily have been changed to Pittsburgh or Passaic without calling for any other alteration in the story. The characters spoke as if they had never heard any kind of language except what came out of a television set. This indicates that something is way out of focus.

There are two qualities that make fiction. One is the sense of mys- 38 tery and the other is the sense of manners. You get the manners from the texture of existence that surrounds you. The great advantage of being a Southern writer is that we don't have to go anywhere to look for manners; bad or good, we've got them in abundance. We in the South live in a society that is rich in contradiction, rich in irony, rich in contrast, and particularly rich in its speech. And yet here are six stories by Southerners in which almost no use is made of the gifts of the region.

Of course the reason for this may be that you have seen these gifts 39 abused so often that you have become self-conscious about using them. There is nothing worse than the writer who doesn't *use* the gifts of the region, but wallows in them. Everything becomes so Southern that it's sickening, so local that it is unintelligible, so literally reproduced that it conveys nothing. The general gets lost in the particular instead of being shown through it.

However, when the life that actually surrounds us is totally ig- 40 nored, when our patterns of speech are absolutely overlooked, then something is out of kilter. The writer should then ask himself if he is not reaching out for a kind of life that is artificial to him.

An idiom characterizes a society, and when you ignore the idiom, 41 you are very likely ignoring the whole social fabric that could make a meaningful character. You can't cut characters off from their society and say much about them as individuals. You can't say anything meaningful about the mystery of a personality unless you put that personality in a believable and significant social context. And the best way to do this is through the character's own language. When the old lady in one of Andrew Lytle's stories says contemptuously that she has a mule that is older than Birmingham, we get in that one sentence a sense of a society and its history. A great deal of the Southern writer's work is done for him before he begins, because our history lives in our talk. In one of Eudora Welty's stories a character says, "Where I come from, we use fox for yard dogs and owls for chickens, but we sing true." Now there is a whole book in that one sentence; and when the people of your section can talk like that, and you ignore it, you're just not taking advantage of what's yours. The sound of our talk is too definite to be discarded with impunity, and if the writer tries to get rid of it, he is liable to destroy the better part of his creative power.

Another thing I observed about these stories is that most of them 42 don't go very far inside a character, don't reveal very much of the character. I don't mean that they don't enter the character's mind, but they simply don't show that he has a personality. Again this goes back partly to speech. These characters have no distinctive speech to reveal themselves with; and sometimes they have no really distinctive features. You feel in the end that no personality is revealed because no personality is there. In most good stories it is the character's personality that creates the action of the story. In most of these stories, I feel that the writer has thought of some action and then scrounged up a character to perform it. You will usually be more successful if you start the other way around. If you start with a real personality, a real character, then something is bound to happen; and you don't have to know what before you begin. In fact it may be better if you don't know what before you begin. You ought to be able to discover something from your stories. If you don't, probably nobody else will.

Working with the Text

1. O'Connor contrasts her definition of a "story" with other prose forms, such as "a reminiscence, an episode, an opinion, an anecdote." What is her idea of a story? How does it differ from those other forms?

2. What does O'Connor mean when she says, "it is the peculiar characteristic of fiction that its literal surface can be made to yield entertainment on an obvious physical place to one sort of reader while the selfsame surface can be made to yield meaning to the person equipped to experience it there"? Which sort of reader are you?

3. What does O'Connor mean when she says, "when one writes a fantasy, reality is the proper basis for it"? How does her example of Kafka's "The Metamorphosis" illustrate her point?

4. O'Connor is known for her sharp sense of humor, and this essay is a good example of it. Which lines do you find funny? Why?

5. Who is O'Connor's audience? What is O'Connor's attitude toward her audience? What general message does she seem to be delivering to them? How do you suppose they reacted? How would you?

Working beyond the Text

1. What do you think of O'Connor's account of writing her story "Good Country People"? Has it ever occurred to you that fiction writers might not know what's going to happen in their stories until it happens? In the library, try to find other writers' accounts of how they wrote some of their works and compare what they say to O'Connor's account. (See, for example, the series of collections of *Paris Review* interviews with famous writers.)

2. Find a copy of O'Connor's story "Good Country People" and compare your understanding of it to her explanation. Do you feel the story works the way she says it does? Try reading another of her stories (such as "A Good Man Is Hard to Find," "Everything That Rises Must Converge," or "Parker's Back") to see if it "works" in a similar way.

3. Have you ever tried to write a short story? Having read O'Connor's essay, do you want to try? What advice does she give that seems most useful?

4. O'Connor asserts that, "Fiction writers who are not concerned with . . . concrete details are guilty of what Henry James called 'weak specification.'" Have your writing teachers given you similar advice about "concrete details" and "strong specification"? What did they tell you? How might O'Connor's advice apply to your own writing, though it is nonfiction?

Puttering in the Prose Garden: Prose Improvement for Fiction Writers

David Huddle

Born in 1942, David Huddle teaches creative writing and literature at the University of Vermont. His many books include collections of poetry and short stories, notably *The High Spirits*. In this chapter from his book *The Writing Habit* (1991), which addresses aspiring writers about a wide range of issues, from how to make time for writing to how to assess and improve prose style, Huddle discusses four styles of language in fiction writing—four ways of rendering "reality" in language—and weighs the value and limitations of each kind.

Today's conventional wisdom, particularly around graduate writing programs, is that what a young fiction-writer must do to achieve success is find his or her own voice. "Finding one's own voice" has a nobler sound than "trying to sell a few stories," and I suppose that, to the extent that it's too vague a notion for anybody to do anything much on the basis of it, the idea itself is harmless. My concern is that it may discourage some young writers from carrying out work essential to their apprenticeship. One can do what one pleases in the name of trying to find one's own voice, or do nothing in the hope that one's own voice will suddenly arrive, like a lightning bolt to the throat. I'd like to suggest a more practical approach for serious story-writers and novelists. 1

In the fiction I read nowadays, I find four categories of prose, and I think of them on a kind of evolutionary scale of development. 2

Basic Prose is an honorable category. The writer of it can use language in a correct and acceptable manner. It is the minimum level of performance for any fiction-writer who hopes to have any success at all. But many aspiring fictioneers (which is to say, students paying tuition to graduate writing programs) haven't mastered it. There are two distinguishing features of Basic Prose, the first of which is not particularly interesting: its correctness. One often feels that writers of Basic Prose are probably language bigots; they wince if you split an infinitive or end a sentence with a preposition; they hate it when you say "hopefully." Correctness is what matters. But it is the second distinguishing feature that is the crucial one in thinking about the consequences of Basic Prose: language has no particular connection to subject matter. As we go up the evolutionary scale in categories of prose, we find that the relationship between language and subject matter deepens, intensifies. But at this level, language and subject matter, though together on the page, don't have anything to do with each other. Here's an example of Basic Prose, the first paragraph of a novel published by W. W. Norton & Company in 1968: 3

If a man's name is not Bormann or Beck or Mueller, but once was, the month of May has a double significance in history. For it was in May that a war never to be surpassed in ferocity—if civilization is to survive on this planet—ended in Europe. And in a May twenty years later a special kind of justice began to grind to a halt. This was the justice of the law books, which trailed the Bormanns and Becks and caught some of them and sent them to prison for crimes against humanity. It did not catch them all, and as the May debate on the German Statute of Limitations ended, pseudonymous men in hiding places all over the world began to breathe a little easier. In Bonn and Mannheim and Dusseldorf for a few more years the courts will be picking at the last ugly threads of the concentration camp cases and tying them up in neat packages and stamping them with official seals. But for the most part, the purge is over.

> Bynum Shaw
> *The Nazi Hunter*

The reader of this passage is being told about experience without ₄ being given much of a feeling for it. There may be a kind of stylishness here (consider, for instance, the syntax of the first sentence), but it is a style willed into being by the author without adequately considering content. Functionally weak, this style is all authorial ego.

Window-Pane Prose is not only an honorable category, it is also a ₅ desirable one. Here language is utterly functional. Language is on the page only for the purpose of allowing the reader access to the experience of the fiction. This language is modest. It may be graceful language, but it never calls attention to itself. It stays out of the way. Here are examples, first paragraphs of stories by two distinguished contemporary story-writers:

> The campus security guard found her. She wore a parka and she lay on the foot-bridge over the pond. Her left cheek lay on the frozen snow. The college was a small one, he was the only guard on duty, and in winter he made his rounds in the car. But partly because he was sleepy in the heated car, and mostly because he wanted to get out of the car and walk in the cold dry air, wanted a pleasurable solitude within the imposed solitude of his job, he had gone to the bridge.

> Andre Dubus
> "Townies"
> *Finding a Girl in America*

The house was not itself. Relatives were visiting from the country. It was an old couple this time, an old couple who could not sleep after the sun was up and who began yawning as soon as dinner was over in the evening. They were silent at table, leaving the burden of conversation to their host and hostess, and they declined all outside invitations issued in their honor. Cousin Johnny was on a strict diet.

Yet wanting to be no trouble, both he and cousin Annie refused to reveal any principle of his diet. If he couldn't eat what was being served, he would do without. They made their own beds, washed out their own tubs, avoided using salad forks and butter knives. Upon arriving, they even produced their own old-fashioned ivory napkin rings, and when either of them chanced to spill something on the table cloth, they begged the nearest Negro servant's pardon. As a result, everybody, including the servants, was very uncomfortable from the moment the old couple entered the house.

Peter Taylor
"Guests"
Happy Families Are All Alike

Window-Pane Prose is usually just as correct as Basic Prose 6
(though its correctness is not as visible), but Window-Pane Prose gives a reader immediate and clear access to the experience of the story. Language is wholly at the service of subject matter. Window-Pane Prose writers depend on the human drama to carry their stories; their discipline is a particularly saintly one: they must be so fluid, deft, and precise that no one notices their work, the making of the sentences through which the reader "sees" the story.

Personable Prose is language with a definite personality, and that 7
personality becomes a part—usually a somewhat small part—of the story. Sometimes we think of the personality of the prose as the "voice" of the author. More often we think of it as connected with the personality of a character in the story. One of the main advantages of Personable Prose is that the reader will be attracted to the personality of the language. I suppose it is possible for a reader to be put off by the personalities of some proses, but in the case of a writer like J. D. Salinger, a reader is usually so charmed by the language that he fails to notice some of the story's short-comings (mushy philosophy, for instance). It's probably fair to say that Personable Prose is the largest category of writing by successful American story-writers. Here are two examples, again first paragraphs of stories:

When he was eighteen and was leaving home for the first time, Ralph Wyman was counseled by his father, principal of Jefferson Elementary School and trumpet soloist in the Weaverville Elks Club Auxiliary Band, that life was a very serious matter, an enterprise insisting on strength and purpose in a young person just setting out, an arduous undertaking, everyone knew that, but nevertheless a rewarding one, Ralph Wyman's father believed and said.

Raymond Carver
"Will You Please Be Quiet, Please?"
Will You Please Be Quiet, Please

We are a family that has always been very close in spirit. Our father was drowned in a sailing accident when we were young, and our mother has always stressed the fact that our familial relationships have a kind of permanence that we will never meet with again. I don't think about the family much, but when I remember its members and the coast where they lived and the sea salt that I think is in our blood, I am happy to recall that I am a Pommeroy—that I have the nose, the coloring, and the promise of longevity—and that while we are not a distinguished family, we enjoy the illusion, when we are together, that the Pommeroys are unique. I don't say any of this because this sense of uniqueness is deep or important to me but in order to advance the point that we are loyal to one another in spite of our differences, and that any rupture in this loyalty is a source of confusion and pain.

> John Cheever
> "Goodbye, My Brother"
> *The Stories of John Cheever*

Whereas Window-Pane Prose gave us clear access to the experience of its story, Personable Prose pulls us closer to the experience by exposing us immediately to personality. The relationship between the reader and the story is a more intimate one. 8

Mega-Prose is extremely heightened language, language of greater density and energy, more pronounced rhythmic qualities, richer textures of sound. Mega-Prose aims for intensity. Mega-Prose, like Personable Prose, reflects personality, but in this case personality has been souped up. The quality of mind it reflects is quickness, allusiveness, quirkiness, liveliness in general. Here are four examples: 9

Iactura vigoris non fortuita est: agitur semper unum antitetrahedron. This dust of poppy, fitchet, bone is in an exact precession with which the gods are intimate but not our rough minds. Who, seeing a mother on her knees before the mammillaria of Cybebe, the Arvals flouring a calf for the knife, the standards of Quirinus in white mist around the watchfires, could believe that the gods are as indifferent as gravity. I huddle upon the wild rose, wait with the moth upon the wall, still as time.

> Guy Davenport
> "C. Musonius Rufus"
> *Da Vinci's Bicycle*

Here it is sweltering. Claire wears the diaphanous and Josie (I have seen) rolls her shorts to sausages, airs those legs all across town. I fan. I think. Listen to droplets fall from Momma's air conditioner in her lair above the garage. *Gnats should festoon such a love as mine.* He's written on vellum, "How could *my* hard heart matter when love is itself a diamond set in bone?" Which I tell Claire, floating in, saying,

"Rhythmically, you know, such care, I swear it cools the insides of my arms."

Eve Shelnutt
"Descant"
The Formal Voice

Talmudic scholar, master of cabala, Isaac felt vulnerable to a thousand misfortunes in New York, slipped on an icy street, lay on his back and wouldn't reach for his hat. People walked, traffic screamed, freezing damp sucked through his clothes. He let his eyes fall shut—no hat, no freezing, no slip, no street, no New York, no Isaac—and got a knock against the soles of his shoes. It shook his teeth. His eyes flashed open, darkness spread above him like a predatory tree, a dozen buttons glared and a sentence flew out, beak and claws, with a quality of moral sophistication indistinguishable from hatred: "What's-a-matta, fuckhead, too much vino?" He'd never heard of vino, but had a feeling for syntax—fuckhead was himself. He said, "Eat pig shit," the cop detected language, me-it became I-thou and the air between them a warm, viable medium. He risked English: "I falled on dot ice, tenk you."

Leonard Michaels
"Isaac"
Going Places

Blind people got a hummin jones if you notice. Which is understandable completely once you been around one and notice what no eyes will force you into see people, and you get past the first time, which seems to come out of nowhere, and it's like you in church again with fat-chest ladies and old gents gruntin a hum low in the throat to whatever the preacher be saying. Shakey Bee bottom lip all swole up with Sweet Peach and me explainin how come the sweet-potato bread was a dollar-quarter this time stead of dollar regular and he say uh hunh he understand, then he break into this *thizzin* kind of hum which is quiet, but fiercesome just the same, if you ain't ready for it. Which I wasn't. But I got used to it and the onliest time I had to say somethin bout it was when he was playin checkers on the stoop one time and he commenst to hummin quite churchy seem to me. So I says, "Look here Shakey Bee, I can't beat you and Jesus too." He stop.

Toni Cade Bambara
"My Man Bovanne"
Gorilla, My Love

When we began at the bottom of the evolutionary scale with Basic 10
Prose, we found that the facts of the situation of the story were coming to us as we needed them: we understood the situation, we just didn't

know what it felt like. Here at the top of the scale with Mega-Prose, we find ourselves in situations—all four of these examples, by the way, are beginning paragraphs of stories—where *we know what things feel like before we understand them.* Mega-Prose plunges us so deeply and so immediately into experience that much of what we're doing when we're reading is trying to figure out what the hell is happening in the story. This is the ultimate degree of intimacy between reader and story: the reader has been pulled so far into the story that he is struggling to see the outside of it. If it works, Mega-Prose involves a reader more wholly than the other Proses. Not only does the reader "get" more of the experience of the story, the story also "gets" more of the reader.

"If-it-works" is a shadow that hovers over most stories written in 11 Mega-Prose. It's brittle stuff, and it's hard to make it yield a narrative. My response to Mega-Prose is usually that I like it if, and in direct proportion to, the sense I can make of it. I'm willing to travel some distance through a story in a state of confusion, but after a while I want to be able to start adding things up. So my liking for the four examples is in ascending order: my desire to go on reading is weakest in the Davenport paragraph and strongest in the Bambara.

In setting forth these categories as a set of steps, I do not mean to 12 be suggesting that we story-writers try to work our way up to the top and all of us become Mega-Prose writers. I don't think the world is ready for a stampede of Mega-Prosers.

But if Basic Prose is the only kind I can write, then, yes, I do need 13 to improve myself. There are NO good stories in which there is not some relationship between the language and the experience of the story. The minimally acceptable relationship is that of Window-Pane Prose. If I'm a Basic Prose writer, then I should try writing Window-Pane and/or Personable. In both these latter categories, I'm required to give myself over to the story, as opposed to making the story submit to the one kind of prose I can write. And this "giving oneself over" to the material is one of the big secrets, it seems to me, of writing good stories.

If I write only one or two of the "acceptable" kinds of prose, then I 14 should try to write the kind or kinds that I don't write. For different kinds of stories, a writer will need different kinds of instruments. More stories are available to the writer who can use different kinds of prose. To "stretch" seems to me good advice for any writer at any stage of development, and it also seems to me advice that is in direct contradiction to the notion of "finding your own voice."

It is true that we can see and hear distinctive qualities of language 15 in the work of certain writers, and those qualities are what we might call "voice," or "style." But that kind of voice, or style, is something that, in my opinion, no good writer ever tried for or thought very much about. Style comes so much from the center of personality that it is present, or not present in one's writing in the same way that personality itself is present or not present, authentic or artificial, in every walking-around human being. Though it is commonly thought to be so, conscious refinement of style is not the key that will unlock the power of good writing.

The story-writer whose work seems to me exemplary here is Eudora Welty. Almost every Welty story has a different quality of language. In "Powerhouse," she's writing Mega-Prose, in "Why I Live at the P. O.," she's writing Personable Prose, and in "A Worn Path," she's using a wonderfully clean Window-Pane Prose. Because she can write various kinds of prose, she can handle various kinds of material. How could a young, middle-class white woman write so exuberantly and convincingly about the lives of Black Jazz musicians in "Powerhouse"? The power is in the language, in the author's giving herself over to the language of the subject. 16

So much of the luck of writing depends on uncontrollable forces that even the most arrogant of writers are humble in the face of the work to be done. Style, in that it is, in the deepest sense, *personality*, comes out of these uncontrollable forces. Your best writing is your best self, for better or for worse. That idea is frightening because it may turn out that your best self is not somebody intelligent, wise, generous, sensitive, or honorable enough to make literature. But the idea is also comforting because your best self is the only legitimate resource you have to bring to your writing. You don't have to try to guess what your readers want you to be writing, what sort of style would be most appealing to them. Who you are is what they get, and they can take it or leave it. 17

It is helpful to remember that the writer works for the story— works for the work. If you can let go of self-esteem, self-protection, self-concerns of various sorts, including the selfish concept of the sacredness of "your own voice"—if you can let go of all that, then you can work *with* the work. The work itself will commence a kind of dialogue with you. Once you kick out that passage of grand writing (in which perhaps you felt "your own voice" take flight) and try to find what the story needs to replace it, the story itself can begin instructing you: Look, you began this way, and obviously this is your ending—don't you see what you're getting at? The language itself has powers, and what a prose-writer needs to do is not to seek control over those powers but to find ways to open him- or herself up to them. To find yourself working with the work, collaborating with the language, these are the highest pleasures of the prose garden. 18

Working with the Text

1. In his opening paragraph, Huddle seems to argue against one approach to learning to write fiction and in favor of another. What are the two approaches? Why does he criticize one and advocate the other?

2. What are Huddle's four categories of "prose" in fiction writing? What qualities does each have? What does Huddle's opinion of each category seem to be? Which one does he like the most? Which one do you like the most?

3. What does Huddle mean when he says, "The language itself has powers, and what a prose-writer needs to do is not to seek control over those powers but to find ways to open him- or herself up to them"? What "powers" does language have, and how do writers "open themselves up" to them?

4. Into what category would you place Huddle's prose in the essay? Is it closer to "Basic," "Window-Pane," "Personable," or "Mega-Prose"? What is the relationship of his language and the information he wants to communicate? Point to his own criteria for his four categories and apply them to specific passages from the essay.

Working beyond the Text

1. Find the three examples from Eudora Welty's writing that Huddle mentions as illustrations of Window-Pane Prose, Personable Prose, and Mega-Prose. Examine each story for the qualities Huddle lists for the three categories. Explain his ideas with examples from the three stories.

2. Find your own examples of Huddle's four categories of prose in fiction writing. A good source for examples might be a modern collection of fiction by many different authors, such as a textbook used for introductory literature courses.

3. Try writing one paragraph of a fictional story four times, using each of the four kinds of fictional prose. Employ the qualities Huddle lists for each of the categories, and compare your writing to the examples he provides.

How "Bigger" Was Born

Richard Wright

Richard Wright (1908–1960) became one of the most prominent African American novelists when his novel *Native Son* was published in 1940. Featuring a frustrated African American man forced into violent acts by social forces, the novel was a best-seller and the first novel by an African American available through the Book-of-the-

Month Club. Wright's other works include the autobiographical *Black Boy*. What follows is an excerpt from his critical comments about *Native Son*, first given as a lecture in a New York Public Library in Harlem and later published in a pamphlet. In this writing, Wright reveals the connections between his own life as a black man in America and the experiences of his main character, Bigger Thomas.

I am not so pretentious as to imagine that it is possible for me to account completely for my own book, *Native Son*. But I am going to try to account for as much of it as I can, the sources of it, the material that went into it, and my own years' long changing attitude toward that material.

In a fundamental sense, an imaginative novel represents the merging of two extremes; it is an intensely intimate expression on the part of a consciousness couched in terms of the most objective and commonly known events. It is at once something private and public by its very nature and texture. Confounding the author who is trying to lay his cards on the table is the dogging knowledge that his imagination is a kind of community medium of exchange: what he has read, felt, thought, seen, and remembered is translated into extensions as impersonal as a worn dollar bill.

The more closely the author thinks of why he wrote, the more he comes to regard his imagination as a kind of self-generating cement which glued his facts together, and his emotions as a kind of dark and obscure designer of those facts. Always there is something that is just beyond the tip of the tongue that could explain it all. Usually, he ends up by discussing something far afield, an act which incites skepticism and suspicion in those anxious for a straight-out explanation.

Yet the author is eager to explain. But the moment he makes the attempt his words falter, for he is confronted and defied by the inexplicable array of his own emotions. Emotions are subjective and he can communicate them only when he clothes them in objective guise; and how can he ever be so arrogant as to know when he is dressing up the right emotion in the right Sunday suit? He is always left with the uneasy notion that maybe *any* objective drapery is as good as *any* other for any emotion.

And the moment he does dress up an emotion, his mind is confronted with the riddle of that "dressed up" emotion, and he is left peering with eager dismay back into the dim reaches of his own incommunicable life. Reluctantly, he comes to the conclusion that to account for his book is to account for his life, and he knows that that is impossible. Yet, some curious, wayward motive urges him to supply the answer, for there is the feeling that his dignity as a living being is challenged by something within him that is not understood.

So, at the outset, I say frankly that there are phases of *Native Son* which I shall make no attempt to account for. There are meanings in my book of which I was not aware until they literally spilled out upon the paper. I shall sketch the outline of how I *consciously* came into possession of the materials that went into *Native Son*, but there will be many things I shall omit, not because I want to, but simply because I don't know them.

The birth of Bigger Thomas goes back to my childhood, and there 7 was not just one Bigger, but many of them, more than I could count and more than you suspect.

The Bigger Thomases were the only Negroes I know of who con- 8 sistently violated the Jim Crow laws of the South and got away with it, at least for a sweet brief spell. Eventually, the whites who restricted their lives made them pay a terrible price. They were shot, hanged, maimed, lynched, and generally hounded until they were either dead or their spirits broken.

Now for the variations in the Bigger Thomas pattern. Some of the 9 Negroes living under these conditions got religion, felt that Jesus would redeem the void of living, felt that the more bitter life was in the present the happier it would be in the hereafter. Others, clinging still to that brief glimpse of post-Civil War freedom, employed a thousand ruses and stratagems of struggle to win their rights. Still others projected their hurts and longings into more naive and mundane forms—blues, jazz, swing—and, without intellectual guidance, tried to build up a compensatory nourishment for themselves. Many labored under hot suns and then killed the restless ache with alcohol. Then there were those who strove for an education, and when they got it, enjoyed the financial fruits of it in the style of their bourgeois oppressors. Usually they went hand in hand with the powerful whites and helped to keep their groaning brothers in line, for that was the safest course of action. Those who did this called themselves "leaders." To give you an idea of how completely these "leaders" worked with those who oppressed, I can tell you that I lived the first seventeen years of my life in the South without so much as hearing of or seeing one act of rebellion from *any* Negro, save the Bigger Thomases.

I made the discovery that Bigger Thomas was not black all the 10 time; he was white, too, and there were literally millions of him, everywhere. The extension of my sense of the personality of Bigger was the pivot of my life; it altered the complexion of my existence. I became conscious, at first dimly, and then later on with increasing clarity and conviction, of a vast, muddied pool of human life in America. It was as though I had put on a pair of spectacles whose power was that of an x-ray enabling me to see deeper into the lives of men. Whenever I picked up a newspaper, I'd no longer feel that I was reading of the doings of whites alone (Negroes are rarely mentioned in the press unless they've committed some crime!), but of a complex struggle for life going on in my country, a struggle in which I was involved.

Let me give examples of how I began to develop the dim negative 11 of Bigger. I met white writers who talked of their responses, who told me how whites reacted to this lurid American scene. And, as they talked, I'd translate what they said in terms of Bigger's life. But what was more important still, I read their novels. Here for the first time, I found ways and techniques of gauging meaningfully the effects of American civilization upon the personalities of people. I took these techniques, these ways of seeing and feeling, and twisted them, bent them, adapted them, until they became *my* ways of apprehending the locked-in life of the Black Belt areas. This association with white writers was the life preserver of my hope to depict Negro life in fiction, for my race possessed no fictional works dealing with such problems, had no background in such sharp and critical testing of experience, no novels that went with a deep and fearless will down to the dark roots of life.

Here are examples of how I culled information relating to Bigger 12 from my reading:

There is in me a memory of reading an interesting pamphlet 13 telling of the friendship of Gorky and Lenin in exile. The booklet told of how Lenin and Gorky were walking down a London street. Lenin turned to Gorky and, pointing, said: "Here is *their* Big Ben." "There is *their* Westminster Abbey." "There is *their* library." And at once, while reading that passage, my mind stopped, teased, challenged with the effort to remember, to associate widely disparate but meaningful experiences in my life. For a moment nothing would come, but I remained convinced that I had heard the meaning of those words sometime, somewhere before. Then, with a sudden glow of satisfaction of having gained a little more knowledge about the world in which I lived, I'd end up by saying: "That's Bigger. That's the Bigger Thomas reaction."

In both instances the deep sense of exclusion was identical. The 14 feeling of looking at things with a painful and unwarrantable nakedness was an experience, I learned, that transcended national and racial boundaries. It was this intolerable sense of feeling and understanding so much, and yet living on a plane of social reality where the look of a world which one did not make or own struck one with a blinding objectivity and tangibility, that made me grasp the revolutionary impulse in my life and the lives of those about me and far away.

But more than anything else, as a writer, I was fascinated by the 15 similarity of the emotional tensions of Bigger in America and Bigger in Nazi Germany and Bigger in old Russia. All Bigger Thomases, white and black, felt tense, afraid, nervous, hysterical, and restless. From far away Nazi Germany and old Russia had come to me items of knowledge that told me that certain modern experiences were creating types of personalities whose existence ignored racial and national lines of demarcation, that these personalities carried with them a more universal drama-element than anything I'd ever encountered before; that these personalities were mainly imposed upon men and women living in a world whose fundamental assumptions could no longer be taken for granted: a world ridden with national and class strife; a world whose metaphysical meanings had vanished; a world in which God no longer existed as a daily focal point of men's lives; a world in which men could no longer retain their faith in an ultimate hereafter. It was a highly geared world whose nature was conflict and action, a world whose limited area and vision imperiously urged men to satisfy their organisms, a world that existed on a plane of animal sensation alone.

So, with this much knowledge of myself and the world gained and known, why should I not try to work out on paper the problem of what will happen to Bigger? Why should I not, like a scientist in a laboratory, use my imagination and invent test-tube situations, place Bigger in them, and, following the guidance of my own hopes and fears, what I had learned and remembered, work out in fictional form an emotional statement and resolution of this problem? 16

But several things militated against my starting to work. Like Bigger himself, I felt a mental censor—product of the fears which a Negro feels from living in America—standing over me, draped in white, warning me not to write. This censor's warnings were translated into my own thought processes thus: "What will white people think if I draw the picture of such a Negro boy? Will they not at once say: 'See, didn't we tell you all along the niggers are like that? Now, look, one of their own kind has come along and drawn the picture for us!'" I felt that if I drew the picture of Bigger truthfully, there would be many reactionary whites who would try to make of him something I did not intend. And yet, and this was what made it difficult, I knew that I could not write of Bigger convincingly if I did not depict him as he *was:* that is, resentful toward whites, sullen, angry, ignorant, emotionally unstable, depressed and unaccountably elated at times, and unable even, because of his own lack of inner organization which American oppression has fostered in him, to unite with the members of his own race. And would not whites misread Bigger and, doubting his authenticity, say: "This man is preaching hate against the whole white race"? 17

The more I thought of it the more I became convinced that if I did not write of Bigger as I saw and felt him, if I did not try to make him a living personality and at the same time a symbol of all the larger things I felt and saw in him, I'd be reacting as Bigger himself reacted: that is, I'd be acting out of *fear* if I let what I thought whites would say constrict and paralyze me. 18

As I contemplated Bigger and what he meant, I said to myself: "I 19 must write this novel, not only for others to read, but to free *myself* of this sense of shame and fear." In fact, the novel, as time passed, grew upon me to the extent that it became a necessity to write it; the writing of it turned into a way of living for me.

But Bigger was still not down upon paper. For a long time I had been writing of him in my mind, but I had yet to put him into an image, a breathing symbol draped out in the guise of the only form of life my native land had allowed me to know intimately, that is, the ghetto life of the American Negro. But the basic reason for my hesitancy was that another and far more complex problem had risen to plague me. Bigger, as I saw and felt him, was a snarl of many realities; he had in him many levels of life. 20

Now, after all of this, when I sat down to the typewriter, I could not work; I could not think of a good opening scene for the book. I had definitely in mind the kind of emotion I wanted to evoke in the reader in that first scene, but I could not think of the type of concrete event that would convey the motif of the entire scheme of the book, that would sound, in varied form, the note that was to be resounded throughout its length, that would introduce to the reader just what kind of an organism Bigger's was and the environment that was bearing hourly upon it. Twenty or thirty times I tried and failed; then I argued that if I could not write the opening scene, I'd start with the scene that followed. I did. The actual writing of the book began with the scene in the pool room. 21

Now, for the writing. During the years in which I had met all of those Bigger Thomases, those varieties of Bigger Thomases, I had not consciously gathered material to write of them; I had not kept a notebook record of their sayings and doings. Their actions had simply made impressions upon my sensibilities as I lived from day to day, impressions which crystallized and coagulated into clusters and configurations of memory, attitudes, moods, ideas. And these subjective states, in turn, were automatically stored away somewhere in me. I was not even aware of the process. But, excited over the book which I had set myself to write, under the stress of emotion, these things came surging up, tangled, fused, knotted, entertaining me by the sheer variety and potency of their meaning and suggestiveness. 22

With the whole theme in mind, in an attitude almost akin to prayer, I gave myself up to the story. In an effort to capture some phase of Bigger's life that would not come to me readily, I'd jot down as much of it as I could. Then I'd read it over and over, adding each time a word, a phrase, a sentence until I felt that I had caught all the shadings of reality I felt dimly were there. With each of these rereadings and rewritings it seemed that I'd gather in facts and facets that tried to run away. It was an act of concentration, of trying to hold within one's center of attention all of that bewildering array of facts 23 which science, politics, experience, memory, and imagination were urging upon me. And, then, while writing, a new and thrilling relationship would spring up under the drive of emotion, coalescing and telescoping alien facts into a known and felt truth. That was the deep fun of the job: to feel within my body that I was pushing out to new areas of feeling, strange landmarks of emotion tramping upon foreign soil, compounding new relationships of perceptions, making new and—until that very split second of time!—unheard-of and unfelt effects with words. It had a buoying and tonic impact upon me; my senses would strain and seek for more and more of such relationships; my temperature would rise as I worked. That is writing as I feel it, a kind of significant living.

The first draft of the novel was written in four months, straight 24 through, and ran to some 576 pages. Just as a man rises in the morning to dig ditches for his bread, so I'd work daily. I'd think of some abstract principle of Bigger's conduct and at once my mind would turn it into some act I'd seen Bigger perform, some act which I hoped would be familiar enough to the American reader to gain his credence. But in the writing of scene after scene I was guided by but one criterion: to tell the truth as I saw it and felt it. That is, to objectify in words some insight derived from my living in the form of action, scene, and dialogue. If a scene seemed improbable to me, I'd not tear it up, but ask myself: "Does it reveal enough of what I feel to stand in spite of its unreality?" If I felt it did, it stood. If I felt that it did not, I ripped it out. The degree of morality in my writing depended upon the degree of felt life and truth I could put down upon the printed page. For example, there is a scene in *Native Son* where Bigger stands in a cell with a Negro preacher, Jan, Max, the State's Attorney, Mr. Dalton, Mrs. Dalton, Bigger's mother, his brother, his sister, Al, Gus, and Jack. While writing the scene, I knew that it was unlikely that so many people would ever be allowed to come into a murderer's cell. But I wanted those people in that cell to elicit a certain important emotional response from Bigger. And so the scene stood. I felt that what I wanted that scene to say to the reader was *more important than its surface reality or plausibility.*

Always, as I wrote, I was both reader and writer, both the con- 25 ceiver of the action and the appreciator of it. I tried to write so that, in the same instant of time, the objective and subjective aspects of Bigger's life would be caught in a focus of prose. And always I tried to *render, depict,* not merely to tell the story. If a thing was cold, I tried to make the reader *feel cold,* and not just tell about it. In writing in this fashion, sometimes I'd find it necessary to use a stream of consciousness technique, then rise to an interior monologue, descend to a direct rendering of a dream state, then to a matter-of-fact depiction of what Bigger was saying, doing, and feeling. Then I'd find it impossible to say what I wanted to say without stepping in and speaking outright on my own; but when doing this I always made an effort to retain the mood of the story, explaining everything only in terms of Bigger's life and, if possible, in the rhythms of Bigger's thought (even though the words would be mine). Again, at other times, in the guise of the lawyer's speech and the newspaper items, or in terms of what Bigger would overhear or see from afar, I'd give what others were saying and thinking of him. But always, from the start to finish, it was Bigger's story, Bigger's fears, Bigger's flight, and Bigger's fate that I tried to depict. I wrote with the conviction in mind (I don't know if this is right or wrong; I only know that I'm temperamentally inclined to feel this way) that the main burden of all serious fiction consists almost wholly of character-destiny and the items, social, political, and personal, of that character-destiny.

As I wrote I followed, almost unconsciously, many principles of 26 the novel which my reading of the novels of other writers had made me feel were necessary for the building of a well-constructed book. For the most part the novel is rendered in the present; I wanted the reader to feel that Bigger's story was happening *now*, like a play upon the stage or a movie unfolding upon the screen. Action follows action, as in a prize fight. Wherever possible, I told of Bigger's life in close-up, slow-motion, giving the feel of the grain in the passing of time. I had long had the feeling that this was the best way to "enclose" the reader's mind in a new world, to blot out all reality except that which I was giving him.

Then again, as much as I could, I restricted the novel to what Big- 27 ger saw and felt, to the limits of his feeling and thoughts, even when I was conveying *more* than that to the reader. I had the notion that such a manner of rendering made for a sharper effect, a more pointed sense of the character, his peculiar type of being and consciousness. Throughout there is but one point of view: Bigger's. This, too, I felt, made for a richer illusion of reality.

I kept out of the story as much as possible, for I wanted the reader 28 to feel that there was nothing between him and Bigger; that the story was a special *première* given in his own private theater.

I kept the scenes long, made as much happen within a short space 29 of time as possible; all of which, I felt, made for greater density and richness of effect.

In a like manner I tried to keep a unified sense of background 30 throughout the story; the background would change, of course, but I tried to keep before the eyes of the reader at all times the forces and elements against which Bigger was striving.

And because I had limited myself to rendering only what Bigger 31 saw and felt, I gave no more reality to the other characters than that which Bigger himself saw.

This, honestly, is all I can account for in the book. If I attempted to account for scenes and characters, to tell why certain scenes were written in certain ways, I'd be stretching facts in order to be pleasantly intelligible. All else in the book came from my feelings reacting upon the material, and any honest reader knows as much about the rest of what is in the book as I do; that is, if, as he reads, he is willing to let his emotions and imagination become as influenced by the materials as I did. As I wrote, for some reason or other, one image, symbol, character, scene, mood, feeling evoked its opposite, its parallel, its complimentary, and its ironic counterpart. Why? I don't know. My emotions and imagination just like to work that way. One can account for just so much of life, and then no more. At least, not yet.

With the first draft down, I found that I could not end the book satisfactorily. In the first draft I had Bigger going smack to the electric chair; but I felt that two murders were enough for one novel. I cut the final scene and went back to worry about the beginning. I had no luck. The book was one-half finished, with the opening and closing scenes unwritten. Then, one night, in desperation—I hope that I'm not disclosing the hidden secrets of my craft!—I sneaked out and got a bottle. With the help of it, I began to remember many things which I could not remember before. One of them was that Chicago was overrun with rats. I recalled that I'd seen many rats on the streets, that I'd heard and read of Negro children being bitten by rats in their beds. At first I rejected the idea of Bigger battling a rat in his room; I was afraid that the rat would "hog" the scene. But the rat would not leave me; he presented himself in many attractive guises. So, cautioning myself to allow the rat scene to disclose *only* Bigger, his family, their little room, and their relationships, I let the rat walk in, and he did his stuff.

Many of the scenes were torn out as I reworked the book. The mere rereading of what I'd written made me think of the possibility of developing themes which had been only hinted at in the first draft. For example, the entire guilt theme that runs through *Native Son* was woven in *after* the first draft was written.

At last I found out how to end the book; I ended it just as I had begun it, showing Bigger living dangerously, taking his life into his hands, accepting what life had made him. The lawyer, Max, was placed in Bigger's cell at the end of the novel to register the moral—or what *I* felt was the moral—horror of Negro life in the United States.

The writing of *Native Son* was to me an exciting, enthralling, and even a romantic experience. With what I've learned in the writing of this book, with all of its blemishes, imperfections, with all of its unrealized potentialities, I am launching out upon another novel, this time about the status of women in modern American society. This book, too, goes back to my childhood just as Bigger went, for, while I was storing away impressions of Bigger, I was storing away impressions of many other things that made me think and wonder. Some experience will ignite somewhere deep down in me the smoldering embers of new fires and I'll be off again to write yet another novel. It is good to live when one feels that such as that will happen to one. Life becomes sufficient unto life; the rewards of living are found in living.

I don't know if *Native Son* is a good book or a bad book. And I 27 don't know if the book I'm working on now will be a good book or a bad book. And I really don't care. The mere writing of it will be more fun and a deeper satisfaction than any praise or blame from anybody.

I feel that I'm lucky to be alive to write novels today, when the 38 whole world is caught in the pangs of war and change. Early American writers, Henry James and Nathaniel Hawthorne, complained bitterly about the bleakness and flatness of the American scene. But I think that if they were alive, they'd feel at home in modern America. True, we have no great church in America; our national traditions are still of such a sort that we are not wont to brag of them; and we have no army that's above the level of mercenary fighters; we have no group acceptable to the whole of our country upholding certain humane values; we have no rich symbols, no colorful rituals. We have only a money-grabbing, industrial civilization. But we do have in the Negro the embodiment of a past tragic enough to appease the spiritual hunger of even a James; and we have in the oppression of the Negro a shadow athwart our national life dense and heavy enough to satisfy even the gloomy broodings of a Hawthorne. And if Poe were alive, he would not have to invent horror; horror would invent him.

New York, March 7, 1940

Working with the Text

1. Why does Wright feel that it would be "pretentious" to "account completely for my own book"? Why shouldn't we expect a writer to be able to "account for" his own book?
2. What are the sources of Wright's novel *Native Son* and the character Bigger Thomas? What sources that he points to seem like obvious choices? What sources are more surprising?
3. What was the process of Wright's work on *Native Son?* What were first steps, middle steps, and final steps? What were some of the difficulties and frustrations? What were the rewards that kept him writing?
4. Wright announces his intentions in the essay and points out the limitations of his abilities to give his audience what it might want. What are his stated intentions? What are the limitations he points to? How does spelling out these things help define his relationship to his material and to his audience?

Working beyond the Text

1. If reading Wright's essay about *Native Son* has made you curious, find the novel and start to read it. Does it fulfill the expectations you had after reading the essay? Is it the kind of book Wright led you to believe it would be?

2. In addition to fiction, Wright also wrote autobiography, including his famous childhood memoir *Black Boy.* You know what he has to say about writing the fictional *Native Son.* How do you think his process might have been similar in writing *Black Boy?* How might it have been different? Compare the styles of the novel and the autobiography.

3. African American poets and novelists writing since Richard Wright have acknowledged him as exerting an immense influence on their work. Use your library to find out what some of the writers have said about Wright, from Amiri Baraka (LeRoi Jones) to Maya Angelou, from James Baldwin to Toni Morrison.

4. Wright connects his artistic creation to his experience of life as an African American. What do other African American authors have to say about the connection between their art and their lives as black people in America? Try to locate essays similar to Wright's by writers such as Toni Morrison and Alice Walker.

UNIT TWO

OTHER AUDIENCES, OTHER RULES

Language and Literature from a Pueblo Indian Perspective

Leslie Marmon Silko

> Leslie Marmon Silko is a Laguna Pueblo Indian best known for her award-winning novel *Ceremony*. Silko has strong ideas about Native American ways of thinking, speaking, and reasoning about the world. In this edited version of a 1979 oral presentation, she explains what she considers the traditional patterns of speech among her friends and family at Laguna, and at the same time gives an illustration of those patterns in the form of her own presentation.

Where I come from, the words that are most highly valued are 1 those which are spoken from the heart, unpremeditated and unrehearsed. Among the Pueblo people, a written speech or statement is highly suspect because the true feelings of the speaker remain hidden as he reads words that are detached from the occasion and the audience. I have intentionally not written a formal paper to read to this session because of this and because I want you to hear and to experience English in a nontraditional structure, a structure that follows patterns from the oral tradition. For those of you accustomed to a structure that moves from point A to point B to point C, this presentation may be somewhat difficult to follow because the structure of Pueblo expression resembles something like a spider's web—with many little threads radiating from a center, crisscrossing each other. As with the web, the structure will emerge as it is made and you must simply listen and trust, as the Pueblo people do, that meaning will be made.

I suppose the task that I have today is a formidable one because 2 basically I come here to ask you, at least for a while, to set aside a number of basic approaches that you have been using and probably will continue to use in approaching the study of English or the study of language; first of all, I come to ask you to see language from the Pueblo perspective, which is a perspective that is very much concerned with including the whole of creation and the whole of history and time. And so we very seldom talk about breaking language down into words. As I will continue to relate to you, even the use of a specific language is less important than the one thing—which is the "telling," or the storytelling. And so, as Simon Ortiz has written, if you approach a Pueblo person and want to talk words or, worse than that, to break down an individual word into its components, ofttimes you will just get a blank stare, because we don't think of words as being isolated from the speaker, which, of course, is one element of the oral tradition. Moreover, we don't think of words as being alone: Words are always with other words, and the other words are almost always in a story of some sort.

Today I have brought a number of examples of stories in English 3 because I would like to get around to the question that has been raised, or the topic that has come along here, which is what changes we Pueblo writers might make with English as a language for literature. But at the same time I would like to explain the importance of storytelling and how it relates to a Pueblo theory of language.

So first I would like to go back to the Pueblo Creation story. The 4 reason I go back to that story is because it is an all-inclusive story of creation and how life began. Tséitsínako, Thought Woman, by thinking of her sisters, and together with her sisters, thought of everything which is, and this world was created. And the belief was that everything in this world was a part of the original creation, and that the people at home realized that far away there were others—other human beings. There is even a section of the story which is a prophesy—which describes the origin of the European race, the African, and also remembers the Asian origins.

Starting out with this story, with this attitude which includes all 5 things, I would like to point out that the reason the people are more concerned with story and communication and less with a particular language is in part an outgrowth of the area [pointing to a map] where we find ourselves. Among the twenty Pueblos there are at least six distinct languages, and possibly seven. Some of the linguists argue—and I don't set myself up to be a linguist at all—about the number of distinct languages. But certainly Zuni is all alone, and Hopi is all alone, and from mesa to mesa there are subtle differences in language—very great differences. I think that this might be the reason that what particular language was being used wasn't as important as what a speaker was trying to say. And this, I think, is reflected and stems or grows out of a particular view of the story—that is, that language *is* story. At Laguna many words have stories which make them. So when one is telling a story, and one is using words to tell the story, each word that one is speaking has a story of its own too. Often the speakers or tellers go into the stories of the words they are using to tell one story so that you get stories within stories, so to speak. This structure becomes very apparent in the storytelling, and what I would like to show you later on by reading some pieces that I brought is that this structure also informs the writing and the stories which are currently coming from Pueblo people. I think what is essential in this sense of story, and story within story, and the idea that one story is only the beginning of many stories, and the sense that stories never truly end. I would like to propose that these views of structure and the dynamics of storytelling are some of the contributions which Native American cultures bring to the English language or at least to literature in the English language.

First of all, a lot of people think of storytelling as something that is ⁶ done at bedtime—that it is something that is done for small children. When I use the term "storytelling," I include a far wider range of telling activity. I also do not limit storytelling to simply old stories, but to again go back to the original view of creation, which sees that it is all part of a whole; we do not differentiate or fragment stories and experiences. In the beginning, Tséitsínako, Thought Woman, thought of all these things, and all of these things are held together as one holds many things together in a single thought.

So in the telling (and today you will hear a few of the dimensions ⁷ of this telling) first of all, as was pointed out earlier, the storytelling always includes the audience and the listeners, and, in fact, a great deal of the story is believed to be inside the listener, and the storyteller's role is to draw the story out of the listeners. This kind of shared experience grows out of a strong community base. The storytelling goes on and continues from generation to generation.

The Origin story functions basically as a maker of our identity— ⁸ with the story we know who we are. We are the Lagunas. This is where we came from. We came this way. We came by this place. And so from the time you are very young, you hear these stories, so that when you go out into the wider world, when one asks who you are, or where are you from, you immediately know: We are the people who came down from the north. We are the people of these stories. It continues down into clans so that you are not just talking about Laguna Pueblo people, you are talking about your own clan. Within the clans there are stories which identify the clan.

In the Creation story, Antelope says that he will help knock a hole ⁹ in the earth so that the people can come up, out into the next world. Antelope tries and tries, and he uses his hooves and is unable to break through; and it is then that Badger says, "Let me help you." And Badger very patiently uses his claws and digs a way through, bringing the people into the world. When the Badger clan people think of themselves, or when the Antelope people think of themselves, it is as people who are of *this* story, and this is *our* place, and we fit into the very beginning when the people first came, before we began our journey south.

So you can move, then, from the idea of one's identity as a tribal ¹⁰ person into clan identity. Then we begin to get to the extended family, and this is where we begin to get a kind of story coming into play which some people might see as a different kind of story, though Pueblo people do not. Anthropologists and ethnologists have, for a long time, differentiated the types of oral language they find in the Pueblos. They tended to rule out all but the old and sacred and traditional stories and were not interested in family stories and the family's account of itself. But these family stories are just as important as the other stories—the older stories. These family stories are given equal recognition. There is no definite, pre-set pattern for the way one will hear the stories of one's own family, but it is a very critical part of one's childhood, and it continues on throughout one's life. You will hear stories of importance to the family—sometimes wonderful stories—stories about the time a maternal uncle got the biggest deer that was ever seen and brought back from the mountains. And so one's sense of who the family is, and who you are, will then extend from that—"I am from the family of my uncle who brought in this wonderful deer, and it was a wonderful hunt"—so you have this sort of building or sense of identity.

There are also other stories, stories about the time when another 11 uncle, perhaps, did something that wasn't really acceptable. In other words, this process of keeping track, of telling, is an all-inclusive process which begins to create a total picture. So it is very important that you know all of the stories—both positive and not so positive—about one's own family. The reason that it is very important to keep track of all the stories in one's own family is because you are liable to hear a story from somebody else who is perhaps an enemy of the family, and you are liable to hear a version which has been changed, a version which makes your family sound disreputable—something that will taint the honor of the family. But if you have already heard the story, you know your family's version of what *really* happened that night, so when somebody else is mentioning it, you will have a version of the story to counterbalance it. Even when there is no way around it—old Uncle Pete did a terrible thing—by knowing the stories that come out of other families, by keeping very close watch, listening constantly to learn the stories about other families, one is in a sense able to deal with terrible sorts of things that might happen within one's own family. When a member of one's own family does something that cannot be excused, one always knows stories about similar things which happened in other families. And it is not done maliciously. I think it is very important to realize this. Keeping track of all the stories within the community gives a certain distance, a useful perspective which brings incidents down to a level we can deal with. If others have done it before, it cannot be so terrible. If others have endured, so can we.

The stories are always bringing us together, keeping this whole to- 12 gether, keeping this family together, keeping this clan together. "Don't go away, don't isolate yourself, but come here, because we have all had these kinds of experiences"—this is what the people are saying to you when they tell you these other stories. And so there is this constant pulling together to resist what seems to me to be a basic part of human nature: When some violent emotional experience takes place, people get the urge to run off and hide or separate themselves from others. And of course, if we do that, we are not only talking about endangering the group, we are also talking about the individual or the individual family never being able to recover or to survive. Inherent in this belief is the feeling that one does not recover or get well by one's self, but it is together that we look after each other and take care of each other.

In the storytelling, then, we see this process of bringing people to- 13 gether, and it works not only on the family level, but also on the level of the individual. Of course, the whole Pueblo concept of the individual is a little bit different from the usual Western concept of the individual. But one of the beauties of the storytelling is that when something happens to an individual, many people will come to you and take you aside, or maybe a couple of people will come and talk to you. These are occasions of storytelling. These occasions of storytelling are continuous; they are a way of life.

Storytelling lies at the heart of the Pueblo people, and so when 14 someone comes in and says, "When did they tell the stories, or what time of day does the storytelling take place?" that is a ridiculous question. The storytelling goes on constantly—as some old grandmother puts on the shoes of a little child and tells the child the story of a little girl who didn't wear her shoes. At the same time somebody comes into the house for coffee to talk with an adolescent boy who has just been into a lot of trouble, to reassure him that *he* got into that kind of trouble, or somebody else's son got into that kind of trouble too. You have this constant ongoing process, working on many different levels.

One of the stories I like to bring up about helping the individual in 15 crisis is a recent story, and I want to remind you that we make no distinctions between the stories—whether they are history, whether they are fact, whether they are gossip—these distinctions are not useful when we are talking about this particular experience with language. Anyway, there was a young man who, when he came back from the war in Vietnam, had saved up his Army pay and bought a beautiful red Volkswagen Beetle. He was very proud of it, and one night drove up to a place right across the reservation line. It is a very notorious place for many reasons, but one of the more notorious things about the place is a deep arroyo behind the place. This is the King's Bar. So he ran in to pick up a cold six-pack to take home, but he didn't put on his emergency brake. And his little red Volkswagen rolled back into the arroyo and was all smashed up. He felt very bad about it, but within a few days everybody had come to him and told him stories about other people who had lost cars to that arroyo. And probably the story that made him feel the best was about the time that George Day's station wagon, with his mother-in-law and kids in the back, rolled into that arroyo. So everybody was saying, "Well, at least your mother-in-law and kids weren't in the car when it rolled in," and you can't argue with that kind of story. He felt better then because he wasn't alone anymore. He and his smashed-up Volkswagen were now joined with all the other stories of cars that fell into that arroyo.

There are a great many parallels between Pueblo experiences and 16 the remarks that have been made about South Africa and the Caribbean countries—similarities in experiences so far as language is concerned. More specifically, with the experience of English being imposed upon the people. The Pueblo people, of course, have seen intruders come and intruders go. The first they watched come were the Spaniards; while the Spaniards were there, things had to be conducted in Spanish. But as the old stories say, if you wait long enough, they'll go. And sure enough, they went. Then another bunch came in. And old stories say, well, if you wait around long enough, not so much that they'll go, but at least their ways will go. One wonders now, when you see what's happening to technocratic-industrial culture, now that we've used up most of the sources of energy, you think perhaps the old people are right.

But anyhow, our experience with English has been different be- 17 cause the Bureau of Indian Affairs schools were so terrible that we never heard of Shakespeare. There was Dick and Jane, and I can remember reading that the robins were heading south for winter, but I knew that all winter the robins were around Laguna. It took me a long time to figure out what was going on. I worried for quite a while about the robins because they didn't leave in the winter, not realizing that the textbooks were written in Boston. The big textbook companies are up here in Boston and *their* robins do go south in the winter. But this freed us and encouraged us to stay with our narratives. Whatever literature we received at school (which was damn little), at home the storytelling, the special regard for telling and bringing together through the telling, was going on constantly. It has continued, and so we have a great body of classical oral literature, both in the narratives and in the chants and songs.

As the old people say, "If you can remember the stories, you will 18 be all right. Just remember the stories." And, of course, usually when they say that to you, when you are young, you wonder what in the world they mean. But when I returned—I had been away from Laguna Pueblo for a couple of years, well more than a couple of years after college and so forth—I returned to Laguna and I went to Laguna-Acoma high school to visit an English class, and I was wondering how the telling was continuing, because Laguna Pueblo, as the anthropologists have said, is one of the more acculturated pueblos. So I walked into this high school English class and there they were sitting, these very beautiful Laguna and Acoma kids. But I knew that out in their lockers they had cassette tape recorders, and I knew that at home they had stereos, and they were listening to Kiss and Led Zeppelin and all those other things. I was almost afraid, but I had to ask—I had with me a book of short fiction (it's called *The Man to Send Rain Clouds* [New York: Viking Press, 1974]), and among the stories of other Native American writers, it has stories that I have written and Simon Ortiz has written. And there is one particular story in the book about the killing of a state policeman in New Mexico by three Acoma Pueblo men. It was an act that was committed in the early fifties. I was afraid to ask, but I had to. I looked at the class and I said, "How many of you heard this story before you read it in the book?" And I was prepared to hear this crushing truth that indeed the anthropologists were right about the old traditions dying out. But it was amazing, you know, almost all but one or two students raised their hands. They had heard that story, just as Simon and I had heard it, when we were young. That was my first indication that storytelling continues on. About half of them had heard it in English, about half of them had heard it in Laguna. I think again, getting back to one of the original statements, that if you begin to look at the core of the importance of the language and how it fits in with the culture, it is the *story* and the feeling of the story which matters more than what language it's told in.   [1979]

Working with the Text

1. According to Silko, how does the Native American "oral tradition" differ from the mainstream American tradition of writing, especially of organizing writing? In what ways is her essay an example of the oral tradition?

2. Silko places "modern" or "family" stories on a continuum with older, more traditional stories such as the Pueblo creation story. Why? What do the two types of story share, and how are they "the same story" for Silko, in spite of anthropologists placing them into two different categories?

3. What are the many uses of storytelling in Pueblo society, according to Silko? Make a list of each of the instances of storytelling she describes. Do all of these uses seem to relate to one overall purpose for storytelling? Does Silko state or hint at an overall purpose?

4. Would you agree with Silko that her oral presentation is "a spider's web— with many little threads radiating from a center, crisscrossing each other"? What is the "center" of her web? What are the various "little threads," and how do they "crisscross each other" throughout the essay?

Working beyond the Text

1. Silko mentions an anthology of Native American literature, *The Man to Send Rain Clouds,* in which she and Simon Ortiz tell different versions of the "same" story about the murder of a state policeman in New Mexico. If the book is available in your school library, read both versions and compare them. How do they relate to Silko's idea that "the story" precedes and supersedes any particular telling of it?

2. Many other Native American writers and also Native American and Anglo critics have written about the "oral tradition," notably novelist N. Scott Momaday. Use the library to find out what others have said about the oral tradition and its importance in Native American life.

3. You have probably been taught to write in a pattern that Silko says she does not intend to use, in "a structure that moves from point A to point B to point C." How have you been told by composition teachers to organize the ideas in your writing? Would you like to try to organize ideas in some other way—as Silko suggests, in a kind of "spider's web," or in some other nonlinear pattern?

Shakespeare in the Bush

Laura Bohannan

Laura Bohannan teaches anthropology at the University of Illinois at Chicago. This popular essay, originally a presentation on the English radio show *The Third Programme,* was later published in the magazine *Natural History* (August/September 1966). In it, Bohannan describes how members of a West African tribe, because of their cultural beliefs and traditions, interpret the story of *Hamlet* very differently from how most Americans and Europeans interpret it.

Just before I left Oxford for the Tiv in West Africa, conversation 1 turned to the season at Stratford. "You Americans," said a friend, "often have difficulty with Shakespeare. He was, after all, a very English poet, and one can easily misinterpret the universal by misunderstanding the particular."

I protested that human nature is pretty much the same the whole 2 world over; at least the general plot and motivation of the greater tragedies would always be clear—everywhere—although some details of custom might have to be explained and difficulties of translation might produce other slight changes. To end an argument we could not conclude, my friend gave me a copy of *Hamlet* to study in the African bush: it would, he hoped, lift my mind above its primitive surroundings, and possibly I might, by prolonged meditation, achieve the grace of correct interpretation.

It was my second field trip to that African tribe, and I thought myself ready to live in one of its remote sections—an area difficult to cross even on foot. I eventually settled on the hillock of a very knowledgeable old man, the head of a homestead of some hundred and forty people, all of whom were either his close relatives or their wives and children. Like the other elders of the vicinity, the old man spent most of his time performing ceremonies seldom seen these days in the more accessible parts of the tribe. I was delighted. Soon there would be three months of enforced isolation and leisure, between the harvest that takes place just before the rising of the swamps and the clearing of new farms when the water goes down. Then, I thought, they would have even more time to perform ceremonies and explain them to me.

I was quite mistaken. Most of the ceremonies demanded the presence of elders from several homesteads. As the swamps rose, the old men found it too difficult to walk from one homestead to the next, and the ceremonies gradually ceased. As the swamps rose even higher, all activities but one came to an end. The women brewed beer from maize and millet. Men, women, and children sat on their hillocks and drank it.

People began to drink at dawn. By midmorning the whole homestead was singing, dancing, and drumming. When it rained, people had to sit inside their huts: there they drank and sang or they drank and told stories. In any case, by noon or before, I either had to join the party or retire to my own hut and my books. "One does not discuss serious matters when there is beer. Come, drink with us." Since I lacked their capacity for the thick native beer, I spent more and more time with *Hamlet*. Before the end of the second month, grace descended on me. I was quite sure that *Hamlet* had only one possible interpretation, and that one universally obvious.

Early every morning, in the hope of having some serious talk before the beer party, I used to call on the old man at his reception hut—a circle of posts supporting a thatched roof above a low mud wall to keep out wind and rain. One day I crawled through the low doorway and found most of the men of the homestead sitting huddled in their ragged cloths on stools, low plank beds, and reclining chairs, warming themselves against the chill of the rain around a smoky fire. In the center were three pots of beer. The party had started.

The old man greeted me cordially. "Sit down and drink." I accepted a large calabash full of beer, poured some into a small drinking gourd, and tossed it down. Then I poured some more into the same gourd for the man second in seniority to my host before I handed my calabash over to a young man for further distribution. Important people shouldn't ladle beer themselves.

"It is better like this," the old man said, looking at me approvingly 8 and plucking at the thatch that had caught in my hair. "You should sit and drink with us more often. Your servants tell me that when you are not with us, you sit inside your hut looking at a paper."

The old man was acquainted with four kinds of "papers": tax re- 9 ceipts, bride price receipts, court fee receipts, and letters. The messenger who brought him letters from the chief used them mainly as a badge of office, for he always knew what was in them and told the old man. Personal letters for the few who had relatives in the government or mission stations were kept until someone went to a large market where there was a letter writer and reader. Since my arrival, letters were brought to me to be read. A few men also brought me bride price receipts, privately, with requests to change the figures to a higher sum. I found moral arguments were of no avail, since in-laws are fair game, and the technical hazards of forgery difficult to explain to an illiterate people. I did not wish them to think me silly enough to look at any such papers for days on end, and I hastily explained that my "paper" was one of the "things of long ago" of my country.

"Ah," said the old man. "Tell us."   10

I protested that I was not a storyteller. Story telling is a skilled art 11 among them; their standards are high, and the audiences critical—and vocal in their criticism. I protested in vain. This morning they wanted to hear a story while they drank. They threatened to tell me no more stories until I told them one of mine. Finally, the old man promised that no one would criticize my style "for we know you are struggling with our language." "But," put in one of the elders, "you must explain what we do not understand, as we do when we tell you our stories." Realizing that here was my chance to prove *Hamlet* universally intelligible, I agreed.

The old man handed me some more beer to help me on with my 12 storytelling. Men filled their long wooden pipes and knocked coals from the fire to place in the pipe bowls; then, puffing contentedly, they sat back to listen. I began in the proper style, "Not yesterday, not yesterday, but long ago, a thing occurred. One night three men were keeping watch outside the homestead of the great chief, when suddenly they saw the former chief approach them."

"Why was he no longer their chief?"   13

"He was dead," I explained. "That is why they were troubled and 14 afraid when they saw him."

"Impossible," began one of the elders, handing his pipe on to his 15 neighbor, who interrupted, "Of course it wasn't the dead chief. It was an omen sent by a witch. Go on."

Slightly shaken, I continued. "One of these three was a man who 16 knew things"—the closest translation for scholar, but unfortunately it also meant witch. The second elder looked triumphantly at the first. "So he spoke to the dead chief saying, 'Tell us what we must do so you may rest in your grave,' but the dead chief did not answer. He vanished, and they could see him no more. Then the man who knew things—his name was Horatio—said this event was the affair of the dead chief's son, Hamlet."

There was a general shaking of heads round the circle. "Had the 17 dead chief no living brothers? Or was this son the chief?"

"No," I replied. "That is, he had one living brother who became 18 the chief when the elder brother died."

The old men muttered: such omens were matters for chiefs and el- 19 ders, not for youngsters; no good could come of going behind a chief's back; clearly Horatio was not a man who knew things.

"Yes, he was," I insisted, shooing a chicken away from my beer. 20 "In our country the son is next to the father. The dead chief's younger brother had become the great chief. He had also married his elder brother's widow only about a month after the funeral."

"He did well," the old man beamed and announced to the others, 21 "I told you that if we knew more about Europeans, we would find they really were very like us. In our country also," he added to me, "the younger brother marries the elder brother's widow and becomes the father of his children. Now, if your uncle, who married your widowed mother, is your father's full brother, then he will be a real father to you. Did Hamlet's father and uncle have one mother?"

His question barely penetrated my mind; I was too upset and 22 thrown too far off balance by having one of the most important elements of *Hamlet* knocked straight out of the picture. Rather uncertainly I said that I thought they had the same mother, but I wasn't sure—the story didn't say. The old man told me severely that these genealogical details made all the difference and that when I got home I must ask the elders about it. He shouted out the door to one of his younger wives to bring his goatskin bag.

Determined to save what I could of the mother motif, I took a deep 23 breath and began again. "The son Hamlet was very sad because his mother had married again so quickly. There was no need for her to do so, and it is our custom for a widow not to go to her next husband until she has mourned for two years."

"Two years is too long," objected the wife, who had appeared 24 with the old man's battered goatskin bag. "Who will hoe your farms for you while you have no husband?"

"Hamlet," I retorted without thinking, "was old enough to hoe his 25 mother's farms himself. There was no need for her to remarry." No one looked convinced. I gave up. "His mother and the great chief told Hamlet not to be sad, for the great chief himself would be a father to Hamlet. Furthermore, Hamlet would be the next chief: therefore he must stay to learn the things of a chief. Hamlet agreed to remain, and all the rest went off to drink beer."

While I paused, perplexed at how to render Hamlet's disgusted 26 soliloquy to an audience convinced that Claudius and Gertrude had behaved in the best possible manner, one of the younger men asked me who had married the other wives of the dead chief.

"He had no other wives," I told him.   27

"But a chief must have many wives! How else can he brew beer 28 and prepare food for all his guests?"

I said firmly that in our country even chiefs had only one wife, 29 that they had servants to do their work, and that they paid them from tax money.

It was better, they returned, for a chief to have many wives and 30 sons who would help him hoe his farms and feed his people; then everyone loved the chief who gave much and took nothing—taxes were a bad thing.

I agreed with the last comment, but for the rest fell back on their 31 favorite way of fobbing off my questions: "That is the way it is done, so that is how we do it."

I decided to skip the soliloquy. Even if Claudius was here thought 32 quite right to marry his brother's widow, there remained the poison motif, and I knew they would disapprove of fratricide. More hopefully I resumed, "That night Hamlet kept watch with the three who had seen his dead father. The dead chief again appeared, and although the others were afraid, Hamlet followed his dead father off to one side. When they were alone, Hamlet's dead father spoke."

"Omens can't talk!" The old man was emphatic.   33

"Hamlet's dead father wasn't an omen. Seeing him might have 34 been an omen, but he was not." My audience looked as confused as I sounded. "It *was* Hamlet's dead father. It was a thing we call a 'ghost.'" I had to use the English word, for unlike many of the neighboring tribes, these people didn't believe in the survival after death of any individuating part of the personality.

"What is a 'ghost?' An omen?"   35

"No, a 'ghost' is someone who is dead but who walks around and 36 can talk, and people can hear him and see him but not touch him."

They objected. "One can touch zombis."   37

"No, no! It was not a dead body the witches had animated to sacri- 38 fice and eat. No one else made Hamlet's dead father walk. He did it himself."

"Dead men can't walk," protested my audience as one man.   39

I was quite willing to compromise. "A 'ghost' is the dead man's 40
shadow."

But again they objected. "Dead men cast no shadows." 41

"They do in my country," I snapped. 42

The old man quelled the babble of disbelief that arose immediately 43
and told me with that insincere, but courteous, agreement one extends
to the fancies of the young, ignorant, and superstitious, "No doubt in
your country the dead can also walk without being zombis." From the
depths of his bag he produced a withered fragment of kola nut, bit off
one end to show it wasn't poisoned, and handed me the rest as a peace
offering.

"Anyhow," I resumed, "Hamlet's dead father said that his own 44
brother, the one who became chief, had poisoned him. He wanted
Hamlet to avenge him. Hamlet believed this in his heart, for he did not
like his father's brother." I took another swallow of beer. "In the country of the great chief, living in the same homestead, for it was a very
large one, was an important elder who was often with the chief to advise and help him. His name was Polonius. Hamlet was courting his
daughter, but her father and her brother ... [I cast hastily about for
some tribal analogy] warned her not to let Hamlet visit her when she
was alone on her farm, for he would be a great chief and so could not
marry her."

"Why not?" asked the wife, who had settled down on the edge of 45
the old man's chair. He frowned at her for asking stupid questions and
growled, "They lived in the same homestead."

"That was not the reason," I informed them. "Polonius was a 46
stranger who lived in the homestead because he helped the chief, not
because he was a relative."

"Then why couldn't Hamlet marry her?" 47

"He could have," I explained, "but Polonius didn't think he 48
would. After all, Hamlet was a man of great importance who ought to
marry a chief's daughter, for in his country a man could have only one
wife. Polonius was afraid that if Hamlet made love to his daughter,
then no one else would give a high price for her."

"That might be true," remarked one of the shrewder elders, "but a 49
chief's son would give his mistress's father enough presents and patronage to more than make up the difference. Polonius sounds like a
fool to me."

"Many people think he was," I agreed. "Meanwhile Polonius sent 50
his son Laertes off to Paris to learn the things of the country, for it was
the homestead of a very great chief indeed. Because he was afraid that
Laertes might waste a lot of money on beer and women and gambling,
or get into trouble by fighting, he sent one of his servants to Paris secretly, to spy out what Laertes was doing. One day Hamlet came upon
Polonius's daughter Ophelia. He behaved so oddly he frightened her.

Indeed"—I was fumbling for words to express the dubious quality of Hamlet's madness—"the chief and many others had also noticed that when Hamlet talked one could understand the words but not what they meant. Many people thought that he had become mad." My audience suddenly became much more attentive. "The great chief wanted to know what was wrong with Hamlet, so he sent for two of Hamlet's age mates [school friends would have taken long explanation] to talk to Hamlet and find out what troubled his heart. Hamlet, seeing that they had been bribed by the chief to betray him, told them nothing. Polonius, however, insisted that Hamlet was mad because he had been forbidden to see Ophelia, whom he loved."

"Why," inquired a bewildered voice, "should anyone bewitch 51 Hamlet on that account?"

"Bewitch him?"   52

"Yes, only witchcraft can make anyone mad, unless, of course, one 53 sees the beings that lurk in the forest."

I stopped being a storyteller, took out my notebook and de- 54 manded to be told more about these two causes of madness. Even while they spoke and I jotted notes, I tried to calculate the effect of this new factor on the plot. Hamlet had not been exposed to the beings that lurk in the forests. Only his relatives in the male line could bewitch him. Barring relatives not mentioned by Shakespeare, it had to be Claudius who was attempting to harm him. And, of course, it was.

For the moment I staved off questions by saying that the great 55 chief also refused to believe that Hamlet was mad for the love of Ophelia and nothing else. "He was sure that something much more important was troubling Hamlet's heart."

"Now Hamlet's age mates," I continued, "had brought with them 56 a famous storyteller. Hamlet decided to have this man tell the chief and all his homestead a story about a man who had poisoned his brother because he desired his brother's wife and wished to be chief himself. Hamlet was sure the great chief could not hear the story without making a sign if he was indeed guilty, and then he would discover whether his dead father had told him the truth."

The old man interrupted, with deep cunning, "Why should a fa- 57 ther lie to his son?" he asked.

I hedged: "Hamlet wasn't sure that it really was his dead father." 58 It was impossible to say anything, in that language, about devil-inspired visions.

"You mean," he said, "it actually was an omen, and he knew 59 witches sometimes send false ones. Hamlet was a fool not to go to one skilled in reading omens and divining the truth in the first place. A man-who-sees-the-truth could have told him how his father died, if he really had been poisoned, and if there was witchcraft in it; then Hamlet could have called the elders to settle the matter."

The shrewd elder ventured to disagree. "Because his father's 60 brother was a great chief, one-who-sees-the-truth might therefore have been afraid to tell it. I think it was for that reason that a friend of Hamlet's father—a witch and an elder—sent an omen so his friend's son would know. Was the omen true?"

"Yes," I said, abandoning ghosts and the devil; a witch-sent omen 61 it would have to be. "It was true, for when the storyteller was telling his tale before all the homestead, the great chief rose in fear. Afraid that Hamlet knew his secret he planned to have him killed."

The stage set of the next bit presented some difficulties of transla- 62 tion. I began cautiously. "The great chief told Hamlet's mother to find out from her son what he knew. But because a woman's children are always first in her heart, he had the important elder Polonius hide behind a cloth that hung against the wall of Hamlet's mother's sleeping hut. Hamlet started to scold his mother for what she had done."

There was a shocked murmur from everyone. A man should never 63 scold his mother.

"She called out in fear, and Polonius moved behind the cloth. 64 Shouting, 'A rat!' Hamlet took his machete and slashed through the cloth." I paused for dramatic effect. "He had killed Polonius!"

The old men looked at each other in supreme disgust. "That Polo- 65 nius truly was a fool and a man who knew nothing! What child would not know enough to shout, 'It's me!'" With a pang, I remembered that these people are ardent hunters, always armed with bow, arrow, and machete; at the first rustle in the grass an arrow is aimed and ready, and the hunter shouts "Game!" If no human voice answers immediately, the arrow speeds on its way. Like a good hunter Hamlet had shouted, "A rat!"

I rushed in to save Polonius's reputation. "Polonius did speak. 66 Hamlet heard him. But he thought it was the chief and wished to kill him earlier that evening. . . ." I broke down, unable to describe to these pagans, who had no belief in individual after-life, the difference between dying at one's prayers and dying "unhousell'd, disappointed, unaneled."

This time I had shocked my audience seriously. "For a man to 67 raise his hand against his father's brother and the one who has become his father—that is a terrible thing. The elders ought to let such a man be bewitched."

I nibbled at my kola nut in some perplexity, then pointed out that 68 after all the man had killed Hamlet's father.

"No," pronounced the old man, speaking less to me than to the 69 young men sitting behind the elders. "If your father's brother has killed your father, you must appeal to your father's age mates; *they* may avenge him. No man may use violence against his senior relatives." Another thought struck him. "But if his father's brother had indeed been wicked enough to bewitch Hamlet and make him mad that would be a good story indeed, for it would be his fault that Hamlet, being mad, no longer had any sense and thus was ready to kill his father's brother."

There was a murmur of applause. *Hamlet* was again a good story 70 to them, but it no longer seemed quite the same story to me. As I thought over the coming complications of plot and motive, I lost courage and decided to skim over dangerous ground quickly.

"The great chief," I went on, "was not sorry that Hamlet had killed 71 Polonius. It gave him a reason to send Hamlet away, with his two treacherous mates, with letters to a chief of a far country, saying that Hamlet should be killed. But Hamlet changed the writing on their papers, so that the chief killed his age mates instead." I encountered a reproachful glare from one of the men whom I had told undetectable forgery was not merely immoral but beyond human skill. I looked the other way.

"Before Hamlet could return, Laertes came back for his father's fu- 72 neral. The great chief told him Hamlet had killed Polonius. Laertes swore to kill Hamlet because of this, and because his sister Ophelia, hearing her father had been killed by the man she loved, went mad and drowned in the river."

"Have you already forgotten what we told you?" The old man 73 was reproachful. "One cannot take vengeance on a madman; Hamlet killed Polonius in his madness. As for the girl, she not only went mad, she was drowned. Only witches can make people drown. Water itself can't hurt anything. It is merely something one drinks and bathes in."

I began to get cross. "If you don't like the story, I'll stop." 74

The old man made soothing noises and himself poured me some 75 more beer. "You tell the story well, and we are listening. But it is clear that the elders of your country have never told you what the story really means. No, don't interrupt! We believe you when you say your marriage customs are different, or your clothes and weapons. But people are the same everywhere; therefore, there are always witches and it is we, the elders, who know how witches work. We told you it was the great chief who wished to kill Hamlet, and now your own words have proved us right. Who were Ophelia's male relatives?"

"There were only her father and her brother." *Hamlet* was clearly 76 out of my hands.

"There must have been many more; this also you must ask of your 77 elders when you get back to your country. From what you tell us, since Polonius was dead, it must have been Laertes who killed Ophelia, although I do not see the reason for it."

We had emptied one pot of beer, and the old men argued the point 78 with slightly tipsy interest. Finally one of them demanded of me, "What did the servant of Polonius say on his return?"

With difficulty I recollected Reynaldo and his mission. "I don't 79 think he did return before Polonius was killed."

"Listen," said the elder, "and I will tell you how it was and how 80 your story will go, then you may tell me if I am right. Polonius knew his son would get into trouble, and so he did. He had many fines to pay for fighting, and debts from gambling. But he had only two ways of getting money quickly. One was to marry off his sister at once, but it is difficult to find a man who will marry a woman desired by the son of a chief. For if the chief's heir commits adultery with your wife, what can you do? Only a fool calls a case against a man who will someday be his judge. Therefore Laertes had to take the second way: he killed his sister by witchcraft, drowning her so he could secretly sell her body to the witches."

I raised an objection. "They found her body and buried it. Indeed 81 Laertes jumped into the grave to see his sister once more—so, you see, the body was truly there. Hamlet, who had just come back, jumped in after him."

"What did I tell you?" The elder appealed to the others. "Laertes 82 was up to no good with his sister's body. Hamlet prevented him, because the chief's heir, like a chief, does not wish any other man to grow rich and powerful. Laertes would be angry, because he would have killed his sister without benefit to himself. In our country he would try to kill Hamlet for that reason. Is this not what happened?"

"More or less," I admitted. "When the great chief found Hamlet 83 was still alive, he encouraged Laertes to try to kill Hamlet and arranged a fight with machetes between them. In the fight both young men were wounded to death. Hamlet's mother drank the poisoned beer that the chief meant for Hamlet in case he won the fight. When he saw his mother die of poison, Hamlet, dying, managed to kill his father's brother with his machete."

"You see, I was right!" exclaimed the elder.   84

"That was a very good story," added the old man, "and you told it 85 with very few mistakes. There was just one more error, at the very end. The poison Hamlet's mother drank was obviously meant for the survivor of the fight, whichever it was. If Laertes had won, the great chief would have poisoned him, for no one would know that he arranged Hamlet's death. Then, too, he need not fear Laertes' witchcraft; it takes a strong heart to kill one's only sister by witchcraft.

"Sometime," concluded the old man, gathering his ragged toga 86 about him, "you must tell us some more stories of your country. We, who are elders, will instruct you in their true meaning, so that when you return to your own land your elders will see that you have not been sitting in the bush, but among those who know things and who have taught you wisdom."

Working with the Text

1. In what way does Bohannan's experience in Africa contradict her original idea that "human nature is pretty much the same the whole world over" and that "the general plot and motivation of the greater tragedies would always be clear—everywhere"? What is the significance of the old man telling her in the end that "people are the same everywhere"?

2. Differences among certain basic cultural beliefs cause differences in the interpretations that Bohannan and her audience give to *Hamlet*. What are some of the beliefs, and what are the differences? How do these differences create different interpretations of certain specific details in the story?

3. What problems are created because Bohannan has to translate the story of Hamlet into another language? What specific words are difficult to translate and lead to misunderstandings?

4. Bohannan's tone in the essay is humorous. Find examples of her humor in which she makes fun of herself, her anthropological "subjects," her entire situation. Why do you think she chooses to present her information in a humorous way? How does it help her communicate her message? How would the essay be different if it were very serious in tone?

Working beyond the Text

1. Bohannan's example presents an extreme case of cultural misunderstanding. The two cultures—Anglo American and West African—are so different that *Hamlet* literally becomes a different story from the one Shakespeare wrote. Can you think of less extreme examples of cultural misunderstandings arising from different cultural beliefs? There may be examples from your own everyday life.

2. If you have made a list of differences in basic cultural beliefs between Bohannan and her African audience, show how their interpretations of another story besides *Hamlet* might differ. Choose a story full of details that might cause confusion. This might include, for example, ghosts, murders, or complicated family relations.

3. Bohannan is an anthropologist talking about misunderstandings between two very different cultural groups. What lessons might her story have for teachers of literature in a more homogeneous setting, such as an American college classroom? What should teachers bear in mind as they attempt to guide students toward what the old man in Bohannan's essay calls "true meaning"?

Notes on Lyrics

Oscar Hammerstein

Oscar Hammerstein (1895–1960) was an Academy-Award-winning Broadway lyricist, half of the famous team Rodgers and Hammerstein. During his career he collaborated on lyrics for such famous Broadway musicals as *Show Boat, Oklahoma!, Carousel* and *The King and I*. In this excerpt from a chapter in his book *Lyrics* (1949), Hammerstein uses the example of writing lyrics for composers to show how literary language is shaped by the necessity to fit its medium, to communicate to an audience, and to be beautiful.

It took me years to learn that I did not play the piano very well. I 1 so enjoyed my own playing. I tackled everything—Victor Herbert, Verdi, Leoncavallo, George Cohan. What expression I could put into their music! What exaltation I felt! My mother thought I had "a lovely touch," she told her friends. But when I became fifteen or sixteen my own friends began to express less sympathetic reactions, and it became clear to me that they were not hearing the same music I thought I was hearing when I played. Remembering this illuminating and disturbing experience, I have misgivings right now as I embark on a discussion of lyrics. I am going to love it, but will you? The hunter gloats reminiscently over the last sabertoothed tiger he has brought back alive. So does the songwriter like to tell of how he has captured a refrain and imprisoned it safely behind thirty-two bars. Both are likely to overrate the spare time of their audience.

One consideration encourages me. Almost every layman I have 2 ever met exhibits a real curiosity about songs and how they are written. It is a standing joke among authors and composers that when they meet people the first question asked of them is, "Which comes first, the words or the music?" Perhaps it is high time that one of us stopped laughing at the classic query and provided a sensible answer to it. There is nothing foolish about the question. A song is a wedding of two crafts, and it is a natural thing to wonder how they meet and live together. Feeling safe on the ground of an interest so frequently expressed, I will start these notes with this subject.

There is, as a matter of fact, no invariable or inevitable method for 3 writing songs. Sometimes the words are written first, sometimes the music. Sometimes two or more collaborators lock themselves in a room and write words and music at the same time. The kind of songs, the individuals involved and the conditions under which they work dictate the process.

Let me say a few words now about the actual writing of lyrics 4 once the subject matter of the song has been determined, and once it has been placed in its proper spot in the telling of the story. I am often asked if I use a rhyming dictionary. I do. I find it a great help and a time saver. The one I like best is Loring's *Rhymer's Lexicon.* A rhyming dictionary, however, should be used as a supplement to one's own ingenuity, and not a substitute for it. I do not open mine until I have exhausted my own memory and invention of rhymes for a word. Attractive combinations of words to make double and triple rhymes are not found in rhyming dictionaries, nor are modern words or colloquialisms which can be used with humorous effect in a song. A rhyming dictionary is of little use and may, in fact, be a handicap when one is writing a song which makes a feature of rhyming. If you would achieve the rhyming grace and facility of W. S. Gilbert or Lorenz Hart, my advice would be never to open a rhyming dictionary. Don't even own one. While I, on occasion, place a timid, encroaching foot on the territory of these two masters, I never carry my invasion very far. I would not stand a chance with either of them in the field of brilliant light verse. I admire them and envy them their fluidity and humor, but I refuse to compete with them. Aside from my shortcomings as a wit and rhymester—or, perhaps, because of them—my inclinations lead me to a more primitive type of lyric. The longer I write, the more interested I become in expressing my own true convictions and feelings in the songs I write. When I was very much younger, I thought that if ever I made all the money I needed out of writing musical comedy, I would then sit back and turn to straight dramatic plays in which I could say whatever I wanted to say and state my reactions to the world I live in. Later on, however, I became convinced that whatever I wanted to say could be said in songs, that I was not confined necessarily to trite or light subjects, and that since my talent and training in the writing of lyrics is far beyond my attainments in other fields of writing, I had better use this medium.

If one has fundamental things to say in a song, the rhyming becomes a question of deft balancing. A rhyme should be unassertive, never standing out too noticeably. It should, on the other hand, not be a rhyme heard in a hundred other popular songs of the time, so familiar that the listener can anticipate it before it is sung. There should not be too many rhymes. In fact, a rhyme should appear only where it is absolutely demanded to keep the pattern of the music. If a listener is made rhyme-conscious, his interest may be diverted from the story of the song. If, on the other hand, you keep him waiting for a rhyme, he is more likely to listen to the meaning of the words. A good illustration is *"Ol' Man River."* Consider the first part of the refrain:

"Ol' Man River,
Dat Ol' Man River,
He mus' know sumpin'

But don' say nuthin',
He jes' keeps rollin',
He keeps on rollin' along.
He don' plant 'taters,
He don' plant cotton,
An' dem dat plants 'em
Is soon forgotten."

"Cotton" and "forgotten" are the first two words that rhyme. 6
Other words are repeated for the sake of musical continuity and design. The same idea could be set to this music with many more
rhymes. "River," instead of being repeated in the second line, could
have had a rhyme—"shiver," "quiver," etc. The next two lines could
have rhymed with the first two, the "iver" sounds continuing, or they
could have had two new words rhyming with each other. I do not believe that in this way I could have commanded the same attention and
respect from a listener, nor would a singer be so likely to concentrate
on the meaning of the words. There are, of course, compensations for
lack of rhyme. I've already mentioned repetition. There is also the trick
of matching up words. "He mus' know sumpin' But don' say nuthin'."
"Sumpin'" and "nuthun'" do not rhyme, but the two words are related. "He don' plant 'taters, He don' plant cotton." These two lines
also match and complement each other to make up for the lack of a
rhyme. Here is a song sung by a character who is a rugged and untu-
tored philosopher. It is a song of resignation with a protest implied.
Brilliant and frequent rhyming would diminish its importance.

Take, as a contrast, the refrain of "I'm in Love With a Wonderful 7
Guy" from *South Pacific*. You will find in it interior rhymes, unde-
manded rhymes and lighthearted similes. The emotion expressed in
this song is so simple that it can afford to wear the decorations and
embroidery of more ingenious rhyming. There is no subtle philosophy
involved. A girl is in love and her heart is sailing. She is sentimental
and exuberant and triumphant in the discovery. The job of the lyric is
to capture her spirit. I think it does. I am very fond of this song.

After rhyming, I would place next in importance a study and ap- 8
preciation of phonetics. Some words and groups of words that look
beautiful in printed poetry are unavailable to one who is writing lyrics
to be sung to music. There is an inexorable mathematics in music—so
many measures in a refrain, so many beats in a measure, and they cannot be ignored. There is rhythm and tempo, and its continuity must be
unbroken. The concessions with which a melody can favor words are
limited. The larynxes of singers are limited. They must be given a
chance to breathe after a certain number of words have been sung, and
if they are building up to a high note at the finish, they must be given a
good deep breath before they attack it. Both the lyric writer and the

composer must worry about all these things. If a song is not singable, it is no song at all.

The job of the poet is to find the right word in the right place, the 9 word with the exact meaning and the highest quality of beauty or power. The lyric writer must find this word too, but it must be also a word that is clear when sung and not too difficult for the singer to sing on that note which he hits when he sings it. Wherever there are vocal climaxes and high notes, singers are comfortable only with vowels of an open sound. A word like "sweet," for instance, would be a very bad word on which to sing a high note. The "e" sound closes the larynx and the singer cannot let go with his full voice. Furthermore, the "t" ending the word is a hard consonant which would cut the singer off and thwart his and the composer's desire to sustain the note. Now and then, when a lyric writer finds a word to which he is very attached, he tries to sidetrack these rules. He may say, "I don't care how many 's's' there are in this line, this is what I want to say and the singer will just have to slow up and sing very distinctly"; or he may say, "I don't care if that word does end with a hard consonant [like the 't' in 'sweet'], that is the only word I can use there and the singer will have to make the best of it." This kind of temperamental defiance is self-defeating because no word, however fine and lofty and exact its meaning may be, is a good word in a song if it is difficult to sing.

Rhyming, phonetics, semantics—all very important. But technique 10 and professional polish do not make a song. They improve it and their absence might ruin it, but there is an element much less tangible that is the deciding factor in a song's life. One evening this summer I was on Arthur Godfrey's television program. He told me that he was continually besieged by young songwriters. He said that almost everyone seemed to have written his one song and wanted to find out how to get it before the public. I told Arthur that I'd had an entirely different experience. Most young songwriters or amateur songwriters of all ages who have approached me have told me that they had at least forty songs—sometimes four hundred songs. Most of them make the point that they can rattle them off very quickly, one a day or as many as anyone would wish. "Songs just come to me," many people tell me. If I met a man with just one song, I would be more interested in him. I believe that anyone who stated sincerely what was deep in his heart could not only write a song, but could quickly get it published because it would be sure to be a good song.

The most important ingredient of a good song is sincerity. Let the 11 song be yours and yours alone. However important, however trivial, believe it. Mean it from the bottom of your heart, and say what is on your mind as carefully, as clearly, as beautifully as you can. Show it to no one until you are certain that you cannot make one change that would improve it. After that, however, be willing to make improvements if someone can convince you that they are needed.

This sounds like simple advice, but no one knows better than I how hard it is to follow. The basic rules are always the hardest ones to observe, even though they seem the easiest. No beginner on the golf course or the tennis courts questions the good sense of his first lesson when he is told to keep his eye on the ball. This seems such an obvious thing to do, and yet no matter how many years you play these games your chief mistake remains taking your eye off the ball. This tendency to skip over the fundamental things and grasp the superficial is the tragedy of man's history from the beginning of time. I do not, therefore, place undue blame on misguided songwriters. They are merely keeping up the tradition of the stupidity of the human race when, instead of writing what they honestly feel, they invent fancy rhymes and foolish jokes and tricky titles and imitative phrases and lines that merely "fill in." I do not blame them if they spend their days trying to get to know someone who knows someone who is the brother-in-law of a publisher. I am just saying that all these things are a waste of time without a good manuscript. Get the right words and the right notes down on paper and, in some way, your song will reach the public. 12

This is a very important thing for writers to remember. You never know when you will be found out if your work is careless. A year or so ago, on the cover of the New York *Herald Tribune* Sunday Magazine, I saw a picture of the Statue of Liberty. It was a picture taken from a helicopter and it showed the top of the statue's head. I was amazed at the detail there. The sculptor had done a painstaking job with the lady's coiffure, and yet he must have been pretty sure that the only eyes that would ever see this detail would be the uncritical eyes of sea gulls. He could not have dreamt that any man would ever fly over this head and take a picture of it. He was artist enough, however, to finish off this part of the statue with as much care as he had devoted to her face and her arms and the torch and everything that people can see as they sail up the bay. He was right. When you are creating a work of art, or any other kind of work, finish the job off perfectly. You never know when a helicopter, or some other instrument not at the moment invented, may come along and find you out. 13

Collaboration is the biggest word in the theater. It is the most important element in theatrical success. Not just the collaboration between an author and a composer, but the total collaboration in every play, the convergence and co-ordination of all the different talents, producing, writing, directing, choreography, acting, scene designing, costume designing, lighting, orchestration, theater management, company management, public relations—the mixture of all these ingredients is essential to every theatrical meal that seeks to make itself palatable to the public. To get along in the theater you must enjoy working side by side with other people. You must be willing not only to give your best to them but to accept their best and give them the opportunity of adding their efforts to yours to their full capacities. 14

One novelist recently stated that she was leaving the theater and ₁₅ returning to writing exclusively for the printed page. She said that she could not stand so many people advising her and helping her and butting in on her work. She did not like the feel of the director's hot breath on her neck. She was right to leave. If you want privacy in your work, and if you want to make your flights of fancy solo, stay away from the theater. The theater is a welding of many arts into one. No one person can be efficient or talented in all these arts, and if any man could write and produce and direct and act and play the music, shift the scenery, design the costumes and, in short, do everything that could be done on one stage and come up with what was literally a one-man show, he would still need one more thing, an audience. You cannot get away from collaboration.

I am discontented with what I have written here. I have not said ₁₆ nearly all I would like to say about lyrics and the plays for which I write them. "I could go on and on" but I don't dare. I feel the self-consciousness of a man who is madly in love with a girl and wants to talk about her but has already imposed too long on his friends' time and politeness. If I have been long-winded, please forgive me my extravagances and indulge my blind infatuation. I'm in love with a wonderful theater.

Working with the Text

1. What are some of the basic principles Hammerstein lays out for writing the kind of lyrics he writes? Which elements of the words seem most important to him and which seem to be less important?

2. What are some of the restrictions on language that a lyricist must deal with that other writers (including novelists and poets) don't need to be concerned with? Why is Hammerstein, as a writer, willing to put up with these restrictions on his writing?

3. Part of Hammerstein's style in the essay is to be "self-deprecating." That is, he often humbly points out his limitations as a musician and as a writer. Point to the many places in the essay where he does this. Why does he do it, do you suppose?

Working beyond the Text

1. Try writing a song or a part of a song. If possible, work with someone else who writes the melody, so that you get the feel for "collaboration" that Hammerstein says is so much a part of most song writing. If you can't come up with an original melody, use one that already exists and write different words to it. Experiment with some of the general principles that Hammerstein lays out, as well as some of the specific rules.

2. Hammerstein is one of the most famous Broadway musical writers of all time. Who was his partner for most of his career? What musicals did he write? What are some of the most famous songs created by this team? Which of his songs did you already know, perhaps without knowing who wrote them? If possible, locate a recording of one of his musicals and listen to it. You might try analyzing one of his famous songs to see if he adheres to the principles of lyric writing explained in the essay.

3. Hammerstein mentions two other lyricists, W. S. Gilbert and Lorenz Hart. Who were they? Who were their partners? What works are they famous for? Why are they considered so great that even Hammerstein says, "I refuse to compete with them"?

4. Hammerstein mentions sometimes using a rhyming dictionary when he writes song lyrics, and recommends a very careful use of it to other song writers. What other reference books might come in handy for a song writer? What reference books do you use when you write, and how do you use them? How might a writer misuse reference books?

5. Do you find any of Hammerstein's advice to song writers good advice for other kinds of writers? Which advice? Why? Try taking his advice when you work on your next essay. Be prepared to explain which advice you used and how it worked for you.

Acknowledgments

GLORIA ANZALDÚA "How to Tame a Wild Tongue" from *Borderlands/La Frontera: The New Mestiza* by Gloria Anzaldúa, copyright © 1987 by Gloria Anzaldúa. Reprinted with permission from Aunt Lute Books.

LAURA BOHANNAN "Shakespeare in the Bush" from *Natural History*, August/September 1966, copyright © 1966 by Laura Bohannan. Reprinted by permission of the Author.

DENISE CHÁVEZ "Heat and Rain" from *Breaking Boundaries: Writing and Critical Readings*, edited by Asunción Horno-Delgado, Eliana Ortega, Nina M. Scott, Nancy Saporta Sternbach; copyright © 1989 by the University of Massachusetts Press. Used with permission.

LOUISE GLÜCK "The Education of the Poet" from *Proofs and Theories* by Louise Glück, copyright © 1994 by Louise Glück. First published by the Ecco Press in 1994. Reprinted by permission.

STEPHEN JAY GOULD "The Median Isn't the Message" from *Bully for Brontosaurus: Reflections in Natural History* by Stephen Jay Gould, copyright © 1991 by Stephen Jay Gould. Reprinted by permission of W. W. Norton & Company, Inc.

Gerald Graff "Other Voices, Other Rooms" from *Beyond the Culture Wars: How Teaching the Conflicts Can Revitalize American Education* by Gerald Graff, copyright © 1992 by Gerald Graff. Reprinted by permission of W. W. Norton, Inc.

GAIL GRIFFIN "Vocation" from *Calling: Essays on Teaching in the Mother Tongue* by Gail Griffin, copyright © 1992 by Gail Griffin. Reprinted by permission of Trilogy Books.

OSCAR HAMMERSTEIN II "Notes on Lyrics" from *Lyrics* by Oscar Hammerstein II, copyright © 1985 by the Estate of Oscar Hammerstein II. All Rights Reserved. Reprinted by permission.

EVA HOFFMAN "Exile" from *Lost in Translation: A Life in a New Language* by Eva Hoffman, copyright © 1989 by Eva Hoffman. Used by permission of Dutton Signet, a division of Penguin Books USA Inc.

BELL HOOKS "Talking Back" and "Keeping Close to Home: Class and Education" from *Talking Back* by bell hooks, copyright © 1989 by bell hooks. Reprinted by permission of South End Press.

DAVID HUDDLE Puttering in the Prose Garden: Prose Improvement for Fiction Writers" from *The Writing Habit* by David Huddle, published by the University Press of New England, copyright © 1994 by David Huddle. Reprinted by permission of the Author.

IAN JOHNSON "The Imagined Nostalgic Consumer Utopia" from *A Student's Guide to First-Year Composition*, 15th ed., edited by Buffington, Ransdell & Ryder; copyright © 1994 by Burgess International Group, Inc. Reprinted by permission of Burgess Publishing, Inc.

JUNE JORDAN "Nobody Mean More to Me than You and the Future Life of Willie Jordan," copyright © 1985 by June Jordan. Reprinted with permission of the Author.

JULIE JUNG "The Pleasures of Remembrance: Raking in Circles and Other Unexpected Delights," copyright © 1996 by Julie Jung. Reprinted by permission of the Author.

ROBIN TOLMACH LAKOFF "The Groves of Academe" from *Talking Power* by Robin Tolmach Lakoff, copyright © 1990 by Robin Tolmach Lakoff. Reprinted by permission of Basic Books, a division of HarperCollins Publishers, Inc.

URSULA K. LE GUIN "Bryn Mawr Commencement Address" from *Dancing at the Edge of the World* by Ursula K. Le Guin, copyright © 1986 by Ursula K. Le Guin. Used by permission of Grove/Atlantic, Inc.

ALAN LIGHT "About a Salary or Reality?—Rap's Recurrent Conflict from *South Atlantic Quarterly*, 90:4 (Fall 1991), copyright © 1991 by Duke University Press. Reprinted with permission.

REGINALD LOCKETT "How I Started Writing Poetry" from *California Childhood: Recollections and Stories of the Golden State*, copyright © 1988. Reprinted by permission of Creative Arts Book Company.

AUDRE LORDE Chapter 3 from *Zami: A New Spelling of My Name* by Audre Lorde, copyright © 1982 by The Crossing Press. Reprinted by permission of The Crossing Press.

MIN-ZHAN LU "From Silence to Words" from *College English*, April 1987, copyright © 1987 by the National Council of Teachers of English. Reprinted with permission.

EMILY MARTIN "The Egg and the Sperm: How Science Has Constructed a Romance Based on Stereotypical Male-Female Relationships" from *Signs: Journal of Women in Culture and Society*, 16–3, copyright © 1991 The University of Chicago. Reprinted by permission of The University of Chicago Press.

BARBARA MELLIX "From Outside In" from *The Georgia Review*, Summer 1987 issue, copyright © 1987 by The University of Georgia; copyright © 1987 by Barbara Mellix. Reprinted by permission of Barbara Mellix and *The Georgia Review*.

MARK CRISPIN MILLER   "Deride and Conquer" from WATCHING TELEVISION, Todd Gitlin, Editor, copyright © 1986 by Mark Crispin Miller. Reprinted by permission of Pantheon Books, a division of Random House, Inc.

SARA MOSLE   "Writing Down Secrets" from *The New Yorker*, September 18, 1995, copyright © 1995 by Sara Mosle. Reprinted by permission of the Author.

INGRID MUNDARI   "Language as Image Maker" from *The Translation of Memory*, edited by Eve Shelnutt, copyright © 1990 by Allyn & Bacon. Reprinted by permission.

FLANNERY O'CONNOR   "Writing Short Stories" from *Mystery and Manners* by Flannery O'Connor, edited by Sally and Robert Fitzgerald, copyright © 1969 by the Estate of Mary Flannery O'Connor. Reprinted by permission of Farrar, Straus & Giroux, Inc.

SIMON ORTIZ   "The Language We Know" from *I Tell You Now: Autobiographical Essays by Native American Writers*, edited by Brian Swann and Arnold Krupat, copyright © 1987 by The University of Nebraska Press. Used by permission of The University of Nebraska Press.

PAUL PACENTRELLI   "How to Sound Erudite" from *The Toronto Globe and Mail*, August 6, 1993, copyright © 1993 by Paul Pacentrelli. Reprinted by permission of the Author.

KIT YUEN QUAN   "The Girl Who Wouldn't Sing" from *Making Face, Making Soul/Haciendo Caras: Creative and Critical Perspectives by Feminists of Color*, edited by Gloria Anzaldúa, copyright © 1990 by Gloria Anzaldúa. Reprinted with permission from Aunt Lute Books.

ELAYNE RAPPING   "Needed: A Radical Recovery" from *The Progressive*, January 1993, copyright © 1993 by Elayne Rapping. Reproduced by permission of *The Progressive*.

F. D. REEVE   "What's the Matter with Poetry?" from *The Nation*, May 24, 1993, copyright © *The Nation* Company. Reprinted with permission from *The Nation* magazine.

ADRIENNE RICH   "Of Woman Born: Motherhood as Experience and Institution" from *Anger and Tenderness* by Adrienne Rich, copyright © 1986, 1976 by W. W. Norton & Company, Inc. Reprinted by permission of the Author and W. W. Norton & Company, Inc.

RICHARD RODRIGUEZ   "Aria: A Memoir of a Bilingual Childhood," copyright © 1980 by Richard Rodriguez. Reprinted by permission of Georges Borchardt, Inc., for the Author.

MIKE ROSE   "The Politics of Remediation" from *Lives on the Boundary: The Struggles of America's Underprepared* by Mike Rose, copyright © 1989 by Mike Rose. Reprinted with permission of The Free Press, a division of Simon & Schuster.

LESLIE MARMON SILKO   "Language and Literature from a Pueblo Indian Perspective" from *The Story and Its Writer*, 2nd edition, edited by Ann Charters, copyright © 1979 by Leslie Marmon Silko. Reprinted by permission of The Johns Hopkins University Press.

NANCY SOMMERS   "I Stand Here Writing" from *College English* April 1993, copyright © 1993 by the National Council of Teachers of English. Reprinted with permission.

SUSAN SONTAG   "On AIDS" from *AIDS and Its Metaphors* by Susan Sontag, copyright © 1988, 1989 by Susan Sontag. Reprinted by permission of Farrar Straus & Giroux, Inc.

JONATHAN STRONG   "Books and Silence from *American Literature*, 68:1 (March 1996), copyright © 1996 Duke University Press. Reprinted with permission.

DEBORAH TANNEN   "Men and Women Talking on the Job" from *Talking from Nine to Five* by Deborah Tannen, Ph.D., copyright © 1994 by Deborah Tannen, Ph.D. Reprinted by permission of William Morrow & Company, Inc.

ELLEN ULLMAN   "Getting Close to the Machine" from *Harper's Magazine*, June 1995, copyright © 1995 by Ellen Ullman. Reprinted by permission of the Author.

VICTOR VILLANEUVA, JR.   "Whose Voice Is It Anyway? Rodriguez' Speech in Retrospect," from *English Journal*, December 1987, copyright © 1987 by the National Council of Teachers of English. Reprinted with permission.

JAMES BOYD WHITE   "The Invisible Discourse of Law" from *Heracles' Bow: Essays on the Rhetoric and Poetics of the Law*, copyright © 1985 by The University of Wisconsin Press. Reprinted by permission of The University of Wisconsin Press.

PATRICIA WILLIAMS   "The Death of the Profane" from *The Alchemy of Race and Rights: The Diary of a Law Professor* by Patricia Williams, copyright © 1991 by the President and Fellows of Harvard College. Reprinted by permission of Harvard University Press. "Hate Radio" from *Ms. Magazine*, March/April 1994; copyright © 1994 by *Ms. Magazine*. Reprinted by permission.

ABIGAIL WITHERSPOON   "This Pen for Hire" from *Harper's Magazine*, June 1995, copyright © 1995 by *Harper's Magazine*. Reproduced by special permission. All rights reserved.

RICHARD WRIGHT   Selections from How *"Bigger"* Was Born by Richard Wright, copyright © 1940 by Richard Wright, renewed © 1968 by Ellen Wright. Reprinted by permission of HarperCollins Publishers, Inc.

Index of Authors and Titles

461